SECURITY AND DEFENCE: PACIFIC AND GLOBAL PERSPECTIVES

Edited by

Desmond Ball and Cathy Downes

Sydney
Allen & Unwin
Wellington London Boston

© Desmond Ball & Cathy Downes 1990

First published in 1990.
Allen & Unwin Australia Pty Ltd
An Unwin Hyman company
8 Napier Street, North Sydney, NSW 2059 Australia

Allen & Unwin New Zealand Ltd
75 Ghuznee Street, Wellington, New Zealand

Unwin Hyman Ltd
15-17 Broadwick Street, London W1V 1FP, UK

Unwin Hyman Inc.
955 Massachusetts Avenue, Cambridge, MA 02139 USA

National Library of Australia
Cataloguing-in-Publication entry:

Security and defence: Pacific and global perspectives.

  Bibliography.
  Includes index.
  ISBN 0 04 442161 3.

1. Security, International. 2. Australia -
Defenses. 3. Pacific Area - National security.
I. Ball, Desmond, 1947- . II. Downes, Cathy,
1959- .

327.1

Printed by Chong Moh Offset Printing Pte Ltd, Singapore

CONTENTS

TABLES

FIGURES

ABBREVIATIONS AND ACRONYMS

AABNCP	Advanced Airborne National Command Post (US)
ABCA	The ANZUS partners, and the United Kingdom and Canada
ABM	Anti-Ballistic Missile
ACPERS	Assistant Chief of the Defence Force (Personnel) (Australia)
ADF	Australian Defence Force
ADFILS	Australian Defence Families Information and Liaison Service
ADI	Australian Defence Industries
AEROTECH	Aerospace Technologies
AEW&C	Airborne early warning and control
AFSATCOM	US Air Force Satellite Communications System
AII	Australian Industry Involvement
ALCM	Air-Launched Cruise Missile
AMRs	Australian Military Regulations
ANZAC	Australian and New Zealand Army Corps
ANZUS	Australia, New Zealand, United States
APC	Armoured Personnel Carrier
ArFFA	Armed Forces Federation of Australia
ARL	Aeronautical Research Laboratories
ASADPO	Australian Strategic Analysis and Defence Policy Objectives
ASAT	Anti-Satellite
ASC	Australian Submarine Corporation
ASEAN	Association of South East Asia Nations
ASIS	Australian Secret Intelligence Service
ASROC	Anti-submarine rocket
ASSP	Assistant Secretary Service Personnel
ASW	Anti-Submarine Warfare
ATA	Aerospace Technologies of Australia Ltd
ATB	Advanced Technology Bomber (US)
AUSTRADE	Australian Trade Commission
AWACS	Airborne Warning and Control System
C-in-C	Commander-in-Chief
C^3	Command, Control and Communications
C^3I	Command, Control, Communications and Intelligence
CAFE	Conventional Armed Forces in Europe
CBM	Confidence Building Measures
CDBS	Command Data Buffer System (US)
CDF	Chief of the Defence Force (Australia post-1984)

CDFS	Chief of the Defence Force Staff (Australia pre-1984)
CEP	Circular Error Probable
CFE	Conventional Forces in Europe
CGS	Chief of the General Staff
CIA	Central Intelligence Agency (US)
CINCSAC	Commander-in-Chief, Strategic Air Command (US)
CIWS	Close-In Weapons System
CJFA	Commander, Joint Forces, Australia
CMP	Counter-Military Potential
CST	Conventional Stability Talks (Europe)
CTB	Comprehensive Test Ban
CW	Chemical Weapons/Warheads
DCP	Defence Co-operation Program (Australia)
DFDC	Defence Force Development Committee (Australia)
DFRB	Defence Force Retirement Benefits Scheme (Australia)
DFRDB	Defence Force Retirement and Death Benefits Scheme
DFRT	Defence Forces Remuneration Tribunal
DFSC	Defence Force Structure Committee (Australia)
DOCCC	Defence Operational Concepts and Capabilities Committee (Australia)
DoD	Department of Defense
DPM	Draft Presidential Memorandum (US)
DSCS	Defense Satellite Communications System (US)
DSTO	Defence Science and Technology Organisation (Australia)
EEZ	Economic Exclusion Zone
EHF	Extrememly High Frequency
ELF	Extremely Low Frequency
EMP	Electromagnetic Pulse
EMT	Equivalent Megatonnage
EOKA	*Ethniki Organoziz Kypriakou Agoniston* (Cyprus)
ET	Emerging Technologies
EW	Electronic Warfare
FBM	Fleet Ballistic Missile Submarine
FEBA	Forward Edge of the Battle Area
FLN	*Front de Liberation Nationale* (Algeria)
FLNKS	*Front de Libération Nationale Kanak et Socialist* (New Caledonia)
FLTSATCOM	US Navy Fleet Satellite Communications
FOFA	Follow-On Forces Attack
FULK	*Front Uni de Libération Kanak* (New Caledonia)
FY	Fiscal Year
FYDP	Five Year Defence Program (Australia)

GAF	Government Aircraft Factory
GDP	Gross Domestic Product
GNP	Gross National Product
GPS	Global Positioning Satellite (US)
GWEN	Ground Wave Emergency Network
HQADF	Headquarters, Australian Defence Force
HUMINT	Human Intelligence
IAEA	International Atomic Energy Agency
ICBM	Intercontinental Ballistic Missile
ICP	Indochinese Communist Party
ICRC	International Committee of the Red Cross
IDC	Inter-Departmental Committee (Australia)
INF	Intermediate-range Nuclear Forces
IRA	Irish Republican Army
IRBM	Intermediate-Range Ballistic Missile
JCS	Joint Chiefs of Staff (US)
JGGRS	Joint Geological and Geophysical Research Station (Alice Springs, Australia)
JIO	Joint Intelligence Organisation (Australia)
JMOP	Joint Military Operations and Plans (Australia)
JSTPS	Joint Strategic Target Planning Staff (US)
KOPASSANDHA	Army para-commando unit (formerly RPKAD)
KOPKAMBIT	*Komando Operasi Pemulihan Keamanan dan Ketertiban* (Operational Command for the Restoration of Security and Order)
KOSTRAD	*Komando Cadangan Strategis Angkatan Darat* (Army Strategic Reserve Command)
KPNLF	Khmer People's National Liberation Front
KPRP	Kampuchean People's Revolutionary Party
LCCs	Launch Command Centres
LFs	Launch Facilities
LNOs	Limited Nuclear Options
LOW	Launch on Warning
LPAR	Large Phased Array Radar
LPRP	Lao People's Revolutionary Party
LTBT	Limited Test Ban Treaty
LUA	Launch Under Attack
MAOs	Major Attack Options
MAP	Mutual Assistance Programme (New Zealand)
MARSAR	1977 ANZUS Australian Maritime Surveillance Area
MBFR	Mutual and Balanced Force Reduction Talks
MCP	Mobile Command Post
MDs	Soviet Military Districts

MGT	Mobile Ground Terminal
MICV	Mechanised Infantry Combat Vehicle
MILSTAR	Military Strategic and Tactical Relay
MIRV	Multi, Independent Re-Entry Vehicle
MLRS	Multiple-Launched Rocket System
MOLINK	Moscow-Washington Link ('Hot Line')
MoU	Memorandum of Understanding
MR	Military Region
MRL	Materials Research Laboratories
MT	Megaton
MX ICBM	Missile Experimental Intercontinental Ballistic Missile
NATO	North Atlantic Treaty Organisation
NCA	National Command Authorities
NDU	National Defence University
NGOs	Non-Governmental Organisations
NIE	National Intelligence Estimate (US)
NORAD	North American Air Defense Command
NORCOM	Northern Command
NPD	Non-Provocative Defence
NPT	Nuclear Non-Proliferation Treaty
NSC	National Security Council (US)
NSDD	National Security Decision Directive (US)
NSDM	National Security Decision Memorandum (US)
NSSM	National Security Study Memorandum (US)
NSTL	National Strategic Target List
NTPR	Nuclear Targeting Policy Review (US)
NUWEP	Nuclear Weapons Employment Policy (US)
NWEAMP	Nuclear Weapons Employment and Acquisition Master Plan (US)
NZDF	New Zealand Defence Forces
OMB	Office of Management and Budget (US)
OMG	Operational Manoeuvre Group (USSR)
OMT	Other Military Targets
ONA	Office of National Assessments (Australia)
OPM	*Organisasi Papua Merdeka* (PNG)
OTH	Over the Horizon Radar
OTVDs	Soviet Theatres of Military Operations
PD	Presidential Directive (US)
Penaids	Penetration aids
PGMs	Precision-Guided Munitions
PLA	(China's) People's Liberation Army
PLB	Personal locator beacon
PLO	Palestine Liberation Organisation

PNG	Papua New Guinea
PPBP	Pacific Patrol Boat Program
PPBS	Planning, Programming and Budgeting System
PRK	People's Republic of Kampuchea
PRM	Presidential Review Memorandum (US)
R&D	Research and Development
RIMPAC	Rim Pacific
RISOP	Russian Integrated Strategic Operational Plan
RNOs	Regional Nuclear Options
RNZAF	Royal New Zealand Air Force
RNZN	Royal New Zealand Navy
ROE	Rules of Engagement
RPKAD	Army para-commando unit, now known as KOPASSANDHA
RPCR	*Rassemblement pour la République*
RS-70	Supersonic Reconnaissance Strike Bomber (US)
RSL	Returned Services League
RT	Relocatable Target
SAC	Strategic Air Command (US)
SACEUR	Supreme Allied Commander Europe (NATO)
SALT	Strategic Arms Limitation Treaty
SAM	Surface-to-Air Missile
SAMOS	Satellite and Missile Observation System (US)
SAOs	Selective Attack Options
SAS	Special Air Service Regiment
SCC	Standing Consultative Commission
SDI	Strategic Defense Initiative (US)
SDS	Satellite Data System (US)
SICBM	Small Intercontinental Ballistic Missile
SIGINT	Signals Intelligence
SIOP	Single Integrated Operational Plan (US)
SLBM	Sea-Launched Ballistic Missile
SLCM	Sea-launched Cruise Missile
SNDV	Strategic Nuclear Delivery Vehicle
SPEC	South Pacific Bureau for Economic Cooperation (renamed the South Pacific Forum Secretariat)
SPNFZ	South Pacific Nuclear-Free Zone
SRAM	Short-range attack missile
SRF	Strategic Reserve Force (US)
SSBN	Nuclear ballistic missile submarine
SSN	Nuclear-powered attack submarine
START	Strategic Arms Reduction Talks
TERCOM	Terrain Contour Matching (US)

TTBT	Threshold Test Ban Treaty
TVD	*Teatr Voyennyhk Deystviy* -
	Soviet Theatre of Military Operations
UN	United Nations
USD(P)	Under Secretary of Defense for Policy (US)
VCDF	Vice Chief of the Defence Force (Australia post-1987)
VCP	Vietnamese Communist Party
VPA	Vietnamese People's Army
VSNKh	Soviet Supreme Council of the National Economy
V/STOL	Vertical/Short Take-off and/or Landing Aircraft
VTOL	Vertical Take-off and Landing Aircraft
VWP	Vietnam Workers' Party
WSEG	Weapons Systems Evaluation Group (US)
WTO	Warsaw Treaty Organisation
WWMCCS	World-Wide Military Command and Control System (US)

NOTES ON CONTRIBUTORS

PROFESSOR HENRY ALBINSKI is Professor of Political Science and Director of the Australia-New Zealand Studies Centre at Pennsylvania State University. He has held visiting appointments at the Australian National University, University of Western Ontario, University of Queensland, University of Sydney, Flinders University, University of Melbourne and most recently (1988-89) at the Australian Defence Force Academy. Professor Albinski has published a dozen books and major monographs and nearly 100 book chapters, journal articles and specially commissioned studies. Among his recent works are: *ANZUS, The United States and Pacific Security* (University Press of America for the Asia Society, Lanham MD, 1987); *The Australian-American Security Relationship* (University of Queensland Press, St. Lucia/St. Martin's Press, New York, 1982); and *Australian External Policy Under Labor* (University of Queensland Press, St. Lucia/University of British Columbia Press, Vancouver, 1977). He is presently completing a book length study on American and Australian comparisons and relationships.

PROFESSOR DESMOND BALL is Head of the Strategic and Defence Studies Centre, Research School of Pacific Studies of the Australian National University. He has previously been a Lecturer in International Relations and Military Politics in the Department of Government at the University of Sydney, a Research Fellow in the Center for International Affairs at Harvard University, and a Research Associate at the International Institute for Strategic Studies in London. He is the author of more than 140 academic monographs and articles on nuclear strategy, nuclear weapons, national security decision-making, and Australia's defence policy. His major books include: *Pine Gap: Australia and the US Geostationary Signals Intelligence Satellite Program* (Allen & Unwin, Sydney, 1988); *A Base for Debate: The US Satellite Station at Nurrungar* (Allen & Unwin, Sydney, London and Boston, 1987); *A Suitable Piece of Real Estate: American Installations in Australia* (Hale & Iremonger, Sydney, 1980); and *Politics and Force Levels: The Strategic Missile Program of the Kennedy Administration* (University of California Press, Berkeley, 1980).

DR ROSS BABBAGE is Deputy Head of the Strategic and Defence Studies Centre, Research School of Pacific Studies of the Australian National University. He has held several senior positions in the Australian Public Service, including Head of Strategic Analysis in the Office of National Assessments. He has also led the ANZUS and UN and Force Development Branches in the Department of Defence. He has written extensively on Australian and Pacific Security issues, being author of *Rethinking Australia's Defence* (University of Queensland Press, St. Lucia, 1980) and *Should Australia Plan to Defend Christmas and Cocos Islands?* (Strategic and Defence Studies Centre, Canberra, 1988). He is also editor of *The Soviets in the Pacific in the 1990s* (Pergamon Brassey's, Rushcutters Bay, 1989) and joint editor of *Geographic Information Systems: Defence Applications* (Pergamon Brassey's, Rushcutters Bay, forthcoming). Dr Babbage is completing a book entitled *A Coast Too Long: Planning the Defence of Australia.*

THE HONOURABLE KIM C. BEAZLEY, MP, has been the Minister of State for Defence since December 1984. He is also the current Leader of the House of Representatives. He has served in Parliament since 1980, when he won the Perth seat of Swan. Mr Beazley also served as Special Minister of State from July 1983 until January 1984. He holds Master's degrees from the Universities of Western Australia and Oxford, where he studied as a Rhodes Scholar from 1973 to 1976. He later co-authored the book, *Politics of Intrusion: The Super Powers and the Indian Ocean* (Alternative Publishing Cooperative, Sydney, 1979).

DR CORAL BELL received her Bachelor of Arts and Master of Science degrees from the University of Sydney and her doctorate from the University of London. She was formerly Professor of International Relations in the University of Sussex, and more recently Senior Research Fellow in the Department of International Relations, Australian National University. Her latest book is *Dependent Ally: A Study in Australian Foreign Policy* (Oxford University Press, Melbourne, 1988).

MR FREDERICK BENNETT AM, received his Bachelor of Economics Degree from Sydney University before gaining 10 years experience in the private sector in the petroleum, chemical, timber and transport industries He then joined the Australian Public Service. He has worked for 30 years in the interface between the Australian Government and industry; 15 years as a statistician, economist and programmer with the Australian Bureau of Statistics; 10 years as an industrial economist, policy adviser and trade negotiator with the Department of Industry and Commerce; and 6 years in charge of capital equipment procurement and defence industry policy in the Department of Defence; between 1972 and 1989 in the Senior Executive Service and from 1977 as a Deputy Secretary. In 1988, he was a Visiting Fellow at the Australian National University's Strategic and Defence Studies Centre. He is a Fellow of the Australian Institute of Management, Member of the Economic Society of

Australia, the Australian Institute of Project Management and the Society of Logistics Engineers.

MR ANTHONY BERGIN graduated with a BA and LLB from Monash University and completed an MA at the Australian National University. He worked as a Legislative Research Specialist in the Foreign Affairs Group of the Legislative Research Service from 1980 to 1981, and then became a lecturer at the Royal Australian Naval College at Jervis Bay. When the academic functions of the Naval College were taken over by the Australian Defence Force Academy in 1986, he joined the staff of the Department of Politics at the Academy. His main fields of interest are the law of the sea, marine policy and ocean management, and international relations. He is managing editor of *Maritime Studies*.

MR GARY BROWN has worked as a defence and national security analyst in Parliament House, Canberra, since 1973. He is the author of a number of journal articles and Strategic and Defence Studies Centre Working Papers on topics including higher defence organisation, nuclear weapons detection, the Australian aircraft carrier debate and the Defence Force in industrial action situations. As a Visiting Fellow at the Strategic and Defence Centre in 1988 he wrote an extended study of the Australian-American alliance entitled *Breaking the American Alliance: An Independent National Security Policy for Australia* (Strategic and Defence Studies Centre, Canberra, 1989).

MR GRAEME CHEESEMAN is a Senior Research Fellow at the Peace Research Centre, Research School of Pacific Studies of the Australian National University. He was previously the Defence Adviser to the Parliamentary Joint Committee on Foreign Affairs and Defence where he was primarily responsible for preparing the Committee's reports on *The Australian Defence Force: Its Structure and Capabilities* (1984), *Disarmament and Arms Control in the Nuclear Age* (1986), and *The Management of Australia's Defence* (1987). His present research interests centre on the Australian arms trade and alternative defence strategies and their application to Australia's defence.

MR HAROLD CROUCH is a Senior Research Fellow in the Department of Political and Social Change, Research School of Pacific Studies of the Australian National University, on leave from the Department of Political Science, National University of Malaysia, where he has taught since 1975. He taught political science at the University of Indonesia between 1968 and 1971 and the University of the Philippines in 1983-84. He is the author of *The Army and Politics in Indonesia* (Cornell University

Press, Ithaca, 1978), and co-editor of *Military-Civilian Relations in South-East Asia* (Oxford University Press, Singapore, 1985). He is also the author of *Trade Unions and Politics in India* (Manaktalas, Bombay, 1966) and co-editor of *Malaysian Politics and the 1978 Election* (Oxford University Press, Kuala Lumpur, 1980). His main current interest is in the politics of economic development in Southeast Asia.

DR CATHY DOWNES is a Research Fellow in the Strategic and Defence Studies Centre, Research School of Pacific Studies of the Australian National University. Dr Downes has held appointments as a John M. Olin Fellow at Harvard University's Center for International Affairs and as a University Research Fellow at the University of Melbourne. Her research interests include Military Manpower and Personnel Management, Military Professionalism and Leadership, Defence Decision-Making and Officer Education and Training. Her publications include *Special Trust and Confidence: The Making of an Officer*, (Frank Cass, London, 1980), *High Personnel Turnover: The Australian Defence Force is Not a Limited Liability Company* (Strategic and Defence Studies Centre, Canberra, 1988), *Senior Officer Professional Development - Constant Study to Prepare* (Strategic and Defence Studies Centre, Canberra, 1989), and *Military Manpower - Military Effectiveness* (Macmillan Press, London, forthcoming, 1990). Dr Downes is a Fellow of the British 21st Century Trust and the Inter-University Seminar on Armed Forces and Society.

AIR MARSHAL R.G. FUNNELL AO joined the RAAF in 1953 and graduated from the RAAF College as a pilot in 1956. After attending the RAAF Staff College in 1967, he served in a series of staff positions in the Department of Air and on exchange with the USAF. In 1971-72 he attended the USAF Air War College and, on his return to Australia, commanded No. 6 Squadron at Amberley, Queensland. Since 1975, Air Marshal Funnell has held several senior staff positions, including Head of Military Project Staff, Australian Defence Force Academy Project; Chief of Staff, Headquarters RAAF Operational Command; and Chief of Air Force Operations and Plans. He was appointed Assistant Chief of the Defence Force (Policy) in Headquarters Australian Defence Force, Canberra in April 1985. He was promoted to the rank of Air Marshal and assumed the post of Vice Chief of the Defence Force in June 1986. He was appointed Chief of the Air Staff in July 1987. Air Marshal Funnell is a graduate of the Royal College of Defence Studies, London and holds a Masters Degree in Political Science and a Graduate Diploma in Administration.

MR DAVID HEGARTY is a Senior Research Fellow in the Strategic and Defence Studies Centre at the Australian National University. In the 1970s he lectured in Political Studies at the University of Papua New Guinea, then in the early 1980s became a senior analyst in the Office of National Assessments working on South Pacific political and strategic affairs. He edited *Electoral Politics in Papua New Guinea: Studies on the 1977 National Election* (University of Papua New Guinea Press, Port Moresby, 1983), and has written extensively on security issues in the South Pacific with a book, *South Pacific Security*, currently in preparation.

MR GARY KLINTWORTH is a Senior Research Fellow in the North East Asia Program, Research School of Pacific Studies of the Australian National University. In 1986-87 he was a Defence Fellow at the Strategic and Defence Studies Centre. He previously worked as a Strategic Analyst in the Joint Intelligence Organisation and specialised in developments in North East Asia and Indochina. He has recently completed a study of Vietnam's involvement in Cambodia entitled *Vietnam's Intervention in Cambodia in International Law* (Australian Government Publishing Service, Canberra, 1989).

DR GREGORY LOCKHART is a Research Fellow in the Department of Pacific and Southeast Asian History, Research School of Pacific Studies of the Australian National University. He is a graduate of the Royal Military College Duntroon and the University of Sydney. As an Army officer he served in Papua New Guinea and Vietnam, and as a scholar he has worked as a school teacher and a university lecturer. His main interests span Southeast Asian and Australian history, and he has been revising his doctoral dissertation for publication with Oxford University Press (East Asia) under the title *The Origins of the People's Army of Vietnam*.

MR GEOFFREY JUKES is a Senior Fellow in the Department of International Relations, Research School of Pacific Studies of the Australian National University. After graduating from Oxford he joined the UK Foreign Office (1953-56), then the Ministry of Defence (1956-65) and finally the Arms Control and Disarmament Research Unit of the Foreign and Colonial Office from 1965 until appointment to his present post in 1967. He has worked primarily in the areas of Soviet defence and foreign policy, especially in relation to the Indo-Pacific region, and Russian and Soviet military history, particularly the two World Wars and the military intervention in Afghanistan, and has a number of publications in these fields. He is currently engaged in research into the scope and likely impact of the new emphasis on the Pacific region in

Soviet foreign policy, the recently-announced changes in Soviet military doctrine, the Soviet military career structure, and the re-evaluation of Stalin's war leadership.

MR ANDREW MACK has lectured in sociology at the London School of Economics, and worked as a Producer on the international current affairs programme 'The World Today' of the BBC World Service. In 1972, he was appointed as Research Director at the Richardson Institute for Conflict and Peace Research, and in 1975 as Lecturer in International Politics at Flinders University, South Australia. In 1984, he joined the Strategic and Defence Studies Centre of Australian National University as a Senior Research Fellow (Arms Control, Disarmament and Peace Research), before being appointed at the end of that year as the Head of the newly established Peace Research Centre. Mr Mack is the co-editor (with Desmond Ball) of *The Future of Arms Control* (Pergamon Press, Sydney, 1987), co-editor of *Imperialism, Intervention and Development* (Croom Helm, London, 1979), co-editor of *Israel and Palestinians* (Ithaca Press, London, 1975) and co-author (with Anders Boserup) of *War Without Weapons: Non-Violence in National Defence* (Frances Pinter Publishers, London, 1974).

MR JAMES RICHARDSON is a Professorial Fellow in the Department of International Relations, Research School of Pacific Studies of the Australian National University. He was educated at the Universities of Sydney and Oxford, and has held fellowships at Harvard University's Center for International Affairs, and Balliol College, Oxford. Mr Richardson joined the British Foreign Office's Arms Control and Disarmament Research Unit in 1965. In 1967, he returned to Australia to take up an appointment as Lecturer in the Department of Government at the University of Sydney. In 1975, he was appointed Professor of Political Science in the Faculty of Arts of the Australian National University, and in 1985 joined the Department of International Relations in the Research School of Pacific Studies. His major research interests include international crisis diplomacy, great power relations in international relations, US foreign policy and arms control and Australia's foreign relations. His published works include *Germany and the Atlantic Alliance* (Harvard University Press, Cambridge Mass., 1966).

DR HUGH SMITH is Senior Lecturer in the Department of Politics, University College, University of New South Wales at the Australian Defence Force Academy where he teaches courses on international relations and on legal and moral problems of international violence. He has written a wide range of articles on defence, foreign policy and military affairs and has been Convenor of the Australian Study Group on Armed Forces and Society since 1977. Dr Smith is also Director of the recently established Australian Defence Studies Centre at the University College.

DR CARLYLE THAYER is a Senior Lecturer in the Department of Politics, University College, Australian Defence Force Academy in Canberra. Dr Thayer was educated at Brown University and holds an MA in Southeast Asian Studies from Yale and a PhD in International Relations from The Australian National University. Before joining the staff at the Defence Academy, Dr Thayer taught at the Royal Military College, Duntroon (1979-85). He has held visiting fellowships at the ANU's Strategic and Defence Studies Centre, Harvard's Center for International Affairs, Yale University, the Institute for Security and International Studies at Chulalongkorn University, and at the Institute of Southeast Asian Studies in Singapore. Dr Thayer has written widely on the domestic and foreign policies of the three Indochinese states. His most recent publications include (with Ramesh Thakur) *The Soviet Union as an Asian-Pacific Power: Implications of Gorbachev's 1986 Vladivostock Speech* (Westview Press, Boulder Colorado, 1987), and *War by Other Means: National Liberation and Revolution in Vietnam* (Allen & Unwin, Sydney, 1989).

Dr GRANT WARDLAW is a Senior Criminologist with the Australian Institute of Criminology in Canberra. He is a specialist on terrorism, special warfare, public order and drug law enforcement. Dr Wardlaw has lectured regularly at universities and military academies in a number of countries and during 1988 was a Visiting Scholar at the US Defense Intelligence College, Washington DC. He is the author of *Political Terrorism* (Cambridge University Press, Cambridge, 1982) and other books, chapters, and articles in his areas of interest.

MR THOMAS-DURRELL YOUNG is a National Security Analyst in the Strategic Studies Institute of the US Army War College, having recently completed his PhD in International Relations in the Programme for Strategic and International Security Studies at the Graduate Institute of International Studies, University of Geneva, Switzerland. He holds a BA from California State University, Long Beach, an MA from the School of Advanced International Studies of the Johns Hopkins University, and a Certificat d'études supérieures es sciences politiques (études internationales) from the Graduate Institute of International Studies. His publications include more than twenty articles on antipodean defence issues. His dissertation is entitled 'An Analysis of, and Commentary on, the Australian, New Zealand and United States Defence Relationship, 1951-1986'.

FOREWORD

It is now widely understood that defence planning in Australia must be based on a coherent national strategy. It is also widely understood that such a national strategy cannot be defined in a political and economic vacuum. Strategy which cannot combine the wider objective reality with a high level of political perception is doomed to be shortlived as a basis of defence planning.

It is less well understood that although Australia's security environment is unique, unique solutions to the strategic problems are unlikely to be found by minds which are not well grounded in strategic concepts, military histories and nations' strategic perspectives even though at first sight such experiences may not seem wholly relevant.

Nevertheless the problem for those in the defence community is that increasingly their contribution to the debate on the defence of this nation will be grounded not simply on professional excellence in their particular field but on their understanding of the broad aspects of defence planning. They have before them the military example of those outstanding staff officers of the 1920s and 1930s who broke their hearts and reputations trying to convince their political masters that the national strategy (based as it was on the strategies of other nations and other particular circumstances) was flawed; and that consequently the nation's defence planning could well produce the nation's destruction.

The task now is not to convince political masters that they require a national strategy. The task is to provide advice which clearly posits strategic concepts in the political and economic milieu in which policy is developed.

This book is very much a handbook of Australian national strategy. Its authors and in particular its editors are names well known for their contribution in recent years to a lively and sophisticated debate of defence issues in this country. At a time when defence issues have not appeared as a high priority on the national agenda we have been well served by an unwillingness on the part of the academic community to let the debate lapse into a torpor which would have deprived those with formal responsibility for defence planning of the essential underpinning of public support.

For students of Australian defence issues this product of that intellectual ferment provides a great deal. It provides background on the strategies which underpin the policies of the powers which dominate the central balance. It introduces the student to analyses of strategies and technological developments which, while not specific to our immediate environment, impact upon it. The book deals with unconventional strategy. It provides essential background to the components of Australian national strategy and defence planning. It situates the product of the latter in a regional setting.

Despite the fact that the authors necessarily paint a broad canvas, this book will nevertheless prove useful in developing the unique solutions that our unique strategic circumstances require. It arrives in the midst of great upheaval in the central balance. Perspectives based solely on anticipated outcomes in the central balance may blind us to the continuing realities of the region in which we live. Despite vigorous efforts in the past to define international events in our region as a result of the competition of the superpowers, reality has always crept through. If we are to maintain an appropriate approach to our circumstances it needs to keep creeping through.

The book has brought together the wider political, strategic, and economic environment in which defence planning must occur. As such it is a major contribution to the Australian defence debate.

Kim C. Beazley
January 1990

PREFACE

Australia's security and defence circumstances are unique. Australia is far from the central areas of superpower contention, yet it is nevertheless closely and formally allied to the leading superpower and hosts critical US strategic command and control facilities on its territory. Australia is geographically adjacent to the most economically dynamic region of the world, but in no significant economic, political or cultural dimension is it part of it. East Asia, Southeast Asia and the Southwest Pacific are very much regions with their own security sensitivities and vulnerabilities - which Australia must understand yet can influence only rarely and selectively. Australians occupy small fringes of the largest island continent in the world, but have yet to come to grips with designing and establishing a national security policy for securing the country.

Those who are involved in the development of national security policy in Australia, those concerned with studying it, and those who are party to the more general public debate need to be informed about an increasing range of global political and economic developments, to be open-minded and far-sighted enough to comprehend both the negative and positive implications of those developments, and to appreciate Australia's unique strategic circumstances. There is much to be learnt from overseas thought and experience - whether it be the writings of the classical strategists such as Clausewitz, the role of arms control in enhancing global stability, or regional cooperation among the ASEAN countries. Australia can neglect overseas security perspectives and developments no more than it can afford to neglect overseas economic, political, social and cultural developments. We are not suited to isolationism. On the other hand, to fully understand and exploit our unique strategic circumstances, our arguments and policy frameworks must be home-grown.

Until the publication of *Strategy & Defence: Australian Essays* by George Allen & Unwin Australia in 1982, there was no single text or collection of readings, written from an Australian perspective or addressing issues of Australian concern, which was available for people interested in national security. That volume was intended to fill that gap. As Admiral Sir Anthony Synnot, then the Chief of Defence Force Staff, noted in his Foreword:

> It is only now that a wide-ranging group of essays dealing with various aspects of Australian strategy is being brought together in one volume....

> They are by Australian academics prominent in the
> fields of international relations, military strategy and defence
> policy.... I commend this volume to all who are interested in
> the security of Australia and its interests.

This new edition builds upon this commendation. It retains an
unabashed Australian perspective, but it adopts a broader approach to
the concepts of strategy and security.

The factors involved in national security are myriad and wide-
ranging. Indeed, the very concept of security has broadened in scope
throughout the 1980s. Military capabilities by themselves are less
relevant as compared to economic, social and even environmental
considerations. Australia has also become more aware of its strategic
interests in the region - whether it be the maintenance of sustained rapid
economic growth in Northeast Asia, peace in Cambodia, or political
stability in Papua New Guinea and the Southwest Pacific.

The implementation of Australia's defence policy of greater self-
reliance has also raised new issues for policy-making and public debate.
Although the basic concepts for planning the defence of Australia have.
been fairly clearly articulated,[1] and their broad thrusts generally
accepted within the defence community, there nevertheless remain
important points of contention. What is the relationship between
greater self-reliance and maintenance of the US connection? Should
Australia withdraw from ANZUS? Are regional defence contingencies
more probable than those directly involving Australian territory? Is the
Australian defence posture too defensive, or, on the other hand, might
not some Australian policies and programs contribute to heightened
suspicion and increased arms acquisition in the region - and hence
diminish Australia's security? Are Australia's security and defence
decision-making processes properly structured for designing a viable
posture for the defence of Australia?

These issues cannot be adequately addressed without lively and
informed public debate. Australian defence policy is inevitably affected
by developments in the civil sector - whether it be the social causes of
officer dissatisfaction and resignation or aspects of State Emergency
Service legislation. Indeed, given Australia's enormous size yet limited
economic and population resources, a self-reliant posture for the defence
of Australia has to be a national effort requiring broad public support
and participation. This can only be achieved through informed public
debate.

---

[1]   See Paul Dibb, *Review of Australia's Defence Capabilities*, (Australian Government
Publishing Service, Canberra, 1986); and Kim C. Beazley, Minister for Defence, *The
Defence of Australia 1987*, (A White Paper presented to Parliament on 19 March 1987),
(Australian Government Publishing Service, Canberra, 1987).

This volume is intended to serve that debate. It is designed as a handbook for students - at Australian military staff colleges as well as at universities - and for those more generally interested in security and defence matters.

Part I provides a comprehensive coverage of general strategic concepts and issues. It includes discussion of the classical European strategists and their work, developments in Soviet and US strategic policies since 1945, the future of the global strategic balance, trends in conventional warfare and technologies, revolutionary war and political terrorism, the strategy of non-provocative defence, and arms control.

Part II is concerned with selected issues in Australian defence policy. These include the strategic options available to Australian defence planners, the arguments for and against the ANZUS alliance and the US connection more generally, the adequacy of the Australian defence policy-making structure, legal aspects of the employment of the Australian Defence Force, personnel issues, the role of Australian science and industry, and the place of the Defence Force in Australian society.

Part III discusses security developments in the region. It includes specific discussion of recent developments in New Zealand's security and defence policies, of developments in China, Indonesia, Papua New Guinea and the Southwest Pacific, and of the interests and policies of the superpowers with respect to the region.

Notwithstanding the comprehensive coverage of this volume, no single book can provide the last word on the subject. The issues involved in security and defence are too myriad and too complex, and they are continually evolving. People wishing to be involved in the public debate on these issues must read further afield - and think critically about this reading. The extensive bibliography prepared for this volume is designed to guide this further reading and thought.

The preparation of this volume was heavily dependent upon the skills of Mrs Elza Sullivan, a member of the support staff of the Strategic and Defence Studies Centre. Mrs Sullivan prepared the typescript for submission to the publisher, and carried many of the editorial burdens which ought more properly to have been our own. We are very grateful to her.

Desmond Ball and Cathy Downes
Strategic and Defence Studies Centre
Australian National University
Canberra
December 1989.

STRATEGIC CONCEPTS

CHAPTER 1

INTRODUCTION TO STRATEGIC THINKING

Air Marshal R.G. Funnell AO

The aim of this chapter is to introduce readers to strategic thinking, how strategic thought has developed, particularly over the last two centuries, and how individual thinking on strategy and related subjects can be developed. The word 'strategy' has come to be used widely in a diffused sense to indicate a general plan to achieve a specified or assumed objective. We hear of marketing strategies, campaign strategies, match strategies and the like. However, here strategy is brought from its derivation in ancient Greek - *strategos* meaning a general - into the modern era and defined simply as the art of high military command. This can, in turn, be defined as the art of planning and directing the operations of major military forces. The Australian Joint Service definition of military strategy is that it is 'the art and science of employing the armed forces of a nation to secure the objectives of national policy by the application of force, or the threat of force'. In the modern era that art and science are not and cannot be the province solely of military commanders. As Earle observes:

> In the present-day world, strategy is the art of controlling and utilising the resources of a nation - or a coalition of nations - including its armed forces to the end that its vital interests shall be effectively promoted and secured against enemies, actual, potential or merely presumed...The highest type of strategy - sometimes called grand strategy - is that which so integrates the policies and armaments of the nation that the resort to war is either rendered unnecessary or is undertaken with the maximum chance of victory.[1]

A second definitional issue needs to be addressed. The difference between tactics and strategy should be made explicit. The traditional differentiation has been that military strategy encompasses military planning and manoeuvre until such time as combat begins at which time tactics take over. However, in recent times, a different and more useful categorization has been increasingly used which separates conflict into three levels - strategic, operational and tactical. The strategic is concerned with the employment of all of a nation's armed forces in the larger totality of a nation's security, foreign and domestic policies; the operational with the employment of forces in a campaign; and the tactical with forces actually in contact with the opponent.

This categorization of conflict warrants further explanation. The tactical level is the level at which combat is actually joined. It is also the area which is very definitely the province of the military. It is impossible for anyone who has not been trained for, and participated at, that level of military art to truly appreciate what occurs there. Moreover, no matter how detailed and deep a person's studies might be, unless that person has actually participated in air combat, for example, it can be argued that it is impossible to develop a full expertise in this extremely complicated aspect of warfare. In like fashion, it is impossible except for those who have been involved - as full participants - in land and naval warfare, at the tactical level, to be expert in those aspects of warfare. At the strategic level of war, in contrast, people outside the military profession can, and do, develop real expertise in strategic matters. It may even be that people, other than military personnel, are likely to be most expert at this level of war due to their background, experience and training. It is not necessarily the case that military members cannot or should not attempt to be experts at the strategic level of war. It is merely to say that it may be easier for others to achieve the necessary level of expertise .

The key level of strategy for most military professionals is that between the tactical and strategic, namely, the operational level of war. In this area resides the essence of military art and science. Expertise at the operational level of war should be the aim of every career military officer, for it is the operational level of war which both guides tactics and informs strategy. At the operational level, the strategist needs to be able to see clearly that which is necessary and feasible in strategic terms and translate it into that which is necessary and feasible in tactical terms. Consequently, one needs to have a deep appreciation of military equipment, military personnel, military psychology and military history. To be effective at this level, one's view must have the perspective that comes from deep knowledge of this broad range of subjects.

In the study of strategy and strategy-making, it can be asserted that strategy at a national level does not predate the existence of nations and that the nation-state system is a product of the 15th and 16th centuries. For example, Martin van Creveld in *Command in War* asserts that 'strategy in the sense that Napoleon, Jomini and Clausewitz made classic hardly existed before their time'.[2] Van Creveld's point recognises the fact that, before Napoleon, the technology to exercise strategic command had not been developed. With limited knowledge of the strength and disposition of the enemy's forces and limited knowledge of the disposition and perhaps the strength of one's own, commanders found great difficulty in deploying and employing forces strategically to achieve their objectives. Politicians, for their part, were able to operate at a grand strategic level but, for the military commander, the application of strategy was beyond the technical means available to him. O'Neill has remarked that 'the strategy we read of in connection with the wars of the Greeks and Romans is little more than grand tactics' and that until the Napoleonic period 'writing and discussion [on strategy] had been intuitive and conducted at a relatively low level of scholarly analysis'.3 It is interesting to note that strategy, in the way it is used today, was first defined in the Oxford Dictionary in 1825, that is in the immediate post-Napoleonic era.4

The Napoleonic Wars provided the background to, and in most respects, the very medium by which strategic thought developed throughout the 19th century. Moreover, the spill-over into this century has been considerable. Indeed, there can be little doubt that Napoleon's genius at the strategic and operational levels of war was a major catalyst for the development of modern strategic thinking. His two most influential interpreters were Jomini and Clausewitz and, because so much of today's thinking is based on their work, this chapter dwells on their efforts at some length.

General Antoine Henri Jomini was born in Switzerland in 1779. After organising battalions in the Swiss Army, his early writings on tactics brought him to the attention of the French and he was appointed aide-de-camp to Marshal Ney whom he accompanied on the Jena and Eylau campaigns and to Spain. After a period as director of the historical section of the French General Staff, he participated in the Russian Campaign of 1812, acting as Ney's Chief of Staff. After failing to receive promotion, he crossed the lines and served as a Lieutenant General in the Russian Army. After the war, he became military tutor to the Russian Imperial Family and helped to found the Military Academy in Moscow in 1832. He wrote widely after 1815 on both military history and strategy until his death in 1869. His most famous work was *Précis de l'Art de la Guerre* published in 1837.

General Carl Maria von Clausewitz, born in 1780, was a Prussian military officer who fought as a very young man against the French in the Revolutionary Wars. He became a disciple of Scharnhorst at the War College which Scharnhorst opened in 1801. He also participated in the campaign of 1806, fought for the Russians in the winter campaign of 1812 and again with the Prussians in the campaigns of the next three years, ultimately serving as Chief of Staff of an Army Corps in the lowlands operations which concluded at Waterloo in 1815. Subsequently, he became Director of the War College, a largely administrative post, but one which gave him the opportunity to think and write about war. His widow assembled his papers into the single work for which he is famous, *Vom Kriege* (*On War*), which was published a year after his sudden death from cholera in 1831.

In assessing the contributions of these two strategic thinkers and, indeed, the works of other writers on strategy, it is useful to have a set of criteria against which judgements can be based, knowledge ordered, and understanding enhanced. In his analysis of Clausewitz's *On War*, Michael Handel has used a framework of four questions which offer a useful structure for the study of the works of strategic thinkers:

1. How does the work reflect the spirit of a given time and its problems?

2. What is the theory (or theories) it advances to explain or solve specific contemporary problems?

3. How was the work interpreted in different periods and circumstances?

4. In what ways has the theory become obsolete?[5]

In relation to Handel's first question of how does the strategist's work reflect the spirit of a given time and its problems, it has already been observed in the case of both Jomini and Clausewitz that their writings were substantially a product of the time. Their analyses were essentially catalysed by political and social, as well as the strategic, changes brought about by the French Revolution and the subsequent Napoleonic Wars. Indeed, it has been argued, particularly in Clausewitz's case, that it is these very conditions of change which Clausewitz uses to develop a more explanatory theory of war as a social and political phenomenon. In contrast, in the writings of Jomini we find the quintessential response to the age of rational enquiry and scientific method of which he was surely a part. As Howard observes of Henry Lloyd whom he describes as a pioneer before the pioneering Jomini:

> Education, penology, law, political economy, agriculture, the applied sciences, in all these fields pioneers were working...to establish universally valid principles which would replace unthinking adherence to traditional patterns of behaviour as a guide to action. One human activity, however, still awaited its Montesquieu, its Newton.[6]

For Handel's second question, the advancement of theory or theories, again, it is possible to identify distinctive approaches taken by Clausewitz and Jomini. In rejecting the philosophy that man and societies were regulated by 'the dictates' of 'an omnipotent Deity transmitted through an ecclesiastical corporation',[7] Jomini joined a tradition of thought which recognised that man was part of a world whose operation was ordered by, and which could be explained through observation and critical analysis of, certain immutable and consistent laws of science. Therefore, the rationalists argued, man's activities should be just as regulated. Through the examination of the campaigns of Frederick the Great and Napoleon, Jomini sought to deduce a set of universally applicable principles which could be expected to pertain in future conflicts. From his analysis, he developed a number of maxims which he believed governed all operations of war, and which, if followed, offered the greatest chance of success, principal amongst which were:

1. To throw by strategic movements the mass of an army, successively, upon the decisive points of a theatre of war, and also upon the communications of the enemy as much as possible without compromising one's own.

2. To manoeuvre the engaged fractions of the hostile army with the bulk of one's forces.

3. On the battlefield, to throw the mass of the forces upon the decisive point, or upon that portion of the hostile line which it is of the first importance to overthrow.

4. To so arrange that these masses shall not only be thrown upon the decisive point, but that they shall engage at the proper times and with ample energy.[8]

Jomini went on to abstract a multitude of concepts which flowed from these maxims. For example, having identified that each opponent functions along a line of operations from their base, Jomini then defined a variety of such lines - concentric, eccentric, interior, exterior - depending upon geography and the disposition of the enemy.

If Jomini was more concerned with abstracting and ordering geographical and logistic evidence, Clausewitz was, in turn, more fascinated by war's moral and political features. While Jomini sought to abstract historical experience as a guide to the future, Clausewitz sought to explain reality by developing a theoretical ideal type of war. Having defined war as 'an act of violence intended to compel our opponent to fulfil our will', he argued that if taken to its logical conclusion, every war should result in total victory for one of the opponents. For Clausewitz, this was 'absolute war'.[9] In seeking to explain the difference between war in the abstract and war in reality, Clausewitz formulated a series of 'intervening variables', which Handel sees as some of his most creative concepts. To Clausewitz, wars were not carried to their logical extreme because of: (1) the political guidance which rationally relates ends to means in war; (2) the asymmetry of the superiority of the defence over the offence; (3) the lack of information as well as uncertainty and friction; (4) the tendency of human nature to make worst case assumptions about the enemy, and play it safe in the absence of clarity and sufficient information; (5) the fact that all military forces cannot be concentrated in space and time simultaneously; and (6) the fact that results in war are rarely final.[10]

Through these concepts and their development, Clausewitz identified and catalogued key characteristics of battle, for example, his notion of 'friction':

> Everything in war is very simple, but the simplest thing is very difficult. The difficulties accumulate and end by producing a kind of friction that is inconceivable unless one has experienced war...Countless minor incidents - the kind you can never really foresee - combine to lower the general level of performance, so that one always falls far short of the intended goal...the military machine...is basically very simple and therefore seems very easy to manage. But we should bear in mind that none of the components is of one piece: each part is composed of individuals, every one of whom retains his potential for friction...A battalion is made up of individuals, the least important of whom may chance to delay things and sometimes make them go wrong.[11]

In this observation, Clausewitz not only identifies the reality that even the most simple of natural or learned of human actions in war becomes difficult to perform, but he also alludes to the notion of uncertainty. It is an implicit recognition that the elements of accident, chance and human fallibilities and frailties exist in war which mock efforts to impose certainty upon the battlefield.

However, these insights on the nature of battle are subsumed in significance to Clausewitz's observations on the relationship between war and politics. In establishing a rationale for war ('The only source of war is politics'[12]), Clausewitz explores the rationality, as opposed to the functionality, of war:

> Clausewitz views war as a rational instrument of national policy. The three words 'rational', 'instrument' and 'national' are the key concepts of his paradigm. In this view, the decision to wage war 'ought' to be rational, in the sense that it ought to be based on estimated costs and gains of the war. Next, war 'ought' to be instrumental, in the sense that it ought to be waged in order to achieve some goal, never for its own sake; and also in the sense that strategy and tactics ought to be directed towards just one end, namely towards victory. Finally, war 'ought' to be national, in the sense that its objective should be to advance the

interests of a national state and that the entire effort of the nation ought to be mobilized in the service of the military objective.[13]

If Jomini can be described simplistically as an analyst, Clausewitz can be described as a philosopher. Jomini sought to understand war through simplifying and clarifying it; Clausewitz sought the essence of war and found that it was not simple and clear, but dark, mysterious, complex and dynamic. If doctrinally Jomini searched for answers, Clausewitz searched for a framework for asking the right questions. While making different contributions, the writings of both Jomini and Clausewitz have had a significant impact upon the development of strategic thought and even the conduct of war. How their works have been interpreted and applied in subsequent eras forms the third part of Handel's framework of analysis.

Jomini's teachings were by far the more influential in the period to 1870. Indeed, as a skilful polemicist and a diligent correspondent, and being blessed with longevity, he moulded the doctrines of the French, Prussian, British, Russian and American armies. In Clausewitz's case, an 1867 survey of military literature concluded that he was well-known but little read. Little has changed 120 years later. Shy, in his essay on Jomini, declares that 'if there can be such a thing as a joke in military history, surely a small one is the belief that...*On War* became the bible of the Prussian Army, the source of their great victories of 1866 and 1870, and soon thereafter the chief military theory of the Western world'.[14] In truth, Clausewitz was little read and little understood. Few German officers bothered to read *On War* from its publication in 1832 through to the Second World War. Clausewitz was influential, not through his writings, but through his key interpreters and, most significantly, not at the strategic, but at the operational and tactical levels of war.

Jomini's influence on the American military was due mainly to the efforts of Dennis Hart Mahan, Dean of the Faculty at the United States Military Academy, West Point. Although there is no direct evidence that Dennis Mahan had a similar effect on his son, there is no doubt that Alfred Thayer Mahan took Jomini to sea. The three major ingredients of Jomini's *Art of War* - the principle of concentration, the value of the central position and use of interior lines of operation, and the close relationship between logistics and operations - were adapted by Mahan the younger to form the framework of his own conceptions of maritime strategy.[15] Mahan was to become the prophet of sea power and naval strategy, and a man of great and continuing influence. Margaret Sprout contends that 'no other single person has so directly and profoundly influenced the theory of sea and naval strategy as Alfred Thayer Mahan'.[16] The remarks of Henry Stimson, US Secretary of War 1940-45, are often quoted and were palpably true: 'the peculiar psychology of the Navy Department...frequently seemed to retire from the realm of logic into a dim religious world in which Neptune was God, Mahan his prophet, and the United States Navy the only true Church'.[17]

Mahan's two great works, *The Influence of Sea Power upon History 1660-1783* and *The Influence of Sea Power upon the French Revolution and Empire, 1793-1812*, were published in 1890 and 1892 respectively. They constituted a naval history of Britain towards the end of the age of sail and set out to correct the fact that, until he wrote, 'the control of the sea was an historic factor which had never been systematically appreciated and expounded'.[18] His work is almost pure Jomini in that he sought to determine the fundamental truths of naval warfare 'which remain constant, and being therefore of universal application, can be elevated to the rank of general principles'.[19] Moreover, Mahan's teachings remain greatly influential in the contemporary era.

In the air too, Jomini had his disciples. His emphasis on rational enquiry and the elucidation of underlying principles seems to have found favour in those areas of warfare dominated by technology. The thinking of the American, Billy Mitchell, and the Englishman, Hugh Trenchard, are testaments to this. The seminal thinker on air power was the Italian, Giulio Douhet, who borrowed widely from Clausewitz, Jomini, Mahan and others, to develop the most coherent and systematic of the early writings on air power. In his major work, *The Command of the Air* (1921), he developed and postulated a number of General Principles of Aerial Warfare. This search for principles has been a continuing theme in air power doctrine to this day.

In contrast to Jomini, Clausewitz's influence has been less direct, although in some areas of military thought and action, and in some eras, it has been considerable. His most influential interpreter in the 19th century was General Helmuth von Moltke (the Elder), Chief of the German General Staff from 1857 to 1887 and victor over the Austrians in 1866 and the French in 1870. Moltke adapted Clausewitz's thinking to develop systems of command, organisation, training and operations which have served the German armed forces superbly from his day until this. He created the General Staff system and introduced the *Auftragstaktik* - a task oriented command system which decentralized authority to where the fighting was, but within a complete and widely-understood operational design. He recognized the revolution in warfare that was occurring through technological developments such as the telegraph, railroad and breech-loading weapons and adapted strategy to it.

Although Moltke explicitly endorsed Clausewitz's contention that the objective of military action was the achievement of a desired political result, in his writings and by his actions, one can see a blurring between strategy and operations. His belief that once war broke out the military became dominant in determining national policy reveals this confusion. The stormy relationship between Moltke and Bismarck during the 1870 War was a certain outcome of their widely differing views. Murray considers that:

> Moltke's writings clearly suggest confusion between strategy and operations. Indeed, Moltke may have emphasized the operational sphere of war (lying between strategy and tactics as defined by Clausewitz) in German military thought in order to exclude political interference from military operations.[20]

As far as Germany was concerned, the most unfortunate outcome of this emphasis was a virtual neglect of the strategic level of war. The German Army's approach to war at the levels of operations and tactics from the time of Moltke has been Clausewitzian. However, at the strategic level in the two World Wars, the Germans ignored him. Murray remarks that:

> The tragedy for Germany was that...slipshod thinking, passing all too often for strategy, helped launch the Second and Third Reichs on two great world wars that Germany had little prospect of winning. Ironically, the tactical and operational skills of the German officer corps then ensured that both wars would last almost to the point of destroying not only Germany but also western civilization. Clausewitz would not have been pleased with what his pupils had wrought.[21]

Murray also found that in contrast, the British and Americans had tended to concentrate on the political, the strategic and the logistic in warfare. Insulated by the sea from the land battle, they were predisposed to think in terms of the long haul. For the Prussians and then the Germans, war meant an immediate land battle and, if this was lost, then so too was the war. An interesting parallel with modern times is found in the Israeli Defence Force. Israel is in a similar situation and, therefore, it is probably not surprising that at the operational and tactical levels the Israelis are so similar to the Germans and so generally Clausewitzian. Unfortunately, too, they seem to have neglected Clausewitz in matters of strategy.

Clausewitz was also highly influential with the French, but once again their reading was unfortunately partial. The passages of *On War* which were most eagerly read were those where he emphasized moral factors in war and the relative insignificance of material elements.[22] Clausewitz's strictures which were neglected included those which referred to the power of the defensive. Indeed, Joffre, for example, emphasized the very opposite. This particular line of thinking reached its imbecilic high point in the words of de Grandmaison, the French Army's Director of Operations, who believed that 'we have...to cultivate with passion everything that bears the stamp of the offensive spirit. We must take it to excess: perhaps even that will not go far enough'.[23] In 1913, de Grandmaison drew up the Regulations for the Conduct of Major Formations which included the famous words: 'The French Army, returning to its traditions, recognizes no law save that of the offensive'.[24]

It would be a mistake to conclude that it was only through the French that the spirit of the offensive came to the fore in military thinking. Colmar von der Goltz and Friedrich von Bernhardi in Germany and Colonels Henderson and Maude in Britain, put a similar, if less extreme, stress on the value and power of the offensive.[25] Also it would be wrong to draw too direct a connection between the emphasis on the offensive and the tragic losses of The Great War. Howard points out that:

> ...the worst losses were those due not to faulty doctrine but to inefficiency, inexperience, and the sheer organizational problems of combining fire and movement on the requisite scale.[26]

However, critics of Clausewitz, particularly men such as Basil Liddell Hart, were to blame his influence for the carnage and horror of that monumental struggle. He was labelled the Mahdi of Mass, the Apostle of Violence, as his protagonists and critics alike distorted his aphorism to be strong in general and then at the decisive point. The almost joyful acceptance of casualties was not seen as a consequence of amoral military incompetence but of the moral strength and determination which Clausewitz required of commanders, and the resultant carnage was laid squarely at his feet. His most famous and much misunderstood teaching about the inter-relationship between war and national policy was seen in the liberal West as evidence of naked Teutonic militarism.

To return to Handel and his analysis of strategic thought, his final question addresses the issue of currency: whether the theory or theories advanced by the writer have withstood the test of time, or whether events have invalidated or superseded the theoretical propositions made. There is little doubt that warfare, as known to Clausewitz and Jomini, has been totally transformed in the twentieth century. Yet, in quite different ways, the writings of both strategic thinkers retain considerable value for the contemporary analyst.

Ironically, the work of Jomini, which had the broader influence in the 19th century and which sought to predict and prepare for future conflicts, has survived less well into this century. Arguably, Jomini sowed the seeds of his own obsolescence in his enthusiasm for immutable constants; that there are constants in war is not in dispute, but analysis reveals that those of significance are far fewer than thinkers in the Jominian stream contend. Jomini, like thinkers such as Marshal Maurice de Saxe, Henry Lloyd and Heinrich von Bulow before him, and Alfred von Schlieffen and Basil Liddell Hart after him, bound his observations by the belief that wars could be best understood and their course predicted, if their constants could be discovered and codified. However as van Creveld points out:

> In nature regularities...are assumed to be fixed and immutable. The same cause will always produce the same effect...War, though it does rest on certain regularities - a man struck by a given force at a given spot always dies, and a tank that has run out of fuel always stops - neither consists of these regularities nor always obeys the same ones...The form of war is very largely determined by the character, both individual and collective, of the people who wage it; by the instruments through which it is waged; the environment in which it is waged; and the circumstances under which it is waged.[27]

Thus, while the search for enduring maxims is perennial, and in this Jomini is as relevant today as in the early 19th century, the method, and most of the results it produces, must almost inevitably be fundamentally flawed, particularly at the strategic level of war.

It is evident that revolutionary and evolutionary changes in the political, economic, technological and social dimensions of war in the twentieth century have combined to narrow the relevance of Jomini's precepts. For example, Jomini placed battle at the centre of his strategic thinking and defined strategy as the art of the commander to determine where and how the battle was fought. However, as observed earlier, the mass mobilisation of entire populations and their human, technological and material resources for war, as occurred in the First World War and more completely in the Second World War, has changed the centrality of battle as the key concern of the strategist. Strategy and strategy-making have ceased to be bounded by the battlefield and to be the province of the military commander:

In the aftermath of the Industrial Revolution, the outcome of war was to be determined as much by the existence of an industrial base and war potential as by performance on the battlefield. As William James wrote: '...the intensely sharp competitive preparation for war by the nation is the real war, permanently increasing, so that the battles are only a sort of public verification of mastery gained during the "peace" intervals'.28

In the post-Second World War period, the trend towards mass mobilisation has taken on a new connotation with the preponderance of civil war and wars of revolution and independence. In these conflicts, again, the centrality of battle, as ascribed by Jomini, has been rejected. Battle on a conventional scale is usually sought by one side but is spurned and avoided at all costs by the other, for most of the war. In such conflicts, moreover, there usually is no front line or flanks in the traditional sense. Finally, in the conduct of conventional operations, Jomini's maxims have not proven to be of sufficient flexibility to accommodate the impact of technology upon the modern battlefield. The period in which he wrote can be considered a technological interregnum. Indeed, the weaponry of the pre-Napoleonic and Napoleonic periods, with few exceptions, remained similar. It was how these weapons and their wielders were mobilised, ordered and manoeuvred before, and in battle, which had altered, and it was these changes in strategy and tactics about which Jomini wrote. In contrast, in the 20th century, it has been new weapons, command and control, communications, and logistic support technologies which have increasingly been relied upon to produce the battle- and war-winning 'edges'. These changes have combined to challenge the universal applicability of Jomini's maxims.

If Jomini's method - the scientific approach - constrains and narrows the relevance of his work in other eras, it is Clausewitz's approach to the study of war which allows *On War* to remain current, useful and relevant in the latter half of the twentieth century. For example, although Clausewitz examined, in a comprehensive and detailed manner, the functionalities of war, which are tied to the practicalities of the day, he spread his analysis to study why wars proceed in the way they do, to place the phenomenon of war in a broader social and political context. As van Creveld comments:

> ...the vast majority of existing works on the theory of war are ultimately nothing but glorified cookbooks. They are full of recipes...justified with the aid of a smaller or greater number of examples taken from military history, as to how things ought to

be done...Clausewitz' unique relevance derives from the fact that he does more than provide recipes...Instead he delves into the question as to what cooking is and what purpose it serves, coming up with answers that are able to resist changes in both the foodstuffs employed and the utensils in use. He is less concerned with cooking than with thinking about it, less with making war than with reflecting about it...[29]

While the essence of Clausewitz's work remains relevant to the contemporary era, and in some parts of even greater relevance than at the time of its publication, in other areas, *On War* is just as challenged by change as the works of Jomini. For example, the technological revolutions of the 20th century have challenged the truism of Clausewitz's dictum that the pursuit of policy provides the rationale for the goals of war. Many wars in this century have been started to pursue goals not successfully attained through diplomatic, political or economic means. However, they have frequently acquired a momentum (often technologically-inspired) and logic of their own. As Weigley comments: 'instead of using war as an instrument of policy, nations allowed operational and tactical feasibility to dictate policy'.[30] Equally, the social and political revolutions of this century, and the inherent disorderliness of the modern international system, have combined to challenge Clausewitz's view of war as the instrumental preserve of nation states. For example, enduring non-state actors have established themselves in the international arena and have routinely applied violence and terror in pursuit of their objectives.

Perhaps the most significant change which calls for a reinterpretation of Clausewitz's writings, as those of many other strategists, is the advent of the nuclear age. Although in the cataclysmic destructive power of nuclear weapons we can see perhaps the closest embodiment of Clausewitz's concept of absolute war, the strategist could not envisage the strategic stand-off which would be presaged by the possession of weapons of absolute destruction. For Clausewitz, and indeed other 19th and pre-nuclear 20th century strategists, war could be regarded as a normal condition, a recognition of the inevitability of routinely alternating states of war and peace. Under such conditions, the role and purpose of military strategy is succinct and unequivocal - to deploy, manoeuvre and *engage* military forces with such concentration and power as to bring about an opponent's conditional or unconditional capitulation. Now, for those nations which possess nuclear weapons, as Howard argues, they confront each other with such alternatives before even a shot is fired.[31] This reality is reflected, for example, in the development of flexible response doctrines out of the stand-off and incredibility of mutual assured destruction.

For many non-nuclear states and non-state actors, the strategic maxims of the 19th century writers remain of considerable relevance and pertinence. However, for many other nations, the risks of escalation and the costs of modern war have served to promote the reassessment of strategic concepts of an earlier era, principal amongst which are the notions of force manoeuvre and minimum use of force. As Howard aptly observes:

> As in the days of pre-Napoleonic strategy, the movement of forces once again becomes part of the bargaining process, an indicator of resolution or of willingness to consider accommodation. To that extent classical models have relevance for nuclear as for non-nuclear powers, but the models must be those, not that of Napoleon with his decisive battles nor those of Napoleon's successors with their total wars of attrition, but of Napoleon's eighteenth-century predecessors: men who had much to lose and little to gain from war, who fearfully committed their forces to battle and manoeuvred them cautiously; men with limited resources and often a divided public opinion within their domains.[32]

Endnotes

1   Edward Mead Earle (ed.), *Makers of Modern Strategy: From Machiavelli to Hitler*, (Princeton University Press, Princeton, 1952), p.viii.
2   Martin van Creveld, *Command in War*, (Harvard University Press, Cambridge, Mass., 1985), p.18.
3   Robert O'Neill, 'Introduction to Strategic Thinking', (Paper presented to the Australian Joint Services Staff College, unpublished, circa 1981), p.11.
4   Martin van Creveld, *Command in War*, p.279.
5   Michael I. Handel, 'Introduction' *Journal of Strategic Studies* (Special Issue on Clausewitz and Modern Strategy), Volume 9, Numbers 2 and 3, June/September 1986, p.4.
6   Michael Howard, 'Jomini and the Classical Tradition', in Michael Howard (ed.), *The Theory and Practice of War*, (Cassell, London, 1965), p.6.
7   *Ibid.*, p.5.
8   Antoine de Jomini, *Précis de l'Art de la Guerre* in Adrian Liddell Hart (ed.), *The Sword and the Pen - Selections from the World's Greatest Military Writings*, (Cassell, London, 1978), p.145.

9   Anatol Rapoport (ed.), *Clausewitz On War*, (Penguin Books, Harmondsworth, 1968), p.14.
10   Michael Handel, 'Introduction', *Journal of Strategic Studies*, June/September, p.5.
11   Carl von Clausewitz, *On War*, Michael Howard and Peter Paret (eds. and trans.), (Princeton University Press, Princeton, 1976) p.135.
12   *Ibid.*, p.605.
13   Anatol Rapoport, *Clausewitz on War*, p.13.
14   John Shy, 'Jomini' in Peter Paret (ed.), *Makers of Modern Strategy: From Machiavelli to the Nuclear Age*, (Princeton University Press, Princeton, 1986) p.177.
15   Phillip A. Crowl, 'Mahan' in *ibid.*, p.457.
16   Margaret Tuttle Sprout, 'Mahan: Evangelist of Sea Power', in Edward Mead Earle (ed.), *Makers of Modern Strategy: From Machiavelli to Hitler*, p.415.
17   Quoted in Phillip Crowl, 'Mahan', p.444.
18   *Ibid.*, p.450.
19   *Ibid.*, p.455.
20   Williamson Murray, 'Clausewitz: Some Thoughts on What the Germans Got Right', *Journal of Strategic Studies*, (Volume 9, Numbers 2 and 3), June/September 1986, p.268.
21   *Ibid.*, p.284.
22   Michael Howard, 'Men Against Fire: The Doctrine of the Offensive in 1914', in Peter Paret (ed.), *Makers of Modern Strategy: From Machiavelli to the Nuclear Age*, p.515.
23   *Ibid.*, p.520.
24   *Ibid.*, p.520.
25   See Colmar von der Goltz, *The Nation in Arms*, (London, 1913), Friedrich von Bernhardi, *On War Today*, (London, 1912), G.F.R. Henderson, *The Science of War* (London, 1905), and F.N. Maude, *The Evolution of Infantry Tactics*, (London, 1905).
26   Michael Howard, 'Men Against Fire', p.526.
27   Martin van Creveld, 'The Eternal Clausewitz', *Journal of Strategic Studies*, (Volume 9, Numbers 2 and 3), June/September 1986, p.41.
28   Michael I. Handel, 'Clausewitz in the Age of Technology', *Journal of Strategic Studies*, (Volume 9, Numbers 2 and 3), June/September 1986, pp.55-56.
29   Martin van Creveld, *Command in War*, pp.45-46.
30   Russell Weigley, in Allan R. Millet and Williamson Murray (eds.), *Military Effectiveness*, (Allen & Unwin, Boston, 1988, Volume 1), reviewed by Colonel Michael D. Wyley, *US Marine Corps Gazette*, (Volume 72, Number 9), September 1988, p.78.
31   Michael Howard, *The Causes of War and Other Essays*, (Allen & Unwin, London, Counterpoint Edition, 1983) p.91.
32   *Ibid.*, p.99.

CHAPTER 2

THE EVOLUTION OF UNITED STATES STRATEGIC POLICY SINCE 1945

Desmond Ball

The Beginning of Nuclear Strategy

The relationship between strategic concepts and doctrine and US strategic nuclear force development at the outset of the nuclear age was quite unambiguous. The Manhattan Project and the strikes against Hiroshima and Nagasaki proceeded unencumbered by the musings of any strategists. Yet, the new technology generated a revolution in US strategic thought - as Bernard Brodie observed at the time, the atomic bomb would 'so govern the strategic and tactical dispositions of either side as to create a wholly novel form of war'.[1]

The central strategic concept which emerged, and went essentially unchallenged in the US for some decades, that of *deterrence*, derived from another classic paragraph written by Brodie in 1946:

> Thus, the first and most vital step in any American security program for the age of atomic bombs is to take measures to guarantee to ourselves in case of attack the possibility of retaliation in kind. The writer in making that statement is not for the moment concerned about who will *win* the next war in which atomic bombs are used. Thus far the chief purpose of our military establishment has been to win wars. From now its chief purpose must be to avert them. It can have almost no other useful purpose.[2]

Brodie went on to state that among the requirements for deterrence were extraordinary measures of protection for the retaliatory force so that it might survive a surprise attack, and that margins of superiority in nuclear weapons, or the means of delivering them, might count for little or nothing in a crisis so long as each side had reason to fear the huge devastation which could be visited on its peoples and territories by the other.

With respect to force structure development, however, these observations begged as many questions as they answered. How large a retaliatory force was needed for viable deterrence? Was the possession of one or a handful of protected atomic bombs sufficient? What levels of assured devastation were required before margins of superiority became meaningless? What precise contingencies did the atomic bomb actually deter? What other defence forces should be procured to complement the atomic elements so as to provide deterrence across the whole spectrum of possible national security contingencies? Strategic thinking did not begin to address these questions until the late 1940s, by which time the development of US strategic nuclear forces had proceeded a considerable distance - by 1950, the United States had several hundred atomic bombs and on 31 January that year the Administration formally decided to proceed with the development of the H-bomb. Targeting of the US strategic forces in the late 1940s and early 1950s reflected more the planning and practices of the 8th and 20th Air Forces during the Second World War rather than any consideration of the requirements of nuclear deterrence.[3]

The first serious attempt to define a comprehensive strategic doctrine which could guide US force structure development occurred in 1950. On 31 January, at the same time as he formally approved the development of the H-bomb, President Truman issued a directive to the Secretaries of State and Defense 'to undertake a re-examination of our objectives in peace and war and of the effect of these objectives on strategic plans, in the light of the probable fission bomb capability and possible thermonuclear bomb capability of the Soviet Union'.[4] The subsequent review, generally known as NSC 68, was prepared by a State-Defense Policy Review Group. Four 'possible courses of action' were considered by the Group: continuation of current policies and programs; isolation; preventive war; and a rapid build-up 'of the political, economic and military strength of the free world'. After extended discussion, the first three of these were rejected: a continuation of current policies would only lead to further deterioration of America's relative military strength as the Soviet nuclear program developed; isolation would deprive the US of the supplementary strength of its allies and hence only enhance the relative position of the Soviet Union; and preventive war would probably be unsuccessful, as it was unlikely that the Soviet Union 'would wait for such an attack before launching one of its own'. The recommended course of action was therefore a broadly-based and rapid build-up which would include a 'substantial increase in expenditures for military purposes'. The conclusions of NSC 68 were accepted by the National Security Council 'as a statement of policy to be followed over the next four or five years' at a meeting on 29 September 1950.[5]

NSC 68 as such, however, had little impact on US strategic force development. To begin with, as one critic has observed, it was '[when] viewed as a call to action rather than policy analysis...an amazingly incomplete and amateurish study'. The discussion of alternative basic national security policies was not at all objective but, rather, addressed 'two straw options (isolation and war), one unacceptable choice (continuation of current policies), and the obviously desired solution (a rapid political, economic, and military build-up)'. Moreover, the authors of NSC 68 had 'deliberately avoided including specific recommendations for program expansion or estimates of cost'.[6] In any case, the Korean War broke out in June 1950 and NSC 68 passed from the deliberations. The total personnel strength of the US armed forces, for example, went from 1,461,000 in June 1950 to 3,636,000 as at 1 July 1952.[7] The development of the US atomic arsenal also proceeded apace, passing 1,000 bombs in 1952, but without either any strategic guidance or any current planning contingency to inform it.

Massive Retaliation

The formulation of a basic and comprehensive national security policy was regarded by President Eisenhower, who took office on 20 January 1953, as one of the most urgent and important tasks of his Administration. In May 1953, he inaugurated 'Operation Solarium', which has been described as 'an effort to determine future national security policy in the broadest sense'.[8] The product of this study was NSC 162/2, which was approved by President Eisenhower on 30 October 1953, and which laid the foundation for the doctrine of 'massive retaliation' announced by Secretary of State Dulles in his historic address before the Council of Foreign Relations on 12 January 1954:

> The way to deter aggression is for the free community to be willing and able to respond vigorously at places and with means of its own choosing.
>
> Now, so long as our basic concepts in these respects were unclear, our military leaders could not be selective in building our military power...Before military planning could be changed, the President and his advisers, represented by the National Security Council, had to make some basic policy decisions. This has been done.
>
> And the basic decision was...to depend primarily upon a great capacity to retaliate instantly by means and at places of our own choosing.[9]

The doctrine of massive retaliation required that the US maintain and be prepared to use effective means to make aggression too costly to be tempting. As such, it made explicit the two essential elements of all deterrence notions - capability and credibility. On capability, the clear guidance that was provided to the military leaders responsible for 'building our military power' was that US forces must be survivable against a Soviet first strike (and hence able to 'retaliate'), must be sufficiently large as to inflict 'massive' devastation, and must be capable of high and continuous alert rates so as to respond 'instantly'. It was the responsibility of declaratory policy to ensure that the posture was credible, that there was no doubt in the mind of any potential adversary about the American willingness to execute the strategy.

As it happened, there was in fact reasonable cause for concern about both elements of the doctrine. First, the work of Albert Wohlstetter and others at the RAND Corporation in the early- and mid-1950s showed quite clearly the potential vulnerability of the US strategic forces even to the much smaller Soviet forces - in 1956 the Strategic Air Command (SAC) had about 1650 strategic bombers capable of striking the USSR (consisting of some 1300 B-47s, some 250 B-36s, and about 100 B-52s), while the Soviet Union had less than 150 bombers capable of reaching the United States, but almost the entire SAC force was based in peacetime at only 30 lightly defended bases in the US, and had only another 70 bases overseas available to it in wartime.[10] Secondly, massive retaliation lacked credibility. Before 1954-55, the US could have launched a nuclear attack on the Soviet Union with virtual impunity, but by the time of Dulles' announcement the Soviet Union was developing a capability to deliver bombs on the US itself, and, as this capability increased, massive retaliation became increasingly incredible.

These points formed the substance of vigorous criticism of the doctrine, in response to which Secretary Dulles and other members of the Administration made a series of 'clarifying' and 'explanatory' statements which, as Bernard Brodie pointed out, 'amounted virtually to a retraction'.[11] However, this backtracking was not reflected in the US force structure development. As Brodie also observed,

> If one examines the course actually pursued by national defense policy and military programming over the next several years [i.e. 1954-59], it was the original speech which stood and not the retraction...Developments in our military force structure...were in the direction of increased rather than lessened dependence on massive retaliation.[12]

The Kennedy Administration:
Flexible Response and Counterforce Options

The Kennedy Administration came into office on 20 January 1961 determined to rectify this situation. Both President Kennedy and Defense Secretary McNamara had personal predilections against the inflexibilities they perceived in extant US strategic nuclear policy - as expressed, for example, in Kennedy's criticism during the 1960

Presidential campaign that the current US posture provided no choices other than 'humiliation or holocaust'. In this, they were fully supported by their chosen advisers - in the President's case, General Maxwell Taylor, his Special Military Representative; and in McNamara's case, a highly articulate group of analysts from the RAND Corporation, including William Kaufmann, Alain Enthoven, Charles Hitch, Henry Rowen, and Daniel Ellsberg. Moreover, this group of analysts had unquestioned confidence in the ability of management techniques such as the Planning, Programming and Budgeting System (PPBS), Systems Analysis, and Cost-Effectiveness studies to generate force structure designs that precisely reflected the strategic guidance. And the Kennedy Administration was perfectly placed in terms of the techno-logical evolution of ICBM and SLBM systems to impose its doctrinal predilections on the US strategic force posture.[13]

When the Kennedy Administration took office, the US was just entering the 'missile age'; only about a dozen ICBMs were operational, all of which were slow-reacting, radio-guided, liquid-fuelled, extremely vulnerable Atlas D missiles, and only two FBM submarines had been deployed (with Polaris A-1 missiles). Under Eisenhower, about 1,100 strategic ballistic missiles had been programmed; about 20% of these were the first-generation Atlas and Titan ICBMs, later phased out of the missile inventory, and about 10% were Mobile Minuteman ICBMs, later withdrawn from the program because of cost and technical problems. Only some 800 missiles were the strategically viable, second-generation Polaris and hard-silo Minuteman missiles. By the time of President Kennedy's assassination, in November 1963, this figure had been more than doubled - to over 1,900 strategic ballistic missiles, consisting of 54 of the storable liquid-fuelled, large payload Titan II ICBMs, 656 Polaris SLBMs, and 1,200 Minuteman ICBMs (cut back to 1,000 the following year). The decisions of the Kennedy Administration essentially determined the size and character of the US strategic missile forces for the next two decades.

Most of these decisions were made in 1961. In a Special Message to Congress on 28 March, President Kennedy announced the decision to limit the Titan program to 54 Titan IIs - and, though it was not explicated, to limit the US strategic missile forces essentially to smmall, relatively low-payload missiles. The decision to limit the Polaris program to 41 submarines (656 SLBMs), rather than the 45 that the Navy was seeking, was made by Secretary McNamara on 22 September 1961. The FY 1963 defence budget, presented to Congress on 18 January 1962, contained authorisation for 800 Minuteman ICBMs, and projected a total force through FY 1968 of 1,200. Although the formal decision to limit the number of Minuteman to 1,000 was not made until 5 November

1964, it is believed that Secretary McNamara had personally decided no later than December 1961 that 1,000 would be sufficient.

The period during which these decisions were being taken was one of extraordinary excitement from the point of view of the development and refinement of strategic concepts and doctrines. The debate both within and outside the Administration was relatively thorough and comprehensive, and broached the essential rationales of the strategic forces. At least within the Administration, there was from the beginning a sufficient consensus in the argument to provide some general illumination in force-structure issues: the US strategic forces must be capable of more than merely surviving a Soviet first strike and inflicting unacceptable damage on the Soviet urban-industrial system; the delivery vehicles must be sufficiently survivable and sophisticated to permit a range of alternative retaliatory strikes, including some relatively limited ones. However, the clarification and implementation of the concepts, and the delineation of compatible targeting plans in the Single Integrated Operational Plan (SIOP), at the time the principal missile decisions were made, was still quite tentative and rudimentary. The progress made in only eight months or so was very impressive, but the work was still more than six months away from completion; it had certainly not proceeded to the point of providing any specific basis for determining the size and character of the US strategic forces.

McNamara's introduction to strategy occurred within the first week of his taking office, when he was given a formal briefing by William Kaufmann on a series of studies which had been undertaken by the RAND Corporation and the Air Staff during 1959-60 and which pointed to the strategic utility of counterforce strikes which held attacks on cities and population to a minimum. He was an immediate convert to this particular 'no cities' version of counterforce strategy, and on 6 March 1961 ordered the preparation of a draft memorandum revising US basic national security policies, including an examination of 'the assumptions relating to counterforce strikes'. The section on 'objectives and general war', the final draft of which was completed by mid-May, was prepared by Daniel Ellsberg and stressed the necessity of providing the President with a variety of options from which to choose in the event of nuclear war. At the same time, the Joint Chiefs of Staff were also ordered to 'prepare a Doctrine which, if accepted, would permit controlled response and negotiating pauses in the event of thermonuclear war'. This study, prepared by Lt. Col. Robert P. Lukeman, also argued for strategic flexibility and graduated options. These papers were then embodied in the Department of Defense's *Guidelines for Planning*, which included a draft *Policy Guidance on Plans for Central War*, which in turn became the basis of the 1961 revision of SIOP.

The SIOP inherited from the Eisenhower Administration had contained only one plan, under which the United States would launch all its strategic nuclear delivery vehicles (SNDVs) immediately upon the initiation of nuclear war with the Soviet Union. The single National Strategic Target List (NSTL) predominantly included Soviet and satellite cities; no strategic reserves were to be retained; and there was no provision for the preservation of command and control capabilities. As Daniel Ellsberg has observed, 'If the SIOP [of 1960-61] were activated, we would have hit every city in the Soviet Union and China in addition to all military targets'.[14] Expected Soviet, Chinese and satellite fatalities were estimated by the Joint Chiefs of Staff (JCS) at 360 to 425 million people.

In place of this single option, a new strategic policy was drawn up which was rather more flexible. For example, China and the satellite countries were separated from the Soviet Union for targeting purposes; Soviet strategic forces were separated from Soviet cities on target lists; strategic reserves were to be held by the United States; US command and control systems were to be protected, to allow 'controlled response'; and Soviet command and control was to be preserved, at least in the initial stages of any nuclear exchange.

With regard to any nuclear exchange with the Soviet Union, the SIOP was given five options, plus various sub-options, with US attacks to proceed along the following spectrum:

I   Soviet strategic nuclear delivery forces, including missile sites, bomber bases and submarine tenders.

II   Other elements of Soviet military forces and military resources, located away from cities - for example, air defences covering the US bomber routes.

III   Soviet military forces and military resources near cities.

IV   Soviet command and control centres and systems.

V   If necessary, all-out 'spasm' attack.

Sub-options included such things as use of air/ground burst weapons; clean/dirty bombs; larger/smaller warheads; civil defence/evacuation. There was also provision that Options I and II be exercised in preemptive fashion 'in response to unequivocal strategic warning of impending major Sino-Soviet Bloc attack upon the US or its allies'.[15]

Initial work on the national guidance for the revised SIOP, done mainly by Daniel Ellsberg and Frank Trinkl, under the direction of Alain Enthoven, was completed by late summer 1961. It was then taken up by

Henry Rowen and General Maxwell Taylor, and formalised in the autumn of 1961. The JCS studied and approved the strategic change in late 1961, and it was officially adopted in January 1962. To provide the Soviet Union with the option of fighting a 'controlled' nuclear war Moscow was specifically separated out from other targets on the NSTL in late 1961. Final approval was given to specific targets, ground-zero areas marked, and specific bombs and missiles allocated to the targets - all prepared by the JSTPS - at a meeting between McNamara, his deputy Gilpatric, and the United States' most senior military officers at SAC headquarters in the last week of June 1962. The new SIOP, formally designated SIOP-63, came into effect on 1 August 1962.[16]

The adoption of the no-cities version of the counterforce strategy was supported by two strategic developments of the early 1960s. One was the development in 1960-61 of photographic reconnaissance satellites, which by September 1961 had provided complete photographic coverage of the Soviet Union. Two US satellite programs were involved. The most well-known is the Air Force's KH-1 SAMOS (Satellite and Missile Observation System), which involved the radio transmission of photographs from the satellite to several ground stations around the world. The first of these KH-1 satellites, SAMOS II, was successfully launched on 31 January 1961; however, the resolution of the photographs obtained in this way was relatively poor, and in any case SAMOS II was only operational for about three weeks, which was not sufficient to fully cover the Soviet Union (and the next successful SAMOS was not launched until 22 December 1961). The much more important program was that of the CIA, which launched a series of KH-4 (Corona) satellites under the cover of the Air Force's 'Discoverer' biosatellite program. These CIA satellites used recoverable capsules for retrieving the photographic intelligence which, together with the lower altitudes at which the satellites were orbited, provided much greater resolution. The first of these satellites was launched on 19 August 1960 and recovered next day; subsequent successful recoveries were made from six satellites launched between November 1960 and September 1961, by which time the 'missile gap' myth of 1958-61 had finally been laid to rest. The National Intelligence Estimate (NIE) of mid-September 1961 estimated that the Soviet Union had less than 10 ICBMs operational.

These satellites provided the first fully comprehensive mapping of the Soviet Union - the Intercontinental Ballistic Missile (ICBM) and Intermediate Range Ballistic Missile (IRBM) bases, the submarine ports, air defence sites, Army and Air Force bases, etc. - without which the 'no-cities' version of counterforce strategy could not have been implemented.

The second development was the acknowledged attainment of clear and overwhelming US strategic superiority - to which the satellite photographs directly certified. At the end of 1961, when the strategic basis of the 1962 SIOP was completed and accepted by the JCS, the Soviet Union had only 4 SS-6 ICBMs operational, whereas the US had 54 ICBMs and 5 FBM submarines with 80 Polaris SLBMs. At the end of 1962, the respective figures were 30 Soviet ICBMs as against 200 US ICBMs and 144 US SLBMs. Moreover, the NIEs of late 1961 and late 1962 projected a US superiority of between 2:1 and 4:1 by the mid-1960s. A counterforce strike by the United States in the early 1960s could perhaps have fully disarmed the Soviet Union.

Despite these developments, McNamara quickly began to backtrack from his no-cities position. The second Draft Presidential Memorandum (DPM) on strategic forces, for example, prepared in late 1962, represented a distinct retreat from his earlier position. It stated, for example, 'we do not want a comprehensive damage limitation posture'.

The reasons for McNamara's apparent retreat from counterforce and no-cities were several. First, within the United States there was much criticism of the first-strike implications of the counterforce strategy. As one former McNamara aide is reported to have said: '... there could be no such thing as primary retaliation against military targets after an enemy attack. If you're going to shoot at missiles, you're talking about first strike'.[17] The question was unnecessarily complicated because of the Administration's ambiguity on whether US policy completely ruled out striking first. President Kennedy had said in March 1962, for example, that:

> Khrushchev must NOT be certain that, where its vital interests are threatened, the United States will never strike first.[18]

A second factor was the Soviet reaction. In their public statements at least, Soviet spokesmen denied the possibility of controlled counterforce warfare. Avowed Soviet strategy was to strike against military targets, governmental and administrative centres and cities simultaneously and immediately on the outbreak of general hostilities. Whether in fact the Soviets would accept the US strategy was an open question; McNamara himself actually believed that any nuclear attack by the Soviet Union on the United States would include an attack on the major urban areas of the United States. In any case, it was argued, while Soviet missiles were few and vulnerable and US forces numerically so superior, the Soviet Union could not afford to play 'games' of controlled 'tit-for-tat' with each other's missiles. And as the Soviet force grew larger and became hardened and dispersed,

McNamara believed the destruction of any large number of missiles would be 'unfeasible'.

A third factor was the unfavourable reaction of West European allies. McNamara had first described the 'no-cities' strategy to them at a secret session of NATO in Athens in May 1962; the audience was reportedly incredulous. In June, Secretary of State Rusk made a three-day tour of six Western capitals to explain to West Europe's leaders the new US policy. But he met with frustration; the NATO allies were obviously unwilling to accept the implications of the no-cities strategy, especially for small, independent European nuclear capabilities. Not only did the 'no-cities' strategy deny the Europeans nuclear independence and fail to consider the different targeting priorities of the European governments; it also raised the spectre of separating European security from that of the United States and, by removing the threat to Soviet cities, of removing *pari passu* the deterrent to a Soviet attack on Europe, and even of the possibility of fighting a nuclear war over European territory while leaving the Soviet and US homelands unscathed.

But, most importantly, McNamara decided to withdraw from the 'no-cities' policy for bureaucratic reasons. By the time of the development of the FY 1964 budget in late 1962, it was clear to McNamara that the Services, particularly the Air Force, were using his declared policy of 'no-cities' counterforce as a basis for requesting virtually open-ended strategic weapon programs - both more Minuteman missiles and procurement of a force of supersonic reconnaissance-strike (RS-70) bombers. He thus came to place more stress on Assured Destruction capabilities (although by defining the Assured Destruction criteria conservatively he could still procure sufficient forces to allow a Damage-Limiting mission), and in January 1963 he directed William Kaufmann to give a briefing to some dozen Air Force generals to the effect that they were no longer to take the avowed US strategy as a criterion for strategic force proposals. In separating declaratory policy from actual policy, McNamara was to a large extent using strategic doctrine as a weapon in the continuous intramural bureaucratic battles over military programmes and Defense (and Service) budgets.

From Counterforce to Assured Destruction

McNamara did not move immediately to a wholesale acceptance of Assured Destruction; rather, declaratory policy from 1964 through 1966 included both Assured Destruction and Damage Limitation as basic US strategic objectives.

The development of the concept of Damage Limitation was principally the responsibility of General Glenn A. Kent (USAF), who headed a study group which McNamara had initially established in the summer of 1962 to undertake a comprehensive analysis of various alternative strategic policies which were available to the United States and the weapons systems and force levels which each implied. The results of a pilot survey were ready in July 1963, and the full study, entitled *Damage Limitation: A Rationale for the Allocation of Resources by the US and USSR*, was published on 21 January 1964.

In a memorandum dated 12 March 1964, McNamara asked for an amplification of the January study and requested 'that the Services conduct studies during the next six months that would focus attention on "damage limitation" and "assured destruction"'. These studies were integrated by the Weapons System Evaluation Group (WSEG) in a two-volume study known as WSEG No.79 and formally entitled *Analysis of General Nuclear War Postures for Strategic Offense and Defense Forces*, dated August 1964. The project was formally completed on 8 September 1964 with the preparation of *A Summary Study of Strategic Offense and Defense Forces of the US and USSR*.

The Kent study and the associated analyses formed the basis of McNamara's discussion of US strategic nuclear policy in his FY 1965 and 1966 defence budget statements. In his FY 1965 statement, submitted to Congress in January 1964, McNamara stated that:

> Comprehensive studies of alternative US strategic retaliatory force structures employed in a nuclear exchange with a wide range of possible Soviet forces and under a wide variety of assumptions pertaining to the outbreak of war and United States and Soviet operational factors [have] found that forces in excess of those needed simply to destroy Soviet cities would significantly reduce damage to the United States and Western Europe. And the extent to which damage to ourselves can be reduced depends importantly on the size and the character of our own forces, particularly by the surface-to-surface missiles such as Minuteman that can reach their targets quickly...While a cities-only strategic retaliatory force would, in our judgement, be dangerously inadequate, a full-first-strike force is, on the basis of our estimates of the Soviet nuclear strike forces in the fiscal year 1967-69 period, simply unattainable...Thus, a damage-limiting strategy appears to be the most practical and effective course for us to follow. Such a strategy requires a force considerably larger than would be needed for a limited cities-only strategy. *While there are still some differences of judgement on*

just how large such a force should be, there is general agreement
that it should be large enough to ensure destruction, singly or in
combination of the Soviet Union, Communist China and the
Communist satellites as national societies, under the worst
possible circumstances of war outbreak that can reasonably be
postulated, and, in addition, to destroy their war-making
capability so as to limit, to the extent practicable, damage to this
country and to our allies.[19]

The concepts of Assured Destruction and Damage Limitation
were described by McNamara in his FY 1966 defence budget statement
presented to Congress in February 1965:

The strategic objectives of our general nuclear war forces are:

1. to deter a deliberate nuclear attack upon the United States
    and its allies by maintaining a clear and convincing
    capability to inflict unacceptable damage on an attacker,
    even were that attacker to strike first;

2. in the event such a war should nevertheless occur, to limit
    damage to our populations and industrial capacities.

The first of these capabilities (required to deter potential
aggressors) we call 'Assured Destruction', i.e., the capability to
destroy the aggressor as a viable society, even after a well
planned and executed surprise attack on our forces. The second
capability we call 'Damage Limitation', i.e., the capability to
reduce the weight of the enemy attack by both offensive and
defensive measures and to provide a degree of protection for the
population against the effects of nuclear detonations.[20]

However, these studies and resultant concepts and doctrines
had little impact on US strategic nuclear force development. For one
thing, this elucidation of strategic criteria never proceeded to the point
of providing any specific bases for strategic weapons procurement. As
McNamara testified in 1964, there were 'still some differences of
judgement' on what the size of the US missile force should be. The final
decision to limit the Minuteman force to 1,000 missiles was formally
made by the Department of Defense on 5 November 1964 and upheld by
President Johnson in a meeting with the Joint Chiefs of Staff, Secretary
McNamara, Deputy Secretary Vance and the Director of the Bureau of
the Budget, Kermit Gordon, on 22 December 1964. The Damage
Limitation project was in hand to inform this decision, but the
overwhelming weight of evidence points to the actual decision to limit
the Minuteman program to 1,000 missiles having been made by

McNamara and his key aides some years before then, and for quite other reasons. As General Kent himself has stated, the Damage Limitation project provided little more than a rationalisation of the predetermined force level.

By 1965, in fact, McNamara had already moved to substantially down-play the Damage Limitation aspect of avowed US strategic policy, and by 1967 it was all Assured Destruction.

The first formal definition of Assured Destruction was given to Congress by McNamara in his FY 1966 budget statement of 18 February 1965:

> A vital first objective, to be met in full by our strategic nuclear forces, is the capability for Assured Destruction. What kinds and amounts of destruction we would have to be able to inflict in order to provide this (capability) cannot be answered precisely. But, it seems reasonable to assume the destruction of, say, one-quarter to a one-third of its population and about two-thirds of its industrial capacity...would certainly represent intolerable punishment to any industrialised nation and thus should serve as an effective deterrent.[21]

From the point of view of the relationship between concepts and US force development, there are two especially noteworthy aspects of the conceptual transition from counterforce to Assured Destruction that took place under McNamara's stewardship. The first is that the force procurement requirements of the former, no matter how imprecisely formulated, are obviously much different from those of the latter; indeed, some aspects of the Assured Destruction posture, with its necessary emphasis on urban targeting, are likely to be quite incompatible with those of the extreme 'no-cities' version of counterforce. The second is that the force posture designed in 1961-62 remained essentially intact at the end of the 1960s.

Second, the criteria on which Assured Destruction was defined did not themselves remain static. In McNamara's FY 1968 budget statement, presented to Congress on 23 January 1967, the required levels of destruction were reduced to 'one-fifth to one-fourth of its [the Soviet Union's] population and one-half to two-thirds of its industrial capacity'.[22] This reduction in the destruction levels did not represent any philosophical reconsideration of the requirements of viable deterrence; rather, it represented a more accurate reflection of US capabilities against the Soviet urban-industrial target structure.

SIOP-5: Expanding Options and Escalation Control

The developments in US strategic policy from the early 1970s through to the mid-1980s were in many respects a direct procession from those which occurred under Secretary McNamara in 1961-62 - but which he was later to disavow. Again, however, it is difficult to correlate these policy developments with the developments in the US strategic force structure during this period.

In mid-1972, without public announcement, President Nixon named his National Security Adviser, Henry Kissinger, to chair a top-level inter-departmental group 'to come up with additional nuclear war options'. The resultant report, National Security Study Memorandum (NSSM)-169, completed in 1973, recommended that US strategic nuclear employment policy be modified to provide for a wide range of options, including at least some 'selective' attacks on Soviet military targets.[23] NSSM-169 led directly to the development of National Security Decision Memorandum (NSDM)-242, signed by President Nixon on 17 January 1974, and which in turn authorised the Secretary of Defense to promulgate the *Policy Guidance for the Employment of Nuclear Weapons* and the associated *Nuclear Weapons Employment Policy* (NUWEP), signed by Secretary Schlesinger on 4 April 1974. These documents were the basis of changes to action policy, in terms of the 'new' targeting plans that were given effect in SIOP-5 of 1 January 1976, as well as to declaratory policy, as reflected in the enthusiastic pronouncements made by Secretary Schlesinger throughout 1974-75.

NSDM-242 began as follows:

> I have reached the following decisions on United States policy regarding planning for nuclear weapons employment. These decisions reflect both existing political and military realities and my desire for a more flexible nuclear posture.
>
> ...The fundamental mission of US nuclear forces is to deter nuclear war and plans for the employment of US nuclear forces should support this mission.[24]

The memorandum directed that further plans 'for limited employment options which enable the United States to conduct selected nuclear operations' be developed and formally incorporated into the SIOP. Much of the public debate of NSDM-242 was concerned with the re-emphasis in these plans on the targeting of a wide range of Soviet military forces and installations, from hardened command and control facilities and ICBM silos to airfields and army camps.[25] This re-emphasis, however, was much more declaratory than substantive since, as described above, the SIOP had, at least since 1962 and including the period when Assured Destruction was avowed policy, contained most of these counterforce targets. A more novel aspect of the memorandum was the notion of targeting those Soviet assets that would be critical to Soviet postwar recovery and power. NSDM-242 directed that an objective of US targeting doctrine should be the 'destruction of the political, economic and military resources critical to the enemy's post-war power, influence and ability to recover...as a major power'.[26]

The concept of Escalation Control was central to the policy outlined. It was essential that the National Command Authorities (NCA) be provided with the ability to execute its options in a deliberate and controlled fashion, throughout the progress of a strategic nuclear exchange. The memorandum directed that the United States must have the potential to 'hold some vital enemy targets hostage to subsequent destruction' and to control 'the timing and pace of attack execution, in order to provide the enemy opportunities to consider his actions', so that 'the best possible outcome' might be obtained for the United States and its allies. NSDM-242 introduced the notion of 'withholds' or 'nontargets', that is, things that would be preserved from destruction. Some of these, such as 'population *per se*', have now been exempted absolutely from targeting; others, such as the centres of political leadership and control, were exempted only for the purpose of intrawar deterrence and intrawar bargaining, and strategic reserve forces (SRF) are to be maintained to allow their eventual destruction if necessary.[27]

Specific quantitative objectives derived from these concepts were set out in the *Nuclear Weapons Employment Policy* signed by Secretary Schlesinger on 4 April 1974 and subsequently known as NUWEP-1. NUWEP-1, for example, contained the requirement that the SIOP forces be able to destroy 70% of the Soviet industry that would be needed to achieve economic recovery in the event of a large-scale strategic nuclear exchange.[28]

Despite some initial expectation that the administration of President Jimmy Carter and Secretary of Defense Harold Brown would move to change US policy back toward something more like Assured Destruction, the concepts and doctrines embodied in NSDM-242 and NUWEP-1 were essentially retained, and indeed further refined, through the development of successive annual variants of SIOP-5. The documentary reappraisal of NSDM-242 began with the preparation of Presidential Review Memorandum (PRM) -10, *Comprehensive Net Assessment and Military Force Posture Review*, which was signed by President Carter on 18 February 1977, just four weeks after he assumed office.[29] This five-month interagency study, supervised by Samuel P. Huntington for the president's national security adviser, was a comprehensive assessment of the Soviet-American global power relationship. This assessment included a study entitled *Military Strategy and Force Posture Review* (prepared largely by the Office of the Assistant Secretary of Defense for International Security Affairs), which considered details of the military balance and alternative military strategies - including strategies for possible nuclear war with the USSR.[30]

PRM-10 was completed in late June 1977 and, together with its attendant reports, was considered by a cabinet-level group, chaired by Zbigniew Brzezinski, the national security adviser, on 7 July. The PRM-10 conclusions were more sanguine and optimistic than most observers had expected. The study assumed the deployment of Trident SLBMs, the Mark 12A warhead on the Minuteman III ICBMs, the development of cruise missiles, and the continued development of the MX ICBM. Assessing the impact of a major nuclear war between the two superpowers, the study found that, at a minimum, the United States would suffer 140 million fatalities and the USSR 113 million and that almost three-quarters of their respective economies would be destroyed. In such a conflict, the report concluded, 'neither side could conceivably be described as a winner'. The report stated that neither side would have an advantage in launching a limited nuclear attack against the other's land-based ICBM forces - and, in fact, that 'whichever side initiates a limited nuclear attack against the ICBM forces of the other side will find itself significantly worse off' in terms of surviving numbers of missiles and missile warheads. The study in addition found that US antisubmarine warfare (ASW) capability was significantly better than that of the USSR; it also found that even after a Soviet missile attack against US air bases, the surviving US bomber force would be larger than that now possessed by the USSR. Finally, it noted that 'Mr. Carter has decided that U.S. missiles and bombers must be able to destroy about 70 per cent of the Soviet Union's so-called recovery resources, meaning the economic, political and military facilities critical to the functioning of society'.[31]

On 24 August 1977, following further intensive review of PRM-10 and the attendant *Military Strategy and Force Posture Review* by NSC officials and the Departments of Defense and State, and extended debate in the Special Coordination Committee (dominated by Zbigniew Brzezinski, Secretary of State Cyrus Vance, and Secretary of Defense Brown), President Carter issued Presidential Directive (PD) -18, *U.S. National Strategy*. PD-18 both codified certain aspects of existing US strategic policy and called for further study of other aspects. Most important from the viewpoint of targeting policy, PD-18 reaffirmed the continued use of NSDM-242 and NUWEP-1 in 'the absence of further guidance for structuring the U.S. strategic posture'.[32] It insisted that the

United States maintain the capability to inflict 'unacceptable damage' on the USSR even if that nation struck first with nuclear weapons. It instructed the Pentagon to develop options for limited nuclear responses by the United States. It directed that a 'reserve' of strategic forces be maintained, safe from attack, for use if nuclear war became relatively extended. And it stated that US forces should be strong enough to ensure that any possible nuclear war would end on the most favourable terms possible to the United States.[33] Finally, it directed that three further major studies be undertaken: a Nuclear Targeting Policy Review (NTPR), a modernization of the ICBM force study, and a strategic reserve force study.[34]

The NTPR was an interagency study headed by Leon Sloss in the Pentagon. Undertaken in two principal phases, the first was completed and forwarded to the Secretary of Defense in December 1978, and the second remained uncompleted when the study group was disbanded in the spring of 1979. Numerous supporting studies were commissioned during 1978, on such topics as the history of US targeting plans, Soviet and Chinese views on nuclear war and nuclear weapons employment policies, the possibility of targeting the Soviet population, targeting economic and political recovery assets, regionalization of the Soviet Union, the C^3 constraints on escalation control, and the question of war termination.

The NTPR reached several important conclusions. The primary systems acquisition requirement identified was that the C^3I system that controlled the SIOP forces should have greater endurance than the present system. It also suggested that more options should be added to the SIOP to give the strategic forces 'greater flexibility in targeting than they presently have'.[35] More specifically, it suggested that relatively less emphasis be accorded to the destruction of the Soviet economic and industrial base and that greater attention 'be directed toward improving the effectiveness of our attacks against military targets'.[36] It also suggested that there be some modification of the SIOP to reflect better the political aspects of nuclear targeting. As one White House official stated at the time:

> In the past nuclear targeting has been done by military planners who have basically emphasized the efficient destruction of targets. But targeting should not be done in a political vacuum.
>
> Some targets are of greater psychological importance to Moscow than others, and we should begin thinking of how to use our strategic forces to play on these concerns.[37]

The NTPR formed the basis of a new Presidential Directive drafted in early 1979. Although the NSC staff pressed for the formal acceptance of this draft, there was opposition from the State Department and from some elements within the Pentagon. Thus, it was shelved for more than fifteen months - until it was retrieved just prior to the 1980 Democratic Convention, revised, up-dated and formally signed by the president on 25 July as PD-59.[38] As Secretary Brown emphasized, 'PD-59 is not a new strategic doctrine; it is not a radical departure from US strategic policy over the past decade or so. It is, in fact, a refinement, a codification of previous statements of our strategic policy. PD-59 takes the same essential strategic doctrine, and restates it more clearly, more cogently, in the light of current conditions and current capabilities'.[39]

Although PD-59 represented no major changes to the targeting guidance as previously set out in NSDM-242 and NUWEP-1, there were at least three noteworthy features of the Carter directive. First, within the area of economic targeting, the directive de-emphasized the concept of targeting to impede Soviet economic recovery in favour of greater emphasis on targeting the Soviet economic war-supporting infrastructure.

Second, PD-59 emphasized that the preplanned target packages in the SIOP should be supplemented by the ability to find new targets and destroy them during the course of a nuclear exchange. While Soviet strategic nuclear installations and economic and industrial facilities would remain essentially fixed during wartime, there would be much movement of Soviet conventional military forces (including second-echelon formations) and much of the Soviet political and military leadership would presumably be relocated.

Third, PD-59 recognized that the current US C3 system was inadequate to support any policy of extended nuclear war fighting. It stated that the strategy embodied in the directive 'imposes requirements in the strategic command, control and communications system, and... improvements in our forces must be accompanied by improvements to that system. The needed improvements lie in the areas of increased flexibility and higher assurance of command-and-control survivability and long-term endurance'.[40]

PD-59 also authorized the issue of a new *Nuclear Weapons Employment Policy*, variously referred to as NUWEP-2 or NUWEP-80, and issued by Secretary of Defence Brown in October 1980.[41] An especially noteworthy feature of NUWEP-2 was the downgrading of the requirement set out in NUWEP-1 for the destruction of Soviet economic recovery assets. Rather, NUWEP-2 gave priority to targeting Soviet military capabilities, including both nuclear and conventional forces, and to targeting Soviet military and political leadership and, within the category of economic targets, to targeting war-supporting industry rather than Soviet economic recovery capabilities. NUWEP-2 served as the basis for SIOP-5F and SIOP-5G, which took effect on 1 October 1981 and 1 October 1982 respectively.

With respect to the US strategic nuclear force posture there were three principal developments which took place contemporaneously with these policy developments of the 1970s. One was that the number of deliverable warheads in the US strategic nuclear forces was more than doubled, and although the average yield of these warheads decreased substantially, this allowed an increase in the number of certain targets that could be covered in the Soviet Union. The second was the introduction of the Command Data Buffer System, which greatly enhanced the targeting flexibility of the Minuteman III force. And the third was the increasing resources that were allocated to improving the survivability, endurance, responsiveness and capacity of US command, control and communications (C^3) systems. Each of these related to significant aspects of the conceptual and doctrinal developments of the 1970s, but none of them were in fact determined by those developments.

At the beginning of the 1970s, the US had slightly less than 5,000 deliverable warheads, made up of one of each on the 1,910 ICBMs and SLBMs in the US strategic ballistic missile force and about 2,800 bombs and Hound Dog air-to-surface missiles carried on the FB-111 and B-52 bombers. By 1976, this figure had more than doubled, to more than 10,000 deliverable warheads, due principally to the deployment of the Minuteman III ICBMs and the Poseidon SLBMs with three and ten Multiple Independently Targetable Re-entry Vehicles (MIRVs) respectively (which together accounted for 6,610 warheads). This increased greatly the number of conventional military targets (such as airfields, Army bases, ports, rail marshalling yards, tank concentrations, etc.), and economic and industrial facilities (such as petroleum refineries, power stations, factories, etc.) that could be attacked by the SIOP forces, as well as enhancing the flexibility with which US planners could approach the Soviet target base. However, the development of MIRVs was essentially a product of the period when Assured Destruction was the ascendant philosophy. The notion of using a single missile to deliver accurately each of several warheads along separate trajectories was conceived and suggested to the military simultaneously by a number of individuals and groups within the US technical community in 1962-63, and was accepted within the Department of Defense in 1964. The decisions to proceed with the engineering development of a Mark 12 MIRV system for the Minuteman and with a larger version of the Polaris B-3 SLBM (later renamed the Poseidon C-3) which would also carry MIRVs, were both formally taken in the autumn of that year. Although it received some support because of its possible counterforce and war-fighting attributes, the determinate strategic consideration within the Pentagon was its utility as a penetration aid in the event of the deployment of a large Soviet ABM system.[42] The first group of ten Minuteman III ICBMs (with the Mark 12 MIRV) became operational in June 1970, about a year later than the original target date, and the first patrol of a Poseidon submarine began on 31 March 1971[43] - several years before the doctrinal reassessment began to take effect in the mid-1970s. The great increase in US warheads produced by the deployments of the Minuteman IIIs and, most especially, the Poseidons, posed something of a problem for US military planners: most of these warheads lacked a sufficient yield/accuracy combination to be used against Soviet ICBM silos, and the major Soviet population centres were already covered to the point where additional warheads had little marginal value. The end result was that the great bulk of Soviet targets in the SIOP came to be made up of non-strategic military installations, military and quasi-military production and R & D facilities, and industrial centres. The broad spectrum of targets described by Secretary Schlesinger in his 1974 policy declaration were much more the consequence of this force development than of any conceptual or doctrinal initiatives. As Dr Perry was to testify in February 1979, the policy declarations from Secretary Schlesinger to Secretary Brown had no operational impact: 'The targeting policy is based on the force we have'.[44]

The second important force posture development of this period was that of the Command Data Buffer System (CDBS). In March 1974, Secretary Schlesinger testified that $33m included in the FY 1975 defence budget 'to complete development and to continue procurement of the Command Data Buffer' was the largest single item of expenditure related to 'the new targeting doctrine'[45] - which is itself quite a revealing observation about the relationship between doctrine and force development! The CDBS enables crews in Minuteman III launch control centres to retarget the missiles in about 20 minutes by electronic means, a process which previously required the physical insertion of new target tapes into each missile's computers, which took up to 36 hours. This new retargeting system greatly enhanced the flexibility and war-fighting capability of the Minuteman III force, and jelled nicely with the needs of the so-called Schlesinger doctrine. However, the design of the CDBS had actually evolved during the late 1960s. The program was first announced by Secretary Laird in March 1971,[46] and installation of the CDBS had begun (at the 90th Strategic Missile Wing, Francis E. Warren Air Force Base, Wyoming) in November 1972.[47] The system was in fact first proposed as an aid to SAC missile maintenance officers involved in retargeting the ICBMs during the periodic SIOP revisions. It was only much later that its strategic utility was appreciated.

The other significant element of force structure development in the 1970s consisted of an extensive array of measures designed to enhance the endurance, survivability, capabilities, flexibility and responsiveness to the National Command Authorities of the US command, control and communications (C3) and related strategic intelligence systems. The most important particular projects were the reorganisation and modernisation of the World Wide Military Command and Control Systems (WWMCCS); the procurement of Boeing 747 aircraft for the Advanced Airborne National Command Post (AABNCP); development and deployment of the Defense Satellite Communications System (DSCS), the Satellite Data System (SDS), the Navy's Fleet Satellite Communications (FLTSATCOM) system and the Air Force's Satellite Communications (AFSATCOM) system; installation of the MOLINK satellite hotline between Washington and Moscow; and improvements in the US ability to detect and process information concerning enemy ICBM and SLBM launches. Secretary Schlesinger testified in 1974 that these measures, together with the procurement of the CDBS, constituted the only development efforts required by his 'new targeting doctrine'.[48] As noted above, the primary systems acquisition requirement identified in the Nuclear Targeting Policy Review of 1977-79 was that the C3 system for the SIOP forces 'should have greater endurance than the present system'.[49] However, it is very difficult to identify any particular C3 project that derived from or was affected in any specific way by the policy revisions of the mid- and late-1970s. Most of the C3 developments associated with current strategic policy and doctrine were in fact initiated in the late-1960s, during the depths of Assured Destruction, when the demands of doctrine on the C3 system were much simpler. It remains the case that, the intensity and complexity of the activity in recent years notwithstanding, the expenditure on strategic C3 was higher in the 1960s than it ever reached in the 1970s.[50] Moreover, these developments derived from a variety of different impulses and were generally subject to little overall coordination. They certainly did not arise from, or proceed, as integral parts of any coherent US strategic posture. The single most important milestone in US C3 development was the DoD Directive 5100.30, signed by Deputy Defense Secretary David Packard on 2 December 1971. That directive vested overall control of the US armed forces in the National Command Authorities, which consists 'only of the President and the Secretary of Defense or their duly deputised alternates or successors', and defined the chain of command as being 'from the NCA through the Chairman of the Joint Chiefs of Staff [*direct*] to the executing commander'. It redefined the principal missions of the WWMCCS to make the system more responsive to the needs of the NCA, and it ordered 'a very vigorous ... effort to improve the reliability and survivability of the nation's early-warning, post-attack assessment, and communications capability'.[51] An immediate result of this was the Pentagon's request in early January 1972 for a fleet of seven AABNCP aircraft.[52] But DoD Directive 5100.30 was a product, more than anything else, of the communications failures and patent lack of C3 responsiveness that had been exhibited in the USS *Liberty*, USS *Pueblo* and EC-121 spy plane incidents of 8 June 1967, 23 January 1968 and 14 April 1969 respectively. It was only as the subsequent inquiries progressed that concern developed about the survivability and responsiveness of strategic C3 systems - but that was still before any substantive revision in US strategic doctrine had begun.

The initiative for the satellite developments lay elsewhere: these principally reflected the pull of technological potential. Satellites had been developed in the late-1950s and 1960s for a wide range of early-warning, surveillance and communications purposes, and as the capabilities of the sensors improved, and the number and bandwidths of channels was increased, it was natural to incorporate the advances in new 'requirements'. The revolutions in computer processing and microcircuitry offered increasingly broad and attractive menus, and strategic concepts provided no effective criteria for determining how much was enough.

The Reagan Administration: Through SIOP-6 to SIOP-6F

In the eight years of the Reagan Administration, the connections between developments in strategic policy, force structure and technological innovation were perhaps more purposeful, complex, and difficult to disentangle than in any other period in US post-war history. The Reagan Administration made a deliberate effort to more closely align force structure development with strategic policy, and, most particularly, strategic nuclear weapons employment policy - albeit in a methodologically less formally structured fashion than had pertained under Secretary McNamara's subscription to Systems Analysis and PPBS. And there was a more deliberate effort to harness technological innovation in support of particular policies and doctrines - albeit policies which were frequently ill-conceived and technologies which were frequently based on wishful thinking as much as practicable science and technology.

A new review of targeting policy was begun by the Reagan Administration in the spring of 1981, under the general direction of Fred Iklé, the Under Secretary of Defense for Policy (USD(P)). In a conscious effort to improve the integration of Nuclear Weapons Employment

Policy with other elements of US strategic nuclear policy, the Reagan Administration produced a *Nuclear Weapons Employment and Acquisition Master Plan* (NWEAMP).[53] This was closely followed, in October 1981, by National Security Decision Directive (NSDD) - 13, prepared as a successor to PD-59. On 29 March 1982, Secretary of Defense Caspar W. Weinberger issued the *Fiscal Year 1984-1988 Defense Guidance*, the nuclear employment policy portion of which directly reflected NSDD-13:

> Should deterrence fail and strategic nuclear war with the USSR occur, the United States must prevail and be able to force the Soviet Union to seek earliest termination of hostilities on terms favourable to the United States.
>
> The United States must have plans that assure US strategic nuclear forces can render ineffective the total Soviet military and political power structure...and forces that will maintain, throughout a protracted conflict period and afterward, the capability to inflict very high levels of damage against the industrial/economic base of the Soviet Union...so that they have a strong incentive to seek conflict termination short of an all-out attack on our cities and economic assets.
>
> US strategic nuclear forces and their command and communication links should be capable of supporting controlled nuclear counterattacks over a protracted period while maintaining a reserve of nuclear forces sufficient for trans- and post-attack protection and coercion.[54]

Finally, in July 1982, Secretary of Defense Caspar Weinberger issued a new NUWEP, designated NUWEP-82. The guidance contained in these documents was then used to develop a new SIOP, in which increased attention was accorded the requirements of nuclear weapons employment in a situation of prolonged or protracted nuclear conflict.[55] This new SIOP, formally designated SIOP-6, took effect on 1 October 1983.

The model effort at achieving consistency between strategic policy and force structure concerned the development and design of the strategic C[3]I architecture. NSDD-12, entitled *Strategic Communications*, was promulgated as a complement to NSDD-13 in October 1981.[56] NSDD-12 stated that strategic C[3]I systems should receive at least as high a budgetary priority as the 'more highly visible' weapons systems.[57] *The Fiscal Year 1984-1988 Defense Guidance* called for the expenditure of $18 billion on strategic C[3] systems over the five year period, with specific objectives being 'assured reliable performance in peacetime, including exercises; capability to execute the SIOP during or after an attack; [and]

support to continue operations over a protracted period of conflict'.[58] A specific requirement was that the strategic C3I system should have sufficient survivability and endurance to support US strategic policy and forces through some 180 days of protracted nuclear war. Particular 'modernization and improvement' programs included strategic communications systems, such as development and deployment of the Extremely Low Frequency (ELF) communications system, the MILSTAR satellite communications system, and the Ground Wave Emergency Network (GWEN) system; mobile command posts for the NCA, SAC and NORAD headquarters, and critical satellite systems; improved 'indications and warning systems'; and satellite mission control capabilities.[59]

The Reagan Administration's strategic C3I modernization and improvement program can be divided into two phases. The first was designed to rectify deficiencies in the extant strategic C3I posture to ensure that US strategic forces could be employed in a reliable and informed fashion for some 12-24 hours following a Soviet first strike. This essentially unobjectionable objective was by and large achieved. However, most of the elements of this phase had been initiated before the Reagan Administration took office. The ELF system for communicating with submarines, for example, had been initiated by the US Navy in the 1960s. NSDD-12 itself was a reaffirmation of PD-53, entitled *National Security Telecommunications Policy*, signed by President Carter on 15 November 1979, and PD-58 on *Continuity of Government*, signed by President Carter on 30 June 1980. With the notable exceptions of the mobile command post for the NCA and the ELF communications system, most of the strategic C3I systems funded by the Reagan Administration had been supported by the Carter Administration.[60]

In contrast, the second phase of the program, which was designed to provide C3I connectivity through a protracted conflict, was not only much more a requirement of the strategic policy of the Reagan Administration, but was also technically much more problematical. As General David C. Jones stated on his retirement as Chairman of the Joint Chiefs of Staff in June 1982, 'it would be throwing money in a 'bottomless pit' to try to prepare the United States for a long nuclear war with the Soviet Union'.[61]

The Strategic Defense Initiative (SDI), announced by President Reagan on 23 March 1983, represents the best recent example of military technical innovation in response to national policy. As originally described by President Reagan, SDI was a long-term research and development (R&D) program designed to explore the possibility of using defensive capabilities 'to counter the awesome Soviet missile threat' in order to decrease, and ultimately eliminate, both the threat of

Soviet ballistic missile attack against the United States and the US reliance on the threat of retaliation by offensive nuclear weapons as the basis for deterrence of a Soviet nuclear attack.[62] This goal was subsequently codified in NSDD - 85, entitled *Eliminating the Threat From Ballistic Missiles, and signed by President Reagan on 25 March 1983.*

Neither the President's speech of 23 March 1983 nor NSDD-85 presented coherent or cogent guidance on the strategic merits of this objective. Rather, they presented 'a vision of the future'[63] unencumbered by strategic argumentation, in which the conditions of successful deterrence, the problems of transitioning from a primarily offensive to a primarily defensive posture, and the technical feasibility of the objective were simply not addressed.[64] It soon became clear that while SDI could provide significant protection for the strategic offensive forces and possibly also a significant level of damage limitation - although in both cases less cost-effectively than other less glamorous measures - there was no way in which it could provide the complete shield which would make ballistic missiles obsolete. The demands which policy had imposed upon technology were simply unfeasible.

The most interesting and complex connections between strategic policy, force structure and technical innovation undoubtedly obtained in the Reagan Administration with respect to the development of a new strategic nuclear weapons employment policy in 1985-88 - i.e., more specifically, the development of policy guidance, objectives and capabilities for SIOP-6F, which went into effect on 1 October 1989.[65] SIOP-6F represents the most radical change in both the structure and substance of the US strategic nuclear war plan since the preparation of SIOP-63 in 1961-62.

The basic policy of 'targeting those assets which are essential to Soviet warmaking capability and political control' was described by President Reagan in January 1988 as follows:

> Our strategic forces and associated targeting policy must, by any calculation, be perceived as making nuclear warfare a totally unacceptable and unrewarding proposition for the Soviet leadership. Accordingly, our targeting policy:
>
> • Denies the Soviets the ability to achieve essential military objectives by holding at risk Soviet warmaking capabilities, including both the full range of Soviet military forces and the war-supporting industry which provides the foundation for Soviet military power and supports its capability to conduct a protracted conflict; and

- Places at risk those political entities the Soviet leadership values most: the mechanisms for ensuring survival of the Communist Party and its leadership cadres, and for retention of the Party's control over the Soviet and Soviet-bloc peoples.[66]

The new targeting policy and SIOP reflects a much greater emphasis by the Reagan Administration on the ability to destroy the Soviet political and military command and control system at any point in a strategic nuclear exchange; the development of new Soviet capabilities, and most particularly mobile or relocatable systems; changes in the US force structure, such as the introduction of new bombers and cruise missiles, as well as new warhead designs and new sensor systems for locating Soviet targets; and new computer capabilities which permit rapid retargeting of the US strategic nuclear forces.

The requirement to target the Soviet leadership and its command and control system is not itself novel. As noted above, a major attack option has been dedicated to this target set since SIOP-63. Until now, however, this target set has been regarded as a 'withhold' - i.e. an option to be reserved until the later phases of a strategic nuclear exchange in order to enhance escalation control, both by preserving the Soviet ability to conduct discriminate and controlled nuclear strikes as well as allowing the possibility of negotiating war termination between the US and Soviet national command authorities. The new plan, however, provides the option for prompt attack of the Soviet command and control system at the outset of a strategic nuclear exchange.

The emphasis accorded counter-leadership and counter-command and control capabilities is also new. The destruction of underground leadership bunkers and command sites is a prime objective of the MX ICBM and the Trident II D-5 SLBM. The large, 9MT B-53 warhead has been reactivated for the specific purpose of destroying deeply buried command centres.[67] In September 1988, the Secretary of Defense formally authorised the development of new earth-penetrator warheads which could be deployed on both MX ICBMs for prompt attacks against underground bunkers and command facilities as well as on cruise missiles for 'follow-on' attacks.[68] New ballistic missile penetration aids (penaids) are also under development to ensure that the ABM system around Moscow cannot prevent destruction of leadership and command facilities in the Moscow area.[69] And new sensor systems (including airborne and satellite Signals Intelligence (SIGINT) systems) are under development to provide a capability to locate Soviet leadership and C³I facilities that are not used in peacetime but are designed to begin functioning during a nuclear exchange.

US target planners have become particularly concerned about the proliferation of mobile or relocatable targets (RTs) in the Soviet Union. In 1984, there were more than 4,000 mobile targets in the National Strategic Target List.[70] With the development of the land-mobile SS-25 and rail-mobile SS-24 ICBMs and new mobile command and communications facilities, not only has this target set increased but it also includes several hundred weapons and facilities which have the highest priority in the SIOP. In December 1986, the Director of Central Intelligence Mobile Missile Task Force Intelligence Requirements and Analysis Working Group reported that new capabilities were required to deal with these mobile targets:

> Our current capability to meet adequately the demands placed upon our limited resources, to address effectively the mobile missile problem, is limited.
>
> A true capability to locate, identify and track mobile missiles for the purpose of targeting is evolutionary.
>
> [It] will require significant enhancement of our present capabilities.[71]

In 1986-87, the US Air Force developed a *Strategic Relocatable Target Capability Program* that was later incorporated in a Defense Department-wide *Master Plan for Relocatable Targets* that 'is keyed to the development of sensors, C³I architectures, and force structure necessary to put at risk these Soviet targets in the future'.[72]

The requirements to locate RTs immediately prior to and during a nuclear exchange has led to the development of new sensor systems, including the **Aurora** Mach-5 Stealth reconnaissance aircraft,[73] more advanced geostationary SIGINT satellites such as the *Magnum* launched in January 1985 and the new *Mentor*; the KH-12 *Ikon* real-time digital imaging satellite;[74] and the *Lacrosse* radar satellite system.

The requirement to destroy these mobile targets has greatly enhanced the importance of new bombers in the US triad. As General John T. Chain, the Commander in Chief of the Strategic Air Command (CINCSAC) asserted in July 1987:

> The capability of the manned bomber to penetrate enemy airspace and search out and destroy relocatable targets, particularly the highly threatening mobile ICBMs, is essential.[75]

And as the US Air Force has argued,

> Because of the increased Soviet emphasis on mobile ICBM delivery systems and command centres, the manned bomber's

real-time potential for locating and destroying relocatable systems is vital to the maintenance of a viable triad.[76]

According to Thomas E. Cooper, Assistance Secretary of the Air Force for Research, Development and Logistics, consideration has been given to modification of the B-1B bomber so that it can accept operational tasking against some relocatable targets.[77] However, while the use of the B-1B for this purpose remains problematical, it is clear that locating and destroying RTs is a prime objective of the B-2 Advance Technology Bomber. As General Chain noted in July 1987,

> The highly flexible Advanced Technology Bomber, with a low-observable design, will penetrate enemy airspace and hold all types of targets, both fixed and relocatable, at risk. This is tremendously important given the growing portion of the Soviet target base that will be relocatable in the next decade.[78]

And as US Air Force officials recently stated,

> With its projected capability to dash into the Soviet Union undetected,...the B-2 [will] be able to roam the strongholds of the mobile Soviet missiles and look for targets.[79]

In addition, rapid retargeting concepts and techniques have been developed to permit the use of Minuteman ICBMs and Tomahawk Land Attack SLCMs 'to place and keep Soviet mobile target systems at risk'.[80] Finally, new 'soft kill' weapons, utilising enhanced electromagnetic pulse (EMP) and microwave emissions designed to destroy the electronic mechanisms in above-ground mobile missile and command and control systems, are also under development.[81]

The most significant change in the structure of the SIOP is that, instead of being an essentially static plan consisting principally of preplanned options, an adaptive planning process is being instituted in which retargeting will be a continuous, real-time process. As Major General Richard B. Goetze, Deputy Chief of Staff for Strategic Planning and Analysis, Strategic Air Command, has reported,

> We are pursuing adaptive planning capabilities - capabilities which will allow future planning systems to respond on a real-time basis to changes in policy, threat, and forces. Numerous initiatives are underway to reduce the time required to build the SIOP or modify it during a crisis. Innovative planning systems and procedures that will maximize force effectiveness are currently being brought on-board. As we enter the 1990s, the time required to build the SIOP can be expected to be reduced from months to weeks or even days. The time required to

retarget sorties in a conflict will be reduced from a few days to a few hours, and in some cases, to a few minutes. This will have a substantial impact on our operational units. Unit planners must be prepared to perform sortie maintenance or respond to retargeting orders on a daily basis. Aircrews, for example, may be required to react to changes in targeting information or intelligence updates about changes in enemy defenses while enroute to the target area. This is particularly important given the dynamic nature of the evolving threat, e.g. the SS-25. The bottom line is that we can expect today's rigid preplanned SIOP, requiring months to build and change, to be a thing of the past.[82]

As General Goetze observed, deterrence based on 'a warfighting plan' has now been instituted in US strategic nuclear policy to the extent that the technical capabilities of the late 1980s permit.[83]

Conclusion

The historical record not only suggests very strongly that strategic concepts and doctrines have played very little role in US strategic force structure developments; it also reveals something of the extent to which the strategic concepts and doctrines are the dependent variables, and of the nature of that particular relationship. In addition, it indicates some of the principal factors that are actually involved in force structure development.

Any impact that strategic concepts and doctrines have had on US force structure development has never been direct or sustained. There are, however, two general notions which warrant consideration. First, the sophisticated strategic calculus, largely originating at the RAND Corporation in the 1950s, which argued the necessity for a survivable, second-strike nuclear retaliatory force, was invoked in the decisions of early 1961 to accelerate the Polaris and silo-based Minuteman programs. Second, throughout the 1950s and early 1960s there was a generally accepted assumption, so fundamental to the thinking of both military and civilian strategists that it was frequently unarticulated, to the effect that the US required a substantial degree of strategic nuclear superiority over the Soviet Union. However, it was never made clear just how this 'superiority' was to be measured. By themselves, general principles of 'survivability' and 'superiority', though they might act as signposts, could not serve as guides to the determination of specific force levels or force characteristics.

At the other extreme, it is possible to find some specific force structure decisions that derived directly from the acceptance and/or declaration of a particular strategic concept or doctrine. Perhaps the clearest examples were the recommendations of the Fletcher Committee, a group of analysts and scientists set up by the Secretary of the Air Force, Eugene Zuckert, in mid-1961 to review the changes in the Minuteman missile system that were required by the policy change from 'massive retaliation' to 'controlled flexible response'. Many of the qualitative improvements that were effected in the Minuteman II (LGM-30F) missile, the first 10 of which were officially declared operational in October 1965, were the direct result of recommendations of the Fletcher Committee: whereas previous plans allowed the Minuteman force to be launched only in squadrons (of 50 missiles) it was now given a selective, individual launch capability; and whereas the Minuteman IA (LGM-30A) missile could only be programmed with a single target, the LGM-30F was given a target selection capability of eight targets. But examples such as this are very few and far between.

The developments in strategic policy during the latter years of the Reagan Administration were more complex. In many cases, policy guidance and technological promise were mutually reinforcing. Most of the improvements in strategic C3I systems that were required by NSDD-12 and NSDD-13 in October 1981 had been initiated by previous Administrations, and most especially the Carter Administration. In contrast, the Reagan Administration did establish new policy objectives which required the modification or revivification of extant technologies (such as the B-1 bomber) as well as new innovations (such as earth-penetrating weapons, third-generation EMP and microwave weapons, and the Lacrosse radar satellite system). Some of the new technologies sought by the Reagan Administration were simply unfeasible (such as strategic defences which would render ballistic missiles obsolete and C3I systems which could support a protracted nuclear war).

More generally, insofar as there is any identifiable relationship between strategic concepts and doctrine on the one hand and US strategic nuclear force development on the other, it is very much one in which military technology is the determinate variable. With respect to strategic policy, it is easy to establish this in a negative sense. It is obvious, for example, that certain counterforce strategies were impossible to pursue before technology provided the means of locating enemy missile silos and bomber bases and the means of accurately delivering relatively large numbers of high-yield nuclear weapons. Hence, little serious thought was given to counterforce strategies before the late 1950s (following the deployment of U-2 reconnaissance aircraft and, from August 1960, surveillance satellites; large numbers of strategic nuclear delivery vehicles; and the H-bomb). And strategies involving controlled and flexible responses were not possible until the development of sophisticated command and control systems, multiple targeting memories, and individual and selective missile launch capabilities. But the positive side of the relationship is more interesting: viz., that which technology permits is frequently adopted as doctrine. This certainly seems to have been the case with some of the more significant elements of the so-called Schlesinger doctrine, and at least partially, the retention of that doctrine by the Carter Administration. By 1977, most of the strategic force requirements of a strategy of controlled, limited, counterforce operations, together with the necessary command and control arrangements, were already emplaced; unless one were persuaded as to their counterproductive arms control impact, there would have been little point in dismantling them and denying oneself the potential options and flexibility they allowed.

This is not to suggest the operation of any pure form of technological determinism. For one thing, it begs the question as to where the impetus for technological development derives. There are some instances, such as the development of the H-bomb in the late-1940s and early-1950s and, perhaps, the pursuit of more accurate ballistic missile guidance systems in the 1960s, where the professional interest of the scientific and technical community was paramount. But this community is only one of the many interested groups that contribute to the decision-making process, and it is certainly far from being the most powerful.

There are in the US weapons acquisition and force development process a wide range of quite disparate groups and individuals, each with their own peculiar loyalties, interests, perspectives and predilections, and each with some semi-autonomous power-political base from which they work to promote their respective positions. The most important of these 'quasi-sovereignties' is of course the President, but the outcomes are generally shaped less by presidential directives than by adversary processes involving a complex interaction of all the participants[84] - the White House staff (and especially the President's National Security Adviser), the Secretary of Defense and his principal civilian assistants, the military chiefs and their respective services, and the Office of Management and Budget (OMB). Studies of the major US force development decisions of the 1950s through the 1970s - the decision to develop the ICBM, the decision to deploy a long-range strategic ballistic missile force of 1,000 Minuteman ICBMs and 656 SLBMs, and the decision to develop the MIRV - all indicate that the outcomes were, more than anything else, the product of intra-mural bargaining, negotiation and compromise between these quasi-sovereignties, with the quality of the arguments and the strategic analysis being decidedly secondary to the political power of respective adversaries.[85]

Strategic concepts and doctrines are themselves not the product of any abstract reflection on national interests. Rather, they are more typically products of the technological and bureaucratic-political environments in which they are developed and advanced. And insofar as they have a role in US nuclear force structure development, it is as instruments to be employed in the intra-mural bargaining rather than as signposts to indicate development.

This is not a novel conclusion:[86] the generally expedient and partisan character of American strategic thought was an implicit theme in Bernard Brodie's *Strategy in the Missile Age,* and one to which he returned in his last writings. However, it is one that deserves wider recognition, for it offers hope to those rationalists who might despair at the failure of US strategic force development to reflect the evolution of strategic concepts and doctrines. For if those concepts and doctrines are appreciated for their instrumental value, to be employed in adversary situations ranging from budget discussions through weapons acquisition processes to international arms control negotiations, then strategic analysis in a broader sense will in the end come closer to realising its intended impact - and that will include its impact on US strategic nuclear force development.

Endnotes

1   Bernard Brodie (ed.), *The Absolute Weapon: Atomic Power and World Order,* (Harcourt, Brace and Company, New York, 1946), p.83.

2   *Ibid.,* p.76.

3   See Anthony Cave Brown (ed.), *Operation World War III: The Secret American Plan 'Dropshot' for War with the Soviet Union,* (Arms and Armour Press, London, 1979).

4   See Samuel F. Wells, 'Sounding the Tocsin: NSC 68 and the Soviet Threat', *International Security,* (Vol.4, No.2), Fall 1979, pp.124-25.

5   *Ibid.,* pp.134-38.

6   *Ibid.,* p.139.

7   Samuel P. Huntington, *The Common Defense: Strategic Programs in National Politics,* (Columbia University Press, New York, 1961), pp.59-61.

8   *Ibid.,* p.73.

9   *New York Times,* 13 January 1954.

10   See A.J. Wohlstetter, F.S. Hoffman, R.J. Lutz and H.S. Rowen, *Selection and Use of Strategic Air Bases,* (The RAND Corporation, Santa Monica, California, R-266, April 1954); and A.J. Wohlstetter, F.S. Hoffman and H.S. Rowen, *Protecting US Power to Strike Back in the 1950's and 1960's,* (The RAND Corporation, Santa Monica, California, R-290, 1 September 1956).

11   Bernard Brodie, *Strategy in the Missile Age,* (Princeton University Press, Princeton, New Jersey, 1959), p.249.

12   *Ibid.,* pp.249, 263.

13   For a fuller discussion of developments in strategic policy and force structure during the Kennedy Administration, see Desmond Ball, *Politics and Force Levels: The*

Strategic Missile Program of the Kennedy Administration, (University of California Press, Berkeley, 1980).

14   *International Herald Tribune*, 9 May 1978.

15   *Operation Plan USCINCEUR NO 100-6*, 15 June 1962, cited in 'How to Blow Up the World', *New Statesman*, 27 June 1980, p.97. See also Alfred Goldberg, *A Brief Survey of the Evolution of Ideas About Counterforce*, (The RAND Corporation, Santa Monica, California, RM-5431-PR, October 1976), p.25.

16   Scott D. Sagan, 'SIOP-62: The Nuclear War Plan Briefing to President Kennedy', *International Security*, (Vol.12, No.1), Summer 1987, p.39.

17   Henry L. Trewhitt, *McNamara: His Ordeal in the Pentagon*, (Harper & Row, New York, 1971), p.115.

18   *Newsweek*, 9 April 1962, p.32.

19   Senate Appropriations Committee, *Department of Defense Appropriations, 1965*, pp.31-32.

20   Senate Armed Services Committee and Senate Appropriations Committee, *Military Procurement Authorization, Fiscal Year 1966*, p.43.

21   *Statement of Secretary of Defense Robert S. McNamara before the House Armed Services Committee on the Fiscal Year 1966-70 Defense Program & 1966 Defense Budget*, 18 February 1965, p.39.

22   *Statement of Secretary of Defense Robert S. McNamara before a Joint Session of the Senate Armed Services Committee & the Senate Sub-committee on Department of Defense Appropriations on the Fiscal Year 1968-72 Defense Program and 1968 Defense Budget*, 23 January 1967, p.39.

23   For a fuller discussion of the strategic developments of this period, see Desmond Ball, *Deja Vu: The Return to Counterforce in the Nixon Administration*, (California Seminar on Arms Control and Foreign Policy, No.46, December 1974).

24   Cited in Jack Anderson, 'Not-So-New Nuclear Strategy', *Washington Post*, 12 October 1980, p.C-7.

25   See for example, Senate Foreign Relations Committee, *US-USSR Strategic Policies*, (Top Secret hearing held on 4 March 1974; sanitized and made public on 4 April 1974), pp.18-19.

26   *Washington Post*, 12 October 1980, p.C-7.

27   *Ibid*.

28   House Appropriations Committee, *Defense of Defense Appropriations for 1978*, (U.S. Government Printing Office, Washington, D.C., 1977), Part 2, p.212. See also *Los Angeles Times*, 2 February 1977, p.1.

29   Lawrence J. Korb, 'National Security Organization and Process in the Carter Administration', in Sam C. Sarkesian, (ed.), *Defense Policy and the Presidency: Carter's First Years*, (Westview Press, Boulder, Colorado, 1979), Chapter 11.

30   See Robert G. Kaiser, 'Global Strategy Memo Divides Carter's Staff', *Washington Post*, 7 July 1977; Hedrich Smith, 'Carter Study Takes More Hopeful View of Strategy of U.S.', *New York Times*, 8 July 1977, p.1; Richard Burt, 'U.S. Study Asserts Russians Could Not Win Nuclear War', *International Herald Tribune*, 7-8 January 1978.

31   *International Herald Tribune*, 7-8 January 1978, and Charles Mohr, 'Carter Orders Steps to Increase Ability to Meet War Threats', *New York Times*, 26 August 1977, pp.1, 8.

32   House Armed Services Committee, *Hearings on Military Posture and H.R. 1872*, (Washington, D.C., 1979), Part 3, Book 1, p.9; *Aviation Week and Space Technology*, 6 March 1978, p.16.

33   Mohr, 'Carter Offers Steps', pp.1,8.

34   House Armed Services Committee, *Hearings on Military Posture and H.R. 1872*, Part 3, Book 1, p.437.

35   See testimony of William J. Perry, Senate Armed Services Committee, *Department of Defense Authorization for Appropriations for Fiscal Year 1980*, (Washington, D.C., 1979), part 1, pp.298-199; House Appropriations Committee, *Defense Appropriations for 1980*, Part 3, pp.116-117.

36   Testimony of Perry, Senate Armed Forces Committee, *Department of Defense Authorization for Appropriations for Fiscal Year 1980*, Part 1, p.497. See also *Air Force Magazine*, March 1979, p.52; and 'Statement of Harold Brown on the Defense Budget before the Senate Foreign Relations Committee', 19 September 1979, mimeo, pp.19,20.

37   See Richard Burt, 'Pentagon Reviewing Nuclear War Plans', *New York Times*, 16 December 1977, p.5.

38   Desmond Ball, 'Counterforce Targeting: How New? How Viable?' *Arms Control Today*, 11, No.3, (February 1981), pp.2,6.

39   Harold Brown, 'The Objective of U.S. Strategic Forces', Address to the Naval War College, Washington, 22 August 1980 (official text, U.S. International Communications Agency), p.5.

40   Senate Armed Services Committee, *Department of Defense Authorization for Appropriations for Fiscal Year 1982*, (Washington, D.C., 1981) Part 7, p.4210.

41   Senate Foreign Relations Committee, *Nuclear War Strategy*, pp.15-16.

42   See Ted Greenwood, *Making the MIRV: A Study of Defense Decision Making*, (Ballinger Publishing Company, Cambridge, Massachusets, 1975), Chapter 2.

43   *Ibid.*, p.10.

44   House Armed Services Committee, *Hearings on Military Posture and H.R. 1872*, Part 3, Book 1, pp.24-25.

45   Senate Foreign Relations Committee, *U.S.-U.S.S.R. Strategic Policies*, 4 March 1974, p.29.

46   *Statement of Secretary of Defense Melvin R. Laird before the House Armed Services Committee on the FY 1972-1976 Defense Program and the 1972 Defense Budget*, 9 March 1971, p.67.

47   *Development of Strategic Air Command 1946-1976* (Office of the Historian, SAC Headquarters, 21 March 1976), p.166.

48   Senate Foreign Relations Committee, *U.S.-U.S.S.R. Strategic Policies*, 4 March 1974, p.29; and *Report of the Secretary of Defense James R. Schlesinger to the Congress on the FY 1975 Defense Budget and FY 1975-1979 Defense Program*, 4 March 1974, pp.72-77.

49   See testimony of Dr William J. Perry, Senate Armed Services Committee, *Department of Defense Authorization for Appropriations for Fiscal Year 1980* (Part 1), pp.298-99; and House Appropriations Committee, *Department of Defense Appropriations for 1980*, (Part 3), pp.116-117.

50   *Report of Secretary of Defense Harold Brown to the Congress on the FY 1981 Budget, FY 1982 Authorization Request and FY 1981-1985 Defense Program*, 29 January 1980, p.71.

51   *Aviation Week and Space Technology*, 6 March 1972, pp.12-13.

52   *Aviation Week and Space Technology*, 17 January 1972, p.11. See also *Statement of Secretary of Defense Melvin R. Laird before the House Armed Services Committee on the FY 1973 Defense Budget and FY 1973-1977 Program*, 17 February 1972, p.73.

53   'Why C3I is the Pentagon's Top Priority', *Government Executive*, January 1982, p.14.

54   Michael Getler, 'Administration's Nuclear War Policy Stance Still Murky', *Washington Post*, 10 November 1982, p.A24.

55   Robert Scheer, *With Enough Shovels: Reagan, Bush and Nuclear War*, (Random House, New York, 1982), p.12; and Robert Scheer, 'Pentagon Plan Aims at Victory in Nuclear War', *Los Angeles Times*, 15 August 1982, pp.1, 23.

56   Jeffrey Richelson, 'PD-59, NSDD-13 and the Reagan Strategic Modernization Program', *The Journal of Strategic Studies*, (Vol.6, No.2), June 1983, pp.131, 139.

57   'Why C3I is the Pentagon's Top Priority', *Government Executive*, January 1982, p.14.

58   Donald C. Latham, Assistant Secretary of Defense (Command, Control, Communications and Intelligence), *Surviving and Enduring Communications, Command and Control: A Major Element in Deterrence and War Fighting*, (Briefing notes, August 1982).

59   *Ibid.*

60   Samuel F. Wells, 'A Question of Priorities: A Comparison of the Carter and Reagan Defense Programs', *Orbis*, Fall 1983, p.661; and Richelson, 'PD-59, NSDD-13 and the Reagan Strategic Modernization Program', p.142.

61 George C. Wilson, 'Preparing for Long Nuclear War is Waste of Funds, General Jones Says', *Washington Post*, 19 June 1982, p.A3.

62 *Text of President Reagan's Address on National Security*, March 23, 1983, Washington, D.C., pp.8-9.

63 *Ibid.*

64 See Desmond Ball, 'U.S. Strategic Concepts and Programs: The Historical Context', in Samuel F. Wells and Robert S. Litwak (eds), *Strategic Defenses and Soviet-American Relations*, (Ballinger Publishing Company, Cambridge, Massachusetts, 1987), pp.1-35.

65 For further discussion of SIOP-6F, see Desmond Ball and Robert C. Toth, 'Revising the SIOP: Taking War-Fighting to Dangerous Extremes', *Intercontinental Security*, (Vol.14, No.4), Spring 1990, pp.65-92. In 1987-88, when the national guidance for the new SIOP was prepared, it was generally referred to as SIOP-7. However, the Bush Administration decided to stress the continuity in the target planning process and designate the new plan as SIOP-6F - partly in anticipation of criticisms of some of the novel departures in the new plan (such as concern with prompt destruction of the Soviet leadership) which were already being voiced.

66 President Ronald Reagan, *National Security Strategy of the United States*, (The White House, Washington, D.C., January 1988), p.14.

67 'Last of the Titans', *Bulletin of the Atomic Scientists*, September 1987, p.62.

68 Warren Strobel, 'U.S. To Make Nuclear Bomb That Burrows', *Washington Post*, 13 September 1988, p.A16; and Tim Carrington, 'Carlucci Orders Move for Development of "Earth-Penetrating" Nuclear Weapon', *Wall Street Journal*, 13 September 1988, p.5.

69 'Countering Star Warski', *Bulletin of the Atomic Scientists*, (Vol.43, No.9), November 1987, p.55; *Aviation Week and Space Technology*, 28 September 1987, p.17.

70 *Air Force Magazine*, December 1984, p.23.

71 Cited in Gregory A. Fossedal, 'U.S. Said to be Unable to Verify Missile Ban', *Washington Times*, 18 November 1987, p.6; and Rowland Evans and Robert Novak, 'What About the Hidden SS-20s?', *Washington Post*, 18 November 1987, p.25.

72 Edgar Ulsamer, 'Missiles and Targets', *Air Force Magazine*, July 1987, p.69; and *Aviation Week and Space Technology*, 7 March 1988, p.15.

73 See T.A. Heppenheimer, 'Revealed!: Mach 5 Spy Plane', *Popular Science*, November 1988, pp.70-73, 114-116.

74 'Tracking Mobile Soviet Weapons Seen as KH-12 Task', *Aerospace Daily*, 17 April 1985, p.269.

75 General John T. Chain, 'Strategic Fundamentals', *Air Force Magazine*, July 1987, p.67.

76 *Air Force Magazine*, October 1986, p.49.

77 'Countering Mobile Targets a B-1B Task?' *Defense Electronics*, March 1986, p.18.

78 General Chain, 'Strategic Fundamentals', p.67.

79 Cited in R.S. Dudney, 'Strategic Forces At The Brink of START', *Air Force Magazine*, February 1988, p.43.

80 *Defense Nuclear Agency, Fiscal Year 1986, Program Document: Research, Development, Test and Evaluation, Defense Agencies*, (Supporting Data for DNA Fiscal Year 1986 Budget Estimates, Submitted to Congress January 1985), p.409; *Defense Nuclear Agency, Fiscal Year 1987, Program Document: Research, Development, Test and Evaluation, Defense Agencies*, (Supporting Data for DNA Fiscal Year 1987 Budget Estimates, Submitted to Congress February 1986), p.67; and 'Fast Targeting For Minuteman', *Defense Week*, 18 March 1985, p.5.

81 Theodore B. Taylor, 'Third-Generation Nuclear Weapons', *Scientific American*, (Vol.256, No.4), April 1987, pp.22-31; 'A Third Generation of Nukes', *Time*, 25 May 1987, p.36; and H. Keith Florig, 'The Future Battlefield: A Blast of Gigawatts?' *IEEE Spectrum*, (Vol.25, No.3), March 1988, pp.5054.

82 Major General Richard B. Goetze, 'SIOP - A Plan For Peace', *Combat Crew*, January 1987, p.15.

83 *Ibid.*, p.13.

84 William T.R. Fox, foreword to Michael H. Armacost, *The Politics of Weapon Innovation: The Thor-Jupiter Controversy*, (Columbia University Press, New York, 1969), p.vii.

85 See Edmund Beard, *Developing the ICBM: A Study in Bureaucratic Politics*, (Columbia University Press, New York, 1976); Desmond Ball, *Politics and Force Levels: The Strategic Missile Program of the Kennedy Administration*; and Ted Greenwood, *Making the MIRV: A Study of Defense Decision-Making*.

86 Bernard Brodie, *The Development of Nuclear Strategy*, (ASIC Working Paper No.11, Centre for Arms Control and International Security, UCLA, February 1978).

CHAPTER 3

THE DEVELOPMENT OF SOVIET STRATEGY

Geoffrey Jukes

At the end of the Second World War in 1945 the Soviet Union had armed forces totalling 11.365 million men.[1] However, their configuration was that of a very strong regional, rather than a global power, namely very large ground forces supported by predominantly short-range tactical air forces and a navy mostly devoted to guarding the army's coastal flanks. The strategic bomber force was small, while the navy had little high seas capability. Amphibious forces were improvised as needed, usually for relatively small and short-range operations, and there were no nuclear weapons. In short the Soviet Union lacked most of the attributes of the other country elevated by the war to superpower rank, the United States; and unlike the United States, the Soviet Union had suffered enormous casualties and devastation. The wartime alliance had been at best a shotgun wedding, and with Germany and Japan, at least, temporarily deleted from strategic equations, the realities of strategy and the ideological definition of the strongest capitalist country as the main enemy, combined to identify the United States, the only country capable of attacking the Soviet Union, as the potential antagonist to be *deterred*.

Since that time the history of Soviet strategy is one of slow but sustained growth, progressively from regional to global power status, involving the acquisition of capacities to project power at a distance which are similar in kind, though not necessarily in scale or detail, to those of the United States. The process has not been mere mimicry of the United States, and has not been based on crash programs. It has resulted in approximate overall parity in the superpowers' capacity to destroy each other, but significant differences in their abilities to handle lower-order contingencies.

The post-war situation was unprecedented in Russian history in that the major perceived antagonist, the United States, was a country which possessed the resources needed to strike at the USSR from a distance, in the shape of its navy and air force, but was itself inaccessible to the main traditional Russian instrument of military power - its army. The first phase of development, from 1945 until Stalin's death in 1953, involved massive manpower reductions (to 2.874 million in 1948)[2] coupled with a major effort to acquire the capital-intensive forces needed to meet the new situation. Strategic needs included nuclear weapons, and the first successful test took place in 1949. The delivery systems for them, first bombers and later missiles (apart from the TU-16

Badger medium bomber) capable of reaching US or allied bases around the Soviet periphery, but not the US itself, were not completed in Stalin's lifetime. However, a comprehensive air defence system, including radars, aircraft, artillery and surface-to-air missiles, was largely in place by 1953.

Prodigious naval expansion was planned, of both surface and submarine forces. Initially this force was to protect the Baltic and Black Sea coasts against Anglo-American amphibious assault, but ultimately was intended to mount a high seas challenge to trans-Atlantic traffic, both with aircraft carriers and with longer range submarines (the *Zulu* class). Especial progress was made in cruiser building. Large numbers of the smaller surface units (destroyers, frigates and corvettes) and of medium-range submarines (the *Whiskey* class) were built, at construction rates never attempted before or since.

The political concepts underlying Stalin's strategic views were simple. General war with a threatened and militant capitalism was ultimately inevitable; Soviet forces should be prepared for it and where possible advantageous positions should be taken in advance - the satellisation of Eastern Europe, for example, provided a buffer zone for defence and a forward base for a theatre offensive. Soviet policy was to avoid any appearance of weakness which might tempt an attack, but also to avoid confrontations which might provoke it.

So when in 1948 the Western allies extended the West German currency reform to their sectors of Berlin, Stalin sought to exploit the city's location deep inside the Soviet occupation zone by declaring all rail, road and waterway access routes from the West as simultaneously closed for repair. The allies decided to supply Berlin by air - a possibility Stalin had either not considered or dismissed as impossible. Apart from sporadic harassment, however, the airlift was not interfered with, and Soviet officers were not withdrawn from the Berlin Air Safety Centre - had they been, the airlift could have operated only in daylight and might have failed, thus causing the allies to escalate the crisis. As Stalin had never formally declared a blockade, he was able in 1949 to make a face-saving withdrawal by declaring the surface access routes repaired and reopened.

Another instance of his opportunism and caution occurred later that year, when North Korean leader Kim Il-Sung proposed to invade South Korea. Kim assured Stalin that South Korea could be wholly defeated and occupied before the United States could act, and when Mao Zedong backed Kim's assessment Stalin endorsed and facilitated the undertaking.[3] The invasion was launched in June 1950, but the US reaction was stronger and faster than expected, and the expected quick victory did not materialise. Stalin not only declined to contemplate

Soviet intervention, leaving it to China to send 'volunteers', but also withdrew all Soviet advisers with the North Korean forces, for fear that the capture of any of them would reveal Soviet complicity. Although he died before an armistice was concluded in 1953, Stalin clearly preferred failure of the venture to confrontation with the United States and its allies.[4] But interpreting the strong US reaction as possibly presaging a general war, he increased the manpower of the armed forces by a one-year increase in the term of conscription.[5] The measure was not publicly announced, for fear that the West would interpret it as a move towards Soviet initiation of general war, and decide to attack first. This measure, probably coupled with a more rigorous attitude towards exemptions, more than doubled the size of the armed forces compared to 1948, and by 1955 they stood at 5.463 million.[6]

Stalin died in March 1953, and the new 'collective leadership' initiated comprehensive reviews of all his policies. While these were under way a leadership struggle resulted in the political ascendancy of Nikita Khrushchev, who not only pursued reduction of military manpower and defence expenditure, but also made two important doctrinal innovations. The first was to proclaim that global war between capitalism and socialism was not inevitable[7] (making definitive the position towards which Stalin had appeared to be moving shortly before his death) and the second was to claim that if it did break out it would inevitably be nuclear from the outset or from a very early stage.[8] The majority of Soviet military leaders apparently endorsed both propositions, but it gradually became apparent that they did not share the conclusion Khrushchev drew from them, that military strength would henceforth be measured in nuclear-warheaded missiles, and hence conventional forces had become relatively unimportant. Khrushchev's reasoning appears to have been that the achievement, in the late 1950s, with bombers from 1955, and a small force of intercontinental ballistic missiles (ICBMs) from 1957, of an ability to destroy American cities comparable to that which the US had had against Soviet cities since the late 1940s, constituted effective military parity. Therefore, accordingly, the United States, deterred from nuclear attack on the Soviet Union by the certainty of devastating retaliation, would also be deterred from lesser military actions against Soviet interests, including those against Soviet-backed Third World governments or revolutionary movements.

In thus equating deterrence with parity and overestimating the spillover effects of nuclear deterrence into situations where threats to use nuclear weapons would not be credible, Khrushchev was not wholly or primarily concerned with strategic logic. He was influenced by the heavy costs of Stalin's programs and attracted by the possibilities of attaining parity more cheaply through arms control and disarmament agreements which would reduce force levels. Negotiations for these would carry a bonus of political parity, presenting the Soviet Union as an equal opposite number to the most powerful capitalist country.

Initially he found an ally in Marshal G.K. Zhukov, the most outstanding of the Red Army's wartime generals, who appears to have shared widespread military concern[9] that Stalin's doctrines, especially their denigration of surprise attack, had prompted programs and force structures inappropriate to nuclear war. As Defence Minister from May 1955 to late October 1957 Zhukov oversaw a wide-ranging professional debate on nuclear war which resulted in substantial alterations in doctrine and force structure, manpower reductions of about 1.84 million, motorisation of the Ground Forces, major changes and cuts in naval construction, the establishment of an integrated Air Defence Force and considerable progress towards the creation of a strategic missile force. However, his streamlining of military organisation included reducing the numbers and influence of the Party-appointed Political Officers in the armed forces, and this was probably the main reason for his dismissal.[10]

Following Zhukov's departure, Khrushchev espoused ever more fundamental disarmament proposals, culminating in advocacy of General and Complete Disarmament in 1959-60 and a speech in January 1960 in which he announced a further cut of one-third in manpower, designed to reduce it from 3.6 to 2.4 million by the end of 1961. In consequence, a number of leading military officers signified their dissent at various times. They included the Commanders-in-Chief of the Warsaw Pact and of the Ground Forces, the Chief of General Staff, the highest ranking Armoured Forces officer and Zhukov's successor as Defence Minister, Marshal Malinovski. The 1960 manpower reduction was quietly cancelled in early 1961, after the incoming Kennedy Administration announced plans to increase US and NATO conventional forces, and another reduction which Khrushchev foreshadowed in 1963 never eventuated. Khrushchev was overthrown in October 1964, and reassessments made by the new leadership produced strategic and tactical doctrines that have only recently begun to be challenged under Gorbachev, and force structure, size and equipment which still prevail.

Two essential premises of Khrushchev came immediately under challenge. One was his belief in 'minimum deterrence' - that provided the Soviet strategic nuclear force was large enough to destroy the United States, it did not matter if its US counterpart was several times as large. In the early 1960s, when missile accuracy was sufficient only for attacks on large and indefensible targets such as cities, Khrushchev's argument might have been valid. However, by 1964 actual and foreseeable improvements in accuracy implied that missile forces would, before long, be able to attack each other. The prominence of counterforce targeting in US doctrinal statements from 1961 onwards also indicated that when the option became available the United States would take it up. The size of one force therefore became a determinant of the size of the other. Possibly in Khrushchev's last months in office, but more likely in the early months of the succeeding Brezhnev-Kosygin regime, the Soviets began a build-up which by the end of the 1960s gave them both more and larger ICBMs than the United States.

The second Khrushchevian assumption to be jettisoned was the one that war would inevitably be, or swiftly become, nuclear, with its corollary that the size of the conventional forces therefore mattered little. An alternative argument, that in nuclear war conventional forces would need to be large because of the heavy losses they would face, had been stated or hinted at more than once by Malinovski himself.[11] Moreover, there had been guarded references to the possibility that even in a general war there might be theatres in which nuclear weapons were not used.[12] By the end of 1966, doctrine had been modified to envisage emergence of alternative scenarios once an approximate parity at strategic nuclear level had been reached. These included the possibilities that even in a general war the superpowers might not use nuclear weapons at all, or might use them only on the territory of allies.

This raised delicate issues. Alliance systems exist to further mutual interests, and, for both Western and Eastern Europe, military alliances rest upon the assumption of a threat which cannot be neutralised without the extended deterrence provided by a superpower. Any indication that the superpowers might use their allies' territory as a jousting-ground raises doubts as to whether alliance may be more dangerous than neutralism, and occasional American references to the possibility of a nuclear war fought only in Europe have invariably aroused anxious reactions there.[13] The Soviets have carefully avoided any public reference to world war scenarios in which the superpowers do not share the devastation inflicted upon their allies. There are, nevertheless, indications that from the mid-1960s Soviet strategy came to cater for such a possibility.

Underlying this was an assumption that the United States would not in all circumstances be deterred from the use of nuclear weapons by a mere threat of destruction, as long as it believed it could inflict greater destruction upon the Soviet Union. But if faced, as it had not been in previous crises such as Cuba 1962, with a threat of *equal destruction*, the United States would be deterred from attacking Soviet territory (and, of course, *vice versa*), leaving the outcome of a war to be decided by campaigns around the Soviet periphery. Massive forces would be involved in these, but nuclear weapons would be either not used or employed only against enemy forces and infrastructure within the theatre.

Acceptance of this scenario, as opposed to the 'deterrence only' policy of Khrushchev, was a triumph of strategy over economics, because it imposed a very costly 'two-track' requirement for defence spending. The first involved increasing strategic nuclear forces to the point where the threat of at least equal destruction could be posed, while the second necessitated comprehensive upgrading of conventional forces so as to win if possible, and at least not lose, the peripheral campaigns. Not only that, the interdependence of the two policies was total. It would be pointless to win on one and lose on the other, so any future move along either track by the much richer Western alliance countries would somehow have to be countered. The need to win a theatre war in Western Europe regained the importance it had had under Stalin, even though the advent of ICBMs and sea-launched ballistic missiles (SLBMs) had deprived it of the rationale that capture of west European airfields would much reduce US capacity to attack Soviet home territory. Moreover, to it had been added a need to provide for possible simultaneous campaigns along the southern and eastern borders. Given the technological dynamism and economic resources not only of the US, but of its major allies in Europe and Japan, the adoption of the two-track policy could well involve permanent strategic and economic overstretch.

Nevertheless, by the end of 1966[14] the policy had been adopted. It was pursued for at least ten years without apparent misgivings about its viability, for several more years after signs of doubt first became apparent in 1976, and was only finally subjected to serious re-evaluation after Gorbachev came to power in 1985.

There is no hard evidence as to why this was so; but the mid-1960s were a period of optimism about the Soviet future and of relative disunity in the American alliance system. In 1966 France had withdrawn from the peacetime military structure of NATO, and NATO bodies, including the Headquarters and the Defence College, had had to move to other countries. The initial twenty-year term of the NATO Treaty would expire in 1969, and in some countries the possibility of withdrawal was being discussed. The European NATO members were uneasy about US involvement in Vietnam, and unresponsive to American suggestions that they should join in it. Moreover, there was discord in Japanese-US relations over the non-return to Japan of Okinawa and other islands. On the mainland the Cultural Revolution appeared likely to weaken China's position internally and reduce its influence internationally as well as among foreign Communist parties; and finally the post-war economic boom in the capitalist world was beginning to flag. Meanwhile the Soviet economy was maintaining higher growth rates than most non-Communist countries, and the circumstances of the time may well have suggested to the Brezhnev-Kosygin Politburo that the two-track solution would become more affordable as time passed because of economic growth on the one hand and weakening of the adversary alliance system on the other. A third 'track', the pursuit of partial detente with the United States, was probably also expected to keep costs within bounds.

However, events turned out differently. The Warsaw Pact invasion of Czechoslovakia in 1968 ended discussion about secession from NATO. The small border war with China in 1969 created a major additional force commitment on the Sino-Soviet border, and, by prompting a Chinese rapprochement with the US, raised for Soviet defence policy the spectre of a tacit Sino-US-Japanese alliance to be confronted in the future. The Okinawa problem was resolved by mid-1971; while America's withdrawal from Vietnam in 1973, though locally a victory for a Soviet ally, removed another source of friction from US relations not only with the NATO and Japanese allies, but also with China. Pursuit of detente initially served its purpose of cost-containment, in the shape of the Strategic Arms Limitation Treaty (SALT) and associated agreements of 1972, which set upper limits to numbers of strategic nuclear weapons and to defences against them (anti-ballistic missiles). The process appeared to move further when Brezhnev and President Ford signed in 1975 a SALT II agreement which, if ratified, would have brought about actual reductions. But Soviet insistence that detente did not apply to the Third World, support for the Marxist FNLA in Angola and Dergue in Ethiopia demonstrating that the insistence was not merely one of philosophical definition, and the continuing modernisation of the conventional forces, accompanied in some cases, particularly the Ground Forces, by increases in their size, were widely seen, especially in the United States, as attempts to exploit detente. Allegations were made, and widely believed in the West, that under cover of detente the Soviets were pursuing military superiority, or had already attained it in some respects. It was argued that a 'window of opportunity' would open for them in the early 1980s, in which they would be able to attack the United States with a good chance of success. Like the 'bomber gap' of the mid-1950s, or the 'missile gap' of 1958-60, the 'window of opportunity' later proved not to exist. However, belief that it might come to do so, and the other factors mentioned above, had reduced the prospects that the US Congress would ratify the SALT II agreement almost to vanishing point even before 1978 when the Soviet-supported Vietnamese invasion of Kampuchea and the direct intervention in Afghanistan led the Carter administration to bury detente for the rest of its term of office.

While detente was withering away, so was the growth rate of the Soviet economy. Indeed, the factors which held favourable for the Soviet leadership in the mid-1960s had by the mid-1970s largely vanished, while those making the two-track solution more of an economic burden increased over time.

There are some signs that by 1976 the Brezhnev Administration had begun to be concerned at the costs of a defence budget which for ten years had been permitted to increase at a higher annual rate than the GNP as a whole. The only publicly available figure ever given for Soviet defence expenditure is a one-line entry in the annual Budget, and, like those of many less secretive societies, it manifestly does not cover anything like all defence costs. Attempts by Western analysts to assess the impact of defence on the Soviet economy come up with widely differing results, largely dependent on what assumptions are made to begin with, but most cluster in the area of 11 to 13 per cent of GNP. Without entering into arguments between economists, it is sufficient to note here that the Soviet Union maintains a military establishment differing in detail from, but overall broadly equivalent to, that of the United States, and therefore likely to have roughly similar total costs. It does so on an economy which is at most 60 per cent as productive as the American, and may even be below 50 per cent if account is taken of recently-released figures showing Soviet industry using far more raw materials and energy for a given level of output than do the industries of the advanced capitalist economies.[15] A figure of 6 per cent of GNP is a fair average for US defence spending over a long period, and it is therefore not unreasonable to assume that maintaining a broadly equivalent defence establishment has over the past twenty years cost the much smaller Soviet economy between 10 and 12 per cent of GNP. It cannot be proved that current Soviet economic problems result solely or primarily from excessive defence spending, but an annual level of peacetime expenditure proportionately twice as large as that of the US, three to four times that of most other NATO countries, and ten times that of Japan is likely to have contributed to them, by competing with the civilian sector for resources, particularly skilled scientific and engineering manpower, precision machinery and scarce raw materials, and by tying up a substantial proportion of young males in largely unproductive activities for two or, in some cases, three years (a longer period than is usual in those advanced industrial countries which have not abolished peacetime conscription) between their departure from school and entry to the labour force.

In April 1976, the Defence Minister, Marshal Grechko, a professional soldier, as had been his predecessors since 1955, died suddenly, and was quickly replaced by Dmitriy Ustinov, a senior politician with extensive experience in defence industry. If the intention was to apply a financial brake, Ustinov was not necessarily the most obvious person to do it, but he was undoubtedly the Politburo member by far most qualified to do so. As People's Commissar (Minister) for Armaments from 1941 to 1957 he had been in charge of the arms and ammunition industries throughout the War, Stalin's post-war programs, and their post-Stalin re-evaluation. In 1957 he had become a Deputy Prime Minister and in 1963 he had been promoted to First Deputy, and appointed Chairman of VSNKh, the Supreme Council of the National Economy. Leaving these posts in 1965 he had been made a Secretary of the Central Committee of the Party, responsible for coordinating and directing research, design and production in defence-associated industries. His experience was therefore unparalleled; but so it had been in 1967, when the post of Minister of Defence had previously fallen vacant. On that occasion the incumbent, Malinovski, had suc-cumbed only after a long terminal illness, during which it had been leaked to the Moscow diplomatic circuit that Ustinov would succeed him. However, Grechko had been appointed instead, the inference being that the senior military had made representations that the post should continue to be held by a professional soldier. The post may well have gone to Grechko also because Brezhnev knew him well, having been in 1943 the chief political officer of the 18th Army, which Grechko commanded. In 1976 the suddenness of Grechko's death left no time for the senior military to lobby over the succession. Ustinov, an honorary Colonel-General since 1944, was immediately promoted to Army General on becoming Minister, and three months later given the highest military rank, Marshal of the Soviet Union.

Ustinov's close association with defence production had encompassed two long periods when military demands on the economy were especially heavy - the war years and the period of high expenditure from 1965 to 1976 - but it had also covered the post-war Stalin programs, where expenditure, though high, had been restrained by the competing demands of recovery from war devastation, and the very comprehensive post-Stalin review. His political stature ensured a hearing for military views at the highest level, but also lent particular authority to him in relation to the military establishment. It is not known what his 'mandate' was, but by 1981 it was possible to deduce that over the five years since his appointment the annual rate of growth of the defence budget had slowed, so that it was being held approximately constant as a proportion of the GNP. This remained the situation until he died in December 1984, whereupon the post was once again entrusted to a career soldier, Marshal Sokolov.

Brezhnev had died in December 1982, and though his successor, Andropov, indicated an intention to tackle problems of the economy, his health failed before he could embark on anything substantial. Chernenko, who followed him, was even more briefly in office, and his achievements were commensurate. Nevertheless, there was an episode in Chernenko's brief reign which indicated that military-political relations might be less than ideal. It concerned the Chief of General Staff and second-highest member of the military hierarchy, Marshal Nikolai Ogarkov.

Ogarkov first became known outside military circles when as First Deputy Chief of General Staff he was senior military member of the Soviet delegation to the SALT talks. In 1977 he was appointed Chief of General Staff (*ex officio* a First Deputy Minister of Defence) and promoted to Marshal. His appointment was significant in three respects. First, he was the senior military officer with most experience of negotiating the strategic balance with the Americans. Second, on appointment, his post, hitherto ranked third in the military hierarchy, after the Minister and the Commander-in-Chief of the Warsaw Pact forces, was elevated to second position. Third, he had a stronger technological and staff background and less field command experience than his predecessors - of his 38 years in the service since 1938, the first 10, including the war, were spent as an engineer officer, and 18 of the rest in staff appointments. As Chief of General Staff, he implemented a major reorganisation of the Ground Forces, under which a new intermediate command level was introduced between the field commands (Military Districts in the Soviet Union, and Groups of Forces in East Germany, Poland, Czechoslovakia and Hungary) and the General Staff in Moscow. The new TVDs (*Teatr Voyennykh Deystviy*, Theatre of Military Operations) replicated a command structure which had been tried early in the Second World War but abandoned in April 1942 in favour of direct control by Stalin and the *Stavka* (GHQ), then re-established in the Far East in 1945 for the brief campaign against Japan. Its reintroduction resulted from the information revolution. Improved communications made it possible for a field commander to control a larger area, while increased mobility of both Soviet and adversary forces made it desirable for him to do so. Moreover, the devolution of some responsibilities to an intermediate level reduced the risk of system overload in attempting to direct several fast-moving campaigns in widely-separated theatres from Moscow. The TVD system placed several Military Districts under one commander. From north-west to south-east they are Western (Leningrad, Baltic, Belorussian and

Carpathian MDs, with Headquarters in Minsk), South-Western (Kiev and Odessa MDs, HQ in Kiev), Southern (Transcaucasus, Turkestan and Central Asian MDs, HQ in Tashkent); and Far Eastern (Siberian, Transbaikal and Far Eastern MDs, HQ in Ulan Ude). The first, Far Eastern, was established in 1978, and the others on 1 December 1984. There are also maritime TVDs (OTVD), one for each fleet. The existence of TVD commands is not officially acknowledged,[16] but the nature of a TVD is officially defined as:

> A part of the territory of a continent with the coastal waters of an ocean, the internal seas and air space (continental TVD), or the waters of one ocean, including islands situated in it, adjacent seas, coastal belts of mainlands and the air space above them (oceanic TVD), within the bounds of which military operations may be initiated and waged by a strategic grouping of armed forces (ground, air or naval). The boundaries and composition of a TVD are determined by the military-political leadership of a state (coalition of states).[17]

The definition goes on to refer to the existence of three NATO TVDs, and to describe the Arctic, Atlantic, Indian and Pacific Oceans as 'historically established' OTVDs, but makes no reference to Soviet counterparts. A TVD is distinguished from a 'Theatre of War', which has no clearly defined boundaries and may comprise several TVDs. It is clear from the above definition that a TVD is a precisely defined area and is considered 'strategic' in scale, placing it in the same hierarchical bracket as, though subordinate to, the General Headquarters/General Staff, and above a Military District, which in wartime becomes a 'Front' (Army Group), the formation that marks the upper limit of the category of 'Operational Art', intermediate between tactics and strategy.

In addition to making this major structural innovation, Ogarkov wrote several articles and booklets in which he lobbied for an even greater orientation of the civil economy towards military needs. In one, for example, he declared that China's rapprochement with the US and Japan presented a threat to the Soviet Eastern frontiers, and advocated greater peacetime organisation of the civilian economy to facilitate rapid transition to a war footing.[18]

It would seem that his importunities and high public profile were too much for the Chernenko Politburo. A decision to remove Ogarkov was probably taken in September 1984, and was certainly implemented in November, because when the three new TVD commands came into being on 1 December, Ogarkov was found to be commanding the largest of them (the Western). This could not be termed dismissal or disgrace. Indeed, it is the largest field command in the entire history of the Soviet Army, extending from the Baltic (perhaps even from the North coast) to the Carpathians, and including control over a Fleet as well as large ground and air forces. But it does not carry with it the First Deputy Ministerial status of his previous post, and from being second in the military hierarchy, Ogarkov is no longer even in the top twenty. The demotion of the military's most vocal advocate did not silence him. In 1985 he published a small book in which he affirmed that the general crisis of capitalism was deepening, imperialist aggressiveness increasing, and the Reagan Administration 'conducting irresponsible preparation for a world nuclear war'.[19] Ironically, between the dispatch of this tract to the censors on 28 February and its approval for printing on 8 April, an era to which such rhetoric would prove unacceptable dawned with the election as General Secretary of Mikhail Gorbachev.

There is little positive evidence between Ustinov's appointment in 1976 and Ogarkov's removal in 1984 as to the state of military-political relations during the later Brezhnev years and the two interregnums. On the one hand, cordiality may be assumed from the way in which the two highest Soviet decorations, Hero of the Soviet Union and Hero of Socialist Labour, came to be dispensed almost as birthday presents to senior officers. On the other, the war in Afghanistan, like unsuccessful wars anywhere, was bound to create some tension between politicians, dissatisfied at the military's inability to end it successfully, and senior officers resentful of the restraints imposed by politicians. Another factor making for a more detached relationship between the political and military leaders was the mere passage of time. Under Stalin the post-war defence structure had largely been dominated by senior officers who had been his closest associates in the *Stavka* (GHQ) during the War. Khrushchev, a Lieutenant-General, had replaced them with his own wartime associates, particularly from Stalingrad (by mid-1960 the Minister of Defence, Chief of the General Staff and all the Commanders-in-Chief were from this background, including Gorshkov who, ironically, since he was to give the Soviet Navy its first true high seas capability, saw all his war service on rivers, from the Volga at Stalingrad to the Danube). As was mentioned earlier, Brezhnev's war service with Grechko was a factor in the latter's acceptability as Minister of Defence; and Ustinov, though a civilian, had spent his entire career in defence industry and held an honorary general's rank since 1944. In addition the military had been able to count on the personal vanity of Brezhnev. The Party leader has always been *ex officio* Chairman of the supreme politico-military decision-making body, the Defence Council. Its precise composition is not known, but its military members are a minority. The Chairman's authority derives from his Party status, whether or not he holds a military rank. Lenin did not hold one, Stalin took one only when he was already Supreme Commander-in-Chief, and Khrushchev retained his wartime rank of Lieutenant-General; but Brezhnev took Marshal's rank in 1976, and had himself given the 'Order of Victory', an award otherwise given only in 1945, to the very highest Soviet commanders and their Allied counterparts such as Eisenhower and Montgomery. He also had himself given the order of 'Hero of the Soviet Union' four times, to equal Zhukov's awards, if not his record. These military predilections were consistent with a benign approach to the heavy costs of the two-track solution.

By 1985, therefore, the military had enjoyed priority access to national resources for almost all the 44 years since the German invasion, and probably did not foresee the implications of a new General Secretary who had done no military service, had no personal or institutional ties to the military, and was a sceptic about the relevance of military solutions to national or global problems.

The initial military reaction to Gorbachev's proclamations of *perestroika* (reconstruction) and *uskoreniye* (acceleration) in 1985 was ambivalent. The need for reconstruction of personal attitudes was not queried. Soviet military journals are always replete with exhortations to greater efficiency, and neither their number nor their content changed significantly in 1985, so the attitude presumably was that no more needed to be done. The military press made no references to the need to reconstruct institutions or to accelerate processes, nor did the Minister, Marshal Sokolov or the Chief of General Staff, Marshal Akhromeyev, make more than routine references to the new Party line.

However, as Gorbachev made his message more explicit, its implications became harder to ignore. His 'Political Report' delivered to the 27th Party Congress at the end of February 1986 differed sharply from those of the Brezhnev era.[20] In the foreign affairs field, for example, Brezhnev's country-by-country catalogue treatment was abandoned in favour of an orientation to issues, including the imperative need to coexist peacefully, cooperating as well as competing, with a capitalist world which so far from being in decline has not yet reached its zenith. The emphasis on globalism and interdependence was accompanied by stress on the inapplicability of military solutions to world problems, and on the need for restraint in conduct of international relations. Mention of the military was sparse, comprising brief references to the existence of parity, the need to maintain it, preferably at reduced levels, the risk that if weapons stocks continued to grow even parity could cease to be a factor of stability, and the need for improved discipline in the Soviet armed forces.

A few months later, in a major speech at Vladivostok,[21] Gorbachev outlined a view of Soviet attitudes to the Asia-Pacific region in which he again denigrated the importance of military factors. He stated that the region was not as militarised as Europe, and should not be allowed to become so, made small, but important, political concessions to China on three of the four issues which China says impede normal relations (reduction in Soviet forces stationed in Outer Mongolia, agreement that on riverine sections of the Sino-Soviet border the frontier should run down the centre of the main channel, not along the Chinese bank, and preliminary indication of willingness to withdraw Soviet forces from Afghanistan), and hinted at a possible reciprocal gesture in the event of US withdrawal from Philippines bases. As in the Congress speech, the strategic implications lay less in the details than in the decline ascribed to the military factor in international relations.

Major weapons systems take on average about ten years from formulation of a requirement to start of production and may then be in service for twenty or more years, so policy changes initiated by Gorbachev in 1985 cannot yet be reflected in hardware procurement. There are, however, indications of change in the way existing forces are used. For example, Soviet naval deployments away from home waters have been reduced substantially since 1985,[22] withdrawal of troops from Afghanistan began in May 1988, some reduction has been made of forces stationed in Outer Mongolia, and the Intermediate-range Nuclear Forces (INF) agreement with the United States has abolished a class of nuclear weapon which accounts for 3 to 4 per cent of all nuclear warheads. In addition some steps have been taken towards political solutions of problems of Sino-Soviet relations, and pressuring Vietnam to accelerate withdrawal of troops from Kampuchea. These actions may serve as a prelude to mutual force reductions along the Sino-Soviet border.[23]

Another indicator of policy changes in Soviet politics is the extent to which a new leadership replaces functionaries appointed by its predecessor. It is not Soviet practice either to retire senior officers at a fixed age, or to rotate them between posts at preset intervals. For example, by 1985 Admiral Gorshkov was aged 75 and in his 29th year as head of the Navy, and General Yepishev, at 77, was in his 23rd year as head of the Main Political Directorate. In this situation, personalities become closely identified with particular policies, and replacement of a large proportion of the highest-ranking officers in a relatively short period suggests the introduction of new policies.

Comparison between the two periods 1982-4 and 1985-7 suggests that there has been a significant increase in the rate of replacement since 1985. The top of the military hierarchy, taken as consisting of the Minister, his First Deputies (3) and Deputies (10), the TVD Commanders (4), Commanders of Military Districts (16), Air Defence Districts (2), Groups of Forces stationed abroad (4) and Fleets (4), and the corresponding Heads of Political Directorates (39), comprised 77 posts before the three new TVD commands (Western, South-Western and Southern) were established on 1 December 1984, and 83 after that date. In 1982, 11 of the posts definitely changed hands and one may have done so (i.e., the change was identified in 1982, but may have taken place in the previous year). In 1983 there were seven definite and one possible changes. In 1984, the figures leapt dramatically to 30 definite and one possible. Of this number, 18 took place in the last month of the year, and were accounted for by unusual events, six changes were not replacements but resulted from the creation on 1 December of new posts (three new TVD commanders and their Chief Political officers) and filling of the resultant vacancies accounted for another six. In addition the Minister (Ustinov) and the Commander-in-Chief of the Air Force (Kutakhov) both died in office during December; Ustinov's death resulted in four changes[24] and Kutakhov's in one. Total replacements in the three years were, therefore, 48 definite and three possible, or 31 and three if the unusual circumstances of December 1984 are discounted. Over the four years 1985-89 there were 74 replacements (17 in 1985, 14 in 1986, 27 in 1987 and 16 in 1988-89); none of these resulted from creation of new posts and only two from death in office. The 1982-84 changes affected seven of the top 16 posts, but four of the seven changes resulted from the two deaths in office. From April 1985 to March 1989 15 of the 16 posts changed hands (the Minister, all three First Deputies, nine of the 10 Deputies, including the Commanders-in-Chief of four of the five armed services, and the Head of the Main Political Directorate). So did all four TVD Commands, every Military District, Group of Forces and Fleet, and one of the two Air Defence (PVO) Districts. At the highest level (the Minister, Deputies and Main Political Directorate) the changes do not constitute a generational shift. The average age of the 'new' group, 63 years, is only five years younger than the 'old'. Rather they represent the emergence of a more 'managerialist' trend. Past writings[25] by the Minister, Army General D.T. Yazov, for example, indicate a long-standing interest in efficient training and 'man management' rather than the more usual line officer's aspiration to write something novel about strategy or tactics, while in a debate among Admirals about naval strategy in 1981-82 Chernavin, then a very recently appointed (November 1981) Chief of the Main Naval Staff, supported its subordination within a single all-force strategy,[26] rather than the more autonomist view espoused by his then chief, Gorshkov.[27]

The importance of personalities is underlined by Yazov's own case. As far as is known, he and Gorbachev first met only in July 1986 during Gorbachev's visit to the Soviet Far East, Yazov then being Commander of the Far Eastern Military District. Six months later Yazov was brought to Moscow as Deputy Defence Minister for Personnel. In the light of later events it seems clear that the move was intended as a prelude to his succeeding the then Minister, Marshal Sokolov, in due course; because in May 1987, when a German light aircraft landed in Red Square, after flying unmolested from Helsinki through the most heavily-defended Soviet air space, Sokolov resigned, and Yazov succeeded him, a mere five months after appointment to the most junior Deputy Ministerial post. A 'quality before quantity' viewpoint appears to have been expressed yet again in the appointment to the Personnel post vacated by Yazov of Army General D.S. Sukhorukov, commander since 1979 of the elite Airborne Forces with which much of his career has been spent.

Apart from the managerialist aspect in the spate of new appointments, several (Yazov, the Chief of General Staff, Army General N.A. Moiseyev, the Chief Inspector, Army General M.I. Sorokin, the Head of Civil Defence, Army General V.L. Govorov, and the Head of the Main Political Directorate, Army General A.D. Lizichev) have in their backgrounds a spell of service in command in the Far East. This, too, may have 'quality before quantity' implications because it has been recognised since the 1930s that Soviet forces in the Far Eastern theatre, unlike those in Europe, can expect to be outnumbered, particularly difficult to reinforce or resupply, and therefore required to fight with especial efficiency and economy of resources. However, it may merely reflect a tendency to give officers regarded as of high potential some experience in that theatre during their careers. In any case, the pattern of new senior naval appointments is different. The Commander-in-Chief, Chernavin, and his First Deputy, Kapitanets, are both former Northern Fleet commanders, while the senior naval Political Officer, A.I. Sorokin (First Deputy Head of the Main Political Directorate) was formerly the chief political officer of the Northern Fleet. The Pacific Fleet's rise from last to second place in importance among the four Fleets is too recent to have been reflected at the highest command levels; the Chief of Main Naval Staff, Makarov, formerly commanded the Baltic Fleet, and his predecessor, Yegorov, the Northern. Only the Chief of the Navy's Political Directorate, Vice-Admiral V.I. Panin, has a Pacific Fleet background, and that neither recent nor senior.[28]

In Gorbachev's speech at the 27th Party Congress a statement about the need to tighten military discipline was among the few references made to the military. It was followed from early June 1986 by a rise in military press articles attacking shortcomings and corruption among senior officers,[29] which has since developed into a steady stream of assaults on incompetence, disregard of duty, cover-ups, bribery, corruption, waste, and all forms of 'non-regulation' (*vneustavnyye*) relations within the forces, down to harassment of newly-inducted conscripts by older ones.

In none of his speeches or writings did Gorbachev specifically mention reductions in current defence spending, but they were implicit in his depictions of a present in which military solutions are irrelevant to global problems, and of a preferred future in which a climate of restraint prevails in international relations, the Soviet Union's included. Interdependence precludes carrying competition to excess, nuclear weapons are reduced and ultimately abolished, and a doctrine of 'reasonable sufficiency' (undefined, but obviously connected with the retention of strategic parity at lower levels of expenditure) becomes the basis of defence procurement.[30] Some of his known supporters have been more specific. An authoritative article in the Party journal *Kommunist* in January 1988[31] stated flatly that neither in Western Europe nor the United States are there any 'politically influential forces' which intend to attack the Soviet Union; that anti-Soviet elements in the West have shifted their ground from military to economic, and see their best prospects as lying in the 'economic exhaustion of socialism in the process of an arms race, particularly by imposing upon it undue military expenditure'; that the US, having failed to 'provoke the Soviet Union into creating its own SDI program', is making 'insistent calls to increase the conventional armaments of the US and of NATO as a whole' which 'are clearly aimed at evoking a massive response from the Soviet side'; and that the 'exhaustion strategy' also includes attempts to ignite regional conflicts with the aim of getting the Soviet Union involved in them. The clear implication of these statements is that the Soviet Union should avoid arms races and involvement in regional conflicts (specifically mentioned were existing commitments to Afghanistan, which Soviet forces have since left, Nicaragua, Angola, Ethiopia and Mozambique).

The authors also referred to the need for a shift from war-fighting capacity to deterrence,[32] implying that it had not yet taken place. Very soon thereafter an anonymous reviewer of a book by Yazov, writing in the military-political journal *Armed Forces Communist*, implied that it had, when he claimed (inaccurately) that 'for the first time in history the task of preventing war is openly expounded in military doctrine',[33] and in the next issue of the same journal the Commander-in-Chief of the Strategic Rocket Forces[34] endorsed the claim, stating: 'The new Soviet military doctrine, aimed at reducing the danger of outbreak of a nuclear-missile war...has a clearly expressed defensive character'.

The problem with such statements is that they do not differ significantly from previous descriptions of Soviet doctrine. The anonymous reviewer of Yazov, for example, went on to quote a passage from the book which said 'after repelling the attack, troops and naval forces must be capable of waging a decisive offensive. The transition to it will take the form of a counteroffensive...'. This passage, apparently referring to conventional forces, does at least imply some modification of the offensive-oriented theatre strategy which has dominated Soviet thinking almost totally since 1945, but the reviewer goes on to quote Lenin to the effect that 'if...we were to give a promise...never to undertake certain action that might in the military-strategic respect appear offensive, then we would be not only fools, but criminals'. Maksimov in his article, in turn, follows his reference to the 'new doctrine' by saying 'In the event of an attack, our armed forces must be ready...to deal a crushing rebuff to the aggressor in any conditions of warfare', a statement which can be paralleled in any number of pre-1987 texts.[35]

At mid-1988 the 'new doctrine' could not be said to have been spelt out in any form which radically distinguished it from the old. 'Reasonable sufficiency' remained undefined, and calls for radical reform of military thinking came from outsiders rather than from the military itself. At a lower conceptual level, military indoctrination in the armed forces retained elements long discarded from Gorbachev's speeches and writings, such as the 'General Crisis of Capitalism',[36] and the contention that the US is actively planning 'preventive war' against the Soviet Union.[37] It is, of course, normal for a military caste to take a more hawkish view of the world than does the society in general, and to be slow to respond to changes in the political climate, even where, as in the Soviet armed forces, political control is tight. This results not so much from military conservatism as from the plain fact that the structure and equipment of an armed force, procured to implement a particular set of ideas on the likelihood and nature of a future war, cannot be changed as quickly as a political leader's mind.

Of all the armies which fought in the Second World War the Soviet Army has been the most dominated by its experience, particularly by the tank, the primary agent of its most traumatic defeats and its most overwhelming victories. The dominance of 'Blitzkrieg'-type thinking, coupled with the perceived need in a future war to overrun Europe quickly, so as to push the United States back to 'arm's length', has given to Soviet doctrines for theatre warfare a much greater offensive orientation than those of NATO, even after NATO's adoption of the 'air-land battle' concept. The initial military exposition of the 'new doctrine', essentially the old one, with a preceding defensive phase added, does not necessarily indicate military disagreement with the new doctrine. It is an inevitable consequence of the way the Soviet armed forces are at present equipped and trained. Gorbachev, while emphasising that authority in matters of peace and war rests firmly with the political leaders,[38] has so far avoided usurping the professionals' role by making detailed pronouncements on strategy, such as contributed to the military's alienation from Khrushchev after 1960. The large-scale replacements of military leaders have led to many retirements but to few dismissals or demotions, so that more officers have gained by them than have lost, and imposition of higher performance standards is likely to be welcomed by the more competent as much as it is resented by the less.

While the military will no doubt be less than enthusiastic about a decline in funding from the high levels to which they became accustomed under Brezhnev, the precedent of 1955-57, in which reduction was traded for modernisation, suggests that military hostility is not inevitable. Despite two decades of modernisation, Soviet forces retain a higher proportion of old weapons than do the US forces, and any of its major and many of its minor allies.[39] Scrapping of older weapons, and their replacement by smaller numbers of modern ones (which, contrary to widespread impressions, is precisely what happened to the Soviet Navy under Gorshkov[40]) would enable the Soviet military to fulfil its major function - retention of overall strategic parity - more cheaply and more professionally satisfyingly through higher cost-effectiveness. But retention of parity depends largely on the readiness of the much richer and technologically more dynamic US alliance countries to continue accepting balance of power as the theoretical framework of their relations with the Soviets. Military spokesmen are therefore not slow to point out that future Soviet action is conditional upon that of others.[41] This keeps open the option of a change of line if, for example, arms control negotiations fail in their purpose of keeping down the cost of parity by restraining the expenditure of potential adversaries.

In his speech on 28 June 1988 at the 19th Party Conference, Gorbachev's references to strategy-related foreign policy objectives included arms reductions (elimination of nuclear weapons by 2000 AD, scaling down of arms levels, withdrawal of forces stationed abroad), 'defence sufficiency'[42] and the 'non-offensive doctrine'. There was nothing new about these, but his prescription for the development of Soviet defence - one sentence only, in a speech of 137 paragraphs - confirmed more precisely than any previous utterance the 'quality before quantity' aspects of the changes in the military hierarchy. He said that its effectiveness 'must henceforward be assured primarily by qualitative parameters, both in terms of technology and military science[43] and in terms of the composition of the armed forces'.[44] Defence Minister Yazov spelt out the implications of this in an article[45] published in August 1988. The objective is to produce forces whose combat preparedness would guarantee effective defence 'under any development in the international situation, any reductions in forces and armaments, or any other organisational and technological measures'. Reliance on quality is dictated 'first, by the need to make irreversible the positive tendencies' in world development (i.e. to avoid giving ammunition to opponents of disarmament), second by possibilities the 'new political thinking' provides for ensuring international security and peace by means other than military strength, and third, by the increasing expense and decreasing effectiveness of reliance upon 'quantitative indicators', i.e. sheer numbers. It relates to all three aspects of the defence structure - technology, military science (i.e. strategy, operational art and tactics) and personnel. Technology must above all 'radically enhance the reliability' of equipment as well as improve its combat performances; military science must develop new concepts appropriate to a defensive doctrine, and improve the training of cadres and subordinate personnel. 'Scientific' (i.e. scholarly) work in the Armed Forces must be better organised and led, and given better technical infrastructure; the gap between theoretical and technical research must be narrowed, their productivity increased, and the time taken to apply theoretical conclusions, scientific recommendations or technical innovations reduced. Personnel matters include not only improvement and intensification of training, but strengthening of discipline, and greater 'democratisation'.

The practical effects of these injunctions will take months if not years to become apparent. However, their general thrust is unmistakably towards forces which must be more efficient because they will be smaller, and must reorient themselves away from the emphasis on the land offensive which Second World War experience made dominant ever since 1945. Yazov gave an oblique indication of what might be entailed when, in a routine order for the celebration of 'Tank Men's Day'[46] he stated that the Party's directives for primary reliance on qualitative parameters 'demand new approaches in the matter of ensuring reliable security for the Soviet state and its allies', a hint that the relative importance of the tank was to decline.

This was confirmed in Gorbachev's speech to the United Nations General Assembly on 7 December 1988,[47] in which he announced a number of unilateral arms reductions. Armed forces manpower would be cut by 500,000 by the end of the 1990s; six Tank

Divisions would be withdrawn from Eastern Europe (East Germany, Czechoslovakia and Hungary) and disbanded by the end of 1991; assault landing troops and river crossing equipment would also be withdrawn from these countries, leading to a reduction of 50,000 men and 5,000 tanks. All army divisions stationed outside the USSR would be restructured to be clearly defensive following the reduction in tanks and other offensive-associated equipment. Divisions in the European USSR would also be reduced, so that cuts would total 10,000 tanks (including the 5,000 to be removed from Eastern Europe), 8,500 artillery systems, and 800 combat aircraft. Forces stationed in the Asian USSR would also be reduced, though by how much was not specified, and 'a major portion' of those stationed in the Mongolian People's Republic[48] would be brought home.

On the same day there were two indications that the policy of unilateral reduction was not entirely endorsed by some senior military. An article by Admiral Chernavin, Commander-in-Chief of the Navy, appeared under the significant title of 'Restraint must be Mutual'.[49] In it he denied US and Japanese estimates that the Soviet Pacific Fleet was still increasing, stating that since 1984 it had been reduced by 57 ships, and denounced increases in US naval activity near Soviet shores and planned increases in Japanese forces. And, even more significantly, Yazov's principal deputy (and most important 'survivor' from the pre-Gorbachev Defence hierarchy) Marshal Akhromeyev, the Chief of General Staff, resigned. While he did so officially 'for health reasons', he had indicated on a visit to the United States in July 1988[50] that he favoured negotiated and mutual, rather than unilateral, reductions. It therefore seems probable that, like a predecessor in 1960, Marshal Sokolovski, he resigned because he disagreed with a political decision not to subject manpower reductions to an international bargaining process. Compared to the reductions effected under Khrushchev, those proposed by Gorbachev are relatively modest. They are also geared to reducing the image of a conventional force threat to Western Europe which has done so much to preserve NATO's cohesiveness, and the initial Western response has therefore been welcoming but guarded.

Gorbachev's speech also included references to making public the experience in converting some defence plants to civilian production, and an agenda of items to be pursued with President Bush. These (a treaty on 50 per cent reductions in strategic nuclear weapons while continuing to observe the ABM Treaty, i.e., limiting US pursuit of the Strategic Defence Initiative, a treaty banning chemical weapons, and negotiations to reduce conventional forces in Europe) contained no new initiatives.

At the end of 1988, therefore, the outlines of the new Soviet defence policy were beginning to become apparent. In conformity with a general downplaying of the military factor in international relations, Soviet military 'presences' abroad were to be reduced (that in Afghanistan eliminated completely except for a small number of advisers), the switch to an at least initially defensive theatre doctrine was about to be implemented on a modest scale, stress was being laid on improved efficiency to make up for reductions in numbers, and further cuts in nuclear and conventional forces would continue to be pursued. There were some signs of military restiveness, but no indications that they were uncontainable at this stage.

Endnotes

1   N.S. Khrushchev, speech of 14 January 1960, in *Pravda*, 15 January 1960.
2   *Ibid.*.
3   N.S. Khrushchev, *Khrushchev Remembers*, (Penguin, Harmondsworth, Vol.I, 1977), pp.393-394.
4   *Ibid.*.
5   First disclosed publicly by Marshal Grechko in 1967. Discussed in G. Jukes, 'Changes in Soviet Conscription Law', *Australian Outlook*, September 1968.
6   N.S. Khrushchev, speech of 14 January 1960.
7   *Ibid.*.
8   E.g. in speech of 7 August 1961, *Pravda*, 8 August 1961.
9   First publicly expressed by Major-General N.A. Talenski, Editor of the General Staff periodical *Military Thought* in its September 1953 issue.
10 In his memoirs Khrushchev claims that Zhukov had voiced Bonapartist aspirations to other officers. *Khrushchev Remembers: the Last Testament*, (Andre Deutsch, London, 1974), p.14.
11 For example, speech of 15 January 1960, *Red Star*, 16 January 1960 and pamphlet 'Vigilantly Stand Guard in Defence of Peace', Voyenizdat, (Moscow, 1962), pp.25-26.
12 For example, by Marshal V. Sokolovsky and Major-General M. Cherednichenko in *Red Star* 28 August 1964, and Colonel-General S.M. Shtemenko in *Nedelya*, issue of 31 January-6 February 1965.
13 E.g. *The Economist* 24 October 1981, p.51, and *The Times*, 6 November 1981, p.1.
14 See M. MccGwire, *Military Objectives in Soviet Foreign Policy*, (Brookings Institution, Washington, DC, 1987) for a full discussion of the evidence.
15 I am indebted for this point to a paper by Paul Dibb, Australian Department of Defence, given at the 1988 IISS Conference.
16 It can, however, be inferred from the protocol order of obituary signatures, in which, beginning with that of Defence Minister Ustinov (*Red Star*, 22 December 1984) a new group of signatories, all Marshals or 4-star Generals, began to appear, senior to the Military District commanders, but not part of any pre-existent organisation.
17 *Voyennyy Entsiklopedicheskiy Slovar* (Military Encyclopaedic Dictionary), (Military Publishing House, Moscow, 1983), p.732.
18 *Kommunist*, July 1981.
19 N.V. Ogarkov, *Istoriya Uchit Bditelnosti* (History Teaches Vigilance), (Military Publishing House, Moscow, 1985).
20 'Report of the Central Committee', 25 February 1985; *Pravda*, 26 February 1985.
21 M.S. Gorbachev, speech of 28 July 1986, *Pravda*, 29 July 1986.

22   *Far Eastern Economic Review*, 30 June 1988, p.11.

23   A possible hint of this occurred in the speech made by Gorbachev in Vladivostok on 28 July 1986 (reference to detente measures not affecting third parties).

24   Ustinov was succeeded by his principal 1st Deputy Sokolov, by Petrov, Commander-in-Chief Ground Forces, Petrov by Ivanovskiy, Commander of Belorussian MD, Ivanovskiy by Shuralev, a promoted 1st Deputy Cdr of Soviet forces in Germany.

25   For example, in *Krasnaya Zvezda* (Red Star) 2 April 1978, 23 November 1979, 24 November 1981, and 9 July 1983.

26   *Morskoy Sbornik* (Naval Anthology), January 1982.

27   In his articles 'Navies in War and Peace', published at intervals in *Morskoy Sbornik* during 1972-73, translated as document reference CRC 257 by the Centre for Naval Analyses, Washington D.C., and both editions of his book *Morskaya Moshch Gosudarstva* (Sea Power of the State), (MOD Publishing House, Moscow, 1976 and 1979).

28   All career details have been taken from the primary sources-based index of senior Soviet military officers maintained in the Department of International Relations, ANU so are not further sourced.

29   Beginning in *Armed Forces Communist*, No.12/1986, with an article by the then Chief Inspector, Army General V L Govorov, in which officers criticised by name included a Major-General and several Colonels.

30   For example, 'Military doctrines...should be strictly the doctrines of defense. And this is connected with such new or comparatively new notions as the reasonable sufficiency of armaments, non-aggressive defense, the elimination of disbalance and asymmetries in various types of armed forces, separation of the offensive forces of the two blocs, and so on...'. M. Gorbachev, *Perestroika: New Thinking For Our Country and The World*, (Collins, London, 1987), pp.142-3.

31   V. Zhurkin, S. Karaganov, and A. Kortunov, 'Challenges of Security - Old and New', *Kommunist*, No.1/1988, pp. 42-50.

32   *Ibid.* 'The level of adequacy of the USSR's military power in the European theatre was formerly determined by the requirement to repel any aggression, to smash any possible coalition of hostile states. Today the task is stated differently in principle; to deter, to avert, war itself. This task requires in its turn a rethinking of many traditional postulates of military strategy and operational art, beginning with re-evaluation of the quantitative requirements for various types of weapons (for example, of tanks), the character of manoeuvres, and so on.'

33   'Kommunist Vooruzhennykh Sil' 3/1988, pp. 88-92.

34   Army General Yu. Maksimov, 'Kommunist Vooruzhennykh Sil', 4/1988, pp.27-33.

35   For example, Malinovsky, Defence Minister 1957-67: 'the best means of defence is warning the enemy of our strength and our readiness to smash him at the very first attempt to commit an act of aggression'. 'Bditelno stoyat na strazhe mira' (Vigilantly stand guard in defence of peace), (MOD Publishing House, Moscow, 1962), p.25. Brezhnev: 'Any possible aggressor well knows that in the event of an attempt at a nuclear-missile attack on our country he will receive an annihilating retaliatory blow'. Materials of XXIV Party Congress, (Moscow, Politizdat, 1971), p.81. Ogarkov: (1) 'Soviet military doctrine has always proceeded and still proceeds from the principle of retaliatory, that is, defensive, actions.' (2) [the socialist countries] 'maintain the vigilance and combat readiness of their armed forces at a level which ensures the crushing defeat of any aggressor who would dare to attack the countries of socialism.' Marshal N V. Ogarkov, 'Istoriya uchit bditelnosti' (History Teaches Vigilance), (MOD Publishing House, Moscow, 1985) p.77 (1), p.95 (2).

36   'Kommunist Vooruzhennykh Sil', *Armed Forces Communist*, No.8/1988, p. 53.

37   E.g. V.V. Serebryannikov, 'V.I. Lenin on the Aggressiveness of Imperialism', (MOD Publishing House, Moscow, 1988), and review of it in 'Kommunist Vooruzhennykh Sil', No.8/1988, pp.85-6.

38   For example, '...in the Army, the State Security Committee, and in every other government department, the Party wields the highest authority, and has a decisive

voice politically'. *Perestroika: New Thinking for our Country and the World*, (Collins, London, 1987), p.128.

39   For example, the T54 tank is of 1949 vintage; the T55 a slightly modified mid-1950s version of it. Where they fought the British Centurion (e.g. in Korea and the Middle East) they proved inferior in most respects; the Centurion has long vanished from the British (and Australian) armies, but T54/55s are a substantial part of the inventory of lower-readiness Soviet divisions, and are front-line tanks in some Warsaw Pact armies.

40   Comparison of successive annual issues of *Janes' Fighting Ships* shows that the Soviet Navy was at its largest in the early 1960s; it now comprises much smaller numbers of vastly more effective ships, like all other major and many minor navies.

41   All Soviet utterances claim that the Soviet Union has always stood for disarmament, but has been frustrated by Western, especially US opposition. Descriptions of the US attitude range from allegations that the USSR is fighting for peace against a US aspiration to start a nuclear war (S. Tyushkevich, 'Armed Forces Communist' 8/1988, p.86), to Ogarkov's less apocalyptic statement in 1985 ('History Teaches Vigilance', p.94) that in then imminent arms talks success depended on the degree of US sincerity, or the (non-military) position of Zhurkin, *et al* (*Kommunist*, No.1/1988) that the US aspires to 'exhaust' the USSR by inciting it into an arms race.

42   Still undefined, apart from the statement '...reasonable sufficiency, that is a level necessary for strictly defensive purposes' in his book *Perestroika: New Thinking...*, (Collins, London, 1987), p.204

43   In Soviet terminology 'military science' is the entire system of knowledge about war; it includes the theories of strategy, tactics, military structure, training, war economics and supply. *Voyennyy Entsiklopedicheskiy Slovar* (Military Encyclopaedic Dictionary), (MOD Publishing House, Moscow, 1983), p.136.

44   TASS Telex E510-001, 28 June 1988, paragraph 50.

45   *Red Star*, 9 August 1988.

46   *Red Star*, 11 September 1988.

47   *Soviet News*, London, No.6455, 14 December 1988.

48   Soviet forces stationed in Mongolia are estimated at four divisions, *London Times*, London, 8 December 1988, p.1.

49   *Red Star*, 7 December 1988.

50   *The Age* (Melbourne), 9 December 1988.

CHAPTER 4

THE FUTURE OF THE GLOBAL STRATEGIC BALANCE

Desmond Ball

The global strategic relationship between the United States and the Soviet Union, commonly referred to as the strategic balance, is fundamentally characterised by complexity, change and uncertainty. Change in the political dimension tends to be somewhat cyclical, with periods of detente and constructive dialogue interspersed with periods of tension, distrust and hostile rhetoric. With respect to the techno-logical dimension, change has been continuous since 1945, albeit with variations in pace, direction, and net impact on strategic stability.

Within the Soviet Union, the political, economic and social reforms instituted by General Secretary Mikhail Gorbachev promise changes more fundamental in scope and implication than anything since Stalin's betrayal of the Lenin/Trotsky revolution half a century ago. The likely consequences of Gorbachev's efforts for the global strategic relationship are impossible to foretell. Should they succeed - and success is far from assured - they could produce a Soviet Union more satisfied with its place in the world, more concerned about the rectification of internal problems and inequities, and more interested in competing with the West in terms of economic and technological achievements rather than military prowess. Alternatively, a more robust economy and technological infrastructure could support a strategic challenge to the West which is more balanced and more difficult to contest.

In the United States, the Bush Administration will pursue many of the policies instituted by the Reagan Administration but the necessity to confront the budget deficit will require substantial adjustments in trade policies and government expenditures. Significant real growth in US defence expenditure is unlikely through the next decade or so.

It is likely that the Strategic Arms Reduction Talks (START) between the United States and the Soviet Union will produce a major reduction in strategic nuclear delivery vehicles (SNDVs) and warheads of a scale and character quite unprecedented in the history of the US-Soviet nuclear competition. It is possible that arms control and disarmament with respect to nuclear weapons will proceed beyond the 50 per cent reductions in certain categories already accepted in START, and perhaps even proceed to address nuclear weapons in other categories and theatres.

Technological research and development during the 1980s has been extraordinarily dynamic and fecund.[1] In the field of engines, propellants and power plants, advances range from small but highly efficient turbofan engines such as the 66 kg engine capable of carrying US cruise missiles with 170 kt warheads over distances of more than 3,000 km, to new fast-burn rocket propellants which enable large (around 200,000 kg) two or three-stage ballistic missiles to burn out and deploy their re-entry vehicles (RVs) before leaving the atmosphere, to space-borne nuclear reactors capable of generating hundreds of kilowatts or even several megawatts of power. In the field of guidance or navigation systems, the Advanced Inertial Reference Sphere installed on the MX ICBM is currently capable of achieving an accuracy in terms of Circular Error Probable (CEP) of some 100 metres over a range of 11,000 km and promises a CEP of 75 metres by the mid-1990s, while long-range cruise missiles equipped with Terrain Contour Matching (TERCOM) and Global Positioning Satellite (GPS) systems should be able to achieve CEPs of less than 10 metres by the late 1990s.

In the case of nuclear warheads, so-called third generation weapons are being developed which selectively enhance certain types of energy, such as electromagnetic pulses (EMP), neutrons, or microwaves,[2] as well as 'earth penetrating' warheads designed to penetrate several tens of metres of rock before detonating in order to destroy hardened underground missile silos, bunkers and command posts.[3] New command, control, communications and intelligence (C3I) systems include communications systems operating at both the extremely low frequency (ELF) and extremely high frequency (EHF) ends of the radio spectrum; various mobile command posts (MCPs) and satellite ground terminals (MGTs); and more sophisticated real-time digital imaging electro-optical satellite photographic intelligence systems (such as the KH-12 *Ikon*) and geostationary signals intelligence (SIGINT) satellite systems (such as the *Magnum* and *Mentor* satellites), and new radar satellites (such as the recently-launched *Lacrosse* satellite). With respect to strategic defence technologies, the US Strategic Defense Initiative (SDI) has failed to realize President Reagan's vision of making ballistic missiles obsolete,[4] but it has prompted the more rapid development of various new directed energy and kinetic energy weapons techniques, very high speed data processing systems, and ground- and space-based sensor systems, as well as enhancing anti-satellite (ASAT) capabilities.

This chapter describes the basic US and Soviet strategic nuclear policies and doctrines; assesses the current state of the strategic balance;

and provides some assessment of the likely state of the balance in the mid-1990s, as projected according to current trends and as it might look under some START regime.

Soviet Strategic Nuclear Policy and Doctrine

The most fundamental objective of Soviet strategic policy, as of US strategic policy, is the deterrence of nuclear war:

> War with the employment of nuclear weapons can undermine the very foundation for the existence of human society and inflict tremendous damage to its progressive development. Therefore, the most important requirement for progress in our time is the prevention of a new world war.[5]

However, unlike US strategic policy, the Soviet view of deterrence involves neither the notion of 'assured destruction' or 'unacceptable damage', nor that of limited or controlled nuclear options.[6] Rather, deterrence of nuclear attack is best achieved by the ability to successfully wage a nuclear war - the better the Soviet forces are equipped and trained to fight a nuclear war, the more effective they will be as a deterrent to a nuclear attack on the USSR. If deterrence fails, these forces will then be used purposefully and massively for military victory.[7]

Soviet discussions of nuclear war invariably stress the importance of the initial nuclear strikes and of seizing the initiative in those strikes. As Marshal Moskalenko wrote in 1969:

> In view of the immense destructive force of nuclear weapons and the extremely limited time available to take effective countermeasures after an enemy launches its missiles, the launching of the first massed nuclear attack acquires decisive importance for achieving the objectives of war.[8]

During the 1960s and 1970s the notion of anticipating and pre-empting the attack was pervasive throughout the Soviet literature. For example, a Soviet military text on *Marxism-Leninism on War and Army* stated that:

> Mass nuclear missile strikes at the armed forces of the opponent and at his key economic and political objectives can determine the victory of one side and the defeat of the other at the very beginning of the war. Therefore, a correct estimate of the elements of the supremacy over the opponent and the ability to

use them before the opponent does, are the key to victory in such a war.[9]

Another Soviet text on *Scientific Technical Progress and the Revolution in Military Affairs* stated that:

One of the decisive conditions for success in an operation is the anticipating of the enemy in making nuclear strikes, particularly against the enemy's nuclear missile weapons.[10]

It is clear, however, that Soviet political and military leaders must have been uneasy about reliance on pre-emption. Although the vulnerability of the Soviet strategic forces allowed the leadership little choice in the matter, the forces and the strategic C^3I system which supported them were quite ill-suited to a pre-emptive posture. During the 1950s and 1960s, the KGB maintained physical custody of Soviet warheads and kept them separate from the delivery vehicles.[11] The warheads and launchers were not mated even during the Cuban Missile Crisis in October 1962. Until the late 1970s, only a very small proportion of Soviet strategic nuclear delivery vehicles were held on alert - perhaps 25 per cent of the ICBM force, 10 per cent of the SLBMs, and none of the Soviet strategic bombers, or about 17 per cent of the total number of Soviet SNDVs. Further, technical considerations - including missile fuelling procedures and the use of spin-axis ball-bearings in missile guidance systems[12] - meant that the forces could not be held on alert 'for more than a short period of time' and hence the Soviets would 'have been reluctant to place their forces on alert unless they were certain a war was coming'.[13] Yet until the 1980s, the Soviet Union lacked a reliable tactical warning and attack assessment system. The Soviet leadership was dependent upon strategic warning - and principally human intelligence (HUMINT) and signals intelligence (SIGINT) - for foreknowledge that war was imminent, but it could have had little confidence that these sources could have provided the assured, reliable, unequivocal and timely warning that would have been necessary for the Soviet forces to have been successfully employed pre-emptively.

Major changes to the Soviet strategic nuclear posture have been instituted since the mid-1970s, providing the Soviet leadership with further options beyond pre-emption. The day-to-day alert levels of the Soviet ICBMs and SLBMs has increased dramatically. Today, more than 80 per cent of Soviet ICBMs, carrying more than 95 per cent of Soviet ICBM-based warheads, and some 30-40 per cent of Soviet SLBMs - or a total of some 7,200 warheads, or 65 per cent of the total Soviet strategic nuclear warheads - are ready to be launched within a few minutes of a decision by the Soviet leadership.[14] The Soviet tactical warning and attack assessment system has also been markedly enhanced. Three over-the-horizon (OTH) radars were built in the 1970s and a fourth has recently become operational, three of which are designed to provide 30 minutes' warning time of US ICBM launches. (The other one is designed to provide warning of Chinese ICBM launches.) In 1976, the Soviet Union began to deploy infra-red early warning satellites. An extensive network of modern large phased-array radars has also been deployed.[15] Although the attack characterisation and attack assessment capability of this system remains rather weak compared to that of the US strategic C³I system, there is little doubt about its capability to support massive launches in a Launch on Warning (LOW) or Launch Under Attack (LUA) mode. Moreover, a large segment of the Soviet ICBM force has been very extensively hardened since the mid-1970s. More than 800 ICBM silos (i.e. those housing the 139 SS-17s, 308 SS-18s and 360 SS-19s operational as at December 1987) have been rebuilt since 1972, and 'fully one-half of these silos have been totally reconstructed and hardened since 1980'.[16] It is likely that the 400 or so silos rebuilt during the 1970s can withstand some 4000 pounds per square inch (psi) of blast overpressure, while those rebuilt in the 1980s can withstand some 6000-7200 psi - or about three times that of US Minuteman ICBM silos.[17] This represents an extraordinary investment, amounting to more than $20 billion. Further investment has been expended on the development of the road-mobile SS-25 ICBM system and the rail-mobile SS-24 ICBM system, as well as on the construction of hardened pens for those ballistic missile submarines not on station in the protected bastions in the waters near Murmansk and in the Sea of Okhotsk. These investments would not be necessary if the Soviet leadership were prepared to rely only on pre-emption and/or LOW/LUA options. The Soviet leadership now has the option of allowing a large segment of its strategic forces to 'ride out' a limited US counterforce attack involving many hundreds of warheads.

In stark comparison to the United States, the Soviet Union has placed great emphasis on ensuring the survivability of the Soviet leadership during a nuclear exchange - not just of the Soviet National Command Authority (NCA) and armed forces at the national level, but also of the military, political and economic leadership throughout the entire country. Soviet defensive measures include active programs such as anti-ballistic missile (ABM) and anti-aircraft deployments and passive measures such as shelter construction and leadership relocation programs.[18]

The Soviets maintain around Moscow the world's only operational ABM system. The original system, designated ABM-IB, consisted of 64 *Galosh* interceptor missiles deployed in four complexes, six *Try Add* missile guidance and engagement radars at each complex, and the *Dog House* and *Cat House* target-tracking radars south of Moscow. Since 1980 a major up-grading of the system has been underway, with new launchers being deployed for modified *Galosh* interceptors designed to engage targets outside the atmosphere and for new *Gazelle* high-acceleration interceptors designed to engage targets within the atmosphere; associated engagement and missile guidance radars; and a new *Pill Box* large phased-array radar (LPAR) at Pushkino, northeast of Moscow, designed to control ABM engagements. The new ABM system was expected to be fully operational in 1989.[19]

Moscow is also well-protected by extensive strategic and tactical air defence deployments. The first Soviet surface-to-air missile (SAM) defences - based on the SA-1 *Guild* SAM and Yo-Yo radar system - were deployed around Moscow in 1956. Moscow is the centre of the heaviest concentration of SAM-5 *Gammon* missiles, which until recently were the most advanced Soviet SAM. The SAM-5 is designed for long-range, high altitude interception and may also have some antiballistic missile capability.[20] In 1980, the Soviet Union began deployment of the new SA-10 SAM, which is designed to intercept targets with a small radar cross-section, such as cruise missiles. More than half the sites so far constructed are located near Moscow.[21] According to the US Department of Defense, 'this emphasis on Moscow and the patterns noted for the other SA-10 sites suggest a first priority on terminal defense of wartime command and control, military and key industrial complexes'.[22]

With respect to passive measures,

> Soviet commanders and managers at all levels of the Party and government are provided hardened alternate command posts located well away from urban centres. This comprehensive and redundant system, composed of more than 1,500 hardened facilities with special communications, is patterned after similar capabilities afforded the Armed Forces. More than 175,000 key personnel throughout the system are believed to be equipped with such alternate facilities in addition to the many deep bunkers and blast shelters in Soviet cities.[23]

This represents an increase in protective facilities corresponding to some 10,000 additional leadership personnel each year over the past decade. According to the US Department of Defense, the cost of construction, and equipment for these leadership relocation sites over the past 25 years is between 8 and 16 billion rubles, or $28-56 billion if acquired in the United States.[24]

According to testimony of the then Chairman of the Joint Chiefs of Staff, General George S. Brown in 1977, 'the first echelon command-control-communications centers of the Soviet government and armed forces at a national level are dispersed and hardened within an 80-mile radius of Moscow'.25 This includes some 75 underground command posts within Moscow itself. Some of these structures are several hundred metres deep and are capable of withstanding 1,000 psi of blast overpressure.

Although the Soviet leadership now has the options of employing the Soviet strategic nuclear forces in pre-emptive, LOW/LUA and retaliatory modes, there is little evidence of any Soviet plans or efforts concerning the possibility of limited or controlled employment of these forces. Soviet military doctrine remains to seize the initiative, either pre-emptively or promptly in the case of a US limited counterforce attack, and then to move to control events through the period of the conflict. Massive blows against US military, economic-industrial and political-administrative resources and facilities would frustrate or at least degrade US military operations, thus minimising damage to the Soviet Union, and would stun the United States into incapacity and eventual surrender.

Soviet strategic policy and targeting doctrine, together with some quite explicit pronouncements, is to the effect that any nuclear exchange would involve simultaneous and unconstrained attacks on a wide range of targets, which would certainly not exclude C3I systems.

Soviet strategic forces would be used massively rather than sequentially, and against a wide range of nuclear and conventional military targets, command and control facilities, centres of political and administrative leadership, economic and industrial facilities, power supplies, etc., rather than more selectively. Urban areas would not be attacked in pursuit of some arbitrary minimum level of fatalities, but neither would they be avoided if they were near military, political or industrial targets.

The breadth of Soviet strategic targeting is shown in the following quotations:

> The Strategic Missile Forces, which form the basis of the combat might of our Armed Forces, are intended for the destruction of the enemy's means of nuclear attack, his large troop formations and military bases, the destruction of the aggressor's defense industry, the disorganization of [his] state and military command and control, and of the operations of his rear and transportation.26

Very important strategic missions of the armed forces can be the destruction of the largest industrial and administrative-political centers, power systems, and stocks of strategic raw materials; disorganization of the system of state and military control; destruction of the main transport centers; and destruction of the main groupings of troops, especially of the means of nuclear attack.[27]

For the achievement of victory in a present-day nuclear war, if it is unleashed by the imperialists, not only the enemy's armed forces, but also the sources of his military power, the important economic centers, points of military and state control, as well as the areas where different branches of armed forces are based, will be subjected to simultaneous destruction.[28]

Although this wide range of targets would be subject to massive and simultaneous attacks, there are some definite priorities regarding the destruction of particular elements of the US military forces, including most particularly the opposing strategic nuclear forces. As Major-General Dzhelaukhov wrote in 1966, 'strategic rockets are regarded as the most important strategic objectives'.[29] Also in the primary category are strategic bomber bases, Fleet Ballistic Missile (FBM) submarine bases and support facilities, nuclear stockpiles, and strategic command and control centres.[30] The second target category consists of theatre nuclear weapons and associated systems, including tactical and carrier aviation, cruise missiles, tactical missiles, airfields, and tactical command and control systems. The third category consists of other military targets, such as large ground troop formations, tank concentrations, reserve forces, storehouses of arms and munitions, equipment and fuel, naval bases, interceptor airfields, anti-aircraft artillery and missiles, and associated command and control systems and facilities. The fourth category consists of political-administrative targets, such as governmental centres and areas where the political leadership is concentrated. Finally, the fifth category consists of a wide range of economic-industrial facilities - including power stations (perhaps the single most important non-military targets in Soviet war planning), stocks of strategic raw materials, oil refineries and storage sites, metallurgical plants, chemical industries, and transport operations (such as 'rail centres and marshalling yards, bridges, tunnels, train ferries and trains on land, and ports and vessels on the water').[31]

On the basis of these target sets, and the priorities attached to their destruction, it is possible to construct a notional Soviet equivalent of the US Single Integrated Operations Plan (SIOP) - the Russian [or Red] Integrated Strategic Operational Plan (RISOP). The most recent version of RISOP-6, which involves the allocation of about 11,200 strategic warheads and bombs to these target categories in generated and non-generated situations (i.e. where the Soviet forces are intact and on a relatively high level of alert as compared to where they have suffered a US counterforce strike), looks something like that shown in Table 1.

TABLE 1
ALLOCATION OF SOVIET RISOP WARHEADS TO TARGET
CATEGORIES IN GENERATED AND NON-GENERATED
SITUATIONS
DECEMBER 1987

	Generated	Non-Generated
Baseline force	11,184	11,184
Weapons deliverable to target	7,221	5,977
Target Category		
1 Strategic C^{3}I targets	700	700
2 US SIOP forces	2,198	2,198
3 Theatre nuclear forces capable of hitting the Soviet Union	80	80
4 US/NATO conventional/power projection forces	750	500
5 US/NATO administrative/governmental targets	450	300
6 US/NATO economic/industrial (E/I), war supporting and economic recovery targets	1,843	1,249
Reserve warheads (including warheads allocated to targets in China)	1,000	750

US Strategic Nuclear Policy and Doctrine

The United States shares with the Soviet Union a commitment to deterrence as a 'major objective' of national security policy. As President Reagan stated in January 1988,

> America's defense policy throughout the postwar period has been aimed at deterring aggression against the United States and its allies. Deterrence works by persuading potential adversaries that the costs of their aggression will exceed any probable gains. Deterrence is the basis of our military strategy.[32]

Similarly, despite periodic statements of declaratory policy to the contrary, the United States has always accepted that a viable policy of deterrence could not be based on the mere possession of an 'assured destruction capability' but requires an effective 'war fighting' strategy and capability.[33] As President Reagan reiterated in January 1988, 'only by being prepared to wage war successfully can we deter it'.[34] And, again like the Soviet Union, the US strategy in the event that deterrence fails is to limit damage to its military forces and economic and governmental structure. As President Reagan also stated in January 1988,

> The United States,...should deterrence fail, must be prepared to repel or defeat any military attack and end the conflict on terms favourable to the United States, its interests, and its allies.[35]

Although the objectives of Soviet and US strategic nuclear policy are superficially similar at this most general level - *viz*: deterrence, war fighting, and damage limitation - there are some very important differences in the employment policies and force postures which each has developed in pursuit of these objectives. Central to these differences is the fact that whereas Soviet strategic planners believe that the best approach to limiting damage to the Soviet Union is the rapid and wholesale destruction of the ability of the United States and its allies to wage nuclear war, US strategic planners believe that limitation of damage can best be achieved by controlling escalation at the lowest possible levels while ensuring that the outcomes are favourable to the US.

As described in chapter 2, the notion of 'controlled response' was developed by the Kennedy/McNamara Administration in 1961-62, and governed the design of SIOP-63, the Single Integrated Operational Plan or the plan for general nuclear war which came into effect on 1 August 1962. It has been further refined but in all essential respects maintained in the concept of 'escalation control' embodied in successive national guidances such as National Security Decision Memorandum (NSDM) - 242, signed by President Nixon on 17 January 1974, and given effect in SIOP-5 of 1 January 1976; Presidential Directive (PD)-59, signed by President Carter on 25 July 1980; National Security Decision Directive (NSDD)-13, signed by President Reagan in October 1981 and given effect in SIOP-6 of 1 October 1983; and, most recently, the national guidance prepared for the institution of SIOP-6F on 1 October 1989.

An extremely wide range of options for the employment of the US strategic nuclear forces has been developed, beginning with the various Major Attack Options (MAOs) and sub-options of SIOP-63 and greatly supplemented by the numerous Selective Attack Options

(SAOs), Limited Nuclear Options (LNOs) and Regional Nuclear Options (RNOs) which have been generated by SIOP planners since 1974.

The targets in the SIOP are divided into four principal groups, each of which in turn contains a wide range of target types. The four principal groups are the Soviet nuclear forces, the general purpose forces, the Soviet military and political leadership centres, and the Soviet economic and industrial base.

Examples of targets within each category were given by the Defense Department to the Senate Armed Service Committee in March 1980:[36]

1   Soviet nuclear forces:

ICBMs and IRBMs, together with their launch facilities (LFs) and launch command centres (LCCs);
nuclear weapons storage sites;
airfields supporting nuclear-capable aircraft;
nuclear ballistic-missile submarine (SSBN) bases;

2   Conventional military forces:
barracks;
supply depots;
marshalling points;
conventional airfields;
ammunition storage facilities;
tank and vehicle storage yards;

3   Military and political leadership:
command posts;
key communications facilities;

4   Economic and industrial targets:
(a) war-supporting industry;
    ammunition factories;
    tank and armoured personnel carrier factories;
    petroleum refineries;
    railway yards and repair facilities;
(b) industry that contributes to economic recovery:
    coal;
    basic steel;
    basic aluminium;
    cement;
    electric power.

As at December 1987, the US had some 13,446 strategic nuclear weapons. The actual number of these which would be available for employment depends on the assumptions made regarding alert levels - whether the forces are in a normal 'day-to-day' posture or whether they are fully generated. These alternatives are reflected in a basic division of the SIOP into an Alert Response Plan and a Generated Operations Plan. Table 2 shows the allocation of warheads to target categories in both the alert and generated situations as would have obtained in December 1987.

TABLE 2
ALLOCATION OF US SIOP WARHEADS TO TARGET
CATEGORIES IN ALERT AND GENERATED SITUATIONS
DECEMBER 1987

	Generated	Alert
Baseline force	13,446	13,446
Weapons deliverable to target	8,119	5,528
Target Category		
1 Soviet nuclear forces	2,512	2,512
2 Other military forces	1,650	950
3 Military and political leadership	850	600
4 Economic/industrial (E/I) targets	2,107	866
Reserve warheads	1,000	600

These plans, options and associated capabilities permit the US to pursue damage limitation by two different - and not altogether compatible - routes. The first is to limit a nuclear exchange before it escalates to the point of attacks against the leadership and economic/industrial targets in the Soviet Union and the United States. For this purpose, the US has developed an extremely sophisticated strategic C^3I system to support its own nuclear forces; attack options have been designed so that Soviet attack characterisation and assessment systems could clearly determine the specific intentions behind particular, limited US strikes; and plans have been developed to enable the US to 'hold some vital enemy targets hostage to subsequent destruction' and to control 'the timing and pace of attack execution, in order to provide the enemy opportunities to consider his actions'.[37] Insofar as is humanly and technically possible, the Soviet Union would be given every incentive to avoid escalation to major urban-industrial attacks. The preservation from destruction or disruption of Soviet C^3I systems, including most particularly the Soviet National Command Authorities (NCA), the Soviet attack characterisation and assessment systems, and the ability of the Soviet NCA to control its strategic forces, is critical to the success of this approach to damage limitation. As described earlier, there is no parallel to any of this in Soviet strategic nuclear war planning.

The second potential US route to damage limitation, which has been accorded much greater attention since the early 1980s, and which much more closely resembles Soviet strategic planning, is to terminate the exchange by destroying the Soviet political and military leadership and associated command and control system before Soviet plans for massive nuclear strikes could be executed. Plans for a prompt counter-leadership and counter-C3I attack have been incorporated in SIOP-6F.38 New sensor systems have been developed to locate and identify the Soviet leadership and supporting C3I systems throughout the course of a crisis and nuclear conflict - including the KH-12 *Ikon* real-time imaging satellite, the *Lacrosse* radar satellite, and the *Magnum* and *Mentor* geostationary signals intelligence (SIGINT) satellites. Advanced penetration aids (penaids) are being sought to ensure that US ballistic missiles can penetrate the up-graded ABM defence system deployed around Moscow. Development of 'earth penetrating' warheads has been authorised to provide a capability to destroy hardened deep underground command and control bunkers (such as the facilities beneath Moscow and the wartime relocation complex for the Soviet NCA at Sharapovo south of Moscow); and the large 9MT B-53 warhead has been reactivated for the same purpose. The destruction of underground leadership bunkers and command sites is a prime objective of the MX ICBM and Trident II D-5 SLBM systems, and the ability to locate and destroy mobile or relocatable command and control systems is a prime rationale for the B-2 Advanced Technology (Stealth) Bomber program.

Since 1982, US strategic nuclear planners have characterised US strategic nuclear policy as 'war fighting'.39 Deterrence based on a 'war fighting' posture has now been instituted in US strategic nuclear policy and planning to the extent that the technical capabilities of the late 1980s permit.

The Strategic Nuclear Balance

During the 1970s, the Strategic Arms Limitation Talks (SALT) - notwithstanding their deficiencies - provided an effective means of managing the superpower strategic competition. SALT confirmed a situation of approximate parity or 'essential equivalence' in the strategic nuclear balance, placed ceilings on some strategic capabilities and hence removed these from the arena of competition, and established a forum -

the Standing Consultative Commission (SCC) - for clarification and discussion of relevant strategic developments of concern to either side.

Unfortunately, however, the Strategic Arms Limitation agreements did not presage the transformation in international behaviour 'from rather rigid hostilities...[to] restraint and creativity', which Henry Kissinger had announced in Moscow in May 1972.[40] It was another seven years before the SALT II Treaty was signed, in Vienna on 18 June 1979, and then, of course, the ratification procedures were aborted by President Carter in December 1979 when it had become apparent that the consent of the Senate was unlikely to be forthcoming.

Despite the failure to ratify the SALT II Treaty, both the United States and the Soviet Union have by and large continued to abide by its constraints. However, these constraints are far from comprehensive. They apply generally to quantitative rather than qualitative developments in the strategic balance and to only a portion of the nuclear forces in the American and Soviet arsenals. The firmest limits were placed only on the numbers of long-range ballistic missiles - intercontinental ballistic missiles (ICBMs) and submarine-launched ballistic missiles (SLBMs). Indirect, conditional, and rather looser constraints were placed on the payloads these ICBMs and SLBMs can carry, and on the numbers of long-range strategic bombers and their payloads. The constraints do not apply to delivery systems with ranges less than 5,500 km. And the agreements did not address qualitative developments relating to the long-range ballistic missile forces, such as the replacement of older systems with more capable modern ones and improvements in the accuracy with which missile warheads can be delivered - the single most important variable in determining the lethality of a weapon. However, it is with respect to developments in these very areas - missile accuracy and weapons systems of less than intercontinental range - that technology is currently the most dynamic and the implications for the stability of the strategic balance most disturbing.

A concern expressed at the highest levels in the United States in the early 1980s was that, primarily as a result of the continuing improvement of its SS-18 and SS-19 ICBMs, the Soviet Union had achieved strategic superiority over the United States - a superiority amounting to a dangerous 'window of vulnerability'. On 31 March 1982, for example, President Reagan claimed that 'on balance, the Soviet Union does have a definite margin of superiority' in nuclear weapons; and, somewhat less categorically, Secretary of Defense Caspar Weinberger said on 16 April 1982 that 'the Soviets have begun to build an edge of superiority'.[41] These claims could not be substantiated by any objective analysis; they were explicitly disavowed by two of

Weinberger's predecessors, James Schlesinger and Harold Brown, and implicitly by the then Chairman of the Joint Chiefs of Staff, General David C. Jones, who testified that he would not trade US military strength for that of the Soviet Union.42 In April 1983, the President's Commission on Strategic Forces, headed by Lt.-Gen. Brent Scowcroft, effectively 'closed' the 'window of vulnerability' by concluding that the issue had been 'miscast', and that the vulnerability of silo-based ICBMs was quite manageable when considered in the context of the US 'triad of forces' - the ICBMs, SLBMs and bombers.43

Because of asymmetries in the respective Soviet and US strategic nuclear forces, the Soviet Union is ahead in terms of some measures of capability and the United States is ahead in others. In the most critical areas, however, the United States retains significant superiority. Tables 3 and 4 provide a quantitative characterisation of US and Soviet strategic nuclear capabilities as at December 1987.

Overall, the US strategic nuclear force posture remains better balanced than the Soviet posture. The Soviet ICBM force contains more than 60 per cent of the total throw-weight of the Soviet strategic nuclear forces and more than 60 per cent of the total weapons fielded by those forces. On the other hand, the US ICBM force contains only a quarter of the total US throw-weight and only 17 per cent of the total US weapons, with SLBMs carrying one-third of the throw-weight and more than 40 per cent of the weapons, and the long-range bombers the rest.

Although the Soviet Union has more strategic nuclear delivery vehicles (SNDVs) than the United States - 2,475 compared with 2,001 - the larger number of weapons carried by the American vehicles gives the United States a lead in total number of weapons of about 20 per cent - some 13,450 compared with some 11,180. Moreover, US warheads and bombs are generally more accurate than their Soviet counterparts. Some versions of the SS-18 and SS-19 ICBMs have been tested with a guidance system which provides an accuracy measured in terms of Circular Error Probable (CEP) as good as that of the INS-20 on the Minuteman III ICBMs (i.e., about 600 feet), but this guidance system has yet to be deployed on operational missiles. In the case of SLBMs and bomber-delivered weapons, the CEPs of the US systems are generally smaller than those of the Soviet Union by factors of two to five, and more than an order of magnitude in the case of air-launched cruise missiles (ALCMs). The one measure where the US lags is that of megatonnage, where the Soviet Union has a lead of about 35 per cent (some 5,465 MT compared with 4,028 MT), but it should be noted that the Soviet advantage in megatonnage, which was a factor of two in the early 1980s, has diminished through the decade as the large, single 20-24 MT

Table 3: US Strategic Nuclear Forces, December 1987

	Number of delivery vehicles (SNDVs)	Number of warheads (N)	Yield per warhead (Y)	EMT per warhead	CEP (feet)	CMP per warhead	Total number warheads (N)	Total MT (NY)	Total EMT	Total CMP
ICBMs										
Minuteman II	450	1	1.20	1.1	1200	0.78	450	540	495	351
Minuteman III (Mark 12)	220	3	0.17	0.31	600	0.67	660	112.2	204.6	442.2
Minuteman III (Mark 12A)	300	3	0.335	0.48	600	1.34	900	301.5	432	1206
MX (Silo)	30	10	0.35	0.5	325	4.7	300	105	150	1410
Sub-total (%)	1000 (50)						2310 (17.2)	1058.7 (26.3)	1281.6 (24.1)	3409.2 (6.7)
SLBMs										
Poseidon C-3	256	10	0.04	0.12	1450	0.04	2560	102.4	307.2	102.4
Trident I C-4	384	8	0.1	0.22	1450	0.08	3072	307.2	675.84	245.76
Sub-total (%)	640 (32)						5632 (41.9)	409.6 (10.2)	983.04 (18.5)	348.16 (0.7)
BOMBERS										
B-52G (Penetration)	61	4 bombs	1	1	600	2.78	244	244	244	678.32
		4 SRAMs	0.17	0.31	1200	0.17	244	41.48	75.64	41.48
B-52G (Penetration and Standoff)	90	4 bombs	1	1	600	2.78	360	360	360	1000.8
		4 SRAMs	0.17	0.31	1200	0.17	360	61.2	111.6	61.2
		12 ALCMs	0.17	0.31	100	24.23	1080	183.6	334.8	26168.4
B-52H (Penetration)	70	4 bombs	1	1	600	2.78	280	280	280	778.4
		4 SRAMs	0.17	0.31	1200	0.17	280	47.6	86.8	47.6
B-52H (Penetration and Standoff)	20	4 bombs	1	1	600	2.78	80	80	80	222.4
		4 SRAMs	0.17	0.31	1200	0.17	80	13.6	24.8	13.6
		12 ALCMs	0.17	0.31	100	24.23	240	40.8	74.4	5815.2
FB-111	56	4 bombs	1	1	600	2.78	224	224	224	622.72
		2 SRAMs	0.17	0.31	1200	0·17	112	19.04	34.72	19.04
B-1B (Penetration)	32	12 bombs	1	1	600	2.78	384	384	384	1067.52
		12 SRAMs	0.17	0.31	1200	0.17	384	65.28	119.04	65.28
B-1B (Penetration and Standoff)	32	12 bombs	1	1	600	2.78	384	384	384	1067.52
		12 SRAMs	0.17	0.31	1200	0.17	384	65.28	119.04	65.28
		12 ALCMs	0.17	0.31	100	24.23	384	65.28	119.04	9304.32
Sub-total (%)	361 (18)						5504 (40.9)	2559.2 (63.5)	3055.88 (57.4)	47039.08 (92.6)
Total	2001						13446	4027.5	5320.52	50796.44

Table 4: Soviet Strategic Nuclear Forces, December 1987

	Number of delivery vehicles (SNDVs)	Number of warheads (N)	Yield per warhead (Y)	EMT per warhead	CEP (feet)	CMP per warhead	Total number warheads (N)	Total MT (NY)	Total EMT	Total CMP
ICBMs										
SS-11 Sego M2	184	1	1	1	3750	0.07	184	184	184	13.88
SS-11 Sego M3	210	3	0.25	0.4	3750	0.03	630	157.5	252	18.9
SS-13 Savage M2	60	1	0.75	0.83	6000	0.02	60	45	49.8	1.2
SS-17 Spanker M3	139	4	0.75	0.83	1300	0.49	556	417	461.48	272.44
SS-18 Satan M4	308	10	0.55	0.67	800	1.05	3080	1694	2063.6	3234
SS-19 Stiletto M3	360	6	0.55	0.67	1000	0.67	2160	1188	1447.2	1447.2
SS-24 Scalpel	5	10	0.1	0.22	650	0.38	50	5	11	19
SS-25 Sickle	126	1	0.55	0.67	650	1.59	126	69.3	84.42	200.34
Sub-total (%)	1392 (56.2)						6846 (61.2)	3759.8 (68.8)	4553.5 (67.7)	5205.96 (93)
SLBMs										
SS-N-6 Serb	272	2	0.375	0.52	4250	0.03	544	204	282.88	16.32
SS-N-8 Sawfly	292	1	1.0	1	3000	0.11	292	292	292	32.12
SS-N-17 Snipe	12	1	1.0	1	3500	0.08	12	12	12	0.96
SS-N-18 Stingray	224	7	0.2	0.34	2000	0.09	1568	313.6	533.12	141.12
SS-N-20 Sturgeon	80	7	0.1	0.22	1650	0.06	560	56	123.2	33.6
SS-N-23 Skiff	48	4	0.1	0.22	1650	0.06	192	19.2	42.24	11.52
Sub-total (%)	928 (37.5)						3168 (28.3)	896.8 (16.4)	1285.44 (4.2)	235.64 (4.2)
BOMBERS										
Bear A	30	4 bombs	1	1	3000	0.11	120	120	120	13.2
Bear B/C	30	5 bombs	1	1	3000	1.11	150	150	150	16.5
Bear G	40	4 bombs	1	1	3000	0.11	160	160	160	17.6
		2 SRAMs	0.6	0.71	3000	0.08	80	48	56.8	6.4
Bear H	55	4 bombs	1	1	3000	0.11	220	220	220	24.2
		8 ALCMs	0.25	0.4	1500	0.18	440	110	176	79.2
Sub-total (%)	155 (6.3)						1170 (10.5)	808 (14.8)	882.8 (13.1)	157.1 (2.8)
Total	2475						11184	5464.6	6721.74	5598.7

warheads on the SS-18 Mod 1 and Mod 3 ICBMs were replaced by much smaller (.55 MT) multiple warheads.

A wide range of indices have been developed for assessing the strategic balance, but all of them have deficiencies of greater or lesser significance. The two indices of greater general utility are equivalent megatonnage (EMT) and counter-military potential (CMP).

EMT is the most meaningful index of destructive capability against 'soft' or 'area' targets such as urban-industrial areas. Since destructive power does not increase proportionally with an increase in weapon yield, it is necessary to apply scaling factors to the nominal megatonnage of the various weapons in the US and Soviet strategic arsenals. Whenever the yield is equal to or less than one megaton, it is appropriate to raise it to the two-thirds power, reflecting the fact that a nuclear explosion occurs in three-dimensional space, whereas its damaging effects occur only along the dimensions of length and width. Even this discounting will tend to overvalue the destructive capability of large weapons as against combinations of relatively smaller weapons where the destructive capability can be more effectively distributed, so that yield should be raised to the 0.5 power in the case of weapons larger than one megaton.[44]

$$EMT = Y^{2/3} \quad \text{where } Y \leq 1\,MT$$
$$EMT = Y^{1/2} \quad \text{where } Y \geq 1\,MT$$

According to this index, the Soviet Union has a total destructive capability against soft targets which is some 25 per cent greater than that of the US forces (6,720 equivalent megatons compared with 5,320). However, the strategic significance of this lead is problematical, since there is only a finite number of soft targets in both the Soviet Union and the United States. (In the Soviet Union, for example, more than one-third of the population and nearly three-quarters of industrial production is concentrated in three hundred cities.[45])

CMP is a useful gross index of the destructive capability of nuclear weapons against 'hard' or 'point' targets such as ICBM silos or underground command and control centres, although there are several important qualifications to its application in assessment of dissimilar force structures. It is a combined index of the explosive power of these weapons (discounted by an appropriate yield-scaling factor) and the accuracy with which they are expected to be delivered. For weapons with yield equal to or greater than 0.2 MT, the yield should be raised to the two-thirds power. However, in the case of lower yield weapons in a hard target context, the use of 0.66 scaling for yield leads to consistent overestimation of damage probabilities, and hence a scaling factor of 0.8 is used for weapons of less than 0.2 MT.[46]

$$CMP = \frac{Y^{2/3}}{(CEP)^2} \qquad \text{where } Y \geq 0.2 \text{ MT}$$

$$CMP = \frac{Y^{0.8}}{(CEP)^2} \qquad \text{where } Y < 0.2 \text{ MT}$$

The total CMP of the US strategic nuclear forces is currently some nine times greater than that of the Soviet forces. However, it must be noted that some 92 per cent of the US total CMP resides in the bomber force - which could take as long as 6-8 hours to reach its targets in the Soviet Union. In stark contrast, some 93 per cent of Soviet CMP resides in the ICBM force. If CMP is to be used effectively, at least against ICBM silos, or against submarine pens and bomber bases from which the submarines and bombers can quickly be put to sea or relocated to secondary airfields, then only prompt CMP - or the CMP of the respective ICBM forces - is of practical import. The prompt/ICBM CMP of the Soviet strategic nuclear force today is just over 50 per cent greater than that of the US force.

Further, the effectiveness of a given amount of CMP depends on the hardness or blast resistance of the notional targets. In general, Soviet targets are rather harder than their US counterparts. Except for the NORAD headquarters under Cheyenne Mountain in Colorado and perhaps a handful of other underground command and control centres, the hardest sites in the United States are the Minuteman silos, most of which are hardened to about 2,000 psi. By far the great majority of other military targets (OMT), economic/industrial installations, and governmental/administrative centres in the United States have no special protection and would be destroyed by less than 25 psi blast overpressure. On the other hand, as noted above, some 30 per cent of Soviet ICBM silos are hardened to 6,000-7,200 psi, and another 30 per cent to about 4,000 psi. Thousands of Soviet leadership relocation bunkers, military command posts, communications stations and associated control facilities have been hardened to greater than 600 psi, and more than 100 to greater than 1,000 psi. The Soviet Union has also undertaken a program of hardening and dispersing key industrial facilities, to the point where significant counterforce capability must now be devoted to the destruction of the Soviet economic/industrial target set.

It is also important to note that today the Soviet Union maintains at least as many strategic nuclear weapons on alert as does the United States - about 7,200 warheads (even assuming that no Soviet

Table 5: US Strategic Nuclear Forces, 1995

	Number of delivery vehicles (SNDVs)	Number of warheads (N)	Yield per warhead (Y)	EMT per warhead	CEP (feet)	CMP per warhead	Total number warheads (N)	Total MT (NY)	Total EMT	Total CMP
ICBMs										
Minuteman II	450	1	1.2	1.1	1100	0.93	450	540	495	418.5
Minuteman III (Mark 12)	200	3	0.17	0.31	550	0.8	600	102	186	480
Minuteman III (Mark 12A)	300	3	0.335	0.48	550	1.59	900	301.5	432	1431
MX (Silo)	50	10	0.35	0.5	250	7.95	500	175	250	3975
MX (Rail)	50	10	0.35	0.5	250	7.95	500	175	250	3975
Sub-total (%)	1050 (47.9)						2950 (18.8)	1293.5 (19.9)	1613 (19.7)	10279.5 (7.8)
SLBMs										
Trident I C-4	264	8	0.1	0.22	1200	0.11	2112	211.2	464.64	232.32
Trident II D-5	456	8	0.475	0.61	600	1.69	3648	1732.8	2225.28	6165.12
Sub-total (%)	720 (32.8)						5760 (36.6)	1944 (29.9)	2689.92 (32.8)	6397.44 (4.9)
BOMBERS										
B-52G (Penetration)	45	4 bombs	1	1	500	4	180	180	180	720
		4 SRAMs	0.17	0.31	1000	0.24	180	30.6	55.8	43.2
B-52G (Penetration and Standoff)	75	4 bombs	1	1	500	4	300	300	300	1200
		4 SRAMs	0.17	0.31	1000	0.24	300	51	93	72
		12 ALCMs	0.17	0.31	70	49.45	900	153	279	44505
B-52H (Penetration)	75	4 bombs	1	1	500	4	300	300	300	1200
		4 SRAMs	0.17	0.31	1000	0.24	300	51	93	72
B-52H (Penetration and Standoff)	30	4 bombs	1	1	500	4	120	120	120	480
		4 SRAMs	0.17	0.31	1000	0.24	120	20.4	37.2	28.8
		12 ALCMs	0.17	0.31	70	49.45	360	61.2	111.6	17802
FB-111	38	2 bombs	1	1	500	4	152	152	152	608
		4 SRAMs	0.17	0.31	1000	0.24	76	12.92	23.56	18.24
B-1B (Penetration)	50	12 bombs	1	1	500	4	600	600	600	2400
		12 SRAMs	0.17	0.31	1000	0.24	600	102	186	144
B-1B (Penetration and Standoff)	50	12 bombs	1	1	500	4	600	600	600	2400
		12 SRAMs	0.17	0.31	1000	0.24	600	102	186	144
		12 ALCMs	0.17	0.31	70	49.45	600	102	186	2967
B-2	60	4 bombs	1	1	500	4	240	240	240	960
		4 SRAMs	0.17	0.31	1000	0.24	240	40.8	74.4	57.6
		4 ALCMs	0.17	0.31	70	49.45	240	40.8	74.4	11868
Sub-total (%)	423 (19.3)						7008 (44.6)	3259.7 (50.2)	3891.96 (47.5)	114392.8 (87.3)
Total	2193						15718	6497.2	8194.88	131069.8

Table 6: Soviet Strategic Nuclear Forces, 1995

	Number of delivery vehicles (SNDVs)	Number of warheads (N)	Yield per warhead (Y)	EMT per warhead	CEP (feet)	CMP per warhead	Total number warheads (N)	Total MT (NY)	Total EMT	Total CMP
ICBMs										
SS-11 Sego M2	65	1	1	1	3500	0.08	65	65	65	5.2
SS-11 Sego M3	95	3	0.25	0.4	3500	0.03	285	71.25	114	8.55
SS-18 Satan M4	128	10	0.55	0.67	600	1.86	1280	704	857.6	2380.8
SS-18 Satan M5	180	10	0.75	0.83	600	2.29	1800	1350	1494	4122
SS-19 Stiletto M3	266	6	0.55	0.67	800	1.05	1596	877.8	1069.32	1675.8
SS-24 Scalpel	185	10	0.1	0.22	400	0.99	1850	185	407	1831.5
SS-25 Sickle	425	1	0.55	0.67	400	4.2	425	233.75	284.75	1785
Sub-total (%)	1344 (50.4)						7301 (43.7)	3486.8 (46.7)	4291.67 (46.6)	11808.85 (85.4)
SLBMs										
SS-N-8 Sawfly	292	1	1	1	2800	0.13	292	292	292	37.96
SS-N-17 Snipe	12	1	1	1	3300	0.09	12	12	12	1.08
SS-N-18 Stingray	224	7	0.2	0.34	1500	0.15	1568	313.6	533.12	2355.2
SS-N-20	240	7	0.1	0.22	1250	0.1	1680	168	369.6	168
SS-N-23 Skiff	192	4	0.1	0.22	1250	0.1	768	76.8	168.96	76.8
Sub-total (%)	960 (36)						4320 (25.9)	862.4 (11.6)	1375.68 (3.8)	519.04 (3.8)
BOMBERS										
Bear G	70	4 bombs	1.0	1	2000	0.25	280	280	280	70
		2 SRAMs	0.6	0.71	2000	0.18	140	84	99.4	25.2
Bear H	175	4 bombs	1.0	1	2000	0.25	700	700	700	175
		8 ALCMs	0.25	0.4	1000	0.4	1400	350	560	560
Blackjack (Penetration)	40	8 bombs	1	1	2000	0.25	320	320	320	80
		8 SRAMs	0.6	0.71	2000	0.18	320	192	227.2	57.6
Blackjack (Penetration and Standoff)	80	8 bombs	1	1	2000	0.25	640	640	640	160
		8 SRAMs	0.6	0.71	2000	0.18	640	384	454.4	115.2
		8 ALCMs	0.25	0.4	1000	0.4	640	160	256	256
Sub-total (%)	365 (13.7)						5080 (30.4)	3110 (41.7)	3537 (38.4)	1499 (10.8)
Total	2669						16701	7459.2	9204.35	13826.89

bombers are kept on alert, whereas some 30 per cent of the US bomber force is on day-to-day alert).

With respect to the future of the strategic balance, there are essentially two basic possibilities. The first is that the current rates and patterns of US and Soviet strategic force deployments will continue, subject to the broad constraints established by SALT in the 1970s. This possibility is exemplified for 1995 in Tables 5 and 6, where projections have been made from current trends, informed by recent decisions and reasonable assumptions about decisions likely to be made in the next few years. In the US case (Table 5), it is assumed that deployment of the MX ICBM will have been completed (with 50 based in former Minuteman II silos and 50 operating in a rail-mobile mode); that regardless of any decision to proceed with deployment of a new small ICBM (SICBM), it would not be operational by 1995; that the Trident II D-5 SLBM will be operational aboard 19 Ohio-class submarines; that production of the B-1 bomber will be completed; and that some 60 B-2 Advanced Technology Bombers (ATBs) will be in service. On the Soviet side (Table 6), it is assumed that deployment of the SS-25 *Sickle* land-mobile ICBM will continue at the present rate of 50 per year, matched by a compensatory phase-out of obsolete SS-11 and SS-13 ICBMs; that deployment of the large SS-24 *Scalpel* ICBM will proceed at a rate of about 30 per year, matched by a compensatory phase-out of the SS-17 force; and that production of the *Bear* H and *Blackjack* bombers will proceed at a rate of approximately 20 per year. The most noteworthy conclusions are that while both the US and the Soviet Union will enjoy net increases in their numbers of SNDVs and warheads, the Soviet Union will retain its lead in SNDVs and will, for the first time ever, surpass the US in numbers of strategic nuclear warheads and bombs; that the Soviet Union will remain ahead with respect to both megatonnage and EMT; and that, while both the US and Soviet CMP totals increase markedly, nearly 90 per cent of the US figure continues to reside in its bomber force while some 85 per cent of the Soviet figure will reside in its ICBM force, maintaining a Soviet advantage in prompt counter-military potential. Further, about 8,650 US warheads would be maintained on alert, as compared to some 8,290 Soviet ICBM and SLBM warheads, or more than 9,800 Soviet warheads if it is assumed that the Soviets move to place some 30 per cent of their bomber force on alert as well.

The second possibility for the 1990s is that there will be some agreement on 'deep cuts' in US and Soviet strategic nuclear forces, along the lines of the so-called 50 per cent cuts discussed and in part agreed in the Strategic Arms Reduction Talks (START) in 1987. This possibility is exemplified in Tables 7 and 8. There are several important points to

Table 7: US Strategic Nuclear Forces, 50% start

	Number of delivery vehicles (SNDVs)	Number of warheads (N)	Yield per warhead (Y)	EMT per warhead	CEP (feet)	CMP per warhead	Total number warheads (N)	Total MT (NY)	Total EMT	Total CMP
ICBMs										
Minuteman III	148	3	0.335	0.48	600	1.34	444	148.74	213.12	594.96
MX Rail	50	10	0.35	0.5	325	4.7	500	175	250	2350
MX Silo	50	10	0.35	0.5	325	4.7	500	175	250	2350
Sub-total (%)	248 (23.5)						1444 (13.5)	498.74 (9.5)	713.12 (11.2)	5294.96 (7.4)
SLBMs										
Trident II D-5	432	8	0.475	0.61	600	1.69	3456	1641.6	2108.16	5840.64
Sub-total (%)	432 (40.9)						3456 (32.3)	1641.6 (31.2)	2108.16 (33)	5840.64 (8.1)
BOMBERS										
B-52G	60	4 bombs	1	1	500	4	240	240	240	960
		4 SRAMs	0.17	0.31	1000	0.24	240	40.8	74.4	57.6
B-52H	84	4 bombs	1	1	500	4	336	336	336	1344
		12 ALCMs	0.17	0.31	70	49.45	1008	171.36	312.48	49845.6
B-1B	100	12 bombs	1	1	500	4	1200	1200	1200	4800
		12 SRAMs	0.17	0.31	1000	0.24	1200	204	372	288
B-2	132	6 bombs	1	1	500	4	792	792	792	3168
		6 SRAMs	0.17	0.31	1000	0.24	792	134.64	245.52	190.08
Sub-total (%)	376 (35.6)						5808 (54.2)	3118.8 (59.3)	3572.4 (55.9)	60653.28 (84.5)
Total	1056						10708	5259.1	6393.68	71788.8

Table 8: Soviet Strategic Nuclear Forces, 50% start

	Number of delivery vehicles (SNDVs)	Number of warheads (N)	Yield per warhead (Y)	EMT per warhead	CEP (feet)	CMP per warhead	Total number warheads (N)	Total MT (NY)	Total EMT	Total CMP
ICBMs										
SS-18 Satan M5	154	10	0.75	0.83	600	2.29	1540	1155	1278.2	3526.6
SS-24 Scalpel (Rail)	100	10	0.1	0.22	400	0.99	1000	100	220	990
SS-25 Sickle (Land)	248	1	0.55	0.67	400	4.2	248	136.4	166.16	1041.6
Sub-total (%)	512 (47.1)						2788 (31)	1391.4 (29.5)	1664.36 (30)	5558.2 (81.4)
SLBMs										
Typhoon SS-N-20	80	10	0.1	0.22	1250	0.1	800	80	176	80
Delta III SS-N-18	160	7	0.2	0.34	1500	0.15	1120	224	380.8	168
Delta IV SS-N-23	48	4	0.1	0.22	1250	0.1	192	19.2	42.24	19.2
Sub-total (%)	288 (27)						2112 (23.5)	323.2 (6.8)	599.04 (3.9)	267.2 (3.9)
BOMBERS										
Bear H	75	4 bombs	1	1	2000	0.25	300	300	300	75
		8 ALCMs	0.25	0.4	1000	0.4	600	150	240	240
Blackjack	200	8 bombs	1	1	2000	0.25	1600	1600	1600	400
		8 SRAMs	0.6	0.71	2000	0.18	1600	960	1136	288
Sub-total (%)	275 (25.8)						4100 (45.6)	3010 (63.7)	3276 (59.1)	1003 (14.7)
Total	1065						9000	4724.6	5539.4	6828.4

note about the strategic balance under a 50 per cent START regime. To begin with, the respective US and Soviet force structures would not be simply a truncated version of those that would obtain in the absence of START. The sub-ceiling of 4,900 warheads on ICBMs and SLBMs agreed at the summit meeting in December 1987 will require extensive changes in both the Soviet and US force structures, while the proposed counting rules for bomber-carried weapons will provide significant incentives for further changes. For example, the US has proposed that bombers not carrying ALCMs will count as only one weapon whereas bombers equipped with ALCMs will be charged with 10 ALCMs regardless of the number actually carried. Hence, although the B-52G, B-1B and Blackjack bombers could be used as both penetrating bombers and as ALCM carriers, there is a strong incentive to configure them solely as penetrating bombers in order to maximize the number of weapons that can be carried.[47]

Second, although there is a common perception that the objective of START is 50 per cent reductions in strategic nuclear forces - or reductions to a common ceiling of 6,000 strategic weapons - it is clear that because the START counting rules significantly undercount deployed weapons, the actual number of weapons that each side will maintain will be much greater than 6,000.[48] According to the counting rules proposed by the US, for example, a B-1B bomber equipped with 24 weapons and a Blackjack bomber equipped with 16 weapons, if configured for penetration rather than ALCM missions, would each count for only one weapon. Hence, the total number of warheads likely to be maintained by the US and the Soviet Union is around 10,700 and 9,000 respectively - or only 20 per cent fewer than those maintained in December 1987, and in fact no less than those in the US and Soviet strategic nuclear arsenals when the 'deep cuts' were first proposed by President Reagan in May 1982!

Third, although there is a common perception that START is supposed to enhance the stability of the global strategic balance, in fact the postures likely to result from the START process will have intrinsic problems with respect to stability, and the process of transition from current numbers to the postulated START levels could well give rise to further disturbing possibilities. For example, START does nothing to help the survivability of silo-based ICBMs. As at December 1987, the US had 1,000 ICBM silos, threatened by some 5,972 SS-17, SS-18, SS-19, SS-24 and SS-25 warheads - i.e. about six warheads per silo. START would reduce the number of US ICBM silos to some 198, with a further 50 MX ICBMs deployed on 25 trains, which would be threatened by some 2,788 SS-18, SS-24 and SS-25 warheads - i.e. some 12.5 warheads per silo and train!

A similar situation pertains with respect to the SLBM forces.[49] As at December 1987, the Soviet Union maintained 61 SSBNs with 928 SLBMs and 3,168 warheads, while the US had 36 SSBNs with 640 SLBMs and 5,632 warheads. It is likely that START will reduce these numbers to some 17 SSBNs with 2,112 warheads in the Soviet case and perhaps 18 SSBNs with 3,456 warheads in the US case. Given that something like these numbers eventuate, then the anti-submarine warfare (ASW) resources devoted to each SSBN will be increased dramatically - by a factor of two in the case of US SSBNs and a factor of about 3.5 in the case of Soviet SSBNs!

This could well represent the greatest increment in counter-SSBN ASW capability since SSBNs were first deployed more than a quarter of a century ago - comparable to the long-feared but always improbable technological breakthrough that would greatly reduce SSBN invulnerability and hence greatly reduce strategic stability based on the assured destructive capability of SSBN forces.

And, fourth, the US and Soviet force postures that are likely to emerge from the current START process pose significant problems for verification and increase the potential for 'breakout' from the Treaty limits.[50] There are, to begin with, major uncertainties with respect to the number of Soviet ICBMs, SLBMs and bomber weapons that have actually been produced, as opposed to those currently deployed. This could amount to several thousand weapons above and beyond those included in START. In addition, the START counting rules understate the potential weapons loadings for several strategic systems. The SS-18 ICBM, for example, could be loaded with 14 warheads rather than the 10 it is assigned, and this would be virtually impossible to detect through satellite coverage. Similarly, the SS-N-23 Skiff SLBM can be equipped with 10 warheads rather than the four it is assigned. Numerous additional ALCMs could also be produced for subsequent deployment on the Blackjack bombers or on large transport planes. As the Defense Policy Panel of the US House Armed Services Committee has noted,

> In a worst case scenario...,the Soviet Union could generate 4,200 additional ICBM warheads, 4,600 SLBM warheads, and 2,000 additional ALCMs, for a breakout total of about 10,800 additional weapons. While such figures are high [indeed, they would exceed the permitted START total], they are not out of the question and should not be ruled out in planning for U.S. security.[51]

The Future of the Strategic Balance

Although the strategic balance is complex, multi-faceted, and its future subject to major uncertainties, the general direction of development is clear. Although there is a widespread public perception, based on the improvement in the US-Soviet political relationship and the limited progress made in arms control negotiations in 1987-88, that the strategic arms competition is being brought under sounder management, in fact it is tending in the direction of greater instability.

The likelihood of major nuclear conflict between the United States and the Soviet Union remains low. There is much in the strategic relationship which promotes stability or reduces the chance of major conflict. These positive factors include the essential equivalence of US and Soviet strategic nuclear forces; the capacity and the determination of US and NATO forces to deter attack by the Soviet and Warsaw Pact forces; the negotiations between the US and the Soviet Union with respect to arms limitation and crisis management regimes; and, most important, the knowledge that each has of the other's capabilities. Overall, there is a clear comprehension on both sides of the awesome consequences of major nuclear conflict. The prospect of large-scale urban-industrial destruction is a powerful deterrent to any use of nuclear weapons by the superpowers. Nevertheless, the US and the USSR remain adversaries and there is a finite chance that some difference between them affecting the vital strategic interests of one or the other may escalate to nuclear conflict. This possibility is being enhanced by current and foreseeable developments in strategic nuclear technology, strategic policies and plans, and force structures.

The various technological developments with respect to greater missile accuracies, very hard target destruction capabilities, third-generation nuclear weapons systems, and real-time strategic intelligence collection systems, all promise to significantly enhance strategic instability. The increasing capability of both sides to locate and promptly destroy the other's strategic nuclear forces, leadership and associated C^3I systems - though very conditional and far from determinate - greatly increases the incentives to pre-empt in a crisis or to escalate from a lower-level or theatre conflict. There is little evidence that either US or Soviet planners believe that the damage they would suffer from the resultant response of the other side would be anything less than catastrophic, but it would be significantly less than that which would pertain in the event that the other side was allowed to control the escalation process or seize the initiative with a major counterforce or counter-leadership strike.

This logic is being increasingly incorporated in the strategic policies and plans of both the United States and the Soviet Union. The operational plans of both sides have in fact long been based on war fighting strategies. In the case of the Soviet Union, strategic nuclear planning has always been dominated by classic military considerations. There has been little interest in notions of limited nuclear war or escalation control, and none in the concept of 'assured destruction'. In the US case, 'assured destruction' has periodically been avowed as declaratory policy but has never been reflected in the actual war plans (or various SIOPs since 1960). The concepts of escalation control and limited nuclear war fighting have been central to US plans since 1961-62, but during the 1980s these have been increasingly complemented by plans for protracted nuclear war, options for prompt counter-leadership and counter-C3I strikes, and the objective of 'prevailing' in a major nuclear exchange. Since 1982, US strategic nuclear policy has been officially characterised as 'war fighting', and the US posture has increasingly come to resemble that of the Soviet Union. This is not surprising. The logic of damage limitation is compelling. And once one side has accepted the war-fighting approach to deterrence, the logic for the other to do likewise is also compelling. Unfortunately, however, the consequences of a general acceptance of war fighting for stability are recessive. Together with the developments in military technology, the developments in strategic policies and plans are leading to greater instability.

Unfortunately, the arms control process has not ameliorated this situation. The SALT constraints of the 1970s provided no inhibition to technological developments such as greater accuracy, MIRVs, and cruise missile deployments - which increased the number of US and Soviet strategic nuclear warheads from about 5,600 to 2,650 respectively when SALT I was signed in 1972 to some 13,000 and 11,000 in 1988, and greatly increased the lethality of these warheads. Moreover, the reductions proposed in the current START negotiations are likely to further reduce strategic stability as well as require additional expenditures for force modernisation and new verification systems. Completely new approaches to arms control, technological innovation, and strategic nuclear planning are required if these various developments are to be reversed and the global strategic balance made more stable in the 1990s.

Endnotes

1   See Desmond Ball, 'Technology and Geopolitics', in Ciro E. Zoppo and Charles Zorgbibe (eds.), *On Geopolitics: Classical and Nuclear*, (Published in cooperation with

the NATO Scientific Affairs Division by Martinus Nijhoff Publishers, Dordrecht, Boston, and Lancaster, 1985), pp.171-199.

2 Theodore B. Taylor, 'Third-Generation Nuclear Weapons', *Scientific American*, (Vol.256, No.4), April 1987, pp.22-31.

3 Warren Strobel, 'U.S. To Make Nuclear Bomb That Burrows', *Washington Times*, 12 September 1988, p.1; and Tim Carrington, 'Carlucci Orders Move for Development of "Earth-Penetrating" Nuclear Weapon', *Wall Street Journal*, 13 September 1988, p.5.

4 President Reagan, 'Eliminating The Threat From Ballistic Missiles', *National Security Decision Directive No.85 (NSDD-85)*, 25 March 1983.

5 B. Byely (ed.), *Marxism-Leninism on War and Army*, (Translated and published under the auspices of the United States Air Force, U.S. Government Printing Office, Washington, D.C., 1974), pp.9-10.

6 See Desmond Ball, 'Soviet Strategic Planning and the Control of Nuclear War', in Roman Kolkowicz and Ellen Propper Mickiewicz (eds.), *The Soviet Calculus of Nuclear War*, (Lexington Books, D.C. Heath and Company, Lexington, Massachusetts, 1986), pp.49-67.

7 For fuller discussion of Soviet strategic doctrine, see Benjamin S. Lambeth, 'The Sources of Soviet Military Doctrine', in F.B. Horton, A.C. Rogerson, and E.L. Warner (eds.), *Comparative Defense Policy*, (Johns Hopkins University Press, Baltimore, 1974), pp.200-216; Benjamin S. Lambeth, *Selective Nuclear Options in American and Soviet Strategic Policy*, (The RAND Corporation, Santa Monica, R-2034-DDR & E, December 1976); Benjamin S. Lambeth, *The Elements of Soviet Strategic Policy*, (The RAND Corporation, Santa Monica, P-6389, September 1979); and Benjamin S. Lambeth, 'Contemporary Soviet Military Policy', in Kolkowicz and Mickiewicz (eds.), *The Soviet Calculus of Nuclear War*, pp.25-48.

8 Cited in Joseph D. Douglas, Jr and Amoretta M. Hoeber, *Soviet Strategy for Nuclear War*, (Hoover Institution Press, Stanford, California, 1979), p.36.

9 Byely (ed.), *Marxism-Leninism on War and Army*, p.217.

10 Col.-Gen. N.A. Lomov (ed.), *Scientific-Technical Progress and the Revolution in Military Affairs*, (Translated and published under the auspices of the United States Air Force, U.S. Government Printing Office, Washington, D.C., 1974), p.147.

11 Stephen M. Meyer, 'Soviet Nuclear Operations', in Ashton B. Carter, John D. Steinbruner and Charles A. Zraket (eds.), *Managing Nuclear Operations*, (The Brookings Institution, Washington, D.C., 1987), pp.487-489; and Kurt Gottfried and Bruce G. Blair (eds.), *Crisis Stability and Nuclear War*, (Oxford University Press, New York and Oxford, 1988), pp.128-132, and 1954.

12 Donald MacKenzie, 'The Soviet Union and Strategic Missile Guidance', *International Security*, (Vol.13, No.2), Fall 1988, p.36.

13 Marc Trachtenberg, 'The Influence of Nuclear Weapons in the Cuban Missile Crisis', *International Security*, (Vol.10, No.1), Summer 1985, p.158.

14 Meyer, 'Soviet Nuclear Operations', p.494.

15 See Desmond Ball, 'The Soviet Strategic C3I System', in Fred D. Byers (ed.), *The C3I Handbook*, (EW Communications, Inc., Palo Alto, California, First Edition, 1986), pp.206-216.

16 US Department of Defense, *Soviet Military Power: An Assessment of the Threat, 1988*, (U.S. Government Printing Office, Washington, D.C., April 1988), p.46.

17 'Soviets' Nuclear Arsenal Continues to Proliferate', *Aviation Week and Space Technology*, 16 June 1980, p.67; Clarence A. Robinson, 'Soviets Testing New Generation of ICBMs', *Aviation Week and Space Technology*, 3 November 1980, p.28; and 'Navy to Develop New Trident Warhead', *Aviation Week and Space Technology*, 17 January 1983, p.26.

   Most of the US Minuteman ICBM silos are hardened to withstand about 2,000 psi. See Secretary Weinberger's testimony to the Senate Armed Services Committee of 5 October 1981, in *Survival*, (Vol.XXIV, No.1), January/February 1982, p.31.

18 See Desmond Ball, 'The Soviet Strategic C3I System', pp.207-208; and US Department of Defense, *Soviet Military Power: An Assessment of the Threat, 1988*, pp.55-62.

19 *Ibid.*, p.55.
20 Ray Bonds (ed.), *The Soviet War Machine*, (Salamander Books Limited, London, 1980), p.55.
21 US Department of Defense, *Soviet Military Power 1985*, (U.S. Government Printing Office, Washington, D.C., 1985), p.50.
22 *Ibid.*.
23 *Ibid.*, p.52.
24 *Ibid.*, pp.52-53.
25 Letter from General Brown to Senator William Proxmire, 3 February 1977, reprinted in *Survival*, (Vol.XIX, No.2), March/April 1977, p.77; and US Department of Defense, *Soviet Military Power: An Assessment of the Threat, 1988*, pp.59-62.
26 Marshal A.A. Grechco, cited in Leon Goure, Foy D. Kohler and Mose L. Harvey, *The Role of Nuclear Forces in Current Soviet Strategy*, (Center for Advanced International Studies, University of Miami, 1974), p.107.
27 Major-General V. Zemskov, cited in Douglas and Hoeber, *Soviet Strategy for Nuclear War*, p.16.
28 Colonel M. Shirokov, cited in Leon Goure and Michael J. Dane, 'The Soviet Strategic View', *Strategic Review*, (Vol.VIII, No.1), Winter 1980, p.81 (emphasis added).
29 Cited in Douglass and Hoeber, *Soviet Strategy for Nuclear War*, p.75.
30 See Joseph D. Douglass, Jr., *Soviet Military Strategy in Europe*, (Pergamon Press, New York, 1980), p.74.
31 Colonel Shirokov, cited in Goure and Deane, 'The Soviet Strategic View', pp.81-83.
32 President Ronald Reagan, *National Security Strategy of the United States*, (The White House, Washington, D.C., January 1988), p.13.
33 See Desmond Ball, 'The Development of the SIOP, 1960-1983', in Desmond Ball and Jeffrey Richelson (eds.), *Strategic Nuclear Targeting*, (Cornell University Press, Ithaca and London, 1986), pp.57-83.
34 Reagan, *National Security Strategy of the United States*, p.13.
35 *Ibid.*, p.3.
36 US Congress, Senate Armed Services Committee, *Department of Defense Authorization for Appropriations for Fiscal Year 1981*, (U.S. Government Printing Office, Washington, D.C., 1980), Part 5, pp.2721.
37 President Richard Nixon, *National Security Decision Memorandum (NSDM)-242*, 17 January 1974, cited in Jack Anderson, 'Not-So-New Nuclear Strategy', *Washington Post*, 12 October 1980, p.C-7.
38 For further discussion of SIOP-6F, see Desmond Ball and Robert C. Toth, 'Revising the SIOP: Taking War-Fighting to Dangerous Extremes', *International Security*, (Vol.14, No.4), Spring 1990, pp. 65-92. See also footnote 65 in chapter 2 of this volume.
39 See, for example, testimony of General Bennie Davis, Commander-in-Chief Strategic Air Command (CINCSAC), in US Congress, Senate Armed Services Committee, *Department of Defense Authorization for Appropriations for Fiscal Year 1983*, (U.S. Government Printing Office, Washington, D.C., 1982), Part 7, pp.4159, 4241.
40 Hedrick Smith, 'Nixon and Brezhnev Close Talks With Joint Declaration of Peace', *New York Times*, 30 May 1972, p.18.
41 George C. Wilson, 'Weinberger Trim's Reagan's Claim', *Washington Post*, 17 April 1982.
42 *Washington Post*, 3 April 1982; and *New York Times*, 1 May 1982.
43 See 'Report of the President's Commission on Strategic Forces (Excerpts), 11 April 1983', in *Survival*, (Vol.XXV, No.4), July/August 1983, pp.177-186.
44 See Jeffrey T. Richelson, 'Evaluating the Strategic Balance', *American Journal of Political Science*, (Vol.24, No.4), pp.795-819.
45 Secretary of Defense Harold Brown, *Department of Defense Annual Report Fiscal Year 1981*, (U.S. Government Printing Office, Washington, D.C., 1980), p.79.
46 See W.A. Barbieri, *Countermilitary Potential: A Measure of Strategic Offensive Force Capability*, (The RAND Corporation, Santa Monica, California, R-1314-PR, December 1973), pp.5-6.

47   US Congress, House Committee on Armed Services, Defense Policy Panel, *Breakout, Verification and Force Structure: Dealing With The Full Implications of START*, (U.S. Government Printing Office, Washington, D.C., 1988), pp.21-23.

48   *Ibid.*, p.24.

49   See Desmond Ball, 'Some Implications of Fifty Per Cent Reductions in Strategic Nuclear Forces for Sea-Based Systems', in Sverre Lodgaard (ed.), *Naval Forces: Arms Restraint and Confidence Building*, (Sage Publications, forthcoming 1990).

50   See US Congress, House Armed Services Committee, Defense Policy Panel, *Breakout, Verification and Force Structure: Dealing With The Full Implications of START*.

51   *Ibid.*, p.5.

CHAPTER 5

TRENDS IN CONVENTIONAL WARFARE AND TECHNOLOGIES

Ross Babbage

Rapid technological change is having a dramatic impact on the conventional battlefield as we have known it in the past. Perhaps its most obvious effect is the provision of new and better pieces of equipment - aircraft which can fly farther, faster, carry greater loads and turn more tightly; tanks which can move faster, fire more accurately and provide their crews with far greater protection; and ships which can unleash enormous firepower and defend themselves against a wide range of attacks.

But rapid technological change is doing much more than simply upgrading the performance of existing weaponry and equipment. It is also providing completely new operational capacities and new types of equipment. For example, there are now several types of missiles and bombs designed to be launched tens and even hundreds of kilometres from their objectives that can consistently strike their targets with accuracies of less than a few metres. At sea, there are area mine systems that, when deployed on or above the seabed, wait for the noise signature of their allotted ship or submarine target and when it is detected within range, automatically launch a homing torpedo. On the ground battlefield, there are night vision systems that not only make it possible for soldiers to see in the dark but also to detect targets through limited amounts of smoke, dust, cloud, rain and light camouflage. In addition, there are both jet and propeller driven aircraft that can not only fly like conventional aeroplanes but hover and land like helicopters. There are miniature robot aircraft that can fly many kilometres behind the enemy's lines to perform real-time reconnaissance, target acquisition, electronic jamming and even *kamikaze* attacks on tanks, radars, communications centres and other targets. These, and many other types of new technology systems, provide completely fresh means of performing important battlefield tasks. In some cases the new technology systems usefully complement and enhance the capacities of traditional military systems and equipment. However, in other instances new technology systems can effectively replace or supersede long-established traditional military systems and equipment because of their great battlefield efficiency and effectiveness. This has obvious implications for the shopping and 'wish' lists of defence departments.

However, this is still only part of a story. The new technologies are also having a dramatic effect on the way units and formations operate on the battlefield. The best methods for military units to deploy, move, communicate, hide, attack, defend and rest are all being modified, and in some cases altered fundamentally, by the pressures of the new technology battlefield. Undoubtedly many tried and tested strategic and tactical principles will retain validity, but the practical means by which they can be employed most efficiently on the battlefield are, in many cases, being changed markedly. Because the new technologies are changing so fundamentally the realms of what is possible and impossible on the conventional battlefield, it is essential that strategies, tactics and operational doctrines be reviewed and tested frequently to ensure that they keep in touch with the realities of the changing environment.

Key Technologies

What are the areas of rapid technological change that are having the greatest impact on conventional warfare as we have known it in the past?

First, there is a wide range of *highly accurate precision-guidance techniques*. By using various terminal homing technologies, it is now possible to direct rockets, bombs, artillery rounds, mortar rounds and other types of ordnance to impact with great precision upon targets of small dimensions, whether they are stationary or mobile.

The earliest precision guidance technique employed simple visual target tracking and radio control to fly missiles into targets. A more recent technique is for anti-tank missiles and torpedoes to be guided to their targets by commands passed down a fine wire or fibre optic link that is unravelled from the projectile as it speeds away from its launcher. Other missiles carry miniature television or infra-red cameras that transmit pictures back to their launch aircraft (or other launch platform) so that they can be flown into their intended targets. Three other precision guidance techniques use laser beams. In one system, missiles fly automatically down a low-powered 'pencil' beam of laser light projected from the launcher to the target. In the second system, a low-powered laser is pointed at the target, but ordnance can be launched from locations remote from the laser designator (or source of laser 'light') and need only be fired into the general 'basket' area of the target. This type of laser homing ordnance guides itself automatically onto targets that are 'painted' by the laser light projected from the laser designator. Finally, a third laser guidance technique uses a low-powered laser mounted on the missile as a laser radar to home onto an assigned target. Most light air-to-air, light surface-to-air and some anti-ship missiles use infra-red sensing to home automatically on the heat signatures of their targets. Some new anti-tank missiles are being developed to use a similar form of passive infra-red homing.

Then there are radar guided weapons of two main types - those (especially anti-ship missiles) with a complete radar set aboard and those (mainly anti-aircraft and some anti-ship weapons) that home on the radar energy reflected off the target beamed from a powerful radar on the launch platform.

The final important category of precision guidance techniques is used to attack fixed targets (bridges, airfields, etc.) or targets known to be passing a fixed location. These systems rely on very accurate navigation techniques and normally use either very sensitive inertial sensors, navigation systems that operate by reference to ground-, air- or space-based navigation beacons, or sensors that periodically check the projectile's position by comparing a digitised terrain map stored in the missile with the terrain features passing below. All of these long range navigation techniques can be made accurate to a few tens of metres, but for pinpoint precision they are normally accompanied by a supplementary terminal homing sensor - frequently a sense-matching correlation sensor or laser radar which compares a stored digitised 'photograph' of the target with the view below the missile at the end of the mission and then homes automatically onto the spot marked for impact. This type of pattern recognition sensor is being further developed and miniaturised to provide missiles that can be launched into the general area of a target (e.g. an armoured formation) and through the use of small sophisticated millimetre wave radars or infra-red scanners can automatically distinguish tanks and other armoured vehicles from their surrounding environments and home onto the detected images.

It is true that there are countermeasures to many of these terminal guidance technologies and some have encountered reliability problems in service. In overall terms, however, their track record has been very impressive. While some of the current terminally guided weapons are frequently described as being 'smart weapons', many of the newer systems now on the horizon are being called 'brilliant weapons' because of their capacity to acquire and attack programmed categories of target completely automatically. The most immediate consequence of these developments is that if a target can be distinguished from its background environment or its location accurately determined, it is becoming far more likely that it will be hit by the first round of ordnance directed against it.

The second major area of advance concerns the development of a *wide range of more efficient propulsion systems*. For example, the development of very small turbo-fan and turbo-jet engines has been crucial to the success of the new generation of compact medium- and long-range cruise missiles. Moreover, new forms of high density propellants are greatly increasing the speed and range capacities of many forms of tactical rocketry. In the case of medium-sized, medium-range rockets the potential for high speed and sustained power is being expanded considerably with the introduction of integrated rocket/ ramjet designs. New technologies are also greatly improving the fuel efficiency and performance of surface ships, conventional submarines and both jet and propeller-driven aircraft.

In effect, these developments in propulsion systems are providing weapons and weapons carriers (or platforms) with much greater range, speed and fuel efficiency, while at the same time frequently reducing their sound, heat, radar and other media signatures. Thus, on the tactical operational level, when the new propulsion systems are combined with the new terminal guidance technologies, it becomes possible to hit accurately any target that can be acquired and identified, even at very long range. On the strategic level, much of the traditional tyranny of distance, in the sense of isolation, is being replaced by a new tyranny of military accessibility.

The third major field of technological advance is the development of *much more effective conventional warheads*. For example, an increasingly wide range of cluster weapons is becoming available, designed to be dropped over enemy force concentrations, airfields or defensive positions to disperse hundreds of 'minelets' or 'bomblets' of tennis-ball size. Multi-stage warheads are being developed in large sizes to penetrate very hard fixed targets such as underground bunkers and aircraft shelters and in smaller sizes to penetrate the new forms of spaced, composite and reactive armours. Fuel air explosives are another warhead development providing extraordinary high overpressures, almost comparable to those of nuclear weapons, over limited areas. Also, there is evidence to suggest that the latest generation of fuel air explosives has substantially overcome earlier weather and other operating constraints. These warheads possess great potential for mine clearance, for the destruction of shipping, for attacking some categories of hard targets and as anti-personnel weapons against units in entrenchments and in the open.

The primary consequence of these new warhead developments is that if a target can be hit (and that is becoming increasingly easy), the resulting destruction is likely to be far greater for a given warhead volume and weight than has been the case in the past.

The fourth major area of advance has been the development of *far more efficient long- and short-range surveillance, target acquisition and identification technologies*. Satellites now provide the superpowers with the capacity to selectively detect, locate, identify and track a wide range of objects of military significance on the surface of the sea and on the ground using an array of optical, photographic, infra-red, radar and electronic sensors. Other major powers are also gradually acquiring capabilities in this field. For example, Over-the-horizon (OTH) radar possesses the potential to detect and track aircraft, large cruise missiles, some types of surface shipping and possibly fast-moving targets on the ground at ranges between 800 and 3,200 km or even further, by bouncing high frequency radio signals off the ionosphere around the curvature of the earth. Airborne warning and control system (AWACS) aircraft can detect and track aircraft with great precision to ranges of about 600 km, and ground and sea targets at somewhat shorter ranges. At sea, the most dramatic development has been in long-range passive sonar arrays fixed on, or above, the sea bed, or towed behind ships. These systems have demonstrated a capacity to detect and, in general terms, locate surface ships and submarines at ranges of up to thousands of kilometres.

The most immediate consequence of these new surveillance and target acquisition technologies is that it is becoming increasingly difficult to hide on the modern battlefield, especially in the air and sea environments, which has, in the past generated a considerable degree of invisibility for those operating in them.

The fifth major area of advance is the development of *increasingly sophisticated command, control and communications (C3) systems*. Primarily through the exploitation of greatly expanded automatic data-processing capacities, a wide variety of area-surveillance, target-acquisition, classification and locating systems, as well as weapon systems themselves, are being tied together electronically. In practice, it has been found that this degree of automatic system integration can significantly multiply the battlefield effectiveness of a total force.

New technology sixthly has produced some *completely new weapons concepts*. For example, a modular glide bomb system which permits the choice of guidance heads (laser designation, television or infra-red imaging) and warheads (high explosive or cluster) to suit particular missions has been developed. The new technologies have also made feasible a number of sensor-weapons, such as area sea mines described briefly above and an anti-aircraft missile designed to be launched without specific direction when an enemy aircraft appears within range. This weapon is capable of acquiring the aircraft signature autonomously and automatically homing on its target. High-powered laser weapons are also under development primarily to provide a last-ditch point-defence for high-value vessels against anti-shipping missiles.

It is difficult to summarise the overall impact of recent developments in conventional military technology. On the one hand, they provide a greatly increased potential to acquire, identify and track targets, to deliver ordnance over both long and short ranges with high accuracy and speed and to destroy a wide range of objectives with a single hit. But, on the other hand, the new technologies also provide greatly enhanced capacities for a range of countermeasures.

Certainly the nature of conventional warfare as it has been known in the past is being changed radically. The practical implications for particular strategic environments are, however, not easy to determine in advance. A wide range of non-technological variables, such as the levels of constraint applied by local financial, political, bureaucratic, social, geographic and climatic conditions, can all influence the consequences of new technological developments in specific regions. Furthermore, and at least as importantly, a great deal will always depend upon human capacities to perceive the broad consequences of the new developments, to choose selectively from the greatly expanded range of technological options, to operate effectively those systems which are procured, to service and maintain them efficiently and to derive strategies, tactics, structures, doctrines and operational procedures that exploit the potential of the new systems fully. Primarily because of the number and variability of these factors, the practical impact of the new technologies upon particular military structures can be expected to differ greatly. However, despite these qualifications and difficulties, it is possible to derive a series of broad consequential trends that possess a degree of general applicability.

Some Important Implications of New Technological Developments

The Increasing Vulnerability and Declining Cost-Effectiveness of Large and Obvious Weapons Platforms.

Because of the great advances in long-range surveillance and target-acquisition technologies, military platforms that have large radar, magnetic, heat, acoustic, electronic or other media signatures are becoming much easier to detect, identify and acquire as targets. Once acquired as a target, the new precision-guidance, propulsion and warhead technologies are increasing greatly the ease with which objects can be attacked and destroyed at both short and long ranges.

These developments have two important consequences. First, large and obvious weapons platforms are becoming increasingly easy to destroy on the modern battlefield, i.e., they are subject to increasing rates of *active attrition*. A second major consequence is to force large and obvious aircraft, surface ships and armoured vehicles to adopt expensive defensive equipment fits and elaborate defensive operational tactics in attempts to maintain their survivability on the modern battlefield. These defensive reactive measures are very complex and expensive, and many imply a very great degradation in total system cost-effectiveness in the performance of traditional functions. In combination, these less obvious effects of the new technological developments can be termed the processes of *passive attrition*.

(i) Active and Passive Attrition in the Air

In intense battlefield environments, aircraft are now subjected to a wide array of advanced ground-based defensive systems. New generation, light, man-portable, surface-to-air missile (SAM) systems not only possess a greater range capacity and more effective warheads than their predecessors but they are also capable of attacking a target from any direction - even head on. Mobile radar-controlled gun systems and large vehicle-mounted short-, medium- and long-range missile systems are also becoming much more effective. However, it should be noted that the greatly increased lethality of ground-based air defences is not due simply to the vastly increased performance capabilities of individual systems. In order for the effectiveness of ground-based anti-aircraft defences to be optimised over the tactical battlefield, it is necessary to coordinate a mix of several different types of surface-to-air systems, each of which is very effective in performing its specific air-defence function (i.e., a mix of systems effective against low-, medium- and high-altitude targets).

The vastly increased lethality of coordinated anti-aircraft defences has forced tactical aircraft to adopt a wide range of measures to improve their survivability and maintain their mission effectiveness. The response of many Western European air forces is to fly through such well defended areas at extremely low altitudes and very high speeds. This tactic has been designed so that aircraft can penetrate below the coverage of most ground-based surveillance and target-acquisition sensors. The speed of penetration gives the few ground-based systems, that can acquire targets flying at that altitude, insufficient time to react effectively. However, mission profiles requiring high-speed flight at low levels effectively limit range, are very demanding, especially at night or in poor weather, and encourage aircraft designs that are not optimised for the secondary task of air-to-air combat at low and medium altitudes.

A second response is to fly at medium altitudes within the coverage of enemy area air defences where necessary, but to do so only with the assistance of large numbers of air-superiority fighter aircraft and also specialised electronic warfare and defence suppression systems. This requires a direct air-superiority confrontation. Specialised fighter aircraft must cover the fighter-bomber formations and engage in air-to-air duels where this is necessary. In attempts to foil anti-aircraft surveillance, tracking and guidance systems, parts of fighter-bomber weapon loads would be frequently sacrificed to permit the carriage of defensive, underwing electronic counter-measure pods. In some intense battlefield environments, supplementary aircraft are required specifically to perform the task of confusing or jamming enemy surveillance and weapon-guidance radars. In areas where air defences are well coordinated and controlled, it will be frequently necessary for attacking or specialised supporting aircraft to concentrate first upon the destruction of the opponent's surface-to-air systems before the primary targets can be attacked with reasonable safety. The gradual addition of a large number of essential supporting aircraft to those required to make close support or interdiction strike missions in the intense European environment has prompted one prominent United States defence analyst to describe these types of operations as air convoys.[1] The impact of this concept on sortie rates is severe and the complexity and overall expense of mounting this type of operation is clearly much greater than that which was required to perform a similar function in the past.

A recent variant of this concept, most clearly displayed in the United States' new F-117 and B-2 stealth aircraft, is to use a wide range of new materials and design concepts to so reduce an aircraft's radar, electronic, visual, sound and other signatures that the probability of the opponent detecting its penetration is greatly reduced. If flying at low altitude, terrain masking can be employed to further reduce the probability of detection. Alternatively there is also the option of flying very high. The probability of detection at high altitude would still be low and the already difficult task of intercepting aircraft or missiles could be made extraordinarily demanding if, in addition to its stealth characteristics, the penetrating aircraft carried advanced electronic countermeasure systems. These technology developments might provide a relatively high level of security for a new generation of advanced strike aircraft. However, the costs and complexity of this technology are great and are unlikely to become available to any but the wealthiest countries in the medium term.

A third type of air force response to the growing lethality of integrated ground-based anti-aircraft networks involves a partial abandonment of the traditional close air support function and its replacement by strengthened ground-based gun and rocket artillery systems. Under this concept, where air-delivered ordnance is still required in intense battlefield environments, it may be delivered at extended ranges by stand-off, air-launched precision-guided munitions. However, in practice, this does not overcome all of the difficulties associated with traditional types of close air support operations. The acquisition of many categories of ground target from tactical strike aircraft is extremely difficult at stand-off ranges. In order to overcome this problem, at least partially, extensive support technologies are required (e.g. special unmanned aircraft, remotely emplaced sensors, electronic intelligence sensors or purpose-built airborne radars), to provide a remote target acquisition and designation capability. A second major difficulty of air-launched precision-guided munitions delivery into intense battlefield environments is that weapon launch-points may not always be placed beyond the range of an enemy's integrated air defence system. The fluidity of intense modern battlefields may make the accurate identification of secure launch areas extremely difficult.

(ii) Active and Passive Attrition at Sea

The new military technologies are also increasing greatly the vulnerability of large and obvious surface ships. They too are becoming easier to identify at long range and are much more vulnerable to a wide range of anti-ship weapon systems.

In response to the increasing anti-shipping threat, most modern navies have concentrated their resources on what is, in effect, a five-element program to enhance the security of their major surface platforms. The overall effectiveness of this effort is, however, the subject of serious doubt. The first element of the program is to seek to destroy weapon launch platforms before anti-ship weapons are released. In some circumstances it may be possible for a defending naval unit to strike cruise missile-equipped patrol craft, surface shipping, aircraft and submarines before their weaponry can be launched. However, for a variety of reasons, this might not always be possible. Firstly, the offensive elements needed may not always be available to perform this function. Secondly, even if they are available, they may not be authorised to launch this type of pre-emptive attack. Thirdly, it seems likely that in many environments enemy aircraft, surface vessels and submarines could approach the naval force undetected within the maximum range of their weaponry. Thus, it is unlikely that all anti-ship systems will be destroyed before they can be launched in any particular conflict, unless some special circumstances apply.[2]

The second element of the surface naval ship's defensive capability involves the use of carrier-borne aircraft. Naval airborne warning and control systems (AWACS, which with current technology require a large conventional aircraft carrier or shore base from which to operate) and fighter aircraft would attempt to destroy anti-ship missiles in flight. This capability assumes the timely air deployment of AWACS and advanced fighter aircraft with a look-down, shoot-down capability at the time and in the area of missile flight. Even if all of these systems were deployed in advance at appropriate locations and were not saturated by a large number of incoming cruise missiles, they would still be ineffective against very high altitude Mach 2+ missiles and against submarine-launched torpedoes. Again it seems that only in very particular circumstances would it be expected that anti-ship strikes would be defeated at this point.

The third element of the surface ship defensive concept is to employ long-range, ship-borne missiles to destroy approaching anti-ship weapons. Clearly there is no practical means of intercepting long-range self-homing torpedoes, although it may be possible for them to be spoofed. The destruction of anti-ship missiles by long-range ship-borne systems would be possible, although still not easy, if the ship concerned possessed this type of weaponry and if the incoming missile flew at medium-altitude and moderate subsonic or transonic speed. However, in the more likely instance of a missile flying at a very low altitude, it would be difficult for it to be acquired and tracked, since most sea-skimming missiles have a very small radar cross-section and would need to be detected against the 'clutter' of the sea's surface. However, for the purpose of this discussion, if it can be assumed that advanced radar techniques and a high state of crew alertness largely resolve the clutter problem, there would still be serious difficulties arising from the very limited reaction time that would be available. If the incoming missile were detected the instant it broached the horizon (which seems highly improbable), and if it were travelling at between Mach 1 and 2, between one and a quarter and two and a half minutes would remain before impact. If the ship were in a high state of alert, long-range weaponry probably could be fired within that time, but directing the interception of a very fast missile, which may well be taking evasive counter-measures and could be at least partially obscured by sea conditions, would be difficult. These problems would be compounded in the event of a simultaneous, multi-directional attack by several weapons. The long-range interception of very high-altitude anti-shipping missiles presents yet another series of extremely complicated problems.

The fourth element of the surface naval ship's defence is its electronic counter-measure capability. Some active radar homing missiles can be spoofed with chaff[3] and electronic jamming, while some infra-red homing systems can be decoyed with flares. Electro-optical systems can be foiled by aerosols and smoke, and some magnetic and acoustic homing torpedo systems can be defeated by trailed decoys and jammers. However, some wire- and inertial-guided weaponry is not susceptible to the normal types of electronic counter-measures. Moreover, the incorporation of many counter-counter-measures in anti-ship weaponry is reducing greatly the effectiveness of a wide range of current ship-borne electronic warfare (EW) systems. Frequency-agile homing radars, infra-red tuning, infra-red imaging, improved data links, multi-sensor terminal guidance and many other techniques are being employed to decrease anti-ship missile susceptibility to electronic warfare.

The final defence element available to surface shipping is that of close-in weapons systems (CIWS). In order to provide surface ships with a 'last-ditch' defence against anti-ship missile attack, Western navies have deployed the *Phalanx, Shortstop, Goalkeeper* and *Sea Guard* automatic gun systems and the *Sea Wolf* short-range missile system. While in one-only non-manoeuvering or jamming target situations, the capacity of all these systems appears credible, they are, themselves, potentially susceptible to external jamming, spoofing and decoying. Further, because of the short-range nature of these systems, many of the intercepts they have achieved, even in ideal circumstances, have taken place at ranges of 500 metres or less. (The range of *Shortstop's* maximum kill probability is reportedly 300 metres.)[4] It should be noted that if an anti-shipping missile carrying a 550 kg third-generation fuel air explosive warhead is detonated at 300 metres range, the blast effect would be sufficient to destroy most types of ship-borne radio, radar, EW and other external antennae. This would effectively render a ship defenceless to a following missile attack. If detonation occurred at 170 metres or less, the blast effect would be sufficient to sink a moderately-sized ship.

Thus, despite the fact that all of the major naval powers have expended very large sums of money on anti-ship missile defence systems of various sorts, their effectiveness in realistic wartime multi-attack conditions is highly questionable. In a candid statement on surface ship vulnerability, the former United States Director of Defense Research and Engineering, Dr Malcolm Currie, pointed to the extreme difficulty of providing an effective defence even against currently deployed anti-ship missile systems. When discussing this capacity of the Soviet aircraft carrier *Kiev*, he stated that it was not so much its V/STOL aircraft that made the ship so formidable:

> ...rather that it is so heavily armed [with] SS-M-12s, a supersonic cruise missile that can come in [at various] angles and...from a naval point of view - not a strategic nuclear point of view - is next to impossible to defend against.[5]

The technology struggle between offence and defence on and above the surface of the sea is likely to intensify further. On the one hand, advanced navies are refining a number of techniques to further complicate the task of attacking forces finding their targets on the high seas. In addition, quick-reaction, vertically-launched counter missile defence systems are already entering production and high-energy laser point defence systems might be available by the mid-1990s. On the other hand, there are already Mach 2+ integral rocket/ramjet sea-skimming cruise missiles under development in both Europe and the United States, and torpedo-carrying surface skimmers may be developed to avoid close-in weapons systems altogether. In this environment, the survivability of major surface ships in the face of modern multiple anti-ship missile and torpedo attacks is by no means assured.

In addition, it should be noted that the increased vulnerability of large and obvious surface shipping and the defensive reactive measures that have followed have caused a severe degradation in the operational effectiveness of vessels performing their primary assigned roles. In many cases, self-defence considerations have driven the elaboration and expansion of originally simple ship designs into larger and more complex platforms. Yet, even when these extremely sophisticated ships are deployed into high-threat environments, they must be operated in closely coordinated teams if the chances of their survivability are to be maximised. However, this tactic serves to reduce their capabilities to perform most of their originally intended functions to an even greater degree, be they anti-submarine warfare, convoy escort, shore bombardment, attacks on surface shipping or some other task.

Submarine survivability varies greatly, depending upon a large number of factors. Older, large submarines, that are poorly shaped and emit great amounts of noise, are much more easily detected than new, smaller, tear-drop-shaped submarines, which make extensive use of non-magnetic materials in their construction and employ laminar-flow technology to reduce drag and water disturbance. Current types of conventional submarines retain an additional source of vulnerability because of their requirement to cruise for significant periods with their snorkels above the surface of the sea. New types of non-nuclear propulsion system are likely to reduce this requirement greatly.

(iii) Active and Passive Attrition on the Ground

The vulnerability and cost-effectiveness of traditional major items of defence equipment in the ground environment is also in a state of flux. The immediate reaction of many countries' armoured units to the proliferation of light, highly accurate and inexpensive anti-tank weapons has been an intensification of combined arms tactics. As a consequence, it seems extremely unlikely that in the future armoured units will manoeuvre and attack fixed positions in isolation, as occurred during the first hours of the Yom Kippur War, for example. Rather, infantry will travel in close proximity to tanks in mechanised infantry combat vehicles (MICVs) or open-topped armoured personnel carriers (APCs), spraying likely anti-tank missile team vantage points with machine-gun and mortar fire. In addition, self-propelled rocket and/or gun artillery will travel in strength in reasonably close proximity, so as to be able to add weight to the curtain of suppressive fire. If enemy surface-to-air systems can be suppressed in the local region, close air-support aircraft can be expected to operate in coordination. The final integrated component of the modern all-arms ground battlefield team is a mobile gun and/or missile anti-aircraft capability. Thus, in order for modern armoured forces to be effective and survivable in intense battlefield environments, a large number of supportive systems are required to act in coordination in most environments.

The second major reaction of armoured units to the proliferation of light anti-tank weaponry has been to improve standards of armoured protection. Vehicles equipped with conventional solid armour (*AMX 30, Leopard I A1* and *I A2, M-60, T-62*, etc.) are likely to remain susceptible to a very large number of ground- and air-launched anti-tank weapon systems. Those vehicles that are equipped with spaced armour (e.g. *Leopard I A3, Merkava*) gain a degree of protection from the smaller, man-portable shaped-charge weapons. However, composite 'special' or layered armour, which is currently being fitted to *MX1, Leopard II, Challenger*, and, most probably *T-80* and the follow-on Soviet tank, offers a much greater degree of protection. This armour effectively resists all but the largest shaped-charge warheads and most currently deployed tank-gun rounds. A further recent development in armoured vehicle protection has been the deployment of 'active armour' plating. When struck by the molten plume of a shaped charge warhead this armour is designed to explode, deflecting the warhead's effects away from the layers of armour beneath.

The implications of these developments in armour-plating are considerable. It appears that because composite and reactive armours are not excessively expensive, they may eventually be deployed widely on a variety of armoured vehicles. This, in turn, is greatly influencing the types of anti-armour weaponry that will be effective in the future. Some systems have been developed to fly over armoured vehicles and penetrate their armour through the roof, where it is frequently thinnest. Other systems are employing much larger shaped-charge warheads, multi-stage shaped-charge warheads or very fast kinetic energy rounds.

The vulnerability of major ground battlefield weapons platforms in the future will depend at least partly upon the extent to which composite and reactive armour is used and the speed with which effective ground-launched direct-fire anti-tank systems can be deployed. However, it should be realised that even after new types of anti-tank systems are developed, all tanks, regardless of the composition of their armour-plating, will remain vulnerable to many air- and artillery-launched precision-guided munitions, fuel air explosives and anti-tank mines and minelets.

There appears to be a clear, identifiable trend emerging from the nature of the battlefield situation that is confronting large and obvious weapons platforms. Although the offensive capabilities of large surface ships, aircraft and conventionally armoured vehicles are rising, many such weapon systems are also becoming increasingly easy to detect, target and destroy on technologically advanced battlefields. Many of the weapons that can effectively damage and destroy these platforms are relatively cheap to buy and are being procured by a wide range of countries in relatively large numbers. Thus, in future conflicts it can be anticipated that large and obvious concentrations of defence capital will be subjected to multiple coordinated attacks by new generations of anti-systems. In order to enhance their survivability, aircraft, ships and tanks now require the support of increasing numbers of supplementary systems and technologies, and the development of more protective and elaborate operational tactics and doctrines. But even with such heavy supportive technologies and tactics, there are now some tasks that are extremely difficult and expensive for traditional platforms to undertake at all. Thus, the overall impact upon large and obvious weapons platforms performing their traditional battlefield functions is to degrade their survivability, stimulate a quantum jump in their costs and, in many cases, cause a drastic reduction in their operational effectiveness.[6]

The Increasing Utility of Small Units

Because large and obvious weapons platforms are being subjected to higher levels of both active and passive attrition in intense battlefield environments, it is becoming increasingly desirable to disperse military capacities. It is becoming preferable to force an enemy to try and find and destroy many relatively inexpensive platforms rather than a few high value ones. This development is being reinforced by the fact that the range capabilities of many small weapons platforms are being extended greatly and most forms of effective guided firepower are becoming increasingly light and compact. In combination, these factors are having the effect of making small units viable for a much wider range of tasks than has hitherto been the case, especially when they operate in closely coordinated teams. Small units are not only able to threaten and destroy larger units in more situations, but they themselves frequently have a better chance of surviving because of their lower all-media signatures and because small units can frequently be made highly agile. Add to this the relatively low cost of these small units and it becomes clear that in many battlefield environments in the future, the proliferation of small units will be a major feature.

The Increasing Importance of Remaining Untargeted

In the new technology environment, as it becomes more and more easy to hit a target once acquired, and a target hit is more likely to be destroyed, it is obvious that the capacity to remain untargeted is becoming an increasingly central determinant of battlefield outcomes. As has been discussed above, this is stimulating a high level of force dispersal, but it is also encouraging the rapid development of a wide array of stealth technologies and tactics. In terms of equipment, it means the extensive deployment of visual, radar, sound, heat and electronic suppression and camouflage systems. In the field of tactical doctrine, the primary effect is to accentuate the need for dispersal and coordinated movement under the cover of terrain features, vegetation, built-up areas, darkness and poor weather. Where a battlefield function regularly requires a high level of battlefield visibility, remotely controlled or remotely emplaced automatic systems are likely to provide the most desirable means of task performance.

The Increasing Importance of Retaining Target Detection,
Identification and Localisation Systems Unscathed

In order to ensure that target acquisition sensor systems remain untargeted by the enemy, it will be important for defence decision-makers to select systems that can operate in as covert and passive a manner as possible. Thus in the ground environment, intensified activity is apparent in the development of advanced acoustic, seismic, optical and imaging infra-red systems. Imaging infra-red scanners can provide a completely passive 24-hour medium-range target acquisition and tracking capability and are replacing radars in performing some functions. Where active radiation-emitting target-acquisition sensors are necessary (e.g. radars and active sonars), it is highly desirable that they be mobile, employ advanced design techniques to minimise their probability of detection and/or operate as far away from intense battlefield environments as possible. Hence, large airborne target-acquisition radars of various types are designed to be operated mainly from areas well behind the forward edge of the battle area (FEBA). Over-the-horizon (OTH) radar transmitters are also likely to be sited at remote locations.

Non-stop War

Because a large number of new technology systems are being employed either to replace or assist the human eye to perform target-acquisition and weapons-guidance tasks, much of the security hitherto derived from darkness, bad weather and light camouflage is being removed. The gradual lifting of this target-acquisition constraint is having the effect of making modern tactical war a more intense and almost non-stop round-the-clock operation. This has various implications, but on the general level, it has obvious significance in purely human endurance terms. Patterns of sleeping, eating and general human activity are likely to be far more subject to modification to fit the new military requirements. Various forms of drugs may be dispensed to improve peak efficiency, extend human endurance or assist personnel to rest and sleep, even in noisy and uncomfortable environments.

Changing Logistics Requirements

The non-stop nature of modern war and the proliferation and dispersal of mobile small units in some phases of war will necessitate the development of new logistics support concepts. The delegation of a larger amount of authority to lower command levels on this type of continuously active battlefield could, in many environments, be expected to stimulate an increased rate of ammunition expenditure. Alternatively, because of dramatically improved weapon accuracies and warhead efficiencies, far less ordnance should be required to destroy a given number of acquired targets than has been the case in the past. The balance between these competing factors is likely to vary considerably according to operating doctrines, level of training and the nature of the local battlefield environment.

One very important and more obvious consequence of new technology developments will be to make logistics systems much more vulnerable to direct attack. Roads, bridges, railways, tunnels, storage and transit areas are likely to be relatively easy for an enemy to target and destroy, even if they are located deep behind the FEBA. As a consequence, centres and routes of logistics support will need to be concealed where possible, but certainly duplicated and dispersed.

Increasing Scope for Surprise Attack

If there is a means by which a country's long-range surveillance and target-acquisition sensors can be degraded or destroyed, then that country will become increasingly vulnerable to powerful surprise strikes. If, in addition, that country has not concealed, dispersed and protected key elements of its defence structure, then new generations of precision-guided weapons will make it increasingly susceptible to rapid and decisive defeat. If ships, aircraft, armoured vehicles, artillery pieces, communications, command and control facilities, and other units of defence capital are grouped in unconcealed and unprotected concentrations, it is becoming very easy for them to be targeted and destroyed by long-range terminally guided weaponry.

However, if long-range surveillance and target-acquisition sensors are concealed, dispersed, protected and, where possible, duplicated and made mobile, it will be extremely difficult for an opponent to mount a surprise attack. Further, if key elements of the defending country's support base and national infrastructure are also concealed, dispersed, protected and provided with a degree of system redundancy, this will serve to greatly enhance defensive endurance in a manner not likely to be sensitive to an opponent's development of new conventional military capacities.

The Increasing Role for Total Defence Planning

One consequence arising from developments in long-range missile and conventional warhead technologies will be to increase greatly the ease with which large numbers of countries will be able to target and, if they wish, attack the economic infrastructure of opposing states from bases within their own national boundaries. Consequently, modern conventional warfare, even between relatively minor states, is likely to threaten the existence of many aspects of the societies involved. It seems probable that countries will strive to reduce the vulnerability not only of key elements of national infrastructure that support the military defence effort in the most direct sense but also a much wider array of targets, including the major centres of population. These broad security and civil defence considerations are likely to grow more important in planning development of national infrastructure and economic developments.

The Rising Costs of Many Military Systems

In the case of many new and improved conventional military systems, unit costs are rising rapidly. This is particularly so for complex multi-purpose systems that involve numerous integrated technologies. For instance, Ball estimated that the costs of United States fighter aircraft increased between 50 and 80 times from 1940 to 1975.[7] Dudzinsky and Digby support this general view by arguing that the average unit costs of US aircraft carriers doubled in real terms in the decade to 1975 and that the average unit costs of US main battle tanks rose by a comparable proportion.[8]

Certainly the operational capacity of almost all of the new technology systems surpasses that of their predecessors by a significant margin. Because of this, the cost-effectiveness of some of the new systems in some operational environments is difficult to dispute. For instance, while a guided glide-bomb may cost thirty times as much as an unguided iron bomb, it may be able to accomplish tasks that otherwise would require hundreds of iron bombs, multiple aircraft sorties and greatly increased risks to both aircraft and air crews.

Cost/performance trade-offs and high/low technology mixes are already accepted practice in many national security structures. However, the magnitude of the current capital equipment cost expansion is likely to place even greater pressure upon the process of selecting new technology elements in total force structures.

The Increasing Cost-effectiveness of Medium-technology Defensive Structures

Whereas most current defence structures are designed to perform both offensive and defensive functions, this situation may change as a consequence of new technology developments. In particular, there is now increased scope for the development of relatively inexpensive specialised structures for tactical defence. The most desirable selection of defensive technologies is likely to vary greatly according to local conditions. However, in many countries, it should be possible to procure a small number of carefully selected high-technology early-warning, identification and long-range target-detection systems and a large number of medium-technology weapon systems which, when structured into appropriate military units, will provide a highly survivable capacity to defend in depth.

In practice, the selective exploitation of the potential that the new technologies provide is likely to have the effect of enhancing greatly the deterrence and tactical defensive capacity of a wide range of countries. Their impact on the balance of forces on the Korean Peninsula, in the Middle East and in the Scandinavian/Baltic region, for example, is already quite noticeable. For countries whose potential enemies are equipped substantially with new technology weaponry, the utility of war, as distinct from the threat of war, will be reduced greatly.

The Enhanced Capacity of Terrorist Groups

Although national governments will retain a clear superiority in conventional military power, the increasingly light and compact nature of guided firepower will provide non-state groups with means of inflicting violence in a highly discriminating manner from stand-off range. For example, terrorist groups armed with modern anti-aircraft, anti-tank and anti-shipping weaponry will pose a threat of quite a different type to that of the past.

The Partial Replacement of Tactical Nuclear Weapons by Precision-Guided Munitions

The effectiveness of advanced precision-guided weapon systems of various types against small hardened and large unhardened targets will make them a viable alternative to tactical nuclear weapons in the performance of many battlefield functions. The precision accuracy of these weapons serves to reduce greatly the requirements for the enormous quantities of firepower that to date only nuclear weapons have effectively provided. Hence precision-guided munition-equipped forces of moderate size can effectively deter major powers on the tactical level and, if deterrence fails, they can effectively destroy attacking forces, their immediate support and, in many environments, important parts of the national domestic infrastructures. As a consequence, precision-guided munitions may be substituted for tactical nuclear weapons when major powers wish to destroy large concentrations of enemy forces, when major powers wish to enhance a client state's defensive capacity, or when an independent state wishes to enhance greatly its self-defence capacity.

Nuclear weapons, (as well as chemical and biological weapons to some degree), because of their unsurpassed destructive capacity, are likely to retain a level of deterrence potential that exceeds that of any conventional munition. The requirement for this level of deterrence, as well as the prestige and other incentives that are always likely to accompany the possession of nuclear weapons, will most probably thwart attempts to reduce non-superpower holdings. However, because the strict military requirement for this type of highly expensive, large, hard-target destructive capacity is becoming more limited in most environments, pressure for the acquisition of tactical nuclear weapons may decline in many countries.

Conclusion

Both civilian and military defence bureaucracies face a major challenge if they are to exploit fully the potential of the new technology environment. Current and forthcoming developments in conventional weaponry and the possibilities they offer are of an order of magnitude greater than anything experienced in the past. However, the processes of adjusting to the new technology environment are extremely complex. As Currie has pointed out, confronting the challenge of the new technologies involves much more than the simple placement of new technology items on defence equipment shopping lists:

> ...I want to make the point that technology *per se* is not enough...Equally important to technology is its innovative use in the overall military context. That is why I believe that the development of tactics is every bit as important as hardware and must be made an explicit and implicit part of the design evolution and development process.[9]

In recent years we have started to see advances in conventional technologies open dramatic new tactical and strategic possibilities. One of the most celebrated cases has been the rapid development of US operational strategy for the European theatre through the concepts of *Assault Breaker, Airland Battle 2000* and *Follow on Forces Attack* (FOFA). New long range battlefield sensors, advanced tactical ballistic missiles and air launched cruise missiles equipped with terminally-guided submunitions and very rapid and reliable communications, command and control technologies are promising a remarkable capacity to strike the opponents' forces in all weathers several hundred kilometres beyond the FEBA.

However, the best means of exploiting the new technologies and developing appropriate operational strategies, tactics, doctrines and structures will continue to vary greatly according to the nature of the opponent, the local terrain, vegetation, weather and other factors. The lessons which might be available from the experiences of others can be expected to provide only a generalised guide to the requirements of local conditions. Hence, for most countries, the only practical method of resolving the problems satisfactorily will be the initiation of an extensive program of field trials and experiments in an effort to derive solutions most appropriate for the local environment. Flexibility of thought, a high level of originality and a willingness to encourage new ideas will be essential in this process.

The instigation of such a process of reassessing traditional structures, systems, methods and techniques is likely to be difficult in many societies and require a major effort and strong leadership. However, the potential consequences of failure in this field are very serious. In the period ahead, national security structures which have not mastered the new technology environment will become increasingly vulnerable to those which have.

Endnotes

1   This point is made by Steven L. Canby, *Tactical Airpower in Europe: Airing the European View*, (Technology Service Corporation, Santa Monica, California, 1976), p.37.

2   Special circumstances may include an opponent's possession of very few anti-shipping weapons, their carriage in a few large, obvious and highly vulnerable platforms, and missile system malfunctions preventing the launching of the attack, etc.

3   'Chaff' and 'window' are terms used to describe minute slivers of radar-reflecting aluminium or metal-impregnated fibreglass. The operational concept is to fire clouds of chaff into the air, to decoy or confuse an opponent's surveillance, target acquisition and weapon-borne radars.

4   For details see 'International Naval Technology Expo', *International Defense Review*, (Vol.60, No.1), January 1977, p.63.

5   Quoted by E. Ulsamer, 'The New Five-year Defense Plan', *Air Force Magazine*, (Vol.60, No.1), January 1977, p.63.

6   For example, it is becoming extremely difficult and expensive for tactical aircraft to perform close air support tasks in intense battlefield environments. The same can be said of large surface ships performing conventional gunfire support missions adjacent to coastlines occupied by well-equipped enemy forces.

7   See the discussion in Desmond J. Ball, 'Australia's Tactical Air Requirements and the Criteria for Evaluating Tactical Aircraft for Australian Procurement', in Desmond Ball (ed.), *The Future of Tactical Airpower in the Defence of Australia*, (Australian National University, Canberra, 1977), pp.61-65.

8   See their argument in S.J. Dudzinsky and James Digby 'The Strategic and Tactical Implications of New Weapons Technologies', in Robert O'Neill (ed.), *The Defence of Australia: Fundamental New Aspects*, (Strategic and Defence Studies Centre, Australian National University, Canberra, 1977), pp.49-56. This case can also be substantiated by reference to the cost escalation of a number of other weapons platforms and systems. For example, with regard to attack aircraft, see William D. White, *US Tactical Air Power: Missions Forces and Costs*, (Brookings Institution, Washington D.C., 1974), pp.55-59.

9   Quoted in *Aviation Week and Space Technology*, (Vol.104, No.21), 24 May 1976, p.56.

CHAPTER 6

REVOLUTIONARY WAR

Greg Lockhart

A notable feature of the extensive English language literature on revolutionary war since about 1945 is its general confusion. The recurring themes are vague. Revolutionary wars are somehow thought to take place within states. For some reason they encompass widespread popular participation, and they are often related to political revolutions in unspecified ways. Interchangeable terms proliferate. These include guerrilla war, revolutionary war, total war, people's war and insurgency. At the same time, however, the notion that there is a single coherent strategy of revolutionary war is pervasive.

Despite much lip service to Mao Tse-Tung's three stage model in which guerrilla forces finally evolve into conventional armed forces using regular strategies, the literature remains largely rooted in the assumption that revolutionary wars are essentially small-scale, irregular affairs from a strategic point of view. These assumptions are reflected in typical titles such as Robert Taber's *The War of the Flea* and Robert Asprey's 1,622 page study *War in the Shadows*.[1] In these works the decisive importance of the regular dimension of the wars that erupted around revolutions like those in China and Vietnam is not entirely ignored, but it is heavily outweighed by the emphasis on their irregular dimension. And while the predominantly regular wars that erupted around the French and Russian revolutions are rarely mentioned in the literature, one writer has gone so far as to claim that 'revolutionary war is irregular war'.[2]

To this confusion we must add the related problem of mystique. Revolutionary wars are not always successful. In 1982, however, Milton Osborne noted the existence of a 'fatalistic view that Western powers can not really match the challenge posed by Asian communist revolutionary warfare'.[3] He cited Michael Elliott-Bateman's 1967 work, *Defeat in the East*, as a good example of this view, and suggested that the rush to print English editions of the writings of Vo Nguyen Giap and Ho Chi Minh on revolutionary war during the so-called Second Indochina War reflected the cult-following these writers had in the West.[4] Although Osborne was criticising, rather than analysing, this aspect of mystique, his observation nevertheless alerts us to its existence.

The mystique that suffuses the literature on revolutionary war is relatively recent. For about a century and a half after the French Revolution of 1789, the links between revolution, social change, and the prodigious powers that could be unleashed on the battlefield, were widely recognised in the scholarly literature. Revolutionary changes in French society were perceived to have created a new kind of army with unprecedented power: the *levée en masse*, which had an incalculable impact on world history in the course of Napoleon's revolutionary campaigns. With the rise of fascism in the 1930s and the Cold War need to emphasise the monolithic nature of international communism after 1945, however, the scholarly literature became steeped in totalitarian theory.[5]

This theory assumed that single parties were able to impose their dictatorships on societies without popular support. Put another way, totalitarian theory could only explain the success of revolutions, especially those with a socialist orientation, by using conspiracy theories and the plots of secret agents. The idea that there was a single theory of revolutionary strategy which could explain the successful conspiracies of the secret agents thus followed, while the political, social and economic roots of revolution were forgotten. With no way to seriously explain the mobilisation and participation of millions of people in regular as well as irregular revolutionary campaigns in many parts of the world, this major manifestation of revolutionary war thus dropped from view.

At the same time as conventional thinking about revolutionary war reflected this fundamental defect, another serious flaw appeared: the tendency to describe any insurgency in the post-1945 period as 'revolutionary'. In definitional terms, however, it is only possible to call even self-styled revolutionary regimes 'revolutionary' when both their programs and the implementation of their programs are guided by an ideology of social transformation.

To amplify this idea that revolutionary wars must be related to social transformations, the following discussion will therefore explain a number of assumptions. It will move from these assumptions to outline the general features of a number of revolutionary wars, and it will distinguish revolutionary wars from other categories of insurgency. A concluding section will then place the phenomenon of revolutionary war in the context of the current international order.

Meanings and Concepts

In its original Copernican sense, the word revolution was used to describe the lawful and irresistible orbits of the celestial bodies. Here the notion was a cyclical one and in the medieval political realm it implied the inevitable restoration of divinely legitimised kingship after periods of rebellion and illegitimate ursupation. Thus, it was only after the writers of the French enlightenment, such as Rousseau, that the idea was first unleashed that poverty, inequality, injustice and tyranny were not inherent in the human condition, but the results of corrupt and repressive political regimes. It was only after what can be called the 'social question' was brought into the realm of political philosophy in the eighteenth century, that the notion of revolutionary change, of an absolutely new beginning forged in the violent overthrow of the old order, was crystallised in the course of the French revolution.[6]

During the course of the nineteenth century, other layers of socialist meaning were then added to the word. Indeed, the writings of the economic determinists, Marx, Engels and Lenin, ensured that the notions of class struggle and the rise of the proletariat were also high in the minds of the Bolsheviks when they seized power in Russia in the October revolution of 1917. Since the notion of class struggle tended to dissolve the notion of nationalism, the notion of 'world revolution' gained considerable currency from around the late nineteenth century. But when nationalism nevertheless proved to be an intractable reality, the word 'revolution' took yet another turn as it was wedded to Mao Tse-Tung's notion of a revolutionary war of 'national liberation' in the anti-colonial struggles of the post-1945 period.[7] Even within what might be described as the socialist context, the word 'revolution' has many layers of meaning.

But this is not the end of the problem, for there is another fundamentally different political context in which the word 'revolution' has gained currency in the twentieth century: the fascist context. Fascists tend to be structural functionalists, so that when they talk about revolutionary change they tend to refer to the perceived need for a radical change that will impose various constraints to re-establish the harmony of the body corporate in times of perceived political, social and economic disharmony.[8]

Despite the multiple layers of meaning the word 'revolution' has acquired in the nineteenth and twentieth centuries, it can be argued that the basic socialist tendency to espouse fundamental change to the old constraints of the political, economic and social order has essentially remained intact since 1789. With the repeated degeneration of many revolutions into the hollow shells of their former selves in the twentieth century, the idea of the possibility of fundamental change has undoubtedly taken a battering. Yet the idea still runs like a river through the literature of numerous Marxist-Leninist oriented and other political parties in the world today. Therefore, while the fascist conception of revolution is medieval in the cyclical sense, that it tends to call for a return to an ideal state, the body corporate, the socialist conception is modern in the sense that it tends to call for social transformation. And this medieval-modern ideological distinction is important for it permits us to clarify the point that political-military strategies based on notions of social transformation are what make wars revolutionary in a modern sense.

This discussion will therefore discard the fascist notion of revolution as medieval, and aim at the crucial linkage between the social, economic, political and military operations for mass mobilization that can be seen to make wars revolutionary in modern terms. Here the concept of 'total war' is useful for getting at the linkage, because it theoretically suggests the mobilisation of entire societies and their involvement in a multi-faceted conflict.[9] However, it needs to be stressed that 'total war' will not be revolutionary unless the linkage between the social, economic, political, and military operations are guided by a modern revolutionary ideology that is rooted in the notion of social transformation.

Some Revolutionary Wars

At a purely military level, there was nothing fundamentally new about the organisational and strategic concepts which Napoleon used to such devastating effect in the first revolutionary wars, those of the first French Republic. Napoleon's organisation of the first modern 'division' and his use of the bold manoeuvre in highly mobile campaigns had already been prefigured in the military thinking of the old regime.[10] What is thus vital for an understanding of Napoleon's revolutionary successes on the battlefield is the first modern social transformation that underpinned them.

It was only after 1789 when every middle class man had the vote, when commercial life was freed up with the abolition of feudal privileges, when French soldiers could pray, 'God of all justice, take into thy protection a generous nation which fights only for equality',[11] that the revolutionary *levée en masse* became both possible and necessary. When this change in French society threatened neighbouring states to the extent that the Prussians invaded France in 1793, the social transformation was then intensified by the need which the nation had to defend itself. As one scholar has recently argued, a generally observable effect of many social transformations since 1789 is that, because of the foreign interventions they tend to provoke, revolution and war cannot really be separated into discrete categories.[12]

No separation was implied when popular, if not doctrinaire, socialist impulses were first brought into the act of war in France in the famous decree of 23 August 1793, and when the strategy of the revolutionary government in France was theoretically to requisition the entire population and its material resources to defeat the Prussian invaders. The decree said:

> Young men will go to the front; married men will forge arms and transport foodstuffs; women will make tents, clothes, will serve in the hospitals; children will tear rags into lint; old men will get themselves carried to public places, there to stir up the courage of the warriors, hatred of kings, and the unity of the republic.13

This, for the first time, was total war guided by a radical republican ideology. And it was so effective because it made strategic revolutionary links between the political, social, economic, and military changes then under way in French society.

Now hard-swearing non-commissioned officers became generals and citizens' militia units expanded and energised when they were brigaded with seasoned units left over from the old regime. Also, as hastily organised and partly trained formations broke the elaborately drilled lines that had turned eighteenth century battles into minuets, the French army marched in mobile columns, usually columns of threes, and formed the first modern divisions that could march up hill and down dale, as they did for ninety-six hours non-stop on one remarkable occasion during Napoleon's early campaigns in the Italian Alps.14 This was the 'nation in arms'; the culminating political-military category of modern times that was both a cause and effect of the social transformation that underpinned the French revolution and the wars of the revolution between 1789 and 1799.

Another example of how a radical social transformation intensified by foreign invasions shaped the strategy of a revolutionary regime comes from Russia after the October revolution of 1917. In this case, Lenin once commented that the essence of the Russian revolution was 'electrification plus soviet power'.15 What he meant was that, after the decay of the feudal regime in Russia, the revolution offered people the vision of a better life as it promised to redistribute power in the society among the soviets and so facilitate the development of a modern industrialised economy. And it was on this promise of social transformation that the Bolsheviks were eventually able to transform the fighting capacities of the Russian Army for the defence of the revolution.

When the Bolsheviks came to power in October 1917, the Tsar's armies had failed completely in the First World War and had disintegrated. Yet within just five and a half months, about 100,000 men had voluntarily enlisted in the revolutionary army16 to defend the revolution against the White Russian forces and ultimately the counter-revolutionary interventions from England, France, America, and Japan.

There were, of course, problems. In 1919 and 1920, voluntary enlistments were often offset by widespread desertions from the Red Army. Revolutionary zeal proved to be no substitute for training and experience. In the first offensive use of revolutionary war this century, the Red Army also failed to promote a revolutionary uprising in Warsaw in 1920. Nevertheless, by the time it fought its decisive battles against the White Russian forces and had incorporated thousands of experienced officers and non commissioned officers from the old Tsarist Army, the Red Army had a major advantage in morale, numbers, and war *matériel*. And where it was at its best, as in the defence of Petrograd against Judenitch, it was braced by enthusiastic support of the armed workers of the city and exhorted in person by Trotsky.[17]

From the purely military point of view, there was clearly nothing revolutionary about the use of such positional strategies. Furthermore, while the use of wide-ranging strategic manoeuvres may have been revolutionary in Napoleon's day, this was not so in 1920, especially when similar manoeuvres were employed by the counter-revolutionary side also as a concrete response to the vast spaces over which the war was being fought. Indeed, when Trotsky was once pressed by the Bolsheviks to define a doctrine of revolutionary warfare, he replied that apart from the essential requirements common to all kinds of war that soldiers obey orders, oil their weapons, and grease their boots there was no such thing as a doctrine of revolutionary war.[18] In other words, revolutionary leaders must base their strategies on concrete conditions like leaders in any other kind of war. But what was fundamental to the Red Army's final success in 1921 was the revolutionary linkage that the Bolshevik regime was able to make between the radical political, social, and economic changes that occurred in Russian society when the promise of 'electrification plus soviet power' became the hallmark of the Russian revolution.

Thus exemplified in the wars of the French and Russian revolutions is the notion that social transformation itself generates new capacities to wage wars whose strategic linkages may be described as revolutionary. At the same time, the need of these revolutions to defend themselves against foreign invaders intensified the social transformation.

While the interaction between social transformation and new capacities to fight war has remained a feature of revolutionary wars up until the most recent times, it should also be recognised that revolutions and revolutionary wars have an end as well as a beginning. Revolutionary ideals and enthusiasms have a habit of petering out along with the social transformations that give rise to them. It would be hard to describe the wars which France's citizen armies fought for hegemony over Europe as revolutionary after the tyrant Napoleon crowned himself emperor in 1802. Equally, it is arguable as to whether the wars fought by the Soviet Union since the Stalinist period have been revolutionary. Consequently, it may be said that revolutionary wars are not boundless but have finite durations.

Yet this observation should not be allowed to obscure a new strategic element that came into play in the revolutionary wars that shook the world in the post-Second World War period. An important feature of the revolutionary wars which characterised the European decolonisation of Asia and Africa is that they were protracted wars. Here, without being able to look at the programs of even a fraction of the anti-colonial regimes, we must be careful not to suggest that all the anti-colonial wars since 1945 were necessarily revolutionary. As we will see later in the case of Malaya and the Philippines, there were a number of insurgencies in the post-1945 period where there are no serious theoretical grounds for following the generally accepted view that they were revolutionary. Nevertheless, in other countries like China, Vietnam, and Algeria, where revolutionary strategic links were demonstrably made in the various wars of national liberation, it is clear that the revolutionary strategies for social transformation and war depended to an important extent on the strategy of protracted war which Mao Tse-Tung first formulated for the Chinese revolution.

Mao's need to formulate a strategy of protracted war in China was that from its inception in the mid-1920s to somewhere around the mid-1940s the Chinese revolution was virtually synonymous with a guerrilla struggle in a peasant society against a far stronger enemy with a regular army. In China the situation was thus quite different from the French and Russian situations where revolutionary military mobilization had been relatively rapid because it tended to be urban-based and the forces of the old regimes had become ineffective. At any rate, between the mid-1920s and the mid-1940s Mao did not envisage for a minute that guerrilla forces could defeat conventional forces. But, especially after the Japanese invasion of 1937, what Mao did envisage in his extremely influential military writings, On Guerrilla War and On Protracted War,[19] was that the strength of the foreign enemy with his long external supply lines and extensive deployment in the Pacific would eventually be sapped in a protracted struggle. Of course, 'the tactical scheme', as Alexander Atkinson puts it, 'of evasion and withdrawal, of attacking weak enemy elements and avoiding confrontation with strong ones'[20] by poorly armed guerrilla forces would have no major tactical impact on the regular Japanese army, just as it had no major impact on Chiang Kai-shek's regular army before 1937. Yet, such a tactical scheme for guerrilla forces would serve the greater strategic purpose of stimulating mobilization for a patriotic war of 'national liberation' in Chinese society itself. This essential internal function of revolutionary guerrilla strategy needs to be emphasised for it is given virtually no attention in the existing literature.

As the revolutionary guerrilla units move through the society like proverbial 'fish in water', they simultaneously 'mobilise' the masses and 'rely' on them.[21] Mao said:

> The Red Army fights not merely for the sake of fighting but in order to conduct propaganda among the masses, organise them, arm them and help them to establish revolutionary political power.[22]

Mao also said that as well as leading the people in their military enterprise, revolutionary leaders also had to solve 'the problems facing the masses'. These included:

> problems of clothing, food and shelter, of fuel, rice, cooking oil and salt, of health and hygiene, and of marriage. In short, all the problems facing the masses in their actual life should claim our attention.[23]

The strategic linkage between revolutionary social, political, and military operations was thus established in China in a reciprocal political-military process whereby the guerrilla forces were not merely the agents of a political and social transformation, but equally the manifestation of the transformation in the first place. Myriad functional groupings - workers, peasants, students, soldiers, women, and so on - would then be factored into the revolutionary grid of guerrilla mobilization for total revolutionary war. And the fundamental process of mass mobilization in the society, which in view of its ambitious goal of transforming social relationships would have to be a protracted one, and the patriotic resistance war against the invader, would finally mesh in Mao's famous strategy for a protracted three-stage revolutionary war.

The first stage of Mao's revolutionary war is the mobile defensive stage when the guerrillas operate from secure bases in difficult terrain. This coincides with political mass mobilization in the base areas and extensions of it where possible. The second stage is a prolonged holding stage in which guerrilla forces consolidate their political strength and build up their forces. Guerrilla operations are more ambitious and better coordinated at the political and military levels. The establishment of bases in the enemy rear begins. The third stage is then the stage of the general counter-offensive where the enemy's forces are sufficiently divided and weakened by the protracted war. The consolidation of large guerrilla formations into tightly organised divisions of the increasingly regular army parallels the development of provincial and national political structures. The different stage of the war may overlap in different parts of the country. But mobile war tends to give way to positional war and with the defeat of the counter-revolutionary forces, revolutionary government is established in all the land. Such in its barest essentials was Mao's strategy for political-military mobilization and protracted war in a peasant society like China's, as long as it is remembered that the mobilization of mass organisations for internal political purposes is the most fundamental feature of the strategy. In the tumultuous post-1945 period of decolonisation and international political readjustment, it was the major success of this model in China which gave it its wide currency in other peasant societies which the European powers had colonised in Asia and Africa.

In China itself, the third phase of the war brought the revolution to a tumultuous conclusion between late 1946 and 1949 when bold offensive action and positional war were combined to destroy the nationalist armies despite the massive aid they received from the United States. In one seventeen-month period in 1946 and 1947, for example, 640,000 nationalist troops were killed or wounded and well over a million were captured for use on the revolutionary side.[24] Yet this spectacular development of stage three Maoist strategies in China did not necessarily mean that all revolutionary wars based on Maoist thinking in recent times have passed through three stages to victory. Some have been victorious after one stage (Algeria) and others have failed in the third stage (Greece). The adaptation of Mao's protracted war strategies to local circumstances, therefore, is one of the hallmarks of a number of revolutionary warfare successes since 1945.

A glance at the best known Vietnamese writings on revolutionary war, Truong Chinh's *The Resistance Will Win* published in 1947, and Vo Nguyen Giap's *People's War, People's Army* published in the early 1960s,[25] confirms the importance of the Maoist model in Vietnam's revolutionary thinking. As in China, the need for social or, more pointedly, socialist transformation to link political, economic, and military operations in a total revolutionary war was given first priority. However, Vietnamese knowledge of Mao's three stage concept did undergo significant adaptation to local conditions as the revolutionary war evolved against the French (1945-1954) and the Americans (1965-1975). These adaptations have been overlooked in the literature and so are worth noting.

The basic difference between Chinese and Vietnamese strategies revolved around what might be described as the need for tactical involution to reinforce mass mobilization in Vietnam. In contrast to

China, Vietnam was a small country with relatively little space for manoeuvre against highly mobile enemies whose flexible use of riverborne and airborne forces meant that they could reach any part of the country within a few hours. Vo Nguyen Giap's concept of the 'combat village' in which every person and every house in every village was regarded as a military unit thus assumed great political and military importance in Vietnam. At the same time as offering resistance points to the enemy everywhere, the guerrilla forces were able to stimulate political mobilization with 'armed propaganda' in villages at the same time as they were covered by the mass of the population itself.

Another feature of tactical involution in Vietnam was that, in order to keep the initiative in the confined spaces available, it was sometimes necessary to fight for cities, a practice which contradicted Maoist theory. The Tet offensive in 1968 was undoubtedly the most impressive example of this practice. The extensive use of tunnel systems in many areas was another feature of tactical involution, and so too was the extraordinarily complex interaction between the political-military action of guerrilla units at the village level and the political-military action of the regional and regular main force units at the province and national levels. As Vo Nguyen Giap explained in purely military terms:

> If you do not have a guerrilla war then you are unable to have a war of movement; but if you have guerrilla war and do not advance to a war of movement then not only will the strategic responsibility to destroy the enemy's main force be unrealised but you will not be able to maintain and develop the original guerrilla war.[26]

In Vietnam, Mao's three stages ultimately had to be compressed into a series of strategic interactions that overlapped with mass mobilization and pumped the army up in the society. The multi-divisional conventional campaigns that resulted in the fall of Dien Bien Phu in 1954 and the fall of Saigon in 1975 were then the culmination of this process.

Yet the judicious adaptation of Mao's model to Vietnamese conditions was not the only reason for the success of Vietnam's revolutionary war. Especially for a small country like Vietnam, it is important to remember that international support helped shape the revolutionary victory. The Viet Minh and the Viet Cong both gained valuable diplomatic and military support from across the Sino-Vietnamese border in China (after the Chinese revolutionary victory in 1949), the Soviet Union, and the socialist bloc in general. As one shifts one's view from Vietnam's revolutionary anti-colonial struggle to similar struggles in the post-1945 period, it should also be remembered that none of them developed in isolation.

With the British, Dutch and other European imperial powers already in retreat, the Vietnamese defeat of the French at Dien Bien Phu in 1954 reinforced the world trend towards decolonisation. This was noted by the well known publicist of the Algerian revolution, Frantz Fanon, whose extremely radical insistence on the need for violence to redeem both the humanity and the homelands of colonised peoples, led him to applaud the French defeat at Dien Bien Phu and explain:

> The great victory of the Vietnamese people at Dien Bien Phu is no longer, strictly speaking, a Vietnamese victory. Since July 1954, the question which colonised peoples have asked themselves has been 'what must be done to bring about another Dien Bien Phu'.[27]

And as other African revolutionary theorists such as Amilcar Cabral in Guinea-Bissau took similar encouragement from Dien Bien Phu, Algerian journalists and guerrilla leaders travelled to Vietnam and to China to study local techniques of protracted revolutionary war.

This did not mean that the Algerian revolution ever became wedded seriously to Marxism-Leninism. The exigencies of war, and the inward-looking nature of the Algerian National Liberation Front, whose leaders generally tended to be indoctrinated with Islamic thought, largely precluded ideological speculation based on foreign theories. Yet the Algerian struggle for national independence was the crucible of a pragmatic social revolution, and the Front did develop mass organisations in rural areas, especially in the inhospitable Aures mountain region, where Alistair Horne observed that the Front's agrarian policies and two years of war caused 'a profound revolution'[28] in the traditionally conservative consciousness of rural Algeria. Ultimately then, it was this rural revolution structured by Maoist style guerrilla strategies, and supported internationally by countries as far afield as China and others in the immediate border area like Morocco and Tunisia, that shaped the final victory of the Algerian revolutionary war.

The French were able to reduce the level of cross-border support received by the Algerian revolutionaries from Morocco and Tunisia with constructions like the Morice line. With the ruthless use of torture and counter-terror tactics, the French also demonstrated that revolutionary uprisings can be effectively defeated in urban settings. For example, the French defeated the Front's organisations in the battle for Algiers. Further, by 1957 there is no doubt that with the use of sophisticated counter-insurgency techniques such as the deployment of Specialist Administrative Sections and commando patrols, the French were able to place great pressure on the Front's rural organisations.[29] Yet the French never completely sealed the borders, and never rooted the Front's organisations out of the countryside. Without evolving from stage one the Algerian resistance was able to maintain a sufficient level of mass mobilization to keep pressure on French public opinion, still bleeding from the wounds of Dien Bien Phu and the economic costs of colonial wars in a disintegrating empire. Hence, without losing a single major battle, the French were eventually forced to withdraw from Algeria, in much the same way as the Americans were later forced to withdraw from Vietnam.

In the revolutionary wars thus discussed, the basic criterion for inclusion in the category has been a strategy of mass mobilization for total war guided by an ideology of social transformation. There are undoubtedly numerous other wars that could also be placed in this category. For example, an examination of the programs of the Marxist-Leninist or Marxist-Leninist-oriented regimes in countries such as Cuba, Nicaragua, Angola and Mozambique at least just before and after they came to power may well permit their inclusion in the revolutionary war category. At the same time, however, there have been any number of insurgencies in the world in the last forty years which have either failed to realise their original revolutionary potential, or which have been categorised loosely or meaninglessly as revolutionary in the existing literature.

Other Categories of Insurgency

Perhaps the most spectacular example of a recent revolutionary war that failed to realise its early potential was in Greece between 1946 and 1949. The available critiques suggest that the Greek communist party was committed to radical change in Greek society.[30] In any case, communist guerrilla units operating among the population on the Maoist model drove the forces of the weak Athens government out of the mountains in northern Greece. With safe international sanctuaries in Yugoslavia and Albania to train men and obtain supplies, the Greek Democratic Army was fighting in battalion strength by 1947. But then everything went wrong.

For a variety of reasons, the Democratic Army began raiding villages and kidnapping recruits. It thus lost its original popular support. Meanwhile, it lost international support when politics in the communist world saw the Belgrade government seal the border with northern Greece and cut off its aid. With domestic and international support seriously diminished, the democratic forces could not then fight a protracted war. A premature move into Maoist phase three style operations saw them make the fundamental error of trying to hold ground against an increasingly formidable Athens army revitalised by British and American support. Thus by 1949 the revolutionary forces had been defeated.[31] The revolutionary forces in Greece lost at least partly because they became something other than revolutionary under the pressure of unfavourable domestic and international circumstances; strategy had not been integrated with the need for mass mobilization.

Two other insurgencies that are usually described as revolutionary, but whose initial revolutionary credentials are even more doubtful than that of the Democratic Army in Greece, are the insurgencies which occurred in Malaya and the Philippines after the Second World War. In the Malayan case, the Minimum Democratic Program of the Malayan Communist Party in May 1946 was essentially liberal-democratic. Although its platform encompassed vague calls for economic restructuring, its basic thrust was for improved working conditions, civil freedoms, and democratic political rights.[32] In terms of the pre-war British colonial regime, these calls were perhaps revolutionary. However, in terms of the post-1945 situation, when the British were combining programs of political and social change with effective military strategies, it can be argued that the Malayan Communist Party's program was so mild that the party was doomed to isolation from the population from the beginning.

In addition, Chin Peng's Malay Races People's Liberation Army was really only rooted in the Chinese community's immigrant workers, and most of these were relatively recent immigrants. Automatically, Chin Peng's army thus tended to be isolated from the Malay, Indian, and even the well-established Chinese middle class populations. Although the British were then able to confine the variously estimated 5,000 to 10,000 guerrillas to remote jungle areas and wear them down gradually with painstaking sweeps of designated areas, they finally prevailed because they supported such effective counter-insurgency tactics with a number of political and social programs designed to woo the Chinese population.[33]

In the case of the Philippines, the Huks had grown from strength to strength through their anti-Japanese resistance during the Second World War and had come to dominate central Luzon and much of Mindanao with their revolutionary forces by 1950. Yet there is very little evidence to suggest that the anti-Japanese resistance of the Huks was integrated with a rigorously defined modern program of social and political change. The Communist Party of the Philippines was not overtly on the side of the Huks Rebellion before 1948, and thereafter it relied heavily, as one scholar has put it, 'on physical threat rather than ideological persuasion' to enforce its 'iron discipline'.[34] In the early 1950s the Communist Party enjoyed some initial success with the Huks escalating large formation military offensives. However, these also provoked massive military intervention from the United States which completely refurbished the Armed Forces of the Philippines. With no deeply-rooted political base in the society, the Armed Forces of the Philippines were therefore able to turn the situation around within eighteen months and effectively destroy the Huks by 1954. Hence, it is very doubtful that, like numerous others, the post-1945 insurgencies in both Malaya and the Philippines were ever revolutionary in any meaningful sense of the word.

As already observed, the scholarly impulse to characterise almost any guerrilla insurgency as revolutionary was rooted in political and intellectual confusion in the 1950s and 1960s. At a time when a number of genuinely revolutionary insurgencies and wars in countries such as China, Vietnam and Algeria were sending shock waves through the old international order, and when Western governments could only explain their inability to thwart these traumatic changes in terms of 'a new kind of aggression', the reflex was to categorise virtually any insurgency as revolutionary. As late as 1980, Purcell uncritically included such diverse insurgencies as those of the Irish Republican Army, the Palestinian Liberation Army, and the Baader-Meinhof group in Germany along with the wars of the Chinese, Cuban and Algerian revolutions in his popular book *Revolutionary War*.[35] If Purcell had been writing today he would probably have also included such insurgencies as those waged against the Russian occupation of Afghanistan, and against the South African government by the African National Congress even though there is little evidence to suggest that these insurgencies are guided by revolutionary notions of social transformation.

Insurgencies against established authority are as old as the history of warfare itself, and today many insurgencies go on in parts of Southeast Asia, Africa, the Middle East, and Latin America as they have gone on for centuries. Especially in the decades immediately after the Second World War, many of the insurgencies which helped reshape the international balance of power were anti-colonial and nationalist in nature. But unless these insurgencies were committed to strategies of basic political and social transformation, as probably the majority were not, there is no foundation for calling them revolutionary.

Conclusion: Revolutionary War in the Contemporary International Order

Perhaps the two most effective revolutionary insurgencies which exist in the world today are to be found in El Salvador and the Philippines. In El Salvador, possibly 7,000 full time guerrillas control as much as 20 per cent of the country and enjoy significant popular support, partly because of the unpopularity of the regime in power, and partly because the insurgency is guided by a sophisticated Marxist-Leninist oriented strategy of political and social change.[36] Some attempt at liberal reform by the Duarte government and American support for it has so far worked against a revolutionary victory. Yet especially with at least potential support from the Sandinistas in Nicaragua, this revolutionary insurgency continues with a future result which no one can predict.

In the Philippines, the communist movement has transformed itself since its great failure in the 1950s. The Communist Party of the Philippines now stresses the political character of the 'people's army' and has trained its cadres to build bases of mass support, largely on a policy of agrarian revolution and united front organisations in the cities, before advancing to armed struggle.[37] In other words, the communists in the Philippines are now waging a kind of total war in which their multi-faceted operations are linked by a revolutionary strategy of social and political change. By early 1987, the 'New People's Army' was therefore reported to be able to muster some 23,000 guerrillas, and there is no doubt that, at a time of weak and divided central government, it controls large areas of the countryside and enjoys considerable popular support.[38] Therefore, despite a range of factors working against a revolutionary victory (such as American support for the Aquino government, some attempts at liberal reform and the at least arguable difficulties of trying to mount a revolutionary war in an archipelago), it is not unreasonable to suggest that the communist movement in the Philippines is one of the few in the world today which could come to power in the foreseeable future.

However, despite the existence of such on-going revolutionary wars, it can be argued that the international order is more stable today than it has been for a very long time. The current economic crisis in world markets could conceivably affect this stability in profound and unexpected ways and open up new prospects for revolutionary parties. Nevertheless, the series of revolutionary wars and related anti-colonial struggles for national liberation which shook the world from around the end of the Second World War to the fall of Saigon in 1975 was part of a fundamental reordering of political, social, and economic priorities as the age of Western imperialism came to an end in Asia and Africa. The scale and the prominence of the revolutionary wars which figured in this process were so impressive, and the sense of threat they generated in the West was so acute that, for at least thirty years, the English language literature has been very largely unable to come to terms with the phenomenon. But now that the world order has largely adjusted itself to the decline of Western power in Asia and Africa, it should be possible to take a more detached view of revolutionary war and, above all, to be more discriminating about its nature.

This discussion has attempted to detach itself from the totalitarian emphases of the Cold War literature. By going back to the roots of the concept and to the first major manifestation of revolutionary war in the late eighteenth century, it soon becomes clear that the post-1945 preoccupation with the 'guerrilla epidemic'[39] and its organisational and strategic aspects distorts its nature. Strategy is certainly important. But the strategic forms which revolutionary war can take are as various and variable as the specific local conditions and stages of military development they grow out of. The primary nature of revolutionary war cannot be defined in terms of an overarching doctrine of guerrilla strategies or any other strategies for that matter. The notion of revolutionary war can only have meaning in the modern world when a society's political, economic, and military operations for war are strategically linked by an ideology of social transformation.

Endnotes

1   Robert Taber, *The War of the Flea - A Study of Guerrilla Warfare: Theory and Practice*, (Paladin, London, 1970). Robert B. Asprey, *War in the Shadows: The Guerrilla in History*, (2 Vols., Doubleday, New York, 1975). Note that Taber unlike Asprey does not have a moral bias against guerrilla war, and to this extent his work provides a useful introduction to revolutionary war in the post 1945 period.

2   Hugh Purcell, *Revolutionary War: Guerrilla Warfare and Terror in Our Time*, (Hamish Hamilton, London, 1980), p.7. Emphasis added.

3   Milton Osborne, 'Aspects of Revolutionary Warfare with Particular Reference to Southeast Asia', in Desmond Ball (ed.), *Strategy and Defence: Australian Essays*, (Allen and Unwin, Sydney, London, Boston, 1982), p. 170.

4   Michael Elliot-Bateman, *Defeat in the East: The Mark of Mao Tse-Tung on War*, (Oxford University Press, London, 1967).

5   This point has been made by Jonathan R. Adelman, *Revolution, Armies, and War*, (Westview Press, Boulder, Colorado, 1985), pp.8-10.

6   Hannah Arendt, *On Revolution*, (The Viking Press, New York, 1963), Chapters 1 and 2.

7   The amount of writing on socialism in the nineteenth and twentieth centuries is vast. Two start points would be Robert C. Cukcker (ed.), *The Marx-Engels Reader*, (W.W. Norton and Company, New York, 1972), and Mao Tse-Tung's collected works published in various editions by The Foreign Languages Press in Peking since the 1960s.

8   See for example Michael A. Ledeen, *Universal Fascism*, (Howard Fertig, New York, 1962), and Frederico Chabod, *A History of Italian Fascism*, (Weidenfeld and Nicolson, London, 1963).

9   David Marr suggested the applicability of the concept of 'total war' to me in an excellent critique of an earlier draft of this essay.

10   See Clarence Crane Brinton, *A Decade of Revolution 1789-1799*, (Harper and Row, New York and London, 1934).

11   *Ibid.*, p.100.

12 David Marr, 'Vietnam's 1945 Revolution as History', (Paper presented to the Department of Pacific and Southeast Asian History, Australian National University, Canberra, 7 October 1987).
13 Quoted in Clarence Crane Brinton, *A Decade of Revolution*, p.125.
14 Vincent Cronin, *Napoleon*, (Penguin, Middlesex 1976), Chapter 8.
15 Hannah Arendt, *On Revolution*.
16 Katherine Chorley, *Armies and the Art of Revolution*, (Faber and Faber, London, 1943), p.197.
17 *Ibid.*, pp.195-202.
18 Leon Trotsky, *Military Writings*, (Pathfinder Press, New York, 1971), Chapters 1 and 2.
19 Mao Tse-Tung, *On Guerrilla Warfare*, translated and introduced by Samuel B. Griffith, (Praeger, New York, 1962), and *On Protracted War in Selected Military Writings of Mao Tse-Tung*, (Foreign Languages Press, Peking, 1966), pp.187-267.
20 Alexander Atkinson, 'Chinese Communist Strategic Thought: The Strategic Premise of Protracted War', *Journal of the Royal United Services Institute*, (Vol.118), 1954, p.157.
21 Mao Tse-Tung, 'Take Care of the Living Conditions of the Masses and Attend to the Methods of Work', *Selected Works*, Vol.1, (International Publishers, New York, 1954), p.157.
22 Mao Tse-Tung, quoted in Alexander Atkinson, 'Chinese Communist Strategic Thought', p.61.
23 Mao Tse-Tung, 'Take Care of the Living Conditions...', pp.137-8.
24 Robert Taber, *The War of The Flea*, p.55.
25 Truong Chinh, 'The Resistance Will Win', in *Selected Works*, (Foreign Languages Publishing House, Hanoi, 1977); Vo Nguyen Giap, *People's War People's Army*, (Foreign Languages Publishing House, Hanoi, 1974).
26 Vo Nguyen Giap, *Major Experiences of the Party in Leading Armed Struggle and Building Revolutionary Armed Forces*, (Hanoi, 1961), p.41.
27 Frantz Fanon, *The Wretched of the Earth*, (Penguin, Middlesex, 1978), p.55.
28 Alistair Horne, *A Savage War of Peace, Algeria 1954-1962*, (Macmillan, London, 1972), p.407. For a general discussion of ideology see also pp.404-408.
29 *Ibid.*, especially Chapters 9, 10, 15.
30 Robert Taber, *The War of The Flea*, pp.123-125.
31 *Ibid.*.
32 Cheah Boon Kheng, *The Masked Comrades*, (Time Books International, Singapore, 1979), p.26.
33 Robert Taber, *The War of The Flea*, Chapter 9.
34 Lim Joo-Jock with S. Vani (eds.), *Armed Communist Movements in Southeast Asia*, (Gower Publishing for the Institute of Southeast Asian Studies, Singapore, 1984), p.72.
35 *Ibid.*, pp.80-81.
36 See report by Greg Sheridan, *The Australian*, 20 March 1987.
37 Lim Joo-Jock, *Armed Communist Movements in Southeast Asia*, pp.80-81.
38 See Greg Sheridan, *The Australian*, 20 March 1987.
39 For example, see James Eliot Cross, *Conflict in the Shadows*, (Constable and Company, London, 1984), Chapter 1.

CHAPTER 7

POLITICAL TERRORISM

Grant Wardlaw

Groups with little or no direct political power have demonstrated repeatedly over the last two and a half decades that by employing certain tactics, central to which is the directed use of terror, they can achieve effects on a target community which are quite disproportionate to the apparent importance of the attackers or the threat they pose. The widespread use of such tactics by a myriad of groups, and the adoption by nations of either the groups which use them or the tactics themselves as instruments of foreign and domestic policy, coalesce to make political terrorism a major threat to domestic and international harmony. It is a threat which touches some parts of the world more than others, but it cannot be ignored by any.

Defining Terrorism

It is generally agreed that modern terrorism is a major problem and that it presents different and, in many respects, more dangerous threats than did past examples. Moreover, most accept that it is increasing in incidence and costs, and that it is morally indefensible. Despite this consensus, there is little real agreement on just what constitutes terrorism. Defining terrorism has always been a major stumbling block to both rational discussion of the subject and to effective international action against it. Because of the moral and political confusion surrounding it, the search for a value-free definition which could form the basis for objective analysis or effective international agreement has always been problematic.[1]

     Attempts at definition are usually based on the (unstated) assumption that some instances of political violence are justifiable whereas others are not. Even when the actual behaviour is similar in two cases, in one case it will be labelled as terrorism and in the other as something with a positive flavour. Particular acts are described as terrorism not on the basis of the essential features of the acts themselves, but on the basis of the political affiliations of the actors or their motives in committing them. The labels 'terrorist' and 'terrorism' are, thus, extremely ideologically loaded. Furthermore, they are used partially by members of *all* political or ideological persuasions.

In defining terrorism effectively, it is necessary to apply the ideological and moral perspective, having first decided upon whether the act is or is not one of terrorism. As Martha Crenshaw has noted:

> We can develop a neutral definition of terrorism while retaining the ability to make moral judgements about its use in different political circumstances. Labelling an action 'terrorist' is not in itself a moral claim.2

The first distinction we must make is between terror and terrorism. Obviously the use of terror need not be politically motivated. Criminals are more and more mimicking terrorist tactics for personal gain, and there has always been an important element of terror in violent crime. Such a use of terror is essentially different from the programmatic employment of fear-inducing violence as a tactic to force changes to specific policies or political systems.

One possible way to distinguish terrorism from other forms of terror is to emphasise the extra-normal nature of the terror involved. Another is to insist that for an act to fall within the definition of terrorism, its target group (those being coerced) must be distinct from its immediate victims. Thus, an act of violence which is aimed only at an immediate victim is not an act of terrorism, even if that victim is terrorised. The assassination of a head of state, for example, is not an act of terrorism, if its purpose is solely that of removing the person from office. The murder of a policeman as part of a campaign of such murders designed to coerce the security authorities into changing their policies, however, would be classified correctly as an act of terrorism. Building on this basis, political terrorism is defined as:

> The use...or threat of use, of violence by an individual or a group, whether acting for or in opposition to established authority, when such action is designed to create extreme anxiety and/or fear-inducing effects in a target group larger than the immediate victims with the purpose of coercing that group into acceding to the political demands of the perpetrators.3

A number of features of this definition bear comment. First, it recognises the reality that states, their agencies, and individuals or groups acting on their behalf may be terrorists. The use of terrorism is not confined to revolutionary or separatist struggles. A second feature of the definition is that it does *not* include such terms as mindless, wanton, or senseless in referring to terrorist violence. Although these terms are widely associated with terrorism in media reports and many academic analyses of terrorism (and, thereby, in the minds of both the public and governments), it is important to emphasise that terrorism as a tactic need not be irrational and is not usually carried out by individuals with any recognisable mental illness.   Terrorism is not mindless. It is a deliberate means to an end. Terrorism has objectives, a point which is often obscured by the fact that, to the observer, terrorist acts appear random and are often directed at killing those whose deaths appear to have no value to the terrorist cause. The analyst who fails to understand from the terrorist's viewpoint what is achieved by, for example, bombing a building and causing a heavy death toll amongst passers-by, will fail to understand the nature of terrorism. This failure will also lead to a failure to develop adequate counter-strategies, particularly those relating to campaigns designed to alienate the terrorists from actual or potential sympathisers.

The definition, finally, incorporates two further features relating to the psychology of terrorism. It recognises the abnormal quality of the act as perceived by the victim, the target (often a government), and the wider audience (for example, the public or part of it).   What differentiates terrorism from other forms of intentional violence is its apparent randomness and its element of surprise and shock. It is this quality which makes terrorism frightening rather than the actual physical impact of any particular incident.   After all, the number of deaths and injuries resulting from terrorism is relatively modest compared to those caused by other modern social ills. The definition further points to the political context within which terror is employed and which, again, makes terrorism different from other violent acts.

Classification of Terrorists

The literature abounds with typologies which have sought to categorise types of terrorism for analytical purposes. There are many ways in which such classificatory schema can be constructed.   One can concentrate on the location of the act (e.g. domestic versus international), the motives of the terrorists (e.g. insurgent versus irredentist), the type of act (e.g. bombing versus hijacking), whether or not there is backing from a sovereign state, and so on. Inevitably in a field which is so ill-defined and whose boundaries change so quickly, there will be some overlap between categories, however they are constructed. One useful way to classify terrorist groups, however, is as follows:

1   *Revolutionary/Sub-Revolutionary Terrorism* - involves the use of terrorism either to bring about political revolution to overthrow an incumbent regime (revolutionary) or to secure more limited objectives short of total revolution, but involving the incumbent

regime making significant policy changes or concessions (sub-revolutionary). This type of terrorism can be further subdivided into:

(i) Nationalist/Separatist Terrorism - involves the use of terrorism in the furtherance of nationalist, autonomist, ethnic minority, irredentist or separatist aims. Examples from the anti-colonial era include organisations such as the Ethniki Organosis Kypriakou Agoniston (EOKA) in Cyprus, the Front de Liberatione Nationale (FLN) in Algeria, and the Irgun Zvai Leumi in Palestine. Contemporary examples include the Palestine Liberation Organisation (PLO), the Irish Republican Army (IRA), and the Spanish Basque group Euzkadi ta Azkatasuna (ETA).

(ii) Left-wing Revolutionary Terrorism - involves the use of terrorism to transform all or part of an existing system of government. Many of these groups have a Marxist foundation, but often this involves either the development of Marxist thought to suit local circumstances or personal predilections, or only the paying of lip service to orthodox Marxism. Some groups (such as the Sendero Luminoso in Peru) have adopted or adapted a Maoist ideology. For many groups in this category, the aims of the terrorist campaign are relatively well-defined and are tied generally to specific issues or countries. At various times, however, such groups may act at a more diffuse level pursuing more general aims such as the elimination of colonialism or imperialism. For example, the West German Baader-Meinhof group began operations at the more general level but as successive 'generations' of the group evolved as the Rote Armee Fraktion (Red Army Faction) there has been a narrowing of the focus so that terrorist acts are now predominantly targeted on the destruction of NATO and the removal of US troops and nuclear weapons from Europe. Other groups which fall within this category include Italy's Brigate Rosse (Red Brigades), Belgium's Cells Combatante Communiste (Fighting Communist Cells), France's Action Direct (Direct Action), Uruguay's Tupamaros, Argentina's Montoneros, and the Weather Underground in the United States. Within this heading also fall a small number of terrorist groups whose aims are much more nebulous and whose targeting is therefore much less specific and predictable. Such groups, which include the Japanese Red Army (JRA), tend to have a millenarian or global flavour, often aimed at overthrowing the 'whole, corrupt international system' and have only a nebulous concept of what should replace it.

2   *Reactionary Terrorism* - involves the use of terrorism, usually in a domestic context, to prevent social, political or religious changes taking place or to restore conditions to some previous state (real or imagined). Examples include terrorism carried out by the Ku Klux Klan in the United States, the Ulster Volunteer Force (UVF) in Northern Ireland, the Grey Wolves in Turkey, and Mano Blanca (the White Hand) in Guatemala. Such groups tend to be strongly right-wing in political orientation.

3   *Religious/Fundamentalist Terrorism* - involves the use of terrorism to expand the influence of a particular religion, defend it against a perceived attack on its existence or its values, or to 'purify' those within the religion who are seen as undermining its basic values. Terrorism of this sort has historically been associated most frequently with various messianic sects such as the Jewish Zealots in the first century AD, the Taborites, Waldensians, and Anabaptists of the late medieval period, and the Jewish terrorists who in 1984 organised the 'Temple Mount Plot', a conspiracy to destroy Muslim sacred shrines built on Judaism's holiest site, that of the Second Temple. Currently, the most important form of such terrorism is that associated with Islamic fundamentalism. Although their aims can be seen as political (for example, the overthrow of governments), such an interpretation fails to see the importance of the religious dimension. As Amir Taheri notes in his recent book on Islamic terrorism:

> The Islamic Jihad Organisation,...the Party of Allah and the scores of other, much smaller groups using violence and terror to promote their causes, would be insulted if described as political organizations seeking political goals. They recruit their members in the name of Islam and are led by religious officials...Islamic terrorism is a movement quite distinct from other groups using political violence in the Middle East and beyond in the name of nationalism or of one of the many different brands of communism.[4]

4   *Repressive Terrorism* - involves the use of terrorism by a state or its agents to control its own population. Such terrorism may be an extension of a more general system of oppression or repression, is used to consolidate power, to control identifiable minority groups, or to react to a state of insurrection or civil war. A reading of Amnesty International's *Annual Report* for any year will indicate that this is the most pervasive and costly (in terms of human suffering) form of terrorism, and always has been.

5   *State Involvement in Terrorism* - apart from repressive terrorism, the involvement of states in terrorism may be categorised separately because of the implications it has for the development of some forms of terrorism and for the effects it has on the functioning of the international community. The apparent increase in such state involvement has made it a major issue of international relations and security in recent years. There are a number of forms of possible involvement, not all of which are usually called terrorism. One useful scheme for classifying state involvement has been devised by Michael Stohl[5] who divides it into the following groups:

(i)   Terrorist coercive diplomacy - involves coercive diplomacy in which the use or threatened use of violence is carried out:

> ...in an exemplary, demonstrative manner, in discrete and controlled increments, to induce the opponent to revise his calculations and agree to a mutually acceptable termination of the conflict.[6]

As Stohl points out, such behaviour is not usually called terrorism, but it is clear that certain threats and uses of force by states are no different tactically than similar behaviour which if it were not nations involved would definitely be so called. It needs to be emphasised, however, that most instances of coercive diplomacy cannot be classified as instances of terrorism.

(ii)   Covert State Terrorism - this is divided into two subtypes, clandestine state terrorism and state-sponsored terrorism. The former involves the state itself directly participating in acts of terrorism, while the latter consists of the state employing other groups to carry out terrorist acts on its behalf.

(iii) Surrogate Terrorism - again sub-divided into two types. The first, state-supported terrorism, occurs when an interested state supports some third party after it has carried out an act of terrorism which happens to be perceived as being in the interests of the supporting state. The second, state acquiescence to terrorism, occurs when a state quietly approves of or fails to condemn or act against an act of terrorism carried out by a third party. Both of these types of involvement are of the form which might be called 'complicity after the fact' in respect of ordinary crimes and carry with them a different level of moral responsibility than the first two categories. These acts involve the crime of encouraging terrorism by approval or by failure to act, rather than by actively supporting it or organising it.

Contemporary Terrorism

Contemporary political terrorism came of age in the 1960s and 1970s. A wave of spectacular aircraft hijackings and embassy takeovers, together with an almost routine fare of bombings, shootings, and kidnappings ensured that terrorism was given constant media attention.[7] Public apprehension was heightened, minor tactical gains were made by terrorists, and governments slowly began to respond with increased security and a growing resolve not to accede to terrorist demands.

But terrorism has proved to be a dynamic phenomenon which has spread and changed its form, partially in response to the initiatives of governments. Not only have insurgent, revolutionary and separatist groups employed terror tactics against targets within their own countries but, increasingly, they have sought to take their case to the world through the export of violence. Acts of terrorism associated with the Palestinian cause or the issue of the Armenian genocide, for example, have occurred in many countries far removed from the source of the grievance. Groups such as the JRA, with no particular constituency and only a vaguely articulated concept of world revolution, see the whole world as their legitimate battleground and are prepared not only to plan and execute terrorist acts which follow their own program, but are willing to 'contract out' their services for groups with whose struggles or ideals they have sympathy. States are themselves becoming increasingly involved in using or supporting terrorism to further their foreign policy or national security goals. As a consequence of these developments, current international terrorism has the potential for posing much more serious threats to peace and stability on a wide scale than does domestic terrorism or previous forms of international terrorism.

In the late 1970s and early 1980s, the security authorities in a number of countries recorded major victories in counter-terrorist operations, prompting some commentators at the time to claim that the 'war on terrorism' was being won. The hardening resolve of the authorities was demonstrated by the successful and spectacular Israeli raid on Entebbe, the rescue of passengers on a hijacked Lufthansa airliner by West German border guards at Mogadishu, and the breaking of the siege of the Iranian Embassy in London by the British Special Air Service Regiment (SAS). Moreover, it appeared that the pressure exerted on the democracies in Western Europe had been substantially reduced by the arrest and prosecution of the leading members of the Baader-Meinhof Group in West Germany and the decimation of the Red Brigades following a successful campaign by the Italians which involved massive arrests based on confessions and information obtained by 'rehabilitating' captured terrorists. In the Middle East, the Israeli invasion of Lebanon and the subsequent dispersal of the PLO, together with the problems caused by the PLO's own internal divisions, were seen by some as limiting the scope for further large-scale Palestinian terrorism for the immediate future.

Such optimistic predictions have, of course, been rapidly overtaken by subsequent events. These developments have impressed upon the world the reality that terrorism is here to stay and is set to exert even more pressure on the international community and on individual nations. New generations of terrorists have sprung up in Germany and, to a lesser extent Italy, which have more clearly defined goals, appeal to a less nebulous constituency, and have shown the ability to form links in a loose coalition with terrorist organisations in neighbouring countries, thus increasing the range of their activities and their operating distance, as well as providing improved logistic and operational support. As a result, these groups, arguably, pose more of a threat than did their forebears.

In the Middle East, the Israeli excursion into Lebanon and the PLO's problems have not, as anticipated, led to a marked downturn in terrorism emanating from the area. While the invasion led to a significant downturn in Palestinian terrorist operations in Israel for a period after the event, the effect was relatively short-lived and was followed by a period of heightened activity. Outside Israel, there was a dramatic short-term increase in surrogate attacks on Jewish and Israeli targets by European and Latin American terrorist groups. Overall the level of Palestinian terrorist activity in the ensuing two years was little different to that in the pre-invasion period.[8]

Furthermore, the Middle East has seen a resurgence of terrorism, either encouraged or executed by states in the region. Some of this activity has been tied closely to purely national interests, (for example, most of the terrorism carried out with Libyan and Syrian backing or approval). However, increasingly, it is tied to Islamic fundamentalism (especially that backed by Iran or organised by many of the Islamic terrorist groups in the Lebanon).

Elsewhere in the world, established terrorist struggles show no signs of abating (for example, those in Ireland, Spain, Central and South America, and South Africa). In others, terrorism has become an increasing problem (for example, India and Sri Lanka), often with international ramifications.

Although the absolute numbers fluctuate from year to year, there has been a clear trend towards increases in acts of international terrorism in this decade. Not only is terrorism increasing in incidence, it is also resulting in higher casualties. One reason for this is the change in terrorist tactics in recent years. Established major terrorist groups have largely abandoned the embassy takeovers and aircraft hijackings which gained so much publicity in the 1970s. Increased security, refined hostage negotiation procedures, and an increased willingness on the part of governments to refuse to make major concessions, and to use force if necessary to terminate terrorist sieges, have made skyjackings and hostage-takings much less attractive options for terrorists (although there are still some circumstances in which they may be useful from the terrorist's viewpoint). For many terrorists, recourse to such tactics involves too many risks, too great a cost, and insufficient guarantee of a successful outcome.

The result of response to government countermeasures has been the increasing use of the time-honoured methods of the bomb and the bullet, albeit in a more destructive form due to the use of advanced technology weapons and explosives. The use of these methods, together with violent attempts to rescue hostages which result in many deaths if they fail, has meant that more incidents involve death or injury. In addition, the number of such casualties per incident has increased in recent years. The particular weapons being used now, especially car bombs, and the rise in the occurrence of fanatical terrorism in which the bomber is prepared, or even determined, to die has also ensured that the casualties have gone up progressively over time. Thus, according to US State Department figures, the casualties in international terrorist incidents in 1985 were 877 dead and 1,300 wounded, compared with 34 dead and 207 wounded in 1968.[9] It is clear, therefore, that terrorism, particularly of the international variety, is a problem with which we will continue to have to grapple.

Aims of Terrorism

In internal struggles, one of the principal aims of terrorism is to separate the mass of society from the incumbent authorities. According to Thornton, this process of disorientation is one of the most characteristic uses of terror.[10] However, he warns that 'terror is only appropriate if the insurgents (or incumbents) enjoy a low level of actual political support but have a high potential for such support. If their potential is low, terrorism is likely to be counter-productive'.[11] In the latter case, those who use it may discover that terrorism leads to a wave of outrage and revulsion against them, sweeping aside any latent or actual base of public support and sympathy for their political cause. Or, in other conditions, it may lead to spontaneous (and unanticipated) counter-violence and terror with the emergence of vigilante groups or rival terrorist units. The original terrorists may then find themselves sucked into a kind of intercommunal or inter-movement struggle which acts to neutralise their potential effectiveness in influencing long-term policy or constitutional changes.

Terrorist propaganda may be an important element in deciding whether the hostility engendered by terrorism will be directed against the incumbents or the insurgents. A significant finding of the air war studies conducted during and after the Second World War was that it was often not the countries responsible for the bombing that were blamed by the victims. Rather their own governments were blamed for failing to protect them. The aim of terrorist propaganda must be to tip the balance so that it is the government that becomes the target for popular aggression. This is a critical and difficult task, the failure of which has led to the elimination of many revolutionary groups. Often the balance is heavily influenced by the past record and present response of the particular government. If the anger of the populace is directed at the terrorists, it is sometimes possible for them to turn the tide by denying responsibility because the credibility of the government is not sufficient to eliminate doubt as to the truth of the terrorists' claims. An excellent example of this is the way in which the Algerian FLN terrorists managed to avoid responsibility for the Melouza massacre in 1957. In this incident, the male inhabitants of the village of Melouza were murdered by the FLN for rebelling against FLN terrorism, supporting a rival nationalist group and also cooperating with the French Army. Although international opinion was not reversed, the FLN managed to persuade most Moslems in Algeria that it was the French who had committed the murders in order to discredit the FLN. In large part this success was due to the fact that the French had no reputation for honesty in Algeria and the Moslems did not believe their protestations of innocence.

An aim of terrorist tactics which is related to the creation of community disorientation is that of provoking repressive measures of an illegal or unconstitutional nature by the incumbent rulers, or of forcing the intervention of a third party. If the government uses extra-legal methods or methods which restrict or deprive ordinary citizens of their human rights in order to suppress terrorists, they may lose both their legitimacy and public confidence and support.

Probably the best-known theorist on methods of provoking the security forces into heavy-handed over-reaction or illegal behaviour is Carlos Marighela. In his *Urban Guerrilla Minimanual*, Marighela is quite specific about the aim of terrorist tactics:

> From the moment a large proportion of the population begin to take his activities seriously, his success is assured. The

> Government can only intensify its repression, thus making the life of its citizens harder than ever: homes will be broken into, police searches organised, innocent people arrested, and communications broken; police terror will become the order of the day, and there will be more and more political murders - in short a massive political persecution...the political situation of the country will become a military situation.[12]

The Tupamaros in Uruguay explicitly followed Marighela's teachings in attempting to force the government to become repressive to such an extent that a climate of collapse would be engendered which would allow the political arm of the guerrilla movement to pose as the viable alternative and accede to power. In that case, however, only the first part of the scenario came true. In fact repression increased to such an extent that the only remaining liberal democracy in South America disappeared. What replaced it in 1972, however, was not the neo-Marxist regime of the terrorists' dreams, but a ruthless, right-wing, authoritarian government which still exists today.

Another major aim of all terrorism, in some instances the foremost aim, is that of publicity. By staging acts which gain the world's attention, terrorists are able to gain recognition of their cause and project themselves as a group that must be listened to and taken account of. Frightening acts of violence and the ensuing atmosphere of alarm and fear cause people to exaggerate the importance, size, and strength of some terrorist organisations. Because of their numerical inferiority, it is important that terrorist groups indulge in dramatic and shocking violence if they are to be noticed.

The importance of the media as a vehicle for the expression of terrorist messages cannot be overstated. Terrorism and media coverage enjoy something of a symbiotic relationship. Television, in particular, is no longer a medium which simply responds to terrorist events, it is an integral part of them. Because of the vast, instant audience that can be conjured up by television, terrorists have learned to stage-manage their spectaculars for maximum audience impact. This is at least partly the reason for the dramatic increase in the occurrence of hostage and siege situations in the past few years. The drama of the situation can be increased by taking hostages. If certain demands are not met, hostages may be killed, thereby escalating the suspense and forcing the authorities to take the terrorists even more seriously. Such increasing tension also serves to intensify outside pressure on the authorities to give in to all or some of the terrorists' demands. The hostages may well have no real or symbolic value as individuals as far as the hostage-takers are concerned. They may be, and often are, anonymous individuals occupying no positions of power and belonging to no particular nation. For the most part terrorism is aimed at the audience, not the victims. Indeed, as has been claimed often, terrorism is primarily theatre.

Terrorism may also be aimed at causing or hastening a general breakdown in social order, demoralising the citizens and causing them to lose faith in the ability of the incumbent government to maintain order and stability or to guarantee their safety. Particularly when a revolutionary group becomes impatient with the people - on whose behalf they claim to act - because they fail to appreciate or act upon the revolutionary message, they may well turn to terrorism as part of a campaign to politicise and mobilise the populace. In theory, if terrorism can be used to show that a government is powerless to protect its people, or to keep vital functions operating in that the government is forced to switch resources to massive security operations and indulge in repressive measures which affect the lives of ordinary people, there will come a time when the people will revolt against the government. In practice, however, such a strategy often backfires and the use of terrorism may well turn the people, even sympathisers, against the terrorist violence and its perpetrators, and lead to support for the government's efforts to wipe out the terrorists.

There is ample historical evidence that terror alone is not generally an effective weapon for bringing about the overthrow of incumbent governments. The few cases in which terrorism played a major part in bringing sweeping political changes have arisen in certain colonial independence struggles against foreign rule, as in the case of the ending of the Palestine Mandate after the terrorist campaigns of the Jewish Irgun and Stern groups, and the EOKA campaign in Cyprus. However, as Wilkinson has shown in his analysis of these situations, even in these rare cases special conditions prevailed that made terrorism a more potent weapon.[13] First, for various reasons of political expediency and international pressure, the occupying power was unwilling to carry through draconian measures to wipe out the terrorist organisations. In each case, there were also inter-communal power struggles within the colony which rendered a peaceful diplomatic settlement and withdrawal difficult, if not impossible. Finally, where terrorists were successful (for example, in Aden) they already enjoyed considerable support within their own ethnic groups which created great difficulties for the intelligence services in penetrating these groups for information and also provided much active and tacit collaboration and support for terrorist operatives.

A further major aim of specific terrorist operations is to wring concessions from the controlling power. This may take the form of a demand for policy changes (for example, the Austrian government agreed to stop allowing Jewish refugees transit through Austria on their way to Israel in return for the safe release of hostages held by Palestinian terrorists in September 1973), ransom (particularly used by South American terrorist groups), the release of prisoners, or the publication of a terrorist manifesto.

The aims discussed above apply both to domestic and international terrorism. In the latter field, however, there are some additional specific aims when the terrorism is sponsored, or carried out, by states in pursuit of foreign policy goals. Essentially this type of terrorism is aimed at achieving a number of goals in influencing the foreign policy of another government. The goal may be to disrupt or destroy processes of dialogue (such as peace negotiations) which are seen as harmful to the sponsor's interests, to undermine the prestige of an enemy nation by seeking to humiliate it, and to force a target state to respond to a problem in a manner which the terrorist sponsor desires (this may include, as in the domestic case, the attempt to force the target nation to over-react or react inappropriately in its counter-terrorist actions so that the sponsor can use the effects in its propaganda against the target).

In addition to examining terrorism as a phenomenon of international relations, attention is increasingly being focussed on the possibility of terrorism providing an alternative means to dominating situations that normally are influenced by conventional military forces. Many analysts see an emerging role for terrorism as a means of 'surrogate warfare' employed by states against other nations.

There is evidence of a trend towards the development of low-level conflict as an important part of the world strategic mosaic. Early predictions that low-level conflict would replace costly conventional wars seem to have been somewhat overstated in that major conventional engagements still occur (e.g. the Arab-Israeli wars, or the Iran-Iraq war) and show little sign of becoming obsolete. But modes of conflict such as guerrilla warfare and terrorism continue to increase. What is more important is that they are being used not only by insurgents, but by states as well.

Possibly the increased use of low-level conflict is related to the diffusion of power in the world today. Ethnicity and nationality compete as the basis for legitimate political authority. At present, the United Nations is growing by approximately three new nations a year. If this trend continues, we will have 200 independent nations by 1990 and even more by the turn of the century. A good many of these nations will be 'mini-states' which are economically dependent and vulnerable to external pressure. Others may not be classed as mini-states, but still feel unable to exert sufficient influence over their own affairs or those of their region because of the influence of large powers. Resort to the tactics of terrorism, or the formation of alliances with terrorist groups, provides an option which allows such nations, that would otherwise be unable to mount challenges using conventional force, to carry out surrogate warfare against their opponents. Some analysts go further and suggest that even large nations may resort more readily to forms of low-level warfare, including terrorism, in the face of the massively escalating costs of conventional warfare. Once again, predictions of this nature tend to over-emphasise the likelihood or the extent of this development. Nevertheless, there is evidence of a trend in this direction which suggests that more resources need to be devoted to the study of terrorism as an element of military strategy and to the development of appropriate military (as opposed to police) doctrine and countermeasures.

The Future

The growing importance of terrorists, their relationships with states, and the erosion of the monopoly of force traditionally enjoyed by states, suggest some changes in both strategy and ideology for future terrorists. We see in the increasing international links being developed by terrorists of profoundly differing philosophies and values the core of a possible new ideology of terrorism which transcends the traditional ideologies of left and right.[14] At least some groups, in rejecting the nation-state system, also turn away from the commitment to traditional nationalism which has hitherto characterised many major terrorist groups. A new, as yet vague, philosophy of global revolution aimed at transforming the nation-state system is struggling to evolve. The motivation and justification for this philosophy expresses anti-Western, anti-technological, and anti-mass society sentiments, and cuts across many left-right distinctions.

It is ironic that it is the very technology which is now the target of much terrorism. Developed countries, being both the symbols of technology, and the most vulnerable targets because of the importance to the functioning of their societies of fragile technological systems, are most liable to attack. But traditional states which use the power of, for example, oil revenues, to modernise, also subject themselves to assault from both left and right. The left may feel that political and social reforms are not accompanying technological innovation, whilst the right may fear that this same technology threatens traditional leadership and values. The emergence of such factors as Islamic fundamentalist terrorism also makes left-right distinctions irrelevant. Both developed and developing countries, therefore, may have something to fear from the shifting coalitions between left and right, modernists and traditionalists.

It is easy to paint a bleak picture of the future. One can envisage a world faced with traditional nationalistic, and ethnically or religiously motivated terrorists, with states either supporting or creating terrorist groups to further their own foreign policy goals, and with the emergence of a new ideology of terror which transcends traditional classifications and motivations. Moreover, there is a tendency towards fascination with apocalyptic possibilities, which may lead one to under-rate trends which lead to unexciting conclusions. Thus, few analysts see the future of terrorism as being a continuing mosaic of largely unrelated incidents of little real threat, preferring instead to believe in a reduction of terrorism caused by effective international action against it, or uncontrolled escalation toward more horrendous outrages.

It should also be borne in mind that focusing only on possibilities tends to over-emphasise their negative aspects. But a number of the trends in terrorism have produced countervailing trends which may act to attenuate their effects. For example, regimes which have in the past either overtly, or tacitly, supported terrorism, but are now themselves potential targets of terrorism, are re-thinking whether they can stand outside the mainstream of international cooperation to counter terrorism. The behaviour of conservative Arab states provides a case in point which exemplifies the value conflict facing some states. They have supported the national self-determination of the Palestinians against the Israelis and, thus, have given material aid and sanctuary to Palestinian terrorists. But, in fact, they wish to enable the Palestinians to gain more power **within** the international system without undermining its foundations. When their own national interests or prestige have come under attack, these same states have very quickly acknowledged the value of the traditional norms of international behaviour. A number of European states, too, which although not condoning terrorism, acquiesced to terrorist demands or turned a blind eye to terrorist activities directed against other nations, have responded much more firmly when their own sovereignty has been impugned.

It is thus becoming increasingly apparent that most states have re-discovered the value of fundamental norms such as those which guarantee the safety of diplomatic and commercial exchanges. In the wake of a massive increase in attacks against diplomats and business executives, a number of states have seriously questioned whether the pursuit of anti-colonialism and self-determination necessitates the abandoning of traditional standards of state behaviour. The consensus among states seems to have moved toward rejection of those forms of political expression which violate such basic trust.[15] (There still exist, of course, some states whose abuse of the protections of the diplomatic system is quite obvious.)

These developments could be thought to presage a new era of international cooperation against terrorism. But that would be a far too optimistic reading of events. At the international level, the issue will continue to be characterised by rhetorical debates over the definition of terrorism. Efforts to reach accord on very specific aspects of terrorism, such as those already existing on protection of diplomatic personnel and hijacking of aircraft, have more chance of success but do little more than nibble at the edges of the problem. Regional agreements (such as the European Convention on the Suppression of Terrorism) which attempt a reasonably comprehensive coverage of counter-terrorist measures are more likely to be reached than global accords, but here, too, problems such as those relating to the so-called 'political offence exception' make their operation very dependent on the individual circumstances surrounding any particular terrorist incident. The best hope of effective action is probably to be found in bilateral agreements and in less formal exchanges between the free nations' police and intelligence services.

In conclusion, it is clear that terrorism has now become as much a problem of international relations as it is a problem of domestic law enforcement. However, it throws into relief a number of dilemmas facing many states. Terrorism reveals the mutual interdependence of states, since a successful response to it requires the cooperation of other states. But many states, whose cooperation is necessary, often sympathise with the aims of the terrorists, thus inhibiting their responses. Consequently, most of these developments in terrorism itself mean that the spread of targets is increasing and now includes states which have supported some terrorist groups in the past. Faced with such a challenge, these states have moved toward rejection of terrorism, increasing the possibility of more comprehensive international cooperation in the future. Finally, there remains the possibility of a pattern of terrorism conducted by or for states themselves as part of their foreign policy initiatives. All of these developments indicate that terrorism will be one of the major international peacekeeping problems of the future.

Endnotes

1   For discussion of the problems of defining terrorism, see H.C. Greisman, 'Social Meanings of Terrorism: Reification, Violence and Social Control', *Contemporary Crises*, (Vol.1), 1977, pp.303-318; B.M. Jenkins, 'The Study of Terrorism: Definition Problems', in Y. Alexander and J.M. Gleason (eds.), *Behavioural and Quantitative*

    Perspectives on Terrorism, (Pergamon Press, New York, 1981), pp.3-10; and Grant Wardlaw, *Political Terrorism*, (Cambridge University Press, Cambridge, 1982), especially Chapter 1.

2   Martha Crenshaw, 'Introduction: Reflections on the Effects of Terrorism', in M. Crenshaw (ed.), *Terrorism, Legitimacy, and Power: The Consequences of Political Violence*, (Wesleyan University Press, Middletown, Connecticut, 1983), p.5.

3   Grant Wardlaw, *Political Terrorism*, p.16.

4   Amir Taheri, *Holy Terror*, (Sphere Books, London, 1987), pp.2-3.

5   Michael Stohl, 'States, Terrorism and State Terrorism: The Role of the Superpowers', in R. Slater and M. Stohl (eds.), *Current Perspectives on International Terrorism*, (Macmillan/St Martin's Press, London and New York, forthcoming).

6   Alexander George, 'The Development of Doctrine and Strategy', in A. George, D. Hall, and W.R. Simons (eds.), *The Limits of Coercive Diplomacy*, (Little, Brown, Boston, 1971), p.18.

7   For detailed introduction to political terrorism, see J. Bowyer Bell, *A Time of Terror*, (Basic Books, New York, 1978); Walter Laqueur, *The Age of Terrorism*, (Little, Brown, Boston, 1987); Grant Wardlaw, *Political Terrorism*, (Cambridge University Press, Cambridge, 1982); and Paul Wilkinson, *Terrorism and the Liberal State*, (Macmillan, London, 2nd edition, 1986).

8   Bruce Hoffman, 'The Plight of the Phoenix: The PLO Since Lebanon', *Conflict Quarterly*, (Vol.5, No.2), 1985, pp.5-17.

9   *Casualties Caused by International Terrorism, 1968-1985*, (US Department of State, Office for Counter-Terrorism and Emergency Planning, nd.).

10   T.P. Thornton, 'Terror as a Weapon of Political Agitation', in H. Eckstein (ed.) *Internal War*, (Collier-Macmillan, London, 1964).

11   *Ibid.*, p.74.

12   Carlos Marighela, *Urban Guerrilla Minimanual*, (Pulp Press, Vancouver, 1974), p.95.

13   Paul Wilkinson, *Terrorism and the Liberal State*.

14   Stephen Sloan, 'International Terrorism: Conceptual Problems and Implications, *Journal of Thought*, (Vol.17, No.2), 1982, pp.19-29.

15   Martha Crenshaw, *The International Consequences of Terrorism*, (Paper presented at the Annual Meeting of the American Political Science Association, Chicago, 1-4 September 1983).

CHAPTER 8

THE STRATEGY OF NON-PROVOCATIVE DEFENCE: THE EUROPEAN DEBATE

Andrew Mack

Introduction

This chapter examines the case for what has been variously called 'non-provocative defence', 'non-offensive defence', 'defensive defence', 'defensive deterrence', 'structural defensivity' and 'mutual defensive superiority'. Proponents of these approaches disagree on many issues but they also share a number of common assumptions. Of the various labels used to describe the new defensive strategies I have chosen the term non-provocative defence (NPD).[1]

Over the past five years in Europe particularly debate over the fundamental assumptions of NATO defence policy has been gathering increasing momentum. Much of this debate has been conducted in the German scholarly and popular media and as such it has received relatively little attention in either the US or Great Britain. Proponents of NPD argue that the core assumptions of contemporary NATO strategic doctrine are deeply flawed intellectually - on this issue there is considerable agreement within NATO as well. But the critics also argue that NATO's proposed cures may be worse than the disease. Traditional Warsaw Pact doctrine with its emphasis on offensive strategic and force posture is seen as posing even greater risks.

Critique of the Status Quo

Former US Ambassador to the Mutual and Balanced Force Reduction (MBFR) Talks in Vienna, Jonathan Dean, recently argued that '...the advent of US-Soviet nuclear parity has highlighted the increasingly acute inner contradictions of deterrence theory...'[2] Ambassador Dean's remarks would command wide consensus both in Europe and America. However, there is little consensus about diagnosis of the cause of the problem or the appropriate prescriptions for its resolution. Few proponents of non-provocative defence would wish to argue against the proposition that the mutual possession of nuclear weapons induces great caution in superpower behaviour - in other words they accept the existence of what McGeorge Bundy has called 'existential deterrence'. The argument is rather against the theory of deterrence which provides the ostensible rationale for much of NATO's so-called 'flexible response' strategy.

A basic flaw in nuclear deterrence theory is its inability to deal coherently with the problem of so-called 'self-deterrence'. The central thrust of the argument is simple. If it is accepted that nuclear pre-emptive strikes by one side cannot disarm the other side, and that nuclear retaliation is a likely response to nuclear attack, it follows that when one side threatens its opponent with nuclear attack it is, in effect, threatening itself with nuclear attack. In a world where mutual assured destruction remains a probable consequence of any nuclear war, using nuclear threats as a means of deterring conventional aggression is like saying, 'Stop or I will commit suicide'. It is essentially for this reason that deterrent threats may be self-deterring.

Indeed, the central problem with all nuclear deterrence theories is that, no matter how apparently sophisticated, they can provide no criteria for determining who is the more deterred by nuclear threats - the party which is threatened, or the party which makes the threat. This uncertainty, as General Sir Hugh Beach has pointed out, 'imports a very large element of the implausible and the irrational into the whole concept of escalation or first-use.'[3]

Since we are likely to be more concerned about the prospect of ourselves being killed than our enemies being killed, there are *a priori* grounds for believing that we may be more deterred by our own threats than are our enemies. This is particularly true when our threats are made on behalf of others as is the case with so-called 'extended deterrence'. It is one thing to risk suicide by threatening nuclear retaliation in response to aggression against one's own country. It is quite another to risk nuclear suicide for other countries. Yet this is precisely what NATO's 'flexible response' doctrine requires the US to do. The problem with such a posture is obvious. Henry Kissinger argued more than ten years ago, 'It is absurd to base the strategy of the West on the credibility of the threat of mutual suicide'.[4]

NATO's nuclear doctrine is no more appealing to the US public today than it was to Dr Kissinger in 1977. In late 1988, a poll taken in the US found that, whereas 77 per cent of Americans supported using nuclear weapons if the Soviet Union attacked the US, only 34 per cent supported US nuclear use to retaliate against a Soviet nuclear attack on America's allies, and a mere 11 per cent supported a US first-use of nuclear weapons if the Soviets invaded Europe in a conventional war.[5] In other words, NATO's nuclear first-use doctrine is overwhelmingly opposed by the voters of the very democracy which would be called on to use the weapons in question.

Threatening to use nuclear weapons on behalf of allies is part of the strategy of so-called 'extended deterrence' - the benefit which America's alliance partners supposedly gain from living under the 'nuclear umbrella'. The doctrine of 'extended deterrence' requires the Soviets to believe that resort by them to conventional aggression could lead to a first-use of tactical nuclear weapons by NATO and that this could, in turn, lead to the use of strategic nuclear weapons.

The lack of credibility of all 'extended deterrent' threats is widely recognised in the strategic community, which is why NATO has consistently aspired either to make its nuclear threats more credible, or to make conventional defence so robust that there was no need to resort to a first-use of nuclear weapons.

One response to the problem of enhancing the credibility of 'extended deterrence' has been to argue for increased 'coupling' between NATO Europe and the US. If the Soviets could be made to believe that an attack on Europe was also an attack on the US, deterrence would be enhanced. For Europe and America to be more tightly 'coupled', there needed to be a 'seamless web' of escalatory options between conventional defence and tactical nuclear weapons, on the one hand, and between the tactical weapons which would be used on European soil and the strategic nuclear systems based in the US and on American missile-firing submarines, on the other hand. Much of the conservative US and European opposition to the Intermediate-range Nuclear Forces (INF) Treaty arose from concern that the removal of US INF weapons (the Ground-Launched Cruise Missile and the Pershing II missile) would create a gap in the 'seamless web' and thus tend to 'decouple' the US from its allies and in so doing undermine deterrence.

The doctrine of 'limited nuclear war' was also a response to the credibility problem which was inherent in the 'extended deterrence' strategy. To make nuclear threats more credible, nuclear weapons had to be made more usable; nuclear war had to become more thinkable.

Making nuclear war more thinkable meant in effect lowering the nuclear threshold - eroding the 'firebreak' which constrains escalation from conventional weapons to tactical nuclear weapons. Part of the essential incoherence of NATO security policy lies in the fact that it seeks to achieve contradictory goals simultaneously. On the one hand, lowering the nuclear threshold was necessary to enhance the credibility of 'extended deterrence'. On the other hand, the imperatives of crisis stability and escalation control required the nuclear threshold to be as high as possible. Seeking to maximise one objective undermined the other.

It is also clear that the stress on 'coupling' tactical (European) nuclear weapons to strategic (extra-European) weapons could be disastrous if deterrence failed. An all-out strategic exchange is the worst possible outcome of any nuclear war. From this it follows that if deterrence fails, the highest priority strategic objective must be to keep any nuclear exchanges as limited as possible. But the stress of 'coupling' was intended to signal to the Soviets precisely the opposite message - giving them an incentive for strategic pre-emption.   Thus, the requirements for 'extended deterrence' and for prudent war-fighting, if deterrence nevertheless fails, are antithetical. The pursuit of one goal subverts the other.

The doctrine of 'limited nuclear war' is flawed in other respects, not least because the Soviets have consistently rejected the rules of the 'game' laid down by NATO.   There can thus be no guarantee that 'limited' and 'controlled' nuclear strikes by NATO will not lead to unlimited strikes being unleashed by the Soviets in response. Moreover, all 'limited' nuclear war scenarios assume, of necessity, that command, control, communication, surveillance, targeting and damage-assessment capabilities will all continue to function adequately enough during nuclear exchanges to permit the control of any intended escalation process by either side. Yet there is now considerable literature - the findings of which have never been seriously challenged - which suggests that such assumptions are wholly unwarranted.[6]

But even if it is assumed that 'limited' nuclear options could be controlled, and that the Soviets would 'play' by Pentagon rules, NATO's policy still cannot escape the paradoxes of self-deterrence.   Only if nuclear wars can be 'won' can the dilemma of self-deterrence be escaped. As Colin Gray has argued, a credible 'extended deterrence' strategy requires 'a capability to win wars'.[7] But Gray also argues that such a capability must 'at minimum' include effective strategic defences - capable of defending the civilian population not just missile silos. Yet no analysts believe that it is possible to build such defences for the foreseeable future - if ever. And even the most perfect strategic defences could not cope with hand-delivered 'suitcase' bombs. Without nuclear pre-emption and leak-proof strategic defences, nuclear wars cannot be won and there is no escape from the paradox of self-deterrence.

This is not to suggest that the assumptions of 'flexible' response would *necessarily* turn out to be wrong in practice. The point is simply that there is no way of knowing in advance whether the logic of deterrence or that of self-deterrence will prevail in a crisis.

Insofar as this is true, much of the baroque edifice of deterrence theory - including many of the assumptions which underpin the concepts of 'extended deterrence', 'intrawar deterrence', 'escalation dominance', 'limited nuclear options' and so forth - simply collapses.

But whatever problems inhere in deterrence theory/doctrine, the reality of 'existential deterrence' - i.e. the great caution which the mere existence of nuclear weapons engenders in the superpower relationship - is not in question. Because of this it probably does not matter that NATO deterrence doctrine is predicated on arbitrary and unprovable assumptions. NATO's nuclear threats may not have very much credibility but, as Robert Jervis has argued, '...only a little credibility may be required'.[8]

The obvious point, as I have argued elsewhere, is that:

> ...a threat which may have a relatively low probability of being carried out, but which imposes catastrophic costs if it is, may be quite as effective a deterrent as a threat which has a higher probability of being carried out, but where the costs of deterrence failing are commensurately less.[9]

What does matter is that the weapons systems and strategies designed to enhance the credibility of 'extended deterrence' may be destabilising - i.e. they may undermine crisis stability and crisis control and in so doing increase the risks of inadvertent war.[10] This is so because, even if 'prevailing' or 'winning' a nuclear war is an unrealisable goal, damage-limiting pre-emptive strikes may appear to be a rational, if desperate, contingency strategy for either or both sides *if (but only if) war appears inevitable, i.e. if deterrence is already perceived to have failed.*

The logic which underpins the incentive to pre-empt was neatly illustrated in a homely example by Tom Schelling some thirty years ago:

> If I go downstairs to investigate a noise at night, with a gun in my hand, and find myself face to face with a burglar who has a gun in his hand, there is danger of an outcome that neither of us desires. Even if he'd prefer to just leave quietly, and I'd like him to, there is a danger that he may think I want to shoot, and shoot first. Worse, there is a danger that he may think that I think he wants to shoot. Or he may think that I think he thinks I want to shoot. And so on. 'Self defense' is ambiguous, when one is only trying to preclude being shot in self-defense.[11]

The consequence of using nuclear weapons in such a situation will be disastrous, but it may be perceived to be relatively less disastrous for the side which pre-empts and in so doing succeeds in destroying much of its opponent's offensive arsenal. Thus, the mere possession by both sides of vulnerable counterforce nuclear weapons can create incentives for starting the very wars these weapons are intended to deter. The greater the ratio of 'time-urgent hard-target' nuclear weapon systems on one side, to vulnerable counter-force (or vital command, control and communication) systems on the other, the greater the incentive to pre-empt. A recent study by Robert Glasser argues that in 1990 (compared with 1985) '...the incentives for the US to pre-empt to cut national fatalities have increased enormously.'[12]

New Approaches to Conventional Defences

The perceived need to find non-nuclear solutions to the problems which inhere in 'extended deterrence' has generated a number of proposals for boosting NATO conventional defence capabilities. Two such approaches are discussed here. Both emphasise the role of so-called 'emerging technologies' (ET) in enhancing conventional defence capabilities. The first emphasises offensive 'Deep Attack' missions; the second stresses more defensively-oriented strategic concepts.

Deep Attack

Proponents of Deep Attack strategies argue for an increased stress on so-called 'emerging technologies' (ET) directed towards offensive 'Deep Attack' missions (sometimes called 'Deep Strike') against second echelon Warsaw Treaty Organisation (WTO) armoured units, airfields, C³I installations etc., which are located deep in enemy territory. 'Deep Attack' technologies will, it is argued, greatly enhance NATO's ability to locate, target and destroy or disable forces of the WTO deployed far from the Forward Edge of the Battle Area (FEBA). Support for 'Deep Attack' concepts also reflects 'dissatisfaction with what was widely regarded by the US Army as an excessively reactive defence doctrine.'[13] NATO has always had both the capability and intention to attack static targets (e.g. airfields and railway marshalling yards) deep in WTO territory. ET capabilities will enhance that capability and, in theory, enable mobile forces to be destroyed as well.

Critics of Deep Attack disagree strongly with the shift away from NATO's traditionally more defensive strategic stance. They argue on a number of grounds against the Deep Attack philosophy, which is embodied in the NATO planning concept known as Follow-On-Forces Attack or FOFA, in the US Army's Air Land Battle doctrine and, more broadly, in the new 'competitive strategies' approach which is gaining increasing support in the Pentagon.[14]

First, the critics question that the systems will deliver munitions as effectively as claimed over such long ranges.[15] The key problem here is that the tasks of target-acquisition and damage-assessment become increasingly difficult as range increases - especially over enemy territory where a wide variety of countermeasures can be deployed. Moreover, Deep Attack strategies would be highly dependent on C³I systems and sensors which are themselves highly vulnerable to attack or counterattack. Steven Canby has summed up these objections succinctly:

> Unfortunately Deep Strike (alias Rogers Plan and FOFA) cannot be effective, in principle or practice. FOFA is a concept beyond the capabilities of technology. Its infeasibility transcends the many limitations of the specific equipment proposed. It is necessarily a preprogrammed, deterministic system. Such systems cannot operate in uncongenial, adaptive and unpredictable environments.[16]

Second, the fact that many of the proposed ET weapons systems are dual-capable will create serious difficulties in both reaching and verifying arms control agreements in peacetime. It could also lead the WTO to believe that a conventional attack which used dual-capable conventional warheads was a nuclear attack - a possibility acknowledged by former Supreme Allied Commander (Europe) (SACEUR) General Rogers.[17]

Third, Deep Attack is predicated on assumptions about Soviet strategy which, it is argued, are outdated. It assumes that in a war with NATO, the Soviets would mass forces for a breakthrough and would need to maintain precise timetables for their advance thus providing targets of opportunity for Deep Attack technologies. But current Soviet strategy is based more on the Operational Manoeuvre Group (OMG) which places high stress on surprise and manoeuvre. This effectively means that the Soviet vulnerabilities which FOFA both assumes and requires will be far less important and targets of opportunity for NATO will be fewer.[18] Fourth, Deep Attack systems are destabilising. The problem with all offensive strategies/force postures is that they may be used either in response to aggression or for aggression. Prudent 'worst case' defence planners need to take the latter possibility seriously and indeed do. Not least of the reasons for Western concerns about Soviet aggression has been the unambiguously offensive nature of the USSR's force posture on the Central Front in Europe.

But offensively-oriented force postures may be destabilising even if they are not seen by opponents as evidence of aggressive intent. Insofar as particular NATO offensive systems are perceived by the Soviets as posing an effective threat to vital Soviet military assets, their destruction will become a vital Soviet wartime objective irrespective of the cause of the war. Since the most effective way to stop certain Deep Attack systems - particularly missiles - is to destroy them on the ground, the very existence of these systems provides the Soviets with an incentive to pre-empt in a crisis. If the Soviets target their Deep Attack systems against those of the US, this will create a US incentive to pre-empt and a Soviet incentive to pre-empt a possible US pre-emption and so forth. When both sides employ offensive strategies there is little if any observable difference between preparations to repel aggression and preparations for aggression. In such a context the interactive 'ratcheting up' of alert statuses may, as Paul Bracken has argued, increase the chances that defensive preparations be seen as offensively intended.[19]

According to the Pugwash Study Group on Conventional Forces in Europe, which has played an active role in analyzing and promoting non-provocative defence, the strategic situation in Europe has been worsening in the sense that changes in the nature of the European conventional balance are antithetical to the requirements of crisis stability. Thus we have:

> ...increased emphasis on time-critical weapon systems; increased numbers of targets for pre-emptive strike; increased numbers of weapon systems that appear to be capable of crippling defences and which thus raise the pressure for pre-emptive attack.[20]

Concern about the incoherence of NATO's nuclear strategy and the destabilising nature of the Deep Attack approach to bolstering conventional deterrence, have been major stimuli to the emergence of non-provocative defence (NPD) strategies. The trend towards new thinking on defence issues has also been encouraged by declining European threat perceptions and by budgetary and manpower constraints on the military.

The Theory of Non-Provocative Defence

Non-provocative defence policies seek to:

- avoid the problems which inhere in attempting to make nuclear 'extended deterrence' policies more credible by lowering the nuclear threshold and making nuclear options more thinkable;

- avoid the different, but equally destabilising, problems which arise when attempts are made to raise the nuclear threshold by increasing conventional deterrence with policies stressing Deep Attack options;

- offer an alternative security policy which provides an adequate deterrent, a defensively-oriented but efficacious war-fighting policy, and which places a high premium on crisis avoidance and crisis stability.

Non-Provocative Defence has been defined as:

The build-up, training, logistics and doctrine of the armed forces...such that they are seen in their totality to be unsuitable for offence, but unambiguously sufficient for a credible defence. Nuclear weapons fulfil at most a retaliatory role.[21]

Notwithstanding the many significant differences between them, all NPD strategies seek to exploit the advantages which accrue to armed forces fighting on their home ground. The advantages include:

- a much better knowledge of terrain for the defender than the invader;
- shorter supply lines and generally better logistics;
- simpler and more robust command, communication, control and intelligence (C³I) systems;
- the possibility for the defence of achieving protection via concealment, while the invader is forced to reveal his position in advancing.

These advantages (there are also disadvantages which I will examine later) have long been recognised by students of strategy. In the Europe of the 1980s, two additional factors enhance the efficacy of defensive strategies.

First, the increased urbanisation and afforestation of Central Europe - particularly Germany - greatly complicates the task of land invasion from the East. As David Gates has pointed out, some 60 per cent of the Bundesrepublik is now wooded, urbanised or otherwise obstructed terrain. This phenomenon is particularly marked along the strategically crucial borders with East Germany and Czechoslovakia.[22] Second, the technological revolution in surveillance, target-acquisition and damage-assessment capabilities - coupled with the development of precision-guided munitions (PGMs) - acts as a powerful force multiplier for the defence. NPD strategies call for PGMs and associated surveillance and target-acquisition systems to be used over relatively short ranges and over allied territory. Such systems do not, therefore, confront the same target-acquisition and damage-assessment problems as the long-range ET systems being advocated for Deep Attack missions, nor are they as vulnerable to spoofing and other types of countermeasure which an enemy can more easily deploy on his home territory.

A Non-Provocative Defence Model

Outlined below is a schematic NPD model for NATO. It borrows from a number of different models which have already been proposed. It is considerably oversimplified and is intended simply to illustrate some of the tactical principles of NPD. It is in no sense meant as a blueprint for an actual force posture. There are a number of elements in the model:

- a 5 km 'fire barrier' zone along the border with virtually no defending troops within which intruding enemy forces would be subjected to intense fire barrages 'from artillery rockets (MLRS), mortars, attack drones and a wide variety of intelligent passive munitions';[23]

- a net of concealed and protected light infantry dispersed behind the fire barrier some 20-100 km deep (the depth of the net varies among NPD strategists);

- networks of concealed short-range and medium-range (20 to 100 km) PGMs loaded with different types of munition and separated from the infantry which provides their target-acquisition data;

- a C^3I network linking the infantry and the remote-fire weapons;

- a strong emphasis on 'passive' defences designed to slow down the enemy's advance and/or channel his forces in particular directions which favour the defence. Such defences could include forests, canals, trench mines and other man-made passive barriers.[24]

The 'fire barrier' provides the first line of defence. The primary task of the light infantry concealed behind the fire barrier is surveillance and target-acquisition for the remotely-fired PGMs. The infantry know the terrain and by visual observation of invading armour they can note target coordinates which are transmitted to the concealed PGMs. Target-acquisition is also aided by concealed sensors spread across the front.

The PGMs are single-shot systems - cheap launchers and expensive munitions. Artillery, by contrast, has expensive launchers and cheap munitions. Because artillery is fired repeatedly it reveals its position - which renders it vulnerable. However, because the PGMs are remotely controlled, their firing does not reveal the position of the infantrymen who launch them. Protection for the defence is achieved primarily by concealment and dispersion rather than concentration and point defence. The goal is to deny the enemy targets to shoot at.[25] The position of the missile is, of course, revealed when it is fired but this is of no consequence since, unlike artillery, it will not be fired again.

The reliance on PGMs has a number of important tactical implications:

- the high 'kill' probabilities which characterise PGMs place a high premium on shooting first;

- in order to shoot first one must have a target - forces which are seen first, get shot at first and, because of the accuracy of 'one-shot kill' PGMs, get destroyed first;

- the attacker must reveal his position when advancing thus becoming a target; the defender may however remain concealed, thus gaining the crucial advantage of shooting first;

- by separating the infantry from their one-shot PGMs and by dispersing them, an efficient NPD strategy can continue to deny the enemy targets to shoot at, while at the same time waging a debilitating attrition campaign against his forces;

- as enemy forces move forward and defensive positions are threatened with being overrun, or as (fixed) ammunition supplies run out, the infantry fall back to other prepared defensive positions; there is thus a tendency for defensive forces to concentrate as the attrited enemy forces advance deeper into the defenders' territory.

What evidence is there that defensive models would be efficacious in practice? Experimental research carried out by Reiner Huber and his colleagues at the Bundeswehr University in Munich provides some striking support for the NPD thesis.[26] The research used a sophisticated computer model to simulate in detail:

> ...all essential interactions affecting the dynamics and outcome of ground battles between battalion-size defending forces and a sequence of regimental-size attacking forces.[27]

Using this system, the Bundeswehr University team war-gamed ten NPD models (they used the term 'reactive defense' rather than NPD) and four models (including current NATO strategy) of 'active defense'. Their modelling experiments revealed that NPD models were up to ten times more cost-effective than the 'active defense' models. This is a particularly interesting finding since, except for directional mines, none of the 'reactive defense' force models which were tested were equipped with the 'smart' PGMs which many NPD strategies assume to be necessary.

What made the standard NATO/Bundeswehr forces so much less cost-effective than the NPD alternatives in the simulations was the high cost of mobility and armour protection.[28] However, Huber and his colleagues were careful to note that their findings were only relevant to the initial stages of a war and that they were useful only in predicting the outcome of particular battles between battalion-sized defending forces and regiment-sized attacking forces. This qualification is important since there is an obvious problem which any attrition strategy of the type described must confront - a problem not dealt with in the simulations in question.

Insofar as the defensive forces are relatively static and dispersed laterally, defenders who are threatened with being overrun in one sector of the defensive net cannot be reinforced by troops from sectors which are not under attack. Attacking points in a defence net which cannot easily be reinforced, the enemy simply has to concentrate enough forces to achieve an eventual breakthrough and thus outflank and envelop the defence. As Canby has noted, 'A passive defence can always be undermined tactically by attacking its non-mutually supporting parts...'[29] It is obviously worth the enemy accepting a very high local attrition rate to achieve such an end.

There are a number of possible responses to this problem. One, advocated by Afheldt, involves the use of longer-range missiles located in rear areas away from the threatened sector of the static defences and able to provide fire support across a wide area of the front. These long-range missile deployments exploit the fact that ET developments enable the defence to concentrate fire power without concentrating forces. Boserup has argued that:

> Functionally, the long-range missiles can be seen as a kind of modern equivalent of the tank formation, only substantially improved. Fire can be concentrated at any point almost simultaneously because it is only the ammunition, not the platform, which is brought to the battle area.[30]

Use of PGMs in this manner is at odds with traditional military wisdom based on Lanchester's famous 'Principle of Concentration', which prescribes concentrating forces to gain numerical superiority in a firefight.[31] However, target coordinates for the long-range missiles may be passed from the concealed light infantry to a more centralised command structure which coordinates the demands for reinforcement and passes them to the appropriate concealed missile batteries which may be up to 100 km away from the battle. (In line with the NPD philosophy of minimising targets for the enemy to shoot at, the missile batteries might be hidden by mounting them in commercial container trucks parked just off the highway.)

Quite apart from very high costs, relatively long-range, 'smart' missiles begin to run into some of the problems which afflict Deep Attack ET systems.[32] The task of hitting targets becomes increasingly exacting as range increases. This is due to the delays which the processes of target-acquisition, transmission of target coordinates and aiming the PGM - plus the missile's flight time to impact - inevitably generate. If the delay is long enough the target will have moved outside the 'footprint' within which the missile's terminal guidance system is effective. Longer range missiles could, however, be used to deliver mines to create mine barriers in front of advancing enemy armour - a task which is less demanding.[33]

Although reliance on long-range missiles in rear areas is very much in line with the no-target philosophy of NPD, it has not been widely supported by NPD analysts. It is seen as relying too much on untested technology and a 'monoculture of weaponry', and as posing command and control problems in effectively linking the infantry net with the remote missile batteries.

In part for the reasons noted above, in part because of cost, and in part because it would require fewer dramatic changes in NATO's force structure, the preferred response of most NPD strategists to the inherent weakness of static defences is the deployment of mobile forces in rear areas. The major task of these 'fire brigade' forces would be to reinforce elements of the relatively passive light infantry nets if they came under sustained attack and could not hold. The task of the attrition net would be to delay the enemy's advance sufficiently to permit the mobile reserve forces to be brought into action. It is conventionally assumed that an attacker needs a 3:1 or 5:1 force ratio advantage over the defence to achieve a breakthrough on a particular front. This means that *ceteris paribus* the offence will have to bring in three to five new fighting units to negate the effect of a single reinforcing unit brought in by the defence.

One of the most developed NPD models, that of Lutz Unterseher's Study Group on Alternative Security Policy, has been described as a 'spiderweb defense'.[34] The infantry nets constitute the 'web' which entangles and slows the intruder. The mobile forces are the 'spiders' which, if necessary, can be brought into play to prevent the intruder from breaking out of the web. In practice, getting the correct balance between 'spider' forces and 'web' forces would obviously be extremely important.

Non-Provocative Air and Naval Strategy

There has been little written by NPD theorists about non-provocative air strategy and still less about naval strategy. Deployment of long-range attack aircraft is seen as destabilising and of dubious efficacy (see below), and in the long run such systems would be phased out in favour of short-range light interceptors and surface-to-air missiles (e.g. *Hawk, Patriot*). The NPD no-target philosophy, the stress on concealment, spoofing and other countermeasures are seen as providing a further degree of protection for the defending forces. There is, however, nothing in the NPD air defence programs which would provide protection against ballistic missile attack. Ballistic missiles mounted with chemical warheads (CW) could have devastating effects on the civilian populations of major cities. This problem is not of course unique to NPD strategies. It applies equally to more conventional defence postures. The CW/ballistic missile threat is a military problem which is resistant to military solutions - insofar as solutions exist, they lie in the realm of politics and arms control.

On the naval side, invasion and long range power-projection platforms (carriers, battleships, nuclear attack submarines, landing craft) tend to be rejected in favour of various coastal defence options - land-based cruise missiles, mines, fast attack craft, helicopters, etc.. Work in this area has, however, been minimal and relatively superficial in comparison with the detailed studies undertaken on NPD land strategies.

The Critique of Non-Provocative Defence Strategies

Defensive strategies, according to their critics, suffer a number of major drawbacks. They concede initiative and surprise to the enemy; they are less efficacious than offensive strategies in actually fighting wars; they cannot win wars; they lack the ability to carry out punishment strikes and hence lack an effective deterrent function. In deliberately eschewing offensive operations - including counter-offensives - defensive strategies simplify the enemy's strategic planning and enable resources which might otherwise have had to be allocated to defence to be allocated instead to the offence and so on.

States which adopt offensive strategies, in contrast, can take the initiative in combat and profit from launching surprise attacks; they can win wars; their ability to threaten punishment enhances their deterrent effect and their ability to strike deep into the enemy's homeland causes him to divert resources to homeland defence.

Let me consider these objections in turn.

1   *Strategic Surprise/Initiative.* The advantages of strategic surprise are overstated in an era of highly sophisticated surveillance devices - a Pearl Harbour-type attack would be inconceivable in Europe today. It is true that a Soviet 'bolt-out-of-the-blue' attack without mobilisation and in a period of non-crisis might surprise NATO, but such an attack is so implausible that few defence planners take it seriously.

Prospects for a successful surprise attack have also been diminished by the confidence-building measures (CBMs) agreed to by both sides at the Stockholm Conference in 1986. These were specifically designed to make surprise attack more difficult. More far-reaching CBMs may be adopted if the current Conventional Forces in Europe (CFE) talks succeed. (CFE was formerly known as the Conventional Stability Talks.)

The claim that NPD concedes the initiative to the offence is also rejected by its proponents. Grin and Unterseher, for example, have argued that:

> Having the initiative does not necessarily mean being continuously one step ahead of the opponent. Rather it means being the one who defines the situation...In the SAS [Study Group on Alternative Security Policy] concept it is possible to define the situation with relatively moderate dynamics. The web structure makes it possible to frustrate an adversary's plans and break his momentum. This can be done directly - attrition everywhere and no easy bypass - and indirectly: by creating a constantly changing problem pattern in cooperation with spider forces.[35]

2   *NPD is Less Militarily Efficacious than Offensive Strategy.* Sweeping generalisations about the relative warfighting efficacy of offensive versus defensive strategies will almost always turn out to be false,[36] while attempts to determine under which conditions one strategic mode may be superior to another can at best be suggestive.[37] The introduction of new weapon systems or defensive technologies may tilt the offence/defence balance of advantage one way or the other over time. Thus, it is generally agreed that during the late Middle Ages the defence prevailed over the offence, whereas between 1450 and 1525, with the introduction of efficient mobile artillery, the balance of advantage had swung back to the offensive.[38]

A more recent example of how changing technology can shift the relative balance of advantage from offence to defence is found in the history of Israel's wars with the Arab states. In June 1967, Israel launched a classic series of offensive, pre-emptive air strikes against the Egyptian Air Force - 300 out of 340 Egyptian aircraft were destroyed within three hours, most of them on the ground. This is often cited as an example of the efficacy of offensive operations - as indeed it was. But in 1967 conditions were particularly propitious for offensive operations by Israel. The Israeli offensive was aided by the fact that Egypt had no airborne early warning and control

(AEW&C) capability to detect attacking Israeli aircraft and coordinate its fighter defences.

In 1982, 15 years after the June War, Israel was again fighting an air war with an Arab state. Yet in the air battles over the Lebanon, Israel fought what tactically was a defensive attrition war against the Syrian Air Force. The Israelis waited for the Syrians to fly into Lebanese air space before responding - they rejected the 1967-style offensive option of attacking Syrian air bases on Syrian soil.

There were a number of reasons for Israel's shift in tactics. First, the Israeli government had no desire to widen an unpopular war by the sort of escalation that direct attacks against Syrian territory would have involved. Second, Syrian air bases were far better defended in 1982 than had been the Egyptian bases in 1967. Third, Israel's capability for fighting a defensive air war was far greater in 1982 than it had been in the earlier war. In 1982, unlike 1967, Israel had sophisticated AEW&C aircraft and highly effective air-to-air missiles (US-made *Sidewinder* and *Sparrow* and Israeli-made *Shafrir II* and *Python 3*) at its disposal. In the aerial engagements over Lebanon the Syrians lost 87 aircraft; the Israelis none. In other words, improvements in defensive technology and tactics made fighting on the tactical defensive far more effective for the Israeli Air Force in 1982 than it could have been in 1967.

A critical variable in these shifts in the offence/defence balance of advantage is technological change and a key question for NATO is whether or not on balance the revolution in surveillance, target-acquisition capabilities and precision-guided munitions favours the defence (as NPD proponents claim) or the offence (as proponents of Deep Attack claim). Since, as noted earlier, almost all the new technologies work more effectively when deployed over short ranges and friendly territory, than at a distance over hostile territory, there are at least *a priori* grounds for believing that NPD strategies will benefit from the technological revolution more than offensive strategies.

There is also some research which supports this assumption at least with respect to airpower:

> ...one careful study has concluded that NATO aircraft attacking enemy airfields will lose as many aircraft as they knock out on the ground. However, NATO's air defences on the central front are expected to shoot down four or five enemy aircraft for each NATO aircraft that is lost in air combat.[39]

In other words, in this example at least, the defensive mode is four to five times more cost effective than the offensive.

3 *Inability to Win Wars.* NPD strategies cannot, it is argued, actually win wars since they make a virtue out of proscribing the very capabilities necessary to achieve victory. Even if defensive strategies can repel an attack, there is nothing to stop the enemy retreating to his secure homeland sanctuaries in order to recuperate, mobilise more forces and return to the offensive. However, as I have argued elsewhere:

> Success in war may be achieved either by destroying an opponent's military capability to wage war or his political capability. Defensively-oriented strategies contribute to the latter objective. Offensive strategies, on the other hand, threaten the national sovereignty of the target state and hence may well increase its national resolve - and hence political capability - to wage war.[40]

Prosecution of a war against a nation which only has a defensive capability makes the war a necessarily limited one for the aggressor, since the survival of the aggressor state is not in question. For this reason, it is frequently difficult to mobilise the full resources of the nation to the war-fighting cause. The prosecution of the war thus has to compete for resources with the pursuit of other national goals. Herein lies the basis for domestic opposition to the war. It is this domestic opposition which undermines the political capability of the state to wage war.[41]

The argument that NPD strategies cannot win wars is only compelling if one accepts the unpersuasive equation of 'victory' with the imposition of a military defeat on the enemy. The Vietnamese were never in a position to pose a military defeat on the US by invading and occupying the US. But that reality was, paradoxically, more a strategic strength than a weakness. It is even possible to prevail politically after being defeated militarily. The FLN resistance fighters were soundly defeated by the French in Algeria but they nevertheless won - i.e. they achieved the objective of their war of independence which was to expel France from Algeria.

4 *NPD Strategies Do Not Provide an Adequate Deterrent.* If deterrence is inadequate, aggression may be encouraged and the risk of war consequently increased. Critics argue that not only do NPD strategies prevent the imposition of military defeat on the enemy, but they also preclude deterrence-by-punishment. This is largely

true, but it does not follow that the deterrent function of NPD strategies is inadequate. Deterrence may be achieved by a number of different means and punishment is only one of them.

Non-provocative defence strategies rely on the deterrent effect of an enemy being denied his wartime objectives. Deterrence-by-denial is predicated on the assumption that the anticipated cost of waging war and not winning will constitute a sufficient deterrent against aggression. This may not be universally true, but there are good reasons for believing that it is true for Europe, over which hangs the shadow of nuclear weapons. Moreover, as John Mearsheimer has argued,

> ...deterrence broadly defined is ultimately a function of the relationship between the perceived political benefits resulting from military action and a number of non-military as well as military costs and risks.[42]

The question of the non-military costs of aggression is largely ignored by the critics of NPD, yet they are crucial. The Soviets are well enough aware that over-extension is the primary cause of imperial decline. Russia played a critical role in bringing down the over-extended Napoleonic and Nazi empires and the Soviets closely observed the decline of the equally over-extended empires of Europe.

During the past few decades it has also become increasingly clear to Moscow that complex, modern industrialised societies simply cannot be run effectively by brute coercion - the active cooperation of citizens is vital. (It is on this fact above all others that non-military defence strategies must depend for their ultimate effect.[43]) So the political disincentive for invading Western Europe for a Soviet Union, which has growing problems controlling Eastern Europe, need hardly be underlined.

Deterrence-by-denial may be seen as imposing lower costs on the aggressor than deterrence-by-punishment and/or deterrence-by-war-winning. It could, therefore, be argued that the latter two approaches constitute more powerful deterrents. But if the anticipated imposition of a certain level of costs is a sufficient deterrent, then the threatened imposition of higher levels of cost is pointless. Moreover, as I shall argue later, offensive strategies designed to enhance deterrence may increase the risk of war by inadvertence.

5   *NPD Strategies Simplify the Enemy's Strategic Planning.* If NATO had
     a purely defensive strategy, WTO war planners could concentrate
     entirely on offensive operations. There would thus be no need for
     them to deploy forces to defend WTO territory and the WTO's
     strategic planning would be considerably simplified. At present
     NATO's offensive capabilities force the WTO states to devote
     considerable resources to homeland defence with correspondingly
     less available for offensive operations.

     There is no doubt that this particular effect of the 'structural
     incapacity for offence' is a major military weakness of the purely
     defensive NPD models. One elegant solution to this problem has
     been suggested by Albrecht von Muller, whose NPD model
     incorporates what he calls a 'conditional retaliation capability'
     embodied in mobile armoured forces deployed behind the attrition
     net. In a pre-war situation these mobile forces are insufficiently
     powerful to pose any offensive threat to WTO forces. If, however,
     the WTO forces attack first they will suffer considerable attrition as
     they attempt to penetrate NATO's defensive barriers. This attrition
     will change the balance of mobile forces in NATO's favour. 'From
     this it follows', von Muller argues, 'that - in conditional
     dependency on a preceding attack by the other side - far-reaching
     counterattacks could become an option for the defender.'[44]
     Recognition of this fact would force WTO planners to allocate
     resources to defending WTO territory. The 'conditional retaliation
     capability' could also provide NATO with a limited degree of
     deterrence-by-punishment and provide forces to regain NATO
     territory occupied by the enemy - which purely passive defences, of
     course, cannot do.

6   *Non-Provocative Defence in Rejecting Nuclear Weapons Undermines
     Deterrence.* Here it is claimed that in rejecting nuclear deterrence
     NPD strategies increase the threat to a NATO which is outgunned
     in conventional forces by the Warsaw Pact. In fact most NPD
     proponents, with the exception of a few British advocates and those
     who support non-military or civilian defence, see nuclear weapons
     as playing an important role in NATO strategy.[45] However nuclear
     weapons are not seen as an integral part of NATO's broad
     spectrum of war-fighting capabilities, but simply as a deterrent
     against nuclear use by the USSR. Most NPD theorists support a no-
     first-use of nuclear weapons stance for NATO and almost all would
     want tactical nuclear weapons completely removed from Europe.
     The preferred NPD basing mode option for nuclear weapons is
     submarines.

Critics argue that such a posture will undermine deterrence. But no convincing arguments have been adduced to show how the Soviets will have a greater incentive to contemplate unprovoked aggression if nuclear weapons are relegated to a minimum deterrent instead of a war-fighting role.

It is also argued that NATO's threats to use its sea-based strategic nuclear weapons in the context of a land war in Europe are not very credible. This may well be true but nuclear threats are not very credible now. As noted earlier, however, the credibility of threats is only one element in the deterrence equation. The other is the level of costs imposed if the threat is carried out. It is the unthinkably large - and invariant - cost factor which makes nuclear deterrence robust even when nuclear threats are not very credible.

The mutual possession of nuclear weapons by the superpowers may in fact strengthen the argument for defensive strategies. Anders Boserup argues that the mere existence of nuclear weapons has profoundly changed the nature of conventional war in Europe: 'Should it come to war the overriding concern of the belligerents would be to avoid or to limit escalation...'[46] From this perspective the existence of nuclear weapons makes the classic Clausewitzian prescription of escalation to maximum force levels a recipe for disaster. In such a situation - which Boserup describes as 'sub-nuclear' - the defence has two critical tasks. One is to fight as effectively as possible to avoid being defeated. The other is to decrease the risk of the nuclear threshold being crossed - which means abjuring from offensive escalation. Only NPD strategies, it is argued, can satisfy both demands.

Crisis Avoidance and Crisis Stability

The discussion thus far has been centred almost entirely with the debate about relative efficacy of NPD versus more traditional strategies as modes of waging war. However, although critically important, war-fighting ability is not the only criterion by which a security policy should be judged. Equally important is its ability to prevent war.

As already noted, proponents of traditional strategies claim that they provide a more credible and effective deterrent against aggression than the NPD alternatives. Proponents of NPD, for their part, argue that their preferred policies provide an adequate deterrent against aggression and that no more than this is necessary. They also claim that NPD strategies are far superior with respect to preventing inadvertent war. There are a number of reasons for this.

First, NPD strategies signal to the WTO NATO's unambiguously defensive intentions. Such strategies and their attendant forces postures act to dispel the suspicion, tension and hostility which are the natural concomitants of highly offensive strategies - as NATO's reactions to the highly offensive WTO doctrine demonstrate. Reduced tension, suspicion and hostility minimise the probability of crises occurring in the first place. Second, defensive strategies remove entirely all incentives for an opponent to resort to pre-emptive or preventive war - i.e. they enhance both crisis avoidance and crisis stability. Third, with NPD, full mobilisation of NATO forces will not be perceived as provocative. This is of considerable importance since:

> The great fear, shared by NATO generals of all nationalities, is that political leaders would waste time fretting about appearing provocative and withhold authority to make some essential movements until it is too late.[47]

Fourth, defensive strategies complement broader policies of common security. Indeed they are an integral part of many common security proposals. Preventing inadvertent war is the central objective of all common security proposals. Fifth, defensive strategies facilitate progress in arms control since they enhance crisis stability. Indeed NPD strategies, if adopted mutually, become a form of arms control.

Sixth, if adopted mutually, defensive strategies eliminate incentives for arms races. If one side's force posture cannot be used for aggression then if its defensive capability is strengthened by adding new weapons, this will pose no threat to the other side and will require no response. If, however, both sides have offensive force structures, adding weapons to increase the offensive capabilities of one side creates new targets for the other side - and an incentive to build countervailing systems to destroy them. This is a recipe for arms racing.

Proponents of offensive and proponents of defensive strategies each accuse the other of promoting policies which increase the risk of war. The former argue that NPD is at best naive, at worst a form of appeasement; it undermines deterrence and so increases the risk of aggression. NPD proponents counter by arguing that offensive strategies undermine crisis-avoidance policies by fuelling suspicion of hostility and encouraging 'worst case' assumptions to prevail. They also undermine crisis stability by increasing incentives for pre-emption in crises when war appears either likely or inevitable, and for rapid escalation if the threshold to violent conflict is crossed. Thus, offensive strategies designed to enhance deterrence may increase the risks of inadvertent war.

If it makes sense to choose a security policy at least in part in terms of its probable success in avoiding war, the critical question then becomes, 'What is the most probable cause of war in Europe?' The answer to this question seems to command near-universal consensus among strategic analysts. Insofar as there is any risk of war in Europe it does not derive from unprovoked Soviet aggression against NATO. Given the existence of nuclear weapons and a finite possibility that they might be used, the possible costs of aggression vastly outweigh any possible benefits. The least improbable cause of war is a crisis sliding out of control and plunging the two alliances into a violent conflict that neither originally sought.

If this line of reasoning is accepted, it follows that, at least with respect to avoiding armed conflict, the highest priority security task should not be the enhancement of an already adequate deterrent, but the reduction of the risk of war by inadvertence. There is no doubt that NPD strategies are superior in this regard.

Non-Provocative Defence as a Unilateral or Bilateral Policy

Over the past four years NPD concepts have gained increasing support and become part of the mainstream European security discourse (especially in Germany and Denmark). In December 1986, the North Atlantic Council stated that armed forces should 'focus on the elimination of the capability for surprise attack or for the initiation of large scale offensive actions.'[48] Support for the idea of reducing offensive forces has also come from West German Foreign Minister, Hans Dietrich Genscher, who told a conference in St Paul, Minnesota in December 1987 that, 'No country should have the capability for attack, all should be capable of defence only.'[49] The German Social Democrats firmly support the concept of non-provocative defence. It is also worth noting that '...many of the components of "non-offensive" defence are already being incorporated into NATO strategy.'[50]

However, for a variety of reasons, it is most unlikely that NATO will unilaterally adopt an unambiguously defensive posture. This is partly for the serious doubts (noted above) which NPD strategies continue to raise and partly for political reasons. Not only would gaining NATO-wide consensus on a shift to a defence-dominant force posture be almost impossible to achieve, but the idea of defence-in-depth which all NPD strategies embrace is unlikely to be acceptable to Bonn for some considerable time. As Mearsheimer has pointed out:

> ...successive West German governments have made it unequivocally clear that they will reject any strategy that requires NATO to surrender territory, however temporary it

may be and to fight major battles in the heart of West Germany.[51]

The discussion thus far has reviewed some of the arguments for and against the adoption of NPD unilaterally. It has assumed that the WTO states continue to maintain their traditionally offensive strategy. Indeed, to understand the strategic logic which underpins NPD policies one must assume that the other side's strategy is offensive. However, there is no doubt that a shift on both sides towards defence-dominant force postures would be far preferable to their unilateral adoption by NATO alone. As Boserup, one of the leading European NPD theorists, put it recently:

> Attractive as the concept of non-offensive defense was in principle, it had a hard case to make when presented from a unilateralist perspective. There was no way to prove that more defensive postures in the West would ever be copied in the East. Many therefore saw it as an unsound gamble, with real military risks and only hypothetical political benefits.[52]

In the early 1980s, most proposals for NPD argued the case for unilateral adoption by NATO of a defensive policy, not least because there seemed little prospect that the Soviets would be willing to change a traditionally highly offensive doctrine which had a clear military logic. The Soviets know that they cannot afford a long drawn out war with NATO since the potential mobilisation base of the economically far stronger NATO powers would enable them to prevail in the long run (assuming the war stayed conventional). Traditional Soviet doctrine has, therefore, always stressed the necessity of imposing a rapid defeat on NATO forces on European soil so that Soviet forces could reach the Atlantic seaboard as swiftly as possible to cut-off American reinforcements. Only a highly offensive strategy can achieve such a goal.

By 1986, however, there were signs of what seemed to be a remarkable change in attitude on the WTO side. Meeting that year in Budapest, the Pact states proposed the idea of a mutual reduction in offensive capabilities. In May 1987, leading Western European NPD analysts, Boserup, von Muller, von Bulow and Nield, plus von Hippel from the US, were invited to the Soviet Union for consultations on NPD strategies. Also in May that year the communique of the WTO Political Consultative Committee meeting in Berlin stressed the need to:

> ...ensure the mutual withdrawal of the most dangerous offensive weapons from the zone of direct contact between the two military alliances and to reduce the concentration of armed

forces and armaments in this zone to an agreed minimum level.[53]

In September 1987, Mr Gorbachev, in an article in *Pravda*, wrote of the need to create a force structure that 'suffices for the prevention of possible aggression, but is insufficient for attack'.[54] In September 1988, Soviet Defence Minister Yazov argued in the *Bulletin of the Atomic Scientists* in support of mutual force reductions which would leave:

> ...both sides with such numbers of armed forces and weapons as would be sufficient for defense but insufficient for offensive purposes...At any stage we are prepared for mutual reductions in offensive arms - above all - tactical nuclear weapons, strike tactical aircraft, and tanks.[55]

Yazov's public affirmation of support for the Gorbachev line was interesting since he has been described as being among those who 'vigorously oppose substantive changes in Soviet military doctrine.'[56]

In December 1988, Mr Gorbachev announced that Soviet military forces would be cut by 500,000 troops and 10,000 tanks (including half of those in Eastern Europe). In January 1989, he stated that the Soviet military budget would be cut by 14.2 per cent and the output of the defence industry cut by a fifth. A number of East European states have also indicated their intention to initiate defence cuts. These actions are consistent with the Soviet leadership's new stress on defensiveness and common security and may well also be a response to Western demands that the Soviets back up their conciliatory words with deeds.

There is no doubt, however, that sectors of the Soviet military oppose both unilateral defence cuts and a shift away from the traditionally highly offensive Soviet force posture. Some elements in the military, while paying lip service to the idea of a defensive strategy, seek to maintain powerful forces for counter-offensives. Such forces are, of course, identical to those needed for aggression. But, at least at the political level, this approach seems increasingly to be rejected. In January 1989, Karpov, the Soviet Deputy Foreign Minister, told a press conference that:

> After the war, our experience was reflected on the assumption of a combination of a defensive national doctrine and methods of offensive combat operations...We have reconsidered that assumption...there are now no considerations of major offensive operations. Our defense involves...standing firm and making the transition to the political settlement of conflicts.[57]

Pressures for Soviet offensive doctrine to be changed have come from the increasingly influential Moscow 'think tanks', such as the Institute for the USA and Canada. Mr Gorbachev has been strongly supportive, but who will prevail in the long term in the conflict between the military traditionalists and the new reformers is difficult to say. It is worth noting, however, that a shift to a more defensive force posture and cuts in the defence budget would not only improve relations with the West, which the Soviets clearly desire, but would also release desperately needed investment funds and other resources for the revitalisation of the stagnant civilian economy.

There is some evidence that thus far, at least, Mr Gorbachev's line seems to be prevailing. The idea of unilateral defence cuts, for example, had been strongly and publicly opposed by Defence Minister Yazov and by former Chief of Staff Akromeyev. Yet the strong military opposition did not prevent such cuts being announced by Mr Gorbachev.

Conclusion

Given that both the Soviets and NATO are publicly committed to the idea of reducing the capabilities both for surprise attack and for large scale offensive operations, prospects for successful negotiations on these points at the new Conventional Forces in Europe talks might appear to be good. There remain real difficulties, however. NATO is still suspicious about Moscow's apparent change in strategy and the Pact states find NATO's stance on offensive systems quite unsatisfactory.

In January 1989, the Soviets released for the first time detailed figures of their troop and forces levels in Europe. In doing so the Soviets were conceding publicly just how great an imbalance exists between the WTO and NATO forces in certain categories of offensive weapons - most obviously tanks. Moscow says it is prepared to reduce the asymmetries which work in its favour but NATO must be prepared to cut back in areas where Moscow claims the West has a clear advantage: frontline strike aircraft, combat helicopters, anti-tank weapons and naval forces. NATO disagrees about some of the Soviet figures but this is only part of the problem.

NATO currently seems only to want cuts in forces which can 'seize and hold territory' - e.g. tanks and other offensive systems where the Soviets have an advantage. NATO is resistant to the idea of strike aircraft and missiles which can strike deep into an enemy's territory being controlled. NATO also rejects the idea that its powerful naval forces should be taken into account in assessing the European balance - even though naval strike aircraft could be used in the European theatre.

NATO's negotiating position is made extremely difficult by the deep disagreements on a wide range of strategic issues which continue to divide the allies. It would be unfortunate to say the least if these differences prevent NATO from making some of the concessions which will be necessary on both sides if an agreement is ever to be reached at the CFE talks in Vienna and if military forces are to be restructured so as to reduce the risk of inadvertent war in Europe - the only risk of any consequence today.

Endnotes

1   This term has the virtue of a high level of generality - i.e. it covers just about all the different approaches under discussion.   A force structure could have a limited offensive (or counter-offensive) capability and still be non-provocative - though it would not be purely defensive or non-offensive.

2   Jonathan Dean, *Watershed in Europe: Dismantling the East-West Military Confrontation*, (Lexington Books, Lexington, 1987), p.13.

3   General Sir Hugh Beach, 'On Improving NATO Strategy', in Andrew J. Pierre (ed.), *The Conventional Defence of Europe: New Technologies and New Strategies, (Council on Foreign Relations, New York, 1986), pp.160-1.*

4   Henry Kissinger, 'The Future of NATO', in Kenneth Myers (ed.), *NATO: The Next Thirty Years*, (Westview, Boulder, 1978), p.8.

5   The poll is part of a study called 'Americans Talk Security' and was reported in *Defense News*, 2 January 1989, p.2.

6   See, for example, Desmond Ball, *Can Nuclear War Be Controlled?* (Adelphi Paper No.169, International Institute for Strategic Studies, London, 1981) and 'Controlling Theatre Nuclear War', *Working Paper No.138*, (Strategic and Defence Studies Centre, Australian National University, Canberra, 1988); Paul Bracken, *The Command and Control of Nuclear Forces*, (Yale University Press, New Haven, 1973); and Bruce G. Blair, *Strategic Command and Control: Redefining the Nuclear Threat*, (Brookings Institution, Washington D.C., 1985).

7   Colin S. Gray, 'War-Fighting for Deterrence', *The Journal of Strategic Studies*, March 1984, p.11.

8   Robert Jervis, *The Illogic of American Nuclear Strategy*, (Cornell University Press, Ithaca, 1984) p.156.

9   Andrew Mack, 'Conclusion' to Desmond Ball and Andrew Mack (eds.), *The Future of Arms Control*, (Pergamon Press, Sydney, 1987), p.312-3.

10   See *ibid.* for a detailed argument of why this is the case.

11   T.C. Schelling, 'The Reciprocal Fear of Surprise Attack', (The RAND Corporation, P-1342, Santa Monica, California, 28 May 1958), p.1.

12   Robert D. Glasser, *Nuclear Pre-Emption and Crisis Stability, 1985-1990*, (Canberra Papers on Strategy and Defence No.37, Strategic and Defence Studies Centre, Australian National University, Canberra, 1986), p.70.

13   Boyd D. Sutton *et.al.*, 'Deep Attack Concepts and the Defence of Central Europe', *Survival*, (Vol.XXVI), March/April 1984, p.2.

14   Peter Arnold, 'Long Range Defense Program Gaining Pentagon "Support"', *Washington Times*, 14 November 1988, p.4.

15   See, for example, Steven L. Canby, 'The Conventional Defense of Europe: the Operational Limits of Emerging Technology', *Working Paper No.55*, (International Security Studies Program, Smithsonian Institution, The Wilson Center, April 1984).

16   Steven Canby, 'Can Non-Provocative Defence Provide Atlantic Security?', in Frank Barnaby and Marlies Ter Borg (eds.), *Emerging Technologies and Military Doctrine*, (Macmillan, London, 1986), p.216.

17   See Philip Williams and William Wallace, 'Emerging Technologies and European Security', *Survival*, (Vol.XXVI, No.2), March/April 1984, p.786.

18   See Christopher Donnelly, 'Soviet Operational Concepts in the 1980s', in *Strengthening Conventional Deterrence in Europe*, Report of the European Security Study, (St. Martin's Press, London, 1983); and Canby, 'The Conventional Defence of Europe'.

19   Bracken, *The Command and Control of Nuclear Forces.*

20   *Pugwash Newsletter*, (Vol.23, No.4), April 1986, p.113.

21   Cited in Barnaby and Ter Borg, *Emerging Technologies*, p.276.

22   David Gates, 'Area Defence Concepts: the West German Debate', *Survival*, July/August 1987, p.302.

23   Albrecht von Muller, 'Structural Stability on the Central Front: A Plaidoyer for a Systematic Integration of Doctrine, Procurement and Arms Control', (Max Planck Institute, Starnberg, 1985), p.11. One NPD strategy which relies almost entirely on the 'fire barrier' concept is that of Col. Norbert Hannig. See his 'Deterrence by Conventional Weapons: the David-Goliath Principle', in Hylke Tromp (ed.), *Non-Nuclear War in Europe: Alternatives for Nuclear Defence*, (Groningen University Press, Groningen, 1984). In most other NPD models the 'fire barrier' plays no role.

24   Although the military utility of passive defences is widely recognised and highly cost effective, they are politically difficult to implement in Germany because, like the Berlin Wall, they are seen as physical manifestations of the division of the two Germanies. The fact that the Germans are so willing to sacrifice military utility for political symbolism suggests that they are very relaxed about the military threat from the East. Interestingly there has not been a great deal of emphasis on disengagement zones in the NPD literature.

25   See Anders Boserup, 'The Strategy of Non-Offensive Defence', *Working Paper No.2* (Peace Research Centre, Australian National University, Canberra, 1986), for an extended discussion of the no-target goal.

26   Hans W. Hoffman, Reiner K. Huber and Karl Steiger, 'On Reactive Defense Options: a Comparative Systems Analysis of Alternatives for the Initial Defense Against the First Strategic Echelon of the Warsaw Pact in Central Europe', (Institut fur Angewandte Systemforschung and Operations Research, Hochschule for Bundeswehr Munchen, Berich Nr. S-8403, November 1984).

27   *Ibid.*, p.2.

28   *Ibid.*, p.19.

29   Canby, 'Can Non-Provocative Defence Provide Atlantic Security?', p.217.

30   Boserup, 'The Strategy of Non-Offensive Defence', p.7.

31   See Robert Nield, 'Implications of the Increasing Accuracy of Non-Nuclear Weapons', *Arms Control*, (Vol.7, No.1), May 1986, for a detailed discussion of this issue.

32   However, target acquisition for the longer range PGMs would be much easier than for strikes against mobile targets deep inside enemy territory since the targets would be identified by NATO forces on their own territory. Enemy countermeasures would also be more difficult to implement when enemy forces were operating on NATO territory rather than their own.

33   Since the position of mines thus delivered cannot be known with any precision such barriers could also cause major problems for the mobile forces of the defence.

34   See John Grin and Lutz Unterseher, 'The Spiderweb Defense', *Bulletin of the Atomic Scientists*, September 1988. For a more detailed discussion of concepts developed by the Study Group on Alternative Security Policy, see Lutz Unterseher, 'Defending Europe: Toward a Stable Deterrent', (Center for Philosophy and Public Policy, University of Maryland, 1987).

35   Grin and Unterseher, 'The Spiderweb Defense', p.30.

36   It is important to note here that although one can talk about defensive **strategies** and **force structures** (those with a 'structural incapacity for offence') one cannot talk about a defensive **weapon** as such. As Richard Nixon once observed, a warrior with a sword and shield is more dangerous than a warrior with a shield alone. The 'defensive' shield is in effect a 'force multiplier' and enhances the offensive capabilities of the warrior.

37   See Jack S. Levy, 'The Offensive/Defensive Balance of Military Technology: A Theoretical and Historical Analysis', *International Studies Quarterly*, (Vol.28, No.2), 1984; and Stephen Van Evera, 'Offense, Defense and Strategy: When is Offense Best?', (Center for Science and International Affairs, Harvard University, March 1987).

38   Levy, 'The Offensive/Defensive Balance', p.239.

39   'NATO's Central Front', *Economist*, 30 August 1986, p.19.

40   Andrew Mack, 'Offence Versus Defence: the Dibb Report and Its Critics', *Australian Outlook*, (Vol.41, No.1), April 1987, p.5.

41   For a detailed exposition of this argument see Andrew Mack, 'Why Big Nations Lose Small Wars: the Politics of Asymmetric Conflict', *World Politics*, (Vol.XXVII, No.2), 1975.

42   John J. Mearsheimer, *Conventional Deterrence*, (Cornell University Press, Ithaca, 1983), p.14.

43   See Anders Boserup and Andrew Mack, *War Without Weapons: Non-Violence in National Defence*, (Schocken, New York, 1975), for an extended discussion of this issue.

44   Albrecht von Muller, 'Conventional Stability in Europe: Outlines of the Military Hardware for a Second Detente', (Max Planck Society, Starnberg, 1987), p.23.

45   British supporters of NPD who reject nuclear weapons include Dan Smith and Michael Randle. Smith is author of 'Non-nuclear Military Options for Britain', *Peace Studies Papers No.6*, (Bradford School of Peace Studies, Bradford, 1982); Randle was one of the major authors of *Defence Without the Bomb*, (Taylor and Francis, London, 1983). On non-military defence see Gene Sharp, *Making Europe Unconquerable*, (Ballinger, Cambridge, 1986); and Boserup and Mack, *War Without Weapons*.

46   Boserup, 'The Strategy of Non-Offensive Defence', p.1.

47   'NATO's Central Front', p.7.

48   Cited in *Non-Offensive Defence*, No.6, May 1987, p.8.

49   Cited in *Non-Offensive Defence*, No.8, February 1988, p.8.

50   Jeffrey Boutwell *et.al.*, *Countdown on Conventional Forces in Europe: A Briefing Book*, (American Academy of Arts and Sciences and Ploughshares Fund, Cambridge, 1988), p.14.

51   John J. Mearsheimer, 'Nuclear Weapons and Deterrence in Europe', in Hylke Tromp (ed.), *Non-Nuclear War in Europe*, (Groningen University Press, Groningen, 1986), p.10.

52   Anders Boserup, 'A Way to Undermine Hostility', *Bulletin of the Atomic Scientists*, September 1988, p.19.

53   Cited in *Non-Offensive Defence*, No.7, September 1987, p.9.

54   Cited in *Non-Offensive Defence*, No.8, February 1988, p.13.

55   Dmitri Yazog, 'The Soviet Proposal for European Security', *Bulletin of the Atomic Scientists*, September 1988, p.9.

56   R. Jeffrey Smith, 'In Moscow, Debate on the Military Role', *International Herald Tribune*, 1 August 1988.

57   'Differing Soviet, NATO Arms Tallies Could Derail Talks', *Washington Times*, 1 February 1989.

CHAPTER 9

ARMS CONTROL

J.L. Richardson

The negotiation of arms control measures in the 1980s has taken place in a quite different political climate from that of the 1960s and 1970s. During those decades, as the Cold War gave way to detente, and this in turn eroded in the tensions of the late 1970s, protracted negotiations led to the achievement of a considerable number of arms control agreements. Although these were of limited scope and in no way amounted to a fundamental change in strategic relationships, they contributed to a general sense that there had been a lessening of the dangers of the nuclear age.

This view of the arms control record was challenged by a school of strategic analysts close to the Reagan Administration, who questioned the value of past agreements and made much of allegations of Soviet non-compliance with some of their provisions. The arms control negotiations of the early 1980s reverted to the rhetorical style of the 1950s: one-sided proposals were advanced in the name of appealing slogans, and Soviet diplomacy which appealed to Western public opinion over the heads of the negotiators, seeking to bring public pressure to bear on the NATO governments to abandon their proposed deployment of intermediate-range nuclear forces (INF), with no countervailing restriction on themselves. There was again a heightened sense of the dangers of the nuclear arms race.

During the second Reagan Administration, however, there was a sudden flurry of ambitious arms control initiatives. At the Reykjavik summit conference, in October 1986, an agreement on radical nuclear arms reductions *appeared* to be within reach, but for the deadlock between the two superpowers over the proposed US Strategic Defense Initiative (SDI). Subsequently the two accepted the principle of the 'zero option' for intermediate-range nuclear forces (INF) and a treaty to eliminate this class of weapons was signed in December 1987.

This chapter seeks to place these paradoxical developments in perspective by returning to the original concept of arms control as it was formulated three decades ago, and by examining some of the problems to which that concept gives rise. The arms control record and the recent developments are then appraised in the light of this discussion.

The Concept

Although some aspects of arms control have earlier precedents, the concept as a whole is new, dating from intensive discussions among policy makers and scholars in the late 1950s of the issues raised by the nuclear age.[1] Unlike many of the ideas generated at that time, it became the basis for substantial policies and, at the same time, it took on powerful symbolic connotations, partly because it was widely regarded as replacing the concept of disarmament. Disarmament negotiations had become a ritual in which the parties, solemnly proclaiming their adherence to utopian goals, advanced deceptively appealing proposals, but made no serious attempt to negotiate practical agreements. In the view of the new strategic analysts, the problems of unrestrained arms competition were too serious to be left to this quasi-negotiation process, but required not only a change of negotiating style but also a new concept. Its essential elements may be summed up as follows.[2]

The Basic Principles of Arms Control

(i)   *The concept* of arms control is broader than that of disarmament - the abolition or reduction of armaments. Arms control includes all limitations on armaments, unilateral as well as negotiated, which are directed towards its essential goals. Thus, in addition to arms reductions, it includes for example, the setting of limits at, or even above, existing levels, the renunciation of specified new weapons systems, and restrictions on the development or use of weapons.

(ii)   *The goals* of arms control are generally taken to be, in order of priority: to reduce the risk of war, especially nuclear war; to reduce its destructiveness, if it should occur; and to reduce the cost of military preparedness. An important implication of this ranking of goals is that disarmament, the reduction of arms, is not *necessarily* desirable: not, for example, if it endangers the primary goal, reducing the risk of war. It is not assumed, as orthodox disarmament doctrine had tended to, that agreed measures of disarmament would *ipso facto* achieve this. In the nuclear age, this ranking of goals is not controversial in principle, but (as discussed below), its application to particular cases may present difficulties.

(iii)   *The continuation of international political conflict* is an explicit assumption of the arms control theory. With respect to the superpower conflict, which formed the focus of most of the early writing, it was postulated that although a settlement of the basic political issues was unlikely, the two powers had an interest in concerting their policies in order to render it less likely that in pursuit of those rivalries they would 'escalate' particular conflicts in ways which would increase the risk of nuclear war. Insofar as the arms competition, or the mode of deployment of nuclear weapons, could increase the incentive to use them in a tense crisis - the incentive to pre-empt - there was a shared incentive to avoid such situations. In the language of game theory, the superpower relationship was not a zero-sum game, cold war rhetoric notwithstanding. In the language of Soviet doctrine, peaceful coexistence was an imperative necessity of the nuclear age, but it did not put an end to ideological conflict.

Arms control theory assumes a continuing need for a military balance between the superpowers. More controversially, it postulates that arms control can be decoupled from the on-going political rivalry to a significant extent. In other words, it does not, as disarmament is often said to do, depend on the prior settlement of the political rivalry. Arms control was not initially advocated as promoting, or depending on, political detente in the way that these came to be linked in public discussion in the 1970s.

(iv) *Arms control has an integral relationship to sound military policy.* This does not imply the acceptance of the military *status quo*, including existing force structures, deployments and plans, but implies a detailed concern with precisely these matters with a view to eliminating those features which could (like the mobilisation plans of the European powers in July 1914) introduce sudden and inexorable pressures towards war which are not understood by political decision-makers. The measures promoting arms control in this sense may be unilateral as much as formal negotiated agreements.

(v) International measures can include *informal understandings* as well as formal agreements. This aspect of arms control thinking can be problematic: for example, is there a tacit understanding that each of the superpowers refrains from directly attacking the other's armed forces? How can such an understanding be substantiated? In principle, it is plausible that there may be an informal acceptance of certain restraints which cannot be part of a formal agreement - in the case of spheres of influence, for example - but it is not clear that there are informal agreements on arms control.

(vi) Although it was not a central tenet of the early arms control doctrine that arms control measures would normally be of *limited scope,* in contrast to the comprehensive agreements typical of traditional disarmament proposals, this is in the spirit of the doctrine. Arms control proposals were seen as a response to *specific* concerns, specific sources of instability, not as part of an endeavour to achieve structural change in the bases of national and international security.

(vii)   Arms controllers advocated greater *public candour* in the arms debate and negotiations. If, as they assumed, the goal of general and complete disarmament, officially proclaimed in the 1960s, was patently unrealistic, continued lip-service to it perpetuated confusion and cynicism in the public debate. Not only should democratic governments promote an informed public opinion as a matter of principle, but uninformed opinion may be more readily manipulated by adversary governments, especially those whose proposals are not subject to critical scrutiny by their own public.

(viii)   Given the focus on the avoidance of nuclear war by the superpowers, arms control writers came to emphasise two more concrete, intermediate goals - *strategic stability* and *crisis stability*. The former refers to a situation, often termed stable mutual deterrence, in which a nuclear 'first strike' is manifestly not a rational policy option for either superpower.   The concept of crisis stability acknowledges the possibility that there could nonetheless, under conditions of acute crisis, be actions which escape the control of the decision-makers, or incentives for a pre-emptive strike if the adversary were believed to be preparing to attack. 'Crisis stability' refers to the situation where both kinds of incentive, to escalate and to pre-empt, are low.

Criteria and Problems

The concept of arms control provides criteria by which specific agreements or proposals may be evaluated, but the application of these criteria may require difficult judgments. For example, a proposal may be well designed to reduce the risk of pre-emption, but its value will depend on whether there is a significant risk of pre-emption in the first place, and on this there may be legitimate differences of judgment. Or a proposal may, to some, appear likely to weaken deterrence, while to others, deterrence may appear sufficiently assured that it can safely be pursued at lower cost.

In general, the effects of arms reductions in decreasing the expected destructiveness of war or the costs of preparedness are easier to determine than the effects of arms control measures on the probability of war. In view of the arcane and controversial nature of judgments about the latter, it is not surprising that the notion of disarmament (arms reductions) has greater political appeal than the austere doctrine of arms control, even though its priority for strategic stability and crisis stability would be widely endorsed.

In principle, there may be trade-offs among the goals of arms control, but in practice, once again, these are difficult to determine, except in extreme cases. For example, it would be widely agreed that the abolition of nuclear weapons would make a great power war more likely as well as less destructive, but how great a reduction in nuclear arms is possible before deterrence is seriously weakened? The answers are widely divergent.

The validity of the theory of arms control has been questioned, and the problems which critics have identified have presented major difficulties for policy makers. The most fundamental of these concern the relationship between arms control and politics. It is often claimed that arms control measures cannot in fact reduce the likelihood of war. The causes of war, it is maintained, are to be found in fundamental conflicts of economic and political interest between states, and arms races and deployments merely reflect these more basic tensions. But while this argument shows that arms control is not all-important, it over-simplifies the complex processes which lead to war. The underlying conflicts may be the main reason for the onset of a crisis, but the decisions taken in crises have multiple causes, which include the characteristics of existing military capabilities, deployments and plans. The historical example of the consequences of mobilisation plans in 1914 shows that decision makers can find themselves trapped with fewer options than they had assumed, or desperately needed. In any crisis between nuclear powers, however acute the political conflicts which might bring it about, the decision makers will have even greater incentives to avoid the final steps to war. Arms control measures may improve their chances of doing so. Consideration of the objection does not negate the importance of crisis stability, but serves to further underline it.

However, measures to enhance crisis stability - except for the original hot-line agreement, which captured the public imagination - tend to be undramatic, and the whole topic lacks political salience, indeed may be repugnant to the general public. Arms reductions or even arms ceilings lend themselves far more readily to political salesmanship, irrespective of their actual consequences. Thanks to such salesmanship, arms limitations since the early 1970s have become inextricably associated in the public mind with detente. As symbols of this state of affairs, they suffered much of the discredit of the detente itself in influential circles in the early 1980s. Moreover, the recent moves towards agreements on arms control have been greeted as a return to detente after the 'new cold war' of the preceding years.

This is entirely contrary to the original logic of arms control. It is precisely in moments of acute conflict that arms control agreements are most needed. And, indeed, there was some acceptance in the early 1980s of the view that arms control negotiations should continue, despite the strained political relations between the superpowers. But the relationship between arms control and detente presents further complexities. *Prima facie*, a period of reduced tension reduces the incidence of crises, and thus the threat of war. If arms control agreements contribute to reducing tensions, this may be as significant a consequence as their contribution to crisis stability - at least in the short run. It is likely, however, that the more fundamental causes of detente are indeed political, at a deeper level - in particular, the consolidation of global relationships since the mid-1960s - such that the artificial revival of a cold war atmosphere in the 1980s did not in fact generate crises as in the Cold War proper. If this is so, then the short-term contribution of arms control agreements to detente need not be disparaged. The primary criteria for evaluating them remain their likely contribution to the three goals stated above.

Certain other problems which have become evident in the contemporary arms control negotiations were already prominent in earlier discussions of disarmament. It was in this context that Hans Morgenthau identified the problem of the ratio: given the different geographical and strategic circumstances of different states, how can agreements establish levels of force acceptable to all parties?[3] Equal levels will not affect each party equally, but asymmetrical agreements tend to raise political objections. Congressional reaction against the unequal numbers of ballistic missiles provided for the SALT I agreement, for example, led to an insistence that future agreements specify equal numbers of delivery vehicles, even though other matters not regulated in the agreement (such as the number of warheads and their accuracy and yield) represent more serious dangers to strategic stability. The same sort of problem underlies the protracted stalemate in the talks on mutual and balanced force reductions (MBFR) in Europe, and reappears in the negotiations over strategic nuclear force reductions.

Problems of verification and compliance have arisen in a variety of contexts. National means of verification have been deemed adequate in the case of the SALT agreements, but have long been the subject of controversy in the case of a projected comprehensive test ban. Some important matters which cannot be verified, such as missile accuracies, have remained unregulated. In the case of the Non-Proliferation Treaty, significant verification procedures have been implemented, providing a degree of assurance of compliance, but no absolute guarantee. The 'unprecedented intrusiveness' of the inspection provisions of the INF

Treaty reflects the perceived need for a higher level of assurance in this context.

A final problem which needs to be noted is technological change. An arms control agreement may be drafted in such a way that it does not address the problems created by new technologies or, even if it attempts to do so, one or more parties may judge that these lead to changes of such consequence that their interests are no longer served by the agreement. In the view of some American analysts, the ABM Treaty, for example, is now called in question on one or both of these grounds.

The Pattern

The arms control agreements since the early 1960s may be grouped under four headings: nuclear testing and non-proliferation; strategic arms limitation; restrictions on deployment; and crisis stability and confidence-building. The principal agreements are listed in Table 1.4 The following comments draw attention to some of the more significant of them.

Testing and Non-Proliferation: The Partial Test Ban Treaty, together with the hot line agreement, symbolised the acceptance by the superpowers of the new approach to arms control and were widely perceived as important steps towards detente. The test ban did not, however, place significant restrictions on arms developments. Moreover, until recently, differences over verification prevented agreement on a comprehensive test ban, or at least provided the ostensible obstacle to agreement, such that the superpowers did not have to confront seriously the question whether a ban would serve their security interests. Subsequently, new obstacles to a comprehensive test ban have emerged in the 1980s.

The Nuclear Non-Proliferation Treaty, the most ambitious multilateral arms control agreement up to the present, has given rise to an extensive literature.[5] Despite its familiar limitations - the absence of sanctions, the absence of clear provisions which would restrain parties from approaching the nuclear weapons threshold, and above all the absence of impediments to determined 'near-nuclear' states which are resolved to acquire their own nuclear option - it is at the centre of the attempt by the superpowers, with the support of the majority of states, to restrict the spread of nuclear weapons. Its verification provisions, implemented by the International Atomic Energy Agency (IAEA) and a network of bilateral safeguards agreements under IAEA auspices, regulate most international nuclear transactions. While the term 'non-proliferation regime' overstates the cohesion of these endeavours,

Table 1: Principal Arms Control Agreements

Testing and Non-Proliferation		
Partial Test Ban Treaty	1963	Multilateral
Treaty of Tlatelolco	1967, 1968*	Regional
Non-Proliferation Treaty	1968, 1970	Multilateral
Threshold Test Ban Treaty	1974, -	Bilateral
Peaceful Nuclear Explosions Treaty	1976, -	Bilateral
South Pacific Nuclear Free Zone	1985, 1986	Regional
Joint Verification Experiment Agreement	1988	Bilateral
Strategic Arms Limitation		
ABM Treaty	1972	Bilateral
SALT I Interim Accord	1972	Bilateral
Biological Warfare Convention	1972, 1975	Multilateral
Vladivostok Accord	1974	Bilateral
SALT II Treaty	1979, -	Bilateral
INF Treaty**	1987, 1988	Bilateral
Restrictions on Deployment		
Antarctica Treaty	1959	Regional
Outer Space Treaty	1967	Multilateral
Sea-Bed Treaty	1971, 1972	Multilateral
Crisis Stability/Confidence Building		
Hot Line Agreement	1963	Bilateral
Hot Line Modernisation	1971	Bilateral
Agreements	1984	Bilateral
Nuclear Accidents	1971	Bilateral
Prevention of Naval Incidents	1972, 1973	Bilateral
Prevention of Nuclear War	1973	Bilateral
Confidence Building Measures	1975	Regional
Confidence and Security Building Measures	1986	Regional
Notification of Launches of ICBMs and SLBMs	1988	Bilateral

---

* The first date is the year of signature; the second (where this is delayed) the year of entry into force.
** In view of the role of intermediate-range nuclear forces in the overall strategic balance, the INF Treaty may be included in this grouping.

would-be proliferators have to act in secrecy and against very considerable opposition. The situation would be very different if there were an entirely *laissez-faire* regime.

Strategic Arms Limitations: The ABM Treaty, prohibiting the deployment of ballistic missile defence systems beyond the two complexes (subsequently reduced to one) originally specified, has major strategic consequences, and accordingly has become increasingly controversial. Its perpetuation of the strategy (or condition) of mutual assured destruction has always aroused misgiving but, for the majority of the arms control community, the condition is seen as inescapable. Indeed, the Treaty's contribution to strategic stability, in closing off the prospect of an offensive-defensive arms race, is seen as the most solid achievement of the SALT negotiations thus far. The Treaty does not seek to prevent research on strategic defence systems, but until the Reagan Administration's recent canvassing of a 'broad' interpretation, it has been generally understood to preclude the development and testing of new systems or their components.6

In the case of the agreements to limit strategic offensive systems (the SALT I Interim Accord and the SALT II Treaty) in contrast, it is their limitations, rather than their positive consequences, which have become more evident. It is true that the quantitative limits in these agreements on nuclear delivery vehicles have introduced greater predictability into one dimension of the strategic arms race, but it is the absence of significant reductions and of constraints on qualitative developments which have come to appear more significant. The indirect benefits of the agreements have turned out to be less than at first seemed likely. For example, it had seemed likely that the intensive negotiations preceding both agreements, and the precision of the agreed statements which complement the articles of the SALT II Treaty, would enhance mutual confidence and open the way to further agreements. However, there was less mutual trust between the superpowers in the early 1980s than for many years, less confidence in strategic stability, and more frequent expressions of concern that the adversary was seeking to achieve a first-strike capability.

Restrictions on Deployment: By and large, these agreements amounted to undertakings not to deploy nuclear weapons or other weapons of mass destruction in remote environments of no immediate strategic interest to the superpowers. Should this situation change, one or other of the agreements will become more significant, but also more controversial.

Crisis Stability and Confidence Building: The agreements under this heading are of greater importance but, being relatively uncontroversial, are little studied. Among the bilateral agreements, the establishment of the hot line is probably the most significant, providing as it does the means of direct communication in an acute crisis, the absence of which had been so prominent a feature of the Cuban Missile Crisis. The 1972 agreement on The Prevention of Naval Incidents imposes certain restrictions on manoeuvres, substantially reducing the number of incidents. Like the agreement on nuclear accidents, it establishes procedures for clarification and communication in the contingencies in question.[7] An agreement to establish a Nuclear Risk Reduction Centre, or Crisis Control Centre, has recently been negotiated but not yet signed. This is expected to provide for the exchange of data, but to be of lesser scope than had been originally envisaged.[8] Any of these measures could prove significant in a crisis, or in averting a crisis, but they do not address the central military problems of crisis stability, such as command and control vulnerability and the pressures to pre-empt.

The Confidence and Security Building Measures in Europe Agreement signed in Stockholm in September 1986 breaks new ground in several ways.[9] The agreement requires all parties to provide advance notice of army, army-air and amphibious military exercises above certain limits and to provide for observation of these exercises by participating states. In addition, up to three inspections per year must be approved, on request, by each participant. However, although they are discouraged, there can still be 'alerts' without prior notification. The agreements will enhance the knowledge of normal military activities within Europe, but whether they can contribute to defusing a crisis is uncertain. The hope is expressed that they may open the way to the discussion of restrictions, as distinct from exchanges of information, in the field of 'operational arms control', a course which may be more promising than the attempt to achieve mutual and balanced force reductions, which have been under negotiation for fourteen years with little progress.

The Decline of Arms Control?

The INF Treaty and negotiations on strategic force reductions have dominated recent perceptions of East-West relations but, taken as a whole, the military policies of the Reagan Administration amounted to a substantial setback for arms control. Although the strategic balance remains stable under normal conditions, a number of trends in the 1980s point towards increasing difficulties for maintaining crisis stability in the future. These include: reduced predictability caused by the proliferation of new technologies, heightened awareness of the vulnerability of command, control, communications and intelligence systems and of the potential dangers of strategic alerts, reduced decision time and the canvassing of launch-on-warning strategies. It is likely that the deployment of the systems envisaged in the Strategic Defense Initiative (SDI) would compound these problems.

The case for a research program on strategic defence is not controversial. Indeed, the possibility of moving away from reliance on mutual assured destruction should be kept under review. Moreover, both superpowers have engaged in research programs, which are not prohibited by the ABM Treaty. The case against the SDI program as pursued by the Reagan Administration is that, in the name of a goal of defending the population which no-one, with the possible exception of President Reagan himself, believed that the SDI could achieve, the Administration made every effort to commit its successors to a deployment which is likely to increase the dangers and costs of the arms race, and which works against some of the most relevant arms control options. It is argued elsewhere that the most substantial argument in its favour, and one which incorporates an arms control perspective, i.e. the thesis of the transition to deterrence based on defensive systems, rests on a number of implausible strategic and political assumptions.[10]

The immediate cost of the Administration's commitment to the SDI is that it rules out both a comprehensive test ban and an agreement not to deploy anti-satellite (ASAT) systems, as well as threatening the continuation of the ABM Treaty. While a comprehensive test ban (CTB) would not end the qualitative strategic arms race, it would considerably slow down some of those developments which endanger crisis stability. At a time when the longstanding verification problems are being steadily overcome, and other arguments against such a test ban treaty which include the need to test existing warheads in order to ensure their reliability are unconvincing, it appears that the main US objection is the need for continued testing in relation to some of the exotic technologies envisaged for the SDI.[11]

Few impending developments are more destabilising than the prospect of the deployment of sophisticated ASAT systems, which could place the superpowers in a position to destroy one another's reconnaissance, communications and early warning satellites, establishing new incentives to pre-empt. Once again, these developments are so closely related to the SDI program that the US is not prepared to consider arms control in this area. As in the case of the CTB, earlier negotiations have been discontinued.

Other manifestations of the Reagan Administration's inclination to prefer the removal of restraints on the arms race to the strengthening of arms control may be seen in the primarily symbolic decision to exceed the SALT II ceiling, and in the manner in which the issue of Soviet compliance with the SALT agreements was raised. Serious concern over compliance might have been taken up, in the first instance, in the institution established for the purpose, the Standing Consultative Commission, and by high-level representations, rather than by public charges which combined matters of serious concern with others which were marginal or questionable.12

The Reagan Administration pursued limited measures relating to crisis stability, but only so long as these did not restrict its pursuit of the qualitative arms race. Thus agreements were reached on the modernisation of the hot line, the establishment of the Nuclear Risk Reduction Centre, and the confidence-building measures in Europe; all of which, however, do little to offset the destabilising tendencies, which proceed unchecked.

The Soviet record during the same period is open to differing interpretations. The unilateral moratorium on nuclear testing, and the less publicised moratorium on ASAT testing, in force since 1982, are consistent with the view that the Soviet Union is prepared to contribute to crisis stability. But they are also consistent with the possibility that the main Soviet concern is to prevent the US from exploiting its technological edge, especially with respect to the SDI.

It is plausible to see Gorbachev's diplomacy as seeking first and foremost to reduce the level of resources needed for Soviet security, and in particular to avoid the further diversion of resources that would be required to counter the SDI. To this end, he is prepared to challenge orthodoxies and perhaps to shake up established structures, but the utopian side to his proposals has been plausibly interpreted as the packaging around a proposed bargain with the US which would limit the SDI to research in the strict sense, in exchange for strategic offensive force reductions which might place emphasis on heavy Soviet ICBMs.13 Such a bargain would promote his larger economic priorities, but would also serve the interests of future crisis stability.

The utopian packaging of disarmament proposals is a sufficiently familiar aspect of Soviet diplomatic style and of negotiations in the UN forum that it is normally discounted in the West. It is assumed that this is a game in which the distinction between rhetoric and practical proposals is well understood by all. It was a matter of consternation among Western governments, however, when an American President delivered his utopian lines with a degree of conviction which suggested that he may have abandoned the conventions, or may not have understood them: the zero option, even the abolition of nuclear weapons, might slip from the world of rhetoric to that of practical reality. European public comment on Reykjavik was muted - unless one construes Mrs Thatcher's public argument with Gorbachev as primarily a signal to the White House - but reflected the same 'bemusement' which was expressed by James Schlesinger, commenting on the US proposal to eliminate all ballistic missiles within ten years: 'At Reykjavik he (the President) was prepared apparently to sacrifice our entire strategic nuclear armament, but unprepared to compromise on outside-the-laboratory testing of SDI'.[14]

Confronted by deadlock at the strategic weapons level, Gorbachev untied the Soviet package to the extent of separating out the INF agreement. In terms of his larger priorities, this could well prove to be a *cul-de-sac*, unless he is able to use the agreement as a springboard for something more far-reaching.

The INF agreement transformed the image of the Reagan Administration, but how does it measure up against the criteria for arms control? An answer will reflect the difficulties of evaluation which were noted earlier. The removal of the Pershings may contribute something to crisis stability, but in itself the agreement will do little to reduce the potential destructiveness of war in Europe, or to reduce the cost of defence. Some European analysts fear that these modest gains will be more than offset by its calling in question the stability of the European military balance and thus the credibility of 'extended deterrence'. For example, the International Institute for Strategic Studies noted that: 'The Reykjavik meeting dramatically and starkly revealed the extent to which Western arms control policies have diverged from NATO strategy'.[15] Rightly or wrongly, the Warsaw Pact conventional forces are perceived as stronger than those of NATO. The crude quantitative data tend to support this perception, even though they do not support the notion of overwhelming Soviet superiority.[16] Moreover it is uncertain, even if new technologies are fully exploited, that NATO's defences can be relied upon to prevent a breakthrough by Soviet tank divisions, whatever the level of spending.

Traditionally, tactical nuclear weapons were regarded as providing a 'manifest mechanism of escalation' which rendered extended deterrence credible. In the late 1970s many in NATO circles came to perceive a danger of the 'decoupling' of European and American security unless this mechanism was reinforced by INF deployments. The sudden removal of these caused alarm, and even more so the possibility that this might foreshadow the removal of further tactical nuclear weapons. Since the time of the Rapacki Plan, the denuclearisation of central Europe has been a recurring theme in Soviet diplomacy, a nightmare of NATO planners and a particular *bête noire* of the West German Christian Democrats. It is true that the opposite logic, that of security through nuclear-free zones and strengthened conventional defence, has its supporters in Europe, but they remain a small minority. In addition to the common dilemma, West Germany faces the additional unhappy prospect that the missiles remaining in central Europe after an INF agreement will be of a range to hit targets only in Germany.

If the INF agreement should lead to a general perception of a military imbalance in Europe, this must have long-term political consequences, especially in the event of any future crisis - in a region which has been remarkably free from crises for a generation. It would seem that the agreement, although advantageous to the West in terms of the relative reduction of military hardware, is not a sound measure of arms control but more in the nature of a gamble. Despite their support for the Treaty, Western European governments were concerned that their vital security interests had been subjected to new uncertainties in the name of arms control.[17]

The accelerating pace of change in the overall geopolitical setting during 1989 provided an entirely new context for arms control. As political reforms in the Soviet Union and Eastern Europe gained unexpected momentum, the intractability of Soviet economic problems became increasingly evident. Soviet foreign policy, it appeared, was driven by economic imperatives: for the first time in the nuclear age the third of the classical goals of arms control - to reduce the cost of defence preparedness - was uppermost in Moscow and also powerful in Washington, given the reduced perception of threat. The reduction in superpower tensions created a climate of high expectations in which a range of arms control agreements suddenly began to appear within reach.[18] At the same time, the sudden violent suppression of the student movement in China in June 1989 served to underline the unpredictability of the process of political reform in communist states, and open political tensions and economic dissatisfaction in the Soviet Union suggest that the new geopolitical constellation could prove to be precarious. To what extent did the prospects for continued East-West rapprochement, and for arms control, depend on Gorbachev's remaining in office, or at least a likeminded leadership? Pressures for Soviet arms reductions would remain, but they might be met less openly and by other means than international collaboration.

Strategic arms limitation remained at the top of the superpower agenda, and here both governments were offering concessions in a way that suggested purposeful movement towards agreement.[19] The same was true of the NATO-Warsaw Pact negotiations at the newly instituted Conventional Forces in Europe (CFE) talks, following Soviet unilateral arms cuts and acceptance of the principle of asymmetrical reductions.

The superpowers were also showing a serious interest in agreement on chemical weapons, but here the prospects were more uncertain, firstly because of American reluctance to forgo the production of a new generation of weapons, and second because of the attractiveness of chemical weapons to a number of Third World governments. On the other hand, the conference between governments and industrial representatives in Canberra in September 1989 demonstrated a willingness to address the formidable verification problems entailed in a chemical weapons ban.

A number of major issues of concern, however, were not yet on the arms control agenda, or only peripherally so. For example, the Missile Technology Control Regime established by certain Western governments in 1987 was of limited effectiveness in checking the proliferation of ballistic missiles. The United States remained averse to contemplating naval arms control and, along with most of the relevant states, was indifferent to regional arms control outside Europe.[20] Where political forces were promoting international accommodation and stability, arms control was assisting to consolidate these gains, but in potentially unstable regions the political and intellectual preconditions for its beneficial impact were not yet present.

These concerns were somewhat alleviated as it became clear that the next item on the superpower agenda was not the 'denuclearisation' of Europe but reductions in the strategic nuclear forces of the superpowers themselves. Should such an agreement be reached, it will contribute to the goals of arms control if its implementation commits the two powers to policies of collaboration in this crucial area. However, in perpetuating the emphasis on quantitative limits, while leaving qualitative changes unrestricted, it will do nothing to control the threats to strategic stability which those changes may entail.

The policies of the superpowers in the 1980s reflected the complex logic of arms control only to a very limited extent. The political sub-culture which dominated American policy was inimical to arms control but favoured strong rhetoric. The Soviet Union, for its part, could not resist the temptation to exploit Western ambivalence and confusion. Above all, the nexus between arms control and strategy was broken, and public candour gave way to the profession of unrealistic goals and misleading symbols.

Endnotes
1   See Hedley Bull, *The Control of the Arms Race*, (Weidenfeld and Nicolson, London, 1961); D.G. Brennan (ed.), *Arms Control, Disarmament and National Security*, (Braziller, New York, 1961); and T.C. Schelling and M.H. Halperin, *Strategy and Arms Control*, (Twentieth Century Fund, New York, 1961).

2   For an earlier version of the present analysis, see J.L. Richardson, 'Arms Control in the Later 1980s: The Implications of the Strategic Defense Initiative', in Desmond Ball and Andrew Mack (eds.), *The Future of Arms Control*, (Pergamon/Australian National University Press, Sydney, 1987), pp.81-84. Arms control is discussed along similar lines by Hedley Bull, 'The Classical Approach to Arms Control Twenty Years After', in Uwe Nerlich (ed.), *Soviet Power and Western Negotiating Policies*, (Ballinger, Cambridge, Massachusetts, 1983), Vol.II, pp.21-30.

3   Hans J. Morgenthau, *Politics Among Nations: The Struggle for Power and Peace*, (Knopf, New York, Fourth Edn., 1967), pp.380-86.

4   The texts of these and other arms control agreements up to 1981, together with brief commentary, are included in Jozef Goldblat, *Agreements for Arms Control: A Critical Survey*, (Taylor and Francis, London, 1982).

5   For the present position, see Jozef Goldblat (ed.), *Non-Proliferation: The Why and the Wherefore*, (Taylor and Francis, London, 1985); Paul F. Power, 'The mixed state of non-proliferation: The NPT Review Conference and Beyond', *International Affairs*, (Vol.62, No.3), Summer 1986, pp.477-91.

6   The arguments relating to the interpretation of the Treaty are discussed in Andrew Mack, *Threats to the ABM Treaty*, (Working Paper No.21, Peace Research Centre, Australian National University, Canberra, 1987).

7   See Sean M. Lynn-Jones, 'A Quiet Success for Arms Control: Preventing Incidents at Sea', *International Security*, (Vol.9, No.4), Spring 1985, pp.154-84.

8   For brief details, see Institute for Defence and Disarmament Studies, *The Arms Control Reporter, 1987*, Section 830 on 'New Suggestions for Arms Limitations', Chronology 1987, pp.850. 187-8.

9   For a discussion of the agreement, see Richard E. Darilek, 'The Future of Conventional Arms Control in Europe', *Survival*, (Vol.29, No.1), January-February 1987, pp.5-20; for excerpts for the text, *ibid.*, pp.79-84.

10   Richardson, 'Arms Control in the Later 1980s', pp.88-95.

11   Glenn Seaborg states that no such tests were carried out when he was Chairman of the Atomic Energy Commission. See Glenn T. Seaborg and Benjamin S. Loeb, 'Make the partial test ban comprehensive', *Bulletin of the Atomic Scientists*, May 1987, p.3.

12   For a discussion of the issues raised by the charges, see Janette Voas, 'The arms-control compliance debate', *Survival*, (Vol.28, No.1), January-February 1986, pp.8-31; also Mack, *Threats to the ABM Treaty*. For a defence of the Reagan Administration's record on arms control, see Colin Gray, 'The Reagan Administration and Arms Control', in Ball and Mack (eds.), *The Future of Arms Control*, pp.45-66.

13   See, e.g., Trevor Findlay, 'The Gorbachev Initiative', *Current Affairs Bulletin*, (Vol.65, No.3), 1987, p.434.

14   James Schlesinger, 'Reykjavik and Revelations: A Turn of the Tide?', *Foreign Affairs*, (Vol.65, No.3), 1987, p.434.

15   International Institute for Strategic Studies (IISS), *Strategic Survey, 1986-1987*, (London, 1987), p.66.

16   See, e.g., *The Military Balance, 1986-1987*, (IISS, London, 1986), pp.223-27.

17   For appraisals by prominent European commentators, see Christoph Bertram, 'Europe's Security Dilemmas', *Foreign Affairs*, (Vol.65, No.5), Summer 1987, pp.942-57; Philip Williams, 'West European Security after Reykjavik', *Washington Quarterly*, (Vol.10, No.2), Spring 1987, pp.37-47.

18   For a discussion of these, see Trevor Findlay, *Arms Control in the 1990s*, (Working Paper No.70, Peace Research Centre, Australian National University, Canberra, 1989).

19   For example, in September 1989 the US abandoned its demand that mobile land-based ICBMs be prohibited, and the Soviet Union abandoned its insistence on linking the proposed agreement to restrictions on strategic defensive systems.

20   For the first major study relating to the northern Asian-Pacific region, see A. Mack and P. Keal (eds.), *Security and Arms Control in the North Pacific*, (Allen & Unwin, Sydney, 1988).

AUSTRALIAN DEFENCE

CHAPTER 10

AUSTRALIAN DEFENCE STRATEGIES

Ross Babbage

Australia's Security[1] Problem

Providing effective security for Australia has been seen as a major challenge ever since the first Europeans landed. Australia's continental dimensions, its remoteness from the major centres of Western civilisation, its small population and limited resources, and its closeness to the vast population masses of Asia have long posed serious problems for the nation's foreign and defence policy planners.

This chapter examines the way Australian security policy has developed to manage the defence and foreign policy dilemmas of the nation's circumstances. Important themes are the evolving nature of relationships with major power allies, the development of greater confidence in Australia's capacity to provide for its own security in its local region, the types of defence contingencies that have driven defence planning, the development of Australia's economic capacity and with it the potential to sustain a defence development program that is impressive by regional standards, and the evolution of close consultative and cooperative defence relations with most of Australia's neighbours in Southeast Asia and the Southwest Pacific.

History of Australian Defence Policy

The first white people to settle on the Australian continent two hundred years ago established small, isolated colonies. They felt remote, exposed and very vulnerable on the other side of the world from 'mother' England. They saw their security as being tied very closely to the progress of the British Empire.[2] Threats were perceived from France and Russia and, although local resources were limited, fortifications were built on the seaward approaches to the major settlements. The Far Eastern operations of the Royal Navy were considered very important for local security .

It was this strong feeling of being British abroad and sense of intimate commitment to the Empire that led volunteers from the Australian colonies to fight alongside British soldiers in the Maori Wars in New Zealand. In 1885, following the fall of Khartoum, the Australian colonies vied amongst themselves for the honour of sending a contingent to the Sudan. In 1899, battalions of Australian Commonwealth Horse were dispatched to the Boer War under the command of Australian officers and in 1900, New South Wales, Victoria and South Australia contributed naval elements to help suppress the Boxer Rebellion in China.

With the outbreak of the First World War in 1914, there was really no question about Australia's commitment. Prime Minister Fisher promised that: 'Australia will stand behind the Mother Country to help and defend her to our last man and our last shilling'.[3] Australia dispatched nearly 330,000 troops overseas and 59,000 died. This was a very heavy sacrifice from an Australian population of five million people (i.e. about one per cent of Australia's population was killed in this conflict).

During the 1920s and 1930s, there was growing Australian concern about Japanese militarism but the country continued to rely primarily on Britain and especially the forces at the British naval base at Singapore for its security. With the outbreak of war in Europe in 1939, Prime Minister Menzies committed Australia to war in similar terms to those of Prime Minister Fisher twenty-one years earlier:

> The peace of Great Britain is precious to us, because her peace is ours; if she is at war, we are at war...The British countries of the world must stand or fall together.[4]

Nearly one million Australians served in uniform during the Second World War and nearly 22,000 lost their lives.

However, with the fall of Singapore, Britain under great pressure at home and Japanese forces pressing further south, Australian perceptions concerning the identity of their major ally changed markedly. Prime Minister Curtin had little hesitation in turning to the United States as the primary guarantor of Australian security.

However, while Australia's great power protector changed during the Second World War, the basic strategic concept remained essentially unaltered both during the war itself and in the years that followed. It continued to be a fundamental assumption that Australia was not capable of providing for its own defence and it needed a major power protector. In order to foster the closest possible security relationship with that ally it was considered important to encourage continued friendly great power, and especially United States, commitments to Australia's region and to dispatch Australian Defence Force elements to support our allies' foreign military actions.

In the late 1940s, the 1950s and 1960s this reasoning paved the way for a further succession of Australian military commitments alongside the forces of Britain and/or the United States in distant theatres. Australian forces participated in the Berlin Airlift, the Malayan Emergency, the Korean War, defending Malaysia against Indonesian confrontation and finally in Vietnam. Many Australians considered that it was better to fight potential opponents in these 'forward defence' theatres than on Australia's own shores. Moreover, these forward military commitments were thought to have the potential of so involving and ingratiating Australia with its great power ally that were Australia itself ever to come under direct threat, the United States response would be assured.

This long tradition of 'forward defence' strategy started to come unstuck in the late 1960s, largely because of changes in the policies and priorities of Australia's major allies. First, the British Government announced the withdrawal of most of its military forces deployed East of the Suez Canal. This heralded the demise of the large British military presence in Malaysia and Singapore. Then, in the early 1970s, the United States began a phased withdrawal of its forces deployed on mainland Southeast Asia and especially from Vietnam. The United States inclination to become militarily involved in Southeast Asia also declined markedly during this period. President Nixon, in Guam on his way home from a visit to Southeast Asia in July 1969, made clear that while the United States would keep its treaty commitments in the region, it expected its Asian allies and friends to provide the main forces for their own defence. Only if threatened directly by the Soviet Union or China could an ally expect the United States to become heavily committed.[5]

This so-called Nixon or Guam Doctrine, together with the British withdrawal from East of Suez, had important implications for Australian security policy. If Australia's major power allies were far less likely to commit themselves actively to the defence of Southeast Asia, there would be few, if any, further opportunities for Australian 'forward defence' commitments into the region alongside United States and British forces. It was clear that any future forward Australian combat operations without heavy United States or British commitments would necessitate greatly increased battlefield and diplomatic risks and have few spin-offs for alliance relations.

A more direct consequence of the Nixon Doctrine for Australia was to condition the United States' security commitment under the ANZUS Treaty. As it was interpreted in Canberra, Washington was signalling Canberra that if Australia were ever threatened by a regional opponent it would need to provide the main forces for its own defence.[6]

These stimuli to rethink the basic assumptions of 'forward defence' were reinforced by yet another parallel development. In the early 1970s most of the countries of Southeast Asia, particularly the ASEAN states, responded to the changed United States and British policies in the region by expanding greatly their capacities to provide for their own defence. This raised additional questions about the relevance of Australia's 'forward defence' concept and strengthened the incentives for a fundamental review of security policy.

Focussing on the Defence of Australia

The conceptual basis for current defence planning was laid with the major reassessment of security policy conducted in the Department of Defence in the early 1970s. That basic policy review concluded that Australia had to take full account of the global nature of United States interests and commitments. As a medium-sized power in a relatively remote part of the world, Australia could no longer rely on the military assistance of its allies in all circumstances and there was, in consequence, a need to place priority on preparing for the direct defence of Australia with a far higher level of self-reliance.[7]

But if Australia was to concentrate on providing for its direct defence primarily with its own resources, what types of threats should it be prepared to defend against? The judgement reached was that Australia is a remarkably difficult target to attack. It is remote from the major centres of global power and strategic competition and surrounded by water which stretches to oceanic proportions on three sides. Many of the same factors that made the early colonists feel isolated and vulnerable were now seen to be extremely valuable defence assets.

A number of countries possess large armies but practically none have the vast quantities of ships and aircraft that would be needed to transport a substantial military force across the sea-air gap that surrounds Australia. Only the Soviet Union and the United States possess maritime forces of the size that would be needed to invade Australia, and even the USSR would have difficulty marshalling the full range of necessary capabilities.[8] Were the Soviet Union to launch a major military operation against Australia, there would be world-wide strategic implications. It is the high risks of these global responses, rather than of the Australian reaction alone, that the USSR would have to weigh against what would seem to be very doubtful benefits. The Soviet Union's primary military forces are most likely to remain heavily tied down in Europe, the Far East and Central Asia.

The major review of Australian security policy in the early 1970s concluded therefore that physical geography and fundamental military considerations provide the country with substantial assurance against major military attack or invasion - at least until other nations develop the major maritime capabilities that would be needed to launch a major assault. It would not be easy for any regional country to develop the massive military capabilities needed to launch a major attack on

Australia. This would necessitate a powerful motivation, require a national mobilisation of manpower and industrial resources and take many years to accomplish. Such preparations would not go unnoticed either in Australia or elsewhere and there would be time to expand Australia's defences to meet the challenge.

It was further concluded that while Australian defence planners needed to address contingencies of major threat, it would be quite unrealistic to dwell on these alone. There was a need to consider a range of circumstances under which limited military operations against Australia might occur, having more political than military objectives.

Australia's defence planners judged that an opponent might consider some types of limited military pressure against Australia to be justified were a serious political dispute to arise and that this possibility should not be overlooked in defence planning. Because the military capabilities needed to launch many types of limited operations against Australia are already held by numerous countries, including some in Australia's region, a serious deterioration in political relations could conceivably trigger such operations at short notice. It was surmised that the Australian Defence Force needed the capabilities necessary to manage such a challenge immediately and the provision of an effective defence against low level contingencies thus became the first priority for defence investment.

It was appreciated that in the event of a serious political dispute, an opponent might not resort to military pressure from the outset. The most likely initial measures would more probably be political, diplomatic and possibly economic. Efforts would be made to rally international opinion to the opponent's cause, boycotts could be imposed against Australia's exports and there could be harassment of Australian diplomats and other Australians abroad. Encouragement and support could also be given to drug runners, illegal immigrants and illegal dealers in flora and fauna whose intensified activities would place greatly increased pressure on Australian customs, immigration and health authorities. Fishing and other civil vessels could be encouraged to operate illegally within the Australian Fishing Zone and possibly engage in rule-of-the-road confrontations with Australian civil and law enforcement vessels. In the course of such a dispute, civilians could be encouraged to land illegally on Australia's offshore islands and reefs, damaging the unmanned weather stations and other installations and destroying the local fauna and flora. Civil aircraft could also be encouraged to penetrate Australian air space without clearance and possibly buzz Australian vessels and coastal and offshore settlements.

Delivering small raiding parties onto Australian territory would not be easy for an opponent based in the local region. The sea-air gap is, in most places, relatively wide and during the wet season (November-April) the weather in the coastal and offshore regions of northern Australia is unpredictable with frequent heavy storms and periodic cyclones. Even during most of the dry season (May-October) the prevailing trade winds are frequently strong, making movements by small craft in open water hazardous. Much of Australia's northern coastline is very rugged with thousands of reefs and islets offshore, extreme tides and dirty water making navigation without local knowledge difficult even in daylight. Nevertheless, once in the coastal environment, numerous potential population and infrastructure targets would be readily at hand and several large rivers provide the potential for small craft to penetrate well inland.

Aircraft could provide another option for delivering small reconnaissance and raiding parties. Small parties could also conceivably be delivered by submarine, but in much of northern Australia their close approach to the coast would be hazardous. Besides, few regional countries possess sufficient submarines to make their routine use in this role seem credible.

Some raiding operations could be increased substantially in scale up to platoon (about 30 troops), company (about 120 troops) or even battalion size (about 1,000 troops). Forces transiting the sea-air gap on this scale would present a larger target for Australian interdiction but once ashore would be capable of undertaking heavy mauling raids on a range of settlements and installations.

Other types of military pressure could include sporadic and small scale air and naval attacks on Australian ships at sea and small scale bombing and strafing raids on northern settlements. An opponent could also lay (or claim to have laid) sea mines in the approaches to Australia's northern ports or its northern coastal waters, for example in the Prince Edward and Endeavour Channels in the Torres Strait Islands.

A confrontation campaign employing these types of operation has the potential to overstretch Australia's present and projected defence capabilities. The opponent's operations could be directed at targets across a frontage of more than 5,000 km from the Cocos Islands to the Great Barrier Reef. This is a vast frontage to defend, about the same distance as from London to Karachi or London to Washington. Were simultaneous operations conducted against PNG, the front could conceivably be even wider, extending from Cocos to Manus Island and New Ireland. By carefully phasing his operations, and periodically concentrating spasms of widely scattered activities into short periods, the opponent could exacerbate Australia's defence problems further.[9]

Providing an effective defence against an opponent's low level operations clearly represents a major challenge for Australia's defence planners. The strategy and operational concepts most appropriate for this remain the subject of considerable debate.

Paul Dibb's major *Review of Australia's Defence Capabilities* in 1986 proposed a layered defensive strategy of denial.[10] This would require, in the first layer, a quality intelligence system to monitor military developments in our region and to render the sea-air gap effectively transparent. The second defensive layer would be composed of aircraft and ships operating offshore tasked with identifying potential air, surface and sub-surface targets in the sea-air gap and possessing a capability to arrest or destroy hostile elements moving towards Australia. The third layer would be composed of air, naval and ground force elements in Australia's northern coastal environment tasked with preventing hostile landings, air attacks and mining operations at the interface between the sea and the land. The fourth defensive layer would comprise ground force elements assigned the task of denying the enemy access to Australia's northern population centres and military and civil infrastructure.

Dibb's layered strategy of denial was criticised by senior military and academic strategists as being too reactive, of conceding the initiative to the opponent and condemning Australia to a long campaign of attrition defence that would be extremely expensive militarily, economically and politically. Some argued that because of the vast and open-ended costs of such a strategy to Australia, an alternative approach was required that would pressure the opponent to rapidly cease his attacks and sue for peace.[11] The Government's *1987 Defence White Paper* endorsed the broad thrust of Dibb's Capability Review but accepted the need for a carefully crafted range of offensive capabilities to supplement those forces designed primarily for denial operations in northern and offshore Australia.[12]

Debate about the relative merits of alternative strategic and tactical concepts for managing low level defence contingencies can be expected to continue for many years. Key issues include the means of preventing such conflicts arising, the most appropriate means of minimising the costs of such conflicts to Australia and maximising those of an opponent, avoiding provocative postures, controlling conflict escalation and devising means of pressuring an opponent to sue for peace at an early stage on terms consistent with Australia's interests.[13] Much work remains to be done to develop coherent strategic and tactical concepts that can be applied effectively with Australia's limited defence resources to the range of contingencies that could arise at relatively short notice in the nation's immediate environment. A great deal of defence analysis and Defence Force exercising and testing is likely to be devoted to these issues through the 1990s.

Australian defence planners acknowledge that while preparations for countering low level contingencies are important, there is potential in the longer term for other, more demanding, threats to arise. The sophisticated and extensive defence resources that would be needed in these higher level contingencies (e.g. fighter aircraft, large combat ships and armoured vehicles) could not be bought and introduced into effective service quickly. Hence, while the Australian Defence Force is presently being developed primarily to meet low-level risk and harassment contingencies, investment is also being made to maintain and develop a carefully selected range of military capabilities which are primarily relevant to larger scale attacks. This is designed to provide a Defence Force capable of responding rapidly and flexibly to a wide range of lower-level contingencies, while at the same time providing a substantial technological, skill and equipment base for expanding the Defence Force speedily should this be required to meet the emergence of a more demanding threat some time in the future.

Exactly how rapidly the present Defence Force would be able to expand to meet the challenge even of low level contingencies remains a source of some controversy. The Australian Army, and to a lesser extent the other two Services, do maintain part-time reserve units. In total, however, these reserve elements number less than 30,000 and very few are trained to standards sufficient for commitment to active operations at short notice. The scale and type of reserve defence units presently maintained by Australia could be said to owe more to historical evolution than to the nation's current strategic priorities.[14]

An important objective of successive Australian governments since the mid-1970s has been to develop national defence capabilities with a high level of self-reliance. The constraints on achieving real self-reliance in a country with Australia's limited financial, industry, manpower and technical resources are well recognised by defence planners. The Defence Force can certainly operate effectively without external assistance for short periods in many environments. But Australia is always likely to depend on substantial external support for the provision of many types of munitions, equipment and other essential supplies in the event of sustained hostilities.

Australian industry does have substantial capability for defence work but it is not able to manufacture much of the more advanced defence equipment on an economic basis. Hence, in order to maximise self-reliance for defence operations, Australian industry is encouraged to concentrate on producing high-usage spare parts and munitions, those items for which Australia has unique requirements, those items that can be produced on an economic basis in Australia (especially those with export potential) and lastly in maintaining sophisticated repair and overhaul capabilities. The practical difficulties and costs of striving for substantially higher levels defence supply self-reliance are likely to limit the scope for major breakthroughs in this field.

While the main priorities for defence procurement, investment and planning now relate directly to the defence of Australia itself, this is not to suggest that the Defence Force cannot and will not be used for other purposes. It can and most likely will. Should circumstances develop in which the Australian government of the day decides that it is appropriate to deploy Australian forces abroad for peacekeeping, emergency evacuation or disaster relief purposes or, alternatively, to bolster the security of a regional friend or ally, the Defence Force will be capable of performing such roles. The important distinction is, however, that the Defence Force will not be designed and developed with the performance of these unpredictable possibilities as a first concern. The priority emphasis in Defence Force development and planning will continue to be on the requirements of defending Australia itself.

ANZUS

The security relationship with the United States continues to play a central role. While international circumstances have changed markedly since the ANZUS Treaty was concluded in 1951 and it is not considered prudent for any nation to rely on the assistance of another in all circumstances, ANZUS continues to provide substantial benefits for Australia. There may be some defence contingencies in which the United States might hesitate to commit combat units to support Australia but in most contingencies enhanced intelligence, equipment and munition supply, technical assistance and training support could be anticipated. Moreover, in many contingencies United States combat elements might be deployed to support Australian forces. Certainly no opponent of Australia could count on Australia not receiving substantial support from the United States. In consequence, ANZUS plays an important role in Australia's deterrence posture.

In peacetime, ANZUS provides a framework for a very wide range of cooperative activities including strategic consultations, intelligence sharing arrangements, combined exercises, and exchanges of defence scientific and technological information.[15] Nearly all of these detailed forms of security cooperation are not related directly to the ANZUS Treaty itself but are governed by separate agreements or memoranda of understanding that have been concluded on a bilateral basis with the United States or within a broader multilateral framework.

This is the case, for instance, concerning the agreements with the United States governing the construction and operations of the joint defence facilities in Australia. The Australian Government has justified the presence of these facilities by arguing that their contribution to early warning of Soviet missile launches, to verifying compliance with arms control agreements and to global deterrence enhances strategic nuclear stability and helps reduce the prospect of global war. The Government acknowledges that the presence of the joint facilities could increase the risks of Australia being targeted by the Soviet Union in a nuclear war but argues that the contribution they make to reducing the prospect of global war commencing outweighs that consideration.[16]

While the risk of global war may appear remote, it can never be completely ruled out. Hence the avoidance of global war and meaningful progress in nuclear arms control and disarmament are not only important objectives of foreign policy, they are also central to Australia's national security policy. Also deserving some priority are civil defence preparations designed to protect those elements of the Australian population most likely to be subjected to direct attack in global war.[17]

Regional Security Cooperation

A third important theme in Australia's security policy is the enduring national interest in encouraging the maintenance of a favourable strategic environment in the surrounding regions. Australian foreign and economic policies contribute significantly to ensuring that PNG, the Southwest Pacific and the ASEAN countries remain relatively free from major instability and external interference. Australia's defence policies are designed to support this endeavour by maintaining a regular program of security consultations, personnel training, combined exercises, visits by defence units and a military assistance scheme (the Defence Cooperation Program) designed to transfer skills, develop expertise and foster a high level of security understanding and cooperation in the region.

Annual expenditure on the Defence Cooperation Program has averaged about $50m in recent years with roughly half this amount being spent on cooperative defence programs with the ASEAN countries. Most of the other half has been spent in Papua New Guinea with the remainder going to the smaller island states of the Southwest Pacific. A major Defence Cooperation Program initiative in recent years has been the provision of purpose-designed patrol boats to many of the island countries in the Southwest Pacific to strengthen their capability for fisheries surveillance, law enforcement and sovereignty control.[18]

A notable element of Australia's security cooperation in Southeast Asia is its active membership of the Five-Power Defence

Arrangement with Malaysia, Singapore, Britain and New Zealand. As part of this arrangement, Australia maintains a permanent defence presence at the Malaysian airbase at Butterworth. Australia contributes 2-3 P-3 *Orion* long range maritime patrol aircraft, an army company to provide airfield security and, in addition, periodically deploys F-18 *Hornet* and F-lll aircraft to the base for major exercises and training.

Conclusion

A notable feature of present Australian defence policy is that those factors which present the greatest challenge to the security of the first white Australians now seem far less daunting and some have been transformed into positive defence assets. Australia is still geographically remote from the major centres of Western civilisation but in the age of almost instant global electronic communications, jumbo jets and very large and fast shipping, the strategic significance of Australia's distant location is much less of a liability. Indeed, Australia's remoteness from the major centres of global competition and possible future battlefields is now in many respects a positive security asset.

Similarly, while Australia's population and industries still appear limited in a comparative international sense, the rapid development of the Australian economy and technological base have reduced greatly the country's sense of vulnerability. Australia is now a technologically advanced and relatively wealthy middle power. Its industry is not sufficiently large to produce all defence requirements domestically. However, it can afford to devote sufficient resources to develop a formidable defence of its vast continental expanses and offshore approaches. For the first time ever Australia is confidently developing the capacities needed to provide for its own defence in the knowledge that any short- or medium-term threat that could emerge from its immediate region could be handled primarily with Australia's own resources.

Australia's security has also been strengthened during the last two hundred years by a growth in the country's international relationships. Close ties have been maintained with Australia's major allies and these links have proved sufficiently flexible to endure many changes of international circumstances. Australia's alliance relationships not only reinforce the nation's security capacity against a wide range of potential threats but also strengthen Australia's confidence in foreign policy dealings. A further important factor has been the gradual development of close relations with neighbouring countries in Southeast Asia and the Southwest Pacific. The fostering of cooperative relations with most of these countries has facilitated wide-ranging joint activities to enhance the security of the region as a whole.

Australia's security stance has thus developed over the last two hundred years into a complex, sophisticated policy conglomerate. It is now based on a broad matrix of economic, military, domestic political and international relations policies. Each of these elements of security policy tends to be mutually reinforcing. If managed with care and balance they have the potential to provide in combination the strength, flexibility and resilience needed to meet the security challenges that may confront Australia in the 1990s and beyond.

Endnotes

1   Security and security policy are defined broadly in this chapter to encompass the range of economic, military, political, diplomatic and social influences that contribute to national well-being and survival.

2   For a short summary of Australian defence concepts and developments in the colonial era see T.B. Millar, *Australia's Defence*, (Melbourne University Press, Melbourne, 1965), Chapter 1.

3   Cited in *ibid.*, p.17.

4   *Ibid.*, p. 21.

5   For details see 'Informal Remarks with Newsmen July 25, 1969', *Public Papers of the Presidents: Richard M. Nixon, 1969*, (U.S. Government Printing Office, Washington, D.C.) pp. 548-49.

6   These and related issues are discussed at greater length in Ross Babbage, *Rethinking Australia's Defence*, (University of Queensland Press, St Lucia, 1980), Chapter 1.

7   The thrust of the major review of Australian defence policy conducted in the early 1970s was spelt out in some detail in *Australian Defence: A White Paper*, presented to Parliament by the Minister for Defence, the Hon. D.J. Killen, November 1976, (Australian Government Publishing Service, Canberra, 1976).

8   For details of the military capabilities of the USSR, US and other countries see The International Institute for Strategic Studies, *The Military Balance 1988-89*, (London, 1989).

9   The challenges that low level contingencies could pose to Australia are discussed in greater detail in Ross Babbage, *Managing Australia's Contingency Spectrum for Defence Planning*, (Working Paper No.108, Strategic and Defence Studies Centre, Australian National University, Canberra, 1986).

10   *Review of Australia's Defence Capabilities*, Report to the Minister for Defence by Mr Paul Dibb, (Australian Government Publishing Service, Canberra, 1986).

11   The major criticisms of the Dibb Review are discussed in Ross Babbage, *Looking Beyond the Dibb Report*, (Working Paper No. 110, Strategic and Defence Studies Centre, Australian National University, Canberra, 1986) .

12   The Hon. K.C. Beazley, *The Defence of Australia 1987*, a White Paper presented to Parliament by the Minister for Defence, 19 March 1987, (Australian Government Publishing Service, Canberra, 1987).

13   For discussion of these issues see Babbage, *Looking Beyond the Dibb Report*.

14   This and related issues are discussed in Babbage, *Rethinking Australia's Defence*, chapter 9.

15   Many of these areas of defence cooperation are discussed in Ernest McNamara, Robin Ward, Desmond Ball, J.O. Langtry and Richard Q. Agnew, *Australia's Defence Resources: A Compendium of Data*, (Pergamon Press Australia, Sydney, 1986).

16   These arguments were spelt out by Prime Minister Bob Hawke on 6 June 1984, *Hansard (House of Representatives)*, 6 June 1984, pp.2982-2989.

17   This view was made Government policy in the 1987 White Paper. See *The Defence of Australia 1987*, p.12. For a more extensive discussion of these and related issues, see Desmond Ball and J.O. Langtry (eds.), *Civil Defence and Australia's Security in the Nuclear Age*, (Strategic and Defence Studies Centre, Australian National University and George Allen & Unwin, Sydney, 1983).

18   For details of the Defence Cooperation Program see Department of Defence, *Defence Report 1987-88*, (Australian Government Publishing Service, Canberra, 1986), pp.51-52.

CHAPTER 11

THE ANZUS ALLIANCE: THE CASE FOR

Coral Bell

Any alliance must be regarded as primarily a shield, constructed against envisaged dangers. So to make a case for any particular alliance, such as ANZUS, one must look essentially at the reality of the dangers envisaged, the prospective effectiveness of the shield, the question of whether any costs it entails outweigh the benefits provided, and whether alternate shields, equally or more effectively, could or should be devised to replace the alliance under examination. This chapter, as specifically a 'case for the defence', will look at those issues as they affect ANZUS, but will leave any countervailing arguments to be presented in the next chapter.

There is no problem at all in determining the nature of the envisaged danger, as far as the Australian public was concerned, when the ANZUS treaty was being drafted. At the time, mid-1951, it was little more than five years since those Australians who had survived the ordeal of captivity by the Japanese had emerged, walking skeletons, from the prisoner-of-war camps. The memory of the bombing of Darwin by the Japanese Air Force was still vivid, as was the recollection of how costly had been the battles to retrieve Papua New Guinea and the Pacific Islands from the swift and efficient Japanese initial conquest. The public mood in Australia *vis-à-vis* Japan was still deeply suspicious and revengeful. When it became clear soon after the outbreak of war in Korea in 1950 that the US intended a lenient peace treaty with Japan (one that would make it an American ally and not preclude the rebuilding of Japanese industrial and, eventually, strategic capacity) the policy-makers in Canberra became determined to require a US security guarantee as their price for going along, without too much protest, with the US-proposed Japan Peace Treaty.

In any event they would have had to acquiesce in the American proposals, so securing the ANZUS treaty as a *quid pro quo* may be regarded as a diplomatic victory of sorts for the Australian policy-makers involved.[1] Their drafting skill is also evident in the fact that a treaty originally designed mostly to fend off possible new dangers from Japan has proved flexible enough for assorted other diplomatic purposes over the subsequent decades. Even during the period of its formulation, the concept of an alternative threat from 'international communism' (seen by many people from 1949 to about 1960 as a monolithic conspiracy directed jointly from Moscow and Beijing) was growing more powerful at least in the minds of the conservative political leadership then in government in Canberra. Equally, the Labor opposition and probably the majority of Australians tended, for most of the 1950s, to see the reviving nation of Japan as a more real future danger. In the early 1960s, especially during the 'confrontation' period, 1962-65, Indonesian ambitions joined with fear of Chinese missionary export of Maoist revolution to provide the most fashionable nightmares, and the 'Peking-Djakarta axis' was much talked of and speculated about. The current convention, defining the Soviet Union rather than China as the more dangerous of the two Communist great powers, really only dates from the 'opening to China' by Kissinger and Nixon in 1971. The sense of Soviet expansionism as the chief problem for the society of states as a whole, including Australia, was increased by a sequence of events from 1975 to 1979: Soviet or surrogate involvement in Angola and Ethiopia, the Soviet missile build-up in Europe, and finally, the invasion of Afghanistan. (Those were the events of Brezhnev's last years as the chief Soviet decision-maker, and the swiftness with which the perception of threat can be changed is apparent in the considerable softening of the Soviet image during Mr Gorbachev's first years in power.)

Long before most of these definitions of the alternative prospective threats in the Australian future, however, there had already been quite a widespread sense in Australia of the United States as prospectively the most useful ally against any eventuality. It emerged clearly as early as the subdued Australian disquiet at the Anglo-Japanese Alliance of 1902, and the Japanese victory over the Czarist Russian fleet in 1905, and still more articulately during the visit of the US 'Great White Fleet' in 1908. It was based on the obvious perception that Australia and the US both lived in the Pacific, whereas Britain lived a whole world away in the North Atlantic, and might some day need to abandon its Pacific commitments. That decision was, of course, temporarily forced upon Britain in the early stages of the Pacific war, 1941-42, and has since found its logical peacetime corollary in the winding-up of empire in that area and elsewhere. The transfer of Hong Kong to China in 1997 will bring down a final curtain on the last substantial relic of the old European ascendancy in Asia.

That will also provide a fitting symbol of a change in Australia's external circumstancces not yet understood by most Australians, and very relevant to the question of whether the US alliance has a future. The whole of Australia's first 200 years of existence as a Western society has been in a phase of history in which the central balance of power has been Western-dominated. Aside from Japan, all the other non-Western powers in the society of states have been pretty much in eclipse, as economic, military and diplomatic forces, during the whole period. But that will not be the case for the third and subsequent centuries of Australia's existence. Asia will be a society of giants, demographically and probably in other respects. China and India are expected to have populations well above the billion mark, and even the smaller societies of Asia, like Indonesia and Japan, will be way above the 100 million mark, whereas Australia is likely to peak at about 27 million. The world balance of power may well centre round the Pacific, since four great agglomerations of power (the US, the Soviet Union, China and Japan) all rub up against each other in the Northern Pacific. But that is not necessarily going to be a comfortable situation for Australia. Indeed, the prospective international environment for Australia, in its third century of national existence, may be less benign, and less quiet, than it was during the first two centuries. In fact during those first two centuries there was only one six-month period of 'clear and present danger' for Australia: the six months from the Japanese attack in December 1941 to the battles of the Coral Sea and Midway in May and June 1942, when Japanese naval and air power were crippled by US carrier forces, and such possibility as there had once been of a Japanese invasion of Australia[2] vanished for the foreseeable future. Only six months serious danger in 200 years requires us to concede that, as nations go, we have thus far had historically a sheltered existence. But it would be an error to assume that this will be a permanent situation. Security is no more a law of nature for Australia than for any other society. The effort to maintain it requires both self-defensive capacity and a reasonable level of diplomatic leverage. Alliance is relevant to both.

This will become clearer if we look in turn at specific varieties of threat that Australian policy-makers have to provide against, both in contemporary circumstances and the foreseeable future. The most useful categorisation is low-level threat, intermediate-level threat and high-level threat.

Low-level threats would be, for instance, sporadic intrusions into Australia's air and naval space by military aircraft, smugglers, drug-runners, boats conducting illegal fishing, sporadic terrorist attack on facilities in Australia or Australian embassies abroad, minor harassment of Australian ships on the high seas, and similar sorts of episodes. In general, they would not be likely to entail the use of large contingents of the armed forces, and the military establishment Australia does or could provide are deemed adequate to cope with them. So the principal usefulness of ANZUS in connection with such episodes is the fact that it eases access to advanced American weapon-systems, like the *Orion* aircraft used for air patrol of the sea-approaches to Australia, radar and sonar systems, patrol boats and other coast-defence craft and various kinds of weaponry for the forces involved. The flow of American intelligence information is also very important for Australia's ability to 'keep tabs' on these low-level threats.

Intermediate-level threats would be more likely to evoke 'consultation' (as prescribed in the treaty) by Australia with its ANZUS partners. This category would include attempted seizure of Australian offshore islands (Cocos and Christmas Islands are much closer to Indonesia than to the Australian mainland), limited lodgements on Australian territory in remote areas like Arnhem Land, a major raid on, for instance, facilities like North West Cape, invasion of Papua New Guinea, or major hostilities between that country and Indonesia, the seizure or secession of an important island under the sovereignty of Papua New Guinea, like Manus Island, a raid on or mining of an Australian port, severe harassment of shipping plying to Australia, or an attempt by an extra-regional power to take over one of the small island states of the South Pacific. None of those possible eventualities is particularly likely: the nearest to being plausible for the foreseeable future would be reasonably substantial hostilities along the border between Papua New Guinea and the Indonesian province of Irian Jaya (the former Dutch New Guinea). It is easy enough to envisage a 'scenario' for such an outbreak: a raid by the anti-Indonesian resistance group, OPM, on a police or army post, who then retreat across the PNG border, 'hotly pursued' by the Indonesians into PNG territory, with subsequent escalating reprisals, and a call by Port Moresby for Australian support. That all this has not happened as yet has been a matter of some commendably prudent crisis-management by all three governments, but no-one can guarantee prudence as a permanent state of affairs.

The other eventualities mentioned remain quite implausible, but that situation may be put down in part to the existence of ANZUS. No-one can, of course, *guarantee* response by some future US Administration to any such episode, but no-one can guarantee *against* it either. Even the shadow of US power could have a deterrent effect on regional policy-makers balancing the potential cost of any such adventure against whatever benefit might be postulated to derive from it. If that beneficial deterrent effect should fail, then the Australian government would need Washington's support, in diplomatic backing and matériel, as acutely as Britain needed American support during the Falklands War.

To sum up all this, one might say that the US connection is useful but not essential to Australia in coping with low-level threats. It would be far more crucial in coping with an intermediate-level threat, though the nature of the US help provided would not necessarily be actual combat forces. Diplomatic backing and supplies would be the vital elements. If we assume that the Guam Doctrine applies to Australia, that might also be as much as could be expected, though some American interpretations leave ambiguous the question of how far the doctrine applies to Australia.

Finally we come to the category of high-level threat, which in my view provides the true justification of ANZUS. However, the actual kind of high-level threat that Australian policy-makers need to contemplate in present circumstances and for the immediate future (the more distant future will be looked at presently) does not much resemble the vision that was certainly in most Australian minds at the time of the signature of ANZUS, and is perhaps the dominant one still, at the grass-roots level. That vision is of direct specific attack on Australia, with bomb or missile devastation, and possibly invasion as apprehended by Canberra policy-makers in 1942. Expert opinion regards that concept as implausible for the foreseeable future. Australia is actually quite a difficult place to invade, largely for geographic reasons. The logistic requirements in sea and air power would be very great. At the present time only the two superpowers could muster them, and neither has any conceivable motive for such an enterprise. By the standards of the region, Australia is a relatively formidable power, strategically speaking, with advanced Western weapon systems which none of our immediate neighbours can match. The only context in which one can plausibly imagine a 1942-style threat would be if, as in 1942, the existing balance of power had been destroyed by war.

The true high-level threat for Australia is in fact the one we share with the rest of the world: the danger of central balance war, war between the superpowers, which would almost certainly involve nuclear exchange. Thus, the most vital of all Australia's vital national interests is simply the preservation of peace between the central balance powers. Given the significance of the central world balance, the case for ANZUS must involve looking at its relevance to the question of how peace between the central balance powers is to be preserved. And for that, in turn, the chief clue is provided by looking at the process by which it *has* been preserved for the past 40-plus years. For the most striking point about the history of the period is that since 1945, despite many, many crises, and despite some erratic decision-makers, the central balance powers have not embarked on hostilities with each other. More than 20 million people have died in, or as a result of, military action during that period, and there are always a considerable assortment of hostilities in progress. But hardly any Russians have died at American hands, or *vice versa*, in more than four decades of almost continuous high tension between the superpowers.

If asked to account for this rather surprising fact, most analysts would perhaps put it down simply to deterrence. But that is rather an oversimplification. The true recipe for avoiding hostilities has been *reasonably prudent crisis-management in a situation of alliance stability and overall deterrence.* All three elements - prudent crisis-management, alliance stability and overall deterrence - have been, and remain, necessary.

ANZUS may be shown to have contributed to all of these essential factors in the avoidance of central balance hostilities. It has been, obviously, part of an alliance-structure remarkably stable by historical standards. (One could say the Western alliance structure as a whole began to be built with the Western European Union treaty of 1947, so it is now about forty years old, though the ANZUS buttress is a few years younger.) The Western alliance-system as a whole has continually been a valuable restraint on such tendencies as have shown up in Washington towards unilateralism or imprudence in various crises. In the Pacific context, one can see the effects, for instance, in British influence in the Korea crisis of late 1950, and both British and Australian influence in the 1954 crisis over Indochina, at the time of Dien Bien Phu. Use of nuclear weapons was contemplated in both instances, and in both the weight of alliance feeling was a major restraint against it.

In more recent years the techniques of anticipating and responding to crises have depended more and more on the system of surveillance by satellite which has totally transformed the underlying defence relationship of the two superpowers, making their strategic dispositions, and any change in them, 'transparent' to each other in a way unparalleled in diplomatic history. The US facilities in Australia, especially Pine Gap and Nurrungar, are essential cogs in the mechanism of that whole system of surveillance and signalling. They are important also (especially Nurrungar) in the monitoring of nuclear explosions, which is the essential basis of verifying compliance with the Partial Test-Ban Treaty and the Non-Proliferation Treaty, along with the agreements achieved in SALT I and SALT II. For no progress in arms control is possible in the nuclear age except where the superpowers are able to check the results through 'national means of inspection'. That official euphemism, which appears prominently in the arms control treaties at present in operation and will certainly figure in those of the future, means surveillance satellites equipped to detect nuclear explosions and missile launches. Nurrungar and Pine Gap are relay-stations which receive such information from the satellites, and transmit it back to the policy-makers in Washington. It is eminently possible that technical progress in the relaying of information directly between satellites will fairly soon phase out the need for Nurrungar (and later maybe even Pine Gap), but until that date the Australian government is entitled to claim (as it does) that the installations play a part in the essential techniques of arms control.

It could also claim (though the argument would not be popular on the left of the Australian political spectrum) that the installations play a relatively substantial part in the third of the factors mentioned, the overall relationship of mutual deterrence. For the three major installations (Pine Gap, North West Cape and Nurrungar) are all part of the global command, control, communications and intelligence network of the United States. The efficiency and reliability of that network is a most crucial part of the mechanism of deterrence: one might say its eyes, ears, voice and nervous system, without which the weaponry would be dangerous rather than effective. Thus, in my view, Canberra could justify the strategic connection with the United States on the ground that Australia's role in providing the real estate for the joint facilities is an important contribution to America's necessary strategic clout *vis-à-vis* the Soviet Union, and thus to the stability of the central balance.

Mutual deterrence must be seen as a psychological relationship, which rests on assumptions by the decision-makers in Moscow and Washington about the war-fighting capacity of the adversary alliance. That is, war-fighting capacity and deterrence are two sides of the same coin, and have been since almost the earliest years of the nuclear age. War-fighting capacity has to be real, and known to be real, for the structure of deterrence to remain viable. The tendency during the first three years of the Reagan period was for various Washington spokesmen to give the impression of enthusiasm for nuclear battle. This unfortunately convinced a lot of people, including many of the critics of the US connection in Australia, that there had been some fundamental change in the American strategic stance, which had transformed, or was transforming, the Australian installations into part of a 'first-strike' system. In reality, all that changed was the tone of Washington oratory. At least since the Eisenhower period, the US has had a large counterforce (i.e. 'war-fighting') capacity, and the proportion of warheads targeted in that mode (about two-thirds, reportedly) has remained much the same throughout the period. The Strategic Defense Initiative (SDI) or 'Star Wars' research might just possibly in time make a true fundamental change in the American strategic posture, from deterrence based on offensive-strike capacity to deterrence based on defensive capacity, or more probably on a mix of offensive and defensive capacity. That at any rate was the vision held out in President Reagan's initial speech in March 1983. If it is ever going to happen, it is probably a long time off (in the twenty-first century), but undoubtedly on the basis of reports of the present technology, all three of the installations in Australia would seem capable of roles in such a system. The technology is changing fast, however, and on present evidence one would say that technological changes which will allow North West Cape and Nurrungar to be phased out are far closer in time than a workable SDI system.

As the final decade of the 20th century approaches many things seem to be changing fast in international politics, so that the shape of Australia's international environment in the 21st century appears beset by ambiguities. In such circumstances a long-lasting alliance like ANZUS is bound to be suspected of obsolescence, especially in view of the fact that New Zealand, one of the original three partners, had been *de facto* suspended in 1985 from the privileges of alliance membership, as far as the US government is concerned, over the issue of visits by nuclear-armed or nuclear-capable ships to New Zealand ports.[3] Clearly, there has emerged a difference of strategic and diplomatic assessments as between the Australian Labor government and the New Zealand Labour government concerning what risks can and should be accepted for the sake of the usefulness, in both global and regional terms, of maintaining the ANZUS trilateral system of consultations. (The suspension, perhaps temporary, of New Zealand does not in fact much affect the fundamental working of the alliance, since almost all its strategic substance consists of the Australia-US connection.)

Differences between Australian and New Zealand government assessments of ANZUS are no new thing. The very first crisis of ANZUS, during the 1951 negotiations to set it up, arose when the New Zealand government developed qualms about entering a treaty of which Britain was not a member. The basic initiative had been an Australian one, with New Zealand 'going along' a good deal less enthusiastically because of the earlier ANZAC agreement of 1944, and a general tradition (probably stemming from 1914) that Australia and New Zealand had identical strategic interests. It was only in 1984 that this traditional assumption began to seem questionable. Yet sharp differences ought to have been visible long before then.

Australia (but not New Zealand) has a substantial Asian neighbour (Indonesia) of uncertain future orientations, capacities and ambitions. Australia (but not New Zealand) has a moral commitment to an ex-dependency (Papua New Guinea) which shares a land-border with that Asian neighbour and only with difficulty avoids conflict with it. Australia (but not New Zealand) has a long coastline facing the Indian Ocean and two island territories there. Australia (but not New Zealand) has a traumatic memory of bombs on its own soil in World

War II, and midget submarines in Sydney Harbour, and six anxious months in which the policy-makers in Canberra believed a Japanese invasion was a real possibility. Moreover, Australia (but not New Zealand) has, for more than twenty years, since 1963, sustained facilities (first North West Cape and then also Pine Gap and Nurrungar) which are unmistakably cogs in the global balance mechanism, far more ambitious and elaborate than anything required by regional threats in the Southwest Pacific.

Thus, one might say retrospectively that Australian assessments and responsibilities in strategic matters had begun to diverge from those of New Zealand at least as early as the 1960s, and the consciousness of threat had been the greater from the early 1940s. So, even with Labour Parties in power on both sides of the Tasman, it has been no real surprise that the two governments' assessments of the best course for their respective countries should be at variance.

From the US point of view, New Zealand has been quite a marginal ally, relevant only to the Southwest Pacific. Australia, increasingly since the early 1960s, has been an important ally in global, not merely regional, terms because of the role of North West Cape, Pine Gap and Nurrungar in its C^{3}I network. The general Western alliance, of which ANZUS is part, has changed its strategic concepts and its military technology quite frequently over its forty years of life. But its strategic function - to maintain a precautionary balance against what otherwise might become overweening power - has not really changed. And it remains an Australian interest.

The Pacific arena appears almost certain to be more, rather than less, important to the central balance in the 21st century than it has been in the twentieth. The four great agglomerations of strategic, economic and demographic power mentioned earlier (the US, the USSR, China and Japan) will all inevitably grow still more formidable, but at differing rates. For example, China's vast area and population and resources (still mostly at a level of development which the Western powers had reached by the early 19th century) will make its future potential capacities rather intimidating to contemplate. One cannot assume therefore that central balance relationships will remain as they are for ever. China and the Soviet Union could conceivably change places by the 21st century, and Japan perhaps swing out of its present relationship with the United States. The dangers against which ANZUS was formulated, and has been maintained, may have been mostly ghosts during the first forty years of the treaty's existence, but they could take on much more solid substance in the next forty years (assuming the alliance persists) and Australia may, in that time, need a shield of sorts more than it has ever done since 1942.

A shield visibly held aloft sends a signal to the potential adversary. For the peace to be preserved, it is important that signals conveyed to potential adversaries should be clear, steady and unambiguous. The whole vast mechanism of NATO, for instance, with its coalition army and battlefield nuclear weapons, may be seen in essence as primarily the means of conveying a clear, steady, *credible* signal that operations which cross a certain line in Europe will be met by certain means. No decision-maker in Moscow for forty years could fail to take that unambiguous signal into account, and the peace has been preserved. But where, as in Korea, an ambiguous signal was inadvertently transmitted,[4] the adversary decision-makers (in Pyongyang and perhaps in Moscow and Beijing) apparently decided to take a chance, and a very bitter and costly local war had in consequence to be fought, to retain an area thus endowed with uncertainty. Similarly, signals which were inadvertently misleading undoubtedly helped precipitate the Argentinian decision to take over the Falklands, and again a hard-fought local war had to be fought to retrieve the consequences of the miscalculation.

Alliances convey a signal. A decision to break an alliance conveys a still more noticeable signal. So it can be argued that the breaking by Australia of its strategic connection with the US would be a far more important signal than the original signing-up in 1951. Then the Pacific was more or less an American lake. The old American (and Australian) adversary, Japan, was still militarily quite prostrate. China had the resources only to operate a short distance outside its own borders, as for instance in Korea. The Soviet Union was still mostly preoccupied with maintaining its strength in Europe. The former Western colonial powers, Britain and France, were still quite powerful in Asia and the Pacific. The islands were still dependencies, under the strategic and political control of the Western powers.

Almost forty years on, all that has changed, and all in the general direction of increased uncertainties. Soviet policy, in Mr Gorbachev's time, has declared a major interest in Asia and the Pacific. China is developing economic muscle which will some time next century give it the capacity to shake the world. Japan has re-established very efficient defence forces, and has the economic capacity to multiply them manyfold, when it takes the political decision to do so. The ties which have kept it in docile relationship with US diplomacy seem to be fraying away through economic frictions. The Western powers have packed up and left Asia, though France retains its rather trouble-making Pacific connections. Most of the Pacific islands have had their sovereignties restored, and thus the right to make their own ways in a dangerous world. The Soviet Navy in the Pacific is rising towards a level which may some day enable it to challenge the 'sea-control' doctrine of the US Navy. Soviet forces now have bases far enough south, in Da Nang and Cam Ranh Bay, for some types of Soviet bombers to reach deep into continental Australia. Even Libya is trying to get into the act, as a determined stirrer of any troubled Pacific waters which it can reach with money and arms and training facilities. The general shape of the world of the 21st century has become fluid and indeterminate. Yet as the end of the century approaches, as when it began, Australia and the US continue to have common strategic interests in the Pacific and in the general global balance, and thus the case for the alliance between them remains strong.

Endnotes

1   The principal actors involved were Percy Spender as Minister for External Affairs and Alan Watt as his Departmental chief. The Prime Minister of the time, Robert Menzies, was somewhat aloof and sceptical.
2   One of Japan's most talented strategists, General Yamashita, did have a plan of invasion, but the High Command, and especially the Navy, were not convinced of its feasibility.
3   Suspension was *de facto* rather than *de jure* since there is no actual provision in the treaty for suspending members. It could therefore be lifted without further formality, given a change of mind by either a future New Zealand government or a future US Administration.
4   In the form of a speech by the then Secretary of State in January 1950 defining the US defence perimeter as excluding South Korea. The attack came six months later, which is about the time necessary to ready that sort of campaign.

CHAPTER 12

THE ANZUS ALLIANCE: THE CASE AGAINST

Gary Brown*

In thirty-eight years since its signature, the ANZUS Treaty has established itself as one of the foundations of Australian national security policy. Indeed, the Treaty has become one of Australia's political sacred cows. It is clear from a study of recent political history and the consistent performance of ANZUS in public opinion polls that termination of the alliance would bring about the certain defeat of any Australian Government which proposed it. ANZUS, unquestionably, represents the will of the Australian people, a fact which legitimises Australian participation while demonstrating that the people are not infallible, especially if given misleading data on which to base their opinion.

This chapter will endeavour to show first, that there has been consistent misrepresentation of ANZUS' benefits; second, that this misrepresentation has had adverse effects on the quality of Australian national security planning from an early date; and third, that the costs to Australia of the alliance are more extensive than are usually admitted. It will also argue that Australian participation in ANZUS has been, in large part, a substitute for the development of national security policies and concomitant supportive structures derived from analysis of Australia's national interest.

The Benefits of ANZUS

A Security Guarantee

> The 'heart' of the treaty is contained in article 4, under which each party recognizes that 'an armed attack in the Pacific area on any of the parties would be dangerous to its own peace and safety'...As in the case of the North Atlantic Treaty, on which this treaty is modelled, the precise action to be taken by each party is not specified. Australia is not bound, and the United States could not accept an obligation, to make an immediate formal declaration of war, which, under the United States Constitution, is the prerogative of the Congress. But, as the

---

* The views expressed in this chapter are the author's and should not be attributed to any other person or organisation.

United States Secretary of State [Dulles] has expressed it, 'our fates have been joined', and the intention is that an attack on one should be regarded as an attack on all, and that all three will resist together.[1]

It is clear from these remarks of the then External Affairs Minister, Mr (later Lord) Casey in July 1951, that ANZUS was represented to the Australian parliament and people as a guarantee of support by the United States should Australia or New Zealand be attacked. Casey's allusion to the NATO agreement (which is actually much more explicit in its reference to the use of armed force than ANZUS), was intended to create the impression that the latter was essentially the same sort of treaty as the former. While a cynical critic might assume that this was little more than the sort of rhetoric frequently used by politicians to persuade the electorate of the virtues of their latest initiative, there is evidence which demonstrates that, by 1956 at any rate, the Government's senior defence advisers had convinced themselves that ANZUS contained a solid security guarantee for Australia.

For many years, a key defence planning document has been that known as the *Strategic Basis*. This document represents the advice of senior defence and foreign policy planners to Government about the strategic circumstances confronting Australia and appropriate policy responses. The 1956 version of this paper concluded that:

> The value of ANZUS as a United States guarantee by treaty of the security of Australia and New Zealand remains undiminished.[2]

This classified advice rendered to government by the Defence Committee, the highest level source of advice available, which asserts the existence of a US security guarantee to Australia and New Zealand, is evidence of private as well as public misinterpretation of the ANZUS Treaty.

This misinterpretation, moreover, persisted intact for at least twenty years. The 1972 Defence White Paper, for example, tabled by the Liberal-Country Party Government of Mr (later Sir William) McMahon, stated unequivocally that 'Article IV of the Treaty is generally accepted to be the assured foundation of Australia's ultimate security'.[3] Generally accepted it was, and is; an assured foundation for Australian security it was not, and is not. The next Defence White Paper, released by the Fraser Liberal-National Party Government in November 1976, was somewhat less effusive about ANZUS, noting that it is not Australian policy, 'nor would it be prudent, to rely on US combat help in all circumstances' though, even then, it considered that ANZUS gave 'substantial grounds for confidence that in the event of a fundamental threat to Australia's security, US military support would be forthcoming'.[4]

In fact, the true nature of the ANZUS 'guarantee' was only spelt out in wholly unequivocal terms first, by the Hawke Government's first Foreign Minister, Mr Hayden, in the course of his report to Parliament on a review of the ANZUS Treaty, conducted soon after the Government came to power, and second, by Mr Paul Dibb, in his 1986 *Review of Australia's Defence Capabilities*. Hayden told Parliament in 1983 that:

> ...the obligation to respond and to assist would not automatically involve the provision of military forces in support of the country subjected to threat or attacks....A range of responses might be available, and it would be up to the other partners to judge which response would be appropriate in a given situation. It may be in certain circumstances that diplomatic action, or political or economic sanctions against the adversary, or the supply of equipment or military logistical support for the ally would be judged a more appropriate response....In other circumstances direct military support may be appropriate.[5]

Thus, Australia's remaining ANZUS partner, the United States, is obliged under the Treaty to give consideration to action in support of Australia if that nation were attacked. Action could range from diplomatic protests to full-scale military intervention. The Treaty gives no guarantees as to the form of action a partner should take, not even the mention of resort to armed forces which is to be found in Article 5 of the NATO Treaty. And, as Hayden made clear, it would be up to the requested partner to determine the nature of action taken in support of its ally. Even blunter was the Dibb *Review*, which stripped away the remnants of the 'guarantee' inteerpretation of ANZUS in a few sentences:

> The ANZUS Treaty provides for consultation in the first instance. *There are no guarantees inherent in it.* It is realistic to assume that the parties will continue to approach each situation in accordance with their respective national interests. [Emphasis added].[6]

Hence in its thirty-eight year history, ANZUS has slid in apparent status from a 'US guarantee by treaty of the security of Australia and New Zealand', or 'the assured foundation of Australia's ultimate security', to the coldly realistic assessment of the Dibb *Review* that 'no guarantees' are inherent in it. What then does the formerly vaunted ANZUS 'guarantee' of Australia's security actually amount to? The following sums up the apparent situation:

- In the event of a 'fundamental' threat to Australia arising - something admitted to be a highly remote contingency, most probably associated with the outbreak of global war - Australia can have 'confidence' that the United States would come to its rescue; and

- For lower-level contingencies, the likelihood of direct US combat support for Australia is much lower. The Guam Doctrine suggests that self-reliance, not alliance, is likely to bring deliverance in conditions associated with lower level threats.

In short, the ANZUS 'guarantee' is most likely to operate against the most unlikely level of threat; conversely, the more probable threat contingencies are those Australia will have to handle by itself. Any discussion of the 'guarantee' at high or 'fundamental' threat levels needs to take account of the fact that in a global war context, Australia's call to the US will have to compete with demands from the NATO allies, Japan, the north Pacific, and the Middle East.

Non-Combat US Support

While combat support at the more credible threat levels is admitted to be unlikely, US assistance could take other forms, ranging from diplomatic or economic initiatives, through to the provision of needed military equipment. The latter option is enshrined in a Memorandum of Understanding (MoU) between the two countries, signed in 1980 by the Carter Administration and the Fraser Government. Paragraph 8 of the MoU lists types of defence items and services which the US makes available to Australia in peacetime. These include weapons systems and equipments, spare parts, munitions, ammunitions, explosives, modification kits, test equipment, specialist services, training, repair services and so on.[7] The agreement then provides that:

> Subject to its laws and regulations and the exigencies of war, the United States will continue to provide logistic support materiel and services of the kind described in paragraph 8 to Australia during periods of international tension or in circumstances of armed conflict involving either or both parties. Such United States support would include the following elements if needed:[8] [Here follows a list, which includes weapons system support, loss replacement, high technology munition supply and other items highly desirable should the Australian Defence Force (ADF) find itself in armed conflict].

The MoU has assumed a place of prominence in ANZUS hagiography and importance in the long-term national security planning process. The *1987 White Paper*, for example, announced that:

> Our agreements with the United States also provide for the supply of munitions and equipment in an emergency, *alleviating the need for large-scale stockpiling by the ADF*. [Emphasis added].[9]

And, in tabling the Paper, the Minister for Defence, Mr Beazley, confidently spoke of Australia's 'guaranteed access to ready resupply of essential warstocks'.[10]

With ADF stockholding policy and planning so closely linked to the MoU, the commitments allegedly entered into by the United States in that document will need to be met should the ADF find itself engaged in active operations against any nation except the very weakest. The advent and rapid proliferation of weapons with high single-shot kill probabilities implies quite high attrition rates in conflicts of relatively short duration. Australia could, thus, require resupply of weapons and/or platforms from the US at short notice should conflict break out with a power itself equipped with precision guided munitions. Although the number of *Harpoon* missiles or *Mk48* torpedoes, for example, held by the ADF is classified, it is apparent, from an examination of Defence's budget estimates papers, that holdings are not large. If Australia is not to find itself in a position similar to Argentina's during the Falklands conflict, unable to follow up early successes because of a weapons shortage, it will most likely require prompt US compliance with the implicit promise of the MoU.

Like the ANZUS Treaty itself, the MoU commits the United States to nothing which it may not want to do at the time. Moreover, the memorandum was varied in a small, but significant, manner when renegotiated by the Hawke Government in 1985. While numerous alterations and additions were made at this time, one of the most important was the alteration of 'would' to 'could' in the same paragraph. Thus, whereas the 1980 agreement said that US support under the MoU would include those items and services outlined, the 1985 version states only that it *could* include them.[11]

Despite its support for ANZUS generally, the Dibb *Review* was able to muster only muted enthusiasm for the MoU on logistic support, stating that it gave 'some assurance' of continued US supply and support in time of conflict.[12] If Australian national security policy and ADF stockholding practice is dependent on our trusting the word of a foreign power with global demands on its economic capacity, military resources and political goodwill, it behoves those who maintain this position to say so explicitly rather than raise a smokescreen of claims supported neither by the Treaty nor its subsidiary agreements.

Distortion of ADF force structure caused by the American alliance has another dimension, namely excessive reliance on the US as a source of matériel. Even a cursory scrutiny of the military inventory reveals a preponderance of US-sourced items. This guarantees our dependence on the weak reeds of ANZUS and the MoU for equipment resupply.

Moreover the ANZUS climate apparently makes source diversification outside the US difficult unless, as with conventional submarines, there are no American suppliers. Since the 1974 order of tanks from West Germany, and excluding the current submarine project, nearly all major equipments - *P3C Orion* and *F/A-18* aircraft, and *Harpoons* for example - have been US sourced.

Intelligence Support and Cooperation

> The United States gains information important to its global maritime intelligence system from Australian surveillance and intelligence gathering activities in an area extending from the eastern Indian Ocean to the South-West Pacific. At the same time Australia has access to the extensive US intelligence resources. This information is not confined to global superpower competition; it also complements Australia's information on political and military developments in our own region.[13]

> Fundamental to the effective development of a self-reliant defence force is comprehensive intelligence cover of our area of primary strategic interest. Whilst we possess significant indigenous capabilities in this field, it is access to complementary US intelligence, and particularly access to US satellite information, which we could not afford to duplicate, that assures us of a comprehensive knowledge of regional developments relevant to our security.[14]

These quotations encapsulate the long-standing Australian Government view on the intelligence benefits of ANZUS. According to this view, Australia and the United States have developed mutually beneficial arrangements for intelligence sharing. In essence, Australia supplies the US with regional intelligence collected from its own sources,[15] and, in return, receives intelligence both on global superpower issues and complementary intelligence bearing on

Australia's region. This intelligence is, according to the Dibb *Review*, not readily replaceable from Australian sources.16

It is very difficult to analyse the effect of intelligence-sharing arrangements, if for no other reason than the 'neither confirm nor deny' wall erected by the intelligence community to protect both legitimate secrets and embarrassing information. As a consequence, there is no way for an external observer to assess, for example, whether or not the US actually provides Australia with information of the value claimed. As Ross Babbage has observed:

> ...reliance upon foreign intelligence services for significant components of the country's priority requirements is highly undesirable. Institutionalized dependence...may render Australia vulnerable to a large number of potentially damaging influences. To illustrate the point, there is considerable scope in this type of relationship for the dispensing country to regulate or modify the flow of information in its own interests. Disinformation might be supplied either unintentionally or otherwise...in some types of situations, foreign sources of information might be suspended arbitrarily or made the subject of bargaining pressures that would not be in Australia's interests.17

The potential for disinformation to impact upon national security decision-making was illustrated (as a potential, not necessarily as a fact), during the US-Libyan confrontation of 1986. In March of that year, it was revealed that the US Central Intelligence Agency and Defense Department were running a disinformation campaign on certain weapons platforms and technology programs, thus establishing that disinformation at least for some purposes was US practice.18 Subsequently, (though not consequently), Bernard Kalb, a senior State Department spokesman, resigned his post in protest at an alleged US disinformation program designed by then National Security Adviser Poindexter, to assist US policy towards Libya by feeding false information about Libyan inspired terrorism to journalists. In the light of this disclosure, the Australian Government's reaction to the US air attack on Libya, launched in retaliation for alleged Libyan complicity in the Berlin night-club bomb outrage, is of interest. Addressing Parliament on 15 April 1986, the Prime Minister refrained from expressing direct support for the US attacks, but mentioned that both he and Mr Hayden had 'been privy to *apparently* compelling evidence of a direct line of command between Libya and the Berlin nightclub bombing' (emphasis added).19 Questioned by Government backbench MP John Scott (Hindmarsh, Adelaide) about his use of the qualifier 'apparently', in the light of Kalb's resignation and other disinformation revelations, Hawke later said only that there was no reason known to the Government for doubting the evidence and that the Government therefore accepted it as genuine.[20] In short, the evidence vindicates Babbage's conclusion that there is a potential for US-sponsored disinformation to influence the policy of allies who cannot verify independently what they are told by Washington.

The risk of disinformation aside, there remain the problems of assuring intelligence feed to support operations should Australia find itself in active conflict and of obtaining the feed without conditions constraining the Government's selection of war aims, rules of engagement, escalation policy and so on. However, notwithstanding his assertion in his May 1987 speech, the Minister for Defence has on at least one occasion claimed that, so far as regional intelligence is concerned, Australia is, for all practical purposes, already self-sufficient:

> We are thoroughly aware of the activities of the Soviet Union in the Pacific, in South East Asia and at Cam Ranh Bay. We are aware of this...because that area is the object of our own independent intelligence gathering activity, which is very substantial....I take this opportunity to remind the House of some of those independent intelligence gathering capabilities....*I stress again that we do not rely on any advice that we receive from anybody else about what is going on in the region.* We have our own intelligence gathering capability and it is very effective. [Emphasis added].[21]

This effectively gives the lie to claims made elsewhere that Australia is incapable of satisfying her essential regional intelligence requirements from her own resources. Material supplied under ANZUS may be useful, but cannot be said to be indispensable.

Exercises and Cooperation

There is an extensive and expensive program of ADF exercises with the United States, all of which, whatever their formal status, can be said to be under the broad aegis of ANZUS. Exercising with a superpower, it is argued by supporters of the alliance, allows Australia to hone its military skills against the very best in technology and on a scale impossible for most nations of comparable size. In the financial year 1985-86, for example, the ADF engaged in 42 distinct exercises, each of which involved more than 100 Army personnel or more than two RAAF combat, transport or surveillance aircraft, or more than one RAN major surface combatant, or more than 200 RAN personnel. Of these, all but six were combined exercises - that is, exercises with elements of foreign defence forces - and these 36 exercises cost the taxpayer some $74.88 million (see Table 1). The 1987 White Paper defined Australia's area of direct military interest as Australia, its territories and proximate ocean areas, Indonesia, Papua New Guinea, New Zealand and other nearby countries of the Southwest Pacific. Of the 36 combined exercises, the majority of which involved the United States, half (including the largest) were conducted outside the area of primary defence interest. Moreover, half of the $75m spent in 1985-86 on combined exercises was spent on exercises held outside this area. Equally interesting is the consumption of nearly 60 per cent of the sum by exercises with the US, as against 0.048 per cent on exercises with Malaysia or Singapore, about 6.8 per cent under the Five-Power arrangements, 1.8 per cent with PNG, 8.8 per cent miscellaneous (principally RAAF participation in RED FLAG 85, exercising F-111s with NATO elements in the US), and 24 per cent with New Zealand.22

Table 1: ADF Exercises in 1985-86

	ADF Alone	US	NZ	Malaysia/ Singapore	Five-Power*	PNG	Other	Total
Numbers:	6	12	10	2	6	2	4	42
Cost ($m):	na	43.535	28.221	9.036	5.094	2.372	6.622	74.88

* Under Five-Power Defense Arrangements (Malaysia, Singapore, UK, NZ and Australia).

Clearly, ANZUS demands are imposing a distortion on the priorities of ADF exercising and especially on the ADF's ability to exercise more extensively inside the area of direct military interest. To make the point another way, it would appear highly desirable for the ADF to be able to exercise with greater frequency and resources inside the area - this does not exclude the possibility of combined exercises with other friendly powers - rather than committing so great a proportion of its limited budget to elaborate large-scale productions conducted in distant environs, such as RIMPAC.

An ANZUS-imposed distortion is apparent also in the choice of capabilities exercised with the US. For example, in 1985-86, no less than three exercises (the SILENT PEARL series), were held in Hawaian waters, and involved Anti-Submarine Warfare (ASW) against a nuclear-powered attack submarine (SSN). An evaluation of the relative merits of air ASW against SSNs and conventional boats concluded that:

ASW sensors and equipment in RAAF P-3Cs are state-of-the-art technology and represent an effective counter to the modern nuclear submarine, but are more limited in respect of the modern conventional boat.[23]

The SSN threat to Australian interests is relatively low. As the Dibb *Review* indicated, it is the conventionally-powered boats which are the more probable threat and the more difficult target, especially because of their quietness relative to SSNs. Logically, therefore, the ADF would be better exercised testing itself against conventional boats rather than nuclear attack submarines. The SILENT PEARL exercises offer an example of exercises superfluous to ADF requirements and represent another case of exercise planning dictated not by national defence priorities but by the availability of the US as a partner and the need to be seen to be exercising frequently with that country to prove once more Australia's enthusiasm for the alliance. It is somewhat ironic that having fitted out the *P3C Orion* aircraft with British and Australian ASW systems - the original US systems being operationally inappropriate for Australia's needs - Australia then exercises them in environments and against targets of marginal relevance to those needs.

Deterrence, Uncertainty and ANZUS

The Dibb *Review* argues that ANZUS still has a deterrent effect on potential aggressors because such 'must take into account possible United States involvement in the defence of Australia'.[24] The 1987 White Paper picked up this theme and the Minister, in tabling it, suggested that:

> The American alliance of course also provides a substantial deterrent. Whilst it would be irresponsible to depend on direct American combat support for our security, the possibility that this would be forthcoming would greatly complicate the offensive strategy of a potential aggressor.[25]

Whether the United States would come to Australia's support, either directly or with intelligence and equipment supplies, will in all cases depend on Washington's assessment of the situation at the time. Neither the ANZUS Treaty nor the MoU obliges the US to do anything of consequence. To give a hypothetical example, should Australia and Indonesia become embroiled in hostilities for some reason, Washington will need to weigh up its priorities very carefully indeed. Both Indonesia and Australia are important regionally to the US, and moreover, each has certain strategic assets - Australia has the US facilities at Pine Gap, Nurrungar and North West Cape; Indonesia controls important maritime chokepoints. The decision is impossible to predict, but there is no certainty that even resupply from the US would be made available to Australia.

The claim that ANZUS helps deter attack on Australian national security interests by generating uncertainty about US intentions in the minds of would-be aggressors may have some substance. However, it is substance which works in both directions, but not with equal force each way. If potential aggressors are uncertain about American intentions, so is Australia. But whereas Australia has made the US alliance a keystone of its national security policy and allowed it to influence ADF stockholding policy, exercise planning and programming and equipment capabilities, and whereas Australia would expect resupply from America during hostilities, none of Australia's regional neighbours have placed themselves in so great a position of dependence upon a single ally. To a potential aggressor, then, US intervention on Australia's behalf is something which *might* happen and which needs to be weighed-up in planning operations against Australia; to Australia, however, US intervention (at least via resupply) is something which *must* happen because current stockholdings are likely to be insufficient for operations over any period or at enhanced levels of intensity.

Any uncertainties about American intentions will complicate an aggressor's planning, but at the same time, such uncertainty would have disastrous consequences for the Government in Canberra and the ADF in the field in the lead-up to operations and once operations had commenced. Will the United States resupply us? When? With what? With how much? On what terms? These questions are significant to potential aggressors; to Australia they are vital.

Influence on Allies

A frequently advanced benefit of the Alliance with the US is that it confers on Australia, an otherwise small-to-middling power of no great consequence beyond its immediate region, influence in the counsels of the most powerful nation on earth.[26] ANZUS does provide an additional conduit for Australia to make representations to the United States on matters of interest or concern. That Australia has, on occasions, made representations in this way would be, to those convinced of the alliance's inherent value, merely further evidence of a healthy working relationship. Indeed, in some cases, there is evidence to suggest that apparently Australia has been able to exert some influence (albeit tardy) on US policy. A case in point concerns the depredations of American commercial fishing interests in the waters of the Southwest Pacific, activities which so soured the perspective of some regional nations that they entered into arrangements with the Soviets instead, because they, unlike the Americans, were prepared to pay for fishing rights. In this case, the Americans heeded Australia's warnings about the serious consequences of illegal US fishing. However, a cynic might argue that it was when the adverse consequences of this fishing came to light, rather than when Australia warned the US, that Washington reacted.

By contrast, in at least two other recent cases, Australia's attempts to exercise influence with its ANZUS ally appear to have been thoroughly and permanently rebuffed. One concerns the Treaty of Rarotonga, otherwise known as the South Pacific Nuclear Free Zone treaty. This treaty was promoted actively by Australia among regional nations, but met with a lukewarm reception in Washington well before it was signed. To address US concerns - which appeared to revolve around the right of nuclear-powered or -armed ships to transit the 'nuclear free zone' set up by the treaty, and around visiting rights for US ships in the ports of signatories - Australia secured the insertion of clauses to protect US interests in these areas. In so doing, it alienated Vanuatu, which declined to sign the final draft because it was seen as too weak. Nevertheless, after lengthy consideration, the United States declined to accede to the relevant protocols of the Treaty.

Of far greater and long-term importance is the matter of US economic policy and its linkage to the Australian-American national security relationship. Since 1986, the US has embarked on a trade war with the European Economic Community, the effect of which has been to undermine traditional markets for Australian primary produce and contribute to a decline in Australia's terms of trade. Despite strong representations at the government-to-government level and the sending of three all-party delegations to the US in the last 18 months, Australia has not been able to achieve any real progress on this issue. It is clear that US decision-makers view the Australian-American national security relationship as separate from its economic relationships. It was reported that Australia had considered cancelling scheduled 1986 ANZUS talks in protest at US trade policies. Secretary of State Schultz, however, 'reacted angrily and said the US could not accept the linking of commercial issues with foreign and defence policy issues. After word of his reaction was sent to Canberra, the boycott idea was dropped'.[27] However, whatever the US view of this matter, it is clear that these two facets of national policy are inseparably linked. If Australia's economic foundation is sufficiently eroded, it will be unable to afford the Defence Force equipment it presently buys from the Americans and its overall ability to address national security problems effectively will decline. While it might be in the short-term American interest to claim a decoupling of economic and national security policies, in the long term, the bill for the latter has to be met via the former. This is as true in Canberra as in Washington.

These two instances demonstrate that, alliance or no alliance, the ability of small powers to influence the decisions of a superpower is limited in the extreme where the superpower has interests of its own engaged. For several years the US Tuna Boat Association appears to have wielded more influence in Washington than either Australia or South Pacific nations; and American agricultural interests obviously outweigh Australia at the moment. Given the great disparity between the two allies in size, power and influence, this conclusion should not be surprising. While Australia may be the 'flavour of the month' in America, the overall perception of Australia in the United States is still at a very low level. So low, indeed, that in a survey, for example, conducted by the Chicago Council on Foreign Relations in 1986, seeking a ranked list of countries in which the US has a 'vital interest', Australia did not score at all, among either the general public or, more significantly, amongst 'opinion leaders'. Countries which did score included India, Poland, and Syria.[28]

The Costs of ANZUS

Most writers in opposition to the ANZUS alliance choose to emphasise its costs, and there is an extensive literature (albeit not always well-informed) outlining them. This section will therefore, very briefly allude to those costs which have substance and which have not been noted, at least implicitly, elsewhere in this chapter.

Credibility and Consistency in Policy

As long ago as the Whitlam Government, it was apparent that there was potentially a conflict between some foreign policy initiatives of the Government and its ANZUS commitment. In supporting the idea of an Indian Ocean Zone of Peace, for example, that Government was taxed by a number of littoral states with gross inconsistency in that Australia hosted (and still hosts) on its Indian Ocean coast the US naval communications station at North West Cape, a prime function of which has always been communications with US ballistic missile submarines (SSBNs). More recently, the present Australian Government attracted analogous criticisms for its advocacy of the Rarotonga Treaty. Similarly, otherwise unexceptionable Australian pronouncements on nuclear disarmament and arms control generally have been greeted with skepticism by some who have pointed out that Australia hosts important US installations suspected of doing much more than contributing to verification, hosts US warship visits under the 'neither confirm or deny' policy with respect to nuclear weapons aboard and is, after all, a treaty partner of a nuclear superpower. While the Government has often responded to comments of this type, the fact remains that the inconsistencies alluded to are not always easy to rationalise, nor would they need to be rationalised were Australia not a party to ANZUS.

Australia a Nuclear Target

It now seems settled, after many years of denial and diversion, that at least the North West Cape, Pine Gap and Nurrungar facilities feature on Soviet target lists. Indeed, in its enthusiasm for the alliance, the Government recently raised the Nurrungar facility to the doubtful honour of being one of the very first targets in the world for Soviet nuclear attack should a superpower war break out. The 1987 White Paper asserted that the US Defense Support Program (which works in Australia through Nurrungar) provides the US with 'its earliest warning of intercontinental ballistic missile attack'.[29] Earliest-warning stations, like Nurrungar, are unlikely in most probable nuclear warfare scenarios to last very long. It can be taken, then, that risk of nuclear attack is a cost of Australia's alliance with the United States.[30] Funds likely to be spent on civil defence measures for communities near the US facilities can also be billed to this account.

Impairment of Sovereignty

Two cases, both involving the North West Cape station, amply demonstrate the potential for impairment of Australian sovereignty as a by-product of the ANZUS alliance. The first is the use of the station in 1973 by the Nixon Administration to place US SSBNs and other forces on a raised condition of readiness without Australian knowledge or consent. The second concerned the updating of certain equipment at the station without proper permission being obtained from Australia. After each case, the Government criticised American behaviour and announced revised procedures to ensure that such lapses could not recur. Doubtless further revisions will be undertaken should lapses of this sort occur again.

Conclusions: ANZUS as a Security Blanket

There is ample evidence to argue that the ANZUS Treaty's principal function is to be a security blanket for both of its remaining partners. For the United States, it represents reassurance that Australia will not 'go bad' and that access to the important facilities on Australian soil will be maintained. For Australia, it represents and appears to realise - nowadays in a form more cautiously expressed, but still effective - an assurance from the United States that Australia will not be left in the lurch should the nation become involved in hostilities. If a major threat materialises, direct US combat support would be awaited with some confidence; if a lesser level contingency confronts the Defence Forces, American assistance under the MoU and intelligence feeds would be the least which would be expected of Australia's ally.

The United States' confidence in ANZUS as a security blanket is unlikely to be misplaced. High levels of public support for the alliance in Australia demonstrate this beyond reasonable question. As noted earlier, the Australian government which proposed to terminate ANZUS would itself be terminated by the electors at the first available opportunity. Yet, there is actually no evidence, declaratory statements for public consumption aside, that the United States would come to Australia's aid in either high or lower-level contingencies because of the ANZUS Treaty. There are, indeed, strong arguments to the contrary. It is true enough that there is little or no evidence that Washington definitely would *not* supply aid as per the MoU or, *in extremis*, direct combat support; but it remains incumbent on those who say Australia should continue the alliance and incur its inevitable costs, to show that these costs are balanced by equally concrete benefits. However, it is clear that the concrete benefits are, in comparison to nebulous 'guarantees' which evaporate under scrutiny, relatively few and by no means dependent on ANZUS as a necessary condition of delivery.

In terminating ANZUS, it is neither necessary nor sensible that Australia declare itself either neutral, non-aligned, or divorced from the Western community. The latter is something which no government can effect in practice. Australia's membership of the Western community of nations is dependent not on alliances, but on fundamental realities beyond the power of governments to alter. Australia, by getting out of the alliance, has the opportunity to take its place in the world as a sovereign, independent nation. In such an environment, it will be up to the government from time to time to make such *ad hoc* cooperative arrangements (such as the Five-Power arrangements), as suit Australia's security requirements. A long-term pact with a superpower which does not provide solid assurances credible over the whole range of contingencies relevant to Australia is no substitute for national security planning and practice developed for Australia's specialised needs.

Those who claim that immediate and severe practical costs will accrue to Australia if we left ANZUS are in error. The US would probably, as with New Zealand, reduce the level of intelligence feed. However, the Minister for Defence is on record about Australia's self-sufficiency in regional intelligence. It would be unlikely to seriously impede the supply of equipment to the ADF in peacetime conditions, for two reasons. First, it is not in Washington's interest to have the ADF run down in capability; and second, vested interests in the US would react poorly to US Government actions which restricted opportunities for further lucrative arms deals with Australia.

The suggestion that the end of ANZUS would cost Australia dearly in terms of the influence it could bring to bear in Washington derives its plausibility chiefly from repetition. It is clear that Australia has, in Washington, just the degree of influence one would expect of a small power making representations to a superpower: as much as the latter cares to grant having assessed its own interests, and no more. Appeals to the alliance and veiled (though empty) hints about the tenure of the US facilities have achieved nothing of note for Australia on US trade policies.

Similarly, claims that the ADF would suffer drastic conse-quences through loss of the ANZUS exercise program are based on a misconception; namely that the ADF needs to exercise frequently and on a large scale with a superpower. In fact, it can be argued that ANZUS exercises consume an altogether disproportionate share of resources devoted to ADF exercises with overseas powers. If Australia is serious about taking an important role in the maintenance of regional security, then much of the $43.5 million spent on ANZUS exercises in 1985-86 could well have been applied to support a comprehensive series of exercises with regional powers, or to the Defence Cooperation Program.

That ANZUS deters through uncertainty may well be true. However, the question is: who is most deterred by uncertainty about whether the US will come to Australia's aid? An American decision to intervene on Australia's behalf *can* be planned for by an aggressor; a decision not to intervene, however, could destroy the basis of ADF planning unless it were conducted *ab initio* on the assumption that no support would be available.

The ANZUS alliance was Australia's price in 1951 for agreeing to a 'soft' Japanese peace treaty. Since then, the alliance has been made to fulfil many different roles, few if any of which have relevance to the maintenance of Australia's security interests. Indeed, by providing ready-made justification for neglect of fundamental national security issues, ANZUS has done the ADF and Australia a great disservice. Because of ANZUS, Australia, for 20 years, followed a policy of 'forward defence' and close cooperation with the United States which resulted in an ADF configured for operations with major allies and incapable of independent operations on any scale in defence of specifically Australian interests. Recent governments, aware, privately at least, that there are no US guarantees, have had to embark on a massive and costly restructuring of the ADF in order to restore its credibility as the defender of Australia, rather than an adjunct of the United States' forces. And even in this exercise they are hamstrung by the need to make concessions to Washington. This long-term distortion of Australian national security planning, and of ADF priorities and capabilities, is a direct consequence of the American alliance.

The costs of the American alliance appear plain and visible, whereas the benefits are vague, unspecific and dubious of realisation in practice. If it is accepted that the partners will act in accordance with their national interests, it is hard to see how documents like the ANZUS Treaty or the MoU, which commit nobody to anything specific, could alter the 'national interest' calculations which Washington would need to perform should Australia seek aid. For Australia to continue to base important aspects of ADF planning, and even some force structure considerations, on so weak a reed, is to give contemporary relevance to the famous Menzies line of faith in the 'great and powerful friend'. Faith, as a personal thing, may indeed move mountains, but it will not supply the ADF when the going gets tough and it is not an appropriate foundation upon which to rest critical aspects of Australian national security.

Endnotes

1   Mr Casey, External Affairs Minister, *Hansard (House of Representatives)*, 13 July 1951, p.1709.
2   *Strategic Basis of Australian Defence Policy*, Report by the Defence Committee, October 1956. Annex, 'Strategic Review', paragraph 36.
3   Department of Defence, *Australian   Defence Review*, (Australian Government Publishing Service, Canberra, March 1972), Chapter 4, Paragraph 25.
4   *Australian Defence*, (Australian Government Publishing Service, Canberra, 1976), Chapter 3, Paragraphs 8 and 7.
5   *Hansard (House of Representatives)*, 15 September 1983, p.900.
6   Paul Dibb, *Review of Australia's Defence Capabilities*, (Australian Government Publishing Service, Canberra, 1986), p.46.
7   *Memorandum of Understanding on Logistic Support Between the Government of Australia and the Government of the United States of America*, (18 March 1980, Paragraph 8. (Hereafter cited as *MoU*, with year as appropriate.)
8   *MoU* (1980), Paragraph 10.
9   Hon. Kim C. Beazley, *Defence of Australia 1987*, (Australian Government Publishing Service, Canberra, 1987), Paragraph 1.21.
10   *Hansard (House of Representatives)*, 19 March 1987, p.1093.
11   *MoU* (1980), Paragraph 10 and body of text. See also *MoU* (1985), Paragraph 10. The 1985 agreement was tabled in Parliament in May that year.
12   Paul Dibb, *Review of Australia's Defence Capabilities*.
13   Hon. Kim C. Beazley, *Defence of Australia 1987*, Paragraph 1.20.

14 Hon. K.C. Beazley, *Self-Reliance - A New Direction?*, Address to the Just Defence Committee, Perth, 23-24 May 1987, p.5.

15 These sources are not inconsiderable. They would include the 'product' of work by the Australian Secret Intelligence Service (ASIS), the Defence Signals Division (electronic intercept at home and abroad), the Joint Intelligence Organisation, the Office of National Assessments and, to a limited extent, even the Australian Security Intelligence Organisation.

16 Paul Dibb, *Review of Australia's Defence Capabilities*, p.46.

17 Ross Babbage, *Rethinking Australia's Defence*, (Queensland University Press, St Lucia, 1980), p.90.

18 David M. North, 'US Using Disinformation Policy to Impede Technical Data Flow', *Aviation Week and Space Technology*, 17 March 1986, pp.16-17.

19 *Hansard (House of Representatives)*, 15 April 1986, p.2269.

20 *Hansard (House of Representatives)*, 24 February 1987, p.278.

21 *Ibid..*

22 Data for these percentages was extracted from *Hansard (House of Representatives)*, 6 May 1987, Answer to Question No.5192.

23 Air Vice Marshal E.A. Radford and Rear Admiral I.W. Knox, 'Land-Based Air Power in Maritime Operations',in Desmond Ball (ed.), *Air Power: Global Developments and Australian Perspectives*, (Pergamon-Brassey's Defence Publishers, Sydney, 1988), p.492.

24 Dibb, *Review of Australia's Defence Capabilities*.

25 *Ibid..*

26 See, for example, John Spender, 'Is the ANZUS Treaty Still Relevant After 31 Years?', *The Australian*, 6 October 1982.

27 Geoff Kitney, 'Canberra Drops ANZUS Boycott Plan', *National Times*, 10 August 1986.

28 'US Versus Them', *Economist*, 14 March 1987, p.33.

29 Beazley, *Defence of Australia 1987*, para 2.10.

30 It has been argued, by the then Foreign Minister Hayden among others, that the risk of nuclear attack is overstressed by ANZUS' critics because 'regardless of the presence of the joint facilities, Australia cannot escape the consequences of a nuclear war'. (*Uranium, the Joint Facilities, Disarmament and Peace*, booklet authorised by the Minister, 4 July 1984, p.16.) While the 'nuclear winter' and other global post-nuclear scenarios remain hypothetical (there being, fortunately, no large-scale empirical evidence), it seems true enough that Australia would not escape unscathed, even were we not targeted. But to imply that enduring the indirect effects of nuclear war is essentially the same as enduring indirect global effects *plus* direct nuclear attack - which is the outcome once the US bases are hit - seems to be gilding the funereal lily a little.

CHAPTER 13

AUSTRALIAN DEFENCE DECISION-MAKING: ACTORS AND PROCESSES

Graeme Cheeseman and Desmond Ball

Change and Continuity in Australian Defence

An understanding of defence decision-making in Australia requires a knowledge of the principal actors involved and the process by which policy decisions are made. It is important also to be aware of the strategic and bureaucratic dimensions of the subject and how these have changed. Over the past decade, Australia's strategic thinking and the structural and power-sharing arrangements which make up the defence establishment have undergone considerable change. At the same time, certain features of Australian defence - most notably its dependent relationship with the United States and the relatively 'closed' nature of the decision-making process - continue to operate and impose certain constraints and limitations on how Australia can act. The first part of the chapter examines these two features against a background of the major changes which have occurred in Australia's defence in recent years. It then describes the principal actors in, and the process of, Australian defence decision-making in the late 1980s, and some of the problems and key issues which presently confront it.

Up until the mid-1960s, a very large area of Australia's national security policy was effectively abrogated to our principal ally. Australia's military forces were developed primarily to fight alongside their British and American counterparts in southeast Asia, and our defence decision-making process was largely concerned with supporting their role. This situation began to change in the aftermath of the Vietnam war and the consequent reappraisal by the United States of its security interests in the Asia-Pacific region. These altered circumstances led Australia to abandon its existing 'forward defence' posture in favour of the strategy of 'self-reliance'. Australia is now responsible for its own security and its military forces are required to maintain the independent capacity to mount operations to defeat hostile forces within an area encompassing the Australian mainland and its territories and proximate waters, Indonesia, Papua New Guinea, New Zealand, and 'other nearby countries of the South West Pacific'.[1]

Although emphasising greater independence in defence matters, Australia's revised security policies continue to be pursued within an overall framework of alliances and agreements of which the most significant are those with the United States. These provide Australia with a range of practical benefits, including the provision of intelligence and access to US training courses and advanced military technologies, as well as a degree of protection against future military threats since a potential adversary must take into account the possibility of direct US military involvement in the event that Australia or its interests were attacked. At the same time, Australia's relationship with the United States tends to detract from our capacity for independent decision-making in some areas and constrains our current efforts to develop a fully self-reliant defence posture since it tends to encourage our preference for state-of-the-art weapons systems, distorts ADF exercise schedules, and imposes inappropriate or unnecessary operational requirements or standards on our armed forces.[2]

The changes in Australia's strategic circumstances paralleled, and were in part responsible for, quite significant changes in the structure of the defence establishment.[3] Between 1945 and 1972, Australia's Defence establishment consisted of a number of separate departments - Defence, Navy, Army, Air Force, and Supply - each with its own Minister and in the case of the Service departments, headed by an executive board which had independent powers and duties. In 1973, as part of the reorganisation of the Defence Group of Departments (the so-called Tange Reorganisation[4]), the Service Departments were amalgamated into the Department of Defence. Under the revised arrangements, the Minister for Defence was solely responsible for the direction of defence policy and for the command and administration of both the Defence Force and the Department of Defence. He exercised these powers jointly through the civilian Permanent Head of the Department and the Chief of the Defence Force Staff (CDFS).

The Secretary was made responsible for the general working of the Defence Department and for advising the Minister on all matters relating to it, including the administration of the Defence Force (this latter responsibility being shared with the CDFS). He was supported in this task by a number of specialist policy units covering the areas of strategic policy and force development, supply and support, defence personnel, resources and financial programs, organisation and management services, and defence science and technology. The CDFS was made the principal military adviser to the Minister and he commanded the Defence Force. He was supported by a Joint Military Operations and Plans (JMOP) Division which operated under the control of a three-star Assistant Chief of Defence Force Staff (ACDFS).

Although the reorganisation was described as an amalgamation of the previous civilian and Service structures, the resultant establishment could be more correctly described as a diarchy since the civilian and military elements of the organisation remained separated and responsible to their respective heads. In order to ensure that policy advice to the Minister reflected the views and concerns of both sides of the diarchy, the architects of the reorganisation superimposed on the formal power-sharing structure a series of informal arrangements and understandings which were later collectively referred to by the Utz Committee as the 'joint process'.[5] These arrangements included:

1   location of Service personnel within the civilian policy units in the Department;

2   making certain appointments responsible to both the Secretary and either the CDFS or the Service Chiefs of Staff (so-called 'dual-hatted' appointments);

3   requiring the organisational elements of both 'sides' of the Department to be 'responsive' to the views and requests of the other; and

4   including representatives of the Services on most of the policy advisory committees that had been established to support the decision-making process.

These basic structural and power-sharing arrangements remain in place today, even though the organisation of the defence establishment has been extensively modified in some areas. The most important changes have occurred in the military side of the establishment, where the emphasis has been on strengthening the role of the CDFS and his joint staff. In 1984, a Headquarters Australian Defence Force (HQADF) was established from the existing joint military staff, and the title of the Chief of Defence Force Staff was changed to the Chief of the Defence Force (CDF) in order to more correctly describe his overall role. The following year saw the creation of a permanent Maritime Headquarters, and in February 1986, the establishment of a Land Force Headquarters and an Air Headquarters. These new headquarters were organised along joint Service lines. They assumed the roles and functions of the previous single Service operational headquarters (which were abolished in 1987), and were placed under the direct command of the CDF. In the same year, a new position of Vice Chief of the Defence Force (VCDF) was established. The VCDF holds the same rank as the Service Chiefs of Staff, he heads HQADF and is responsible to the CDF for the oversight of centralised military planning and policy-making and for the development of joint military input into the force development process.

In 1987, the Service Chiefs of Staff were formally removed from the operational chain of command. Henceforth, the prime responsibility for both the planning and conduct of military operations would lie with CDF and his joint force commanders. An ADF Command Study (the so-called Baker Report) identified the need for a Commander Joint Forces Australia and a subordinate formation to Land Command. The latter, entitled Northern Command (NORCOM), became operational in July 1988. The former position would only become operational in times of war or significant military conflict and would be responsible to the CDF for the planning, conduct and coordination of joint force operations.[6] On the civilian side, most of the central policy units which were established by the Tange reorganisation have been reviewed by the Department and modified or streamlined in order to improve their efficiency and effectiveness. The basic role of these organisations, and their formal involvement in the policy process, however, remain largely unchanged.

An important consequence of Australia's altered strategic circumstances is that national security policy can no longer be equated purely with defence policy. Future assessments of Australia's national interests need to take account of a range of non-military concerns, and there needs to be greater public awareness of, and debate over, different options and strategies. The latter requirement sits uneasily with the restricted and closed nature of the Australian defence decision-making process. There are a number of external bodies and interest groups which are concerned with matters relating to Australia's defence. These include Parliamentary Committees, defence industries and industry groups such as the Defence Manufacturers Association of Australia, various returned services and veterans affairs associations, professional bodies such as the United Services Institutes and the Australian Defence Association, and a number of specialist defence academics and journalists.[7] It is possible to cite instances where individuals and groups from this set have influenced decision-making in Australia, sometimes in some quite crucial ways (such as the decision in late 1975 to establish the Defence Council), but these examples are very few and far between. The Australian defence decision-making process is simply too closed for outsiders to successfully penetrate and, in any case, there are no outsiders with anywhere near the strength of (say) their American counterparts. Allegations of a military-industrial-academic-bureaucratic complex in the Australian context are simply foolish!

The closed nature of the defence decision-making process is enforced by the secretiveness of the defence bureaucracy which, at least until the introduction of freedom of information legislation in the early 1980s, tended to characterise all government departments in Australia. While there has been some improvement in recent years both in public accessibility to Defence and in the release of information, it remains the case that nearly all defence documentation is classified and that much of it can be, and is, prevented from being released by invoking grounds of national security. While there are certain demands of national security where the case for secrecy is undeniable, there is a tendency on the part of the Australian defence establishment to too closely identify the national interest with its own bureaucratic and political interests.

The closed nature of the decision-making process does have one advantage for the student of Australian defence. This is that the participants in it are severely delimited and hence easy to identify. In practical terms, the principal actors are located within the official defence establishment and comprise the Minister for Defence, the Secretary of the Defence Department, the Chief of the Defence Force, and the Chiefs of Staff of the three Services, Navy, Army and Air Force. While there are other important individuals and groups involved in defence issues, these six occupy the key decision-making positions, they are formally responsible for developing Australia's defence policy, and they head the principal organisational interests which are located within the defence establishment.

The Principal Actors

The Minister for Defence is the pre-eminent formal actor in the defence decision-making process. He sits at the pinnacle of the defence establishment and, in accordance with the Westminster theory of Ministerial responsibility, makes the decisions on defence policy. This has substance both in the sense that the Minister selects, or at least endorses the recommendations of his Department, and also to the extent that he is held accountable for those decisions. The Defence Minister's responsibility flows, in general terms, from his authority as a member of the Federal Executive Council as derived from Sections 62 and 64 of the Australian Constitution. His specific responsibilities are laid down in the Administrative Arrangements Orders, which lists the various enactments to be administered by him. Although there are some 20 relevant Acts, the two key ones are the Defence Act 1903 and the Defence Force Reorganisation Act 1975. In the 1975 Act, the Minister's statutory authority is set out in Section 8 as follows:

> The Minister shall have the general control and administration of the Defence Force, and the powers vested in the Chief of Defence Force Staff, the Chief of Naval Staff, the Chief of the General Staff and the Chief of the Air Staff by virtue of Section 9, and the powers vested jointly in the Secretary and the Chief of Defence Force Staff by virtue of Section 9A, shall be exercised subject to and in accordance with any directions of the Minister.

The Act further provides that the Chief of Defence Force Staff and the three Service Chiefs shall in matters relating to their command 'advise the Minister in such manner as the Minister directs'.

The language of the Act is quite unqualified. However, the reality is much more complex as, in practice, there are some very powerful controls on the Minister. First, there are constraints imposed by other Ministers and by Cabinet at large. The policies and interests of such other Ministers as the Prime Minister, the Treasurer and the Minister for Foreign Affairs and Trade, impinge almost daily on those of the Defence Minister. And, as Defence Ministers have increasingly found every year since 1973, budgetary restrictions can be a particularly constraining factor. Second, the Minister is constrained by his own predilections, interests and capabilities. Given the increasing size of the Australian defence establishment and the growing complexity of the issues being addressed, no single Defence Minister could possibly exercise his authority to the limit. In any case, few make the attempt. The demands of a Minister's other party, parliamentary and electorate responsibilities are simply too overwhelming, even for a Minister as knowledgeable and capable as the present incumbent Mr K.C. Beazley.

The Minister is not without non-bureaucratic forms of support, however. Indeed, in the last two decades there has developed a variety of forms of Ministerial assistance which have impinged on the decision-making process. In July 1987, as part of a general restructuring of the Public Service, the Hawke Government established the position of Minister for Defence Science and Personnel. The new Minister was given full responsibility for the Defence Science and Technology Organisation (DSTO), as well as a number of personnel-related matters. Unlike the earlier, largely unsuccessful approach of appointing other Ministers of State as Ministers Assisting the Minister for Defence, the new Minister is not involved in any other portfolio and works solely to the Minister for Defence.

The current Minister for Defence has also made use of Ministerial consultants to review certain aspects of defence policy and make recommendations for change. The best example of this was the appointment in February 1985 of a Senior Research Fellow from the Australian National University's Strategic and Defence Studies Centre and former member of the Department of Defence, Paul Dibb, to undertake a review of Australia's defence capabilities.[8] Other examples have included the appointment in November 1985 of Sue Hamilton from the Office of the Status of Women to report on the problems facing spouses of ADF personnel,[9] and Robert Cooksey from the Australian National University, who examined Australia's defence cooperation program, defence exports and defence industry, and defence facilities.[10]

The contribution to defence decision-making of these particular studies has been quite significant. This may be due to the close personal support and interest that was given to them by the current Minister. Where such interest or support is lacking - as was the case for the 1982 review of Australia's higher defence organisation (the Utz Report), and for the findings of many of the recent Parliamentary reports into aspects of the defence establishment - the contribution is much less significant at least in the short term.

A third form of Ministerial assistance which has been tried was the practice of attaching advisers to the Ministers' private offices. This approach was widely adopted by Ministers in the first Labor Government, including Defence Ministers Barnard and Morrison, although of course it was not originated by them. Previously, and generally since the Whitlam period, Defence Ministers have used their staffs for private secretarial assistance, for Departmental liaison, for electoral and party political duties, and for public relations. In spite of having influenced a number of specific policy decisions, the personal staffs of neither the Barnard nor the Morrison Ministries were able to act as a 'countervailing force' to the bureaucracy. The fundamental reason for this lack of substantive impact is that the powers of Ministerial staffs are quite conditional. They, like the Minister, rely heavily on the Department for much of their information and advice. This problem goes right to the heart of the present Ministerial system and, more particularly, the relationship between the Minister and the permanent bureaucracy.

The defence bureaucracy is itself a conglomeration of disparate individuals and groups, each with their own perspectives, interests and power-political bases. The most important of these is the Permanent Head of the Department. The statutory responsibility of the Permanent Head derives principally from three enactments. The first is the Public Service Act 1922, Section 25(2) of which directs that: The Secretary of a Department shall under the Minister, be responsible for its general working, and for all the business thereof, and shall advise the Minister in all matters relating to the Department. The second is the Audit Act 1901, which (together with related Finance Regulations) makes the Permanent Head accountable for all expenditure of the Department. The third is the Defence Force Reorganisation Act 1975, which vests the Secretary (jointly with the Chief of the Defence Force) with responsibility for the administration of the Australian Defence Force. These enactments are complemented by a Ministerial Directive to the Secretary (issued on 1 November 1985) which describes him as 'the principal civilian adviser to the Minister for Defence' and makes him responsible, *inter alia*, for 'advising on policy, resources and organisation', financial planning and programming within the Department of Defence, and financial administration and control of expenditure.[11]

In addition to this legal authority, the Permanent Head has a large number of other sources of strength. There are, for example, those that arise from his length of tenure. Whereas Heads are 'permanent', Ministers tend to change every two or three years. Not only does this mean that the Secretary is likely to be more expert than the Minister in the subject matter of the portfolio, but it is also likely that the Secretary's loyalties extend beyond any particular incumbent. The limited expertise of the Minister and the other demands on his time mean that the Secretary must also identify the issues to be brought to the attention of the Minister, determine their relative urgency, suggest the solutions and draft the briefs. This privileged access to the Minister and control over who and what he sees enables the Permanent Head to exert considerable influence over defence policy. There are, further, a wide range of tactics which a Permanent Head can, and does, employ in his attempts to ensure that the Minister accepts his recommendations; they include such practices as manipulating the Minister's workload, putting important questions among less significant papers, presenting submissions only shortly before a decision is required, establishing 'off-limit' matters which the Minister must leave to the Permanent Head, reaching agreement with the Heads of other Departments so that no single Minister can overturn it, and presenting the Minister with a *fait accompli*.[12]

Although the Permanent Head is probably the single most important individual in Australian defence decision-making, his role is limited to the extent of the power-political bases of other actors within the defence establishment. These include the Secretary's principal subordinates who are responsible for the day-to-day running of the Department and who, in recent administrations in particular, have had more experience in defence matters. In particular, however, the Secretary is circumscribed, both legally and in working practice, by the authority of the military. There is a tendency in the literature to consider the military in Australia as a single group. In fact, the military is not monolithic, but comprises a number of discrete entities whose interests and perspectives do not always coincide, and who often compete with each other as well as the Secretary and his staff over policies and resources. The important groupings within the military are presently the three single Services - Navy, Army and Air Force - and a Joint Service component comprising the CDF and his joint staff in the Headquarters Australian Defence Force (HQADF). A fourth group, which are currently not involved in the higher decision-making process to a significant degree, but will assume an increasingly important role, are the Joint Force Commanders.

The position of the Chief of the Defence Force (or Chief of Defence Force Staff as it was titled then) was created in the 1973 reorganisation and took over the functions and responsibilities of the previous Chairman, Chiefs of Staff Committee. Unlike his predecessor, the CDF has considerable statutory authority. Section 9 of the Defence Act states that the CDF shall command the Defence Force and shall 'advise the Minister, in such manner as the Minister directs, on matters relating to the command...of the Defence Force'. Section 9A of the Defence Act also states that the CDF (jointly with the Secretary) is responsible for the administration of the Defence Force.

While the CDF has the same formal status as the Secretary, his capacity to influence the defence decision-making process is constrained by a number of factors. To begin with, the CDF does not have full control over a number of policy areas which relate directly to his command responsibilities. In a submission to the 1982 inquiry into the higher defence organisation in Australia, the then CDFS, Admiral Sir Anthony Synnot, stated that:

> At present I have no authority in the central policy areas of personnel and logistics, which directly relate to my command responsibilities, and I have no authority also in other major policy areas where I have more general responsibilities such as strategic policy, force development, and science and technology.[13]

Sir Anthony suggested that the CDFS should command the Defence Force, and have prime responsibility for military strategy, force capabilities, force development, and the organisation of the Defence Force. The Secretary, for his part, would be responsible for financial control, audit, personnel management of civilian staff, budgeting and financial programming, and related departmental matters. Such a basic realignment of authority was not supported by the Utz Committee, which concluded that 'it would be unwise to expand the general jurisdiction of the CDFS for reasons of both principle and practice'.[14] The Utz Committee instead emphasised the importance of the 'joint process' as the means of ensuring adequate military input into the defence decision-making process, and suggested a number of means of improving it. These changes were not adopted by the Department and the issue remains one of contention between military and civilian officials.

The CDF is also constrained by his limited staff support, especially compared with both Defence Central and the Service Offices, by his limited tenure in office and, most importantly, by his association with, and reliance on, the Services for much of his advice and support. Despite their apparent downgrading as part of the 1973-76 reorganisation, the Services and their respective Chiefs of Staff retain considerable formal and informal power in defence policy matters. Section 9 of the Defence Act states that, subject to the overall directions of the Minister, 'the chief of staff of an arm of the Defence Force shall, under the Chief of Defence Force Staff, command the arm of the Defence Force of which he is chief of staff'. The informal power base of the Services stems from the fact that they have retained much of their original organisational and staff structures. They provide the initial input into many key policy areas, exercise considerable autonomy in the implementation of defence policy, and are well represented on the Defence committees. The informal power of the Services is also strengthened by their unquestioned technical expertise in many areas of defence policy. There are few civilian or joint Service organisations within the Australian Defence establishment which can challenge the Services in terms of knowledge of weapons systems specifications or technical performance characteristics. It is difficult to over-estimate the 'authority' which accrues to the military from this; most civilians would prefer to allow Service claims to pass rather than to demonstrate their technical ignorance.

In the overall civil-military relationship, however, the military suffer one major disadvantage - that is, while the civilian chain is made up of career bureaucrats, the military posting system involves frequent rotation of serving officers. Given a normal three-year posting, an officer is really just beginning to settle in at Russell Hill when he must begin preparations for handing over to his successor. This severely handicaps the military in their responding to the opportunities for co-equal participation.

In summary then, the balance of power within the defence establishment in Australia tends to favour the civilian and the single Service elements in the organisation. While both the Minister for Defence and the CDF have considerable formal powers, in practice their capacity to influence defence policy is limited. The constraints on the Minister stem from his isolation from the decision-making process and his reliance on his principal advisers. The CDF is constrained by his association with, and reliance on, the Services: military advice given by the joint organisation is both fragmented and compromised. This balance of power is gradually changing as the role and authority of the CDF and his joint staff are being enhanced but there is still some way to go in this process.

The Formal Process

The current structure of the Australian Defence establishment is characterised by a number of special features. The first noteworthy feature, and one which distinguishes Defence from all other Commonwealth departments is its diarchic structure. As described earlier, the defence establishment comprises two basic components: the Australian Defence Force, which is commanded by the CDF and is made up of the three single Services, the Joint Force Commands and HQADF, and the Department of Defence which is headed by the Secretary and comprises a number of specialist policy support groups.[15] A second, and related, feature of the defence establishment is the 'joint process' which is the means of ensuring that the two halves of the diarchy work together to produce both coherent and broadly acceptable policies and decisions.

An important component of the 'joint process' and a third distinguishing characteristic of the defence establishment is its committee system. The Department makes extensive use of committees to draw together advice from the different organisational interests within the defence establishment. While the committees have no executive role - they provide advice or make recommendations only - they play a crucial role in the policy-formulation process since they provide the framework for consultation on, and resolution of, different views and interests which is, of course, the essence of decision-making.

The Departmental publication, *Senior Defence Committees* (DRB4), lists 96 Defence Committees ranging from senior statutory committees to single Service planning and advisory committees. At the pinnacle of the committee structure is the Council of Defence. Consisting of the Minister for Defence, the Minister for Defence Science and Personnel, the Secretary to the Department of Defence, the CDF and the three Service Chiefs, the Council's official function is 'to consider and discuss matters relating to the control and administration of the Defence Force and of the respective Arms of the Defence Force, referred to the Council by the Minister'. The Council meets only infrequently, however, and limits its activities to general discussions; it is not a decision-making body. The most senior decision-making committee is the Defence Committee. This is chaired by the Secretary to the Department, and has as its members the Permanent Heads of the Treasury and the Departments of the Prime Minister and Cabinet and Foreign Affairs and Trade, the CDF and the three Service Chiefs. The role of the Defence Committee is to advise the Minister on:

1   defence policy as a whole;

2   the coordination of military, strategic, economic, financial and external affairs aspects of defence policy;

3   matters of policy or principle and important questions having joint Service or inter-departmental defence aspects; and

4   such other matters having a defence aspect as are referred to the Committee by or on behalf of the Minister.[16]

In the area of force structure decision-making, the two most important committees are the Defence Force Development Committee (DFDC) and the Defence Force Structure Committee (DFSC). Indeed, as the Defence Committee has declined in importance since the reorganisation, the DFDC has come to play the pre-eminent role in Australian defence decision-making in general. The DFDC is chaired by the Secretary and has as its members the CDF and the three Service Chiefs. The functions of the Committee are:

1   to advise the Minister for Defence, on the development of the Australian Defence Force as a whole;

2   to initiate and review major studies concerned with the development of the ADF;

3   to review the Five Year Defence Program and the annual defence estimates;

4   to review progress in the preparation of proposals and appreciations for submission to Government; and

5   to review other matters of common interest to members and to exchange views.[17]

The Force Structure Committee advises the DFDC on the development of the defence force structure and on equipment proposals and their inclusion in the Five Year Defence Program (FYDP).

This leads to the fourth significant feature of the current defence decision-making structure - the Five Year Defence Program (FYDP). Introduced into the Department of Defence in fiscal year 1971-72, the FYDP provides the programming basis for the flow of Defence proposals through to actual decision. The program is a 'rolling' one in that, at least ideally, any proposal involving expenditure should enter as a Year Five project and 'roll' forward until authorisation for that expenditure is required in Year One, the fifth year of the Program under review. The FYDP is the end product of a much broader Planning, Programming and Budgeting process which is used by the Department to translate Australia's defence objectives and military strategies into a coherent program of activities and capability acquisitions.[18]   The preparation of the FYDP is essentially a political process, just as the

262 *Security and Defence: Pacific and Global Perspectives*

determination of the financial guidance is itself political. As Wildavsky has noted, if politics can be regarded as a conflict over whose preferences shall prevail in the determination of national policy, 'then the budget records the outcomes of this struggle'.[19]

The Politics of the Defence Decision-making Process

In explaining actual decision-making outcomes, the nature of this internal political process is just as relevant as an understanding of the formal FYDP machinery or the structure of the functional organisation. For while necessary, neither organisational charts, nor detailed descriptions of formal processes are ever fully satisfactory explanatory tools. There are always some informal relationships and arrangements which impact substantively on decision-making outcomes, not to mention the inevitable political and bureaucratic-political factors. They are present, for example, in the relationship between the Department of Defence and other departments. Formally, the principal non-Defence departments involved in defence decision-making (Prime Minister and Cabinet, the Treasury, Foreign Affairs and Trade, Finance, and Industry and Technology) are represented on numerous inter-departmental committees (IDCs) with Defence. The formal relationship between these Departments and Defence also involves routine memoranda, discussions with relevant Defence and other departmental officers involved in the defence function, and attendance at meetings. On balance, however, by far the greatest and most important part of the relationship between Defence and these other Departments, takes place at more informal levels. A former Assistant Secretary, Policy Secretariat, was quite explicit on this: 'The inter-departmental relationships are largely ad hoc; more time is spent on the telephone than at inter-departmental meetings'. This judgement is shared by the relevant responsible officers in the other departments.[20]

The same admixture of formal and informal factors operates with respect to decision-making within the Department of Defence itself. In the case of equipment procurement, for example, the formal process is invariably followed.[21] Proposals for new weapons and support systems begin with the preparation by the Services of the basic documentation (the Staff Objective, Staff Target, and Staff Requirement). These are first considered by the Defence Operational Concepts and Capabilities Committee (DOCCC) and then, if endorsed, are progressed through the FYDP machinery (including the DFSC and the DFDC). The proposals are then submitted to the Minister or, if necessary, the Cabinet for approval. Throughout this process, reference is repeatedly made to the 'strategic guidance'. All the proposing documentation for a piece of equipment begins with a justification relating the proposal to the current strategic guidance, which is considered by the DOCCC and the DFSC. And recommendations from the Defence Force Development Committee to the Minister must be framed 'in the context of strategic assessments'.

Despite this formal litany, it is clear that the process also involves a range of informal interactions and influences which may not be conducive to effective policy-making. Sponsors regularly liaise with the Force Development and Analysis Division and other central policy divisions in the preparation of formal submissions. Agreements - tacit and otherwise - are reached between interest groups over support for a particular agenda item or groups of items at forthcoming committee meetings. Briefing papers are written to reflect the institutional interests of the principal actors. And personalities inevitably play a significant role in the consideration and resolution of issues within the senior committees. These factors tend to operate in favour of the civilian and single Service elements of the defence establishment. The civilians control the decision-making process and so are able to set the agenda for debate. Their longer time in office also enables them to become more proficient in the bureaucratic-political skills that underlie the bargaining process. And, of course, they have the final say by virtue of the Secretary's role as principal policy adviser to the Minister.

The Services are able to exert considerable influence because they determine which equipments and weapons systems enter the process, and are able to use their numbers and superior technical expertise to ensure their passage through the programming phase of the FYDP. This position of strength allows the Services to generate outcomes which, while flowing through the formal procurement process in the appropriate way, are often not optimal from the overall perspective of the defence of Australia. The Services have obvious predilections, such as a disdain for local defence industries, and a preference for teeth at the expense of tail, and sometimes tend to follow some rather inimical practices, such as 'gold-plating' and writing staff requirements around their preferred brand names.

The problem is compounded by certain weaknesses in the defence planning system; in particular lack of clarity and coherence in basic defence guidance. For if this guidance, from which all subsequent decisions flow, is fundamentally inadequate, then the informal processes must prevail. Australia's present guidance is provided by two basic documents: the *Strategic Basis of Australian Defence Policy* and the *Defence Force Capabilities Paper*. The *Strategic Basis* is produced every three to five years (the last document being produced in 1989) and draws upon intelligence assessments contained in *Australia's Security Outlook* which is produced by the Office of National Assessments and is endorsed by the National Assessments Board.[22] According to the Utz Report, the purpose of the *Strategic Basis* is 'to produce strategic and policy objectives based on the situations, trends and contingencies of importance to Australia's defence security'.[23] As such, the document is very broadly stated, it has a restricted focus, and its level of generality is too high for it to be anything more than vacuous as a basis for defence planning. The result is that, as a senior Army officer is reported to have said in 1976, the *Strategic Basis* can be used to justify the procurement of any weapon system.[24]

From the single Services' perspective, the resultant freedom from centralised 'guidance' is attractive. Indeed, at this level, it is in the perceived interest of the military that the guidance be vacuous. As Admiral Peek, a former member of the Defence Committee, has said,

> In their contribution to the preparation of the strategic guidance, the individual Chiefs deliberately make it vague and woolly so that they can use it to justify the selection of any piece of equipment they want.[25]

But the absence of centrally developed and quite specific guidance on defence objectives and military capabilities is not conducive to the development of an optimum force structure and one based on joint rather than single Service principles. In recognition of this, the Department has sought to produce the *Defence Force Capabilities Paper* which 'relates the strategic and policy objectives endorsed by the Government more specifically to the development of defence capabilities'.[26]

The *Defence Force Capabilities Paper* is developed by the Force Development and Analysis Division, in consultation with HQADF and the Services. It is submitted to the Defence Force Development Committee for endorsement and then issued, together with financial guidance, to the Services and other resource coordinators for use in the preparation of bids for the Five Year Defence Plan. All proposals for new operational requirements, or new weapons and support systems, are considered by the Defence Force Structure Committee and other review committees against the basic guidance contained in the *Defence Force Capabilities Paper* and the *Strategic Basis*. Thus, the *Defence Force Capabilities Paper* is a key document in the defence planning and policy-making process. In addition to providing the link between defence objectives and requisite forces and capabilities, it also serves as the principal means of directing and controlling the development of defence policy. Without formalised defence guidance of this kind, informal processes are likely to prevail and defence programs and policies run the risk of being incoherent.

In spite of its central importance, it is clear from the findings of successive reviews of the defence establishment that Australia's strategic and defence guidance, and the means of producing it, remain deficient.[27] The situation has improved somewhat with the publication of the Government's policy information paper, *The Defence of Australia 1987*. However, as noted by the report of the Joint Committee on Foreign Affairs, Defence and Trade, the information provided by the 1987 White Paper equates primarily to the level of guidance provided by the *Strategic Basis* paper, and so is not sufficient to facilitate the development of the most appropriate defence force structure and the detailed capabilities that are needed to satisfy Australia's basic defence interests and objectives.[28]

While this fundamental deficiency continues, defence decision-making in Australia will continue to derive, at its very source, from non-formal factors. And where the formal process is subsequently followed, it will be often more a matter of rationalisation, than of rational decision-making. This is not to say that if the Government provided clearer, more precise and less overtly political direction, complete rationality would be achieved. The closed nature of Australian defence decision-making notwithstanding, there are just too many participants for conflict and compromise to be removed completely. The basic legacy of the Tange reforms has been to institutionalise bureaucratic politics within Russell Hill and to ensure that policy outcomes will be determined more by adversary processes than the application of reasoned argument.

Endnotes

1   This area is defined as Australia's 'area of direct military interest'. See Hon. Kim C. Beazley, *The Defence of Australia 1987*, (Australian Government Publishing Service, Canberra, 1987), p.31.

2   Some of the potential costs and disadvantages of Australia's continuing defence relationship with the United States are described in Chapter 12; and Joseph A. Camilleri, *ANZUS: Australia's Predicament in the Nuclear Age*, (Macmillan, Sydney, 1987), Chapters 2 and 3.

3   The most up to date summary of the evolution of the Australian defence establishment since the end of the Second World War is contained in the report of the Joint Committee on Foreign Affairs, Defence and Trade, *The Management of Australia's Defence*, (Australian Government Publishing Service, Canberra, 1987), Chapter 2.

4   Sir Arthur Tange, *Australian Defence: Report on the Reorganisation of the Defence Group of Departments*, (Australian Government Publishing Service, Canberra, November 1973).

5   *The Higher Defence Organisation in Australia: Final Report of the Defence Review Committee 1982*, (Australian Government Publishing Service, Canberra, 1982), pp.23-27.

6   Brigadier J.S. Baker, *Report of the Study into ADF Command Arrangements*, (Headquarters Australian Defence Force, March 1988); Department of Defence, *Defence Report 1987-88*, (Australian Government Publishing Service, Canberra, 1988), pp.1-2.

7   See G.L. Cheeseman, 'Interest Groups and Australian Defence Decision-Making', *Defence Force Journal*, No.35, July/August 1982, pp.23-32.

8   Paul Dibb, *Review of Australia's Defence Capabilities*, (Australian Government Publishing Service, Canberra, March 1986).

9   Sue Hamilton, *Supporting Service Families: A Report on the Main Problems Facing Spouses of Australian Defence Force Personnel and Some Recommended Solutions*, (April 1986).

10   Robert Cooksey, *Review of Australia's Defence Exports and Defence Industry* (Australian Government Publishing Service, Canberra, March 1986); Robert J. Cooksey, *Review of Australia's Defence Facilities*, (Australian Government Publishing Service, Canberra, 1988). Cooksey's report on the Defence Cooperation Program was never released to the public.

11   The current Ministerial directives to the Secretary and the CDF, and to those two officers jointly, are contained in *The Management of Australia's Defence*, pp.372-76.

12   See, in particular, Richard Crossman, *The Diaries of a Cabinet Minister, Volume 1: Minister of Housing 1964-66*, (Hamish Hamilton and Jonathan Cape, London, 1975). A good treatment of the relationship between Ministers and their departments in Australia is contained in Patrick Weller and Michelle Grattan, *Can Ministers Cope? Australian Federal Ministers at Work*, (Hutchinson of Australia, 1981).

13   *The Higher Defence Organisation in Australia*, p.29.

14   *Ibid.*, p.34.

15   The outline organisations and current functions of the defence establishment are given in Department of Defence, *Defence Report 1987-88*, (Australian Government Publishing Service, Canberra, 1988), Appendix 9 FOI Section 8 Statement. See also *The Management of Australia's Defence*, Chapter 3.

16   *Defence Report 1986-87*, pp.146-47.

17   *Ibid.*, 1986-87, p.147.

18   For a more detailed description of the Planning, Programming and Budgeting System used within Defence, see *The Management of Australia's Defence*, Chapters 2 and 6.

19   Aaron Wildavsky, *The Politics of the Budgetary Process*, (Little, Brown and Co., Boston, 1964), p.4.

20   Interview, 1978. For a discussion of the formal and informal networks involved in the intelligence collection and assessment process, see Department of Foreign Affairs, Evidence presented to the Joint Committee on Foreign Affairs and Defence, *Hansard*, 23 April 1987, pp.141-2.

21   For a detailed outline of the formal defence procurement process in Australia together with a critique of the more informal factors, see Desmond Ball, 'The Role of the Military in Defence Hardware Procurement', in F.A. Mediansky (ed.), *The Military and Australia's Defence*, (Longman Cheshire, Sydney, 1979), Chapter 3; and *The Management of Australia's Defence*, Chapter 7.

22   See *Review of Australia's Defence Capabilities*, pp.24-28; and *The Management of Australia's Defence*, Chapters 3 and 6.

23   *The Higher Defence Organisation in Australia*, p.50.

24   Lt T.P. Muggleton, *An Evaluation of the Analytical Infrastructure for Force Structure Decision-making in the Australian Defence Department*, (B.A. (Honours) Thesis, University of New South Wales, Faculty of Military Studies, Royal Military College, Duntroon, Department of Economics, 1976), p.36.

25   Interview, 28 February 1978.

26   *The Higher Defence Organisation in Australia*, p.51.

27   The *Review of Australia's Defence Capabilities* concluded, for example, that:
        Strategic guidance, military concepts, capabilities analysis, and financial guidance are not drawn together under current arrangements. This leads to

inadequate advice being available to Government and also makes it difficult to plan ahead with sufficient clarity.

And,

... the lack of simple procedural clarity and precision in the guidance for determining the priority of core capabilities has tended to frustrate force structure planning. In practice, the force development processes of the senior Defence Committees...take account of strategic guidance, credible contingencies and warning-time/lead-time considerations on an essentially ad-hoc basis, usually in the context of major equipment proposals.

See also *The Management of Australia's Defence*, Chapter 6.

28   *The Management of Australia's Defence*, pp.214-32.

CHAPTER 14

LEGAL ASPECTS OF THE EMPLOYMENT OF THE AUSTRALIAN DEFENCE FORCE

Anthony Bergin

In the hierarchy of topics of interest to students of national security, legal issues are often treated with patronising indifference, cast into the category of necessary-but-boring. However, accompanying the obsessive search for ever greater destructive capabilities in the application of force has been an equally-determined, if less successful, quest for rules, laws, principles and codes of practice, which seek to 'mitigate the hardships and savagery of war' and which aim at combating the 'great danger of war degenerating into excess and indiscriminate violence'.[1] Particularly over the course of the 20th century, the political, economic and social structures of the international system have changed significantly. Equally, the methods of prosecuting war and the availability of destructive capabilities have altered and expanded. As a consequence, the entire concept of modern warfare, its participants, how it starts, how it can be controlled, and how it can be stopped, have undergone significant modifications. In this context, an understanding of the legal justifications and constraints which underpin the employment of military force by the State is of crucial importance to the calculations of defence decision-makers and planners, strategic analysts, and students of national security policy-making and implementation. Australia, both as an international actor, and in the evolving strategies and force structures it is setting in place for the provision of its own territorial defence, confronts a variety of issues raised by the contemporary nature of war and the initiatives taken to constrain the excesses and anarchy which characterise it. It is the purpose of this chapter to examine a number of these issues including the legal basis for the defence power of the Australian government, legal issues relating to low-level operations, the ramifications of changes in international law applicable to armed conflict, and the legal parameters and constraints operating on the Australian Defence Force (ADF) in aiding the civil power.

The Defence Powers of the State

By virtue of the defence power in Section 51(iv) of the Commonwealth Constitution, the Parliament shall, subject to the Constitution, have power to make laws for the peace, order and good government of the

Commonwealth with respect to 'The naval and military defence of the Commonwealth and of the several States, and the control of the forces to execute and maintain the laws of the Commonwealth'. However, the Commonwealth Parliament's power is not, as Lee observes, confined to Section 51 (vi).2 It should be seen in conjunction with other supporting sections of the Constitution, including Section 51(xxxii) which empowers the Commonwealth Parliament to legislate with respect to the control of railways for transportation for naval and military purposes; Section 51(xxxix), the incidental power; Section 52(ii) which gives the Commonwealth Parliament the exclusive power to make laws with respect to matters relating to any department of the public service, the control of which is transferred to the Executive Government of the Commonwealth by the Constitution; Section 68, vesting the command-in-chief of the naval and military forces of Commonwealth in the Governor-General as the Queen's representative; Section 69 which transfers the departments of naval and military defence from the States to the Commonwealth; Section 70 which transfers all powers and functions from the State Executive Governments to the Executive Government of the Commonwealth in relation to those matters within the exclusive power of the Commonwealth; Section 114, which prohibits the States from raising or maintaining any naval or military force; and Section 119 which imposes an obligation upon the Commonwealth to protect the States from invasion and domestic violence.

It should be noted that the title of Commander-in-Chief as held by the Governor-General is purely titular. It seems clear that 'no question of any reserve power lurks within the terms of Section 68 and practical considerations make it essential even were constitutional ones not also to require it, that the Governor-General should have no independent discretion conferred upon him by that section'.3 For reasons which the constitutional commentators Quick and Garran describe as 'historical and technical rather than practical or substantial', Section 68, unlike some other references in the Constitution to the Governor-General, makes no mention of the Federal Executive Council, but the Governor-General must act on the advice of the Minister for Defence. Section 8 of the *Defence Act 1903* provides that the 'Minister shall have general control and administration of the Defence Force' and under Section 9(3), the Chief of the Defence Force is required 'to advise the Minister in such a manner as the Minister directs, on matters relating to the command...of the Defence Force'. Former Governor-General Sir Ninian Stephens has observed: 'it seems that considerations of elegance of drafting, a fear of being regarded in Whitehall as constitutionally naive and a belief that, as it stood, Section 68 clearly required the Governor-General to act only on Ministerial advice' together led to the omission of a reference in Section 68 to the Governor-General 'in council'.4

The defence power is not exclusive to the Commonwealth. The States are empowered to pass legislation relevant to the preparation for war to assist the Commonwealth in the defence of Australia. Particularly in the areas relating to economic organsiation and public safety, the States can introduce legislation relevant to defence. In relation to civil defence, for example, the States have wide powers with respect to evacuation, in which attacks by an enemy are included in the definition of a disaster. By virtue of Section 109 of the Constitution, however, a State law can be invalid to the extent of any inconsistency with a Commonwealth law.

Low Level Operations

The defence power, as it has been interpreted by the High Court, is an elastic concept: its limits expand or decrease depending on the level of defence threat. The defence power, as discussed by various writers, has been regarded as dividing naturally into four phases: wartime, postwar, peacetime and preparation for war. However, Professor Colin Howard has observed that:

> The division of the power into four merging but distinguishable stages rests basically on the assumption that war is always a measure of national defence. This assumption fitted the facts in the first and second world wars but is of course not true as a general proposition. The kind of intervention in which Australia has participated in Korea and Vietnam can be, and has been to some extent, accommodated by postulating a theory of forward defence, the idea that it is better to defend in someone else's country than in one's own. But this reasoning becomes strained where there is no credible military threat because the situation is one of political warfare, which for the present purposes may be defined as warfare undertaken to produce political pressures rather than immediate conquest.5

It is this kind of 'political warfare', designed to produce 'political pressure', which raises legal questions relating to the defence power. In times of war, the normal distribution of powers is suspended and Parliament has jurisdiction to enact, on defence grounds, legislation covering virtually every aspects of the country's life. According to the 'black letter' law, the further the defence power is stretched beyond actual war itself, the more likely it is to be challenged successfully. In times of peace, the defence power will, of course, permit traditional military matters such as the erection of military installations, the manufacture of weapons, the recruitment of personnel, the conveyance of troops wherever required and entering of land for training. But the defence planner will want to know how far the Commonwealth can go in the use of the defence power in situations short of war, to organise resources before the trouble begins. Must legislation enacted under the defence power, to increase the military's position, be in consequence of a factual situation or can it anticipate such a situation? The answer, according to case law, is that the power to pass legislation under the defence power will only come into existence when the threat materialises. It is only in a situation of mounting danger, or hostilities, that the actual operation of the defence power may be extended. This may be a problem in low-level situations because it may be difficult to convince the court that there is a threat. This problem is compounded by the fact that many low-level contingencies may arise at short notice. Moreover, judicial guidance in respect of what would be a valid exercise of the defence power in preparations short of war is virtually non-existent. Given that the most likely contingencies which Australia will face are low-level threats, it would appear that the law lags well behind the facts. For example, the term 'low-level' is unknown in law.

In broad terms, there are two roles for the ADF identified in Section 119 of the Constitution which requires the Commonwealth to 'protect every State against invasion and, on application to the Executive Government of the State, against domestic violence'. In relation to this defence role, the *Defence Act 1903* provides essentially that the Regular Army and Regular Army Supplement may be called out at any time (Section 4). The Emergency Forces, or part of the Emergency Forces, may be called out at any time the Governor-General considers it desirable and by notice in the Gazette calls them out for continuous full-time military service (Section 50D).

The Government, in 1987, passed legislation which affects the call-out of Reserve Forces. Previously the Defence Act provided for the Reserve Forces to be called out only in circumstances of time of war or proclaimed defence emergency. This provision was introduced in 1964 by the Menzies Government. According to the Explanatory Memorandum to the Defence Legislation Amendment Bill 1987, when it was first presented to the House of Representatives, the new Section 50F 'is intended to enable the call-out of the Reserve Forces in situations of low level threat'. The Minister for Defence, Mr Beazley, in his second reading speech on the Bill stated:

If the value of the reserve forces is to be exploited fully in providing an effective defence capability for Australia, then there is a clear case for a legislative provision permitting limited call-out of reserves short of the declaration of a defence emergency. If the concept of a 'total force' is to have any meaning, and, if integration is to be effective, the Defence Force must be able to plan on the employment of any component of the force, including the reserves, in situations which fall far short of a declared defence emergency. I think it is clear that in low level contingencies governments would be understandably reluctant to take the seemingly escalatory step of declaring a defence emergency. Yet, it is precisely during a period of tension potentially leading to low level conflict that some elements of the reserve forces would most likely be required.[6]

A Proclamation made under the new Section 50F must (like proclamations calling out the reserves in time of war or defence emergency) give reasons for the making of the Proclamation. Reserves can be called out in the first instance for a period not exceeding three months but the Governor-General may extend the period for another three months. After 12 consecutive months, a member of the Reserves shall be released from service. The Governor-General will be required to communicate the reasons for the making of the Proclamation to each House of Parliament.

As far as the legal environment in which the military would be required to operate in countering a low-level threat in Australia is concerned, it should be made clear that not all legal problems can be identified in advance. Where they can be so identified, it is preferable that changes take place in response in peacetime. Defence emergencies may not be conducive to good law-making and it must, therefore, be before trouble begins that legal aspects of defence planning and operations are fed into training and operational doctrines.

The most striking aspect of the legal setting in which a force would deploy in Australia is the fact that the Defence Act hardly envisages the possibility of hostilities in Australia, and certainly does not look at the possibility of action being fought in the middle of a civilian population. There exists no Commonwealth legislation which would give soldiers, performing a defence function, authority by way of police powers or power similar to that under State Emergency Service Acts - powers relating to such matters as traffic control, arrest, search, civilian evacuation, guarding, etc.[7] As far as civilians within an area of operation are concerned, the Defence Force Discipline Act 1982, Section 3(1), defines a 'defence civilian' as a person, other than a defence member, who, with the authority of an authorised officer, accompanies a part of the Defence Force that is outside Australia or on operations against the enemy, and who has consented in writing to subject himself to Defence Force discipline. Civilians who accompany a part of the Defence Force which is engaged in warlike operations, would include organisations like the Red Shield and employees of media organisations. Where the military considered it to be essential for the person to become a defence civilian and the person declined to do so, the probability is that the person would not be permitted to accompany the force. This could create potential difficulties with civilian contractors to the military who do not wish to become defence civilians. Where a defence civilian is captured by the enemy, he will usually be entitled to prisoner-of-war status (para A(4) of Article 4 of the Third Geneva Convention). Civilians within an area of operation who are not 'defence civilians' would remain subject to State law. Thus, there would be some level of civil administration, including police, in an area of operations, if the military were attempting to maintain, as far as possible a 'business-as-usual' policy. Close liaison between the police and the military would, thus, be critical in any low-level contingency.

In low-level conflict situations, where the Defence Forces would be operating in areas where they would come into contact with the civilian population, Commonwealth emergency legislation would be appropriate. (As already noted, this may not be politically easy to pass in peacetime.) Such legislation would need to specify what power military personnel would have so that legal uncertainty would be reduced to a minimum. Commonwealth emergency legislation would help overcome possible problems that the military may find with State legislation, for example, in areas relating to State criminal codes. In the absence of Commonwealth legislation which gives police-type powers to the military, the police would no doubt accompany elements of the ADF. Draconian legal measures, involving sweeping legal changes should, however, be resisted if possible. The introduction of such measures early in a conflict may have significant costs, not the least in terms of the degree of cooperation which may be forthcoming from the local community.

Of course, with or without Commonwealth legislation, the States would play a useful role through their own emergency/natural disaster legislation in assisting the ADF to meet low-level threats, for example in matters such as public safety, transport and essential services.[8] It should be remembered, as mentioned earlier, that the defence power is a 'concurrent' power and, while in many circumstances a State could not implement measures of defence, it may certainly introduce measures which complement Commonwealth efforts, for instance, compensation for civilians or volunteers in State Emergency Services assisting the military would be important.[9] This should certainly be the case if troubles are confined to a particular area within a State. State legislative activity would obviously require close coordination between Canberra and the State(s) but, as a matter of policy, many legal issues arising in low-level contingencies would be resolved best at the State level. This would certainly apply, for example, to defence operations on Aboriginal land.[10]

On rules of engagement (ROE), Cabinet would decide policy, although it should be noted that whatever ROE may be in force at the time, under common law, the commander of an ADF unit will have the right to use such force in self-defence as may be deemed necessary to protect the lives of the people under his command.

In situations of low-level conflict, it would be preferable (and probable) to lease or hire whatever the ADF required under normal commercial arrangements. However, requisition may be necessary. Here, Section 67 of the Defence Act provides the power for the requisition of any 'vehicle, horse, mule, bullock, aircraft, aircraft material, boat or vessel or any goods',[11] provided that regulations have been made under Section 124 (i)-(r) to prescribe the manner of recompense. (Just terms of acquisition of property is required by Section 51 (xxxi) of the Constitution, otherwise requisition is invalid.) If regulations are made (and they have not to date), power under Section 67 is exercisable not just in 'time of war' but under any other circumstances. Section 69 of the Defence Act confers powers in relation to the use of any lands for 'training, maneouvres, or other naval, military or air force exercises or purposes'. Under the Lands Acquisition Act 1955, the Commonwealth has the power to acquire interest in land (including buildings) for any defence purpose. The Airlines Agreement Act 1981 (Schedule clause 19) provides for the Minister to call upon the two main Australian airline fleets in time of war or 'immediate danger' to the Commonwealth. There is nothing in the legislation relating to QANTAS, but as the owner of QANTAS, the Commonwealth would simply charter the fleet. In a situation where the Navy wished to use merchant vessels in times of emergency, there do not appear to be any particular legal problems (although there could well be considerable administrative ones). Compulsory purchase is empowered by the Defence Act, Section 63(f), subject to an authorisation by Order in Council.[12] Section 41 of the Naval Defence Act 1910 also gives power to the Commonwealth to acquire, build and maintain ships, vessels and boats for naval defence or services auxiliary to naval defence, although this section would not be available for the compulsory acquisition of same. Requisition under Section 67 of the Defence Act requires notice to be served on the owner, which may limit the ability to requisition under this section to Australian-owned vessels and may not extend to all

Australian registered vessels if those vessels are not also Australian-owned.[13] It should also be noted that a merchant vessel which forms part of the fleet, or operates directly in furtherance of military operations, can be attacked without warning.[14] Crew on such vessels must, if captured, be treated as prisoners of war.

Two other areas of law which are relevant to low-level operations should be noted. These are industrial and administrative law. In operating among the civil community, the ADF would, in a low-level conflict, have to accept the fact that as far as the trade unions are concerned, industrial law, as it currently operates, will continue to be in force. Federal and State awards will apply and workers will continue to exercise all their normal industrial rights, including the right to strike. The military, who may want to rely on the provision of essential services by union members will, no doubt, find it irksome that there are all sorts of conditions in awards relating to overtime, shift work, work breaks, weekend work and so on. World War II showed that, even in grave emergencies, there will be workers unhappy with their lot and seeking to press for what they consider to be their industrial rights. Particularly, therefore, in situations short of war, defence planners and decision-makers must expect there will be no automatic shutdown of the normal industrial law system.

Administrative law is concerned with the procedures for administrative decision-making and the means by which aggrieved citizens can seek review of administrative decisions. Defence decision-making in any emergency will require the use of wide discretionary powers by many administrative officers. The last two decades have witnessed an extraordinary expansion of both the statutory and judge-made laws regarding the rights of the citizen to bridge the gap between himself and the State. This has arisen largely in response to the rapid growth of the ambit of administrative power over the public. At the Commonwealth level, three statutes which embody important changes in administrative law are the *Administrative Appeals Tribunal Act 1975,* the *Ombudsman Act 1976* and the *Administrative Decisions (Judicial Review) Act 1976.*[15]

In order to understand the reach of administrative law, a few aspects where administrative law might be relevant in the defence context may be mentioned: liberty of the subject and laws relating to aliens; immigration; passports; freedom of movement; the security of information; import control; the harnessing of private industry in furtherance of defence purposes; calculation of compensation for the use of civil assets; the regulation of working conditions; and equal opportunity legislation. In fact, it is difficult to think of areas of administrative discretion that are not caught within the scope of administrative review. The entrenchment of both bureaucratic and judicial processes of review is a fact, and from the defence planner's view, this does constitute a problem - a problem which may require, in any emergency, an even more draconic legislative and regulatory reversal than was the case in World War II.

International Law Applicable in Armed Conflict

The Geneva Conventions Act 1957 incorporates the Geneva Conventions of 1949 into Australian domestic law. In 1978, Australia signed two Protocols entitled *Protocols Additional to the Geneva Conventions of 12 August 1949 relating to the Protection of Victims of Armed Conflict*. Protocol I is concerned with armed international conflict and Protocol II with non-international armed conflict. Australia announced on 11 March 1986 that it would proceed with ratification of the Protocols. In this announcement, by the then Acting Minister for Foreign Affairs, Senator Gareth Evans, and the Deputy Prime Minister and Attorney-General, Mr Lionel Bowen, it was stated that Australia had been a party to the Geneva Conventions which deal with the treatment of the sick and wounded, prisoners of war and civilians in time of war since 1958. They pointed out that the Geneva Protocols extend the protections spelt out in the Conventions to non-international conflicts, deal in greater detail with matters such as civil defence, and tackle questions of the means and methods of warfare which the framers of the Convention had not felt themselves able to do. In particular, the Protocols prohibit indiscriminate attacks on civilian targets and require the selection of weapons to limit the effects, as far as possible, to the military target they were directed at. The Ministers said that insofar as the Protocols would improve the level of international legal protection available to Australian defence personnel and civilians in any future conflict with another party to them, there was every reason to ratify and encourage other nations to do likewise.

Against this background, Australia will introduce legislation necessary to implement certain provisions of Protocol II in domestic law. According to a senior official in the Attorney-General's Department, Mr L.J. Curtis, this will include the incorporation in the legislation of offences breaches and grave breaches of the Protocol I as described in Article 85 (these include matters such as launching indiscriminate attacks against civilian targets, the provision of penalties appropriate to such offences, and the conferring of jurisdiction on appropriate courts to deal with such offences).[16] This legislation will also deal with the legal protections to be given to persons accused of offences arising out of armed conflict (Article 75.4), the issuing of special identity cards to certain persons (such as medical personnel) as provided for in Article 18(3) and Annex 1, and the regulation of the use of certain detailed radio and light signals by medical units and transports under Articles 6 and 7 and Annex 1.

The legislation will be difficult to draft. One 'grave breach' in Article 85 of Protocol I which legislation must proscribe concerns 'practices of apartheid and other inhuman and degrading practices involving outrages upon personal dignity, based on racial discrimination'. The Geneva Conventions require that they apply 'to all cases of declared war or any other armed conflict...even if a state of war is not recognised' by one of the parties (Article 2). The same article provides that 'although one of the powers in conflict may not be a party to the present convention, the powers who are parties thereto shall remain bound by it in their mutual relations'. The ADF would then be bound to apply the provisions of the Conventions and as a signatory Australia has undertaken to discharge its obligations under the Protocols. The Conventions come into force when the armed conflict commences and, prior to this, acts committed by the opposing forces against persons or property would be regarded as criminal offences under relevant State or Commonwealth laws. The determination of the commencement of the armed conflict would need to be settled by a tribunal, similar to ones established to determine the status of captured persons (Article 5 of the Third Geneva Convention).

Article 5 of Protocol I establishes, for the first time, procedures for the designation of Protecting Powers to observe compliance with the Conventions and the Protocol, requiring the International Committee of the Red Cross (ICRC) to offer its good offices to the parties to a conflict to facilitate designation of a Protecting Power (i.e., a state that agrees to look after the interests of one state in the territory of another). It authorises the ICRC to ask the Parties to agree to look after the interests of the Parties to give it lists of at least five acceptable Protecting Powers and requires them to provide such lists within two weeks. If no Protecting Power can be agreed upon, it obligates the Parties to the Conflict to accept an offer by the ICRC (should it make an offer) to substitute for a Protecting Power. A state cannot, however, be compelled to accept a Protecting Power. While it would be expected that Australia would appoint a Protecting Power to oversee military activities on Australian territory, it may well be that an enemy would not agree to such an appointment.

In Protocol I, there is a chapter of articles (chapter VI) dealing with 'Civil Defence'. These articles establish that civil defence must be looked at from the view point of protecting civilians and not from the viewpoint of helping the war effort. Civil defence personnel cannot be used for any war-related activities and, if they are, they lose their special civil defence protection. (Civil defence organisations are now entitled to a distinctive sign, the equilateral blue triangle on an orange background.) This will involve practical difficulties in most Australian contingencies in that specific functions which define civil defence overlap military activities of a similar kind. Civilian civil defence units may perform activities outside defence civil defence tasks (at least if these additional tasks do not include acts harmful to the enemy under Article 65 - see below) and this will not deprive the organisation of its future protection when it reverts to being exclusively assigned to civil defence tasks. However, if military personnel have been assigned to civil defence, they are forbidden, for the duration of the conflict, from performing combat or combat support duty. Civilian civil defence personnel lose their special protection, i.e, they may be prevented from carrying out their tasks, if they commit acts harmful to the enemy. The following are not, under Article 65, considered as acts harmful to the enemy:

- civil defence tasks carried out under the direction or control of military authorities;
- civilian defence personnel cooperating with military personnel in the performance of civil defence tasks, or where some military personnel are attached to civilian civil defence organisations;
- where the performance of civil defence tasks may incidentally benefit military victims, particularly those who are *hors de combat*.

But does this mean that a civil defence unit (or an individual civil defence worker) who engages in an act(s) harmful to the enemy could not return to legitimate civil defence functions? The best interpretation here would be that:

> ...the protection should cease as long as there is a reasonable connection with the commission of acts harmful to the enemy. In the case of a unit having consistently engaged in acts harmful to the enemy, such connection could probably only be broken by some kind of reorganisation, personnel reshuffle or the like....It is in the interest of any Party to make sure that the other Party can trust that protection is not abused.[17]

The protocols could thus pose problems in the Australian context in that civil defence must be related to humanitarian purposes.[18]

Finally, the Protocols create specific responsibilities and obligations for Contracting Parties in regard to the observance of the

Protocols particularly by force commanders. Article 87, for example, notes that:

1 The High Contracting Parties and the Parties to the conflict shall require military commanders, with respect to members of the armed forces under their command and other persons under their control, to prevent and, where necessary, to suppress and to report to competent authorities breaches of the Conventions and of this Protocol.

2 In order to prevent and suppress breaches, High Contracting Parties and Parties to the conflict shall require that commensurate with their level of responsibility, commanders ensure that members of the armed forces under their command are aware of their obligations under the Conventions and this Protocol.

3 The High Contracting Parties and Parties to the conflict shall require any commander who is aware that subordinates or other persons under his control are going to commit or have committed a breach of the Conventions or of this Protocol, to initiate such steps as are necessary to prevent such violations of the Conventions or this Protocol, and, where appropriate, to initiate disciplinary or penal action against violators thereof.

Article 86(2) goes on to state:

> The fact that a breach of the Conventions or of this Protocol was committed by a subordinate does not absolve his superiors from penal or disciplinary responsibility as the case may be, if they knew, or had information which should have enabled them to conclude in the circumstances at the time, that he was committing or was going to commit such a breach and if they did not take all feasible measures within their power to prevent or repress the breach.

Moreover, under Article 82:

> The High Contracting Parties at all times, and the Parties to the conflict in time of armed conflict, shall ensure that legal advisers are available, when necessary, to advise military commanders at the appropriate level on the application of the Conventions and this Protocol and on the appropriate instruction to be given to the armed forces on this subject.

The main function of the legal adviser is to advise the commander on the application of the Conventions and Protocols. Commanders would not be bound to follow the legal officer's advice on legal matters, although one imagines most would. The implications of Articles 82 and 87 are, of course, significant in terms of the training and instruction in the law of armed conflict necessary for the ADF, and the requirements for military legal staff to achieve a very high level of knowledge of the Protocols in order to advise operational commanders. However, the institution of legal advisers in armed forces raises a great number of problems which have not been solved or even touched by Article 82. For example, in which phase of the process of decision-making in the military field does the legal adviser find his proper place? Should he be incorporated into the military hierarchy, and, if so, at what level? Who is finally responsible for a decision which has been taken on his advice or against his advice?[19]

Aid to the Civil Power

Aid to the civil power is defined in Defence Instructions as 'Defence Force aid to the Commonwealth and/or State Governments and their civil authorities in their performance of law enforcement tasks'.[20] It is to be distinguished from 'aid to the civil community' which is 'the provision of Defence Force personnel, equipment, facilities or capabilities to perform tasks which are primarily the responsibility of civil authorities and organisations and for which the civil community lacks the necessary equipment or resources'.[21] This covers such items as Defence Force assistance to private organisations and individuals in fighting bush fires, defusing bombs, flood relief, etc. There are no particular legal problems posed when the Defence Force is used in aid to the civil community. (There may arise, however, problems if the military are seen to be 'taking business' from legitimate business enterprises in the performance of these tasks.) The Defence Instruction on 'Aid to the Civil Community' distinguishes various categories of assistance and provides certain administrative procedures to be followed. For example, the Instruction points out that requests which have political implications 'are to be referred to HQ ADF's Joint Military Operations and Plans Section which will consult with the sources concerned and obtain legal, financial and policy clearance as necessary'.[22]

The possible application of armed force is the main criterion in distinguishing aid to the civil power from aid to the civil community. However, as Brian Beddie points out, the two definitions do not in fact point to situations which are clearly differentiated from one another:

> Indeed, the definition of aid to the civil community includes the definition of aid to the civil power. Civil authorities performing law enforcement tasks are still civil authorities in terms of the

definition of assistance to the civil community and, like other civil authorities, they may lack equipment and resources. In itself it may not matter that one definition is included in the other. But in the context of the Defence Instructions, it does matter. This is so because aid to the civil power is governed by a set of procedures which is quite different from the set governing assistance to the civil community.[23]

It should also be remembered that some members of the ADF are required to enforce Commonwealth law and protect Commonwealth interests in the course of their normal duties in situations which have nothing to do with aid to the civil power. Examples are to be found in a wide range of offshore legislation flowing from Section 51(6) of the Constitution, the Fisheries Act, Continental Shelf (Living Resources) Act, and the Customs Act, which govern members of the Navy and, to a lesser degree, the Air Force. The powers of enforcement given to defence personnel are not uniform and need greater attention.[24]

While neither the Constitution nor the Defence Act refer explicitly to aid to the civil power, both contain sections dealing with the concept. For example, Section 119 provides that 'The Commonwealth shall protect every State against invasion and, on the application of the Executive Government of the State, against domestic violence'. Section 51 of the Defence Act provides:

> Where the Governor of the State has proclaimed that domestic violence exists therein, the Governor-General, upon the application of the Executive Government of the State, may, by proclamation, declare that domestic violence exists in that State, and may call out the Permanent Forces and in the event of their numbers being insufficient may also call out such of the Emergency Forces and the Reserve Forces as may be necessary for the protection of that State, and the services of the Forces so called out may be utilised accordingly for the protection of that State against domestic violence....Provided always that the Emergency Forces or the Reserve Forces shall not be called out or utilised in connexion with an industrial dispute.

Although Section 119 uses the world 'shall', Section 51 of the Defence Act replaces the world 'shall' with 'may'. It would be up to the Commonwealth to decide how to use its discretion to respond to a State's request, for as Lee comments:

> If the conclusive decision is vested exclusively in the State it would provide the State with an uncontrolled access to the Commonwealth military resources. The Commonwealth's

power to determine the amount of force to be committed is more consistent with the better view that it is for the Commonwealth to determine for itself the existence of domestic violence on receipt of the State's application.[25]

In the role of protecting the States against domestic violence, the Defence Forces operate under restrictive conditions. These are detailed in Australian Military Regulations (AMR) Part V, AMRs 398 to 415 (inclusive). Air Force Regulations Part IX, and Naval Instructions have similar requirements, the main elements being:

- **Call-Out:** The requirement for a call-out in accordance with Section 51 of the Defence Act;

- **Requisition:** The requirement for a requisition in writing from the civil authority before providing aid;

- **Magistrate:** The requirement for a magistrate to accompany the forces and remain as near as he can to the commander;

- **Request:** The requirement for the magistrate to assess the situation and, where he considers that the situation demands the active interference of the military forces, request the commander to take action. Such a request should preferably be in writing;

- **Action:** The requirement that the commander shall have absolute discretion as to whether action will be taken and, if taken, the nature and extent of such action;

- **Emergency:** The requirement that, in extraordinary cases of immediate and pressing danger which, in the opinion of the commander, demands his immediate interference, he shall take such action as he thinks necessary, although he has not received a requisition from a civil authority or a request from a magistrate.

Regulations applying to State-initiated call-outs should 'as far as possible' be observed in the case of Commonwealth initiated call-outs (AMR 415). Section 63(1)(f) of the Defence Act which states that the Governor-General 'may do all matters and things deemed by him to be necessary and desirable for the efficient defence and protection of the Commonwealth or of any State' is the link back to the power in the Constitution for the Commonwealth to protect itself and its interest and property and would justify the use of the Defence Force in an operational role.[26] There have been two occasions where the Commonwealth has initiated a call-out of part of the Defence Force to protect its interests against a threat of domestic violence. The first occasion was in Papua New Guinea in 1971, when there was a threat to law and order on the Gazella Peninsula (in the end it was not necessary to send troops), and the second was in Sydney at the time of the bombing outside the Hilton Hotel in 1978.[27]   In the contemporary situation, Commonwealth initiated call-outs seem much more likely than State initiated call-outs. As Beddie states:

> In a country like present-day Australia internal violence with which the police are unable to cope is likely to be linked to international terrorist activity. In addition, whatever the source of the violence, it is difficult to imagine that widespread disorder in any State could fail to infringe Commonwealth laws and harm Commonwealth property and interests.[28]

Brigadier Ewing, a former Director of Army Legal Services, has argued that in a deteriorating security situation, the Defence Forces may, in the first instance, be involved in assisting civil authorities to supplement civil capabilities for dealing with armed violence:

> In low level contingencies, hostile actions against Australia may, in law, simply begin with actions that breach Commonwealth or State laws. Examples are breaches of customs and quarantine regulations and unauthorised incursions into Australian sea space, air space or coastal territory. They may even extend to apparently isolated acts of criminal violence such as arson, sabotage or terrorism before the distinctly military threat becomes evident, that is, uniformed bodies of armed men with distinguishing uniforms and under the orders of foreign national authorities. Thus where the situation involves or appears to involve no more than isolated breaches of Australian or State law, Governments are shown as unlikely to authorise dedicated military operations, at least in the first instance, as distinct from specialist defence assistance in aid to the civil power.[29]

It is submitted, however, that in a situation where it was clear that the threat is external, it would be improper to call-out the Defence Force in aid to the civil power. The call-out of the ADF would be based on the power conferred by the Constitution for the Commonwealth to protect itself and its interests and property.[30] Reliance could then be placed on Section 63(1)(f) of the Defence Act.[31]

After the Sydney Hilton bombing, the Prime Minister appointed the Hon. Mr. Justice Hope to conduct a review of protective security. His *Review* contains a number of important recommendations.[32] In a proposed new Section 51 of the Defence Act, Mr Justice Hope set out three sets of conditions under which members of the armed forces may be used to protect Commonwealth interests and laws. Before a Minister can recommend that the Governor-General authorise the use of the Defence Force, there must be a requisition by a Commissioner of Police in a non-self-governing territory or by the Government of a State or self-governing Territory. In any final legislation, it will have to be made clear whether the Governor-General acts on the advice of the respective Minister or the advice of the Executive Council, for this may have some political significance: 'if the authorisation requires approval of the Executive Council of which all Ministers are members, it would be understood to carry the approval of the Government as a whole'.[33]

Mr Justice Hope was also concerned about possible misuse of the Defence Force in suppressing domestic violence and he recommended that in certain circumstances the call-out would have to be reported to Parliament. This seems a reasonable suggestion, although it may not satisfy those who raise the possibility of a military coup. (The only response one can make to this fear is to say that legal machinery will not be much help in a major political crisis. Even with a Bill of Rights, the courts would not win against a government determined to embark on a course which overthrows those laws and conventions which assist the running of a constitutional system.)

Mr Justice Hope recommended greater legal protection for members of the Defence Force in aid of the civil power. At present, the soldier's responsibilities in an aid to civil power situation, under the civil and criminal law, are the same as any other citizen. But the soldier is there as part of a military force subject to military orders. He may use such force as is necessary, and if excessive force is used, he is legally liable under the general law. What is 'excessive' cannot be determined in advance and that can be no comfort for the soldier when he may leave himself open to conviction for murder if he misunderstands the law. What is reasonable force in the circumstances will be extremely difficult for the soldier to know. As Professor Blackshield points out:

> To some extent the flexible case-by-case processes of the common law judgement may be acceptable as a substitute for precise regulation, in advance, of the legal rights and liabilities of citizens and soldiers; but it seems unlikely that either citizens or soldiers would be content to leave their rights and liabilities solely at the mercy of judicial wisdom-after-the-event.[34]

As far as the law of self-defence is concerned, the matter has been settled by the High Court in *Viro v R*;[35] an accused soldier who has used excessive force in self-defence will be guilty of manslaughter, not murder. However *Viro v R* does not fully resolve the dilemma of the soldier when employed in aid of the civil power. In many instances, the soldier is involved in the defence of somebody else or in the protection of government property: what is his position if he kills a person in order to prevent him inflicting harm on a third person, such as a terrorist attempting to kill a visiting foreign dignitary?[36] The answer is problematic, although the better view would be that the manslaughter doctrine should be preferred whether it be involved in the context of self-protection or in the context of prevention of crime.[37] On a defence of superior orders, Section 14 of the Defence Force Discipline Act 1982 states:

> A person is not liable to be convicted of a service offence by a reason of an act or omission that:
>
> (a)   was in execution of the law; or
>
> (b)   was in obedience to (i) a lawful order; or (ii) an unlawful order that the person did not know, and could not reasonably be expected to have known, was unlawful.

The question of superior orders does not affect the liability of the superior officer who gave the illegal order. Such an officer 'would be liable in civil, criminal and military courts for the consequences of any illegal orders he may give'.[38]

Justice Hope added the important proviso that members of the ADF in giving aid to the civil power shall act only as part of the Defence Force and shall be individually liable to obey the orders of their superior officers as if they were being used for the naval, military or air defence of the Commonwealth of the several States. Leaving to one side the very good reasons why the police, and not the military, should be used in internal security,[39] the suggestion that the Defence Force should have the powers of police officers in aid to the civil power raises a number of legal policy issues. First, as Robin Evelegh has observed in relation to the situation in Northern Ireland:

> ...the military need more clarity in their powers than the Police, or at least the Police in normal times. The military come in to suppress disorder, after abandoning their other duties quite suddenly. Their officers will have had some necessary training in the law, while the legal knowledge among the junior ranks is probably confined to what can be gleaned from detective serials on television. Most important, the military do not possess the years of collective experience of operating the law that resides in a Police force.[40]

Second, and related to the last point, is the fact that it is not exactly clear what limits may be placed on the police officer's powers to use force, search, patrol, and guard, arrest and set up road-blocks, etc. What is clear, and must be emphasised here, is that police powers are very limited. For example, there is no legal right for police to set up a road-block and question those in cars. The Defence Force may be crippled in their operations, not by the lack of draconian legal powers, but by the lack of minor laws such as giving the soldier the right to demand the production of driving licences and vehicle documents. In any internal security situation where it is felt desirable to use the ADF, the States may have to grant extra powers to police and soldiers in advance. Certainly what is needed is some legislation which spells out the rights, duties and obligations of those members of the ADF called out in aid of the civil power. (Here it may be worth examining the possibility of granting the ADF similar immunities as State authorities acting in suppressing disorder.) Such legislation is best introduced in quiet times, rather than waiting for a dangerous situation to develop. Neither soldiers, nor citizens, should be placed in a position of legal uncertainty when the Defence Force is called out. Northern Ireland has proved that legal uncertainty can be by itself a source of physical conflict because it leads to unpredictability in military and police responses to disorder.

Mr Justice Hope recognised the current military regulations dealing with aid to the civil power are an echo of a by-gone era. The regulations assume that internal disorder will take the form of riot control. In rewriting the regulations, it is important to remember that the ADF and the civil community need to know what to do in a crisis - the regulations should, therefore, be clearly and briefly stated when soldiers are thrust into a situation of countering terrorism. The written instructions may be the only legal support to go by. Justice Hope's recommendations are now under active consideration by Government and amendments to the Defence Act are expected in the near future.

Finally, one area where government and military decision-makers need to exercise caution is in the use of Defence Forces in industrial disputes. (Five of the six occasions where States have asked for Commonwealth assistance of one kind or another were based on a threat to civil order caused by industrial strikes.[41]) While there are no particular legal difficulties involved in the call-out of troops for this purpose (provided the Emergency Services and Reserves are not used, Section 51 of the Defence Act), there are good policy reasons why the use of armed forces 'in connexion with' industrial disputes should be approached with great caution.[42]

The legal aspects of the preparation for and employment of military force have not attracted a great deal of research interest in Australia, despite the fact that the legal framework, in which low-level conflict in Australia would take place, will impact significantly on the operational environment. Appropriate emergency legislation, at the

Commonwealth level, needs to be set in place so that there is no risk that flawed legislation will be introduced during the heat of any national emergency. Defence planners may find some assistance in examining the Canadian Emergencies Act which was first presented to the Canadian Parliament in June 1987. The Emergencies Act includes safeguarded and appropriately limited exceptional powers to deal with four types of postulated national emergencies. It ensures that the exceptional powers granted by Parliament will be no more than what is needed for the emergency at hand. The four types of emergency are:

- **Public Welfare Emergencies**, including severe national disasters or major accidents affecting public welfare, which are beyond the capacity or authority of a province to handle;

- **Public Order Emergencies**, which constitute 'threats to the security of Canada', are so serious as to be national emergencies and are beyond the capacity or authority of a province to handle;

- **International Emergencies**, which arise from acts of intimidation or coercion or the use of serious force or violence that threatens the sovereignty, security or territorial integrity of Canada or any of its allies;

- **War Emergencies**, which include real or imminent armed conflict against Canada or its allies.

The Canadian initiative is worthy of study in the framework of improving the legal setting for the defence emergency employment of military forces in Australia.

Endnotes

1   Michael Glover, *The Velvet Glove - The Decline and Fall of Moderation in War*, (Hodder and Stoughton, London, 1982), p. 11.
2   H.P. Lee, *Emergency Powers*, (Law Book Company, Sydney, 1984), p. 10. For a very good discussion on the defence power see Chapter 11.
3   Sir Ninian Stephen, 'The Role of the Governor General as Commander-in-Chief of the Australian Defence Forces', *Defence Force Journal*, (Number 43), November/December 1983, p. 8.
4   *Ibid.*, p. 8.
5   Colin Howard, *Australian Federal Constitutional Law*, (Law Book Company, Sydney, 3rd Edition, 1985), pp. 487-488.
6   Parliament of Australia, *Hansard (House of Representatives)*, 18 March 1987, p. 1050.
7   Some assistance to the military as far as denying access to land may be found in the Crimes Act (Commonwealth) 1914, Section 80, which allows certain areas to be declared 'prohibited places'. See also Defence (Special Undertakings) Act 1952, Sections 7 and 8, (prohibited areas), Section 14 (restricted areas). Certain powers of arrest and search of unauthorized persons in prohibited areas are given, see Section 20 (search), Section 23 (arrest). The Crimes Act 1914, Section 84 provides for arrest of persons in or about prohibited areas. The Defence Act 1903, Section 82(3) creates the

offence of trespassing on any building or land set apart for the Defence Force. This section empowers any member of the Defence Force to arrest without warrant any person he believes has committed an offense against Section 82. The Crimes Act, Section 84A provides that a Defence Member while acting in the course of his duty may cause the search of a person, his belongings and any bag or other article in his possession without warrant, if he has reasonable grounds for suspecting that person to be in possession of evidence of any offence against Part VII of the Crimes Act when that person is (a) about to enter or leave the Commonwealth; (b) has been in or near, or has passed over a prohibited place (c) is behaving or has behaved in a suspicious manner; and is in possession of evidence of an offence against Part VII of the Crimes Act and may, without warrant, detain the person for that purpose. On controlling road traffic, a prohibited area under the Defence (Special Undertakings) Act 1952 may only be declared if the road is used exclusively for the purpose of a defence special undertaking (Section 7(2)). On evacuation, the States natural disaster legislation allows a designated authority to order an area to be evacuated. (Western Australia does not have such legislation); see *Northern Territory Disasters Act 1982* (NT); *State Counter Disaster Organisation Act 1975* (Queensland); *State Emergency Services and Civil Defence Act 1972* (NSW); *State Disasters Act 1980* (SA); *Victorian State Emergency Service Act 1981* (Victoria); and *Emergency Service Act 1976* (Tasmania). The Executive power is limited to the powers of the Commonwealth under the heads of power granted the Constitution and statutory backing is required for any action involving executive interference with the life, liberty or property of citizens. Given this and that there is not Commonwealth emergency legislation and that the States have wide civil defence legislation, the best course with regard to evacuation would be to rely on State legislation.

8 See H.P. Lee, *Emergency Powers*, Chapter V, for a discussion of state emergency and natural disaster legislation.

9 Commonwealth employees under the *Compensation (Commonwealth Government Employees) Act 1971* would be covered.

10 Despite legal powers given to aborigines to keep others off their land, the evidence would appear to be that they have co-operated in the training of the ADF on aboriginal land in the Northern Territory. For an excellent discussion of this issue see Graeme Neate, *Legal Aspects of Defence Operations on Aboriginal Land in the Northern Territory*, (Working Paper Number 136, Strategic and Defence Studies Centre, Australian National University, Canberra, September 1987).

11 It should be noted that the Defence Act 1903, Section 64 provides for 'control' not acquisition of railways in time of a proclamation of war.

12 *Commonwealth v Colonial Ammunition Co. Ltd.*, (1924), 34 CLR 38.

13 See Section 14(a) of the *Shipping Registration Act 1981* which enables registration on the Australian register of foreign-owned vessels under demise charter to Australian operators. Those vessels would not appear to come within Section 67 of the Defence Act. For an examination of requisition powers, see R.N. Baker, 'The Compulsory Acquisition Powers of the Commonwealth', in R. Else Mitchell (ed.), *Essays on the Australian Constitution*, (Law Book Company, Sydney, 2nd Ed., 1961), pp. 193-220.

14 See Georg Schwarzenberger, *International Law: The Law of Armed Conflict*, (Stevens and Sons Limited, London, 1968), Volume 2, p. 382.

15 In 1983, the Ombudsman Act was amended to incorporate the office of the Defence Force Ombudsman. The Defence Force Ombudsman has power to investigate administrative action relating to the service of a member of the Defence Force. Although the Defence Force Ombudsman may not investigate administrative actions taken by a Minister, he may investigate action leading to that action. The Defence Force Ombudsman may not investigate action taken under the Defence Force Discipline Act 1982. If the Defence Force Ombudsman is of the opinion that an action is unreasonable, unjust, oppressive or improperly discriminatory, or was in accordance with a rule of law or practice but the rule or practice is unreasonable, unjust, oppressive or improperly discriminatory, he may report to the Department.

16 L.J. Curtis, Keynote address to the Conference on Prospects for International Humanitarian Law in Today's World, Adelaide, 19th September 1986, pp. 17-18.
17 Michael Bothe, K. Josef Partsch and A. Waldemar, *New Rules for Victims of Armed Conflicts*, (Martinus Nijhoff, The Hague, 1982), p.413.
18 See Major General K.W. Latchford, 'Civil Defence - its New role and Functions' in J.O. Langtry and Desmond Ball (eds.), *A Vulnerable Country? Civil Resources in the Defence of Australia*, (Australian National University Press, Canberra, 1986), pp. 501-511.
19 See Michael Bothe *et.al.*, *New Rules for Victims of Armed Conflicts*, p. 501.
20 Defence Instructions (General) OPS)1-2 'Defence Force Aid to the Civil Power - Situations other than counter-terrorist operations - Policy and Procedures', (22 September 1978).
21 Defence Instructions (General) OPS 05-1, 'Policy and Procedures for Defence Force Assistance to the Civil Community', (20 October 1978).
22 Defence Instruction General, OPS 05-1, p. 5.
23 B.D. Beddie, 'Aid to the Civil Power', in Hugh Smith (ed.), *Law, Change and the Services*, (Royal Military College, Duntroon, Faculty of Military Studies, Department of Government, 1984), p. 65.
24 These are discussed at length in W.R. Edeson, 'The Effect of Maritime Legislation and Legal Constraints on Enforcement', (Paper presented at the 8th RAN Legal Conference, HMAS WATSON, January 1983). This legislation is referred to in a short paragraph headed 'Special Authorisations' in the Defence Instruction on Aid to the Civil Power. For a criticism of this practice, see B.D. Beddie, 'Aid to the Civil Power', p.49.
25 H.P. Lee, *Emergency Powers*, p.205. There has been one case whereby a State application was made under Section 119. This was in Queensland in 1912 and the application was rejected. See B.D. Beddie and S. Moss, *Some Aspects of Aid to the Civil Power*, (Royal Military College, Duntroon, Faculty of Military Studies, Department of Government, Occasional Monograph Number 2, 1982), pp. 8-20.
26 See M.J. Ewing, 'Military Aid to the Civil Power', *Defence Force Journal*, (Number 57), March/April 1986, p. 26.
27 See B.D. Beddie and S. Moss, *Some Aspects of Aid to the Civil Power*, pp. 51-65.
28 B.D. Beddie, , 'Aid to the Civil Power', p.55.
29 M.J. Ewing, 'Military Aid to the Civil Power', p.25.
30 In his second reading speech on the Defence Legislation Amendment Bill 1987, the Defence Minister, Mr Beazley, referring to the amendment to permit the reserve forces to be used in situations short of defence emergencies states that 'the reserves will be employed only in tasks of direct national defence in responding to an *external* (emphasis added) threat to Australia's security. It [i.e., the new call-out powers] is not relevant to call-out in aid of the civil power. Such assistance would be effected under Section 51 of the Defence Act...' *Hansard (House of Representatives)*, 18 March 1987, p.1050.
31 M.J.Ewing, *Defence Force Journal*, (Number 57), 1986, p.25.
32 Mr Justice R.M. Hope, *Protective Security Review*, (Australian Government Publishing Service, Canberra, 1979).
33 B.D. Beddie and S. Moss, *Some Aspects of Aid to the Civil Power*, p.69.
34 A.R. Blackshield, 'The Siege of Bowral - The Legal Issues', *Pacific Defence Reporter*, (Volume 4, Number 9), March 1978, p.10.
35 (1978) 141 C.L.R., 88.
36 H.P. Lee, *Emergency Powers*, pp.239-240.
37 *Ibid.*, p.241.
38 Mr Justice Hope, *Protective Security Review*, p.169.
39 See Grant Wardlaw, *Political Terrorism*, (Cambridge University Press, Cambridge, 1982), Chapter 10.
40 Robin Evelegh, *Peace Keeping in a Democratic Society*, (C. Hurst and Co., London, 1978), p. 152.
41 See B.D. Beddie and S. Moss, *Some Aspects of Aid to the Civil Power*, p.77.

42   A plan was prepared under the Fraser Government for use of the armed forces to replace strikers during industrial disputes. The plan was cancelled by the Hawke Government. See Gary Brown, *The Australian Defence Force in Industrial Action Situations: Joint Service Plan 'Cabriole'*, (Working Paper Number 115, Strategic and Defence Studies Centre, Australian National University, Canberra, 1986).

CHAPTER 15

DEFENCE FORCES PERSONNEL

Cathy Downes

Periods in the history of war can be distinguished when innovations and reforms in the mobilisation, deployment, and engagement of military manpower have altered the course of battles and wars. Equally, there are periods in which technological developments in weaponry, logistics, communication, and intelligence systems have changed the balance of force in a variety of conflicts. In almost all senses, the 20th century has been the century of technology. In issues of Western security and defence, the seductiveness of technological 'fixes' for problems of military strategy and operations has led frequently to a discounting of the role of military manpower and a ready acceptance of the proposition that people are an elastic, plentiful and readily available resource. For strategists, the seemingly pedestrian concerns of military manpower evince, at best, a passing and indifferent interest.[1] For budget analysts, military manpower is seen as an unrepentant black hole which swallows up financial resources with few quantifiable measures of productivity or economy. For technologists, manpower is the deficiency to be compensated for, the inefficiency to be overcome.

Yet, despite this wealth of disdain, it is argued that the burden of success in modern war will continue to rest as much, if not more so in many cases, with the wielder as with the weapon or the strategy. Most nations cannot rely upon being able to effectively man their military forces at short notice and with parsimonious investment. Moreover, despite the unceasing efforts of scientists to make people redundant on the modern battlefield, it is the new generations of weapons, in concert with the diverse nature of contemporary conflicts, which have created the demand for more highly skilled, trained and intelligent, if numerically smaller, military manpower bases. Many of these conditions are evident in the approaches taken to manning and personnel management in the Australian Defence Force (ADF). This chapter will examine the recent record of manning the ADF, outline how the Department of Defence is structured in relation to the manpower and personnel function, and discuss a number of economic and technological trends which hold the potential to significantly influence the structure and composition of the future ADF.

The Contemporary Record

The size and character of Australian military forces has been determined by a number of influences. Australian forces have been primarily armed and manned to reflect the reliance of Australian security policy upon strategies of forward defence and the formation of reliant partnerships with larger allies. Force structures and manning levels have also reflected the essential compromises which all governments make in matching the dedication of resources to the insurance policy of defence and the levels of perceived and assessed threat to the security of the nation. Finally, force postures have often been determined as much by the inertia of existing force levels and organisation as by changes in strategy or international affiliations.

However, the enunciation of the Guam Doctrine by US President Nixon and the conclusion of Australian involvement in Vietnam provided a watershed both in terms of the development of Australian defence strategies, and in the force structures and manning levels designed to support those strategies. The 1960s had witnessed the steady expansion of the ADF from a volunteer, regular force of 47,000 in 1960 to a force of 84,250 (including 16,200 National Servicemen) in 1970.[2] Within days of being elected in 1972, the Labor Government halted all further inductions of National Servicemen, and offered those still serving the option of discharge in preference to completing their term of service. As a consequence, the ADF declined in size from its 1970 peak to 67,500 in 1974.

With a return to an all-volunteer force, the Government implemented a number of initiatives in service conditions which had been recommended during the tenure of its predecessor. These included a new and simplified pay structure, the establishment of a Committee of Reference on Defence Forces Pay, the introduction of pay principles more in line with those applying in the civilian community, and increases in the levels of remuneration (the recommendations of the Kerr-Woodward Report), the introduction of a new Defence Forces Retirement Benefits (DFRB) Scheme (the recommendations of the Jess Report), the extension of coverage of the Defence Services Homes Act and an increase in the size of loans offered, improvements in the range of resettlement benefits, and the introduction of a $1,000 re-engagement bounty.[3]

Collectively, this package of pay and conditions, although seen as necessary to recruit and retain a credible manpower base, contributed to a blow-out in defence expenditure on manpower. For example, in 1971-72 Defence Forces pay and the DFRB scheme accounted for 35 per cent of defence expenditure. In 1973-74, this had risen to 42 per cent of the Defence budget. Similarly, the total military and civilian manpower costs as a proportion of defence expenditure increased from 50 per cent in 1971-72 to 61 per cent in 1973-74. Commensurably, there was a significant decline in expenditure on the acquisition of capital equipment, which had accounted for 37 per cent of the defence vote in 1967-68. In 1973-74 it represented a bare 7 per cent of expenditure.[4]

While these figures do not provide a complete picture, they are demonstrative of the imbalance which had developed between categories in defence expenditure during this period. Under forward defence strategies, a greater priority had been attached to the commitment of troops; the requirement to update and maintain weapons and equipment arsenals was eschewed.

With the shift in strategic postures from forward defence to self-reliance and defence in-depth, correcting this imbalance has become a dominant influence on the determination of defence resource priorities. Moreover, the new strategies have called for a far greater commitment to capital equipment resourcing than merely the updating of existing systems. However, Australia has re-entered the capital procurement business at a time when the processes of research, development, manufacture and purchase of weapon systems and platforms have increased significantly in complexity, lead-times and cost. In order to develop force structures which are appropriate to the new strategies, there has been a requirement to significantly increase expenditure on capital procurement. This could be achieved through a considerable expansion of the defence budget, or failing that, through a reordering of allocation priorities, in which resources from other areas were redirected into capital procurement. In fact, both options have been employed.

Although, the strategic premises had not been fully developed and clarified, this resource strategy was enunciated in the 1976 *White Paper on Australian Defence* which called for a substantial increase in defence expenditure. While the goals set proved to be overly ambitious, the policy of reordering resource priorities in favour of capital equipment became accepted. The policy direction was confirmed by the in-coming Labor Government in 1982. For example, between FY 1982-83 and a peak in 1986-87, expenditure on new capital equipment grew by $1,193,196 million. By contrast, ADF salaries and allowances, over the same period, grew by $374,922 million.[5] Procurement of new equipment rose from 15.2 per cent of the defence budget in 1982-83 to 25.7 per cent in 1986-87, while ADF salaries and allowances declined from a 33 per cent share to 26.5 per cent of the budget.[6] (See Figure 1: Defence Function Expenditure by Category.) Finally, manning ceilings have been imposed and adjusted downwards. For example, the strength of the ADF on 30 June 1982 was listed as 73,185. In 1988, the average strength of the ADF was 70, 181.[7]

Although it has been necessary to redress the earlier imbalance between resources devoted to the procurement of capital equipment and personnel, there are finite limitations on the extent to which the latter can be used to subsidise the former. Where the introduction of capital equipment occurs in response to a change in role, unless another role is abandoned, that introduction will create a manpower demand. Where new equipment replaces old, there is every expectation that a significant part of the additional manpower required can be met from the pool of labour released by the decommissioning of obsolete units. However, it is likely that any pool so generated will be insufficient or inappropriately trained. This occurs because capital equipment projects themselves generate a demand for manpower, and accurate and complete estimates of manpower requirements tend not to be provided in capital procurement bids.

The manning pipeline is not only responsible for generating the required number of skilled and trained operators and maintainers. It is expected to produce teams of trained, experienced and competent project managers, planners and analysts. The failure to maintain a consistent and healthy commitment to capital procurement has created a hump of systems obsolescence. As a consequence, the ADF is now faced with managing several large projects not consecutively, but at the same time. This serves to increase the pressure on the constrained manpower resource to generate the required project staffs. The case of the Navy is illustrative. Within a very short time frame, the RAN must provide staffs for seven substantial capital equipment programs - the *Oberon* submarine replacement project, the *ANZAC* ship program, the guided missile destroyer modernisation project, the guided missile frigate follow-on project, the survey motor launch program, the *Sea-Hawk* helicopter project, and the mine countermeasures vessel project. In addition, other projects are being studied which may include the procurement of a helicopter support ship and a second underway replenishment ship.[8] Unless the ADF can provide staffs of sufficient size, competence and tenure, the risk is substantially increased that these and other projects will run over-time and over-cost, as has occurred in past projects.[9]

In order to keep the costs of any equipment bid to the minimum, the associated manpower costs are often under-estimated or excluded. In addition to the salaries and allowances of the estimated number of operators, maintainers and project staffs for any proposed weapon system, there are a series of flow-on costs including additional postings, the training and/or retraining of personnel, extra instructors, and

Figure 1. Defence function expenditure by category

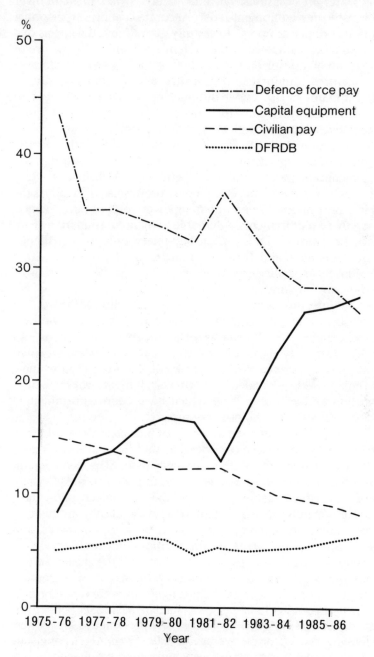

Source: Department of Defence, Defence Reports 1975–86 (Canberra, Australian Government Publishing Service).

increases in, or relocation of, support facilities and support personnel. These outlays are, on occasions, not adequately costed in manpower estimates prepared for equipment bids. Accurate costing of personnel requirements also depends upon successfully quantifying the effects of a number of variables - estimates of the system's reliability, the nature of the technology involved (for example, whether the system has remove-and-replace features, automated diagnostics and is user-friendly or unfriendly), estimates of use under different operating conditions and scenarios, anticipated workloads to be carried by support units, unit structures (combat-to-support ratios), and how personnel management policies are determined.[10]   It is difficult to predict and quantify accurately the manpower requirements and costs which are derived from the interaction of these variables. Therefore, it is difficult to fully incorporate such expenses in equipment proposals.   Finally, the difficulties inherent in quantifying the manpower costs of new weapon systems leave these requirements vulnerable to manipulation in the Five Year Defence Program (FYDP). When budgetary pressures challenge the acquisition schedule, and there is a reordering of priorities within the FYDP, loosely specified manpower costs can be deferred or sometimes they can 'slip' indefinitely.

The underestimation of, and low priority afforded to, manpower costs in capital equipment bids can result in manpower requirements exceeding the allowances set in budgetary allocations. As a consequence, despite being unable to effectively influence the capital procurement process, Service manpower planners are required to meet the total manning needs generated by capital equipment projects, out of a vote allocation and manning level which have been constrained in order to free resources to fund those very projects.

By constraining manpower at a time of increased demand for it, this resource strategy has placed considerable, and in a number of cases excessive, pressures upon the ADF manpower base. The demands on the constrained manpower resource, when combined with the effects of a number of restrictive personnel policies and societal changes, have contributed significantly to a substantial increase in the number of members resigning prior to completing their career appointments, and to others not opting to re-engage for an additional term of service. A sustained trend of increasing personnel turnover rates has resulted, which is only the latest in a succession of such trends. As a percentage of total strength, 7.14 per cent of the ADF resigned or were discharged in 1982-83. This had risen to 13.17 per cent in 1987-88. 12.03 per cent of male officers in 1987-88 resigned, as against 6.68 per cent in 1982-83, and as against the ten-year historical average of 8.78 per cent.[11] Changes in rates for particular categories show even more marked changes. For example, the resignation rate for Naval Engineer Lieutenant Commanders in 1985-86 was 16 per cent as compared with the 8.3 per cent average for Lieutenant Commanders. The 10-year average for male sailors in 1985-86 was 11.7 per cent. In that year, the discharge rate for sailors in the Radio Operator Teletype category was 19.6 per cent and for the Air Technical Weapons Electrical category, 18.1per cent. [12]

Despite the consistency of a six-year trend, efforts to establish high levels of personnel turnover as a cause for concern and action were rejected and dispelled. The requirement to maintain the impetus of the capital procurement program, for one, tended to ensure that issues, which have shown the capacity to draw off funds from that program, receive such treatment. Moreover, accounts of increased occupational mobility in society, growth in employment opportunities, the Vietnam hump of retirees and the increased number of women in the ADF (who usually have higher turnover rates than men) all offered plausible explanations for the increase. The reluctance to discern and address the numerous concerns which underpinned the increase in personnel turnover has served to increase the magnitude of the problem and the scale of response required to have an impact upon it.[13]

One of the more substantive responses was the appointment, after the 1987 General Election, of a junior Defence Minister, responsible for Defence Science and Personnel. However, the dictates of broader Government social and economic policy, the Government's traditional distrust of, and disinterest in, the military institution, and its refusal to sanction ADF policy which could be construed as precedent-setting (particularly in conditions of employment matters), particularly ensure that the capacities of the Minister to take action in a timely and effective manner are heavily circumscribed.

Other responses have included the drawn-out implementation of the the Hamilton Report on Supporting Service Families, with the establishment of the Australian Defence Families Information and Liaison Service (ADFILS) which is designed to assist in the provision of community and dependant education support for military families. In addition, a National Consultative Group of Service Spouses was created which, along with other Wives Associations, is forming an identifiable interest group to monitor official action and to press for reforms in the treatment of the military family. In 1987, the Government passed legislation which created the Defence Housing Authority, a statutory body with the powers to efficiently and effectively manage the Defence Force housing stock. In late 1988, the position of Assistant Chief of the Defence Force (Personnel) (ACPERS), was created in HQADF with responsibilities which include ADFILS and the development of ADF aspects of Service personnel policies and procedures.

In October 1987, the Senate referred the issue of Defence Force personnel turnover to the Joint Committee on Foreign Affairs, Defence and Trade. The Defence Sub-Committee received a total of 226 written submissions (compared with the 35 and 26 submissions prepared respectively for its two preceding inquiries), resulting in a substantial body of previously unavailable evidence being amassed. The Committee tabled its 434-page report in November 1988, making in total some 48 recommendations. In May 1989, the Government presented its response to the Committee's Report. It demonstrated a telling need to deflect the criticisms of the Report by seeking to have the Report portrayed as limited to negativisms and redundant in light of on-going and aggressive Government initiatives.[14] However, the main planks of what was somewhat importantly described as the Government's 'ADF Personnel strategy' were predictably governed by the same set of political, financial and bureaucratic constraints and prohibitions as those outlined above. As a consequence, despite considerable progress in addressing some of the personnel concerns of ADF members, there has been little advance towards a cogent, flexible and comprehensive manpower and personnel strategy which reflects the underlying relationships between the manning and personnel management of the ADF and between the ADF manpower base and defence strategy, force structure and weapons acquisition.

Department of Defence Personnel and Manpower Planning Structures

The structures and policy processes designed to support, or which have an influence upon, Defence Forces personnel are complex and multifaceted. There are three principal groups within the Department of Defence which contribute to policy-making and the implementation of policy in regard to manpower planning and personnel management. These are the Single Service staffs in Army, Navy and Air Force Offices, the military staffs in Headquarters ADF (HQADF), both responsible to the Chief of the Defence Force, and the primarily civilian staffs in Defence Central, responsible to the Secretary of the Department. These individuals and organisations, in significant part, interact and function through a series of policy and advisory committees composed of both public servants and military staff members. As with any bureaucracy, the organisational configuration of divisions, branches, directorates and committees which make up these groups is the subject of regular amendment and adjustment. Thus, the structures outlined are those in effect at the time of writing.

Army, Navy and Air Force Offices and HQADF. Within each Service Office there is a separation of responsibility between manning and personnel management. Manpower planning is primarily undertaken within the Offices of the Chief of the General Staff, and the Chief of the Air Staff, while a 1987 change brought Naval manpower planners into the Naval Personnel Division. In contrast, Single Service personnel management policies in the main, and their implementation, have been the responsibility of staff directorates under the Assistant Chiefs of Staff (Personnel) for each Service. (See Figure 2: Military Staffs for Personnel.) This latter set of staffs make a significant input into a whole range of personnel management issues including recruitment, selection, education, training, postings, promotions, career and branch/unit/category structures, pay and allowances, conditions of service, personnel records, ombudsman and parliamentary questions, reserves and cadets, removals, housing, and religious, legal, and health matters.

Within the personnel staffs, there is a further division of labour between those directorates which are concerned with the recruitment, training, career management and employment of Service personnel, and those which deal with the personal and welfare issues affecting Service members. Close links are maintained between the first group of directorates and the manpower planning and recruiting staffs, the latter of which are grouped under a Director General of Recruiting who currently reports to the head of Defence Central's Human Resources Division. Individual Service directors of recruiting are also accountable to their respective Assistant Chiefs of Staff (Personnel).

HQADF, since its creation in 1984, has gradually assumed greater responsibility for the coordination of policies between the Services and for the promulgation of policies which are common to all three. With the increasing emphasis upon standardisation and joint policies, HQADF has tended to gather a number of functions under its umbrella. For example, when the Industrial Division of Defence Central was disbanded in 1987, its Service Conditions Branch was transferred to HQADF, with the responsibility for preparing the ADF's cases to the Defence Forces Remuneration Tribunal and advising the Department of Industrial Relations on ADF allowances not in the nature of pay.[15] Similarly in 1987, when the Training and Education Policy Branch of the Policy and Administration Division (later renamed Human Resources Division) was divided, the military section was transferred to HQADF. These functions have now been drawn together under the auspices of ACPERS.

Defence Central. Deputy Secretary (Budget and Management) is responsible for five functional divisions of which four deal mainly with manpower and personnel matters: Management Improvement and

Figure 2. Military Staffs for personnel

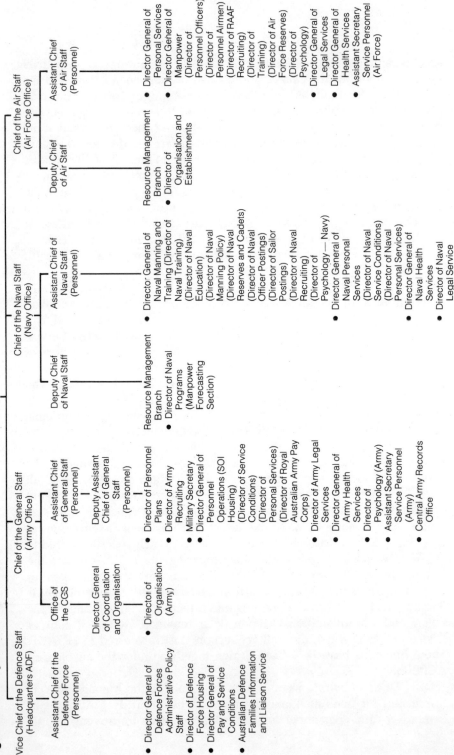

Figure 3: Defence Central Staffs for personnel

Secretary
Deputy Secretary (Budget and management)

Management Improvement and Manpower Policy Division

- Administrative Services Branch
- Organisation and Structures Branch
- Productivity Improvement Branch
- Manpower Computing Centre
- Manpower Policies and Strategies Branch

Human Resources Division

- Service Personnel (Navy)
- Service Personnel (Air Force)
- Service Personnel (Army)
- Director General Recruiting
- Civil Personnel Branch
- Defence Industrial Branch

Inspector General Division

- General Investigations and Reviews
- Management Audit

Policy Co-ordination Division

- Co-ordination and Liaison Branch
- Legislation Branch
- Defence Security Branch
- Public Information Branch

Resources and Financial Policy Division

- Financial Programs Branch
- Resources Policy Branch
- Resource Planning (Navy) Branch
- Resource Planning (Army) Branch
- Resource Planning (Air Force) Branch
- Resource Planning (Central) Branch
- Resource Planning (Capital Procurement) Branch
- Special Adviser Financial Accounting Management

At the time of writing a review was under way to rationalise the areas of responsibility for manpower and personnel matters between Deputy Secretary (Budget and Management) and ACPERS, which may result in revised arrangements.

Manpower Policy, Human Resources, Inspector General and Policy Co-ordination. (See Figure 3: Defence Central Staffs for Personnel.)

The Human Resources Division is primarily responsible for administering and managing the civilian departmental workforce. Until 1989, the Division also contained a Services Personnel Policy Branch which was tasked with the development of personnel policies which affected all three Services and a Defence Industrial Branch to monitor and advise HQADF staffs on the preparation of Defence Force submissions to the Defence Force Remuneration Tribunal. Each Service Assistant Chief of Staff (Personnel) had an Assistant Secretary, Service Personnel (ASSP) attached to his office, who reported to the First Assistant Secretary, Human Resources. The ASSPs acted as the Secretary's representative and as the vote coordinators for appropriations relating to particular manpower programs in that Service Office. They were also responsible for approving advice and responses made by the Service Office to Ministerial, Parliamentary, Ombudsman and other inquiries and for advising and assisting their Service ACPERS.16 Under the 1989 *Structural Review of Higher ADF Staff Arrangements* (the Sanderson Report), the Services Personnel Policy Branch has been transferred to and incorporated in an expanded HQADF Personnel Division which has three branches - Personnel Co-ordination, Administration and Training, and Pay and Conditions. Under the new structure, the Assistant Secretary Service Personnel positions have been abolished with their functions being incorporated in a Defence Central integrated Administration and Finance Branch.

The Management Improvement and Manpower Policy Division has three main branches. The Manpower Policy and Strategies Branch is primarily tasked with the analysis and scrutiny of current and future manpower requirements and the preparation of manpower statistical bulletins. The Organisation and Structures Branch deals with the review of establishment levels in ADF units, while the Productivity Improvement Branch is responsible for conducting management improvement investigations and the preparation of annual Departmental management improvement plans. The Policy Co-ordination Division has a Coordination and Liaison Branch which prepares submissions, speeches and reports for delivery by the Ministers, the Secretary and the CDF, acts as the departmental liaison point with the Parliament and provides the secretariats for the higher Defence Committees. (The Division also has Legislation, Defence Security and Public Information Branches.)

The Defence Committees. There are over 90 Higher Defence, Defence Central and Single Service Office committees, some 40 of which

Figure 4: Defence Committees with a personnel input*

Senior Defence Committees
- Defence Committee (Statutory)
- Council of Defence (Statutory)
- Chiefs of Staff committee (Non-Statutory)
- Defence Force Development Committee (Non-Statutory)

Principal Subordinate Committees
- Consultative Group
- Force Structure Committee
- Defence Housing Policy Committee
- Services Personnel Policy Committee
- Defence Forces Audit Policy Committee
- Defence Forces Pay and Conditions Committee

Other Defence Central Committees
- Personnel Management Advisory Committee
- Defence Manpower Electronic Data Processing Steering Committee
- Services Health Policy Committee

Other Defence Related Committees
- Defence Force Retirement and Death Benefits Committee
- Services Canteens Trust Fund
- Services Health Consultative Group
- Defence Forces Scales of Accommodation Committee
- Defence Hospitals Policy Committee
- Committee for Employer-Support of Reserve Forces
- Defence Housing Authority Defence Liaison Committee

Army Office Committees
- CGS Advisory Committee
- Appointments and Promotions Committee
- Army Reserve Advisory Council
- Army Reserve Appointments and Promotions Committee
- Army Reserve Retention and Selection Committee
- Promotions and Selection Committee
- Army Programming and Estimates Committee
- Army Structure Committee
- Army Works Committee
- Long Term Students and Exchange Committee

Navy Office Committees
- CNS Advisory Committee
- Naval Health Benefits Society Management Committee
- RAN Staff Requirements Committee
- Naval Mobilisation Committee
- Navy Programs and Estimates Committee
- RAN Central Canteens Board
- RAN Relief Trust Fund Committee
- RAN Ship Hospitality Committee
- RAN Uniform and Clothing Committee

Air Force Office Committees
- CAS Advisory Committees
- Manpower Allocation Advisory Group
- Air Force Programming and Estimates
- Air Force Requirements Committee
- Annual Flying Hours Conference
- Employment Standards Committee
- Exchange Program Review Committee
- Works Priority Committee

Source: Department of Defence, *Senior Defence Committees*, (DRB 4, 5th Edition, 1988)

have either representation from personnel staffs or have a functional relevance to manpower planning and personnel management. (See Figure 4: Defence Committees with a Personnel Input.) The Secretary of the Department, or his representatives, chair four out of the five most influential committees - the Defence Committee, the Defence Force Development Committee, the Consultative Group and the Force Structure Committee. Recently, the Assistant Chief of the Defence Force (Personnel) has assumed the chairmanship of two key personnel committees - the Defence Forces Pay and Conditions Committee and the Services Personnel Policy Committee.

The separation of policy formulation and implementation staff work in the Department is mirrored in the division of committees into those responsible for executive policy consideration and those established for the day-to-day management and operation of activities. The committees are further divided into two types: those in which personnel and manpower issues are but one factor in a broader equation - for example, in the Consultative Group which reviews the FYDP and annual draft budget estimates - and those for which manpower and/or personnel is the main focus of their deliberations. The degree of influence exerted, and diversity of interests represented by the various actors, differs in each group of committees. For example, in the senior committees, it is evident that there is considerable inequality of influence. The weight of policy guidance and the personal predilections of key actors combine to ensure that manpower and personnel issues are not usually treated as first order priorities, but rather assume the routine status of encumbrances. In contrast, in those committees specifically raised to address manpower and personnel management issues, there is a certain measure of equality of influence amongst the representatives. This changes both the character and outcomes of their deliberations.

The Policy Process. The processes of policy formulation and implementation are facilitated primarily through the interaction of these three sets of actors. For example, as noted in Chapter 13, under the provisions of a Ministerial Directive (as well as the Public Service, Defence and Audit Acts), the Secretary of the Department is held accountable for the provision of advice on policy, resources and organisation, for the financial planning and programming of all elements of the defence outlay, and for the financial administration and control of expenditure. These provisions furnish the Secretary and his staff members with the formal authority to support the task of proposing policy and administrative action but also, as importantly, the task of scrutinising and monitoring the policy proposals of Single Service and HQADF staffs. This task involves, in the first instance, ensuring that such policy options are in accordance with rules of financial propriety and provide an efficient and effective utilisation of resources. Second, policy proposals need to be scrutinised and further developed in such a way as to ensure that they fall within the confines of Federal and State legislation and the dictates of Government policy. Third, policy staffs, through their own experience and communication, contribute to the development of policy proposals in a manner which they believe is likely to receive the concurrence of 'interested' Departments and, if necessary, are capable of surviving a Cabinet vote. The achievement of these goals is, in part, facilitated through the processes of consultation and communication achieved through the Defence Committee System.

Officially, the committee system '...helps to draw together the joint and separate responsibilities of the various components of the Defence organisation, both civil and military....Committees provide a formal mechanism for officers charged directly, or by delegation, with particular Defence functional responsibilities to consult with others whose responsibilities will be affected by the actions under consideration'.[17] In practice, the committees represent a microcosm of the methodology of Defence decision-making, both in terms of functions and the manner in which decisions are derived. For example, in a bureaucratic sense, the committees provide a forum not only for the dissemination of information, but also for the articulation of competing viewpoints and the expression of influence. Moreover, behind the venue of formal committee meetings, an array of informal and semi-formal coalitions or groupings have evolved which seek to work out bargaining positions in preparation for such meetings. For example, there is a Defence Forces Manpower Group which, while having no formal recognition in the committee system, meets to determine negotiating positions to be taken by manpower actors in the Consultative Group.

The trend towards centralising policy formulation authority and activity, set in motion by the creation of a unified Department of Defence and Defence Central policy staffs, has continued through the agency of the particular manner in which the HQADF has developed. As the Headquarters has accumulated functions, a shift in the influence over policy formulation has occurred, initially at the expense of Defence Central, but latterly at the expense of the Single Service Offices. If the trend continues, the Single Service Offices will be almost solely responsible for policy implementation, and only one source of input into the policy formulation process. The effects of this trend towards decentralised policy implementation and centralised policy-making have not yet all been revealed. For example, the process is experiencing what can be described as real growing pains. Although the HQADF has been assuming greater and broader influence in policy formulation, it, like Defence Central, is dependent to a significant degree upon the provision of relevant information by the Single Service staffs which have been rationalised to accommodate the growth in the centre. However, centralisation of policy functions is driven not only by the efficiencies achieved through standardisation. As defence decision-making, particularly in the manpower and personnel management area, is more influenced by agencies external to Defence (such as the Government Departments, including Finance, Foreign Affairs and Trade, Industrial Relations, Employment, Education and Training, and a variety Federal legislation, including the Administrative Appeals Tribunal Act, the Administrative Decisions (Judicial Review) Act, the Ombudsman Act, and State legislation), Single Service staffs separately are poorly placed to identify, develop and carry through policy options and positions which can survive the gauntlet of external concurrence.

In many respects, activities in support of personnel management and the manpower base (as well as other areas of defence activity) are not well served by this overall process of decision-making. In a general sense, the process operates according to most of the usual maxims of bureaucratic practice: the Laws of Longevity (power goes with permanence, impermanence is impotence and rotation is castration); the Laws of Inversion (it takes longer to do things quickly, it's more expensive to do things cheaply, and it's more democratic to do things secretly); and the Law of Information (the way in which information is provided, manipulated or withheld is the key to controlling events)[18] - all of which ensures that many decisions made are not necessarily solutions to the problem or issue under consideration, but rather the resolutions of the compromises, negotiations and manoeuvres of actors of unequal influence. Moreover, the employment of bureaucratic stratagems, complicated channels of communication and the weight of information to be collected and analysed, results in a decision-making process which is frequently slow and unwieldy. As a consequence, by the time many personnel issues are addressed they have attained problem or even crisis status. Indeed, most are not considered *until* they fall into this category. The system must then respond to a crisis, in part of its own making, with an urgency which is anathema to it.

The defence decision-making process, because of its problem-oriented and concurrence-seeking nature, is less than well-equipped to identify, anticipate and respond to change in a timely and effective manner. However, the assessment of future trends highlights a number of issue areas which will require substantial responses before they become problems. The final section of this chapter considers two such sets of future trends which are significant in terms of personnel management and manpower planning in the ADF.

Future Trends: Occupations and Employment

Particularly in the post-World War II period, most armed forces have, to greater and lesser degrees, undergone a process of civilianisation in which there has been a convergence of technical and managerial skills and organisational formats between military and civilian sectors.[19] This trend is illustrated by the declining proportion of military personnel employed in the combat arms, and the increasing proportion of military members employed in combat-support and support occupations. Other evidence is provided in the adoption of business management techniques, industrial wage determination methods and associational forms of representation in employment issues, the housing of military families in civilian communities, and the expanded employment of women.

As a consequence of this broadly-based shift, Western armed forces, including the ADF, are significantly more vulnerable to changes which are occurring in civilian employment structures and social practices. Over the last five years, the Australian economy has undergone considerable restructuring. Moreover, its future world competitiveness will depend upon following trends, already well established in other industrialised nations, towards a substantial expansion in employment sectors concerned with information work. Other economic trends of significance include the growing complexity of products and production methodologies, the increasing use of machines to undertake physically demanding, hazardous and repetitive tasks, and the use of information technology to reduce administrative and supervisory tasks.[20]

The substance of these trends will generate considerable change in the demand for people in particular occupations, the type of training and educational experiences required to prepare them for employment, and the efforts of employers to recruit and retain specially skilled and qualified people. The evidence of one study, on the nature of quantitative change, predicts the requirement for single-skilled craftsmen and support and personal service workers in production industries will decline, while the demand for all types of professionals, engineers, technologists, multi-skilled technicians and craftsmen will increase.[21] (See Figure 5: Occupational Trends.) As these changes occur, there will be an increase in the demand for employees in the Australian workforce who are computer literate, who have a high level

Figure 5: Occupational Trends*

Expanding Occupations

All Professions (electronic engineers, progress, planning engineers, chemists, surveyors, architects, instructors, accountants, solicitors and other professional workers)

Support Services (part-time) (clerks, cashiers, office machine operators, secretaries, telephone and telegraph operators)

Personal Services (part-time) (security guards, porters, kitchen hands, caretakers, cleaners, cooks, bar staff)

Engineers, Scientists and Technologists (civil, mechanical, electrical and electronic engineers, physicists, technologists, progress, planning production and other engineers, architects and surveyors)

Technicians (technicians, draughtsmen, laboratory assistants)

Multiple-Skilled Craftsmen (in engineering, electrical and electronic trades, woodworkers, painters, decorators, bricklayers)

Service Industries

Production Industries

Managers and Administrators (production, sales, personnel managers, proprietors and partners)

Technicians, Craftsmen (technicians, laboratory assistants, transport inspectors)

Operatives

Support Services (full-time) (clerks, cashiers, office machine operators, typists, salespersons)

Personal Services (full-time) (porters, housekeepers, bar staff, kitchen hands, cleaners, security guards, caretakers)

Single-Skilled Craftsmen (in engineering, electrical and electronic trades, miners, skilled textile and clothing workers, painters)

Operatives (Riggers, electroplaters, bakers, butchers, printers, mine, quarry workers, gas, coke and chemical workers, semi-skilled textile, construction and transport workers, boilermen)

Support Services (clerks, cashiers, office machine operators, secretaries, salespersons (distribution), commercial travellers)

Personal Services (security guards, porters, housekeepers, kitchen hands, caretakers, cleaners, bar staff)

Contracting Occupations

*Source: A. Rajan, R. Pearson, *UK Occupations and Employment Trends to 1990* (Sevenoaks, Butterworths, 1986) p. 188.

(i.e., tertiary) of general education and who have well developed, relevant intellectual capabilities. Another study of socio-economic trends observes that such sought-after capabilities will in the future include intellectual skills of logical and integrative thought; entrepreneurial competencies of efficiency and productivity; and social skills of self-control, adaptability, and perceptual objectivity.[22] Until such time as, and even after, the educational system can function to produce employees who have developed such skills and qualities, Australian employers are developing strategies to procure and retain the type of people they regard as essential to the operation of their businesses. For example, increasingly, employers are competing for employees through the development of flexible and total remuneration packages which are responsive to the lifestyle stage, career aspirations and personal preferences of the individual employee. Such packages reflect a variable balance between salary, superannuation and other benefits such as loans, vehicles, child-care, parenting leave, accommodation and other allowances. They also tend to be based upon performance-related pay standards which are reflected, for example, in accelerated promotion and merit bonuses.[23]

Because of the increased requirement for fiscal efficiency and productivity in the operation of the ADF, the pursuance of policies which lead to civilianisation and the more complete reliance of the ADF upon high-level technologies, the trends and developments in civilian practices outlined will have significant ramifications for military personnel management and manpower planning. Most obviously, the ADF is, and will be more so in the future, in direct competition with business and industry to recruit and retain employees who are highly trainable and who have developed, or who have the potential to develop, the intellectual, entrepreneurial and social skills and knowledge which are needed by both military organisation and civilian enterprise alike.

However, it is not at all certain that the ADF is equipped to win this competition in the future. For example, at a time when more civilian employers are moving to individually-tailored, total remuneration packages, the ADF has been required to harness its military remuneration system (based upon the All of One Company principle which ties pay primarily to rank with some limited occupational pay banding) to a civilian industrial wage-fixing system, which because it operates through confrontationist, collective bargaining and primarily upon 'payment to come to work' principles, is increasingly non-responsive to occupational and employment developments. The ADF is required to operate with a wage determination system which offers little flexibility in demonstrating to employees the value placed by the organisation upon occupational specialties which are crucial to the performance of its missions, and which cannot recognise easily the differences in the value of the occupational qualifications of its employees. As a consequence, '...military pay becomes especially attractive to personnel possessing the less valuable skills, while it fails to satisfy those possessing the more valuable skills...the armed forces end up paying some of their workers more than they need to and others less than they ought to'.[24] This situation makes a significant contribution to increasing personnel retention difficulties, both in terms of losses of highly skilled and valued employees and the retention of less qualified and valued workers. Finally, because of the system's inherent rigidities, it will be difficult for the ADF to offer the same flexibility of initiatives as the civilian enterprises against which it must compete for the type and quality of manpower it requires.

Future Trends: Military Technology

Military technological advances have been, and will continue to be, fuelled by three fundamental goals. These are the objective of developing and sustaining a qualitative edge in weaponry and equipment as a countervailing weight against a numerically superior opposition; the aim of multiplying the force projection which can be achieved by a given number of military combatants; and, finally, the motive of reducing the number of people required to man military forces. The application of military technology to attain these goals has contributed significantly to the rationale for the procurement of highly sophisticated, technologically complex and exponentially more powerful weapon systems, and platforms from which to launch them, by the ADF.

Technological advances will continue to aim at reducing the number of people needed to undertake a variety of tasks, particularly those which are repetitive, routine, or physically demanding or hazardous. Trends are to replace people with machines (for example, robotics and remotely piloted vehicles), to enhance the capabilities of people (for example, automatic data processing) and to increase the power projection achievable for a given number of people. However, the areas in which manpower savings have been, and look likely to be achieved, are discrete and concentrated primarily in the combatant component of military forces. Moreover, these economies are, in the main, offset by the increased requirement for technicians behind the forward edge of battle to maintain technologically sophisticated weapon systems and platforms. In fact, technological advances have resulted as much in a relocation of manpower demand as in an overall reduction.

In some cases, this relocation has occurred in a qualitative as well as quantitative sense. For example, the replace-and-repair logic of consumer durable, black-box technology and associated self-diagnostics programs is to permit lower-skilled, as well as fewer, technicians in forward areas, while laser optics for instance, are employed so that weapon systems are easier to operate by lesser qualified personnel and still achieve a given level of performance. At the same time, the application of complex technologies has served to increase and expand the specialisation of effort, knowledge and skills of rear-area maintenance and administration manpower requirements. The range of higher-skilled technical occupations has expanded, while the technical complexity of many existing jobs has also grown.[25] Finally, the dependence of the ADF upon these specialised occupations has spread to encompass almost all areas of operation. The skill and manpower mix generated by these trends is summarised as: fewer or the same number of military personnel per unit of equipment being required in forward areas and more military and civilian personnel being employed in rear areas; and the same or marginally decreasing skill demands for forward operators and increasing and specialised skill and knowledge requirements for rear-area maintainers and workers.[26]

However, as a consequence of newer generations of technologies, counter-trends are developing concurrently with the shifts outlined above. For example, modern weapons and equipment are a combination of a number of interrelated sub-systems of mechanical, electromechanical, hydraulic, pneumatic, electric, and heating/cooling devices and computer hardware and software. The ability to fully exploit new technologies and achieve the full potential of new weapons systems and equipment will depend increasingly upon multi-skilled, rather than single-skilled, tradesmen, who are capable of understanding how each sub-system is integrated into the whole. Also, as technological advances extend the penetrability and distance over which force can be projected, support and combat support areas of military operations will become increasingly vulnerable to attack. As a US Air Force report comments, this vulnerability '...will require a modification of...current support strateg[ies] and the dispersal of aircraft and resources away from main-operating bases to improve their survivability'.[27] The nature of envisaged Australian areas of operation already requires the adoption of such dispersed deployment strategies. Moreover, because of a lack of war stocks, and the time and recalibration penalties associated with the return of faulty or damaged equipment to southern-based repair depots and return of repaired items to the north, it is likely that the ADF will increasingly rely upon fix-forward maintenance concepts. However, the employment of such strategies and concepts will be dependent upon increased numbers of military (as opposed to civilian) technicians who are multi-skilled and who can operate without substantial base support.

In terms of manpower planning and personnel management, a number of significant implications flow from this range of trends. First, the shifts towards specialisation, and the need for multi-skilling, generate a requirement to recruit a greater number of entrants who have the aptitude, basic education and intellectual qualities to complete training for such occupations. As already noted, given the growing similarity of demands between civil and military sector employment, the ADF will face even greater competition in recruiting such people. Moreover, improvements in systems capability are a substantial component of investment in high-technology capital procurement projects. Yet, a key assumption which underwrites the achievement of such advances is a given level of operator and maintainer performance. Failure to recruit and train entrants of sufficient calibre and in sufficient numbers will result in reduced performance standards and a resultant reduction in return on capital outlay.[28]

Second, the training required to ensure that operators, maintainers and supervisors can function effectively is likely to continue to expand in length, intensity of manpower consumption and expense. This, in turn, will increase the 'value-added' worth of military personnel not only to the ADF but also to civil sector enterprises. As a consequence, the spend-money-in-order-to-save-money arguments of initiatives to retain valuable military personnel will become even more compelling. Moreover, any increase in multi-skilling will not only be value-added in the sense of investment in training. The commissioning of weapons and equipment which maximise force multiplier effects and minimise numerical manpower demands, but which increase the requirement for higher-level and multi-skilled operators and maintainers, serves to increase the scale of loss of capability incurred if the ADF cannot successfully retain such people.

Third, new generations of weapon systems and equipment, both as a consequence of greater complexity and the tendency to under-estimate numerical and qualitative manpower increases, and over-estimate potential manpower savings, in weapons proposals, have tended to create increased demands upon the manpower base. If genuine and lasting manpower economies are to be achieved in the future development of the ADF, there is a requirement to ensure that manpower planning and training factors are incorporated earlier and more fully into the weapons acquisition process. It may also entail consideration of a change in the priority attached to performance parameters of new weapon systems over those of their reliability and maintainability, in that systems with high reliability and maintainability war-time quotients reduce the manpower costs of training, maintenance and logistics. Equally, the evaluation, inclusion and retention, in weapons proposals, of training aids packages may well assume a new priority in addressing the increased length and expense of both operator and maintainer training programs.

As noted in the introduction, military manpower and personnel management has frequently been disregarded by strategists and weapons procurers as a presumed and available constant, and treated by budget analysts and technologists as a problem to be solved. As a consequence, for example, the development of an Australian strategic posture in the 1980s has taken place without a full assessment of the force structure and manning implications of various strategic alternatives. There has been little consideration, for example, of the weight of contribution, in overall performance terms, attributable to manpower as opposed to weapons in a variety of conflict scenarios. The difficulties of evaluating and incorporating manning and personnel management considerations early and fully in the capital procurement program has engendered a cart-before-the-horse circumstance in that a major force modernisation program has been undertaken without sufficient reference to the manpower and personnel needs which underwrite its success as much as the direct input of financial resources. As Admiral Zumwalt Jr., the US Chief of Naval Operations in 1970-74, recognised: 'Keeping up the quantity and the quality of naval personnel was a *prerequisite* for any modernization plan' [emphasis added].[29] There is a fundamental rationale which underpins the necessity of attaching a significantly higher priority and profile to the examination, evaluation and inclusion of manpower and personnel variables in strategic, force capabilities and defence logistics decision-making:

> In the end it comes down to cost: the cost of recruiting and paying young people with potential, the cost of training them, the cost of losing experienced people versus the cost of keeping them, and the opportunity costs associated with higher personnel costs - fewer new ships and aircraft, fewer new weapons and lower readiness rates.[30]

Endnotes

1   Gregory D. Foster, 'Manpower as an Element of Military Power' in Gregory D. Foster, Alan N. Sabrosky, William J. Taylor Jr., (eds.), *The Strategic Dimension of Military Manpower*, (Ballinger Publishing Company, Cambridge, Mass., 1987), p. 13.

2   Department of Defence, *Defence Report 1973*, (Australian Government Publishing Service, Canberra, 1973), Table 2, p. 34.

3   *Ibid.*, pp.15-16.

4   Department of Defence, *Defence Report 1975*, p. 15; and *Defence Report 1967*, (Australian Government Publishing Service, Canberra, 1967), p.10.

5   Department of Defence, *Defence Report 1986-87*, (Australian Government Publishing Service, Canberra, 1987), p.105.

6   *Ibid.*, p.106.

7   Department of Defence, *Defence Report 1987-88*, p.92, and Department of Defence, *Defence Report 1985-86*, (Australian Government Publishing Service, Canberra, 1986), p. 137.

8   General Peter C. Gration, 'The Australian Defence Force - Current Issues and Future Prospects', Paper presented to the Strategic and Defence Studies Centre Bicentennial Conference, *Australia and the World: Prologue and Prospects*, 6-9 December 1988, p. 10.

9   See Parliament of Australia, Joint Committee on Public Accounts, *Review of Defence Project Management, Volume I - Report, Volume II - Project Analyses*, (Australian Government Publishing Service, Canberra, 1986, Report Number 243).

10   Martin Binkin, *Military Technology and Defence Manpower*, (Brookings Institution, Washington, D.C., 1986), pp.38-68.

11   See Parliament of Australia, Joint Committee on Foreign Affairs, Defence and Trade, *Personnel Wastage in the Australian Defence Force - Report and Recommendations*, (Australian Government Publishing Service, Canberra, 1988), pp.12-73.

12   Assistant Chief of the Defence Force (Policy), 'ADF Manpower - Consideration of Wastage and Retention', (Headquarters, Australian Defence Force, Canberra, ACPOL 132/1987), pp.3-8.

13   See Cathy Downes, *High Personnel Turnover: The Australian Defence Force is not a Limited Liability Company*, (Canberra Papers on Strategy and Defence Number 44, Strategic and Defence Studies Centre, Australian National University, Canberra, 1988).

14   The Hon. David Simmons MP, Minister for Defence Science and Personnel, Ministerial Statement in Reponse to the *Personnel Wastage in the Defence Force*, Report of 10 November 1988 by the Defence Sub-Committee of the Joint Committee on Foreign Affairs, Defence and Trade, 11 May 1989.

15   For a discussion of the establishment of the DFRT see David Quick QC, 'An Independent Arbitrator: The Defence Force Remuneration Tribunal' in Hugh Smith (ed.), *Rewarding the Defence Force*, (Australian Defence Studies Centre, Australian Defence Force Academy, Canberra, 1987).

16   John Robson, 'Role of ASSPs and ASP-AF in Particular', (Internal Paper, Service Personnel Branch - Air Force, Department of Defence, Canberra, 7th May 1986), p.2.

17   Department of Defence, Directorate of Departmental Publications, Departmental Administrative Instruction No. 2/86, 16th April 1986) paras. 3,7, pp. 1-2).

18   Jonathan Lynn and Anthony Jay (eds.), *The Complete Yes Minister - The Diaries of a Cabinet Minister by the Right Hon. James Hacker MP*, (BBC Books, London, 1984).

19   See Charles C. Moskosand and Frank R. Wood (eds.), *The Military - More than Just a Job*, (Pergamon-Brassey's International Defense Publishers, Washington, D.C., 1988).

20   Joseph M. Marchello, 'Education For a Technological Age', *Futures*, (Volume 19, Number 5), October 1987, pp.555-565.

21   A. Rajan and R. Pearson, *UK Occupations and Employment Trends to 1990*, (Butterworths, Sevenoaks, 1986), pp.166-188.

22   A. Rajan, *et.al.*, 'Officer Corps in the Future: Socio-Economic Trends in UK to 1995', (Institute of Manpower Studies, University of Sussex, Brighton, 1987, Crown Copyright), pp.148-149.

23   Joellen Munton, 'Annual Salary Review 1988', *Portfolio*, October 1988, pp.42-44.

24   Martin Binkin and Irene Kyriakopoulos, *Paying the Modern Military*, (Brookings Institution, Washington, D.C., 1981), p. 39.

25   See Martin Binkin, *Military Technology and Defence Manpower*, pp. 3-10.

26 William E. DePuy, 'Technology and Manpower: Army Perspective', in William Bowman, Roger Little and G. Thomas Sicilia (eds.), *The All-Volunteer Force After a Decade - Retrospect and Prospect*, (Pergamon-Brassey's International Defense Publishers, Washington, D.C., 1989), pp.122-130.

27 John W. Roberts, 'Technology and Manpower: Air Force Perspective', in *ibid.*, p.153.

28 For a discussion of the system-equipment-human performance equation see William E. DePuy, 'Technology and Manpower: Army Perspective', p.131.

29 Admiral E. R. Zumwalt Jr., *On Watch - A Memoir*, (Quadrangle/New York Times Book Co, New York, 1976), p.127.

30 Robert R. Murray, 'Technology and Manpower: Navy Perspective', in William Bowman, Roger Little and G. Thomas Sicilia (eds.), *The All-Volunteer Force After a Decade*, p.147.

CHAPTER 16

DEFENCE INDUSTRY AND RESEARCH AND DEVELOPMENT

Fred Bennett

Introduction

The need for a defence industrial base varies with the strategic situation of each country and with the stances taken in its international and defence policies. The same factors affect the nature of the base required, and the means available to develop and sustain it. In Australia's case, the principal determinants of need are its geographic position and the current strategy of self-reliant defence within a framework of alliances. Given Australia's geographic isolation, complete self reliance would require a full mobilisation base, i.e., the ability to equip and support the Australian Defence Force (ADF) in military operations independent of equipment, component and consumable supplies from overseas sources. An industrial base of the scale and at the level of technical sophistication required would be beyond Australia's financial, technical, scientific and workforce capacity. Participation in alliances reduces the industrial base required to more manageable proportions by providing access to a range of modern military equipment and the fruits of defence science and technology in the Western world. It enables arrangements to be made for assured logistic support. It enables the Government to be highly selective in the industrial capabilities which are supported for defence purposes.

Such capabilities were identified in the 1987 Defence White Paper as 'The capacity to maintain, repair, modify and adapt defence equipment to the Australian environment, independently of overseas sources....This requires Australian involvement in design, development and production to acquire the necessary detailed knowledge, skills and facilities'.[1] On the basis of this role, Australian defence industry includes those industrial activities which provide support to the ADF and the Government factories, dockyards and depots operated by the three Services. Of course, the scope of this definition depends on the scale of defence force activity. In a major contingency requiring full-scale mobilisation, virtually all manufacturing industry, the major part of the transport and construction industries and much of agriculture and the tertiary sector would be part of defence industry. In peacetime, or lesser contingencies, the scope is much more limited.

Scope of Defence Industry

Almost all repair, maintenance and modification of defence equipment is currently carried out in Australia. Most food, fuel and other consumables, uniforms, field equipment and motor vehicles used by the ADF are produced in Australia. For complex capital items such as aircraft, armoured vehicles, electronic equipment and missiles, Australia relies more heavily on imports. However, most major capital items are now either partly manufactured, or assembled, in Australia. Where there are special needs which cannot be met by equipment designed for use in the defence forces of other nations, products have been developed by Australian scientists and produced by industry from a mix of local and imported components. In terms of expenditures with Australian manufacturing industry, in 1987-88, Defence spent some $1,770 million on manufacturing. The budget appropriation items for this expenditure are provided in Table 1.

Table 1: Defence Expenditure in Australia: Manufacturing 1987-88*

Category	$ Million
Purchase of Manufactured Products	
Major Equipment Projects	637
Other New Equipment and Stores	188
Weapons, Armament, Ammunition and Explosives	85
Rations	49
Liquid Fuels and Lubricants	113
Replacement Equipment and Stores (including hire)	283
Office Requisites and Equipment	31
Furniture and Fittings	20
Repair and Overhaul	245
Support for Defence Industry	
Munitions Production	44
Aerospace	25
Shipbuilding	50
Total	1,770

* **Source:** Department of Defence, Additional Budget Estimates (March 1988)

The Defence Industry Pyramid

The Australian defence industry sector can be depicted as a pyramid with the ADF at the apex and industrial establishments arranged in descending order of association with the Defence Forces. See Figure 1 for a diagrammatic representation of defence and defence-related industries. At the highest level are the fleet bases, workshops and

Figure 1: Australian Defence Industry Pyramid

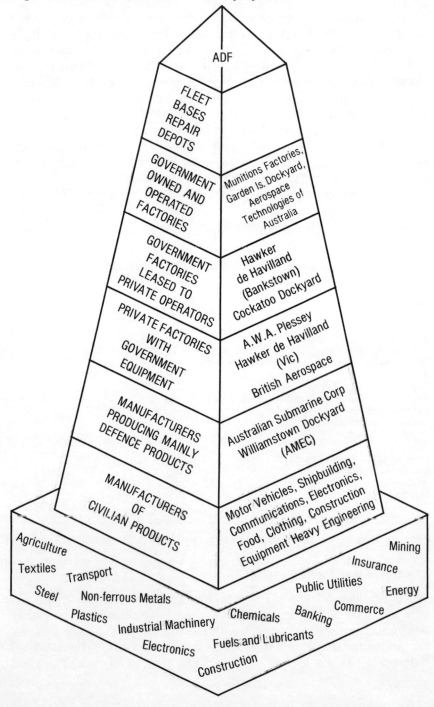

depots run by the ADF. These establishments carry out intermediate, and in some cases, depot-level maintenance. Examples of the latter include *F-111* aircraft maintenance at RAAF No. 3 Aircraft Depot, Amberley, and *Leopard* tank servicing at the Royal Australian Electrical and Mechanical Engineers Depot, Bandiana. At the next level are the Government-owned and -operated establishments. The main group consists of the nine factories and dockyards currently operated by the newly-established Australian Defence Industries (ADI). These ADI establishments produce explosives, propellants, ammunition, ordnance, small arms and clothing, and carry out ship repair, modernisation and maintenance. There is also another Government-owned company, Aerospace Technologies of Australia (ATA), which operates two factories in Melbourne.

There are several other Government-owned but company-operated establishments. For example, Hawker de Havilland Ltd. operates the aircraft factory at Bankstown which is largely Government owned. A number of privately owned establishments use Government equipment for defence work. For some of these, such as Hawker de Havilland (Victoria), A.W.A., and Plessey, defence work is a major part of their total business. In 1987, Defence began to dispose of this equipment where it is not regarded as essential for self-reliant support of the ADF. There are other enterprises which are entirely privately-owned, but rely heavily on defence work, including for example the Australian Marine Engineering Corporation which recently acquired the Williamstown Naval Dockyard and the Australian Submarine Corporation in Adelaide. Below these companies are enterprises which operate primarily to serve the civilian market, but which also produce products for the ADF. The motor vehicle, construction equipment and communications industries are good examples. Finally, the whole pyramid is supported by the general industrial base of the nation.

The Decline and Recovery of Defence Industry

Australia is a small nation with a relatively small manufacturing sector - less than 20 per cent of GDP. The defence budget is also small by international standards. In 1986-87, for example, $7 billion was appropriated for defence and two-thirds of that was spent on manpower and operating costs. This left some $2 billion for capital equipment. By way of comparison, this latter amount is not much more than one hundredth of the sum spent by the United States on defence capital equipment. At this level of expenditure, production of equipment for the ADF is on a small scale and orders for particular items of major equipment are sporadic. It is therefore not feasible to maintain the capability for design and production of a full range of front-line weapons systems, such as aircraft, warships, ordnance, radar and communication systems.

These limitations were keenly felt in the 1970s when a significant trough in defence expenditure occurred. In the capital equipment area, expenditure feel from 12 per cent of defence appropriations in 1970-71 to less than 5 per cent in 1974-75. As a result of this fall off, there was substantial excess capacity in defence industry throughout the decade. After a time lapse, considerable rationalisation of both public and private sectors took place. Equipment expenditure recovered in the latter half of the 1970s rising to 15 per cent by 1979-80, and continued to rise in the 1980s reaching a peak of 27 per cent in 1986-87. However, the recovery did not bring immediate benefits for Australian industry, primarily because from 1975-76 to 1984-85, expenditure going overseas surged. Growth in expenditure in Australia was much less until 1985-86 when the pattern was reversed as more Australian projects came on stream. See Figure 2.

The growth in overseas expenditure was due to the acquisition of major items of equipment such as frigates, medium artillery and missiles of existing overseas production lines. For the large purchase of 75 *F/A-18* aircraft, a substantial Australian industry program was developed, including final assembly and test of the aircraft, but most of the work was done in the United States. These equipments appeared at the time to be relatively cheap because of the high value of the Australian dollar and the high start up cost of dormant Australian capacity.

Australia's need for a strong defence industry for self-reliant defence in combination with a declining defence industry sector posed a policy dilemma. As the 1987 White Paper explained: 'While a substantial commercial workload can provide a base from which to bid for defence orders, the inverse is rarely true. The peacetime requirements of the ADF are usually too small and, particularly for the acquisition of new equipment, too infrequent and too limited in duration, to provide a viable long term base workload for individual firms or industry sectors'.2 It has now been recognised that if Australia is to have a strong defence industry, an internally competitive, export-oriented manufacturing sector is necessary.

For many years Australian manufacturing industry was not well adapted to this role. Its scope was restricted to the protected domestic market by a regulated exchange rate and capital market, a relatively high wage structure and the long-term side-effects of protection. In the 1980s, deregulation of the exchange rate and financial sector, and

Figure 2. Defence expenditure on capital equipment

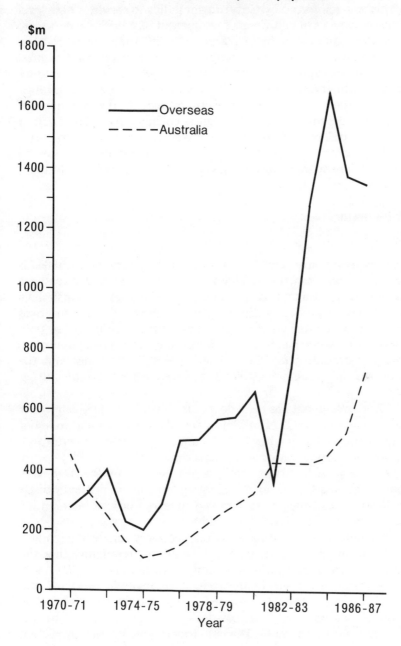

policies to make Australian industry more competitive began to take effect. This was reinforced by Government policy to require a high level of Australian content in new defence equipment. By 1988, projects were already under way to construct frigates and submarines in Australia to overseas designs. Other major projects were in hand for the local production, or assembly, of trainer aircraft, helicopters, minehunter vessels, light artillery, small arms, radios, motor vehicles and long-range surveillance radar. When these were added to the program of Australian work on the *F/A-18* fighters, they have produced a resurgence in defence production. However, Australian industry's traditional problems of shortages of skilled manpower, industrial disputes and low manufacturing productivity still remain as limiting factors.

The Major Sectors

Aerospace

The aerospace industry, employing some 14,000 persons in 1985, is dominated by two companies, Hawker de Havilland and Aerospace Technologies of Australia, and the maintenance divisions of Australia's domestic and international airlines. Between them, these enterprises account for 80 per cent of employment in this sector. Although the bulk of the industry's work has been in maintenance and repair of aircraft, the assembly programs for the *F/A-18*, *Pilatus PC-9* trainer and the *Blackhawk* and *Sea Hawk* helicopters have increased the manufacturing share.

The Government has been deeply involved in the industry. For example, it owns ATA, QANTAS and Australian Airlines and much of the equipment used by Hawker de Havilland, while most of the research to support the industry is done in Government research laboratories. Up to 1987, most maintenance work, contracted out by the ADF, was done on a cost-plus basis under trading agreements which subsidised the overhead costs of the contractors and involved official intervention in detailed aspects of company management.

The industry has all the elements necessary for the design and production of simpler aircraft, or parts of complex aircraft, including the manufacture of modern composite-material airframes and engines, and aircraft assembly and test. In the past, it successfully designed and produced items such as the *Ikara* guided missile and the *Jindivik* pilotless target aircraft. Forays into aircraft design and production, with the *Nomad* light transport and *Wamira* trainer were, however, not commercially successful, because production and design costs were too high. In terms of the space industry, the sector is small and mainly consists of manufacture of ground equipment for satellite systems.

The industry's main value for defence is the maintenance, repair and modification work it performs for the ADF. The life extension programs, for example, carried out on the *Mirage* fighters and *Macchi* jet trainers produced both economic and strategic benefits. Assembly and test programs on the *F/A-18*, *PC-9*, *Blackhawk* and *Seahawk*, and the manufacture of selected generic components and sub-systems in Australia, were designated under the Government's Australian Industry Involvement policy which aims at fostering future support and modification capabilities for those aircraft.

During the 1970s, activity in the industry declined and the major private companies incurred losses. However, by 1978-79 Hawker de Havilland was making profits and by the early 1980s, so was the Commonwealth Aircraft Corporation.[3] However, the Government-owned and -operated Government Aircraft Factory (GAF) made consistent losses. In 1987, the industry experienced a major rationalisation with Hawker de Havilland taking over the Commonwealth Aircraft Corporation, and the GAF being corporatised by the formation of Aerospace Technologies of Australia, which is a wholly Government-owned company, managed by an independent board. Government policies towards the aerospace industries have also changed. In 1986, a new trading agreement was negotiated between the Commonwealth and Hawker de Havilland to provide for more maintenance work to be done on a fixed-price basis and to end the Government's commitment to support the company's overheads. With the establishment of ATA, the Government announced its intention that the company should fully cover its operating costs through sales revenue.

The economics of the aircraft industry are dominated by research and development costs which require long production runs for commercial success. It is also a heavily subsidised industry worldwide. As the Bureau of Industry Economics observed:

> In many cases the development of the industry is premised on defence or prestige rather than commercial grounds. The international industry appears to be severely afflicted with politically induced excess capacity, especially in the production of airframes.[4]

In these circumstances, the industry has relied mainly on maintenance and modification work, sub-contracted assembly and testing of aircraft, and manufacture for export with the support of the offsets program. Yet, a more venturesome spirit in the restructured industry was indicated in 1988-89, when both Hawker de Havilland and ATA were seeking to enter into international risk-sharing ventures for development of new aircraft.

Ship-Building and Ship-Repair

Australian naval ship-building and ship-repair capability is widely dispersed from Cairns to Fremantle. In addition to the Navy's fleet bases, recently active yards have included North Queensland Engineers and Agents in Cairns, Carrington Slipways and their subsidiary Ramsey Fibreglass in Newcastle, Garden Island and Cockatoo Island Dockyards in Sydney, the Australian Marine Engineering Corporation at Williamstown in Melbourne, the Australian Submarine Corporation (ASC) and Eglo Engineering in Adelaide, and Australia Shipbuilding Industries in Cockburn Sound. There is also a geographical shift taking place as naval support capability is developing in Western Australia, following the announcement of the Minister for Defence's decision to locate half of the fleet in that State. The development of the naval base at HMAS *Stirling* is continuing and a shiplift with capacity to take vessels up to destroyer size is under construction in Cockburn Sound.

The industry has complete design and construction capabilities for smaller vessels such as minehunters, patrol boats and survey vessels. For larger vessels such as the Fleet Underway Replenishment vessel, HMAS *Success*, submarines and frigates, overseas designs have been used to save time and reduce risk, but substantial local design work is involved in adapting the designs to incorporate Australian requirements and product content. A complete range of refit, repair and modification capabilities exists, including weapons and sensor refurbishment and calibration at Garden Island. Garden Island and, to a lesser extent, Williamstown are capable of installing such systems and testing them in operation. The shipyards have extensive links with other industries, especially heavy engineering and electronics. For example, torpedo tubes for the new submarines will be built at the Ordnance Factory, Bendigo; Garden Island will assemble the diesel engines; and the weapons system will be assembled and tested in Sydney before installation.

Activity and employment in the industry are cyclical, rising and falling at each yard as contracts are let and completed. The industry passed through a turbulent period in the 1980s, when major reductions in capacity took place. The State Dockyard in Newcastle was closed in 1987, employment was run down at Cockatoo Island upon completion of HMAS *Success* and the Commonwealth Government recently announced that the lease at Cockatoo Island would not be renewed beyond 1992. In addition, in an effort to reduce costs, and improve their competitiveness, substantial manning reductions took place at the remaining major yards. These fluctuations, the traditional attitudes and rivalry of the many craft unions in shipyards and the tradition of confrontation on the waterfront as a whole, has created a very difficult industrial relations climate in the industry. Closure of the State Dockyard and the privatisation of Williamstown Dockyard were largely due to the effects of that climate. Smaller yards with fewer unions have tended to be more successful and in 1988, reductions in the number of separate unions were being pursued at the major yards. This resulted in protracted industrial disputes at Williamstown and the ASC construction facility in Adelaide.

In the late 1980s, after a lean period, the industry has on its books, or in prospect, Australia's largest peacetime naval building program. With improved efficiency resulting from the process of rationalisation in recent years, and the greater competitiveness enjoyed by manufacturing industry as a whole, the industry has better prospects, but their realisation depends on continued improvements in productivity and industrial relations.

Munitions

The seven major munitions factories, currently operated by Australian Defence Industries (ADI), comprise the bulk of the munitions industry in Australia. In 1988, their planned employment was approximately 5,000 employees, more than half of them being located in the ordnance, ammunition and explosives factories in Melbourne. The remainder were spread between Sydney, Bendigo, Lithgow and Mulwala. ADI also operates the Government Clothing Factory in Melbourne, a Production Development Facility at Salisbury and the Guided Weapons and Electronics Support Facility at St Marys, South Australia. The ADI factories are capable of manufacturing a wide range of ordnance, small arms, ammunition and rocket motors, and of carrying out precision engineering for ship-building projects. In 1988, the factories were engaged in the production of 105 mm Howitzers for Australian and New Zealand Armies; a new family of 5.56 mm small arms; a range of propellants, explosives and ammunition; a number of major components for warships; and work for civilian projects including the North West Shelf oil and gas development.

The industry, like most other defence industries, faces problems of peaks and troughs in workload. As far as practicable, orders, placed by the ADF are matched with capacity by consultation between the ADI and the ADF, but the scope for this is limited by the need to avoid uneconomically small batches and by financial constraints to cope with the surge in demand that could occur. Peacetime under-utilisation is also a problem because the amount of ammunition used for training is only a small fraction of that needed in conflict. This is a particularly serious problem for the manufacture of propellants and explosives, for example, where annual peacetime demand is also a small proportion of the minimum economic plant capacity.

Although these difficulties are real, ADI's greatest problems were cultural in origin. Over a long period the munitions factories became inward-looking enclaves, insulated from market stimuli and lacking incentive for efficient performance. Transformation of this culture has been initiated by a program of management reform to engender a more commercial spirit in factory management and employees. For example, until 1987-88, the factories were subsidised under an accounting system which concealed the true cost of their products. From July 1988, commercial accounting systems and full-cost costing were applied. ADI's income is now to come from sales revenue with a small increment to fund certain identified uneconomical strategic capabilities sponsored by the ADF. Capabilities without a clear strategic basis are being eliminated and overmanning reduced. The effects of the transformation have been dramatic. ADI, while still the Office of Defence Production, committed itself to an overall productivity increase of 30-50 per cent between 1985 and 1991. By 1988, an increase of 25 per cent had already been achieved. Operating subsidies had been reduced from nearly $70 million in 1985 to less than $20 million in 1988. Export orders rose from less than $5 million in 1983 to $45 million in 1987.[5]

Electronics

The electronics industry is a particular example of the problems of small scale and domestic market orientation of Australian manufacturing industry. The industry is very small by international standards; its turnover in 1986 was estimated at $US1.13 billion.[6] It is much smaller in total than many international companies; for example, the US company, NEC had a sales of semi-conductors alone of $US2.8 billion in the same year.[7]

Based on consumption of components, the combined defence and aerospace sector is relatively small, making up 11 per cent of the total industry. However, in the late 1980s, this sector has grown rapidly, both in size and importance, as a number of major communications and surveillance, and weapon systems projects, with a high electronic content, have come on stream. A number of areas in the industry are important for defence. A review of the industry in 1983 by the Defence Industry Committee concluded that the following areas were particularly relevant to defence: microcircuit design and fabrication, communications technology, sonar, microwave and millimetric radar, optoelectronics, systems engineering, magnetism and degaussing, training and operational simulation and maintenance support.[8]

The industry is almost completely dependent on imported components. Moreover, there is a high degree of overseas ownership. Subsidiaries of multinational companies, competing in the world market, accounted for two-thirds of employment in the defence sector in 1987.[9] They have been attracted to invest in Australia by tariff protection, Government programs to encourage local content, such as the Australian Industry Involvement program for defence purposes, and by the procurement strategy of Telecom, which encouraged the establishment of local manufacturing capability for telecommunications equipment. Telecom and Defence have provided the main domestic market for a number of years. As they have shifted from one preferred source of technology to another, new subsidiaries of multinational firms have been established, or marketing subsidiaries have extended into production. Reflecting this history, the industry is highly fragmented, with individual firms having difficulty in obtaining a stable workload of sufficient size to ensure their viability, independent of their overseas parent. Moreover, the ability of small firms to fund the levels of research and development necessary for future success in such a technologically-dynamic industry is particularly con-strained. Consequently, the industry is also heavily dependent on imported technology, usually obtained through intra-corporate channels. Defence examples of such transfers include the *Raven* tactical radios and the combat system for the new submarines. In these circumstances, Government intervention has been necessary to establish electronic industry capabilities for strategic purposes. For example, Defence Department funding has supported the production of integrated circuits and hydrophone arrays, and the development of electronic warfare and electro-optical capabilities in industry.

Problems of Defence Industry

In the 1980s, Australian defence industry has a dual character of tested technical strength and competitive weakness. The technical strength of defence industry, its ability to absorb, apply and adapt advanced technology, in fields of importance to defence, makes a major contribution to national security. Defence industries have developed capabilities at the cutting edge of technology in the fields of aeronautical, mechanical, electronic, chemical and software engineering and the integration of complex systems. They have acquired these capabilities through participation in production or assembly and training in maintenance, diagnosis and correction of faults. Defence industry supports modern aircraft, ships, armoured vehicles, missiles and surveillance systems and their propulsion systems, weapons and sensors. The capabilities of industry in these respects are unsurpassed in the region.

On the other side of its dual nature, defence industry faces many serious problems. It is small because it depends almost entirely on the Australian defence market. It is fragmented by the division of that market along State lines, or between subsidiaries of multinational corporations. Productivity is relatively low in industries where economies of scale are important. Capacity utilisation is low and traditional sectors such as shipbuilding and aircraft have outdated work practices. Many of the quality assurance systems, demanded by defence customers, have been lacking. In a field where product differentiation is the order of the day, Australian industry has few products of its own to market; nor can it benefit from continuity in product development. It is dependent on technology developed overseas or in government laboratories. It has a single customer which, being an arm of the government, is cumbersome to deal with. It has often suffered from poor industrial relations. Finally, its capacity to export is inhibited by the high value of the Australian dollar and by tight controls on exports of defence equipment.

Lack of economies of scale is illustrated by the aerospace and shipbuilding industries. For example, two *FFG Class* frigates are being constructed in Australia for the RAN, compared with 47 constructed in the United States for the US Navy. Some benefits of scale have been achieved by ordering major ship components, such as propulsion systems and weapons off the same production runs as the ships produced in the US, but this cannot apply to labour-intensive tasks, such as hull fabrication and fitting out. Seventy-five *F/A-18s* are being finally assembled for the RAAF at ATA compared with 1,100 produced by McDonnell Douglas, plus possibly 500 of an upgraded version in the future. Low capacity utilisation is widespread. Moreover, the differing rates of utilisation can be so great in some areas, for example filling artillery shells with explosives, that periodic small production runs have to be organised just to maintain the competence of the workforce and maintain safety standards.

Shipbuilding provides an example of the effect of work practices on productivity. Traditionally, work in Australian shipyards was demarcated between many different worker classifications. In Garden Island, for example, there were members of 14 blue collar unions, some of which had their own internal classifications. Fine sub-division of work reduces productivity because one worker will be idle for part of the time waiting for others in different classifications to complete their tasks. In competing countries, one worker would perform the tasks carried out by several different Australian work classifications. In 1988, negotiations were under way in the Conciliation and Arbitration Commission to substantially reduce job demarcation in the Dockyard. A trial was being conducted of two redesigned job classifications - Ship Repair Tradesman and Ship Repair Assistant. The introduction of the latter concept, in the semi-skilled area, enabled the Dockyard to operate with 310 people where it previously employed 650. Through this approach, and from improved matériel supply, the Dockyard recorded a lift in productivity of 11 per cent in 1987-88, albeit at the short-term cost of schedule delays caused by industrial disputes.

Specifications for Defence products commonly call for more stringent standards of reliability, durability and ruggedness than are requested for commercial products. They also require the manufacturer to demonstrate that satisfactory quality assurance systems are in place. To some extent, there is a move away from the formal requirements of military specifications, especially for electronic components and products, but the requirement for quality assurance systems is increasing. However, few manufacturers have been able to meet these standards. In announcing the new submarine contract, Defence Minister Beazley noted that many Australian firms would benefit from the massive transfer of technology which would ensue from the contract, but added that: 'To successfully apply these technologies and skills a significant upgrading of quality assurance is needed in many Australian firms'.[10] To assist with the necessary upgrading, the Commonwealth Government authorised a wide range of agencies to give accreditation to firms' quality assurance systems.

The obvious way to escape many of the limitations of the Australian market is to export, but Australian defence industry has had few exportable products. Successes such as *Ikara*, *Jindivik* and *Barra* became well known because they were exceptional. There have been small-scale successes such as generators for military vehicles, propellants, pyrotechnic and target ranges. There is potential in products such as minehunters, tactical radio, water purification, infra-red surveillance, and in several Defence Science and Technology Organisation (DSTO) inventions, including missile decoys and the Laser Airborne Depth Sounder system. Restricted export franchises were negotiated for some overseas designs, manufactured in Australia under licence, and these enabled 105mm Howitzers and the *Steyr* individual weapons to be sold to New Zealand. There are also regional prospects for exports of the *PC-9* pilot training aircraft. In total, however, exports of final products, designed and manufactured by Australian firms, have been a small proportion of total defence exports and a much smaller proportion of equivalent imports.

Defence industry shares these features with the civilian manufacturing sector. In 1985, Australian imports of 'science based differentiated products'[11] exceeded exports by a factor of eight to one. To put this performance in perspective, the ratio for Canada was two and a half to one, and in the United Kingdom, imports equalled exports. Exports exceeded imports by one half in the US, by a factor of two in the Federal Republic of Germany and by a factor of four in Japan.[12] For 'mature industries', including shipbuilding and ordnance, Australian imports exceeded exports by a factor of four; the countries listed above, again, out-performed Australia, but by slightly lesser margins.[13]

Statistics of private defence research and development and outlays are lacking, but an idea of the limits to that expenditure can be gained from statistics on research and development (R&D) for all manufacturing industry. In 1981-82, expenditure on high technology R&D by all manufacturing industry in Australia was little more than $100 million. In 1985-86, with the powerful stimulus of a 150 per cent taxation concession (reduced to 100 per cent in the May 1988 Economic Statement), it had doubled and was forecast to grow by a further 25 per cent in 1986-87.[14] That would take it to close on $300 million. In the event that defence industry accounted for as much as 10 per cent of the total, its R&D expenditure would amount to only $30 million. By way of comparison, Commonwealth Government outlays on defence science and technology in 1986-87 was $184 million.[15] The extent of reliance on Government R&D is apparent. Yet a further perspective can be provided by one American corporation - United Technologies - which invested the equivalent of more than $1 billion in R&D in 1987.[16]

Policy Responses

By 1988, new policies and management approaches were being introduced to overcome many of the problems outlined above, and to take advantage of opportunities presented by the general improvement in the competitiveness of Australian manufacturing, occurring through the floating of the Australian dollar, deregulation of financial markets and the national wages accord with the trade union movement.

Defence industry has long chafed under government controls on defence exports. This is a sensitive policy issue, involving international obligations to restrict the manufacture and export of defence matériel as well as diplomatic and domestic political considerations. However, Robert Cooksey, in his report on *Australia's Defence Exports and Defence Industry*, recommended that the limiting guidelines in force should be replaced by a revised criteria in which '...the onus be placed on those opposing particular exports to establish their case'.[17] In June 1988, after long debate within the Government, lobbying by trade unions and industry councils, and intervention by the Defence Industry Committee, the view of the Minister and Department of Defence prevailed and a new export policy, which largely met industry's request, was announced. The policy focussed on goods that are lethal, or of major military significance, thus freeing many products previously controlled. It placed the onus of proof less on the exporter to justify approval and more on the Minister and officials to justify disapproval of exports. It presumed that approval will be given where allies would supply comparable equipment. It provided for explicit published guidelines and required an official response to an application within 21 days.

The issue of arms exports will continue to be one of extreme political sensitivity. This was illustrated immediately after Mr Beazley's announcement of the policy, in the public comment by the then Minister for Foreign Affairs and Trade, Mr Hayden that: '...matters of principle and moral commitment' would remain dominant to him.[18] Moreover, Cooksey's estimates that 'Implementation of key recommendations could lead to a doubling of defence exports, to around $500 million in three to five years'[19] were disputed and Mr Hayden dismissed the estimate adding that 'media hype could undermine talks with the United States on disarmament'.[20]

Moreover, in considering what the outcome will be, it should be noted that the exporter of defence products faces formidable obstacles. Global excess production capacity exists because, for strategic reasons, many countries maintain uneconomic capabilities. It is a common practice to seek exports to reduce the cost burden, avoid workload peaks and troughs and maintain employment. This leads to many forms of aggressive marking including subsidies for R&D, production costs, training and support, offers of counter-trade, political pressure, bribery, denigration of competing products and violation of intellectual property rights.[21] In addition, many markets are closed by overt or covert 'buy-national' policies, such as the Buy America Act. Further complexities for products embodying high technology arise from controls designed to avoid leakage of military and dual-use technology to the Soviet Bloc. As Jacques Gansler has observed: 'Very little of traditional economic theory appears applicable to the overall field of international arms trade. Most of the decisions are politically driven...'.[22]

The Department of Defence advises exporters on how best to approach markets influenced by these various strategies, and sponsors industry missions to key buyers in the major markets. The Government also makes representations to prevent new marketing tactics from being introduced, or to modify their effects on Australian exporters. In 1987 and 1988, for example, an active lobbying program was carried out with the US Administration, the Congress and major US defence contractors against the large number of trade restrictions then being considered by the Congress. Despite the best efforts of the Australian and other Governments, it is realistic to expect that severe barriers to defence exports will remain for the foreseeable future.

Cooksey recommended that a new marketing arm, AUSDEX, be established within AUSTRADE to promote defence exports. He argued that greater support should also be given to defence exporters by the ADF through the conduct of demonstration trials and the collection of market intelligence by Defence Attaches abroad. The Government did not establish AUSDEX; however, ADF support was included in a package of export assistance measures announced in October 1986 to assist Australian manufacturers of defence products to demonstrate and market their products in other countries.[23]

On other aspects of defence industry policy, the main theme running through Cooksey's recommendations was that there should be more detailed planning of the development of defence industry by the Department. He proposed that Defence should produce: 'a detailed and authoritative paper which translates long-term strategic defence planning into precise industry objectives and/or measures to encourage maximum participation by Australian industry'.[24] Programs should then be directed to selectively develop the precise industry capabilities required. This has been called the 'centre of excellence' approach, under which selected companies or government factories are designated as centres for the production of certain kinds of strategically important defence equipment or supplies.[25] Ammunition is a common example. The government pays for the intellectual property, machinery and establishment costs and, if necessary, subsidises production losses. Contracts to supply the product in question are directed to the centre of excellence, often on a cost-plus basis.

There has been much debate about the extent to which the development of defence industry should be planned by Western governments in this way. Advocates usually argue that the imperfections of the defence market are so great that market forces cannot be relied upon. As Gansler commented:

> The free-market system is not operating to achieve economically efficient or strategically responsive behaviour in the area frequently referred to as the 'military industrial complex'.[26]

However, these arguments have not been accepted by the US, UK or Australian governments who have moved to increase the role of competition in defence procurement and to rely more on market forces for the allocation of resources in defence industry and less on detailed planning by defence departments. They have judged that imperfectly competitive firms would be more efficient than government-sponsored monopolies.

This judgement has taken account of the perceived failings of the centres of excellence approach. It was seen to lead to cost overruns, excessive prices for components and spare parts and failure of equipment supplied to meet performance specifications. President Reagan's *Blue Ribbon Commission on Defense Management* in response recommended that '...DoD should greatly increase its use of truly effective competition, using as a model the competitive buying practices of major corporations and their suppliers'.[27] In Britain, the introduction of competitive procurement and the substitution of fixed-price contracts for cost-plus contracts are at the core of the defence industry reforms of the Thatcher Government. The two key principles of the approach of the Procurement Executive are: '...to make use of competition wherever reasonable and practicable and act in a commercially astute manner'.[28] The implementation of these principles include 'alignment-with-industry discussions' which are talks undertaken to give industry early guidance on the performance the armed forces would like to have and enable firms to plan their own commercial development programs. Tenders are called on the basis of Critical Point Specifications which include some mandatory requirements relating to necessary operational features, safety and interfaces, but which allow '...the greatest flexibility for firms to bid equipments that they designed for exports'.[29]

Although the balance has swung in favour of competitive tendering in Australia, centres of excellence cannot be completely discarded. Direct government support of some key strategic capabilities will still be necessary. As the financial resources available to support such centres are limited, very few will be able to be afforded: priorities will need to be carefully defined and closely adhered to, but where domestic competition is not possible, the stimulus of overseas competition needs to be applied as far as practicable.

To provide these capabilities to support the ADF in the longer term, both the competitive sector of defence industry and the centres of excellence need to be involved in aspects of the design, development and manufacture of defence equipment. It is important that production of equipment be planned and controlled in Australia, rather than from abroad. For example, Australian engineering standards and components can be designed-in at the beginning, avoiding the delay and expense of substitution at a later stage. Recognition of this policy has been demonstrated by the Government's requirement that the prime contractor for the new submarines and ANZAC ships is an Australian, or in the latter case Australian/New Zealand, enterprise.

When major items, such as aircraft, ships, weapons and sensors, are procured from overseas, selective Australian involvement in these aspects is arranged under the Australian Industry Involvement (AII) policy. Production of high usage replacement parts and consumables, and of items representative of generic technological capabilities, is given high priority when work is designated to be done in Australia for this purpose. Work designated under the AII policy may receive assistance with initial capital costs, and for a few high priority capabilities, with recurring costs. A further element of the AII policy is the defence offsets program under which benefits to the value of 30 per cent of the overseas content of imported equipment are required to flow to Australian industry. Those benefits may take the form of technology transfer, design or production work, or access to overseas markets.

A variety of other forms of Government assistance is provided to Australian defence industry. For example, it is desirable that Australian industry gains maximum advantage from Australian scientific advances. Under the Australian Ownership and Control of Information guidelines, where sensitive new technology, which has been developed in Australia, is being used on a defence project, access is restricted to Australian nationals and to firms which can demonstrate that their operations are controlled by Australians. When calling for competitive tenders, the Government assists Australian industry to bid by publishing information on how to do business with the Department of Defence and on forward plans for procurement of equipment. The Defence Science and Technology Organisation (DSTO) also provides briefings on its forward research programs. Finally, defence industry benefits from all forms of assistance available to industry generally. This includes import tariffs, production bounties and the 20 per cent Government purchasing preference, the 100 per cent R&D tax concession, and export assistance through AUSTRADE. A purchasing preference greater than 20 per cent can be given where justified for strategic purposes.

To widen opportunities for Australian industry to export, the Government has also sought to enter into collaborative procurement arrangements with other countries. Collaboration has been achieved with the UK on the *Barra* sonarbuoy and the *Ikara* anti-submarine weapons system and on joint development of the *Nulka* anti-ship missile defence system with the US. Arrangements to foster future collaboration have been made with Sweden in the context of the submarine contract and negotiations are under way with other countries.

Research and Development

As already noted, research and development is mainly carried out by the Defence Science and Technology Organisation (DSTO). It is Australia's second-largest research organisation with a staff of 4,300 in 1988. About 1,000 of them are professional scientists and engineers. The Organisation has five main objectives: maintenance of a technology base; advice to the Department of Defence; support of the ADF; conception of new equipment and systems; and fostering defence industry.

DSTO's key resource is its technology base, which comprises 'the knowledge, expertise, accumulated experience of its staff and the facilities available to them'.[30] This base requires continuous renewal to keep up with the rapid advance of technology and to remain relevant to changing defence needs. Current development projects such as the *Jindalee* Over-the-Horizon-Radar, the *Kariwara* towed array, the *Lads* laser depth-sounding equipment and the *Nulka* missile decoy are fruits of the technology base laid down in earlier years. The advice given by DSTO applies to many activities of the Department. For example, it played a crucial role in the planning and execution of procurement projects for fighter aircraft, submarines, frigates, minehunters and a range of electronic equipment. The Chief Defence Scientist, Mr Henry d'Assumpcao, described DSTO's role in this context as follows:

> Advice to the Defence organisation embraces all matters scientific but focusses on helping Defence to be a smart buyer (selecting the most appropriate technology for our often unique requirements) and a smart user (maximising the effectiveness of equipment).[31]

Also, d'Assumpcao sees DSTO's role as contributing to supporting the:

> ...development, in concert with Australian industry, of equipment to meet unique Australian needs or to exploit commercially attractive Australian defence innovations; modification of defence materiel purchased from overseas; and integration of defence equipment from many sources.[32]

In this role, the Organisation solves problems faced by the ADF in keeping equipment operational and extending its life, contributing greatly to the effectiveness of the ADF and the safety of its personnel.

DSTO is organised into five major laboratories which carry out integrated research and engineering (up to the stage of technology demonstration) and are organised on product or system lines. They are:
* Aeronautical Research Laboratory (ARL), Fishermans Bend, Victoria (aircraft and aircraft systems);

- Electronics Research Laboratory (ERL), Salisbury, South Australia (electronic warfare, information technology and military communications);

- Materials Research Laboratory (MRL), Maribyrnong, Victoria (defence materials, underwater weapons systems, sea and land vehicles and life sciences);

- Surveillance Research Laboratory (SRL), Salisbury, South Australia (electro-magnetic surveillance including the experimental *Jindalee* radar at Alice Springs);

- Weapons Systems Research Laboratory (WSRL), Salisbury, South Australia (guided and unguided weapons systems, sonar systems, propulsion systems and ballistic weapons).

New Priorities for DSTO

DSTO's R&D capabilities are a scarce resource in strong demand. Like other areas of government, the Organisation has been under tight human resource constraints: its staff numbers have been successively reduced from 6,000 in 1974 to 4,300 in 1988. As a result, additional resources have only been applied to new and high priority research tasks by adjusting priorities. This is a difficult and slow process in research establishments because it commonly takes many years for a scientist to acquire knowledge and expertise in a particular field and the established human capabilities may not be well matched with the new high priority tasks. New research priorities emerged in the 1987 Defence White Paper and, to meet these within the tight constraints on its human resources, DSTO was reorganised, with the new structure coming into effect in 1988. The new priorities place greater emphasis on intelligence and surveillance, over-the-horizon-radar, mine countermeasures, mobility, towed acoustic arrays and command, control and commu-nication systems. There has also been a fall in the share of DSTO's resources directed to the support of its technology base.

To meet these needs, there has been an expanding emphasis on science and a move away from engineering development. The general rule has been adopted that DSTO will only take development to the stage of technology demonstration; industry will have to carry out engineering development. This shift has been reflected in the abolition of the Advanced Engineering Laboratory and the creation of the Surveillance Research Laboratory. There has also been a shift in the balance of DSTO's workforce in favour of researchers, with corresponding reductions in support staff. Finally, a search has begun for ways to contract more work out to industry and involve industry more directly in defence R&D.

Fostering Industrial Development

Despite all the difficulties of commercial development, scientific innovations can be the basis of highly profitable industrial developments on a large scale. The spin-offs from the US space program which provided a foundation for the electronic microcircuit industry in so-called Silicon Valley in California is an oft-quoted example. With this in mind, DSTO's functions were amended in November 1986 to give greater emphasis to fostering industrial development. At the same time, the DSTO laboratories were seeking ways of obtaining funds additional to those appropriated by the Government. The conjunction of these two forces led to an active search for new commercial links between DSTO and industry.

Several forms of arrangements are under consideration, including the establishment of trust funds to enable the laboratories to reinvest income earned by selling their expertise and use of their facilities to industry. Also considered were the licensing of 'ferrets' - representatives of private companies who would be located in DSTO to identify research tasks with commercial potential; and the establishment of one or more DSTO companies to market DSTO skills and technology. The last suggestion originated with ARL, which proposed the establishment of AEROTECH, a company owned by ARL which would have skills in marketing and finance and be tasked with selling ARL's expert services and technology. The AEROTECH proposal was supported by the 1986 review of DSTO by the Australian Science and Technology Council and Cooksey went further in recommending the establishment of similar companies with MRL and the Defence Research Centre at Salisbury.

All of these ideas were considered by the Joint Parliamentary Committee on Public Accounts in its 1987 review of DSTO. It conditionally supported the ARL and Cooksey recommendations and proposed that the Department of Industry, Technology and Commerce undertake a detailed examination of the 'ferret' system.[33] While noting the gap between R&D conducted by DSTO and the marketing of the results of that work, the committee recommended that the laboratories be allowed to retain part of the income generated by commercialisation of their R&D efforts. Following her appointment in 1987 as Minister for Defence Science and Personnel, Ms Kelly also strongly emphasised the need to commercialise the DSTO's innovations more effectively and streamline the transition from research to industrial production to enhance DSTO's contribution to the development of export industries.

It remains to be seen whether the new attempts to close the gap between research in government laboratories and successful marketing of the results of that research will succeed any better than past ones. It may be that the most effective solution would be for research on the development of new defence systems to be undertaken by scientists employed in industry under an arrangement like the Cardinal Points Specification System used in the UK and described above. The other tasks of maintaining the technology base, advising Defence and supporting the ADF, on which 85 per cent of DSTO's resources are employed, would remain with DSTO. In one stroke, this approach would eliminate the present institutional gap between research and commercial exploitation. It would, of course, be necessary, in some cases, to give the firm involved direct access to DSTO's technology base. This could be done by seconding key scientists from DSTO, or by locating corporate scientists within DSTO for the duration of the project. Contracting out research, as is currently done by DSTO, offers similar benefits but it is on a small scale ($7.2 million in 1986-87) and its effectiveness in fostering the development of new and exportable products could be limited unless the contracted research covered the whole of the development of a new defence system, rather than part of it.

Australian defence industry is almost wholly dependent on technology developed overseas, or in government laboratories. This dependence, and the associated corporate culture, are serious disadvantages in the fiercely competitive international defence market. The planned withdrawal of DSTO from the engineering development phase of new defence systems will provide industry with a better opportunity to develop its own technology and improve its competitive position. Moreover, it is evident that where the object is industrial development, it is more efficient if the research is undertaken by an organisation with a dominant business, rather than scientific, culture.

However, it needs to be recognised that, at best, the funds for research flowing to industry from a reallocation of part of DSTO's work or the technological advantage gained from better arrangements to commercialise the results of that work would have a marginal impact on the competitive position of Australian defence industry. The scale of DSTO's work on new systems is just too small to make a major impact. To succeed in export markets, Australian defence firms need to emulate their overseas competitors, and make the development of proprietary technology their top investment priority. The most encouraging sign in 1988 was the rapid growth occurring in high technology R&D in manufacturing industry generally, albeit from a minuscule base by international standards.

Endnotes

1   Hon. Kim C. Beazley, *The Defence of Australia 1987*, (Australian Government Publishing Service, Canberra, 1987), p.76.
2   *Ibid.*, p.75.
3   Bureau of Industry Economics, *The Australian Aerospace Industry: Structure, Performance and Economic Issues*, (Australian Government Publishing Service, Canberra, 1986, Research Report 20), p.370.
4   *Ibid.*, p.368.
5   These improvements were mainly achieved through work on the *Hamel* gun and Small Arms Replacement projects, which include export orders to New Zealand, and sub-contracts for naval ship construction and engineering work. Department of Defence, Office of Defence Production, *Draft Corporate Plan 1988-89 - 1997-98*.
6   BIS Shrapnel, *Report into the Australian Electronic Components Industry*, (Prepared for the Communications Equipment Industry Strategy Co-ordinating Committee, November 1987), p.67.
7   *Ibid.*, p.57.
8   Department of Defence, Defence Industry Committee, *Study of the Australian Electronics Industry*, (Canberra, September 1983).
9   Extracted from the *Directory of Australian Industry Defence Capability*, (Canberra, November 1987).
10 Minister for Defence, *News Release*, 18 May 1987.
11 These products include aircraft, professional and scientific equipment, electrical industrial machinery, radio, TV and communications equipment, electrical apparatus and supplies, industrial machinery, drugs and medicines.
12 Department of Industry, Technology and Commerce, *Annual Report 1986-87*, (Australian Government Publishing Service, Canberra, 1987), p.11.
13 One of the 'notable success stories' in expanded exports in 1986-87 was Hawker de Havilland with exports valued at $96 million or 55 per cent of its turnover. These exports comprised components for aircraft manufactured by Boeing and Airbus Industries, and engine overhauls. *Ibid.*, p.13.
14 *Ibid.*, p.14.
15 Commonwealth of Australia, *Commonwealth of Australia, 1987-88 Budget Papers*, (Commonwealth Government Printer, Canberra, 1987, Paper No.3).
16 United Technologies, *Annual Report 1987*.
17 Robert J. Cooksey, *Review of Australia's Defence Exports and Defence Industry*, (Report to the Minister for Defence, Australian Government Publishing Service, Canberra, 1986), p.5.
18 Quoted in the *Canberra Times*, 16 June 1988.
19 Robert J. Cooksey, *Review of Australia's Defence Exports and Defence Industry*, p.3.
20 Quoted in the *Australian Financial Review*, 17 June 1988.
21 Jacques S. Gansler, *The Defense Industry*, (Massachusetts Institute of Technology Press, Cambridge, Mass., 1980), p.211.
22 *Ibid.*, p.212.
23 Minister for Defence, *News Release*, Number 151, October 1986.
24 Robert J. Cooksey, *Review of Australia's Defence Exports and Defence Industry*, p.9.
25 Eldon J. Healey, Assistant Deputy Minister (Materiel), Canadian Department of National Defence, interviewed in *Aerospace & Defence Technology*, March-April 1988.
26 Jacques S. Gansler, *The Defense Industry*, p.1.

27   President's Blue Ribbon Commission on Defense Management, *A Quest for Excellence - Final Report to the President by the President's Blue Ribbon Commission on Defense Management*, (US Government Printing Service, Washington, D.C., June 1986), pp.62-63.
28   Ministry of Defence, *The Procurement Executive*, (Her Majesty's Stationery Office, London), p.10.
29   See D.G. Kiely, 'The Evolving Pattern of Naval Weapons Procurement', *Journal of Naval Science*, (Volume 10, Number 1), p.6935.
30   Department of Defence, *Defence Report 1986-87*, (Australian Government Publishing Service, Canberra, 1987), p.76.
31   H.A. d'Assumpcao, *The Australian* (Defence Supplement), 15 May 1987.
32   *Ibid.*.
33   Parliament of Australia, Joint Parliamentary Committee on Public Accounts, *Report Number 280*, (Australian Government Publishing Service, Canberra, 1987), p.vii.

CHAPTER 17

THE DEFENCE FORCE AND AUSTRALIAN SOCIETY

Hugh Smith

History

Armed forces have always played an important role in white Australian society. British troops landed with the first fleet in 1788 and remained in the colonies until 1870. To some, the Redcoats were jailers and oppressors, to others, they were upholders of order and protectors of property. British forces also represented a guarantee of protection against attack by imperialist powers such as France, Germany and Russia. Some settlers, nonetheless, believed the colonies should look more to their own defences and a few even voiced the suspicion that Britain might not always be at hand to defend them. Despite these occasional doubts, loyalty to the British Empire remained strong. There were volunteers to fight alongside Britain in the Crimean War, though none were accepted. Some 2,600 troops took part in the Maori Wars beginning in 1863 and a similar contingent went to the Sudan in 1865. Over 16,000 Australian volunteers served in the Boer War from 1899 to 1902. In the great test of loyalty to Britain in 1914-18, over 330,000 men - out of a total population of some 5 million - chose to fight in a war which posed no direct threat to Australia.

A volunteer tradition had become firmly established. When the colonies first began to raise their own forces in the 1850s, there had been no thought of a standing army. Militia forces - volunteer civilians willing to undergo occasional military training - appeared both adequate and appropriate. In the event of a major threat, it was accepted that the militia, together with a small number of permanent staff officers, would provide the basis for an army made up of citizens. These people might lack the usual trappings of the military but they would bring to the business of war qualities and skills learnt in the bush, together with a natural resourcefulness and bravery.[1] Once the war was over, they could return to their civilian occupations. A militia force also seemed better fitted to a society which considered itself egalitarian and democratic. The creation of a large and permanent officer elite would have set some Australians above others and raised the spectre of undue military influence on the government.

The performance of Australian troops in the Great War confirmed the faith of Australians in the effectiveness of the citizen soldier. The heroism and endurance of Australians at Gallipoli - though a costly and unsuccessful operation - inspired many to believe that Australia had come of age as a nation.[2] In France, the fighting qualities of the Australian soldier were highly regarded by Allied commanders, though the Australian Imperial Force (AIF) also prided itself on being more democratic and less authoritarian than its European counterparts. Most officers were recruited from the ranks, and leadership was regarded as something to be earned by ability rather than granted by status. General Monash could declare after the war that 'there was no officer caste, no social distinction in the whole force'.[3] The war also confirmed Australia's preference for the volunteer, although the two referendums of 1916 and 1917 saw the proposals for conscription defeated by only 71,000 and 156,000 votes respectively out of a total electorate of 2.3 million.

The picture of the all-conquering 'digger' may have been romanticised in some degree, but it remained influential. The soldiers who returned from the Great War were 'an elite with the aura of heroes'.[4] They now looked to society to reward, or at least recompense, them for what they had done. Already during the war, associations had been formed to promote the interests of returned soldiers and the first legislation was passed in 1917 with the Australian Soldiers' Repatriation Act.[5] One form of reward was preferential employment by State and Federal governments, a policy which persisted through World War II. The benefits accorded to veterans may have been no more than they deserved, but a certain resentment developed on the part of those who, in the austere inter-war years, missed out on employment or paid higher taxes to support returned servicemen. The issue of recompensing those who had risked their lives for their country and the dependents of those who had given their lives became a permanent feature of Australian politics.

The Second World War placed burdens on the whole nation. Volunteers came forward, but by 1943, the government felt compelled to extend conscription for military service beyond mainland Australia to a defined area of the South West Pacific. The demands of diplomacy and the practicalities of conducting war in Australia's own region overcame - in a temporary and partial fashion - the traditional reliance on volunteers.

The establishment of the Australian Regular Army in 1948 marked the end of an era. With the onset of the Cold War and rapid advances in military technology, a permanent fighting force became necessary and the foundation was laid for the emergence of a military profession in Australia. Within two years, Australian servicemen were in action in the Korean War. To promote Australia's defence preparedness, the Menzies Government introduced a compulsory military training scheme which operated from 1951 to 1959. Australians were familiar with compulsory peacetime training schemes (these had operated between 1911-15 and 1919-29), and the great majority accepted the need for the new system which did not require overseas service. Many people saw it as instilling desirable qualities such as discipline and moral fibre in the youth of the day while the government saw benefits in the enhancement of physical fitness.6

By the late 1950s, however, the National Service Scheme had proved cumbersome, costly and inappropriate. It was abandoned but, following an expansion of the armed forces in 1963, a new selective scheme, based on two years service, was introduced in 1964, to meet what Prime Minister Menzies called Australia's 'deteriorating strategic situation'.7 In 1965, the Government committed regular troops and, in 1966, conscripts, to fight alongside the United States in Vietnam. By 1972, some 17,424 conscripts had served in Vietnam.8 While most Australians supported involvement in Vietnam up to 1969, majority opinion rejected conscription for service in the war.9 Widespread and occasionally intense opposition developed, taking the form of protest marches, demonstrations, burning of draft cards and the like. The chief target of such protests, however, was neither the Australian soldier nor the armed forces - thought the latter did not escape unscathed - but the policy of the Government.

Defence and Society

The way in which Australia has gone about the business of war and defence reflects the nature of Australian society. It is not simply that society funds the armed forces and determines defence policy, but that there exists a constant interaction between those citizens in uniform and the rest of the population. As in other Western democratic nations, the armed forces are an integral part of society, rather than a detached and unresponsive instrument.

Recruits to the Australian Defence Force (ADF) are drawn from society and reflect its values and educational levels. The 70,000 personnel currently in uniform have frequent dealings with civilians - public servants, politicians, state authorities, the police and so on, as well as with community organisations and their local communities. Another 27,000 citizens are members of the Reserve Forces and regularly put on uniform to carry out their training obligations. Over half of all ADF personnel are married and many have children - a total of approximately 100,000 dependants. These 'service families' lead a fairly nomadic existence, but still need such things as housing, education for their children and employment for spouses - matters which bring them into close contact and sometimes conflict with the civilian community.

Nor should the ex-soldier be forgotten. The National Service Scheme operating from 1965 to 1972 conscripted 63,970 men into the forces for a period of two years.[10] Since that time around 7,000-9,000 personnel have left the ADF each year - well over 110,000 up to 1988. Many of these have joined the Returned Services League (RSL) which has over 1,500 sub-branches around Australia and a membership of approximately 250,000 ex-service personnel, together with several thousand serving members. In addition, there are over 20 organisations such as the Vietnam Veterans Association, Legacy, War Widows Guild and the Regular Defence Force Welfare Association, as well as organisations for those who served in particular units or operations. The RSL estimates that it has only about half of its potential membership. This suggests that at least half a million Australian citizens once wore uniform - about 1 in 20 of the population over the age of 18.

Defence, moreover, is a factor to be reckoned with in the Australian economy. In addition to those in uniform, there are more than 36,000 full-time civilian employees of the Department of Defence, including nearly 5,000 full-time staff in Canberra and about 10,000 workers in the eleven factories and one dockyard managed by the Department. Defence is the largest single employer in the country, not counting those public servants involved with defence in Departments such as Treasury and Foreign Affairs and Trade. Expenditure by the Defence Department within Australia in 1987-88 amounted to $2,775 million on salaries (plus $558 million on death and retirement benefits), $2,061 million on operating costs and $2,092 million on capital equipment and facilities.[11] This accounted for 9.4 per cent of the Federal Budget and 2.5 per cent of the nation's gross domestic product.[12] Defence spending must compete primarily with social security, health and education - matters which directly affect most Australians. If Australia's economic circumstances do not improve markedly in the next few years, continuing pressure on defence budgets seems probable. This will be true regardless of which political party holds office.

Australian society interacts most directly with its armed forces in terms of personnel and budgets; it influences the training and equipping of the ADF more indirectly through government policies and strategy. But all of these interactions take place in a social and political context that is unique to Australia and includes factors such as perceptions of the historical role of the armed forces, attitudes to the 'digger' and the returned soldier, beliefs about conscription and the volunteer, and the general acceptance - or otherwise - of ADF activities within Australia (such as training, aid to the civil power and, potentially, operations on Australian soil). The social and political context will also determine whether in broad terms those in the ADF feel appreciated by, or alienated from, the rest of society

Consideration of this kind are not the traditional stuff of military strategy but they shape Australia's armed forces and its defence policy just as surely. The rest of this chapter will examine four main areas: (i) the transition of individuals between society and the ADF; (ii) the sociology of the military, in particular, the extent to which it reflects society at large; (iii) public attitudes towards the ADF and its functions; and (iv) defence and the ADF in the political arena. A final section considers the place of the military in Australian society.

Transition: Recruitment and Separation

Since 1971, the ADF has replenished its ranks from volunteers at a rate varying between 6,000 and 10,000 a year. The economic climate, unemployment, civilian wage levels as well as demographic trends influence the number of volunteers willing to put on uniform, though the relationship between hard economic times and high numbers of applicants for the ADF is not a straightforward one. The social climate - including attitudes to discipline, willingness to undertake long training, and the desire to serve one's country - has changed much in recent years and might be expected to make the ADF a less attractive proposition for young men and women.[13] Nonetheless, there exists considerable interest in service life. In 1987-88, inquiries to recruiting offices numbered 199,469 of whom, 39,181 made formal applications to join up. From the 30,692 selected for interview, 8,483 ultimately enlisted.[14]

Conscription as a means of filling military ranks has been off the political agenda since the end of Australia's involvement in the Vietnam war in 1972. The ADF leadership itself favours a smaller, well-equipped, professional force, rather than a more numerous force which demands experienced manpower to train. But the public, at large, continues to be attracted to the idea of compulsory military service - at least in principle. Polls asking whether the respondent was 'in favour of the re-introduction of compulsory military service' have indicated support ranging between 59 per cent (1978) and 52 per cent (1985). Majorities in favour of 'compulsory military training for young men' were even greater, varying between 61 per cent in 1977 and 66 per cent in 1980.[15]

The transition from the armed services to civilian society tends to be a particular concern of the ADF when separation rates are higher than average and highly skilled personnel are being lost. Separations have risen steadily from 9.4 per cent of total strength in 1983-84 to 13.2 per cent in 1987-88. It is difficult to assess how much this is due to dissatisfaction with the Defence Force and how much to the pulls of civilian life.[16] Certainly, personnel policies and pay levels play a part, although the skills which some have acquired while in uniform make them eagerly sought after by employers.

Such losses can create severe problems for the ADF, but the effect of these separations on society must be judged as marginal. Though some former officers have gone on to important positions in the law, politics and business, ex-military personnel constitute only a small fraction of the workforce. In general, the transition from soldier to civilian is an easy one for the individual, reinforcing the view that soldiers remain citizens despite their distinctive lifestyle and code of discipline.[17] Some controversy exists over the lasting psychological effects of service in the Vietnam War.[18] A Veterans Counselling Service has been established but the relatively small number involved - some 47,000 served in Vietnam - has meant that the returned soldier has been much less prominent than after 1918 or 1945.

Sociology of the Defence Force

The nature and functioning of the Defence Force as a social group is important for a number of reasons. Military effectiveness depends at least as much on intangibles, such as a sense of purpose, *esprit de corps*, and levels of training, as on numbers and hardware. The advice given by the military to governments also reflects the attitudes, outlook and education of the personnel concerned as well as their interaction with civilian counterparts. Therefore, the sociological make-up of the ADF cannot be ignored. It is determined partly by the individuals who enter the armed services, but also by the personnel policies, institutions and functioning of the Defence Force.

Personnel Policies

If there is one area which reinforces the fact that the ADF remains inextricably connected with society at large, it is the service family.[19] Housing must be provided, either on-base or off, but the expectation is that it will be comparable with community standards. Wives of servicemen, like increasing numbers of women in the community, are seeking work in order to continue their own careers, to make ends meet, or simply for their own satisfaction. Whatever the reason, difficulties arise as husbands are posted from one location to another every two years or so. Children's education, especially in the high school years, is also a major concern of families as they move around the country, a problem aggravated by differing educational systems in the States. Nor, of course, are service families spared the problems such as separation, divorce and juvenile delinquency which are to be found in society at large.

Family pressures certainly constitute one of the major reasons for resignation and failure to re-engage.[20] A whole range of allowances and subsidies is paid to alleviate the social and personal turbulence experienced by service personnel and their families. As noted in Chapter 15, the Australian Defence Families Information and Liaison Staff and a Defence Housing Authority have been established to tackle some of these problems. Moreover, in planning any major new military establishment such as the RAAF Base at Tindal in the Northern Territory, or the projected move of the RAN from Sydney, the ADF cannot ignore the social consequences for service personnel and their families. There is a constant pressure to expend resources and to change posting practices in order to minimise problems for service families and the ADF must draw a fine balance between military effectiveness and the welfare of personnel.

Another clear reflection of society can be found in the increasing employment of women by the ADF over the last ten years:[21]

	1977	1982	1978
Female personnel	3,790	4,326	6.239
% of total personnel	5.4	6.0	8.8
Female officers	379	583	818
% of officer corps	3.9	5.8	7.9

About 35 per cent of all positions in the Defence Force are now open to women compared with 8 per cent in 1983.[22] Female officer cadets have been admitted alongside their male counterparts to HMAS *Creswell* since 1979, to Office Cadet School Portsea since 1985, and on the latter's closure, to Royal Military College Duntroon since 1986. When officer education was concentrated in the Australian Defence Force Academy in 1986, all three Services admitted female cadets.

The reason for these changes is not the extensive difficulty of recruiting suitable males to the ADF, but rather the tendency of the Defence Force to follow general community patterns, albeit at some distance behind. Nonetheless, certain limits are observed as can be seen over the question of women undertaking combat or combat-related duties. The *Sex Discrimination Act* of 1984 specifically exempts the ADF from the obligation to treat women equally in respect of combat and recent Cabinet decisions have maintained the existing prohibition. The chief reason given has been community values and expectations.

Institutions and Individual Rights

In recent years, the ADF has adopted a number of institutions and procedures inspired by civilian practice. The crucial matter of determining service pay and allowances in the nature of pay, for example, has been removed from the Minister for Defence and is now in the hands of an independent Defence Force Remuneration Tribunal (DFRT). The establishment of the Tribunal in 1985 was designed to give the ADF 'access to processes which apply to the community at large' and it was 'required to have regard to decisions of and principles established by the Conciliation and Arbitration Commission'.[23] Decisions of the Tribunal are binding and a right of appeal exists. The Tribunal has thus put the ADF more on a par with the civilian workforce in terms of procedures and rights.

The DFRT has some advantages over its predecessor, the Committee of Reference, which required decisions by the Minister, first, to conduct an inquiry and, second, to accept its recommendations. The new tribunal is independent of the government and must hold a review every two years; its determinations, moreover, have the force of law. Nonetheless, the attempt to bring the method of remunerating the ADF into line with the rest of the community has its costs. The Tribunal must in effect apply principles and concepts developed in the civilian wage-fixing arena to the special circumstances of military service. The notion of overtime, for example, does not readily equate with the traditional military concept of being on duty and under discipline 24 hours a day, seven days a week. Similarly, urgent measures to retain skilled personnel cannot easily be instituted through the DFRT, which was circumvented in the case of the Pilot Retention Bonus in 1988. At the same time, of course, members of the ADF lack many of the freedoms enjoyed by civilians such as the right to form an industrial union, to withdraw labour, to take a second job and to resign as they choose.

The ADF appears to have lost a degree of autonomy and privacy in the setting of its rewards. It is compelled to argue for benefits in terms of civilian principles while trying to assert the distinctiveness of the military life. The change from the old paternalistic approach towards the armed forces is most clearly manifested in the fact that in open forum the Chief of the Defence Force is responsible for putting the ADF case to the DFRT in opposition to that of the Commonwealth Government. Society may wish to compel the ADF to follow community practice in this way - and to an extent this is inevitable - but there is likely to be an intangible price to pay in terms of morale, retention and recruitment.

The formation of the Armed Forces Federation of Australia (ArFFA) in October 1984 was not unrelated to dissatisfaction with pay and conditions. While earlier attempts to establish such an organisation in the 1970s had failed, attitudes in the 1980s had moved towards greater acceptance of collective action. Like any industrial organisation, ArFFA seeks to improve conditions of service on a collective basis, but its constitution expressly renounces the intention to strike or interfere with the chain of command.[24] Though its membership is only some 3,000, the Federation has been recognised by the Defence Force and has been permitted to make its own submissions to the DRFT. The Federation has some of the advantages of a trade union in that it can push its politics publicly, and persistently, criticise government decisions and involve itself in electoral politics.[25]

The *Defence Force Discipline Act* (1982) which came into force in 1985, also reflects changes in the world outside the military. The Act was intended to bring the three Services under the same disciplinary code, and to modernise a fairly antiquated and complex system of military discipline which relied for its authority on a number of outdated British Acts of Parliament. It was also concerned - in line with community standards - to protect the rights of individual Service members by, for example, overhauling procedures for hearing cases and reducing reliance on such vague charges as 'conduct to the prejudice of good order'.[26] The impact of social changes was also evident in the need to deal with offences involving possession and use of drugs. More broadly, the new Act was considered necessary to counteract the gradual shift of disciplinary power - resulting from the outmoded character of the old system - away from the Defence Force and into the hands of civilian authorities.

The rights of individual Servicemen and women were also to the fore in the establishment of the position of Defence Force Ombudsman in 1983. Service personnel have few substantive rights in relation to their employment, lacking a legally enforceable contract and holding their positions at the pleasure of the Crown. The Defence Force Ombudsman is able to investigate any matter of administration relating to service in the ADF and most commonly deals with complaints about postings, promotions, discharges and eligibility for allowances.[27] Service personnel have thus been extended a measure of protection which civilians have taken for granted.

Some changes, of course, cut both ways. In 1985, for example, legislation was introduced to permit the garnisheeing of service pay which had previously been exempt because of the special nature of military service, including frequent absence on courses or overseas postings. Such considerations were now seen as less relevant to the repayment of debts and the new rules were designed in part to assist service personnel to obtain loans more readily in the commercial market. Where procedures and practices akin to those in civilian life are adopted, Service personnel can expect some loss of privilege alongside the gains.[28]

Civilianisation of the Military?

It is one thing to point to ways in which the ADF reflects the society of which it is a part; it is another to argue that the military has become more civilianised. Yet, in several important respects the military profession has come to resemble is civilian counterparts. First, many technical and professional tasks in the ADF are essentially comparable with those found in civilian life. Moreover, the management of any large organisation requires particular skills and knowledge whether it is military or civilian. Second, decision-making in the ADF, while retaining its hierarchical form, has become increasingly based on committees and on specialist advice. This tends to cut across military rank in that authority depends less on superior status and experience than on specialist knowledge and the ability to coordinate different interests and points of view. In the area of policy advice and administration, Service personnel are expected to acquire the skills of the bureaucrat and committee member. Finally, there are many functions for which the Services now employ civilians. In some cases, it is cheaper to use civilian staff for tasks such as gardening, secretarial work or even guard duties. In other cases, the Services simply do not have, or cannot spare, personnel with the necessary skills.

All this could be considered of little consequence if the traditional roles and ethos of the military were untouched. Yet, there are questions even here. The growth of technical specialisation and the importance of management in the ADF - together with greater focus on personnel rights and on rewards comparable with civilian occupations - has caused some to suggest that the combat ethic in the armed forces is under threat. As more and more personnel become managers and technicians, the 'warrior' may be giving way to the 'bureaucrat in uniform'; the military - once an institution in society - may be turning into an occupation more or less like any other.[29] These trends will be all the stronger at a time when prospects of conflict seen remote.

Functions and Public Attitudes

The formation of public attitudes toward armed forces is a complex matter. The two previous sections have looked at the way individuals interact with the ADF and at the nature of the ADF itself as it reflects the society around it. Other significant factors in forming community views are the activities of the ADF both within Australia and beyond, together with calculated efforts on the part of the ADF to develop its relations with the public and the media.

External Functions

The focus of the external functions of the ADF has changed markedly in recent years. Following a history of combat operations in Korea, Malaya, Borneo and Vietnam, Australia's armed forces have carried out extensive peacetime tasks such as participation in United Nations and Commonwealth peacekeeping operations, development of the Papua New Guinea Defence Force, military assistance to regional states and alliance cooperation. Combat has seemed a relatively remote possibility. The ADF has not been preparing for any particular war or to meet any particular enemy; at most, it seeks a generalised deterrent effect by maintaining a range of combat capabilities.

As an instrument of peaceful diplomacy, the ADF no doubt wins a measure of public support. It appears to be justifying at least part of the funds allocated to it without raising fears about likely threats to Australia. Yet, the potential exists for some adverse public reaction. Military assistance to the Indonesian and Philippine armed forces, for example, has attracted criticism from time to time. Cooperation with the United States, particularly if it involves exercises with nuclear-armed vessels or nuclear-capable aircraft, is another potential source of antagonism. To date, however, such criticism has been limited and sporadic.

Internal Functions

At the present time, the internal role of the armed forces appears to contain much greater potential for political debate and contention, particularly the use of troops for law enforcement or in connection with industrial disputes. There is in Australia a long-standing reluctance on the part of governments to use the armed forces in domestic affairs.[30] The Commonwealth has never acceded to a request from the states for armed forces to deal with what the Constitution calls 'domestic violence' and has only twice called out troops on its own authority to deal with internal violence. The single instance within Australia was the use of troops to protect those attending the Commonwealth Heads of

Government Regional Meeting at Bowral, NSW, in February 1978, after a bomb explosion at the Sydney Hilton hotel.[31] Public support for the action was high, but many commentators pointed to the need to proceed carefully in this area.

One fear was that the threat of terrorism provided only a vague definition of the circumstances in which the use of troops might be justified. Public support for the Bowral action might encourage a government to resort too readily to military action. The relevant laws and conventions were far from clear and a subsequent Review (discussed in Chapter 14) conducted by Mr Justice Hope, in recommending procedures for authorising the use of the ADF, stressed the need to ensure parliamentary control over the use of the ADF in such circumstances.[32] The ADF has its own reasons for approaching such activities with caution. They require training and doctrine markedly different from combat operations and constitute a diversion of effort from other tasks. Moreover, the legal position of the individual soldier acting to uphold law and order is an extremely complex one.

The role of the Defence Force in industrial disputes constitutes a veritable minefield. Colonial forces were used against strikers on a number of occasions in the second half of the 19th century amid great controversy and bitterness.[33] Commonwealth Governments, however, have shown great reluctance to act in this way. In order to avoid one source of controversy, the Defence Act was amended in 1914 to forbid the use of Citizen or Reserve Forces 'in connexion with an industrial dispute'. The major instances of the use of regular troops in this context have been to carry out open-cast coal-mining during the miners' strike of 1949, and to load ships at Bowen in Queensland in 1953, the latter generating considerable controversy.[34] Rather less contentious has been the use of military capabilities to relieve distress caused by industrial action - for example, the use of the RAAF to fly home passengers stranded in New Zealand by a Qantas strike in 1981 and the use of the RAAF in the domestic pilots' strike in 1989.

In the 1979-82 period, the ADF drew up plans for contingencies in which they were called upon to restore essential services to the community, whether in connection with an industrial dispute or not.[35] This would seem a reasonable precaution given the great complexity of such action. But political sensitivities were such that on learning of 'Plan Cabriole', Defence Minister Beazley ordered its immediate abandonment. It is commendable that governments should show great reluctance to even contemplate the use of the ADF in such circumstances. The other side of the coin is that the ADF may in the event be called upon to act with little or no preparation and training. Much depends on the government of the day understanding the inevitable limitations of military forces in dealing with industrial disputes and the potential repercussions for Service personnel.

Public Relations

In recent years, the ADF has become more conscious of the need for improved public relations, not only for recruiting purposes, but also to create a favourable image in the community at large, to engender support for the Defence Force and to demonstrate accountability to the public. The position of Director of Public Information was created at one-star level in 1979 and the Department of Defence now operates one of the largest public relations organisations of any government department. Numerous films, videos, publications, newsletters, media releases and so on are put out each year. Service awareness of the importance of publicity - good and bad - is further illustrated by the requirement that proposals for major projects or activities now contain what might be called a public relations impact statement.[36]

The role of the media has received particular recognition. It is now not uncommon for serving officers to be heard on radio or to appear on television and courses in media awareness are offered to a range of personnel. In 1985 the Chief of the General Staff explicitly called upon Army Commanders to take a greater part in public debate.[37] Significantly, the number of radio, television and newspaper reporters covering defence has doubled over the last decade. The long-standing distrust of the media by Service personnel remains, but there are signs that it is diminishing.

The ADF and the Department of Defence have also been open to greater public scrutiny since December 1982, through the Freedom of Information Act. In 1987-88, for example, 1,599 applications were processed.[38] The great majority are for personnel documents but a small proportion concern potentially contentious issues such as operational activities, equipment selection, land acquisition or defence policy. There are of course limits to publicity. Certain information must be kept confidential for reasons of national security or commercial practice and there is a natural tendency on the part of Defence to over-classify material.

Relations with the media in time of combat is another difficult area for which the ADF has been attempting to prepare contingency plans. It is unlikely that the public, and especially the media, will ever be fully satisfied with the amount of information which is released. Nonetheless, the ADF has acted on the belief that public support, or at least public understanding, is a major asset and has been willing to adopt a distinctly higher public profile in recent years.

Defence in the Political Arena

The community finally relates to the ADF through the political arena. This includes both the formal institution of Parliament and the informal activities of lobby groups and political movements. The focus here will not be on decision-making, but rather on prevailing attitudes and ideas towards defence and the ADF.

Parliament

The general level of interest in, and debate on, defence issues in Parliament has increased markedly in recent years. Parliamentary questions on defence, for example, have averaged over 210 each year in the 1980s compared with 70-80 per year in the 1970s. This appears to reflect a greater concern with the defence of Australia and a more independent strategic outlook than in earlier times. Though there is broad bipartisan agreement on defence, in particular the need to maintain the ANZUS Alliance with the United States, a range of issues have stimulated the interest of members of Parliament - from the aircraft carrier-replacement to the acquisition of land in the Bathurst-Orange-Cobar region, from defence cooperation to service conditions.

Parliamentary committees, notably the 28-member Joint Committee on Foreign Affairs, Defence and Trade and the 6-member Senate Standing Committee on Foreign Affairs, Defence and Trade, have provided many opportunities for parliamentary investigation - as have a range of other committees. These vary from Estimates Committees to the Senate Standing Committee on Constitutional and Legal Affairs, which examined proposed legislation designed to permit conscientious objection to particular wars.[39] Numerous military and civilian personnel give evidence to these committees and from time to time parliamentarians visit ADF installations.

The impact of these activities is difficult to assess. It certainly creates a more informed climate on defence issues and may produce some indirect pressure on governments to change policies or practices. On occasions the effect is more discernible. Investigation by the then Senate Foreign Affairs and Defence Committee into the Army's proposal to acquire land for training in the Cobar region of NSW, for example, stimulated considerable debate in both public and official circles and may have contributed to the eventual abandonment of the project.[40] The Public Works Committee's examination of the proposal to build the tri-service Defence Academy also stirred up considerable opposition, including much within the Defence Force itself, but in this instance the project continued despite an adverse report by the Committee.[41]

One particular area of Parliamentary interest has been conditions of service, no doubt reflecting a greater awareness that Service personnel have votes and that concentrations of them exist in marginal constituencies.[42] The appointment of a junior Minister for Defence Science and Personnel in 1987 can be seen as a response to problems in the area of service conditions, though the more cynical might see it as relieving the Defence Minister of a particularly onerous area of his portfolio. The Joint Committee on Foreign Affairs, Defence and Trade report on personnel wastage has also prompted both government and opposition to profess their concern with conditions for ADF personnel and their families.

Lobby groups in the defence area are of various kinds and do not focus only on defence policy itself. The activities of the Armed Forces Federation of Australia have been mentioned but it is only one of several groups, including the Returned Services League, which focus on conditions of service in the ADF. Another focus for pressure groups of concern to the community is defence industry. While there is nothing resembling a military-industrial complex in Australia, much political lobbying has been conducted in recent years by overseas firms seeking contracts and by State governments seeking employment opportunities for their own State. The new submarine project and the ANZAC Ship Frigate project, for example, saw intense rivalry between NSW and South Australia and NSW and Victoria to secure orders for their shipyards.

The Public Arena

In recent years, defence has attracted greater interest not only in political circles but among the general public. Defence has not become a major election issue, but it has given rise to a series of running debates. Four main areas of contention may be identified. One is service conditions, where there are complex interactions between the Defence Force and society at large and where greater activism inside and outside the ADF is very much in evidence. A second area concerns the impact which defence activities have on local communities. Changes in defence policy have brought proposals for major land acquisitions, for the transfer of RAN facilities from Sydney to Jervis Bay, for the creation of the new RAAF base at Tindal and so on. All such developments stimulate both local support and local opposition.[43] In addition, some uses of the armed forces by the government can produce or exacerbate political conflict. The so-called 'spy-flights' over Tasmania during the dams dispute in 1983 were a classic example of the ADF becoming entangled in a political dispute.

Other areas of public debate involve the ADF less directly. The US Alliance has attracted little opposition in the mass media and has the broad and continuing support of the population. But it does entail numerous forms of cooperation between Australian forces and their US counterparts. ADF facilities have been employed to assist the US in many ways, for example, the B-52 reconnaissance flights staged through Darwin, MX missile testing or visits by US warships - all matters which have attracted vocal opposition. Several hundred ADF personnel serve in the various US strategic communications facilities in Australia which are also targets for protest from time to time.

More broadly still, the peace movement in Australia has enjoyed something of a revival in the last decade. Fuelled by issues such as uranium mining, the US strategic communication facilities, visits by nuclear-powered and -armed ships, as well as wider issues like French nuclear testing, nuclear-free zones and the global arms race, the peace movement has gained the support of a vocal and persistent minority. It has received backing from scientists, academics and writers as well as some sections of the mainstream churches. It has seen the acceptance of peace education in many schools and the establishment of a Peace Research Centre at the Australian National University. In the 1984 election, the Nuclear Disarmament Party received 640,000 first preference votes in the Senate and, in the 1987 election, the anti-nuclear movement secured the election of a second Senator. The ADF itself has rarely been the target for peace activists, but many demonstrations, placards and slogans seen in recent years have carried a clear anti-military message which may one day be directed against Australian forces.

The Place of the Military in Australian Society

Australians do not consider themselves a war-like people, despite the fact that they have been at war for more than one year in three since Federation. War has been something which originates in Europe or Asia and which draws in Australia for reasons of historical attachment and strategic calculation. Australians have not gone to war out of national pride or ambition, though their performance on the battlefield has been occasion for favourable comparisons with other nations and, as in 1915, for a celebration of nationhood. But war, by and large, is treated as a job, a practical business. Australia's armed forces are seen as a necessity, but not a particularly welcome one.

Historically, the business of war has been regarded as a matter for all citizens. Until the formation of the Regular Army, citizen forces provided the bulk of Australia's military effort. Even since that time, the

National Service Scheme of 1951-59 and the selective conscription system of 1965-72 have ensured the presence of large numbers of citizen-soldiers in the Army. There remains in the community a hostility towards military values of the traditional, authoritarian kind and even a certain suspicion towards soldiering as a full-time career. It is an anti-militarism directed not at the individual soldier, or the ADF as such, but at the possibility that the business of war, and preparation for war, might be taken from the people and placed in the hands of an elite. It is an anti-militarism which might be termed 'democratic militarism' - a belief that all citizens should be able to take part in the business of war.[44]

Australia's military forces have, in fact, remained broadly representative of the wider society. The officer corps has been recruited from a variety of backgrounds and has steadily increased the number of women officers. It does not see itself as a superior caste set above the other ranks. Nor is the officer corps part of an 'establishment' as in those countries where strong links exist between government, a social elite and the military. Partly in consequence, the military profession does not enjoy a high status in Australia.[45] It is seen as a worthy occupation - provided it does not succumb to militarist values - but as one which enjoys no special merit or privilege. In the final analysis, most Australians believe any citizen could leave his peacetime occupation and fight in defence of the country.

At the same time, the ADF has developed in ways which reflect changes in the community at large. Greater attention is being paid to the education of the officer corps. New institutions have provided Service personnel with rights more akin to those of other citizens. The problems of Service families are being recognised and addressed. Commensurate with these changes, the ADF has adopted a higher profile in the political arena and in the community. Interaction between the armed forces and the community is more extensive than ever before in peacetime. Australia's defence force is an integral part of the society which sustains it, a fact of life which defence planners and strategists cannot ignore.

Endnotes

1   See Jane Ross, *The Myth of the Digger*, (Hale & Iremonger, Sydney, 1985), pp. 14-24.
2   This idea is discussed in K.S. Inglis, 'The ANZAC Tradition', *Meanjin Quarterly*, (Volume 24, Number 1), 1965, pp.25-44; and G. Serle, 'The Digger Tradition and Australian Nationalism', *Meanjin Quarterly*, (Volume 24, Number 2), 1965, pp.149-158.
3   Cited in S. Encel, *Equality and Authority*, (Cheshire, Melbourne, 1970), p.434.

4   N. McLachlan, 'Nationalism and the Divisive Digger', *Meanjin Quarterly*, (Volume 27, No.3), 1968, p.306. McLachlan argues that the 'digger' legend has been a profoundly divisive force in Australian society.

5   Details of the origins and activities of the Returned Services League can be found in G.L. Kristianson, *The Politics of Patriotism*, (Australian National University Press, Canberra, 1966); and P. Sekuless and J. Rees, *Lest We Forget*, (Rigby, Dee Why West, NSW, 1986).

6   See the speech introducing the legislation by the Minister for Labour and National Service, Harold Holt, reprinted in J.M. Main, *Conscription: The Australian Debate, 1901-70*, (Cassell Australia, Melbourne, 1970). Details of the scheme can be found in N.T. Shields, 'National Service Training, 1950-1959', in R. Forward and B. Reece (eds.), *Conscription in Australia*, (University of Queensland Press, St Lucia, 1968).

7   *Ibid.*, p.137.

8   Frank Frost, *Australia's War in Vietnam*, (Allen & Unwin, Sydney, 1987), p. 1. See also Jane Ross, 'Australian Soldiers in Vietnam: Product and Performance', in P. King (ed.), *Australia's Vietnam*, (Allen & Unwin, Sydney, 1983).

9   M. Goot and R. Tiffen, 'Public Opinion and the politics of the polls in *ibid.*, pp. 140-44. See also H.S. Albinski, *Politics and Foreign Policy in Australia: The Impact of Vietnam and Conscription*, (Duke University Press, Durham, North Carolina, 1970), pp. 193-202.

10   For details see M. van Gelder, 'Australia's Selective National Service Training Scheme 1965-72', *Defence Force Journal*, (No.19), November-December 1979, pp. 49-55.

11   Figures taken from the annual Department of Defence, *Defence Reports*, (Australian Government Publishing Service, Canberra).

12   Department of Defence, *Defence Report 1987-88*, (Australian Government Publishing Service, Canberra, 1988), p.108.

13   See the surveys conducted by Australian National Opinion Polls for the ADF: 'Community Attitudes Towards Australia's Defence Force', October 1980; 'Young People's Attitudes Towards Australia's Defence Force', September 1984; and 'Public Attitudes to Defence', September 1987.

14   Department of Defence, *Defence Report 1985-86*, (Australian Government Publishing Service, Canberra, 1986), p.141.

15   D. Campbell, *Australian Public Opinion on National Security Issues*, (Working Paper Number 1, Peace Research Centre, Australian National University, Canberra, 1986), pp.29-30.

16   Cathy Downes, *High Personnel Turnover: The Australian Defence Force is not a Limited Liability Company*, (Canberra Papers on Strategy and Defence No.44, Strategic and Defence Studies Centre, Australian National University, Canberra, 1988), Chapter 1; see also Joint Committee on Foreign Affairs, Defence and Trade, *Personnel Wastage in the Australian Defence Force - Report and Recommendations*.

17   There are, however, some difficulties in adjusting to civilian life. See D. Maclean, 'The Officer in Retirement: The Time of Transition', in H. Smith (ed.), *Perspectives on the Military Career*, (Department of Government, Faculty of Military Studies, University of New South Wales, Canberra, 1985).

18   B. Borman, 'Review: The Vietnam Veterans Ten Years On', *Australian and New Zealand Journal of Psychiatry*, (Vol.16, No.3), September 1982, pp.107-27.

19   For a discussion of these issues see Sue Hamilton, *Supporting Service Families: A Report on the Main Problems Facing Spouses of Australian Defence Force Personnel and Some Recommended Solutions*, (Department of Defence, Canberra, 1986); and H. Smith (ed.), *The Service Family*, (Department of Government, Faculty of Military Studies, University of New South Wales, Canberra, 1982).

20   N.A. Jans, *Careers in Conflict: Report of a Study of Service Officers' Careers and Families in Peacetime*, (Canberra College of Advanced Education, Canberra, 1988); and 'Main Findings of the Service Officers' Careers Studies', *Defence Force Journal*, (Number 65), July-August 1987, pp. 4-12.

21 Figures taken from the annual *Defence Reports*, (Australian Government Publishing Service, Canberra). The 1985-86 edition refers for the first time to 'Personnel Statistics' rather than 'Manpower Statistics'.

22 Minister for Defence, *News Release* No.93/87, 11 June 1987.

23 Minister for Defence, *News Release* No.7/85, 17 January 1985.

24 P.T.F. Gowans, 'The Armed Forces Federation of Australia: A Major Change in Direction in Defence Industrial Relations', *Journal of the Royal United Services Institute of Australia*, (Vol.8, No.2), June 1986, pp. 23-29. See also, G. Pratt, 'Institution, Occupation and Collectivism Amongst Australian Army Officers', *Journal of Political and Military Sociology*, (Vol.14, No.2), Fall 1986, pp. 291-302.

25 An ArFFA press release shortly before the July 1987 election pointed out that six of the government's most marginal seats had large service populations. *Press Release* PR 9/87, 3 July 1987.

26 G.L. Purcell, 'Perspectives on the New Discipline Legislation', *Defence Force Journal*, (No.52), May-June 1985, pp. 9-14.

27 J.C. Jordan, 'The Defence Force Ombudsman: Genesis, Expectations and Realisations', *Journal of the Royal United Services Institute of Australia*, (Vol.8, No.2), June 1986, pp. 43-50.

28 On the right of Service personnel injured in the course of their employment to sue the Commonwealth and other military personnel, see S. Miller, 'Soldier as a Citizen', *Defence Force Journal*, (No.33), March-April 1982, pp.14-15.

29 See Charles C. Moskos, 'From Institution to Occupation: Trends in Military Organisation', *Armed Forces and Society*, (Vol.4, No.1), November 1977, pp. 41-50; and 'Institutional/Occupational trends in Armed Forces: An Update', *Armed Forces and Society*, (Vol.12, No.3), Spring 1986, pp. 377-382.

30 B.D. Beddie and S. Moss, *Some Aspects of Aid to the Civil Power in Australia*, (Occasional Monograph Number 2, Department of Government, Faculty of Military Studies, University of New South Wales, Canberra, 1982), pp. 72-3.

31 The other instance was the call-out of the Pacific Islands Regiment in Papua New Guinea in 1969-71; in the event the troops were not used. Both episodes are examined in *ibid.*, pp. 51-72.

32 Mr Justice Hope, *Protective Security Review: Report*, (Australian Government Publishing Service, Canberra, 1979), pp. 156-67, 175-78.

33 C. Coulthard-Clark, 'The Military as Strikebreakers', *Pacific Defence Reporter*, (Vol.7, No.11), May 1981, pp.72-3.

34 B.D. Beddie and S. Moss, *Some Aspects of Aid to the Civil Power in Australia*, pp. 39-51.

35 For details see G. Brown, *The Australian Defence Force in Industrial Action Situations: Joint Service Plan 'Cabriole'*, (Working Paper No.115, Strategic and Defence Studies Centre, Australian National University, Canberra, 1986).

36 M.S. Unwin, 'Public Information and the Defence Perspective', in H. Smith (ed.), *Australians on Peace and War*, (Australian Defence Studies Centre, Australian Defence Force Academy, University College, Canberra, 1987) p. 36.

37 *Ibid.*, p.34.

38 See Derek Woolner, 'Parliamentary Debate on War and Peace', in H. Smith (ed.), *Australians on Peace and War*.

39 Senate Standing Committee on Constitutional and Legal Affairs, *Conscientious Objection to Conscripted Military Service*, (Australian Government Publishing Service, Canberra, 1985).

40 Senate Standing Committee on Foreign Affairs and Defence, *Land Acquisition in New South Wales by the Australian Army*, (First Report, Australian Government Publishing Service, Canberra, 1986).

41 Public Works Committee, *Report Relating to the Proposed Construction of a Defence Force Academy in the Australian Capital Territory*, (Australian Government Publishing Service, Canberra, 1979).

42 It was reported in the *National Times*, 25 January 1987, that Defence Minister Beazley's advisers had identified 12 marginal federal electorates containing at least 500 voters who were defence personnel or family members.

43   For an analysis of the relationship between a military base and the local community see H.C. Franklin, 'Townsville: Military Support for Communities', in J.O. Langtry and Desmond Ball (eds.), *A Vulnerable Country?Civil Resources in the Defence of Australia*, (Australian National University Press, Canberra, 1986), pp. 219-50.

44   H. McQueen, *A New Britannia*, (Penguin Books, Harmondsworth, 1970), pp.80-1.

45   P. Boreham, A. Pemberton and P. Wilson, *The Professions in Australia*, (Queensland University Press, St. Lucia, 1976).   The authors do not mention the military profession even in passing.   J. Higley, D. Deacon and D. Smart, *Elites in Australia*, (Routledge & Kegan Paul, London, 1979), contains no reference to the armed services as such, only to senior officials of the RSL.

SECURITY IN THE REGION

CHAPTER 18

NEW ZEALAND

Thomas-Durrell Young

Since the establishment of New Zealand as a colony of Great Britain with the signing of the Treaty of Waitangi in 1840, successive New Zealand governments have strongly adhered to a defence policy based upon the principle of collective security. Either within a British Imperial/Commonwealth framework, or *via* its early strong support for international security guarantees through the United Nations immediately following the Second World War, and later manifested by entering into the ANZUS treaty with Australia and the United States in 1951, a defence policy based on collective security has been a consistent and fundamental assumption supporting New Zealand's security posture. In view of New Zealand's 'security requirements', this policy choice has made sound political and financial sense. As a small, predominantly European country with a population of 3.3 million, with extensive trading links world-wide,[1] and a long tradition of global political interests, to unilaterally provide for the defence of these far-flung interests, let alone to attempt to effect the physical security of the country, could hardly be contemplated. While New Zealand officials have been at pains to discern specific threats during various periods of its history, limited resources and global interests have necessitated the reliance on powerful allies as the *sine qua non* in formulating defence policy.

It is only in light of the historical background that one can fully understand the implications for New Zealand's security which have resulted from the anti-nuclear policy initiatives of the fourth New Zealand Labour Government led by David Lange. In attempting to resolve domestic political exigencies (i.e., the strong anti-nuclear feelings in its party caucus and in some segments of the general population as well) the fourth Labour Government instituted a major change in direction from the traditional approach to defence policy. Despite claims by Government officials to the contrary, the fourth Labour Government altered greatly the conditions by which New Zealand can hope to pursue a policy of strict adherence to collective security with its traditional allies. The purpose of this chapter is to describe and analyse New Zealand's security policies and the posture of the New Zealand Defence Forces (NZDF), prior to the *de jure* end of the ANZUS diplomatic and defence relationships in August 1986. This chapter will then assess the future outlook for New Zealand's security options in light of the Labour Government's policies.

The ANZUS Defence Relationship

Despite the rather austere provisions of the 1951 ANZUS Treaty concerning defence cooperation between the three alliance partners, the defence relationship, which subsequently evolved from the early 1950s, was quite extensive. For a small country like New Zealand, with very limited financial resources to direct toward its defence forces of approximately 12,600 regulars, the ANZUS defence relationship was essential to enabling its armed forces to remain aligned to Western defence standards. At the heart of the ANZUS defence relationship was the principle that in view of the relatively favourable security environment of the Southwest Pacific region, the partners would conduct defence cooperation on the basis of alliance coordination, so as to rationalise their national efforts in defence security. In consequence, prior to the *de facto* break in New Zealand-United States security relations in February 1985,[2] defence cooperation was extensive and by association included the NZDF in numerous Anglo-Saxon standardization and defence cooperation programs and agreements.

In a general sense, the ANZUS defence relationship was unusual in comparison with most Western security arrangements in that there never developed within the alliance any form of bureaucratization. Nevertheless, prior to February 1985 there was an extensive series of regular consultations between Defence officials of the three countries for the purpose of managing defence cooperation (see Figure 1). At the operational level, the three countries had extensive arrangements for the maritime reconnaissance and surveillance of the Southwest Pacific and Eastern Indian oceans as established by the 1951 Radford-Collins and the 1977 ANZUS Maritime Surveillance Area (MARSAR) agreements.[3] The former agreement also provided the basis for contingency planning for the Allied naval control and protection of shipping in the region. For both Australia and New Zealand, close defence ties with the United States also enabled the development of an extensive logistic support relationship through the Foreign Military Sales Program of the individual Services of the US armed forces. This arrangement included assurances for support in contingent circumstances as outlined in the 1982 Memorandum of Understanding on Logistic Support between New Zealand and the United States. Because of the perennially limited financial resources available to the NZDF, these logistic support arrangements with the United States enabled New Zealand to prioritise finances for operational missions, over support requirements.

Figure 1: ANZUS-Sponsored Consultative Meetings

Name	Delegates	Frequency
ANZUS Council	Secretary of State/ Foreign Ministers	annual
ANZUS Military Representatives	CINCPAC/Australian and New Zealand Chiefs of (the) Defence Force (Staff)	annual
ANZUS Officials	Assistant Secretary of State/Foreign Affairs Secretaries and/or Ambassadors	annual
ANZUS Staff Level Meetings	Military delegations led by Brigadier (Equivalent)	semi-annual
ANZUS Seminar	Military delegations led by Colonel (Equivalent), with Major and Lieutenant (Equivalent) participation	semi-annual
ANZUS Exercise Planning Conference	Military working level delegations and held in conjunction with the ANZUS Seminar	annual
Ad hoc fora (e.g., ANZUS Communications Forum, 1984)	Military working-level delegations	as needed

The ability of the armed forces of the three countries to operate with each other, under combat conditions, was fostered through an extensive series of alliance-sponsored exercises, personnel and unit exchanges, and Service-to-Service cooperative arrangements. The results of these cooperative activities were synthesised into a series of ANZUS Documents which governed joint deployments between the three countries' defence forces.[4]

Moreover, the legal basis for defence cooperation with the United States also indirectly enabled the NZDF to attain membership and/or observer status in a series of Anglo-Saxon defence cooperative programs (commonly known as the 'ABCA' arrangements) which includes the ANZUS partners and the United Kingdom and Canada. The purpose of these numerous arrangements (see Figure 2) has largely been to ensure that the five countries' defence forces can operate and support each other should the need ever arise, in addition to rationalizing the individual efforts of the five countries to develop new

Figure 2: New Zealand Membership in Anglo-Saxon Defence/Security Cooperative Arrangements

Program	Status	Purpose
ABCA Armies Standardization Program	Member *via* the Australian Army	Effect doctrinal compatibility
ABCA Navies Standardization Program (Field Z)	Observer Status	Ensure material standardization to facilitate mutual support
Combined Communications-Electronics Board	Member	Ensure communications/electronics compatibility Publishes *Allied Communications Publications*
AUS-CAN-NZ-UK-US Naval Communications Organization	Member	Ensure naval communications (and more recently command and control) compatibility
Air Standardization Coordinating Committee	Member	Effect material, operational and doctrinal compatibility
The Technical Cooperation Committee	Member	Coordinates and encourages defence science research and development in non-nuclear fields
Combined Exercise Agreement	Member	Agreement governing maritime exercises between the five countries in the Pacific/Indian Oceans
UKUSA Treaty	Member	Agreement for signal intelligence cooperation

tactics, doctrines, operating procedures for weapon systems and platforms, etc. The degree to which the free exchange of information under these programs has been high is observed by the fact, for example, that information eligible for exchange extends up to and includes that at the *secret* level of security classification.[5]

In essence, the significance of ANZUS defence relations for New Zealand was twofold. First, the fact that such a high degree of defence cooperation was attained during a peacetime setting served to emphasise the close political alignment and acceptance of joint purpose at the strategic level between New Zealand and its Western allies. Second, the ANZUS defence relationship allowed the NZDF to maintain strict adherence to Western military standards with an ageing equipment inventory, while maintaining one of the lowest defence budgets of any Western Allied country.[6] These ANZUS and Anglo-Saxon defence arrangements provided New Zealand with the best of both worlds in terms of its defence requirements. Since these arrangements were based on the principles of the coordination and rationalisation of national defence efforts, New Zealand gained Allied status without the need to maintain a large order of battle, or to contribute large numbers of its forces to standing ANZUS formations. The sole exception to this rule was the responsibility of New Zealand to maintain a modern and sophisticated maritime surveillance and reconnaissance capability during peacetime.[7] New Zealand's responsibilities for the surveillance of its MARSAR in the South Pacific and this region's general low relevance to the central strategic balance, also resulted in probably the fewest number of port visits by US Navy ships and submarines of any formal US ally.[8] Finally, the ABCA arrangements enabled the NZDF to attain the benefits of defence cooperation with its closest allies, but through the safety and familiarity of these multilateral fora made up of Commonwealth nations; as a 1984 New Zealand Ministry of Defence document declared: the ANZUS defence relationship 'overcomes isolation'.[9]

Changes in Defence Policy

It is perhaps ironic then that in view of the *nature* of the ANZUS defence relationship, and the growing interest by the United States in the Southwest Pacific, as a result of Soviet diplomatic and commercial initiatives to the region during the mid-1980s, that ANZUS security cooperation abruptly came to an end at the period when it had reached its zenith and was becoming more important to the Western security system. The cause of the end of the ANZUS diplomatic and defence relationship was due to the now well-known anti-nuclear policies implemented by the fourth Labour Government. The Labour Party was elected in July 1984 on a campaign platform essentially focussing on economic issues, but also aiming to de-nuclearise New Zealand. Consequently, once in power, the Government stated that it would not allow into New Zealand ports warships which were either nuclear-propelled or capable of deploying nuclear armaments unless it could assure itself that such vessels were not carrying such armaments.[10] The central problem with this policy stance was that it directly challenged the US, British and French policies of neither confirming nor denying the presence of nuclear armaments aboard their ships or aircraft. To date no other US ally has questioned this policy.[11] The formal refusal by the Labour Government in February 1985 to allow an aged conventionally-powered US Navy destroyer to make a port call following the end of an ANZUS-sponsored exercise, because Cabinet could not discern for itself that the ASROC anti-submarine missile system carried by the warship was not nuclear-armed, led to what was to become the end of bilateral defence cooperation with the United States. Following 18 months of fruitless diplomatic exchanges to effect an agreement, the United States formally ended its security commitment to New Zealand and exchanged notes with Australia transforming the ANZUS treaty into a bilateral alliance,[12] albeit with the door left ajar for a future diplomatic *rapprochement*.

In regard to the particular aspects of defence policy advanced by the Labour Government, with two very important exceptions, Labour has continued the major defence themes which have typified the recent evolution in New Zealand's security orientation. As outlined by the 1987 Defence White Paper, the Government claimed that it intended to stand by its commitments to collective security arrangements, continue to redirect the orientation of the NZDF from meeting contingencies in Southeast Asia to the South Pacific (without the assumption of active allied support), improve the self-reliance of its Defence Forces, especially in the areas of logistics and supply support (traditional weaknesses in the NZDF), and work for a closer defence cooperative relationship with Australia.[13] The two principal areas of Labour defence policy which break with the past are the end of New Zealand's support for the concept of nuclear deterrence, and in effect, the disassociation of New Zealand in defence matters from the United States, and even the United Kingdom. In undertaking these fundamental changes, it should also be added that the Labour Government has also succeeded in ending the traditional bipartisan support which has long typified the defence debate in New Zealand.

In general, the implications for New Zealand defence policy as a result of the Government's anti-nuclear stance have been to end its previously close collective security association with the Western alliance system and to drastically limit national options in the defence field. Although some defence cooperation between New Zealand and the United States is still extant at the time of this writing (unspecified communications arrangements and New Zealand's continued membership in apparently all of the Anglo-Saxon defence standardization programs to which the NZDF has been a member), Wellington has become cut off from its principal security benefactor which in recent years has become the most important source for the NZDF in such areas as intelligence, modern defence technical information, assurance of logistic support, etc.

Problems Facing the NZDF

For the NZDF the break in defence ties with the United States could not have happened at a less opportune time. The Defence Forces have long been subject to neglect for reasons of finance, regardless of the political party in power. Since almost all of the NZDF's equipment requirements must be procured from overseas with perennially scarce foreign exchange, proposals for major armaments purchases have traditionally not received sympathetic hearing in Cabinet. For instance, the lack of financial investment in the NZDF and long-term planning by previous governments have resulted in a situation whereby the Royal New Zealand Navy (RNZN) and Royal New Zealand Air Force (RNZAF) are currently facing bloc obsolescence by the 1990s of their frontline weapon systems, i.e., *Leander*-class frigates[14] and *A-4G/K Skyhawk*[15] attack aircraft, while the New Zealand Army lacks many modern combat capabilities such as air defence.[16] Financial constraints have also greatly limited the procurement of modern weapons systems and particularly platforms (for example a naval transport/amphibious lift vessel) which would allow independent combined force deployments by the NZDF. Consequently, the Forces have had to make do with obsolescent equipment, and within a limited defence vote, approximately half of which is consumed by personnel costs. Since in recent years the NZDF has not had to stress developing forces capable of fighting in a high-intensity combat environment, let alone on its own, its relatively antiquated capital equipment and limited capabilities were more or less accepted by New Zealand's allies, particularly with the policy shift outlined in the 1978 Defence Review toward directing the orientation of the armed forces to the South Pacific region.[17]

What is unfortunate for the NZDF at the present juncture in its development, however, is related to the policy decision by the previous National Party government to make the South Pacific its prime area of defence activity. There were numerous compelling rationales for this redirection in New Zealand security policy which included the changing political conditions in the South Pacific and limited financial resources available for defence. As demonstrated by the 1987 Fijian military *coups*, some of the island states of the South Pacific are increasingly vulnerable to domestic turmoil. Additionally, Moscow has expressed a growing political interest in the region, although a permanent naval presence has not yet materialized. Clearly as well, New Zealand officials have been aware that membership in the Western alliance system carries the perhaps informal expectation that each member must be able to make a singular contribution to Western security, if reciprocity in terms of intelligence and technical information is expected. In view of New Zealand's geographic proximity to the South Pacific, its limited defence resources and the growing interest in the region by the Soviet Union have combined to make it an attractive and logical area for defence specialisation. This geographic orientation is facilitated by the fact that New Zealand has had historic political and defence ties to the region,[18] as well as Allied maritime security commitments there.

Yet, in order to achieve this goal of regional defence specialisation, close cooperation with its allies, particularly the United States has been needed. Given New Zealand's limited financial resources and small Defence Forces, the development of greater defence independence in national combined operations has necessitated Allied technical assistance. For example, for the NZDF to prepare doctrinally and choose the optimal defence hardware for independent operations in the South Pacific, it is essential, in terms of finances and resources, to have access to extant staff studies on such topics by their allies. Furthermore, because of the small sizes of the New Zealand Army and the RNZN both are incapable of developing independently operational doctrines and tactics since they need, *inter alia*, access to larger allied formations in order to test new operational concepts.[19]

A potentially more fundamental limitation to realising the goal of a credible regional defence capability with a greater degree of independence by the NZDF is in the area of logistic support, and perhaps surprisingly in view of the wide availability of weapon systems, the procurement of suitable weapon systems. As to the latter point, with New Zealand no longer considered as a formal US ally, the previous expedited procedure for approving arms purchases from US contractors has been lost. This has been demonstrated in RNZAF's $NZ140 million contract with the US firm Lear Siegler for the modernisation of its 22 *A4G/KI Skyhawks*. Such agreements are now subject to a potentially lengthy Congressional approval process in addition to the possibility of disapproval.[20] Although the United States is not the sole possible arms supplier for New Zealand, it is certainly the most logical source for follow-on logistic support, particularly in light of its geographic position and meagre defence supply holdings.[21]

The break in the previously close defence relationship with the United States has destroyed as well the process by which the NZDF have been able to procure supply support from the United States under favourable terms accorded to formal allies. The 1982 Memorandum of Understanding of Logistic Support enabled the NZDF to continue to maintain their traditionally meagre stock holdings by providing *assurances* of follow-on logistic support from the United States in times of international tension, contingent circumstances and general war. While it is the case that the NZDF will most likely be able to obtain whatever matériel and supplies they desire from American sources through commercial contracts or via the Foreign Military Sales Program, the previous assurance of reliability of supply support has been lost. In February 1987, the United States served notice to New Zealand that when this memorandum came up for review in June of that year, it would be allowed to lapse.[22] Considering the important provisions for continued and favourable access to US supply stocks, Defence Minister Frank O'Flynn's ill-considered comment that the termination of this memorandum would have little effect on the NZDF must be held as simply nonsense.[23] Without this memorandum, New Zealand now lacks the assurances necessary to base its defence policy on a higher degree of independence, unless it moves to significantly expand its own support structure and stock holdings. The proposition of increasing New Zealand stocks will be a very expensive undertaking and difficult since New Zealand defence planners have to now attempt to anticipate specific operational requirements and, therefore, project levels of stock holdings which will be challenging at best considering the generally favourable security environment of the South Pacific. Conversely, a closer defence supply relationship with Australia is not without its own particular limitations. Australia's own support and supply structures are themselves limited[24] and perhaps more disconcerting from a New Zealand perspective, the terms of the US Arms Export Control Act prohibit the transfer from Australia to New Zealand of equipment and/or supplies of US manufacture without US Presidential approval.[25] Self-reliance and a credible regional defence orientation for the NZDF, exclusive of the ANZUS defence relationship, therefore, have significant obstacles to overcome.

ANZAC Defence Cooperation

Notwithstanding the problems associated with Australian-New Zealand defence supply cooperation, the loss of close defence ties with the United States has left Wellington with little other choice than to opt for closer defence relations with Canberra. There have long existed close defence ties between the two countries, which have grown substantially since the early-1970s, especially in the areas of consultations (see Figure 3), joint exercises, personnel and unit training exchanges,[26] cooperation in maritime surveillance, intelligence, and defence supply. Indeed, the

Figure 3: Major Australian-New Zealand Defence Consultative Meetings

Name	Delegates	Frequency
Australian-New Zealand Defence Meeting	Delegations led by Ministers of (for) Defence	annual (as a general rule)
Australian-New Zealand Defence Consultative Committee (Joint Coordinating Committee)	Secretaries of Defence/Chiefs of (the) Defence Force (Staff)	annual (as a general rule)
Australian-New Zealand Defence Policy Group	Delegations of senior service and Defence officials	annual/semi-annual
Australian-New Zealand Combined Working Group on Defence Supply	Delegations of senior service, Defence, and Trade and Industry officials	semi-annual
Australian-New Zealand Joint Exercise Committee	Australian Director of Joint Planning/ New Zealand Director of Defence Operations, Training and Plans, and the Deputy Director of Training	semi-annual

move toward closer antipodean defence cooperation is long overdue and in certain areas, such as the joint procurement of equipment and cooperative logistics, greater defence cooperation between the two countries makes sound sense. Nevertheless, substantial obstacles to closer bilateral defence cooperation are obvious. As noted by Ross Babbage, the New Zealand Government's actions regarding the ANZUS alliance have produced the most serious questioning yet to the concept that Australia and New Zealand share a single strategic environment,[27] as given such prominence in the 1983 New Zealand Defence White Paper.[28] It is also difficult to see how the New Zealand Government, which has disclaimed any connection whatsoever with the world strategic balance and nuclear weapons, can reconcile the fact that its closest defence ally, Australia, remains closely tied to the United States in the defence field, which, by virtue of the joint communications and intelligence facilities, includes active participation in the maintenance of the strategic balance. Given the limited Australian defence budget, if choices have to be made by Canberra between its two closest allies, for example, exercising with the US armed forces (which the Australian Defence Force requires) or the NZDF, the choice which will be taken is obvious.[29]

Fundamentally, the problem Wellington faces in attempting to effect greater security cooperation in Canberra, is that the terms of the relationship have been shifted in Australia's favour. In the past, possible Australian domination of the bilateral relationship has been tempered by the fact that with close defence ties with the United States and even Britain, New Zealand had a range of options. Without the previously close defence relationship with the United States and as Britain continues to orient its defence resources to the Western European theatre of operations, the New Zealand Government's policies have limited New Zealand's defence options to the Australian context. Without assurances of follow-on logistic support from its traditional arms suppliers, the United States and the distance from the United Kingdom, one can expect the NZDF to turn progressively more to Australian-manufactured equipment, despite the higher costs traditionally associated with these equipments in order to obtain a limited degree of assurance of follow-on support from Australian industry. Since it is unlikely that the present or a future New Zealand government, irrespective of political persuasion, will move to significantly increase defence outlays to make up for higher equipment costs, the overall level of defence resources for other activities (e.g., operations, overseas training, etc.), will have to decrease.

Outlook

The implications of Labour's security policies for New Zealand's defence posture, therefore, are not encouraging. The most important effect of the Government's policies has been to cast serious doubts over New Zealand's previous commitment to collective security and the Western alliance. By implication, the Government's actions have made New Zealand's status within the Western alliance system ambiguous at best.[30] The United States Administration has made it quite clear that it cannot, and will not, conduct defence relations with New Zealand as a formal ally as long as US Navy vessels are restricted from New Zealand ports by virtue of the anti-nuclear policy. This policy decision has not been without its own particular problems for the United States since in view of many issues in which the two countries strongly agree (e.g., exclusion of the Soviet Union from the South Pacific), Washington has yet to decide how future defence cooperation with New Zealand will be conducted. For the immediate future, however, defence cooperation from the perspective of the United States will be done solely on a case by case basis.[31] Even given a return to power of the National Party or a change to a more accommodating Labour Government, it is unlikely that the United States would agree to a return to the defence relationship *ante* February 1985.

Unfortunately for New Zealand, the anti-nuclear policies of the Government have had the effect of politicizing the ANZUS defence relationship in Washington to a degree to which it has never experienced before. With the decision by the Reagan Administration to restrict defence cooperation with New Zealand in February 1985, it first had to initiate an 'audit' of sorts to discern exactly where cooperation was extant since the non-bureaucratised nature in which defence business had theretofore been conducted resulted in an extremely decentralised security relationship. Now that Washington is generally privy to the extent to which the previous defence relationship had been allowed to grow (largely without direct political oversight and at the working level), efforts to return to the *status quo ante* will be allowed only on the terms acceptable to the United States.[32] Probably most unencouraging of all in terms of the prospect of the re-establishment of full alliance defence ties is the fact that it would be fallacious to assume that Washington would be willing to consider rebuilding a defence relationship with a country which could be prone to the reintroduction of anti-nuclear restrictions which would again challenge the basis for the continued workings of defence cooperation. In brief, the actions of the Government have seriously cast doubt on the reliability and consistent political character of New Zealand as an ally.

The question of New Zealand reliability as an ally has also extended across the Tasman. Officials in the Australian Government have, on numerous occasions, stated their outright disagreement in public with its New Zealand counterparts over the anti-nuclear ship visit policy. The most serious questioning of New Zealand's continued status as a Western ally can be found in Australian Defence Minister Kim Beazley's statement to Parliament of 20 February 1987.[33] In that statement Minister Beazley stated that the Australian Defence Force would begin to pay greater attention to the South Pacific and deploy more maritime air and surface surveillance units to the region. For example, deployments of Royal Australian Air Force P-3C *Orion* long-range maritime patrol aircraft to the region alone are to be doubled from five to ten missions a year. What is of singular import in Beazley's statement is that the region to which he refers has traditionally been a New Zealand responsibility, as delineated by the 1951 Radford-Collins and 1977 ANZUS MARSAR agreements.[34] As Mr Beazley's announcement was made in the full knowledge of the contents of the New Zealand defence review with its stress on a greater regional defence, and which was made one week *prior* to the release of the New Zealand White Paper, Australia's action should be interpreted as manifesting displeasure with the direction in Wellington's security policy and questioning New Zealand's reliability as an ally. Despite Mr Beazley's claims that Australian surveillance efforts would be coordinated with New Zealand, as has been previously governed by a 1975 agreement,[35] it is clear that New Zealand is now being treated as an object, rather than as a subject as it has in the past. It probably would not be going too far to state that New Zealand no longer enjoys full membership in the Radford-Collins[36] and ANZUS MARSAR agreements. With Australia desirous of playing a greater defence role in the South Pacific and given the limited capabilities of the NZDF which will doubtless remain, New Zealand's defence efforts are likely to become seen as an appendage to that of Australia as closer Trans-Tasman defence cooperation grows. After all, without Allied status as it had under ANZUS, and limited national defence capabilities, New Zealand will hardly be in a position to hope to negotiate the terms upon which defence cooperation will take place.

Of course, the above assessment of the future outlook on New Zealand's security policies cannot but have serious repercussions on New Zealand's diplomatic relations with its regional neighbours, let alone its geographically distant traditional friends. With New Zealand's clear dependence on Australia for security and defence-related matters, and with Canberra's increased interest in the region in addition to its greater financial resources, why should regional Pacific island states consider New Zealand as important in a regional diplomatic context? With Australia's greater political interest and defence activities in the South Pacific proper, future New Zealand governments will find it more difficult, over time, to provide a unique contribution to Western security. This in itself must be interpreted as weakening any future New Zealand attempt to restore the *status quo ante* February 1985.

In the final analysis, the current New Zealand Government has succeeded in achieving, perhaps by default, the central diplomatic condition successive post-war New Zealand governments of both political parties have for so long fought strongly against: an ambiguous status in the Western alliance system and a foreign policy bordering on isolationism from its traditional friends and allies.[37] The major challenge to future New Zealand governments must be to attempt to re-establish a semblance of its once close association with the Western alliance system *via* ANZUS, but within the obvious limitations of domestic New Zealand political exigencies.

Endnotes

1 'Exports are vital to our economy - in 1986 exports of goods and services as a share of GDP amounted to 23 per cent', *Appendix to the Journal of the House of Representatives*, (AJHF), 1987, G.4a; see also Ministry of Defence, *Defence of New Zealand - Review of Defence Policy 1987*, (New Zealand Government Printer, Wellington, 1987), p.26.
2 *New York Times*, 6 February 1985.
3 See, for example, Thomas-Durrell Young, 'Australia Bites off More than the RAN Can Chew', *Pacific Defence Reporter*, (Vol.12, No.9), March 1986, pp.15-17.
4 The mechanics of defence cooperation between the two countries is outlined in New Zealand Ministry of Defence, *Background Briefs for Minister of Defence*, (Wellington, July 1984), Brief 2, 'ANZUS', *passim*.
5 Information available on the ABCA arrangements is scarce, albeit extant. See *Army Research, Development and Acquisition Magazine*, (Vol.23 No.1), January-February 1982, *passim*; Australian Army, *American, British, Canadian, Australian Armies (ABCA) - Standardization Program*, (Canberra, n.d.); J.F. Koek, 'A Guide for International Military Standardization: ABC Armies' Operational Concept, 1986-1995', *Defence Force Journal*, (No.5), July-August 1977, pp.51-55; *The Air Standardization Coordinating Committee*, (ASCC Management Committee, Washington, DC, 1984); John K. Walker, *Responses-Synopsis of Questionnaires and Some Observations - Air Standardization Coordinating Committee*, (The RAND Corporation, Santa Monica, California, April 1982); *ABCA Navies Field Z Management Manual*, Part 1: General, (Naval Quadripartite Standardization Office, Washington, DC, 1984); Robert Howell, 'Aus-Can-What?', *Signal*, (Vol.37 No.1), (September 1982), pp.35-37; and *AUS-CAN-NZ-UK-US Naval Communications Organization*, (Permanent Secretariat, NAVCOMMS Organization, Washington, DC).
6 Defence expenditures as a percentage of GNP in New Zealand have had difficulty maintaining a 2 per cent level since the early 1980s. In 1985, for example, New Zealand defence expenditures as a percentage of GNP was 1.9 per cent, as compared to 2.9 per cent for Australia and 6.6 per cent for the United States. See US Arms Control and Disarmament Agency, *World Military Expenditures and Arms Transfers*, (U.S. Government Printing Office, Washington, DC), various years.
7 David Filer makes the perceptive observation that funds have been forthcoming from New Zealand governments in the 1960s for this requirement. See David Filer, *The New Zealand Armed Services: Their Development in Relation to Defence Policy, 1946-1972*, (MA Thesis, University of Canterbury, Christchurch, 1972), pp.98-99, 130-131.
8 In 1981, four US Navy vessels visited New Zealand; in 1982 the number of visits dropped to two; and, in 1983, only one US warship did so. In contrast, twelve US nuclear-propelled attack submarines paid visits to one RAN base, HMAS *Stirling*, in 1982. See Desmond Ball, 'The ANZUS Connection: The Security Relationship Between Australia, New Zealand and the United States', in T.J. Hearn (ed.), *Arms, Disarmament and New Zealand*, (Department of University Extension, University of Otago, Dunedin, 1983), pp.66, 69.
9 New Zealand, *Background Briefs*, Brief 2 'ANZUS', p.7.
10 These diplomatic developments are documented in, Michael McKinley, *The ANZUS Alliance and New Zealand Labour*, (Canberra Studies in World Affairs No.20, Department of International Relations, Australian National University, Canberra, 1986), pp.33-49.
11 See US Congress, House of Representatives, Committee on Foreign Affairs, Subcommittee on Asian and Pacific Affairs, *Security Treaty between Australia, New Zealand, and the United States*, (U.S. Government Printing Office, Washington, DC, 1985), pp.155-156.
12 See the Exchange of Notes between the United States and Australia in Department of Foreign Affairs, *Backgrounder*, (538), 20 August 1986, pp.XII-XIV.

13   New Zealand Ministry of Defence, *Defence of New Zealand - Review of Defence Policy 1987*, p.31.

14   See Thomas-Durrell Young, 'New Zealand's Dilemmas', *United States Naval Institute Proceedings*, (111/8/990), August 1985, pp.5056.

15   See Thomas-Durrell Young, 'New Zealand Air Power Requirements and Force Determinants', *Air University Review*, (Vol.37 No.3), May 1986, pp.82-92.

16   See Thomas-Durrell Young, 'New Zealand Army', *The Army Quarterly and Defence Journal*, (Vol.115 No.3), July 1985, pp.272-276.

17   New Zealand Ministry of Defence, *Defence Review 1978*, p.7.

18   See B.M. Poananga, 'New Zealand and the South Pacific: Defence and Strategic Questions', in *New Zealand and the South Pacific*, (Department of University Extension, University of Otago, Dunedin, 1981), pp.43-50.

19   See New Zealand, *Background Briefs*, Brief 2 'ANZUS', p.4; and New Zealand Ministry of Defence, *ANZUS Exercises*, (Wellington, n.d.).

20   See the *Evening Post* (Wellington), 27 February 1986.

21   It was reported in the New Zealand press in 1986 that the NZDF had war reserves stock for only two days in cases of 'sustained' contingencies. See Simon O'Dwyer-Russell, 'End of the Road for ANZUS?', *Jane's Defence Weekly*, (Vol.6 No.7), 23 August 1986, p.231.

22   *Washington Post*, 3 February 1987.

23   *Evening Post* (Wellington), 4 February 1987.

24   T.B. Millar writes that Australian reserves are adequate for only short periods and in low level situations. T.B. Millar, 'Australian Defence Policies in the 1980s', in Desmond Ball (ed.), *The ANZAC Connection*, (George Allen & Unwin, Sydney, 1985), p.31.

25   Section 3 (c) (1) (A) (ii) of Public Law 90-629, as amended.

26   In 1986, for example, 70 per cent of the NZDF's overseas training took place in Australia. *AJHR* 1986 G. 4. *Defence*, p.9.

27   Ross Babbage, 'The Future of the Australia-New Zealand Defence Relations', (Paper delivered at the seminar on New Zealand Defence Policy, Victoria University of Wellington, 9 December 1986), p.9.

28   *AJHR* 1983 G. 4a, *Defence Review 1983*, pp.16-17.

29   A point stated by the then Australian Foreign Minister Mr Hayden during a very well publicised trip to New Zealand in December 1986 where he strongly criticised the Government for its anti-nuclear stand. See the *Press* (Christchurch), 16 December 1986; and the *Dominion* (Wellington), 16 December 1986.

30   It is interesting to note that the Government has gone to great pains to explain that it does not wish to withdraw from the Western alliance system and remains committed to ANZUS - but only in the conventional field. See *Selection of Recent Foreign Policy Statements by the New Zealand Prime Minister and Minister of Foreign Affairs, Rt. Hon. David Lange*, Information Bulletin No.11, (Ministry of Foreign Affairs, Wellington, March 1985), *passim*.

31   See Deputy Assistant Secretary of Defense Karl D. Jackson's statement in US Congress, House of Representatives, Committee on Foreign Affairs, Subcommittee on Asian and Pacific Affairs, *United States Policy Toward New Zealand and Australia*, (U.S. Government Printing Office, Washington, DC, 1987), pp.21-22.

32   See Thomas-Durrell Young, 'What Hope for ANZUS Now?', *Jane's Defence Weekly*, (Vol.6 No.20), 22 November 1986, p.1228.

33   Minister for Defence Kim C. Beazley, MP, Ministerial Statement on Defence Initiatives in the South Pacific, 20 February 1987.

34   New Zealand's region of maritime responsibility is generally within 170° East and 160° West and from just south of the equator to the Antarctica. See Filer, *The New Zealand Armed Services*, p.141; New Zealand Ministry of Defence, Defence Scientific Establishment, *DSE Annual Report 1985-1986*, DSE Misc. 86/1 (Auckland, April 1986), p.36; and the *Star* (Christchurch), 11 February 1985.

35   This agreement was a product of the 1975 Australian-New Zealand Ministerial Defence Meeting which includes provisions for the transfer of operational control of

surveillance platforms to the other country in certain circumstances. See 'Ministerial Joint Communique on Australia-New Zealand Defence Cooperation, 1975', in *Australian Foreign Affairs Record*, (Vol.46 No.7), July 1975, p.419.

36 The 1987 Defence White Paper's discussion of the protection of New Zealand trade is far from reassuring. The question of the vulnerability of New Zealand's shipping 'is lessened by the fact that New Zealand's world trade is very diversified. It can therefore be concluded that although New Zealand is heavily dependent on overseas trade, the diversified nature of this trade, the spread of overseas markets, and the additional factor of the number of export ports serving our overseas trade, means that any substantial interdiction of our trade would pose difficulties for any aggressor'. *AJHR* 1987 *Defence of New Zealand*, pp.26-27. Why would the White Paper go to such lengths to argue that New Zealand's sea communications are effectively secure without national or Allied contingent arrangements unless the Royal New Zealand Navy is no longer a member of the Radford-Collins agreement?

37 A most comprehensive assessment of the Labour Government's handling of defence policy and relations with New Zealand's allies is found in the findings of the Corner Committee. See Report of the Defence Committee on Enquiry, *Defence and Security: What New Zealanders Want*, (Government Printer, Wellington, 1986).

CHAPTER 19

INDONESIA AND THE SECURITY OF AUSTRALIA AND PAPUA NEW GUINEA*

Harold Crouch

Indonesia has always entered into the defence calculations of both Australia and Papua New Guinea (PNG). At times Indonesia itself has been perceived as a threat, while at other times the islands of the Indonesian archipelago have been seen as stepping stones for a possible invasion originating further to the north. In contrast to the 1950s and 1960s, however, Australian governments during the last decade-and-a-half have down-played possible external threats - whether from Indonesia or anywhere else.[1] PNG, in contrast, has sometimes shown considerable nervousness about the intentions of its nearest neighbour and in 1983, the PNG Minister for Defence Mr Epel Tito said that he expected an Indonesian invasion 'in the next ten to twenty years'.[2] Although Tito was quickly moved to another ministry and his statement disavowed by the Prime Minister, his worries were shared by many PNG leaders. In 1984, for example, Mr Aron Noaio claimed during a parliamentary debate that 'Indonesia plans to take over Papua New Guinea', and asked: 'What will we do when the Indonesians kill all the West Irianese and come across our border?'[3]

The fears expressed from time to time by PNG leaders have been felt also by a not insignificant part of the Australian public. Public opinion polls have shown a growth in the proportion of people identifying Indonesia as a likely threat to Australian security. Of the 52 per cent in 1968 who were worried about an external threat, only 6 per cent identified Indonesia as the threat and Indonesia ranked fourth after China, Vietnam and the Soviet Union.[4] However, in 1986, although only 40 per cent expected that Australia would face a military threat in the next ten years, Indonesia was viewed as the likely enemy by 31 per cent of that 40 per cent compared with 21 per cent who were concerned about the Soviet Union and much less in the case of other countries.[5]

The popular perception of Indonesia as a potential security threat arises in part from differences in size and the not unusual wariness of small countries which happen to have large neighbours.

---

* A first version of this chapter was presented at the 13th National Conference of the Australian Institute of International Affairs in Melbourne, 14-16 March 1986. A revised version appeared in *Australian Outlook*, (Vol.40.No.3), December 1986, pp.167-174.

Indonesia's population of 160 million dwarfs Australia's 16 million and PNG's 3.5 million, while its armed forces of 292,000 far outnumber Australia's 70,000 and PNG's 3,000. Further, public fears have been aggravated by common perceptions of Indonesia's past behaviour. During the early 1960s Indonesia, under the leadership of President Sukarno, was usually portrayed as an expansionist power which had acquired West Irian and wanted to take parts of Malaysia. Public opinion had little understanding of Indonesia's arguments in support of its claim to West Irian, or the extremely complex set of circumstances that lay behind the confrontation campaign. The fall of Sukarno and the establishment of the New Order produced a less belligerent public image of the Indonesian government, partly because of the breaking of ties with China and the new, warmer relationship with the West. But old fears were revived in 1975 when Indonesia's invasion of East Timor contributed to the belief that it might one day turn its attention to its southeastern neighbours.

The perception of Indonesia as a potential threat has often been combined with the belief that Indonesia's leaders have been - and perhaps still are - somehow irrational and unpredictable in their behaviour. Both Sukarno and Suharto have sometimes been portrayed as 'mystical Javanese' whose political goals have an inscrutable logic of their own which cannot be understood by rational Western observers. It is feared that Indonesia's Javanese leaders are motivated by a deeply embedded yearning to recreate a kind of idealist vision of the 14th-century *Majapahit* empire in which Java would regain her predominance over neighbouring lands. In support of the view that Indonesia is inherently and irrationally expansionist, it is common to cite the three occasions when Indonesia has taken offensive military action outside her internationally recognised borders. It is interesting to note that General Suharto played a major role in all three cases - as military commander of the West Irian campaign, deputy commander of the confrontation campaign and president when Indonesia invaded East Timor.

The historical record, however, does not give much support for the idea of inherent Indonesian expansionism. Indonesia's policymakers, like those of virtually all other countries, have in fact been guided by more-or-less rational assessments of alternative courses of action and their consequences. All of Indonesia's previous military ventures beyond its own borders had definite immediate objectives and the means chosen, although sometimes proving ineffective in practice, were not obviously inappropriate. Each of the three cases arose from special circumstances and, if history is a guide, provide little support for the conclusion that Indonesia is bent on expansionism and that Indonesian policy is fundamentally irrational.

The West Irian campaign in the early 1960s was a very special case from the Indonesian point of view. Like nationalist movements elsewhere, the Indonesian nationalists claimed the right to inherit the entire territory previously held by the colonial power which, in Indonesia's case, included West Irian. From the Indonesian perspective, the campaign for the 'return' of West Irian was aimed at completing the anti-colonial revolution. The fact that the Irianese were culturally different to the Javanese was seen as no more relevant than the cultural differences between the Javanese and the Acehnese, the Bataks, the Ambonese and the various tribes of Kalimantan. Whether one accepts the Indonesian claim or not, it clearly did not involve external territories.

The *Konfrontasi* campaign against Malaysia, which was launched in 1963, was an entirely different matter but it too offered little evidence to support the view that Indonesia had long-term expansionist goals.[6] Whatever the complex reasons for the campaign - which were as much related to the domestic struggle for power as to external objectives - the goal was not to acquire Sabah and Sarawak for Indonesia. At no time during the campaign did Indonesian forces attempt to occupy these territories. The military's role in the campaign was largely limited to forays by company-sized units into East Malaysian territory where they stayed for a few days before withdrawing again. Indonesia's goal was to break up the Malaysian federation which it regarded as a 'neo-colonial project' imposed by the British in order to prolong their influence in Southeast Asia. Military action by Indonesia was designed, quite rationally in view of the balance of forces, not to occupy Malaysian territory, but to increase the costs for the British in maintaining their position.

It is only the invasion of East Timor in 1975 which seems to give some grounds for fears of expansionism on Indonesian's part. Unlike the case of West Irian, Indonesia had no historical claim to East Timor and, unlike the case of *Konfrontasi*, Indonesia did in fact occupy territory beyond her border and eventually incorporated that territory into the Indonesian state. But did the East Timor case indicate an inherent, irrational urge to expand or was it a rational response to particular circumstances? Several considerations influenced Indonesia's policy towards East Timor but the most basic was its concern that an independent East Timor might become a regional 'Cuba'. It was feared that a government might come to power in East Timor which would adopt an anti-Indonesian stance and perhaps cooperate with other powers hostile to Indonesia in activities harmful to Indonesian security.[7] It could be argued, therefore, that Indonesia might not have intervened militarily if she had been convinced that a strong, stable government in East Timor would establish close and permanent ties with Indonesia, but developments in East Timor during 1974 and 1975 made the emergence of such a government unlikely. Thus, Indonesia intervened in order to ensure that East Timor did not come under a government hostile to Indonesia which might have allied itself with countries such as Vietnam, the Soviet Union or China. The Indonesian government's assessments of developments in East Timor and their likely consequences for Indonesia's own security can, of course, be questioned and its disregard for the rights of the people of East Timor can be condemned, but there appear to be no grounds for viewing the occupation of East Timor as a step in a plan of expansionism which will eventually cover other areas as well. Indonesia was motivated primarily by concern for its own security which it saw as potentially threatened by the possible outcome of developments in East Timor and it acted rationally - in terms of its own objectives - to deal with the threat.

Indonesia's past policies have never been motivated by a simple desire to acquire new territories and there are no grounds for expecting that such objectives are likely to be adopted in the future. The historical record, however, does show that Indonesia has been willing to project military power beyond its own borders when this was believed necessary to achieve what was considered a vital national objective. In taking military measures of this sort, Indonesia was not, needless to say, acting in an unusual way by international standards. To recognise this, however, does not necessarily imply approval of these actions or indicate a lack of concern about the possibility of similar moves in the future. But it is important to avoid confusing general expansionism with limited military measures designed to achieve defined objectives arising from particular circumstances.

The type of military action that any country might take is of course limited by its military capacity. The Indonesian Army was formed in 1945 as a guerrilla force to fight Dutch colonialism and this experience continues to influence military doctrine to this day. Poorly trained and ill-equipped, the Indonesian forces had no alternative to guerrilla warfare which required heavy reliance on local inhabitants. After independence, the Indonesian military continued to be poorly equipped, although efforts were made to re-organise the armed forces and train its officers. In these circumstances, the military leaders realised that the armed forces could not possibly prevent an attack by a well-equipped aggressor so the guerrilla doctrines of the revolutionary period were retained. In the event of an attack, the invader would be allowed to land while the armed forces would retreat to the hinterland where the people would be mobilised. As in the revolution, the

Indonesian forces would carry out guerrilla warfare against the enemy on the calculation that he would eventually find the occupation too costly and withdraw. The basic defence doctrine of the Indonesian armed forces was that of 'Territorial Warfare'. This doctrine required that the Defence Forces, especially the Army, be organised principally along 'territorial' rather than 'functional' lines. The whole nation was divided into territorial commands more or less parallel to the civilian administration. In terms of defence doctrine, a major function of the territorial commands was to maintain contact with the local people so that they could be mobilised quickly to support guerrilla operations, whenever necessary. It may be added, of course, that this territorial structure has also been very convenient for the purpose of political control. Under the territorial warfare doctrine, the main emphasis was on the Army and also the police rather than the Navy and Air Force. The full implementation of this doctrine would have left the armed forces with little capacity for operations beyond Indonesia's borders.

In the early 1960s, the West Irian and Malaysian campaigns required substantial reformation of the territorial warfare doctrine. Operations beyond Indonesia's borders required greater mobility and a larger role for the Navy and Air Force than envisaged in the original doctrine. Supported by aid from the Soviet Union, Indonesia acquired modern ships and aeroplanes while the Army expanded in size and placed greater emphasis on mobile 'functional' units created with the special purpose of carrying out the two campaigns. However, the fall of Sukarno and the collapse of the Guided Democracy system saw the abandonment of *Konfrontasi* and the re-emergence, almost by default, of the territorial warfare doctrine as the basis of defence policy. The new government's emphasis on economic development meant that the armed forces were starved of funds. Modern weapons could no longer be purchased and most of the Navy's ships and the Air Force's aircraft fell into disrepair due to lack of spare parts from the Soviet Union. Meanwhile the Army concentrated fully on its internal security role.

It was only in the 1970s that Indonesia began again to upgrade its conventional capacity. Under the Guam Doctrine announced by President Nixon in 1969, the US placed greater emphasis on building up the armed forces of friendly Asian states, including Indonesia. In the early 1970s, the US provided transport and counter-insurgency aircraft as well as several frigates which had seen service in the Vietnam war. But by the late 1970s, Indonesia's capacity to fight a conventional war remained extremely limited. For example, at the end of the 1970s, Indonesia's air-defence force consisted of sixteen out-of-date Australian-provided *Avon Sabre* fighters while the Navy had three Soviet-made submarines and eleven obsolescent frigates, four of which were about to be withdrawn from service. That the Indonesian military was by no means in good shape was demonstrated most clearly after 1975 when Indonesian forces, overwhelmingly superior in both numbers and armaments, faced serious difficulties in dealing with the Fretilin resistance in East Timor. Reportedly some 20,000 to 30,000 soldiers were required for the Timor campaign and casualties were said to be very high.

The debacle experienced by Indonesian forces in Timor seems to have led to some re-thinking among senior officers about the need to improve the military's fighting capacity. This re-thinking was reinforced by the changing strategic environment in Southeast Asia following the communist victories in Indochina in 1975. Before 1975, there was no real concern in Indonesia about the possibility of Indonesian territory being threatened by aggression from the North. But the American departure from Indochina and the closure of US bases in Thailand removed an important check on Vietnamese power. Despite its very limited naval capacity, Vietnam already had the most powerful military force in Southeast Asia, a fact that was underlined by its occupation of Kampuchea and brief war with China in 1979. Indonesia did not primarily fear a direct attack on Indonesian territory and indeed many Indonesian officers continued to regard Vietnam as a buffer against China rather than a threat against Indonesia. Nevertheless, there was some concern in Indonesian military circles that Vietnam might behave aggressively against Indonesia's ASEAN friends, especially Thailand, and, more importantly from Indonesia's point of view, that disputed territorial claims in the South China Sea might escalate into more serious conflict. Although Indonesia's possession of the Natuna Islands was never in dispute, Vietnam and Indonesia have conflicting claims to part of the Sea which is believed to be oil-bearing. The possibility of conflict with Vietnam in the South China Sea was an important stimulus to Indonesia's increased weapons acquisition program in the early 1980s, especially the expansion of the Air Force and Navy.

It so happened that the changing strategic environment of the late 1970s coincided with the availability of funds. The Islamic revolution in Iran had produced the second world oil 'shock' in the form of a sharp rise in oil prices. Indonesia's foreign exchange earnings increased rapidly and the country was awash with funds which the economy could not easily absorb. While the civilian technocrats in the government would have preferred to invest the surplus funds abroad, military leaders regarded the oil-price increases as a golden opportunity to acquire the modern armaments which they believed were necessary to modernise the armed forces. In this intra-bureaucratic tussle, the military largely had its way, and defence expenditure rose sharply from US$1.47 billion in 1979 to US$2.87 billion in 1982-83, with both the Navy and the Air Force acquiring significant new capabilities.8

The Air Force was one of the main beneficiaries of the re-equipment programme. For example the *Avon Sabres* have been replaced with modern *F-5* fighters while second-hand *A-4 Skyhawk* fighter-bombers were acquired from the United States. Indonesia now has 15 *F-5s* and 32 *A-4 Skyhawks*. In addition 16 British-made *Hawks* were bought which are primarily intended for training but which can, if necessary, be used for shorter-range ground and maritime strikes. In 1986, Indonesia took a major step forward when it ordered twelve ultra-modern *F-16/100* fighters (eight single-seater *F-16As* and four two-seater *F-16Bs* for training). Previously, the United States had been willing to sell the *F-16/100* only to 'front-line' allies such as South Korea, Pakistan and, after considerable deliberation, Thailand. However, after agreeing to sell it to Singapore, a non-'front-line' Southeast Asian state, the way was opened for Indonesia. Indonesian military officers have justified their interest in the *F-16/100* more in terms of keeping abreast of the latest technology than as a necessity for meeting any threat. Indeed, some doubts have been expressed by foreign observers about Indonesia's current capacity to maintain such modern aircraft. The acquisition of a dozen *F-16/100s* will certainly enhance Indonesia's conventional capacity but the expansion of Indonesia's Air Force has to be seen in regional context. At present, Indonesia has only slightly more than half the number of fighters and ground-attack fighter-bombers than Singapore has, and is behind Singapore in the queue for the *F-16/100*. More importantly in the context of the present discussion, Indonesia's Air Force is still small compared to the Australian Air Force with its 22 *F-111* fighter-bombers (which are far superior to Indonesia's *A-4 Skyhawks*), and its eventual acquisition of 75 *F/A-18s*.

The Indonesian Navy has also undergone considerable modernisation since the end of the 1970s. In 1979, the Navy in addition to smaller patrol craft had three submarines and eleven frigates which were all either almost non-operational or already withdrawn from service. In the 1980s, the Russian submarines were replaced by two *Class-209 (Type-1300)* submarines from West Germany, while another is on order. Of the old surface fleet, four World War II-vintage *Jones*-class frigates provided by the US in the 1970s remain, while two of the old Soviet frigates can still be used as well as a Yugoslav frigate for training. In the early 1980s, three modern *Fatahillah*-class corvettes (sometimes classed as frigates) armed with *Exocet* missiles were bought from the Netherlands. In addition, three old, but refitted *Tribal*-class destroyer escorts (also classed as frigates), which had been withdrawn from the

British Navy, were bought in 1985 and the first two of six *Van Speijk* frigates, withdrawn from the Dutch Navy, arrived at the beginning of 1987. Apart from these vessels, the Navy also has fast attack craft, some of which are armed with *Exocet* missiles. Despite these purchases of two new submarines, three modern corvettes and nine second-hand frigates, the Indonesian Navy's capacity to support a major external campaign against a well-equipped enemy is still very limited.

Despite the acquisition of new aeroplanes and ships by the Air Force and the Navy, it is the Army which remains the mainstay of the Indonesian armed forces. Following the end of the *Konfrontasi* campaign and the establishment of the Army-dominated New Order government, the Army, in fact, declined in size from about 300,000 in 1966 to about 180,000 at the end of the 1970s but, during the 1980s, recruitment increased and strength grew again to 228,000 in 1985.[9] It is, however, totally misleading to imagine that Indonesia has 228,000 soldiers waiting in barracks for a command to go into action against an external enemy. Like armies everywhere, combat troops make up only part of the Army while a substantial proportion of personnel are employed in administrative and support duties. However in Indonesia, the Army is also the dominant political power, both providing personnel for the government and acting as its main supporter and protector.

The ideology of the Indonesian armed forces does not portray the military as a professional body concerned only with defence and security. The Indonesian armed forces were founded during a political revolution in which military and political functions were closely intertwined. After the revolution, many military officers continued to believe that the special nature of the Indonesian military's origins entitled them to continue to play a legitimate political role. After a brief interlude in the 1950s when the military withdrew, at least partially, to the barracks, the armed forces returned unambiguously to active participation in politics and administration as a result of the introduction of martial law by President Sukarno in 1957 and they have continued to be directly involved in politics and government ever since. The military formulated the doctrine of the *Dwifungsi* or the Dual Function of the armed forces to legitimise its political role. According to the *Dwifungsi* concept, the Indonesian military is not limited to its defence-and-security function but has an obligation to participate, whenever necessary, in all fields of national life, including the government. Since 1966 this second function has been the predominant one.

The military's role in Indonesian political life is very large indeed. Both the president and the vice president are retired generals while twelve out of thirty-two full members of the cabinet and two out of five junior ministers are military officers, as are the secretaries-general of many government departments. In regional government, about two-thirds of provincial governors and around half of the *bupati* (district heads) are either retired or active military officers. A large number of Indonesia's ambassadors are military men and military officers sit in national and regional representative assemblies as appointed members. In addition, military officers play a big role in the management of state corporations while the nation's dominant 'political party', *Golkar*, was created by the military, is currently headed by a general and enjoys substantial military support during election campaigns. The number of members of the armed forces serving in non-military capacities were more than 21,000 in the mid-1970s but dropped to 17,000 in 1980[10] and, according to unconfirmed reports, had fallen to about 8,000 in 1985 - partly due to the transformation of military officers to civilian status on retirement.

The military's political role, however, is greater than the participation of some of its officers in non-military functions. The Army, together with the other branches of the armed forces, is the indispensable protector of the government. As noted earlier, the territorial organisation of the armed forces not only fitted in with the requirements of the doctrine of Territorial Warfare but also provided the military with a structure through which to exercise political control. Until 1985 the Army was organised into sixteen regional commands with each command covering the area of a province or sometimes, in the Outer Islands, several small provinces. The territory of each regional command was divided into *Resort* commands centred on larger towns, while the *Resort* commands were divided into district commands based in smaller towns and *Rayon* commands at the lowest level. This territorial structure was responsible not only for dealing with civil unrest and other political threats to the regime but was also entrusted with carrying out routine political supervision. Acting as local agents of the national security organisation, the KOPKAMTIB, the territorial commanders had power to act against dissidents and, every five years, played vital roles in ensuring the success of the government party, *Golkar*, in elections. In the 1985 Army re-organisation, the number of regional commands was reduced to ten but their internal-security functions remained largely unchanged.

A large part of the Army's resources, therefore, are devoted to routine internal security responsibilities. Of the Army's 82 infantry battalions, for example, 63 are part of the territorial structure and concerned primarily with internal security and political management. Most of these territorial battalions do not in fact operate as battalions because their members are spread out in smaller territorial units. These forces would not be easily available for use in a conventional external war, partly because they are not specially prepared for that role but most importantly because their territorial functions are vital for the maintenance of internal political stability and the authority of the government. If large numbers of troops were suddenly transferred from territorial duties to a conventional role in order to pursue some external objective, the government would run the risk of not being able to deal with local political upheavals - whether in Java or the Outer Islands - of the sort which have broken out from time to time during the New Order period.

The invasion of East Timor in 1975 and the need to commit some twenty battalions there during the late 1970s imposed a severe strain on the Army's resources at a time when Vietnam was being seen as a possible short-term threat. In response, the Army's size was increased during the early 1980s to its present level of 228,000. Special emphasis was placed on building up a strong combat-ready force capable of engaging in conventional warfare. In 1980 and 1981 two substantial military exercises involving some 30,000 troops from all Services were held in which, for the first time, conventional forces were mobilised to meet an 'enemy from the north' in contrast to earlier internal security-oriented exercises. General Benny Murdani, who succeeded General Mohammad Yusef as Commander of the Armed Forces in 1983, revised Yusef's target of 100 combat-trained battalions, and said that it is necessary to have only twenty combat-ready battalions.[11] The combat-ready battalions are part of the Army's Strategic Reserve Command (KOSTRAD) and the Special Forces Command (KOPASSANDHA, formerly RPKAD). In the past, the regional territorial commands in Java had their own infantry brigades which could be transferred to KOSTRAD whenever required, but in the 1985 reorganisation KOSTRAD was provided with its own forces which are now quite separate from the territorial commands. KOSTRAD now has two divisions - one consisting of three infantry brigades (nine battalions) and the other of two infantry brigades (six battalions) - complete with cavalry, artillery and support forces. Two of the five brigades have an airborne capability. In addition to KOSTRAD's troops, which amount to between 16,500 and 19,000 men, another 5,000 are part of the elite KOPASSANDHA force.[12] In recent years KOSTRAD's forces have been largely occupied in East Timor where, according to General Murdani in late 1984, there were fourteen battalions,[13] although foreign observers usually estimate about twenty. Also, one KOSTRAD battalion operates in Irian Jaya on the PNG border.

The Army's capacity to undertake conventional operations, therefore, has grown during the first half of the 1980s, but as long as a large proportion of KOSTRAD and KOPASSANDHA forces are tied down in East Timor there will not be many combat troops left over for other purposes. Even if the East Timor insurgency does eventually subside, there is no shortage of potential problems elsewhere and the major function of KOSTRAD, as a reserve command, will continue to be to keep forces in reserve to deal with possible future threats to internal security. This does not mean, of course, that Indonesia would never use its KOSTRAD forces to achieve external objectives but the primary concern is likely to remain the maintenance of domestic political stability.

It can be confidently asserted that the growth of Indonesia's military capacity during the early 1980s will not continue at the same rate during the rest of the 1980s. The expansion of the armed forces had been dependent on propitious economic circumstances. The availability of oil funds had made both the weapons acquisition program and the expansion in size possible. But defence expenditure has had to be held back in recent years because of the current world economic recession and especially the fall in oil prices. From US$2.87 billion in 1982-3, estimated defence expenditure has fallen to $2.53 billion in 1983-4 and $2.01 billion in 1986-7.[14] In the 1986 budget estimates, the total budget declined for the first time during the New Order period, signifying a shortage of funds which has affected all areas of expenditure, including defence and security.

In any case, Indonesia's perception of its strategic environment has changed. The concern about Vietnam's motives expressed in some circles in the late 1970s seems to have largely evaporated. In 1979, Yusuf Wanandi, of the government-affiliated think-tank, the Centre for Strategic and International Studies, declared: 'In the long term it is clear that China is a bigger potential threat than Vietnam'.[15] It now appears that Indonesia, especially the Indonesian military, has no real worry about Vietnam's future behaviour. The only direct issue of contention between the two countries, the overlapping claims to part of the South China Sea near the Natuna Islands, has been the subject of long-running negotiations and both sides seem committed to a peaceful settlement. Meanwhile, the Commander of the Armed Forces, General Murdani, has made it quite clear, to the consternation of some ASEAN countries, that he does not regard Vietnam as a threat. During a visit to Hanoi in February 1984 he stated, after surveying the condition of Vietnam's armed forces and the state of her economy, that Vietnam was in no position to launch an 'expedition' against ASEAN and was therefore not a military threat.[16] China, too, is not seen as a direct military threat - at least in the medium-term although it remains the focus of long-term concern. 'It is not a Chinese invasion army we are worried about',

Murdani told a journalist in 1985.[17] Instead China has been seen as a possible source of, in the words of President Suharto, 'subversion and infiltration'.[18]

Indonesia's military leaders, therefore, believe that Indonesia is not likely to face any external threat in the foreseeable future. The main threat, from the military perspective, is not external but rather internal. The Minister for Defence and Security, General Poniman, has said that in coming decades there is little prospect of external invasion but a probability that domestic disturbances might increase.[19] One implication of this expectation is that the main emphasis in the future development of the armed forces should be on the Army, which is directly concerned with internal security, rather than the Air Force and Navy which are concerned primarily with external defence. It is, nevertheless, still likely that the Air Force and Navy will gradually acquire new hardware and upgrade their capabilities in the future but certainly not at the rate of the early 1980s.

Could Indonesia, then, represent some kind of security threat to Australia or PNG? The very raising of this question might be considered offensive in some Indonesian circles but it cannot be denied that it exists in the minds of the public in both Australia and PNG. Indonesia's policies, behaviour and military capacity are naturally examined more closely than those of other neighbouring states because it is only Indonesia which could conceivably, in a worst-case scenario, mount a serious military campaign harmful to Australian or PNG interests. The Australian and PNG habit to periodically discuss the possibility of an Indonesian threat does not so much reflect anti-Indonesian sentiment as indicate a recognition of the facts of geography, demography and capability.

Military threats do not arise of their own accord. Apart from having the military capacity to carry out operations against neighbours with reasonable expectation of success, a threatening power must have a purpose - a goal the fulfilment of which would put the country in a more advantageous position than before the conflict. In the Indonesian case, we must ask not only what it could do but also what purpose beneficial to Indonesia would be served by doing it.

The possibility that Indonesia might try to invade Australia with the intention of occupying the whole, or a large part of, the country can be dismissed out of hand. First, no Indonesian leader has ever given the slightest indication of being interested in such a venture. Second, any benefits to Indonesia from acquiring economically valuable territory such as the Pilbara iron ore mines or the North-West oil-fields, would depend on gaining unchallenged control, but it is inconceivable that seizure of such areas would not be contested vigorously by Australia.

Third, the Indonesian economy could not sustain the costs of a prolonged campaign. And finally, in any case, Indonesia's military capacity simply would not permit such an invasion. An invasion across the sea would require naval and air superiority and a vastly larger land force. But Indonesia's naval and air forces could not provide the superiority needed while its land forces would also be inadequate. Using the conventional assumption that an invading force needs three times as many troops as the defending force, an Australian parliamentary committee in 1981 estimated that a potential - not necessarily Indonesian - invasion force would need around nine divisions to overcome an Australian force consisting of one regular division and two reserve divisions.[20] While the size of the Indonesian Army is such that it could on paper mobilise nine divisions, its practical limit, as explained above, would be no more than two. But no Indonesian government would want to commit all its reserve forces to a permanent occupation army overseas. There are, therefore, no grounds for concern about a full-scale invasion of Australia by Indonesia.

If Indonesia ever took military action against Australia, it would have to be at a level lower than outright invasion. A hostile Indonesia would probably have, or could fairly easily acquire, a capacity to take limited military action against Australia such as, for example, interfering with Australian shipping, occupying the Cocos or Christmas Islands, bombarding coastal areas in the North or even occupying isolated townships for a few hours and damaging facilities. Provocative action of this sort without the protection of air and naval superiority would, of course, invite the possibility of unacceptable Australian retaliation such as could be carried out by Australia's *F-111* bombers. But hostile Indonesian actions would not be initiated as ends in themselves and would have to be directed towards achieving some purpose advantageous to Indonesia. It is difficult to imagine Indonesia engaging in hostile action of this sort except in the context of a wider dispute having its origins other than in the area of actual physical conflict. Indonesia might consider hostile military action against Australia in response to what it perceived as hostile Australian action against Indonesia such as, for example, the provision of support to a separatist movement or similar 'interference' in Indonesia's internal affairs. But it is hard to imagine Australia taking such provocative action in the first place. The only territorial issue between the two countries involves the so-called 'Timor Gap' - the 250 km undetermined sea-bed boundary south of East Timor - but neither side would want to go to war over this. It is, therefore, very difficult to envisage a bilateral issue that would induce Indonesia to engage in limited hostilities against Australia. The main potential source of conflict between Indonesia and Australia does not lie in the bilateral relations between the two countries but in the trilateral relationship which also embraces PNG.

The possibility that Indonesia might one day decide to invade and occupy PNG has a surface credibility and is certainly a source of public unease, especially in PNG itself. In a direct conflict with PNG without the intervention of other powers, Indonesia would control the air and could easily mobilise a land force far superior to PNG's current two infantry battalions. There would be little to prevent Indonesian forces capturing the main towns and eventually taking Port Moresby.

But how would such an invasion serve Indonesia's interests? There is no evidence to suggest that Indonesia's leaders have ever given serious thought to conducting such a campaign which, like the case of an invasion of Australia, would only be economically advantageous if the occupation were largely unchallenged. But it is one thing to invade and another to occupy. Indonesia's capacity to carry out a prolonged occupation of PNG is limited. The Indonesian occupation of East Timor with a population of less than 700,000 required an occupation force of some twenty battalions (more than two divisions) for almost a decade and still ties down a substantial number of troops. The problems of a permanent occupation of PNG with its difficult terrain and a population of 3.5 million would be enormous. Moreover, the level of resistance which an invading force could expect to face when occupying an established independent nation would be much greater than in the case of a colony suddenly released by its colonial master. It should also be remembered that any Indonesian consideration of a move into PNG would almost certainly be in the context of growing resistance in Irian Jaya and the need to commit additional troops there.[21]

Further, the assumption that an invasion of PNG would not involve other powers might not be valid. Indonesia could not dismiss the possibility of an adverse reaction from its international friends such as Australia, the United States and Japan. Australian military intervention would be possible, while it is likely that America and perhaps Japan would apply diplomatic and economic pressure. Although Indonesia is certainly regarded by the US and Japan as more important than PNG, this does not mean that Indonesia would be given a blank cheque to do whatever it liked with PNG. Third-party intervention would not, of course, be automatic but the risk, from Indonesia's point of view, would be high.

A full-scale Indonesian invasion of PNG, therefore, is hard to envisage. While Indonesia has the military capacity to invade, the costs of occupation would be prohibitive, the benefits slight and the risk of third-party intervention high. In any case, Indonesia's leaders, acting on rational calculations, have not shown any signs of being interested in subjugating PNG.

That Indonesia has neither the ambition nor the military capacity to annex PNG does not mean, however, that there are no circumstances under which Indonesia would take military action against its neighbour. Indonesia has not been inhibited in the past, by the abstractions of international law, from taking military action across its borders when it believed that such action was in its interests. In particular, the East Timor case showed that Indonesia has been prepared to take strong action when it felt its own security to be potentially endangered. In what ways could developments in PNG be interpreted by Indonesia as posing some kind of threat to her security interests? Three possible sets of circumstances could be envisaged in ascending order of probability.

One circumstance which would cause deep concern in Jakarta would be the establishment of a government in PNG openly hostile towards Indonesia. While PNG's hostility in itself would probably not be sufficient to spur Indonesia into action, a policy of aiding rebels in Irian Jaya, for example, would certainly bring forth a sharp response from Jakarta. There would also be great consternation if Port Moresby were to establish more than diplomatic and commercial ties with communist countries. If Port Moresby not only adopted a foreign policy of friendship with communist states but also accepted military aid, for example, or went so far as to provide military base facilities, Indonesia's reaction would be hostile in the extreme and some sort of intervention not unlikely. But even then, at least initially, Indonesia would be much more likely to turn to diplomatic and political, rather than military, measures. Such scenarios are remote, however, as PNG is most unlikely to adopt policies of this sort.

A second imaginable circumstance which would worry Indonesia and perhaps lead to intervention in one form or another would be some kind of breakdown in PNG's own political system, perhaps caused by regional dissidence. Indonesia would be worried that a dissident province might seek aid from a big power hostile to Indonesia or even that Port Moresby, in its attempt to control the situation, might seek such aid. In such circumstances Indonesian intervention, if it did eventuate, would most likely be in support of the central government but it could also be imagined that it might seek to gain influence with dissident forces. Much would depend on actual circumstances. Again, Indonesian intervention would not necessarily be military in form. Whatever Indonesia's reaction to an internal crisis in PNG, it can be said, however, that Jakarta has no interest in the political disintegration of PNG. Its basic interest is in the maintenance of a strong government in Port Moresby, friendly towards Indonesia and capable of preserving stability throughout its territory.

The most serious problem in Indonesia-PNG relations relates to Papuan resistance to Jakarta rule in Irian Jaya. The Indonesian government has faced low-level opposition to its rule since Indonesia replaced the UN administration in 1963.[22] The stage-managed 'Act of Free Choice' in 1969 did little to enhance the legitimacy of Indonesian rule in the eyes of either Papuans or the rest of the world. Rebels, organised loosely under the banner of the *Organisasi Papua Merdeka* (OPM), have never posed a serious threat to Indonesia's hold on Irian Jaya but have been a constant source of irritation, especially along the border with PNG. The Indonesian government has asked for PNG's cooperation in preventing PNG territory from being used as a sanctuary by the OPM but PNG governments have sometimes been reluctant and have not always taken consistent action against the OPM. Many PNG leaders, backed by public opinion, have in fact felt no obligation to help Indonesia repress fellow Melanesians while some, such as former Deputy Prime Ministers Iambakey Okuk[23] and John Momis,[24] have expressed strong sympathy for OPM goals. The failure of past PNG governments to take firm measures against the OPM has sometimes led to Indonesian forces themselves illegally crossing the border to take action against OPM activists. While such limited incursions clearly violated international law, they do not, it should be stressed, indicate that Indonesia has larger objectives in mind. If the OPM problem would somehow disappear, much of the friction on the border would disappear with it.

The main danger for both PNG and Indonesia, however, is that, far from disappearing, the OPM movement might expand and pose a greater threat to Jakarta than it has so far. If OPM activity persists at about its present level or even declines, problems will no doubt continue to arise from time to time along the Indonesian-PNG border but they would be unlikely to lead to wider conflict. However, if the OPM resistance becomes more than an irritant and actually challenges Jakarta's grip on Irian Jaya, Indonesia would see its security as seriously threatened and most likely take far-reaching military measures against the rebellion. This would presumably lead to more border-crossings by rebel forces and the increased use of sanctuaries in PNG. It would also most likely lead to a rise in public sympathy and support for the OPM in PNG making it politically difficult for the PNG government to restrict OPM activities. It is in such circumstances that military conflict between Indonesia and PNG could break out with Indonesia taking its own action against what it believed to be OPM sanctuaries in PNG. While isolated small-scale raids followed by rapid withdrawal have been reluctantly tolerated by PNG governments in the past, an increase in the size and frequence of cross-border incursions in the context of a growing OPM insurgency could lead to clashes between Indonesian and PNG forces and a possible appeal by PNG for help from Australia. How Australia would respond to such a contingency is by no means easy to anticipate and would depend a lot on the precise circumstances both on the Indonesia-PNG border and in Australia itself.

Indonesia, PNG and Australia all have an interest in preventing a deterioration in the relations between Indonesia and PNG, but none exercises much influence over the organisation which could potentially upset that relationship. Contrasting views are expressed in Indonesian and PNG, as well as Australian, circles about the nature and potential of the OPM.

Indonesia has always played down popular support for the OPM which is not in fact a cohesive organisation but really a disparate and loose alliance of local dissidents. Initially, Indonesia blamed the Dutch for fostering a small elite which aspired to independence. More recently, Indonesian officials have suggested that the OPM is more a problem for PNG than for Indonesia.[25] It is claimed that the main bases for OPM activities, in fact, lie on the PNG side of the border, while occasional upheavals in the interior of Irian Jaya, often attributed to the OPM, are really cases of tribal warfare of a sort that also breaks out from time to time in PNG. Action against the OPM, it is argued, is therefore as much the responsibility of PNG's security forces as Indonesia's. This Indonesian view attributes what it sees as the OPM's limited popular support to incitement, harassment and intimidation by the OPM itself. If the PNG security forces could deprive the OPM of its sanctuaries on PNG territory, many Indonesians seem to believe that the OPM would wither on the vine. The proponents of this view are mainly Indonesian officials, but it is not difficult to find Australian diplomats whose perception of the OPM is not very different to that of the Indonesian officials.

The alternative view sees the OPM problem as rooted in developments in Irian Jaya. The Melanesian people of Irian Jaya are ethnically and culturally separate from other Indonesians and had no role in the decision to merge with Indonesia. Under Indonesian rule, Melanesians have sometimes held important posts such as governor of *bupati* (district head) but in general the administration has been in the hands of non-Melanesians. In addition, the military role has been large. Since the incorporation of Irian Jaya in 1963, small-scale local rebellions have taken place from time to time in various areas and have been put down by military force. Military operations against rebels have, almost unavoidably, been accompanied by abuses in which ordinary villagers have been killed or wounded, their villages and crops destroyed, and women raped. It is, of course, impossible to know how widespread and frequent incidents of this sort have been, but their occurrence undoubtedly kindles fierce resentment towards the government and undermines the legitimacy of rule by Jakarta.

Indonesian rule has also been accompanied by a steady increase in non-Melanesian immigration to Irian Jaya.[26] Non-Melanesians are usually estimated to make up about a quarter of the present population of about 1.5 million. The majority of the non-Melanesians have come spontaneously from nearby islands and are often prominent in trade. In addition, another 70,000 had come from Java and Bali under the government's transmigration program and been settled in agricultural projects before the commencement of the current five-year plan in 1984. Under the current plan, the transmigration target for Irian Jaya rose very sharply to 137,800 families or 661,000 people, although it was explained that one quarter would consist of 'local transmigrants' and that only 103,000 families or 496,000 people would be brought from Java and Bali. If the planned target were to be achieved, the ethnic balance in Irian Jaya would be changed drastically. Some concern about the high rate of transmigration was expressed in Indonesian academic and military circles[27] - the military critics in particular being worried about the likely growth in Melanesian resentment and the resulting stimulus of OPM activity. But it is now clear that there is no possibility of the target being achieved during the plan period, not so much because the government has taken heed of its critics but as a result of financial cutbacks caused by the collapse of the price of oil in 1986.

The future development of the OPM, then, is likely to have a crucial impact on Indonesia's relations with PNG and, at one remove, Australia. If, as one view sees it, the OPM's real support is limited to the border areas and mobilised largely through harassment and intimidation, the movement is unlikely to grow much beyond its present strength and therefore should not pose insurmountable difficulties in the relations between Indonesia and PNG. But if, as the alternative view sees it, Jakarta's attempts to integrate Irian Jaya with the rest of the country are counter-productive and result in growing resentment against the Indonesian authorities, an expansion of the OPM's popular base and its activities can be expected not only in the border areas but in other parts of the province as well. The OPM's struggle, however, seems unlikely to expand to the point where it could drive the Indonesian armed forces from Irian Jaya - except perhaps in the event of a major regional upheaval elsewhere or some sort of breakdown of the government in Jakarta, neither of which seem very likely at present. A major expansion of the OPM, however, would certainly complicate

PNG's foreign and defence policy and give Australia considerable cause for concern.

This survey of Indonesia's military capacity and security objectives comes to the conclusion that neither Australia nor PNG have grounds to fear any move towards policies of general expansionism on the part of Indonesia. Indonesia has neither the political desire nor the military capacity to subjugate either Australia or PNG, although its military capacity *vis-a-vis* PNG is substantial. No issue in the bilateral relationship between Indonesia and Australia seems to be a potential source of serious conflict. The only potentially threatening issue is trilateral and involves PNG. The danger of conflict on the Indonesia-PNG border depends not so much on the intentions and policies towards each other of the respective governments, but on the future of a non-governmental organisation over which no government exercises control. Neither the Australian nor PNG governments can do a great deal to influence the course of the OPM's development in the long run. The crucial factor lies in conditions within Irian Jaya itself.

Endnotes

1   See the Hon. D.J. Killen, Minister for Defence, *Australian Defence*, (White Paper presented to Parliament of Australia, Australian Government Publishing Service, Canberra, 1976); Joint Committee on Foreign Affairs and Defence, *Threats to Australia's Security: Their Nature and Probability*, (Australian Government Publishing Service, Canberra, 1981); and Paul Dibb, *Review of Australia's Defence Capabilities*, (Australian Government Publishing Service, Canberra, 1986).

2   *The Australian*, 9 September 1983.

3   Mr Aron Noaio in the PNG Parliament on 19 November 1984, quoted in B.D. Brunton, 'Indonesian and Australian Influence on Constitutional Democracy in Papua New Guinea', paper presented at the 13th National Conference of the Australian Institute of International Affairs, March 1986.

4   See D. Campbell, *Australian Public Opinion on National Security Issues*, (Working Paper No.1, Peace Research Centre, Australian National University, Canberra, 1986), p.27.

5   *The Australian*, 6 June 1986.

6   The main study of *Konfrontasi* is J.A.C. Mackie, *Konfrontasi: The Indonesia–Malaysia Dispute, 1963-1966*, (Oxford University Press, London, 1974).

7   For discussion of Indonesia's motives, see M. Leifer, *Indonesia's Foreign Policy*, (George Allen & Unwin for the Royal Institute for International Affairs, London, 1983), p.155; J. Dunn, *Timor: A People Betrayed*, (Jacaranda Press, Queensland, 1983), pp.109-110; and H. McDonald, *Suharto's Indonesia*, (Fontana Books, Victoria, 1980), pp.193-4.

8   Information on military hardware and expenditure is largely taken from *The Military Balance*, (The International Institute of Strategic Studies, London, various years).

9   *Tempo* (Jakarta), 11 May 1985; *The Military Balance, 1986-1987* gives 216,000.

10   D. Jenkins, *Suharto and His Generals: Indonesian Military Politics 1975-1983*, (Cornell Modern Indonesia Project, Cornell University, Ithaca, 1984), p.198.

11   *Tempo*, 15 May 1983.

12   For further details, see D. Jenkins, 'Indonesia's Armed Forces and Irian Jaya', Paper
     presented at the 13th National Conference of the Australian Institute of International
     Affairs, March, 1986.
13   *Sinar Harapan* (Jakarta), 18 December 1984.
14   *The Military Balance 1986-1987*, p.155.
15   *Tempo*, 13 October 1979.
16   *Tempo*, 25 February 1984.
17   *Asiaweek*, 11 October 1985.
18   *Tempo*, 13 November 1982.
19   *Indonesia Reports*, (No.5), 14 February 1985.
20   See *Threats to Australia's Security*, p.31.
21   When asked about possible Indonesian designs on PNG, one senior Indonesian
     general replied, only half-jokingly, that Indonesia's armed forces have enough
     trouble controlling Indonesia's own territory without trying to control anyone else's.
     Personal interview, 1982.
22   See R. Osborne, *Indonesia's Secret War: The Guerilla Struggle in Irian Jaya*, (Allen &
     Unwin, Sydney, 1985), p.171.
23   During the 1982 election campaign Okuk, who was still deputy Prime Minister at the
     time, claimed that 99 per cent of thinking people in PNG supported the OPM. See
     ibid., p.171.
24   In a speech at the National Press Club in Canberra in May 1986 Momis, now Deputy
     Leader of the Opposition, said: 'I am convinced that we have no option but to
     weather Indonesian displeasure and support West Papuan freedom'. See *Sydney
     Morning Herald*, 16 May 1986.
25   Based on conversations with Indonesian officials and foreign diplomats in Jakarta in
     late 1985.
26   See Chris Manning, 'Irian Jaya's migrants gain economic clout' and 'Transmigration
     is seen as solution to poverty', *Far Eastern Economic Review*, 30 March 1987, pp.40-43.
27   A team headed by Professor Mubyarto of the Gajad Mada University in Yogjakarta
     prepared a critical report for the Minister for Transmigration in February 1985.   A
     report entitled 'Transmigration program in Irian Jaya should be given a Special
     Treatment so that it could help solve Security Problems' was prepared by the Irian
     Jaya regional commander, Brigadier General R.K. Sembiring Meliala in January
     1983.   See also, I. Bell, H. Feith and R. Hatley, 'The West Papuan Challenge to
     Indonesian Authority in Irian Jaya: Old Problems, New Possibilities', *Asian Survey*,
     May 1986.

CHAPTER 20

INDOCHINA

Carlyle A. Thayer

Indochina comprises the three mainland Southeast Asian states of Vietnam, Laos and Kampuchea. The power of these states may be roughly measured by three indicators: population, the size of military forces and gross domestic product (GDP).[1] Vietnam, with a population nearing 65 million, is the region's second most populous country, ranking after Indonesia (173 million) and before the Philippines (58 million) and Thailand (54 million). Vietnam's military forces, estimated at over 1.25 million (1988), outnumber the combined total of the seven other non-communist Southeast Asian states (1.05 million). The Laotian and Kampuchean armed forces total 55,500 and 40,000 respectively, or less than one-fifth of the armed forces of neighbouring Thailand.

In terms of economic power, as measured by GDP (1986/87 figures), Vietnam ($US 20.4 billion) ranks fifth behind Indonesia ($US 68.4 billion), Thailand ($US 47 billion), the Philippines ($US 35 billion) and Malaysia ($US 30 billion), and slightly ahead of Singapore ($US 20 billion). The combination of figures for Laos and Kampuchea with those of Vietnam does not alter the relative standing of Indochina when compared with its non-communist neighbours. In terms of GDP, Laos and Kampuchea rank second-last and last among regional states. All three countries are indebted and heavily dependent on foreign assistance. Vietnam alone has foreign debts totalling over $US 8 billion.

Since 1975, state power in each of the three Indochinese countries has been in the hands of a communist party committed to building a socialist economic system. Each of the three ruling parties traces its origins to the Indochinese Communist Party (ICP) formed in 1930 and headed by Ho Chi Minh.[2] Historically, the revolutionary movements in Laos and Cambodia lagged behind that of Vietnam. During the ICP's first decade, for example, ethnic Vietnamese living in Laos and Cambodia were targeted for recruitment in preference to ethnic Lao and Khmer. This situation changed somewhat during the Second World War and especially during the anti-French resistance (1945-54) when communist-led nationalist movements and armed forces emerged in each country.

The anti-French struggle was conducted on an Indochina-wide basis in response to French initiatives which had merged the separate countries of Laos, Cambodia and Vietnam into a single 'Indochinese

Union'. French military operations directed against the ICP were mounted on a regional basis, leading Vo Nguyen Giap to conclude in 1950 that:

> Indochina is a single strategic unit, a single battlefield. For this reason, and especially because of the strategic terrain, we cannot consider Vietnam to be independent so long as Cambodia and Laos are under imperialist domination, just as we cannot consider Cambodia and Laos to be independent so long as Vietnam is under imperialist rule. The colonialists used Cambodia to attack Vietnam. Laos and Cambodia temporarily have become the secure rear areas of the enemy and simultaneously their most vulnerable area in the entire Indochina theatre. Therefore, we need to open the Lao-Cambodia battlefield resolutely and energetically.[3]

Prior to 1951, some consideration had been given by the ICP to forming an Indochinese Federation after the revolutionary movements in Laos, Cambodia and Vietnam had achieved victory. However the stark socio-economic differences between the three countries, and the rise of nationalist sentiment led to the dropping of this notion.[4] In 1951 the ICP formally split into three national parties. In Vietnam, the ICP renamed itself the Vietnam Workers' Party (VWP). After a period of reorganisation, the communist movements in Laos and Cambodia emerged, respectively, as the Lao People's Revolutionary Party (LPRP) and the Kampuchean People's Revolutionary Party (KPRP).

The relative strength of these movements was reflected in the terms of the cease-fire agreements reached at the Geneva Conference in 1954. All of Vietnam north of the seventeenth parallel was placed in communist hands. In Laos, the anti-French forces were given control of the provinces of Phong Saly and Sam Neua, while in Cambodia, the revolutionary movement was not assigned any territory. For nearly half a decade after the Geneva Conference, the communist movements in Laos, Cambodia and Vietnam pursued separate paths. During the Vietnam War in the 1960s, however, both communist Vietnamese and American military planning and operations were mounted on a regional basis. Once again Indochina became a single strategic battlefield.

The communist movements in Laos and Vietnam can trace an unbroken line of cooperation and coordination extending over three decades.[5] This is not the case with Kampuchea. Cooperation and coordination developed only in 1970, after the overthrow of Prince Sihanouk and the convening of an Indochinese summit meeting. Nevertheless fundamental differences persisted between the

Kampuchean and Vietnamese communist parties which emerged full blown in the mid-1970s.

After the communist victories of 1975, Vietnam sought to maintain its position as *primus inter pares* in Indochina by forging 'special relations' with Laos and Kampuchea. At the 4th congress of the Vietnamese Communist Party (VCP) in December 1976, for example, the development of special relationships with Laos and Kampuchea was listed second among Vietnam's foreign policy goals. In July 1977, Laos and Vietnam entered into a 25-year Treaty of Friendship and Cooperation under which terms they pledged to consult if faced with the threat of force from a third party. In late 1986, at the VCP's 6th congress, Vietnam's leaders declared that the 'special relations' among the three countries of Indochina were now 'a law governing the survival and development of all three fraternal nations'.

The ultra-nationalist Pol Pot faction in Kampuchea, fearing domination by Hanoi, rejected Vietnamese overtures and turned to China for protection. This, and other factors, precipitated the 'Third Indochinese War'.6 Vietnam invaded and occupied Kampuchea in December 1978 and immediately placed in power a sympathetic faction of the KPRP. In January of the following year, the People's Republic of Kampuchea (PRK) entered into a 25-year Treaty of Peace, Friendship and Cooperation with Vietnam similar to the agreement signed with Laos. Shortly thereafter, in March 1979, Laos and Kampuchea entered into an agreement on economic, cultural, scientific and technological cooperation.

Security Concerns of the Indochina States

For much of the period since the Second World War, military concerns have dominated the national security perspectives of the Party elites in Vietnam, Kampuchea and Laos. In the years immediately following 1975, all three countries were preoccupied with internal security. The government in Laos, in particular, faced several insurgent threats mounted by H'mong tribesmen and anti-communist resistance forces. Vietnam too confronted armed dissidence, mainly by ethnic minority tribesmen in the central highland, and by ARVN remnants. In neighbouring Kampuchea, the regime was mainly concerned with imposing draconian rule over 'new people', the urban and rural population not previously identified with the Khmer Rouge.

After 1977-78, external security concerns came to the fore as the border war between Kampuchea and Vietnam escalated in intensity. In December 1978, Vietnam invaded and occupied Kampuchea. In February 1979, China responded by launching a massive punitive attack on Vietnam's six northern provinces.7 The attack was of limited duration as Chinese forces withdrew the following month. Over the next half decade, however, fighting along the Sino-Vietnamese frontier has waxed and waned in a series of periodic escalations mounted by China in response to Vietnamese military operations in Kampuchea.

Since 1979, Vietnamese military forces in Laos and Kampuchea have been primarily concerned with giving support to the incumbent regime and counter-insurgency operations. In Laos, the main challenges were mounted by domestic resistance groups supported from Thailand and China. Resistance activity in Laos has been desultory and never posed a major threat to the central government. Such is not the case in Kampuchea, where Khmer Rouge guerrilla forces, operating from sanctuaries in Thailand and remote areas of Kampuchea, and supplied mainly by China, constitute a major threat to the Phnom Penh government. Since 1982, the Khmer Rouge has been joined by the military forces of the two non-communist resistance groups, the Khmer People's National Liberation Front (KPNLF) and Armée Nationale Sihanouk, in a nominal coalition.

Given the circumstances just described, it is not surprising that the Party elites of Vietnam, Laos and Kampuchea concluded that their mutual security was dependent not only on the maintenance of their special relations but also their 'strategic alliance' with the Soviet Union. In November 1978, it should be recalled, the Soviet Union and Vietnam signed a 25-year Treaty of Friendship and Cooperation. The USSR remains the main supplier of military equipment and hardware to the three armies of Indochina.

Beginning around 1985-86, a series of external and internal developments occurred which have affected the security outlook of the Indochinese states. On the external front, Mikhail Gorbachev's 'new political thinking' has played a major role in precipitating a reconsideration of long-held assumptions about national security. Gorbachev's initiatives in settling regional conflicts by political means and normalising relations with China has changed the strategic environment affecting the Indochinese states.8 On the internal front, Vietnam's political system has been undergoing a process of regularisation and reform caused by the passing of its original revolutionary generation and the rise of pragmatic reformers.9 The impetus to pursue economic reform in Vietnam, which has firm domestic roots, has now become linked with Gorbachev's *perestroika*. The new pragmatism in Vietnam has affected Laos and Kampuchea.

The pace of change engulfing Indochina since 1985-86 has been startling. For example, academic specialists meeting at separate venues in Washington and Canberra in March 1987, in the wake of Gorbachev's speech the previous July in Vladivostok, were unable to anticipate the scope and pace of change which would shortly unfold.[10] One specialist argued that a Soviet withdrawal from Afghanistan was unlikely in the foreseeable future.[11] Another specialist argued that there were no signs that the Vietnamese were prepared to end the Kampuchean conflict by withdrawing its forces.[12] Other specialists predicted continuing Sino-Vietnamese hostility in the near term.[13]

Within two years of his speech in Vladivostok, Gorbachev had moved resolutely to remove the three obstacles blocking the normalisation of relations with China. The Soviets have reduced their troop strength in Mongolia and have totally withdrawn all military forces from Afghanistan. It would appear that Soviet diplomatic pressure was responsible in part for Vietnamese troop withdrawals from Kampuchea in late 1987, and again in 1988. Moscow and Beijing are now engaged in discussions to reduce troop strength along their common border.

Similar changes have occurred at the regional level. Since 1985 serious fighting along the Sino-Vietnamese border has all but ended. This has fuelled speculation that a *modus vivendi* has been worked out between Beijing and Hanoi. In January 1989, Vietnam and China opened a dialogue at the deputy minister level on settling the conflict in Kampuchea. These developments have been accompanied by a marked improvement in Thai-Vietnamese and Sino-Laotian relations. In addition, Laos and Thailand have negotiated a settlement of their border dispute. Most remarkably, despite the fact that a political settlement in Kampuchea has not been reached, the Thai Prime Minister has hosted a private visit by his counterpart in Phnom Penh, Hun Sen.

On the economic front, the three countries of Indochina are moving rapidly to open up to free market economies. Both Vietnam and Laos have promulgated relatively liberal foreign investment codes; Kampuchea is presently drafting one. Vietnam has signed nearly thirty joint venture agreements with foreign firms since the promulgation of the foreign investment law[14] and is now regularly hosting visits by businessmen from Japan, Hong Kong, Indonesia, Thailand, Singapore, Australia, the Philippines, South Korea and Taiwan. Taiwan is also in the process of establishing a trade office in Ho Chi Minh City. Laos has hosted visits by businessmen from Thailand, while Kampuchea's Hun Sen discussed future cooperation with the Thai Prime Minister during his 1989 visit in such areas as precious stones, timber and tourism.

Vietnam

Changes in the regional strategic environment, coupled with domestic reform within Vietnam, have led to a reassessment of long-held assumptions about national security. The present re-evaluation in Hanoi is also impacting on Party elites in Vientiane and Phnom Penh. Previous notions about the strategic unity of Indochina, the need to forge a militant alliance of the three countries, and the stress on military means to achieve these ends, are coming under challenge. The 'new thinking' in Hanoi reflects Soviet views on this subject. Some elements of Vietnam's leadership have now accepted that political and above all economic factors are more important in maintaining national security than military considerations.[15] These elites argue that the international system is changing as nations - especially those with different social systems - become increasingly interdependent. National security will now be determined, they argue, by expanded regional contacts with the free market economies.

The impact of this 'new thinking' on Vietnam's national security orientations has been quite marked. For example, the preamble to Vietnam's 1980 state constitution is being amended to drop all hostile references to China and US imperialism. In the former case, this change reflects a rethinking of relations with China that has been underway for several years and is now being cautiously implemented. In the case of the US, Vietnam has shifted gears in recent years and appears more cooperative in providing information about US Servicemen 'missing-in-action' from the war, than before. Vietnam's troop presence in Laos has been drastically cut,[16] while recent troop withdrawals from Kampuchea (as distinct from troop rotations) have been confirmed as genuine by western intelligence sources. The Vietnam People's Army is to be pared in size and the officer corps greatly reduced.[17] In a new development, Vietnam has quietly abolished its Indochina-wide economic coordinating commission.[18]

The conflict in Kampuchea (coupled with Chinese threats along the northern frontier) have preoccupied Vietnamese national security managers for over a decade. Vietnam's prime security considerations in Kampuchea have been twofold: to guarantee Vietnam's own territorial integrity from armed attack, and to prevent the emergence in Phnom Penh of a government allied with a power hostile to Vietnam. In practical terms, this has meant preventing the return to power of the Khmer Rouge backed by China, and maintaining in power a government in Phnom Penh which is sympathetic to Vietnam and capable of standing on its own after a Vietnamese troop withdrawal.

Vietnamese national security managers have sought to avoid an open ended military commitment in Kampuchea. They have realised the costs involved of a prolonged stay: an indefinite international aid and trade boycott, continued Chinese military pressures, and the possibility that an extended presence in Kampuchea would arouse anti-Vietnamese nationalist and racist sentiments among the Kampuchean population and override the credit earned by a population initially grateful to be freed from Khmer Rouge control.

It would appear in retrospect that Vietnam's 1984/85 dry season offensive was designed to buy time to build up the PRK and to set the stage for a political settlement. In 1985, Vietnam declared that it would withdraw all its troops by the end of 1990 whether or not a political settlement was reached. In January 1989, in an effort to influence the political dialogue unfolding over Kampuchea, Vietnam brought forward the date of its departure to September 1989 on the condition a political settlement was reached first. Quite clearly Vietnam has come under Soviet pressure to settle the matter in a manner parallel with the Soviet withdrawal from Afghanistan. Significantly, 1990 marks the end of Vietnam's current five-year plan and it is likely that this date was chosen so that Vietnam's economic planners could draw up the next five-year plan secure in the knowledge that the costs of the Kampuchean conflict would be behind them by then.

In summary, Vietnam does not seek to impose a military solution on the conflict in Kampuchea. Vietnam is offering to trade off the total withdrawal of its military forces in return for the cessation of all external military assistance to the resistance forces. Vietnam hopes that this trade off can be achieved within the context of an acceptable political settlement. Such a settlement, in Hanoi's view, would ensure the continued influence of the KPRP in Kampuchean domestic politics. In the event the Khmer Rouge attempted to take advantage of a Vietnamese withdrawal by toppling the PRK, Vietnam would probably view a request by the PRK for assistance sympathetically.

It needs to be stressed that regional developments are still in flux. Conservatives in Vietnam are reluctant to adopt the 'new political thinking' uncritically, and stress the importance of traditional notions of national security based on geography and military might. For the conservatives, a durable settlement in Kampuchea appears a long way off. While hostilities with China have been kept to manageable proportions, the threat along Vietnam's northern border remains real. Negotiations with Beijing on troop reductions and confidence building measures have yet to be conducted. Vietnam's military still appears to be debating what size and composition of the Vietnamese People's Army (VPA) is necessary to ensure 'sufficiency' in defence needs. At the same time, new areas of potential conflict have presented themselves as China develops naval forces capable of conducting operations in the South China Sea. In early 1988, several Vietnamese vessels were sunk after an encounter with Chinese ships in the Spratly Island chain. Although both sides downplayed the incident, there is no sign that this territorial dispute is slated for early resolution.

At present, the regional balance of power is shifting from the polarised alignments caused by Vietnam's invasion of Kampuchea, into a more fluid, multipolar balance in which the role of new actors, such as Japan and China, will become more important, and in which old roles will change as former enemies move to new forms of cooperation. Vietnam's economic dependency on the Soviet Union is unlikely to alter. Indeed, Vietnam's leadership will come under increased pressure to put its own economic house in order as a requirement for continued Soviet aid. In this respect, the advocates of reform in the Soviet Union and Vietnam are natural allies. Vietnam can also expect a drastic lessening of Soviet military aid as its forces withdraw from Kampuchea and as the size of the VPA itself is reduced.

In the post-Kampuchea period, the thrust of Vietnamese national security policy will be focused on regional arrangements, such as an expanded ASEAN, the Zone of Peace, Freedom and Neutrality, and the South East Asia Nuclear Free Zone, to secure and maintain a benign environment conducive to economic development. Vietnam will also develop a more omni-directional foreign policy in the hopes of counter-balancing its dependency on the Soviet Union. Vietnam's relations with countries such as Japan, India, France, ASEAN, Australia and even the United States will be important in this regard.

Kampuchea

During the dry season of 1984/85 Vietnamese forces unleashed their largest offensive since 1979. In a series of operations VPA regulars stormed and occupied all the resistance base camps astride the Thai-Kampuchea border. The Vietnamese and their Kampuchean allies then made determined efforts to seal off the border by erecting anti-infiltration barriers and extensive mine fields. Increasingly, PRK troops took over border duties. The 1984/85 dry season offensive was part of a five-year strategy designed to secure a political settlement of the conflict.

The size of the KPRP has increased from 'several hundred' (1979) to 10,000 (1986), while membership in core organisations has also grown to over 70,000, a fivefold increase since 1981.[19] In the period since 1985, the KPRP has made determined efforts to step up recruitment and improve the quality of party members. At the same time, efforts have also been made to build up the governmental structure at central, province (*khet*), district (*srok*) and sub-district (*phum*) levels. A National Front and mass organisations, for women, workers, and youth have also been expanded. Most importantly, the PRK Armed Forces have been built up to 40,000 and the village based self-defence militia increased to 105,000. Quite clearly the KPRP is seriously preparing to meet the political challenge mounted by the resistance coalition.

The main national security concerns of the PRK are survival during and after the period of Vietnamese withdrawal. The bulk of the Kampuchean population and agriculturally productive rice lands are under the control of the PRK. The PRK's administrative structure appears to function reasonably well given the conditions of internal war and resource scarcity. The domestic policies of the PRK appear reasonably popular. The centrepiece of the PRK political strategy is its policy of national reconciliation and the dismantling of the armed forces and top leadership of the Khmer Rouge. Thus the PRK is pursuing a national security policy of attempting to negotiate a political settlement which recognises its undoubted domestic strengths and, at the same time, isolate its main opponent, the Khmer Rouge. The PRK has been successful in gaining international acceptance that the Khmer Rouge should not return to power following a political settlement. The PRK has been less successful in splitting the resistance coalition and enticing its members, such as Norodom Sihanouk, into an anti-Khmer Rouge alliance.

The PRK must also face the possibility that no political agreement will be reached and that internal conflict will continue. PRK strategists anticipate that they will be able to deal with the threat mounted by the Khmer Rouge on condition that a Vietnamese military withdrawal is accompanied by a cessation of military assistance to the resistance coalition. The PRK strategy would then rest on winning external support and ultimately legitimacy as a result of successful nation-building efforts at home.

Laos

Laos is probably the best placed country in Indochina to take advantage of the changes currently under way in Indochina. For most of the past decade Lao national security managers have been concerned primarily with maintaining internal cohesion, suppressing externally backed resistance forces, and countering political, economic and military pressures from Thailand. At present, the Lao have achieved considerable success. External support for anti-government dissidents has fallen in recent years, and resistance activities have dropped considerably. Relations with Thailand, which plummeted to an all time low in 1987 when the two nations clashed over three border villages, has now improved dramatically. In 1988, as a result of determined efforts by both sides, agreement has been reached to turn the Mekong into a 'river of peace'. In 1989 Laos and Thailand agreed to set up joint patrols along their common border.

Laos is presently ruled by its first generation revolutionary elite. This group will pass from the scene shortly and be replaced by a younger, more technically competent and less ideologically orientated generation. In the post-Kampuchea period, Laos can be expected to maintain its close ties with Vietnam and the Soviet Union. But Laos will also intensify its efforts to open to the market economies of Southeast Asia. A recent agreement with Thailand to build a bridge over the Mekong River would greatly facilitate the transport of goods to this land-locked country. Thai and Japanese business interests can be expected to play a greater role.

Indochina and Australia

In December 1986, Australia was singled out in the Political Report to the 6th congress of the Vietnam Communist Party as one of five countries with which Vietnam wished to develop relations.[20] This friendly reference to a non-fraternal country was unprecedented and reflected the special ties between Hanoi and Canberra forged by the Labor Government after 1983, and based on the policies of the Whitlam and Fraser governments in the period 1972-1978.

Australia has provided aid and other forms of development assistance to Laos, Kampuchea and Vietnam for over thirty years. Initially aid was provided under the Colombo Plan (which also included the Republic of Vietnam). The Whitlam government extended diplomatic recognition and aid to the Democratic Republic of Vietnam in 1973. Diplomatic recognition was extended to Kampuchea in 1975. These policies were pursued by the Fraser government until 1979 when, in the aftermath of Vietnam's invasion of Kampuchea, all aid programs to Vietnam were terminated. In 1981, reacting to widespread evidence of mass atrocities by the Pol Pot regime, Australia followed Britain in withdrawing recognition from the Pol Pot regime.

The election of the Australian Labor Party to government in 1983 brought with it a sharp reversal in policy. Australia, under Foreign Minister Bill Hayden, set out to build a robust relationship with Vietnam and provide it with an alternative to complete dependence on the Soviet Union. Under Hayden, the government resumed indirect aid through multilateral and non-governmental channels, initiated a series of ministerial level exchanges, and undertook efforts to promote trading links.

During the 1983-85 period, Hayden pursued an activist policy in trying to facilitate a peaceful settlement of the conflict in Kampuchea. He visited Hanoi twice and hosted his counterpart, Nguyen Co Thach, once in Canberra. Australia also broke ranks with ASEAN and declined to co-sponsor (although it did vote for) its annual resolution in the UN General Assembly in November 1983. In March 1985, Hayden met privately with PRK Premier Hun Sen during a stop in Ho Chi Minh City. Hayden's initiatives and public comments attracted criticism by ASEAN members, especially Thailand. They were also seized upon by the opposition in the Australian Parliament. Nevertheless, Hayden's stand earned Australia a reputation in Hanoi and elsewhere in Indochina as being 'independent' on the issues in question. Australia, in their eyes, was perceived as an honest broker.

In short, Australia is valued for the political role it can play as a middle power with good relations in the region, with China and the Soviet Union, and as an ally of the United States. Australia's views are solicited and listened to with respect. No doubt the Indochinese countries expect that Australia would, in private, accurately convey their views and concerns to ASEAN, China, the Soviet Union, and the US.

Australia is also valued for its role in providing technical and other development assistance to Laos, Vietnam and Kampuchea. Australia's involvement with Laos predates the formation of the Lao People's Democratic Republic. Australia provides direct assistance to the Lao government for a variety of technical schemes, and Australian Non-Government Organisations (NGOs) are also active.[21] Aid to Vietnam is provided indirectly mainly through UN agencies.[22] Of significance is a scheme under which thirty to forty Vietnamese students study English as a second language in Canberra each year. Australia and Vietnam are involved in facilitating family reunion, family visits, trade and tourism. Australian aid to Kampuchea for humanitarian and rehabilitation purposes is provided through NGOs which operate an office in Phnom Penh.[23] Recent developments include private visits to Australia by PRK officials and the hosting of thirty Kampuchean students in Tasmania for English-language studies.

Since the adoption of the foreign investment codes in Laos and Vietnam, Australian private enterprise has been increasingly active in looking for trade and investment opportunities in Indochina. OTC has won several contracts in Vietnam and Laos to improve tele-communications by installing ground satellite equipment. Alobana, a

Perth-based company, appears to have negotiated Australia's first joint venture in the seafood processing industry.[24] BHP is involved in negotiations for oil exploration rights on an offshore block east of Vung Tau. Westpac Banking Corporation has been approached to open an office in Vietnam. In January 1989 Senator Gareth Evans, Minister for Foreign Affairs and Trade, visited Vietnam and Laos on a familiarisation tour, with trade and investment figuring high on his agenda.

On the political front, Australia was asked to play a role in the settlement of the conflict in Kampuchea, and participated in an international conference held in Paris in mid-1989 to ratify a future political settlement. Australia is also likely to be asked to contribute military personnel to whatever international control mechanism is set up to ensure the implementation of a peace settlement if one is finally reached. The Minister of Defence, Kim Beazley, has reportedly commissioned a study of a commitment of 1,000 men. In the interim, Australia will be lobbied by the Indochina states to continue to support their diplomatic efforts to end the conflict.

Australian concerns about the Soviet-Vietnamese military relationship are likely to diminish in the post-Kampuchea period as the expected cuts in Soviet military aid take place. The Soviet air and naval presence at Cam Ranh Bay will continue to be viewed as a potential threat to Australia. Official Australian statements have been less alarmist than those of the United States government, however. In this respect, it should be noted that except for improvements in the infrastructure, Soviet air and naval assets based in Cam Ranh have remained relatively static since 1984. In September 1988, Gorbachev offered to withdraw Soviet forces from Cam Ranh in exchange for a US withdrawal from its bases in the Philippines. The offer was obviously politically motivated and designed to influence Filipino attitudes. Gorbachev's offer drew a sharp response from Vietnam, however, which pointed out that the Soviet Union could negotiate any deal it liked with the US, but Cam Ranh Bay remained sovereign Vietnamese territory. In future, Gorbachev may make a dramatic gesture and announce the withdrawal of Soviet aircraft and ships from Cam Ranh in a move timed to influence Philippine-US base negotiations. Vietnam, for its part, uncomfortable about the publicity accorded the Soviet presence in Cam Ranh, may move to defuse the issue by inviting other navies to visit the bay. Regardless which direction developments take, Australia's military role in the region, specifically its membership in the Five Power Defence Arrangements and participation in the Integrated Air Defence System, have not attracted critical comment by the Indochinese states. Australia, in the post-Dibb *Review* period, is viewed in Hanoi as a benign regional power whose military forces and regional alliance relations do not pose a threat to the Indochina states.

Endnotes

1   Figures have been taken from *Pacific Defence Reporter 1989 Annual Reference Edition*, (December 1978/January 1989), pp. 177-187.

2   Initially founded in February 1930 as the Vietnam Communist Party; it was renamed Indochinese Communist Party in October of that year at the insistence of the Comintern. See MacAlister Brown, 'The Indochinese Federation Idea: Learning from History,' in Jospeh J. Zasloff, (ed.), *Postwar Indochina: Old Enemies and New Allies*, (Center for the Study of Foreign Affairs, Foreign Service Institute, U.S. Department of State, Washington, D.C. 1988), pp.77-102.

3   Vo Nguyen Giap, *Nhiem Vu Quan Su Truoc Mat Chuyen San Tong Phan Cong*, (Uy Ban Khang Chien Hanh Chinh Ha Dong, 1950), p. 14 cited in Nayan Chanda, *Brother Enemy: The War After the War*, (Harcourt Brace Jovanovich, Publishers, New York 1986), p.120.

4   M. Brown, 'The Indochinese Federation Idea'.

5   Carlyle A. Thayer, 'Laos and Vietnam: The Anatomy of a "Special Relationship"', in Martin Stuart-Fox, (ed.), *Contemporary Laos: Studies in the Politics and Society of the Lao People's Democratic Republic*, (St. Martin's Press, New York and the University of Queensland Press, Brisbane, 1982), pp.245-273; and Zasloff, 'Vietnam and Laos: Master and Apprentice,' in Zasloff (ed.), *Postwar Indochina*, pp.37-62.

6   See Kelvin Rowley and Grant Evans, *Red Brotherhood at War: Indochina Since the Fall of Saigon*, (Verso, London, 1984).

7   For a definitive account see King C. Chen, *China's War With Vietnam, 1979*, (Hoover Institution Press, Stanford, 1987).

8   Carlyle A. Thayer, 'Kampuchea: Soviet Initiatives and Regional Responses,' in Ramesh Thakur and Carlyle A. Thayer (eds.), *The Soviet Union as an Asian Pacific Power: Implications of Gorbachev's 1986 Vladivostok Initiative*, (Westview Press, Boulder, Colorado, 1987), pp.171-200.

9   Carlyle A. Thayer, 'The Regularization of Politics: Continuity and Change in the Party's Central Committee, 1951-1986,' in David G. Marr and Christine P. White (eds.), *Postwar Vietnam: Dilemmas in Socialist Development*, (Southeast Asia Program, Cornell University , Ithaca, N.Y., 1988), pp.177-193.

10   Papers submitted to these two conferences have since been published. See Ramesh Thakur and Carlyle A. Thayer (eds.), *The Soviet Union as an Asian Pacific Power: Implications of Gorbachev's 1986 Vladivostok Initiative*, (Westview Press, Boulder, Colorado, 1987); and Jospeh J. Zasloff, (ed.), *Postwar Indochina: Old Enemies and New Allies*, (Center for the Study of Foreign Affairs, Foreign Service Institute, U.S. Department of State, Washington, D.C., 1988).

11   Donald S. Zagoria, 'The Soviet-Vietnamese Alliance,' in J. Zasloff (ed.), *Postwar Indochina*, pp. 139-140; see also Amin Saikal, 'Afghanistan,' in Thakur and Thayer (eds.), *The Soviet Union as an Asian Pacific Power*, pp.154-156.

12   Nayan Chanda, 'Vietnam and Cambodia: Domination and Security,' in J. Zasloff (ed.), *Postwar Indochina*, p.64; see also Zagoria in *ibid.*, pp.139-140; and J. Zasloff, *ibid.*, p.xvi.

13   William J. Duiker, 'China and Vietnam and the Struggle for Indochina,' in J. Zasloff (ed.), *Postwar Indochina*, p.188; and Zaslof, *ibid.*, p.xvii, and p.188.

14   *Vietnam News Agency*, 19 October 1988.

15   This section is based, in part, on discussions held by the author with Vietnamese government officials in Hanoi in December 1987.

16   Nguyen Quyet, 'Renovate the Contingent of Party Cadres in the Army', Hanoi Home Service, broadcast in three instalments on 7 and 8 November 1988; AFP dispatch from Vientiane, 23 November 1988; and Nayan Chanda, 'Taking a Soft Line,' *Far Eastern Economic Review*, 8 December 1988, p.27.
17   *The Washington Times*, 17 January 1989; Humphrey Hawksley dispatch from Hanoi, *The Australian*, 2 March 1989.
18   Hanoi Radio, 31 January 1989.
19   Michael Vickery, *Kampuchea: Politics, Economics and Society*, (Allen & Unwin, Sydney, 1986), pp.xvii, 78-79, 117-118 and 186.
20   The others were Sweden, Finland, France, and Japan.
21   Governmental aid to Laos, including all forms of bilateral assistance (project, training, food aid and emergency) and Australian contributions to multilateral sources totalled nearly $A 6.4 million in 1987.
22   Australian aid to Vietnam in this form totals over $A 7.4 million.
23   Australia is the largest western donor of aid inside Kampuchea with an annual contribution of nearly $A 4 million.
24   *Vietnam News Agency*, 23 November 1988.

CHAPTER 21

THE SOUTH PACIFIC AND PAPUA NEW GUINEA

David Hegarty

Introduction

For most of this century the South Pacific has been a quiet and isolated backwater in international affairs. Except for a brief period during World War I when Australian and New Zealand forces seized Germany's Pacific colonies (New Guinea, Western Samoa and Nauru), and for an important phase of the Pacific War of 1941-45 when Japan advanced southward and occupied a number of island territories, the region has not been the object of great power interest or rivalry. Small populations on tiny, resource-poor islands, long distances from theatres or likely theatres of conflict, the lack of important communications choke-points, and the absence of exploitable, defence-related mineral and other resources have contributed to the strategic irrelevance of the South Pacific.

Politically the region has been orientated toward the West, a pattern established by the colonial powers - Britain, France, United States, Australia and New Zealand - and maintained beyond the onset of decolonisation in the 1960s and 1970s. The major defence alliance - the ANZUS Treaty - has been regarded as providing a security 'umbrella' for the South Pacific region as a whole and has reinforced Western hegemony. Although France has maintained a little publicised but relatively large security force in its territories since the mid-1960s, the defence of Western security interests has been left to the region's 'wardens', Australia and New Zealand. Security issues within the region have surfaced only occasionally. Anti-colonial rebellions, for example, in the early part of the century were suppressed by respective administering authorities. The controversial transfer of West New Guinea from the Dutch to the Indonesian government in the 1960s led to an increase in Australia's defence effort in its then territory of Papua New Guinea (PNG). In the 1970s, concern over the potential for instability and strife in the newly emerging island states produced a round of contingency planning by defence staffs in Canberra and Wellington. In 1980, troops from the PNG Defence Force, with Australian logistical support, were required to quell a rebellion in Vanuatu in the days following that country's independence.

Nevertheless the regional security environment was regarded almost universally as benign.[1]

A Changing Strategic Environment

(i) Small New States

The first significant change in the post-World War II strategic complexion of the South Pacific occurred with the onset of decolonisation in the 1960s. Beginning with Western Samoa's independence in 1962, the South Pacific witnessed the emergence of nine independent sovereign states, and four states which are self-governing in 'association' with their former administering powers.[2] (See Table 1 for the political status of each state and territory.) All are active in regional affairs and most are participants in international forums, although only five Pacific island states are members of the United Nations. Decolonisation, however, is incomplete. Nine dependencies remain of which perhaps only three, Palau, New Caledonia and French Polynesia, are likely to achieve some form of autonomy or independence before the end of the century.

The island states and territories are small in size and population. With the exception of PNG, which has 3.5 million people and accounts for 65 per cent of the region's population and 84 per cent of its land area, all others qualify for the description of mini-state. All states and territories are economically fragile and face the problems of achieving growth and minimising dependency on foreign aid, capital and expertise. (See Table 2 for selected social and economic statistics.) Only Fiji and PNG have some military capability to defend their territory. Yet these apparent similarities mask a host of diversities among the South Pacific states. Their colonial histories and practices are different. Their traditional political cultures and social structures, broadly defined as Melanesian, Polynesian or Micronesian, have forged different styles of leadership and political behaviour. Their political systems vary from the fluid democracies of PNG and the Solomon Islands, to the monarchical and socially disciplined Kingdom of Tonga, through to, since 1987, a military-backed administration in Fiji. Their economies vary markedly in size and although all exhibit a high degree of openness and dependence, some, particularly those in Melanesia, have a greater potential to achieve viability than others. Such diversities have rendered obsolete the assumption that the region is uniformly similar in political outlook and behaviour.

In their initial years of independence the Pacific island states focused firmly on domestic and regional affairs. Island governments concentrated on adapting the colonial structures they had inherited, on

Table 1: Pacific Island States and Territories - Constitutional Status

Country	Constitutional Status
Forum Members	
Cook Islands	Free Association with NZ (1965)
Federated States of Micronesia	Free Association with the US (1986)
Fiji	Independent (1970)
Kiribati	Independent (1979)
Marshall Islands	Free Association with the US (1986)
Nauru	Independent (1968)
Niue	Free Association with NZ (1974)
Papua New Guinea	Independent (1975)
Solomon Islands	Independent (1978)
Tonga	Independent Monarchy (1970)
Tuvalu	Independent (1978)
Vanuatu	Independent (1980)
Western Samoa	Independent (1962)
Non-Forum	
American Samoa	US Territory
French Polynesia	French overseas territory
Guam	United States Unincorporated Territory
New Caledonia	French overseas territory
Norfolk Island	Australian Territory
Northern Mariana Islands	Commonwealth of the US (1986)
Palau	US Trust Territory
Pitcairn Island	British Territory
Tokelau Islands	New Zealand Territory
Wallis and Futuna Islands	French overseas territory

establishing their own political legitimacy, and on the difficult task of economic development. Decolonisation had proceeded relatively smoothly, except in Vanuatu, where French intransigence and an externally inspired rebellion had traumatised the independence process. Relations between the new states and their former metropolitan powers remained reasonably harmonious. Regionalism became the focus of the new states' foreign policies. Notions such as 'The Pacific Way' were current in an endeavour to engender solidarity and a Pacific identity. The South Pacific Forum, established in 1971, provided an organisation for the island states (including Australia and New Zealand) to discuss political and developmental issues and gave the region a voice in international affairs. The question of decolonisation, particularly in New Caledonia, was frequently on the Forum's agenda, but broader questions of defence and security, and of alignments generally, were rarely discussed. There was a tacit assumption that the exclusion of the

Table 2: South Pacific— select indicators

Country	Land area km²	Sea area km² '000	Population 1986 '000	Population growth rate	GNP US$m	GNP per capita US$m	Trend GDP per cap.%*	Total aid US$m	Aid per capita US$	Aust. aid as % total	Aust. DCP 1987-1988 A$m#
Cook Islands	240	1,830	17	-0.6	21	1,235	1	26.4	155	2.5	—
Fiji	18,272	1,290	715	1.6	1,282	1,793	-1	42.5	59	19.8	0.37
Kiribati	690	3,550	66	1.3	26	393	-2	13.4	203	14.2	0.1
Nauru	21	431	8	0.5	160	20,000	na	na	na	—	—
New Caledonia	19,103	1,740	165	1.2	1,200	7,272	na	206.6	1,387	—	—
Niue	259	390	3	-0.3	3	1,000	na	4.2	1,400	6.4	—
Papua New Guinea	462,840	3,120	3,593	2.6	2,409	772	0.5	263.6	73	81.9	24.0
Solomon Islands	28,369	1,340	286	3.4	126	440	-2	30.2	106	14.6	2.0
Tokelau	10	290	2	na	1	500	na	2.0	1,000	—	na
Tonga	699	596	108	1.6	100	925	2	15.1	139	25.2	1.0
Tuvalu	26	857	8	1.3	4	500	-5	4.4	550	13.6	—
Vanuatu	11,880	680	142	2.9	118	830	-5	24.4	171	23.8	3.4
Western Samoa	2,935	120	165	0.8	110	666	-1	23.3	142	16.3	0.7

*Economic Growth: Trend in the annual percentage change in real GDP *per capita* over various periods from late 1970s to mid-1980s.
#General Defence Cooperation Program (DCP) Assistance to South Pacific an additional $9.0 m (figures exclude Patrol Boat Program).

Sources: *Pacific Economic Bulletin*, Vol. 3, No. 2, December 1988; Muriel Brookfield and R. Gerard Ward (eds), *New Directions in the South Pacific—A Message for Australia*, Academy of the Social Sciences in Australia, Research School of Pacific Studies, Canberra, 1988. Australian International Development Assistance Bureau (ADAB), *Australia's Relations with the South Pacific*, March 1987. R. Babbage 'Australia's Strategic Approach to the Southwest Pacific' Paper presented at the *Strategic Cooperation and Competition in the Pacific Islands Conference*, Washington, May 1989.

Soviet Union from the region minimised superpower rivalry and enhanced security.

(ii) External Power Interests

Throughout the 1980s, however, both the pattern of regional politics and the strategic environment became more complex. The major powers stepped up their level of interest. The Soviet Union, which had been rebuffed by regional states over its invasion of Afghanistan in 1979-80, sought again to extend its influence into the South Pacific. Commercial and diplomatic activity was lifted and Mr Gorbachev's Vladivostok speech of July 1986 confirmed a sharpened Soviet focus on the region. The United States, in response, devoted more policy attention to the South Pacific and patched up some difficulties it had had with island states by signing a Tuna Fisheries Accord. Japan announced in January 1987 a 'new deal' in its relations with island states and foreshadowed new aid packages which would make it the region's most prominent aid donor by 1990. China also raised its interest in regional affairs. A series of high-level visits from countries around the Pacific Rim, from the ASEAN states (Singapore, Indonesia, Malaysia) and from as far afield as the Middle East attested to the region's higher profile. Libya, in an effort to irritate France and Western interests generally, developed links with Vanuatu in 1986 and gave encouragement to small Pacific independence movements especially in the French territories. France became more alert to regional affairs, and the United Kingdom arrested its declining level of interest. India began to take some note of regional politics, and late in the decade Israel established diplomatic relations with all independent South Pacific states.

(iii) Strategic 'Map'

The South Pacific's strategic 'map' has also been changed significantly by a number of important developments. In the late 1970s all countries and territories in the South Pacific declared 200-mile exclusive economic zones. The area of these zones totalled more than 30 million square kilometres, covered much of the South Pacific Ocean, and contained some of the world's most productive tuna fishing grounds. The refusal by the United States to accept the jurisdiction of the island states over migratory species of fish in these zones caused considerable irritation in Island-US relationships. In 1984, the dispute between the United States and New Zealand over the latter's anti-nuclear policies, and the subsequent diminution of the ANZUS Alliance produced not only tensions between the Western allies, but in the Pacific islands themselves a degree of uncertainty over regional security. In 1985 the declaration by the South Pacific Forum nations of a South Pacific Nuclear Free Zone

(SPNFZ) - the Treaty of Rarotonga - was an important if somewhat symbolic assertion by the region of a desire to control its destiny. China and the Soviet Union signed the protocols to the Treaty which invited all nuclear powers to observe its provisions, but the United States, France and the United Kingdom, the traditional friends of the island region, refused to do so. Another important but less publicised strategic development has been the increase in research and exploration for seabed minerals and other oceanographic features undertaken by many of the world's industrial powers.[3]

(iv) Domestic Political Volatility

This decade has also witnessed a trend towards domestic political volatility in the island states and territories.[4] A military *coup* in Fiji in May 1987, which saw Colonel (now Major-General) Rabuka overthrow the democratically-elected coalition government of the Fiji Labour Party and the Indo-Fijian-backed National Federation Party and install an interim administration consisting of many members of the defeated Alliance Party, severely dented the South Pacific's reputation for stability. The *coup* became a benchmark in the assessment of regional stability and highlighted, in an extreme way, the emerging political turbulence and potential for instability elsewhere in the region. In Papua New Guinea, for example, shifting coalition governments, law and order problems, restiveness in the army, and in 1988-89, violence and the threat of secession in the copper-rich North Solomons (Bougainville) Province raised fundamental questions about the country's stability. In Vanuatu, a bitter power struggle between Prime Minister Walter Lini and his former radical colleague but now rival, Barak Sope, led to demonstrations in the capital, the call-out of the island's small military force, the attempted dismissal of Lini's government by the President (Sope's uncle), and an unsuccessful legal action for sedition against the President, Sope and others. Vanuatu consequently has become tense and divided.

The pattern of turbulence has not been confined to the independent countries. In New Caledonia, the on-going trauma of decolonisation has produced an acutely polarised society, intermittent violence, a serious clash in April 1988 between militant *independentists* and French commandos which left more than 20 dead, and in April 1989 the tragic assassination of the Kanak independence leader Jean-Marie Tjibaou. In the US Trust Territory of Palau, factional power plays revolving around the acceptance of the Compact of Free Association, have resulted in political violence, the assassination of one president and the suicide of another. Elsewhere in the Pacific, there have been lesser degrees of turbulence, including industrial strife, parliamentary standoffs and the formation of opposition parties. Even in Tonga there have been stirrings against monarchical rule.

(v) Regional Power Structure

The character of regionalism, which has been assiduously cultivated by the early generation of island leaders, also underwent some changes. The membership of the South Pacific Forum expanded to include the Federated States of Micronesia and the Marshall Islands. The 'clubbish' atmosphere of the Forum was all but dispensed with. A more professional approach to the management of regional problems became apparent. The South Pacific Bureau for Economic Cooperation (SPEC) was renamed the Forum Secretariat, and a number of ideas borrowed from elsewhere, for example, the ASEAN practice of dialogue with aid donors, was implemented. Individually, the island states have begun to diversify their external relationships and although regionalism has remained a major tenet of their foreign policies, many states, influenced by a new generation of leaders, have became more international in outlook.

New tensions however have arisen between Forum members, adding to the long-standing but often muted Melanesian/Polynesian divisions. In 1986, a 'Melanesian Spearhead' group was formed consisting of Papua New Guinea, Vanuatu and the Solomon Islands.[5] The 'spearhead' was designed to promote more strongly the question of independence for New Caledonia and to give the Melanesian states more clout in the Forum. The group also shared PNG's view that Australia and New Zealand have been too influential in the Forum and that the islands themselves should set the agenda for regionalism. The effects of this Melanesian 'caucus' were to cut across the grain of consensus decision-making in the Forum and to stimulate thinking about the formation of a 'Polynesian summit' as a countervailing force. The aftermath of the declaration of the Treaty of Rarotonga also produced divisions. The Treaty, an Australian initiative, designed in large part to harness the strong anti-nuclear sentiment of the region while at the same time preserving Australian and American security interests, found favour with the Polynesian states because the decision to allow ship access remained the prerogative of individual states. For their part, the Melanesian states felt that the Treaty was 'soft' on the question of transit and port visit rights for foreign navies.

The implications for regionalism of the Fiji *coups* have also become apparent. Fiji has lost its status as leader and lynch-pin of the islands region, and PNG has moved to assert its position as the third 'power' in the South Pacific behind Australia and New Zealand. There have been other subtle shifts in the regional power structure. Australia and New Zealand, while still regarded as the major forces and patrons of the region, have lost some relative influence, largely as a result of their reactions to the Fiji *coups*. Other island states were less perturbed by the *coups*, seeing them as an inevitable move to restore indigenous Fijian authority. At the end of the decade, relations between Fiji and both Australia and New Zealand remain strained. New Zealand also lost some relative standing with the Polynesian states over its anti-nuclear foreign policy, although in some sections of Melanesia it was applauded for having taken such a bold and adventurous step as well as for having stood up to the superpower United States. Ironically, having lost some relative political clout, Australia and New Zealand have strengthened defence relations with most countries except Fiji. In particular, Australia strengthened its commitment to the defence of PNG through a multi-purpose quasi-treaty known as the 'Joint Declaration of Principles' governing relations between the two countries. Both Australia and New Zealand have strengthened ties with Vanuatu. Long regarded as the regional maverick because of its radical foreign policy tendencies, Father Lini's government quickly embraced ANZ defence and security assistance when challenged in a domestic power-play by his rival, Barak Sope. France, having been soundly condemned across the region since the 1970s for its nuclear-testing program in French Polynesia and for its refusal to decolonise its territories, quite remarkably has revived its flagging diplomatic fortunes. Careful cultivation of the Polynesian states and the post-*coups* regime in Fiji helped France regain standing, but the major factors in France's improved position have been the regional partnership strategy adopted by the Rocard government (elected in 1988), its progressive stance on decolonisation, and its improved bilateral relations with Australia and New Zealand.

(vi) Security Pressure Points

While increasing interest by external powers in the South Pacific and tensions in both domestic and regional politics have been major features of the 1980s, the region's two security 'pressure points' - the independence struggle in New Caledonia and the situation on the PNG/Indonesia border - have continued to pose policy and security dilemmas. Although quite different and separate issues, these security 'pressure points' have been so regarded because both have required, in the course of the decade, the application of military force to contain the disputants. Also, both have held the potential to escalate and, in certain circumstances, to involve militarily other countries in the region.

At the end of the 1980s there have been only ambiguous signals that these issues were heading towards a more permanent resolution. In

New Caledonia an agreement of June 1988 known as the Matignon Accords set up a framework for economic reform measures to benefit the Kanaks, a system of quasi-federal power-sharing (or power separation) for the pro- and anti-independence communities, and a national referendum on the question of independence to be held in 1998. Whether or not the three signatories to the Accord - the FLNKS, the RPCR, and the French government - can maintain support for the agreement in an atmosphere of deep suspicion and polarisation is problematical.

On the issue of the Papua New Guinea-Indonesia border, there have been developments, including the signing in 1986-87 of a 'Treaty of Mutual Respect, Friendship and Cooperation' between Indonesia and PNG, indicating a greater willingness by both governments to reduce tensions and build confidence in bilateral dealings. The survival, however, in Irian Jaya of a small, nationalist guerrilla movement, the *Organisasi Papua Merdeka* (OPM), which continues its struggle for independence and which at times uses PNG's territory as sanctuary, as well as the continuation of border crossings by Indonesian troops in pursuit of these guerrillas, does not augur well for a settlement of the issue.

The South Pacific 'pattern of islands' has thus undergone considerable change. Security questions have become firmly on the region's agenda. But obviously the region has not become a zone of conflict nor one in which the superpowers or their clients have been engaged (or have had much incentive to engage) in open competition. The absence of such confrontation or of polarizing issues in the South Pacific raises interesting methodological questions about a framework for analysing regional security. Buzan's idea of a 'security complex' which assumes that 'local sets of states exist whose major security perceptions and concerns link together sufficiently closely so that their national security problems cannot realistically be considered apart from one another', may perhaps be usefully applied.6

The South Pacific is no longer as stable as once it was. The different players, from the largest to the smallest, have differing views on regional security. Cross-cutting pressures and tendencies are likely to deepen, making the security outlook somewhat less predictable. It is appropriate, therefore, to consider the differing security perceptions, and those issues likely to disturb or to continue to disturb the regional order. These issues include the Soviet Union's interest in developing influence in the islands' region; meddling in regional affairs by external countries, in this instance by Libya; decolonisation issues, particularly that of New Caledonia; political instability and economic pressures in the island states; and the potential for conflict along the PNG-Indonesia border.

Security Perceptions

Throughout the 1980s divergent, though by no means opposed, views of security amongst the regional states have become obvious. For the island states, the fundamental goal of economic viability and self-sufficiency have shaped their security perceptions. Vulnerability to physical attack (for all except PNG and Fiji) has been accepted as a given. The major 'threat' has been that of continued economic dependence, not only on the vagaries of the international markets, but particularly on the goodwill of aid donors. Allied to this has been threats of illegal exploitation of their 200-mile Economic Exclusion Zone (EEZ) marine resources by foreign companies or countries, and of pollution of the maritime environment by, for example, France's nuclear testing activities. In addition, the threat from natural disasters - cyclones, tidal waves, and probable rises in the sea-level as a consequence of the 'greenhouse effect' - has weighed heavily on many states, especially those low-lying coral atoll countries.

The region's recently-won independent status also affects the island countries' notion of security. Most small states hold to a particularly acute view of sovereignty and are sensitive to perceived interference in their affairs or by perceived patronising attitudes by the 'big brothers', Australia and New Zealand. On occasion what might be regarded elsewhere as normal diplomatic discourse has been regarded at times by some states as a form of 'direction' by the larger regional powers. In other instances, Kiribati, for example, was annoyed at being (as Kiribati saw it) 'lectured' by Australia over the security implications of dealing with the Soviet Union, when Kiribati's foreign and defence review had itself advised the government on such problems.

Domestic political instability that disrupts effective government and development is considered by most states to be next in the ranking of security threats. The next concern is that of external power intrusions into regional affairs. Some island states explicitly, others tacitly, accept a low-key Western hegemonic influence in the region; all seek to discourage superpower rivalry; most discourage a Soviet presence although the once universal antipathy to the Soviet Union is now fading. Vanuatu has been the one state whose ideological orientation has been towards reducing or at least finding some 'balance' to Western influence. In May 1986, Vanuatu's Prime Minister Father Walter Lini described Australia and New Zealand as the biggest threat to the region's security, citing alleged neo-colonialist desires of both these countries to dictate policy in the region, and the 'threat' posed by the existence of Australian and New Zealand military forces 'ready' for duty in the South Pacific. Later, Vanuatu partially backed away from this view by hosting and participating in a New Zealand military exercise and by expressing support for Australia's defence cooperation program. Father Lini's appeal for ANZ security support during the political turbulence in Port Vila in 1988 indicated a greater degree of pragmatism in his security perceptions than previous rhetoric had indicated. While Vanuatu has been most vocal in challenging the conventional view of security, there is a small body of opinion developing around the view that, if the West does not get its house in order (presumably by being more attentive to, and respectful of, small state interests) neither superpower should be allowed to have a presence.

Australia and New Zealand share similar perceptions of security in the South Pacific despite a major divergence of view over whether security is best obtained by participation in, or withdrawal from, a nuclear alliance. Both recognise the island states' primary security concern as that of economic vulnerability. In the ANZ view, lack of economic development leads to social discontent and political instability. Opportunities are thus opened for external meddling, for disruption to the regional security environment, and for political damage to ANZ's security interests. These latter interests are perceived in more conventional terms, such as the protection of sea lines of communication, of territories and of commerce, the exclusion, or at least the limitation, of influence of the potentially inimical external powers or groups, and the facilitation of access to the region by ANZ's defence forces. The ANZ view of their security within the regional security is thus cast essentially in geo-strategic terms.

Regional Security Issues

(i) The Soviet Union

The Soviet Union has made it clear that its primary objective is to establish a position of influence in the South Pacific.[7] Mr Gorbachev's speech in Vladivostok in July 1986 referred to the need to 'lend dynamism' to Moscow's relationships with the South Pacific states and, by listing most of them in his speech, indicated a sharper, high-level focus than had been the case in over a decade. Soviet Foreign Minister Shevardnadze said in Australia in 1986 he expected Soviet practical influence to develop out of its commercial dealings with the islands. In 1989, a senior Soviet diplomat in Australia said that the Soviet Union would build its influence in the region by using Australia (and its good standing with the islands) as a conduit. The Soviets' recent efforts to develop relationships in the region have netted few significant gains, although Gorbachev's reversal of his country's confrontationist approach to international relations has produced a softening of attitude toward the Soviet Union within the region. In 1985, the Soviet Union concluded a one-year agreement with Kiribati to fish for tuna, and in 1987 reached a fishing agreement with Vanuatu on more favourable terms, including the right of port access. On each occasion, the fees offered were well over the price which other distant- water fishing nations were prepared to pay. Neither agreement was renewed because the island states were not prepared to accept the new lower fee offer of the Soviet Union. Soviet officials have continued to explore a possible multilateral fisheries treaty. Soviet trade and commercial delegations visited the region but concluded few deals. Diplomatic activity, however, has been stepped up, a small amount of aid has been delivered (tractors to Vanuatu, but without manuals or spare parts!), and there have been some indications of increased support by Soviet-front organisations for regional 'activists'. A concerted effort has been made to broaden the Soviets' relationships with Australia and New Zealand, one by-product of which was a possible fishing agreement with Australia. Soviet requests to PNG have resulted in permission being granted for a resident mission in Port Moresby - the first such mission in the islands' region.

The Soviet Union's broad strategic objectives in the region are relatively clear. Mr Gorbachev's new style diplomacy notwithstanding, the Soviet Union seeks to extend its access to all parts of the globe (in the case of the South Pacific to an area in which it had had virtually no formal access); to complicate Western alliance management and relationships in what has been a Western regional preserve; and to detach the islands from their commitment to the West. Since the mid-1980s, there has been speculation on the more specific military objectives or at least the potentially important military-strategic gains which could have impelled the Soviet Union to seek a foothold in the islands' region. American officials and others have speculated that an island location would enhance the Soviets' knowledge of military geography, and would allow greater knowledge of the troughs, trenches and underwater peaks of the ocean floor which may be used for submarine deployment and transit or hiding in wartime contingencies. Soviet research vessels have surveyed areas of the South Pacific from south and east of New Zealand, the central Fiji-Tonga-Samoa triangle, east to Tahiti, north to Hawaii and north-west through the Melanesian Archipelago. Much of this research has a naval or military value. Such areas, however, are a long way from likely theatres of operations, although they may be used for hiding or transit purposes. Some areas would be alternative high density shipping lanes in the event of the straits in Southeast Asian waters being closed.

A central South Pacific location may advance Soviet intelligence gathering techniques, although regional signals intelligence (SIGINT) surveillance could be readily obtained from facilities within the Soviet embassies in Canberra and Wellington. Other suggested advantages which might accrue to the Soviet Union from such a location include easier surveillance of US missile and SDI research on Kwajalein, operational benefits for the Soviet space and military satellite programs, support for future Soviet strategic minerals deep sea-mining in the Pacific, and improved Soviet cross-Pacific air traffic capabilities. The Soviet Union could perhaps also be interested in setting up an array of underwater acoustic devices in waters off Vanuatu, presumably to monitor submarines and other shipping. Defence specialists have dismissed the idea, although it is of interest that a decade ago the Soviets reportedly showed an interest in similar monitoring devices in much the same area of ocean. While of interest, these 'objectives' would seem to be currently of less importance than the political and more general strategic objectives. Critics point out that had a location such as Kiribati been of such strategic significance, the Soviet Union would scarcely have quibbled over a million dollars in the renegotiation of its fishing deal.

Governments of the region have responded with caution to Soviet initiatives. Certainly there has been no rush to embrace the Soviet bear. Regional concerns revolve around the potential for superpower competition which an increased Soviet presence and profile would bring; the development by the Soviet Union of constituencies within local politics; the capacities of the small states to withstand the economic and other blandishments of the Soviet Union and their ability to manage a Soviet on-shore presence (in terms of surveillance and counter-intelligence); the problems which would arise should the Soviets insert themselves into local conflict situations; and the Soviets' continuing propensity to use extra-diplomatic methods of political penetration.

(ii) Libya

Libya's interest in the South Pacific has raised considerable alarm in most parts of the region.[8] Contacts have been developed over the past few years between Libya and the *Front Uni de Libération Kanak* (FULK) party in the New Caledonian independence coalition. The FULK party is small and not particularly influential in the overall independence movement. Nevertheless, on a number of occasions young supporters of the FULK have been sent to Libya for training. Of importance also have been the official contacts which developed between Libya and

Vanuatu. After criticising the American bombing raid on Tripoli in early 1986, Father Lini's government in Vanuatu established diplomatic relations with Tripoli. In the following 12 months there were a number of visits by representatives from Libya, some reportedly offering large investment and trade opportunities. A small number of Ni-Vanuatu received training in Libya and some were reportedly involved in the demonstration/riot in Port Vila in May 1988 which brought to a head the struggle for power between the former Vanua'aku Party Secretary-General Barak Sope and Prime Minister Lini. Attempts were made by Libyan officials to establish a Libyan People's Bureau (embassy) in Port Vila early in 1987. But after Australian and New Zealand expressions of concern, extensive press coverage, a dramatic flight by Foreign Minister Hayden to consult with New Zealand's Prime Minister Lange over the issue, and domestic criticism, Prime Minister Lini deferred the establishment of a Bureau. The Libyan connection broadened to include links with the OPM, the small guerrilla movement operating sporadically in the PNG-Indonesia border area, although it is unlikely that Libyan-sourced material support has found its way to the OPM.

Regional concerns revolved around the following: Libyan activity in other parts of the world - including the Caribbean, the Philippines and Thailand - has been aimed at mischief-making and destabilisation, and there was little reason to expect it to be different in the Pacific; encouragement may have been given for some form of terrorist activity; the training of Kanaks in Libya would exacerbate the problem in New Caledonia (Libyan-trained Kanaks took some part in the confrontation with French security forces in April-May 1988); the supply of even a small amount of arms and/or training for the OPM would enhance its capability and thus escalate tension along the PNG-Indonesia border; and the type of training and political indoctrination likely to be received in Libya would be alien to the general ambience of South Pacific politics.

Libya's interest appeared aimed at antagonising the French. Colonel Gaddafi is on record as saying that he will stir unrest in the French territories unless France desists from its resistance to his policies in North Africa. The former Libyan representative in Canberra made it clear that Libya would continue to support the Pacific's independence struggles. By 1989, the heat had gone out of the issue and although both FULK and Sope have had contact with Libyan officials based in Kuala Lumpur, the level of Libyan activity and the amount of assistance provided to the region has been small.

(iii) France and New Caledonia

High on the agenda of regional security as far as many (but not all) of the South Pacific states (including ANZ) are concerned is that of France's role. In French Polynesia, France continues its nuclear testing program at Muroroa Atoll. France justifies its testing program in the Pacific on the grounds that it is maintaining its independent nuclear deterrent and contributing to Western security generally. It sees French Polynesia as a part of France and, despite regional criticism of its testing program, sees no reason to abandon it. France points to studies which show that to date its nuclear testing has not been harmful to the environment and asserts that a French military presence constitutes a stabilising, pro-Western factor in regional security.

The political situation in New Caledonia remains a matter for concern to the region. Most states recognise that the demographic composition of the population in New Caledonia makes for difficulties in decolonisation - the indigenous people, the Kanaks, number only 45 per cent of the population - and that a transfer of power to a minority (assuming the French were willing to do so) would be a unique occasion in colonial history. However, the region wants to see steady and smooth progress towards some form of independence for New Caledonia. The Mitterand Government (1981-86) took steps towards a form of 'independence-in-association'. With the election of the Chirac Government in early 1986, these tentative steps were reversed, financial powers were withdrawn and land reform measures were abandoned. This reversal prompted the South Pacific Forum countries to have New Caledonia reinscribed on the United Nations' list of territories to be decolonised - a step the Forum had been reluctant to take for some years. The Chirac government refused to cooperate, or to listen to advice from outside the islands, including that from Japan and Indonesia.

Politics became acutely polarised. A referendum in September 1987 (boycotted by the Kanaks) resulted in a 58 per cent vote in favour of New Caledonia remaining part of France, but in effect resolved nothing. A new constitution which attempted to 'strait-jacket' New Caledonia's politics by splitting the regions equally between loyalists and *independentists* offered no way out of the impasse. Confrontations took place as riot police dispersed political assemblies. The government felt it necessary to deploy over 8,000 security personnel (for a population of 150,000!) in the territory. The upshot was a series of violent clashes in April-May 1988. In the bloodiest incident, hostages seized by Kanak militants were released by French troops. Overall more than 25 people were killed.[9]

The return of President Mitterand in May 1988, the election of the Rocard government, and the preparedness by Kanak and loyalist leaders to reach an accommodation produced a dramatic turnaround. Dialogue between the various parties led to the Matignon Accords which mapped out a path for constitutional evolution. Despite the tragic assassination (by a militant Kanak) in April 1989 of independence leader, Jean-Marie Tjibaou, there appear to be reasonable prospects for a settlement of the New Caledonian crisis, for France's image in the region to be improved, and for it to normalise relations with the states of the region.[10] Much will depend on New Caledonia's leaders on both sides of politics to contain their militant supporters, and on the development of a bipartisan policy on the territory's future within metropolitan France.

(iv) Political Instability and Economic Pressures

The trend to political turbulence in the South Pacific by the late 1980s has raised a number of general and potential security concerns. An unstable state has a disruptive and detrimental effect on the well-being and general security of its people. In certain circumstances (though not all) an unstable state acts as a magnet, drawing external players, often with no intrinsic interest, into the arena and provides opportunities for meddling. Domestic instability facilitates the development of constituencies by external influences enabling the promotion of sectional, ideological or other causes. Disaffected groups may adopt militant tactics, promote their cause by armed struggle, and seek external patrons. Political instability may lead to unpredictable outcomes, sudden shifts in policies and priorities, perhaps even in alignments. Instability in one or a number of the region's states may disrupt regional and bilateral relationships or networks, thereby inhibiting the development of a security community and inviting competition between the larger external powers.

The destabilising tendencies in the region are multiple and complex. Race and ethnicity are obvious primary causes of tension in the communally-based societies of Fiji and New Caledonia. The *coups* in Fiji in May and September of 1987, for example, cannot be explained simply in terms of race, but they had as their basis the desire by the Fijian coupists and their supporters to prevent Indo-Fijian rule and to restore ethnic Fijian political paramountcy.[11] A military-backed administration is currently in control. But divisions within the Fijian community over the proposed coalition, a looming leadership succession struggle, the prospect that the Indo-Fijians will be permanently second-class citizens, and the fact that some small sections have contemplated armed resistance are clear pointers to future tension.

In New Caledonia, while the large majority of (Melanesian) Kanaks support the movement for independence, the large majority of the other racial and ethnic groups within the territory oppose independence. The history of antagonism between these groups does not augur well for whatever post-colonial settlement is negotiated. Ethnicity plays a different role in the heterogeneous Melanesian societies of PNG, Solomon Islands and Vanuatu. Loyalty to small-scale clans or linguistic units, an antipathy by those units to others around them, and an apprehension about belonging to the aggregate 'nation', has led to parochialism, ethno-nationalism and, at times, secessionism. Such sentiments illustrate the considerable difficulties in the region in building enduring, coherent and legitimate nation-states.

A wide range of economic and social factors have increasingly impinged on political stability. Population growth rates for all countries of the South Pacific are high, with the Solomon Islands, for example, recording 3.3 per cent annual increase. The process of urban drift has continued, unemployment has risen and economic inequalities have increased. Social differentiation, already established in the hierarchical Polynesian societies, has become increasingly apparent and social class tensions have been reflected in political action. Intra-elite power struggles, a growing incidence of corruption, and a perceived 'neglect of the social contract' by political leaders have produced degrees of cynicism and disenchantment in many Pacific island states.

Institutional weaknesses have also contributed to political turbulence. The constitutional provision in PNG, for example, which allows governments to be changed frequently on the floor of parliament has, in that country, disrupted the process of governance.[12] The absence or relative weakness of political parties and the consequent lack of integration and communication between governors and governed, has emerged as a major structural problem in Pacific politics.

Poor economic growth rates in the South Pacific affect both security and stability. Although there is no strong correlation between political instability and levels of economic development, there is a concern in all developing countries that social discontent will rise if rates of economic growth do not increase sufficiently to match both population increase and the public's rising expectations. There are indications in the South Pacific in recent years that the once sound economic growth performance is slipping. According to a number of recent studies, all island countries have experienced negative or stagnant rates of economic growth within the past decade, with the following countries showing a consistently negative trend: Fiji, Solomon Islands, Vanuatu, Western Samoa, Kiribati and Tuvalu. The Solomon Islands' economist Tony Hughes has likened the situation to that of 'climbing the down escalator'.[13] Neither the expansion of government revenue nor productivity in the traditional land and subsistence base can keep pace with the increase in population and the demands for economic services.

There are, however, stabilizing forces at work which offer a counter-balance of sorts to the turbulence. The post-colonial record of the region has been impressive. Most South Pacific societies have demonstrated a capacity over time to accommodate change and their political leadership style remains essentially pragmatic. Constitutional structures and forms have been adapted to some degree to suit local conditions, and in particular have provided for an orderly succession process. Respect for constitutionalism throughout the region remains high in comparison with other Third World states. The opportunities for upward social and political mobility (more so in Melanesia than in Polynesia) represent a stabilizing element in the region's politics. In Polynesia, opportunities for emigration, and the subsequent reverse flow of financial remittances, are important to the maintenance of political order. Instability is by no means endemic and much of the current volatility, therefore, may prove transitory and to be evidence of political adaptation rather than systemic crisis.

(v) The Papua New Guinea-Indonesia Border

The border area between Papua New Guinea and Indonesia has long been regarded as one of the more troublesome security issues of the region.[14] Since the incorporation of what was known as 'West New Guinea' (now Irian Jaya) into the Indonesian Republic - a process which commenced in 1963 and ended in 1969 with an Act of Free Choice - periodic tensions have arisen between the two countries. Sizeable numbers of Irianese, usually members of the Melanesian elite either resisting or disenchanted with Indonesian rule, have sought refuge in PNG. Indonesian military operations against the small Free Papua Movement - the OPM - have often resulted in waves of border crossings by Irianese into PNG. In the course of such operations, Indonesian forces have occasionally crossed the border, drawing sharp diplomatic protests from the PNG Government. Equally, Indonesia has expressed annoyance at PNG's apparent toleration of the OPM's presence and activity on the PNG side of the border. Within PNG, considerable sympathy exists for the notion of a Melanesian 'brotherhood', for the plight of the Irianese people, and for the OPM cause, all of which continues to concern Indonesian policy-makers.

The OPM is small and disorganised but is by no means a spent force. Formed in the early 1960s, initially in opposition to Dutch colonisation but shortly thereafter to oppose Indonesian control, the movement has offered and continues to offer sporadic resistance to perceived external rule. Symbolic protests (e.g. raising the OPM flag), passive resistance, harassment of officials and development projects, sabotage, small-scale attacks on government outposts, occasional kidnappings, underground courier and inter-group communications systems, and rudimentary pamphleteering efforts have characterised OPM activity over the past 25 years in areas stretching from Sorong in the 'Bird's Head' region, Biak off the north coast, the Baliem Valley area in the central highlands, to the Jayapura and Merauke districts of the border area. The OPM groups, however, are small, factionalised, and lacking in ideological coherence beyond a basic nationalist sentiment. Full-time OPM activists probably number less than 500, though there is a large support base (and potential base) amongst the Irianese educated elite in the towns of the province as well as latent village support. The OPM's international support is very small and its linkages, at this stage, to countries and groups likely to provide material support are virtually non-existent. Its military capability is low and generally constitutes no threat to Indonesia's control over the province, though its ability to attack isolated patrol posts, airstrips, mine sites and presumably transmigration settlements raises the proportion and the cost of any Indonesian response.

The border issue has been, and remains, of considerable interest to Australia and to the South Pacific, not only because tensions or hostilities on the border could lead to instability, but because in certain circumstances, all three members of the Indonesia-PNG-Australia 'triangle' could be drawn into conflict. A dispute between PNG and Indonesia, for example, over different approaches to border management and control, could escalate into hostilities with limited exchanges on the border. Military operations by Indonesia in an attempt to rout the OPM might require, on Indonesia's reckoning, cross-border pursuit of rebels and/or incursions into PNG to eliminate rebel sanctuaries - moves which PNG would see as a violation of its territorial integrity. Further, perceptions by Indonesia that PNG, directly or indirectly, was supporting anti-Indonesian rebel activity could lead it to 'teach PNG a lesson' by conducting a punitive operation inside PNG territory. In all three situations above (and we could draw variations of them as well as others), PNG is likely to seek (and to expect) Australian support.

Bilateral relations between PNG and Indonesia plummeted to an all-time low in mid-1984 following an abortive OPM rebellion in Jayapura and the unprecedented wave of over 12,000 Irianese border crossers into PNG. In PNG's view, Indonesia had not satisfactorily explained the circumstances of the exodus, nor had it explained apparent intrusions by troops and aircraft into PNG territory. Subsequently PNG expelled the Indonesian defence attaché from Port Moresby. From late 1986, however, relations between Jakarta and Port Moresby improved markedly. PNG arrested and deported key OPM leaders, and a change of attitude on the part of both governments resulted in the 'Treaty of Mutual Respect, Friendship and Cooperation' being signed in early 1987. The Treaty was designed to widen the scope of the relationship and to situate the border problem as but one of the issues of mutual interest.

However, an OPM raid on an Indonesian transmigration settlement in March 1988 in which 20-30 people were killed and injured sparked another round of border tension. On seven occasions in that year Indonesian troops crossed the border in search of the OPM. PNG troops were deployed to see the Indonesians back across the border, and at least on one occasion shots were exchanged. Bilateral relations were strained again, but the mechanisms for conflict resolution, including that of rapid high-level consultation, together with informal business and political linkages at the elite level, appear to have had some effect in defusing tension.

Conclusion

These adverse trends in regional security should be seen in the context of efforts made by regional and extra-regional states to contribute to a stable environment. Economic assistance to the South Pacific has increased steadily so that some island states are amongst the highest *per capita* recipients of aid in the world. Problems remain in some cases over the islands' capacities to absorb large quantities of aid, and in others over how effectively aid is utilised, but generally the quality and appropriateness of aid has improved. Resource management and protection, especially that of fisheries, has been enhanced by the growing capability of the Forum Fisheries Agency and by increased aerial surveillance by ANZ air forces of the 200-mile EEZs.[15] Consciousness has also grown throughout the region on environmental protection issues.

In more conventional defence and security terms, Australia has raised its assistance under the Defence Cooperation Program (DCP) to a level equal to that provided to Southeast Asia. Port calls by Australian naval vessels and maritime surveillance operations by the RAAF have been increased, and a network of surveillance centres has been developed. Australia continues to provide, at a project cost of $A 62 million, patrol boats to most island states under its Pacific Patrol Boat Project (PPBP). The patrol boats are multi-purpose vessels capable of undertaking surveillance, enforcement, disaster relief, medical evacuation, search and rescue, and general transport functions. New Zealand has expanded its Mutual Assistance Program (MAP) through the training of islanders for the patrol boat program and through an increase in exercises, including with Vanuatu. New Zealand provides regular security briefings to island officials, and then responds to bids from island officials on defence and security projects. New Zealand's rhetorical commitment to South Pacific defence which emerged strongly after the ANZUS fracas, however, has not been matched, to date, by significant expenditure increases in the area. The United States contributes a small amount of military training aid to the region, and France, in its drive to re-establish a position of influence, has provided substantial assistance to Fiji's military forces.

Beyond the Treaty of Rarotonga which brings together all Forum countries in a limited form of arms control, a patchwork of security-related agreements and understandings link islands and metropolitan states. Most, however, are 'supportive' in character, requiring 'consultations' rather than defence commitments. A suggestion for a (NATO-type) Pacific-wide security treaty involving Rim powers and island states, floated by American officials (including former Secretary of State, George Shultz) in the late 1980s, has met with little support. While defence treaties are no longer in vogue, at a more limited level the Australian and PNG Joint Declaration of Principles guiding relations between the two countries includes a defence clause that requires both countries to consult in the event of a perceived security threat. PNG's Treaty of Friendship with Indonesia has also enhanced confidence in the conduct of bilateral relations.

At a regional level, the Forum Secretariat has initiated steps for an exchange of information and intelligence. Liaison and communication on police and criminal intelligence matters has also strengthened. Advocates of a regional peace-keeping force have so far met with an indifferent response. The practical difficulties of membership, financing and command, exacerbated by the *coups* in Fiji, are likely to preclude the establishment of a regular force, but cooperation between select regional states to deal with particular crises is a likely development through the next decade.

The security outlook for the 1990s, however, is one of increasing complexity. While there are no foreseeable threats of a military or invasive kind to the South Pacific, security concerns of a lesser but nevertheless important order are likely to continue. The internationalisation of the South Pacific, the developing mosaic of external interests in the region, some of which will be competitive in nature, could have an unsettling effect on regional security. Further economic pressures and domestic instability will have reverberations across the region. The number of security 'pressure points' may well increase. In circumstances of severe political turbulence, the prospect of intervention by Australian and New Zealand forces will be raised.[16]

The task of security management in the next decade, therefore, will be to address a number of challenges. In Australia's case, attempts should be made to disentangle some of the apparently conflicting or ambivalent attitudes to the region, in particular those which hold that Australia is only proximate to and not really part of the South Pacific. Policy-makers must come to terms with Australia's role as a small power on the international scene, but a major power in its immediate region. This will require a clear delineation of interests and responsibilities combined with a sensitivity to the island states' aspirations. Given the changing patterns of competition and influence, Australia should refine its role as 'gate-keeper' to the region, and develop a coherent strategy for dealing with regional problems. Australia should also constantly monitor its two-pronged strategy for regional security-economic and defence assistance - and give consideration to forms of assistance in crisis conditions as well as non-crisis situations in the island states. The small island states - the 'weak in the world of the strong' - will require continuing strategies for dealing with the asymmetries of power relations in the region, for maximising their sovereignty and room for manoeuvre, and for minimising economic dependency. They will have to cope with the demands of a more variegated region, as well as with the crucial domestic problem of maintaining political cohesion and legitimacy. All states of the region will face the challenge of adapting to, and seizing, the opportunities presented by the larger shifts in world politics; that is, the tendency to multi-polarity and the increasing prominence of the Asia-Pacific region.

Endnotes:

1   Richard A. Herr, 'South Pacific Defence - Regional Security in the South Pacific', in Stuart Inder (ed.), *Pacific Islands Yearbook*, (Pacific Publications, Thirteenth Edition, Sydney, 1978); T.B. Millar (ed.), *International Security in the Southeast Asian and Southwest Pacific Region*, (University of Queensland Press, St Lucia, 1983); T.B. Millar, 'An "Anzac-South-west Pacific Defence Community"?', in T.B. Millar (ed.), *Australian-New Zealand Defence Cooperation*, (Australian National University, Canberra, 1968); June Verrier, 'The Origins of the Border Problem and the Border Story to 1969', Chapter 2 in R.J. May (ed.), *Between Two Nations: The Indonesia-Papua New Guinea Border and West Papua Nationalism*, (Robert Brown and Associates, Australia, Bathurst, 1986).
2   Peter Larmour, 'The Decolonization of the Pacific', in R. Crocombe and A. Ali (eds), *Foreign Forces in Pacific Politics*, (Institute of Pacific Studies, Suva, 1983); and Barrie

Macdonald, 'Decolonization and Beyond', *The Journal of Pacific History*, (Vol.21, No.3), July 1986.

3   Alan Burnett, *The A-NZ-US Triangle*, (Strategic and Defence Studies Centre, Australian National University, Canberra, 1988); Greg Fry, 'Regional Arms Control in the South Pacific', Chapter 8 in Desmond Ball and Andrew Mack (eds.), *The Future of Arms Control*, (Australian National University Press/Pergamon Press, Sydney, 1987); Ramesh Thakur, 'A Nuclear-Weapon-Free South Pacific: A New Zealand Perspective', *Pacific Affairs*, (Vol.52, No.2), Summer 1985; Anthony J. Slayter, 'Tuna and the Impact of the Law of the Sea', and Jon M. Van Dyke and Carolyn Nicol, 'U.S. Tuna Policy: A Reluctant Acceptance of the International Norm', in David J. Doulman (ed.), *Tuna Issues and Perspectives in the Pacific Islands Region*, (East-West Center, Hawaii, 1987); and J. Kotabalavu and D.L. Tiffin, 'Ocean Minerals: Prospects for South Pacific Islands', *Pacific Viewpoint*, forthcoming 1989.

4   David Hegarty, *Stability and Turbulence in South Pacific Politics*, (Working Paper No.185, Strategic and Defence Studies Centre, Australian National University, Canberra, June 1989); David Hegarty, 'Political Stability and Instability in the South Pacific', in H. Albinski, J. Dorrance and F. Mediansky (eds.), *Strategic Competition and Cooperation in the Pacific Islands*, (National Defense University, Washington, D.C., forthcoming).

5   Norman MacQueen, 'Sharpening the Spearhead: Subregionalism in Melanesia', *Pacific Studies*, (Vol.12, No.2), March 1989.

6   See Barry Buzan and Gowler Rizvi, et al., *South Asian Insecurity and the Great Powers*, (Macmillan, London, 1986), pp.7-8; and Barry Buzan, 'The Southeast Asian Security Complex', *Contemporary Southeast Asia*, (Vol.10, No.1), June 1988.

7   David Hegarty, 'The Soviet Union in the South Pacific in the 1990s', in Ross Babbage (ed.), *The Soviets in the Pacific in the 1990s*, (Brassey's Australia, Sydney, 1989); R.A. Herr, 'The Soviet Union in the South Pacific', in Ramesh Thakur and Carlyle A. Thayer (eds), *The Soviet Union as an Asia-Pacific Power*, (Westview Press, Boulder and London,1987); and Paul Dibb, 'Soviet Strategy Towards Australia, New Zealand and the South-West Pacific', *Australian Outlook*, (Vol.39, No.3), August 1985.

8   Denis McLean, 'The External Powers: Other Extra-Regional Powers', in H. Albinski, J. Dorrance and F. Mediansky (eds.), *Strategic Cooperation and Competition;* David Hegarty, *Libya and the South Pacific*, (Working Paper No.127, Strategic and Defence Studies Centre, Australian National University, Canberra, October 1987).

9   Helen Fraser, *New Caledonia: Anti-Colonialism in a Pacific Territory*, (Peace Research Centre, Research School of Pacific Studies, Australian National University, Canberra, 1988).

10   Stephen Henningham, 'Keeping the "Tricolour" Flying: The French Pacific Presence into the 1990s', *The Contemporary Pacific*, (Vol.1, No.1), July 1989.

11   Robert T. Robertson and Akosita Tamanisau, *Fiji - Shattered Coups*, (Pluto Press, Sydney, 1988); Deryck Scarr, *Fiji: Politics of Illusion*, (University of New South Wales Press, Sydney, 1988); Brij V. Lal, *Power and Prejudice: The Making of the Fiji Crisis*, (New Zealand Institute of International Affairs, Wellington, 1988); and Yaw Saffu, 'Changing Civil-Military Relations in Fiji', *Australian Outlook*, forthcoming.

12   David Hegarty, *Papua New Guinea: At the Political Crossroads?* (Working Paper No.117, Strategic and Defence Studies Centre, Australian National University, Canberra, April 1989).

13   A.V. Hughes, *Climbing the Down Escalator - The Economic Conditions and Prospects of Solomon Islands*, (Islands/Australia Working Paper No.88/2, National Centre for Development Studies, Australian National University, Canberra, 1988).

14   R.J. May (ed.), *Between Two Nations*.

15   Anthony Bergin, 'Fisheries Surveillance in the South Pacific', *Ocean and Shoreline Management*, (No.11), 1988.

16   Australia's Defence Minister Kim Beazley has argued that in responding to a request from the Vanuatu government for security assistance in May 1988, Australia had demonstrated its preparedness to take 'those difficult decisions', and 'to match the rhetoric of our commitment to regional security with firm action'. See Kim C.

Beazley, 'Australian Defence Policy', in Desmond Ball (ed.), *Australia and the World: Prologue and Prospects*, forthcoming.

CHAPTER 22

CHINA'S SECURITY

Gary Klintworth

Introduction

China's security outlook and its regional perceptions over the next decade will be shaped primarily by the stresses of modernisation. Countries in the Western Pacific will have to accommodate what has been described as the unfolding of one of the great constructive developments in East Asia, and indeed in world history. China rates as a great Asian, if not global, power because of its sheer physical size, its large population, and its geographical centrality at the hub of East Asia. Moreover, it is the only Asian state with strategic nuclear weapons. It also meets several of the traditional criteria for great power status. China has a substantial economic base and significant reserves of most minerals and other natural resources. Moreover, it is one of the world's largest producers of many basic commodities and manufactured goods.

Yet, China is also one of the most over-populated, poorest and least-developed of nations. Its energy and mineral resources are unevenly distributed. It struggles to support 22 per cent of the world's population on the equivalent of 7 per cent of the world's cultivable land. Measured in terms of per capita GNP, China falls into the least-developed category of states, along with Bangladesh, Ethiopia and Zaire. It has fewer roads, fewer railway lines and fewer trucks per capita than India. China lacks a modern, creative scientific and technical pool; and the proportion of post-secondary educated people is less than that in India, Pakistan, Brazil or Mexico. Its political institutions are weak. Overall, China suffers from an industrial infrastructure and the political and economic habits which are typical of centrally-planned socialist states. Its reform program is entering uncharted waters.

Despite its statistical shortcomings, no strategist can ignore China's size and purposefulness in their calculus of its power and influence. If China can get the balance right between political and economic reforms, its modernisation progress will be strengthened immeasurably. Nationalism, the overcoming of adversity and disunity, and a sense of direction, have long contributed to China's prestige and authority, vital components of its strategic influence. Since 1950, China's record of going to war after declaring that it would do so, has given it the very useful reputation of meaning what it says. If the Chinese Foreign Ministry warns that another state will be 'responsible for all the consequences of its actions', neighbouring states can presume that China is in earnest.

Prior to the Tiananmen killings in June 1989, Australia had developed something of a strategic and defence relationship with China. RAN ships have made visits to Shanghai since the inaugural call of HMAS *Swan* in September 1981; Defence Attaches were exchanged in 1982. There have been regular consultations at a senior level on common regional security concerns, such as the war in Cambodia, the situation on the Korean peninsula, and disarmament and superpower issues. Australia had established a 'special relationship' with China hinged on growing bilateral trade. This relationship is being reassessed in light of the Tiananmen affair and the realisation that China is not a democratic society after all.

China's Modernisation

Chinese leaders have sought to transform China from a backward, over-populated Asian under-developed country, to a modern industrialised and powerful Middle Kingdom. This goal is expressed in terms of quadrupling per capita GNP to $US 800-1,000 by the year 2000, when China will have risen from low income to medium income status. According to Deng Xiaoping, China aims to be approaching the front ranks of the world in terms of GNP by 2000; China would then be in a relatively strong position militarily because even 5 per cent of GNP for national defence would amount to up to $US 50 billion. By 2049, one hundred years after having been established as the People's Republic, Chinese leaders are planning to be close to, or on a par economically with the developed nations.

To achieve this goal, China's leadership has made 'a strategic decision to shift the focus of its work from revolution to economic modernisation'. The agenda does not, however, include political reform and, as Tiananmen has shown, the Party leadership reserves the right to crush dissent.

China has a lot of inherited problems, and modernisation has brought with it a number of new contradictions. There is the Party's instinct to reassert control over innovative managers who might, through tough labour rules, turn a loss-making factory into a profit maker. Rising political expectations have led to student confrontations with a conservative and often corrupt Party machine. Many of China's problems can be categorised as the unavoidable accompaniment of rapid economic development and unprecedented social and political change. Modernisation, inevitably, alienates old institutions and elites, and creates new stresses because it fuels crucial changes in values, attitudes and expectations. Leadership instability has been a recurrent phenomenon, and today is no exception. This reflects a cyclical pattern which has become well established since 1949 and one which will continue as China grapples with the genie of economic reform and a profound reluctance for parallel political reform.

Despite a slowdown in the aftermath of the Tienanmen affair, if China can satisfactorily settle the Deng succession, it is likely to make substantial progress in the next two decades, while the foundations for rapid and equitable growth in the 21st century could also be laid. The task, however, will be complicated by the flux and ferment of reform communism. China may also be too big to ever complete the process of becoming a modernised state. It can attain certain statistical goals by the year 2000 and, in absolute terms, it will have great economic and military influence in the Western Pacific. But until the Chinese Communist Party reforms itself - and that is an enormously difficult contradiction yet to be resolved - China will continue to suffer from the blight of central planning and the stifling of intellectual, literary, scientific and technical creativity.

Defence Modernisation

Defence modernisation is not an urgent priority in China at present. There are several reasons for this, including China's relaxed security outlook, its shortage of resources, and a confidence in the strength of its existing military capabilities. A reassessment of the global balance was followed by the conclusion that with clever diplomacy, China can exploit superpower rivalry to its own strategic advantage.

China's security today is perhaps the most favourable it has been since the mid-19th century. China's judgement is that it faces 'no immediate threat for twenty years'. Li Desheng, a Political Commissar of China's new National Defence University (NDU) in Beijing noted therefore that China's People's Liberation Army (PLA) could 'switch from a war readiness posture of preparing to fight an early major and nuclear war to the normal track of building a regulated and modernised revolutionary army during a period of peace'.[1] China perceives Soviet naval, nuclear and strategic bomber forces in the Soviet Far East as aimed primarily at the US and Japan rather than at China.[2] Soviet Far East ground forces, it believes, are intended to deal with contingencies involving Japan as much as China. In any event, Soviet ground forces are well below European readiness levels. For example, half of the Soviet Far East divisions remain at about one quarter strength.[3] They would require several weeks to fill out with reserves before being ready for a war with China.[4] Soviet ground forces along the Sino-Soviet border number about 450,000, or less than half the figure of 1 million sometimes claimed by China. PLA forces, by comparison, number about 1.5 million, backed by an extensive reserve and militia force.[5]

An important seminar on China's national defence needs in the Year 2000, held in Beijing in July 1986, summed up China's security outlook as follows:

> In today's special international circumstances, people generally hold that it is possible to postpone the outbreak of major war, because the world is now situated in a 'balance of terror' caused by mutual deterrence and containment between the two blocs....This gives time to China to concentrate on economic construction. In order to advance economic construction in a country with a large population and a weak economic foundation, it is natural that defense expenditure must be retrenched.[6]

China's preoccupation with modernising its industrial, agricultural and technical base, has eclipsed any desire to compete directly with, or confront, the superpowers. It has also meant that China will not experiment with political reform. Chairman of the Central Military Commission, Yang Shangkun, observed that China instead:

> must try by every means possible to develop its national economy...everything we do must serve this purpose and all disturbances must be removed....The whole party, the whole army and the whole nation was required to concentrate all financial and material resources on economic construction.[7]

The pressure to reduce defence allocations is reflected in the percentage of government expenditure devoted to defence over the last decade. (See Table 1).

Another factor in China's relaxed approach to defence modernisation is the existing state of its conventional and nuclear forces. Chinese tanks, artillery, fighter aircraft and assorted missiles, are fewer and inferior to Soviet inventories. Chinese military planners, nonetheless, take comfort from the failure of the Soviet effort in Afghanistan and remember the lessons of the Korean War. They believe that the USSR has insufficient reserves to mobilise the 2.7 to 4.5 million-strong force necessary to pose a serious threat of invasion of China and

Table 1: China's Defence Expenditure 1979-1988

Year	Yuan Million ($A 1.00= 2.66 Yuan)	% of Total Government Budget Expenditure
1979	22,270	17.48
1980	19,330	16.00
1981	16,797	15.06
1982	17,635	15.29
1983	17,713	13.68
1984	17,870	11.68
1985	19,148	10.48
1986	20,020	9.30
1987	20,400	8.30
1988	21,526	8.20
1989	24,550	7.49

to cater for a possible war in Europe. As a consequence, they have a reasonable confidence that China can deter a Soviet conventional attack.[8]

At the strategic force level, China has a credible nuclear deterrent force, including a maritime component of perhaps two SSBNs with 12 SLBMs armed with small nuclear warheads and a present range of approximately 2,500-3,000 km.[9] The strategic rocket force includes over 100 medium and intermediate range missiles and at least six ICBMs, some capable of reaching Moscow, Washington DC, or Canberra.[10] Other estimates attribute China with 10-20 limited range ICBMs and 4-8 full range missiles, the latter capable of reaching around the world.[11] Whatever the precise figures, the fact is that both superpowers credit China with some retaliatory strike capability.

While China's strategic rocket forces are a fraction of the size of the superpower arsenals, China's credibility as a nuclear power is magnified several times by its position outside the knot of superpower rivalry. Moreover, some missiles are emplaced in caves and solid rock; or are widely dispersed, often in hardened silos in narrow mountain valleys.[12] Others have alternate basing modes.[13] Some are too carefully camouflaged for satellite reconnaissance to detect. The possibility therefore - however slight - that China could still attack several Soviet or American cities, after absorbing a first strike, gives it a small credible nuclear deterrent capability, adequate for Chinese requirements.

Furthermore, this capability is being improved through an impressive program to ensure that China remains at the forefront of space and missile research.[14]

As the Chinese defence force posture has 'switched from being on an alert or semi-alert status to the orbit of peaceful construction', the necessity of maintaining 'huge numbers of armed forces spending most of the military budget on food, clothing and articles of daily use' has been reduced.[15] China's conventional forces have been cut by 25 per cent (a trend that seems likely to be followed by the Soviet Union, Vietnam, and perhaps even North Korea). Most of the Chinese reduction has been in the army's supporting bureaucratic and political structure, especially the headquarters elements. According to PLA Chief of Staff Yang Dezhi, there were too many administrative levels.[16] In addition, China has reduced units on garrison duty on the Sino-Soviet border and opposite Taiwan. The funds saved by streamlining are being used to pay for research and development on better quality weapons and equipment, new military schools and improved pay and conditions for soldiers. A more efficient vertical chain of command, fewer Military Region (MR) commands, and the reintroduction of a rank structure have been set in place to improve command and control.

Other reforms include the transfer of local and frontier security functions to the People's Armed Police under the Department of Public Security; the transfer of 50,000 of the PLA's Construction Corps engineers and 20,000 Railway Corps personnel to the civilian sector;[17] higher recruitment standards; an improved reservist scheme; the merger of some units such as logistics and supply; an early retirement rule to ensure a more practical ratio of officers to men; and tougher promotion criteria with emphasis on professional qualifications. According to Yang Shungkun, these reforms and budgetary cuts are intended to develop 'a modern regular revolutionary army with Chinese characteristics', to turn the PLA progressively into:

> a contingent of crack troops, smaller in size but more flexible in command, better equipped, more highly trained, quicker in response, and therefore more effective.[18]

As well as troop cuts, the PLA is divesting itself of a substantial portion of its facilities and infrastructure, including airfields, ports, docks, barracks, hospitals, farms, hotels, factories, oil and fuel depots, warehouses and special purpose railway lines. Even more striking is the civilianisation of China's defence industries. Naval factories, for example, switched over 30 per cent of their total output to civilian products in 1984.[19] By July 1986, the Ministry of Ordnance reported that since 1980, it had increased the number of civilian products from 64 to more than 700.[20] A bomb factory in Kunming switched to manufacturing bicycles, while an explosives factory in Zhejiang spends 65 per cent of its time producing clocks and fireworks.[21] The same trend is evident in other Ministries. The output value of civilian products manufactured by China's national defence industries rose from 10 per cent of total production in 1979 to 42 per cent in 1985, and is scheduled to rise to 67 per cent by 1990.[22]

This trend, however, could easily be reversed if Chinese arms sales increase. China has become very active in the world arms trade. Arms sold, or for sale, include a range of missiles such as the Silkworm anti-ship weapon system and CSS-2 intermediate-range ballistic missiles, radar jamming equipment, armoured personnel carriers, tanks (including the T-69), aircraft, including the F-6 (MiG-19), the F-7 (MiG-21), the F-8 fighter and an updated B-6 (Tu-16) bomber, together with a range of options and various calibres of artillery, mortar, small arms and ammunition. By 1985, China was the fifth largest arms dealer in the world, with sales estimated around $US 1.5-2 billion per year since 1980.[23]

Western Technology

China however is still looking to the West for essential defence science and technology and management skills. China needs foreign technology in such key areas as precision manufacturing equipment, advanced electronics, micro-processors, and calibrating instrumentation. A feature of this quest is that it is well defined and very specific. China is buying in critical areas and has sent as many as 20,000 scientists to study in advanced fields at some of the best institutes of learning in the West. It also has an active world-wide collection program for defence technology through Hong Kong and third countries such as Israel. It has obtained advanced defence technology in a wide range of areas. For instance, it has been able to copy modern air-to-air missiles such as the AIM-9L *Advanced Sidewinder*, the AA-2 *Advanced Atoll* and the French *Matra Magic* R-550 infra-red air-to-air missile through third country samples. Purchases of dual-use technology or equipment are also common, notably the US Sikorsky S-70C-2 *Blackhawk* helicopter, one of the most advanced US technology packages supplied to China.

Purchases of large quantities of complete weapon systems are, however, unusual. Experience has shown up the inappropriateness of too much ill-chosen defence technology that is beyond China's ability to absorb, synchronise or maintain. Contracts that have been signed are often bolt-ons to existing or hybridised platforms. For example, there is an armoured personnel carrier built on a Chinese chassis with a Vickers turret and a 25 mm McDonnell Douglas gun.[24]

Until the Tiananmen affair in June 1989, the US was China's best source of defence technology. It could supply very advanced defensive weapons and had a strategic interest in doing so. The US wanted to draw China into a tacitly anti-Soviet consensus through a technology transfer-dependency relationship. Chinese naval and anti-submarine warfare capabilities, although backward, were a potential asset for US naval contingency planning in the Western Pacific. The US Chief of Naval Operations affirmed on a 1986 visit to Beijing that the US wanted to help upgrade China's Navy by selling it gas turbine naval engines, MK-46 anti-submarine torpedoes, and towed array sonar equipment.[25] As well as naval technology, the US offered China gun and artillery shell technology, anti-tank (TOW) and anti-air (I-*Hawk*) weaponry, avionics for the F-8 fighter aircraft, *Vulcan* aircraft guns, transport aircraft (C-130s), and radar and communications equipment.[26] Since June 1989, the US has drawn back from defence cooperation with China, partly in an effort to punish China for its apparent abuse of human rights, but also because in the era of Soviet-US *detente*, China is of less strategic importance than hitherto.

Combined Arms Doctrine

The most significant focus of China's defence modernisation has been on training, tactics and doctrine, on improvements to command, control and communications, and on an upgrading of logistics, mobility and professionalism, all areas in which the PLA has made significant progress at little cost. Exercises now stress joint service and combined arms operations for fighting a 'people's war under modern conditions'. There is a greater use of 'think-tanks' such as the Beijing Institute of International Strategic Studies and the Institute of Strategic Studies in the National Defence University. Seminars on national defence planning now combine academic, military and civilian experts, as well as multi-disciplinary specialists. They are providing a new kind of consultative service to defence policy-makers.[27]

China's defence doctrine is being changed. Rather than being based upon overwhelming manpower in defence, a more modern war-fighting doctrine has been adopted, based on mobility, firepower, more armour and combined arms operations. Beginning in 1983, China's 35 or so field armies have been reorganised to form approximately 25 combined or group armies, which form the building blocks for the new doctrine. A new combined army consists of three infantry divisions, an anti-aircraft division, a tank division and an artillery division, together with anti-tank, engineer, transport and chemical and biological warfare elements.[28] The result is a significant improvement in coordination between different arms, and more firepower. The 'time of the old mainly infantry-based field army has passed', to be superseded by the much more technically diverse combined army. In a mechanised group army in North China for example:

> ...one in every two soldiers is a technician and only one in five is an infantryman; the army is composed of various modern units including infantry; artillery; self-propelled artillery; armour; signals; anti-chemical warfare; engineers; air defence; air and electronic counter-measures.[29]

China's defence strategy now involves positional defence combined with coordinated mobile warfare. The former principle of side-stepping an invasion and 'luring in deep' to fight a protracted people's war inside China has been relegated to a worst-case option.[30] The new concept of 'people's war under modern conditions' envisages a more active forward defence posture. It entails a flexible response to an invasion including actual confrontation from selected positions and counter-strikes with combined arms formations, supported by air operations and, eventually, tactical nuclear weapons.

One reason for the shift in strategy is a realisation that while people's war and defence in depth may be suitable in the thinly populated northwest, the concept may not be practical or feasible in the industrialised northeast. Equally, prospective future border wars, for example, on the Sino-Indian border, or perhaps in the South China Sea will have little or no use for 'people's war'. Rather, there will be a requirement for efficient logistics support, and effective coordination of naval, air and land forces. Joint service exercises in the northwest Pacific in June 1986 reflected the priority attached to these goals. The objective was 'to meet the requirements of future naval warfare' by a quick response in taking the offence and coordinating forces over several thousand nautical miles of ocean.[31] Another exercise involved Chinese Marine Corps forces launching mid-ocean amphibious assaults on islands in the South China Sea.[32]

Despite cuts, China's ground forces are still a formidable defensive force. Combined arms and joint service training, together with infusions of key Western defence technology, have improved the PLA's capabilities. Regional perceptions of China's army have perhaps exaggerated the impact of Western defence technology. The PLA is regarded by neighbouring countries as a rapidly modernising, well-disciplined and professional force, capable of significantly extending China's military reach. By the 1990s, however, if the current approach to strategy prevails, China's ground forces will still be unlikely to be able to push much more than perhaps 150 km beyond China's immediate borders and then for no more than a short period. They will nevertheless be stronger than at present, and well able to launch the kind of limited border attack seen in 1962 against India, and in 1979 against Vietnam.

China's Air Force

China's air force has been compared to the Polish cavalry charging German tanks in 1939.[33] Against Soviet, American and Japanese air defences, there may be something to this view. China lacks the accessories of a modern well-equipped air defence force, for example, with electronic counter-measures, advanced air-to-air missiles, modern aircraft avionics, and look-down radar. Modernisation will be at least an 8-10 year process. Most of China's combat aircraft were initially produced in the 1950s. For example, the F-6, the mainstay Chinese fighter, is based on the MiG-19, which first flew in 1953; the F-7 is derived from the MiG-21, which first flew in 1956. Despite its age, however, the Chinese Air Force has a total of over 5,300 aircraft, the largest in the Asian region. In quantitative terms, China could overwhelm the air defences of small neighbouring states, even if at great relative cost. Moreover, China is the only country in the Western Pacific (apart from the USSR) with a nuclear capable bomber force.

China's old aircraft are being upgraded with Western avionics, missile systems, and other add-on equipment, in itself a very complex design and manufacturing step. Although there may be a suspension of Western defence technology transfers to China in the next year or two following Tiananmen, the flow is likely to resume. Alternatively, China can buy from Israel or Brazil.

Of some significance for China's southern neighbours is the upgrading of China's bomber aircraft - the B-6. The latest version, the B-6D, appeared in January 1987. Updated with electronic navigation equipment, it is armed with two long-range (32 km, Mach 1.4) air-to-surface or anti-ship C-601 missiles which are more devastating than the *Exocet*. Equipped with defensive weapons and ECM equipment, the B-6D, like the Soviet Badgers at Cam Ranh Bay, could yet become a relatively potent symbol of Chinese air power in the Western Pacific.

A new fighter bomber, destined for use by the Navy in a maritime strike role, was unveiled in 1988. Designated the B-7, the aircraft is armed with wing-tip mounted PLB air-to-air missiles and two underwing C-801 anti-ship missiles plus two drop tanks. The B-7, which looks like a cross between the F-18 *Hornet* and the F-4 *Phantom*, is a significant achievement for China's aircraft industries. It will be an important addition to China's ability to project naval and military power well beyond its territorial seas.[34] The Badger aircraft meanwhile is being modified as a tanker, with an inflight-refuelling capability and a receiver system to hook-up with the A-5 ground attack fighter bomber.[35] Once perfected, this capability will extend China's potential radius of air and naval operations. Chinese naval bombers can already 'fly nonstop to the Spratly Islands and back at altitudes as low as 30 meters'.[36] These incremental developments, plus infusions of Western technology and weapons systems, should significantly boost China's regional airpower capabilities by the early 1990s.

China's Navy

But it is China's naval modernisation that will have the most profound visual impact on security perceptions of China by neighbouring countries. Chinese naval authorities have approved 'a long term strategic development plan' which will guide naval modernisation until the year 2000. Priority will be given to a positive off-shore naval capability, to include 'the development of warships, submarines and aircraft',[37] i.e., a navy which can take offensive action and which is not simply relegated to a defensive or passive order.

The present Chinese Navy is the largest small-ship navy in the world. It has the second largest number of submarines, a substantial amphibious force able to lift 30,000 men plus equipment in a regional amphibious assault situation, and a large naval air force. The naval inventory includes nuclear and nuclear attack submarines, seaplanes for special tasks including anti-submarine warfare, maritime patrol aircraft, and 'a new enclosed missile escort destroyer' with modern equipment such as the Chinese designed CPMIEC HQ-61 surface-to-air missile system and Western-style 3D radar with phased-array antenna.[38] Another 'advanced missile carrying escort vessel of modern design and equipment', based on 'all available domestic and foreign' technology, is being built after a novel system of competitive tendering by Chinese naval shipyards.[39] A demonstration of China's modern naval communications occurred in May 1986 when naval combat manoeuvres in the Northwest Pacific were coordinated over several thousand nautical miles. The manoeuvres involved a naval task force and bombers 'brought together quickly from scattered bases on the China coast'.[40]

The requirement for a modern navy with extended strike capabilities reflects the breadth of China's naval interests. These encompass traditional ones such as defence of China's maritime approaches and the security of Chinese territory, including some 6,000 or so offshore islands. There is, in addition, a strong interest by China in becoming a regional naval power. China is undergoing 'a tremendous maritime renaissance of historical significance' and is building the foundations to become a great sea power once again.[41] We should note the May-June 1980 deployment of an 18-ship naval task force on a 8,000 nautical mile voyage to the Fiji-Vanuatu area in the South Pacific to monitor a CSS-4 ICBM test; underwater SLBM tests in 1982 and 1985; the development of SSNs and SSBNs to total perhaps four of each by the late 1990s;[42] an Antarctic expedition by two naval auxiliaries in late 1984; a task group of two ships to Pakistan, Bangladesh and Sri Lanka in January 1986; and a program of large-scale multi-ship, bomber and possibly submarine exercises. Naval manoeuvres near the disputed Spratly Islands in 1987 were followed by the use of naval force to seize several of the islands in 1988. In addition, there is on-going development of new anti-aircraft guided missile frigates, escort vessels, seaplanes, minesweepers, and a modernised fleet air arm equipped with air-to-surface missiles. China also has a Marine Corps which is ready to 'respond to emergencies' and which has 'mastered coordination of loading, transport and escort forces including destroyers, submarine chasers and aircraft'.[43] These developments can be seen as signposts in the transformation of the Chinese Navy from an exclusively coastal force to 'a fleet with blue water pretensions' or at least one which can police 'the Chinese lake' in the South China Sea.[44]

China's growing familiarity and competence in maritime operations and its prestige as a regional naval power have been complemented by a strong merchant shipping fleet. It is now one of the ten largest in the world, and is expanding at a rate which will make it a premier merchant shipping power by 2000. Moreover, China has an impressive capacity for ship-building. It currently produces some 800,000 tonnes of shipping per year in a variety of highly specialised categories which meet advanced world standards.[45]

China's naval technology and capabilities, of course, pale in comparison with those of the US 7th Fleet or the Soviet Pacific Fleet. However, this should not disguise the upward momentum in China's naval development and its regional significance. By the 1990s, a Chinese Navy supported by an air-refuelled fleet air arm, several SSNs and SSBNs and 60-70 modernised main surface combatants is a prospect with important regional implications. Reports of Chinese plans to acquire 'deck-landing aircraft' and up to five 20,000 tonne aircraft carrier vessels suggest China may eventually build or purchase an aircraft carrier capability, subject of course to finance.

China's Strategic Missile Force and Space Program

Spending on China's strategic weapons has continued steadily, neither affected by other priorities nor by any sense of urgency. Missiles, nuclear weapons, satellite systems and space technology have been well-supported, drawing a consistent one per cent per year of China's GNP.

China's substantial experience in rocket and space technology has also enabled it to quickly absorb Western breakthroughs. It has been able to by-pass intermediate phases and make quantum leaps in some areas. China is closely monitoring developments in Soviet and US space weapons research and conducts its own advanced research into chemical lasers and missile tracking instruments. It can match the satellite launch capabilities of the US, USSR and Western Europe, and is offering commercial satellite launch services to several countries, including Australia and the US. This potential, together with multiple-satellite launch and geosynchronous satellite orbit capabilities, suggest that China is well able to acquire the space-based 'eyes and ears' needed for a radically improved intelligence collection and nuclear targeting system.[46]

By the mid-1990s, China will have benefited from a surge of Western technology and scientific information. It could by then have increased the present number of its land based missiles and SLBMs from approximately 100-120 to perhaps 180-200, including 20-30 full and limited range ICBMs and perhaps 2-3 SSBNs with increased-range SLBMs.[47] Old liquid fuelled medium range ballistic missiles will probably be phased out for more accurate solid fuel short range and intermediate range ballistic missiles. Advanced fuel technology, improved accuracy and mobility, some multiple re-entry vehicle weapons, hardened silos, improved reaction time, better concealment and alternative basing modes and a more sophisticated satellite navigation technology, should consolidate the credibility of China's nuclear deterrent by the 1990s.

According to Chinese strategic analysts, China's nuclear deterrent will remain effective for at least 30 years before any space-based ballistic missile defence system becomes deployable.[48] As far as China is concerned, 'an appropriate nuclear offensive and counter-attack capability is sufficient to guarantee the benefits of a deterrent against nuclear attack'.[49]

Defence Modernisation: Outlook and Implications

By the early 1990s, the PLA will be better equipped, more streamlined, with improved command, control and communications, greater mobility and stronger firepower, including, probably, tactical nuclear weapons.

Despite this, China's technical standards will still lag behind those of the superpowers. Such a comparison, however, is of little value in assessing the significance of China's defence modernisation for the security of the Western Pacific. More pertinent would be a comparison between China and India and China's smaller neighbours including Taiwan and Vietnam.

China's growing conventional military strength will add to its sense of security against a threat from the north. This confidence is being boosted by the strategic leverage accruing to China from the nuclear balance between the superpowers, the Sino/Soviet rapprochement, the continuing improvement in the accuracy, reach and reaction times of China's strategic rocket force, and the naval/defence relationship China has allowed the US to nurture in Sino-US relations. The result is increasing superpower acceptance of, and deference to, China's status as a great Pacific power. This has important implications for regional security perceptions and for the leeway it gives China to engage in compellent diplomacy on its southern flanks if the need should arise.

In this context, China's naval modernisation begins to loom large. China's navy is likely to become an active regional force, routinely operating out to distances of 1,000 nautical miles or more into the Western reaches of the Pacific Ocean. Chinese warships will probably build up a schedule of activities, including circumnavigation of Taiwan, probes around disputed offshore islands, amphibious landing exercises, port visits throughout the region, combined air/sea and submarine exercises and more distant voyages into the Indian Ocean.

By the early 1990s, China will be regarded as having an ability to project military power well beyond its immediate borders. This perception will complement China's existing cultural and political influence, and its growing economic interests throughout the Western Pacific. It will qualify China where previously it had been rather incomplete as a regional power, at least in Southeast Asia. This prospect, in conjunction with China's unique situation of being unchallenged by any other great power, could increasingly worry strategists in Tokyo, Hanoi, Jakarta, Kuala Lumpur, and New Dehli.

Conclusions

China's modernisation and its strategic importance, together with that inestimable national quality of resolve and purpose, give China great power status. Not quite a superpower perhaps, but a very important 'big' power. This is an important consideration in the strategic planning of Moscow and Washington, when deciding whether to make concessions on a border demarcation dispute in the case of the USSR, or to give advanced weapons technology in the case of the US. Both superpowers are sensitive to the implications of China's modernisation in the context of their own strategic rivalry. From Beijing's viewpoint, China's international influence can be expected to rise. By the year 2000, China will, it believes, advance up the world table of GNP rankings from its present position of eighth to perhaps third or fourth. Instead of superpower bipolarity, China expects to make up the third leg in a tripolar world. Since the rivalry of the superpowers will be constant, China expects to be in a position to hold the balance. In these circumstances, the US and USSR will be reluctant to challenge China in the Asia-Pacific context, so as to avoid a shift by China at the superpower level. China's suspicion that it might indeed hold this leverage was aroused by the inactivity of the USSR on the Sino-Soviet border when China attacked Vietnam in 1979.

Significantly, neither the USSR nor the US now believe they can sustain their old encirclement strategies against China. Instead, they are prepared to treat China on terms of equality as a respectable and legitimate great Asia-Pacific power. Both, for example, brief China on the state of their relationship with each other; both vie for strategic advantage in Beijing. Both are offering economic cooperation to assist in China's modernisation. Chinese power and influence in the Western Pacific is the chief long-term beneficiary.

The US has tacitly endorsed China's regional security enforcement role as guarantor for Thailand and as a counter to Vietnam, and it has accepted Chinese claims to Taiwan. It was, until recently, assisting in the modernisation of China's air force and navy. The USSR has still to accept the reordering of the Western Pacific between China and the superpowers. Yet the USSR has urged Vietnam to accommodate Chinese interests in Kampuchea, and is likely to give up Cam Ranh Bay. It has been relatively circumspect in North Korea and has counselled India against a re-run of its 1962 war with China. The Soviet Union is also cutting Soviet military deployments in Mongolia.

Sino-Soviet relations are for all intents and purposes already normalised. This has given impetus to Gorbachev's Asia-Pacific diplomacy. More fundamentally, it has eased China's defence burden and could ease complications in Soviet contingency planning in the Far East. This has been of concern to Japan and has added to arguments in Tokyo for a higher regional profile and increased defence expenditure.

Realignment by small actors to a newly emerging order in the Western Pacific can be expected. Burma and Thailand are clear instances of small regional states basing their foreign policies on a centre of gravity in Beijing. South Korea might make a similar move despite the residual problem of China's relations with North Korea. Vietnam now seems prepared to acknowledge China's proximity and importance. But not all countries in the Asia-Pacific would agree with, or acquiesce in, a China dominated Asia-Pacific region: Japan, Indonesia and India for example probably see themselves as alternative centres of power. Hong Kong and Taiwan - the other Chinas - are pessimistic about Beijing's stability and its external responses.

China's modernisation will not have direct security consequences for Australia, New Zealand or Papua New Guinea. However, China's naval modernisation may affect areas of strategic importance to Australia in Northeast Asia, Southeast Asia and South Asia. Provided China can maintain its policies of economic reform and the open door, and subject to the outlook for Hong Kong as 1997 approaches, China's economic modernisation and its interdependence with the Western Pacific should be a stabilising factor for the security of the region and should boost its economic dynamism. This will be of benefit to Australia. However, regional tensions along China's southern border could arise as China tests its status as an ascending power in the Western Pacific, confident that it faces no immediate threat on its Northern or Eastern flanks. A renewal of Sino-Indian tension could prompt the spread of nuclear weapons in South Asia and pressure India into further development of its already substantial naval reach.[50] This could affect ASEAN perceptions and lead to a substantial expansion in the navies of Malaysia, Singapore and Indonesia. Sino/Soviet rapprochement meanwhile could lead to an increase in the underlying distrust between China and Japan. The Korean peninsula and Indochina, on the other hand, should be areas of reduced tension as a direct consequence of China's modernisation, its more relaxed security outlook and the improvement in Sino-Soviet relations. The end of the war in Kampuchea, however, may be followed by a reassessment of China by the ASEAN states in circumstances in which the bridge between them provided by their common security concern about Vietnam is no longer present.

While it is difficult to make confident predictions about the security implications of China's modernisation, several facts seem to be reasonably clear. First, China is likely to make considerable progress towards increasing its GNP in absolute terms. Second, it will be an ascending military and political power of some significance or, at least, regional perceptions will credit China with that status. Third, China is entering a phase when its environment has never been so secure from great power threats. Fourth, China is conscious of the cycles of its history: it believes it is approaching an upward phase. And finally, as

C.P. Fitzgerald remarked: a 'country like China does not shed its ancient mental habits and prejudices overnight, even if there has been a revolution'.[51]

Endnotes

1   *Ta Kung Pao*, 16 February 1986, p.1.
2   Interviews, Beijing, February 1987.
3   Allen S. Whiting, 'The Great Triangle: China, The USSR, and Japan', in Harrison Brown (ed.), *China Among the Nations of the Pacific*, (Westview Press, Boulder, Colorado, 1982), p.51.
4   Harlan W. Jencks, 'People's War Under Modern Conditions, Wishful Thinking, National Suicide or Effective Deterrent', *China Quarterly*, (Number 98), June 1984, pp.306-307.
5   Alastair I. Johnson, 'China Nuclear Force Modernisation: Implications for Arms Control', *Journal of North East Asian Studies*, (Volume 2, Number 2), June 1983, p.15.
6   'Liaowang Views Defence Strategy Seminar', *FBIS-China*, 25 July 1986, p.K3.
7   'Yang Shangkun Discusses PLA Reorganisation', *Liaowang*, Beijing, (Number 27), 8 July 1985, (Foreign Broadcast Information Service Transcript).
8   Monte R. Bullard, *China's Political-Military Evolution - The Party and the Military in the PRC 1960-84*, (Westview Press, Boulder, Colorado, 1985), p.21.
9   *The Military Balance 1985-86*, (International Institute for Strategic Studies, London, 1986), p.113. The range of such missiles could be extended in the future. A limit of 3,000 km confines their usefulness to the Mediterranean or Arabian Seas and secondary cover of the Soviet Far East from the Yellow Sea. However, there is an important prestige factor involved.
10   Robert J. Sutter, 'Chinese Nuclear Weapons and American Interests - Conflicting Policy Choices', in *China's Economy Looks Towards the Year 2000*, (U.S. Government Printing Office, Washington, D.C., 1986), Volume 2, pp.175-176.
11   Robert Wang, 'China's Evolving Strategic Doctrine', *Asian Survey*, (Volume 24, Number 10), October 1984, p.1049.
12   Allen S. Whiting, *Siberian Development and East Asia: Threat or Promise*, (Stanford University Press, Stanford, 1981), p.164.
13   Handbook of the Chinese People's Liberation Army, (U.S. Defense Intelligence Agency (DIA), Washington, D.C., November 1984), pp.72-73.
14   Bradley Hahn, 'China in Space', *The China Business Review*, July-August 1984, p.12; and *South China Morning Post*, 13 October 1986, p.7. See also Craig Covault, *Aviation Week and Space Technology*, 8 July 1985, 15 July 1985, 22 July 1985, 29 July 1985, 5 August 1985, and 12 August 1985.
15   *Jiefangjun Bao*, Beijing, 9 July 1985, *FBIS* Transcript.
16   Yang Dezhi, 'A Strategic Decision on Strengthening the Building of our Army in the New Period', *Red Flag*, 1 August 1985, *FBIS* Transcript.
17   Research Institute for Peace and Security (RIPS), *Asian Security 1986*, (Brassey's Defence Publishers, Tokyo, 1987), p.81.
18   'Yang Shangkun Discusses PLA Reorganisation', *Liaowang*, Beijing, 8 July 1985, *FBIS* Transcript.
19   Tai Ming Cheung, 'China Switches from Defence to Development', *Pacific Defence Reporter*, (Volume 13, Number 5), November 1986, p.27.
20   *Beijing Review*, (Number 30), 28 July 1986, p.4.
21   *South China Morning Post*, 9 July 1986.
22   *Beijing Review*, (Number 15), 14 April 1986, p.4; and *China Daily*, 23 January 1986.
23   *South China Morning Post*, 7 November 1986, and 14 January 1987.
24   See *South China Morning Post*, 7 November 1986, and *MILTECH*, March 1987, p.44.

25 *South China Morning Post*, 14 April 1986; and K. Dumbaugh and R.F. Grimmett, *US Arms Sales to China*, (The Library of Congress, Congressional Research Service, Report Number 85-138F, Washington, D.C., 8 July 1985), p.19.

26 *Xinhua*, Beijing, 2 April 1987, in *FBIS-China*, 3 April 1987, p.B4; *Defence Week*, 5 May 1986, p.13; *International Defence Review*, December 1985, p.1919; and *Wen Wei Po*, Hong Kong, 'China and the US Enhance Military Technology Transfers', in *FBIS-China*, 18 May 1987, p.B3.

27 Zhang Aiping, in *China Daily*, 8 November 1986.

28 'Seminar on National Defence Strategy', *Xinhua*, Beijing, 20 July 1986, in *FBIS-China*, 22 July 1986, pp.K1-2.

29 *Beijing Review*, (Number 18), 6 May 1985, p.19.

30 June Teufel Dreyer, 'China's Military Modernisation', *Orbis*, (Volume 27, Number 4), Winter 1984, p.1015.

31 *Wen Wei Po*, Hong Kong, 10 June 1986, in *FBIS-China*, 10 June 1986, p.W1; and *AFP*, Hong Kong, 3 June 1986, in *FBIS-China*, 4 June 1986, p.K1.

32 *Xinhua*, Beijing, 21 April 1987, *FBIS-China*, 21 April 1987, p.K23.

33 Bill Sweetman, in Gerald Segal and William T. Tow (eds.), *Chinese Defence Policy*, (Macmillan, Hong Kong, 1983), p.71.

34 *MILAVNEWS*, October 1988, p.8; *Asian Aviation*, September 1988, p.62; *Flight International*, 10 September 1988, p.2.

35 *MILAVNEWS*, October 1986, p.10.

36 Li Wei, 'Chinese Naval Airforce has Attained World Levels', *Zhongguo Xinwen She*, Beijing, 28 February 1986, *FBIS* Transcript.

37 *China Daily*, 11 April 1987, p.1.

38 Report in *FBIS-China*, 21 April 1987, p.K23.

39 *Liaowang*, Beijing, 30 March 1987, in *FBIS-China*, 16 April 1987, pp.K28-29.

40 Report in *FBIS-China*, 10 June 1986, p.WI.

41 David J. Muller, *China As A Maritime Power*, (Westview Press, Boulder, Colorado, 1983), p.224.

42 G. Jacobs, *Jane's Defence Weekly*, 9 February 1985, p.222.

43 *Xinhua*, Beijing, 'Report on PLA Navy Modernisation', in *FBIS-China*, 21 April 1987, p.K23.

44 Dreyer, 'China's Military Modernisation', p.1016.

45 *Beijing Review*, (Number 25), 23 June 1986, p.19.

46 Denis Simon, 'The Evolving Role of Technology Transfer in China's Modernisation', in *China's Economy Looks Towards the Year 2000*, (U.S. Government Printing Office, Washington, D.C., 1986), p.283.

47 Richard E. Gillespie, 'China's 2nd Artillery Corps', *The China Business Review*, July-August 1984, p.38.

48 Bonnie S. Glaser and Banning Garrett, 'Chinese Perspectives on the Strategic Defence Initiative', *Problems of Communism*, (Volume 35, Number 2), March-April 1986, pp.40-41.

49 *Guoji Wenti Yanjiu*, 'A New Stage in US-Soviet Disarmament Talks', Beijing, 13 January 1987, in *FBIS-China*, 6 March 1987, p.A3.

50 *The Times of India*, 6 May 1987.

51 C.P. Fitzgerald, 'Chinese Reactions to Tendencies Towards Condominium', in Carsten Holbraad (ed.), *Superpowers and World Order*, (Australian National University Press, Canberra, 1971), p.78.

CHAPTER 23

THE SUPERPOWERS IN THE PACIFIC

Henry S. Albinski

A conspicuous territorial presence shapes the Pacific basin security interests of the United States and the Soviet Union. So does their geographic environment: predominantly maritime for the former, predominantly land-centered for the latter. Their regional interests and objectives are, moreover, driven by their roles as global superpowers with a deep legacy of mutual suspicion and contention. For them, the notion of security is generously proportioned, and subject to the etching of elaborate, conceptual linkages by each. By comparison with the European arena, the context of their rivalry in the Pacific is more complex, less manageable, and thereby more susceptible to instability; factors which impose the need for carefully crafted and adjustable policies. This is not simply a function of the region's distinctive distances and geographical fragmentation, but of the glaring variety of size, strength, resources, cultural inheritances and political dispositions found among resident countries. The aim of this chapter is to draw these strands together and to postulate some of the foreseeable opportunities, constraints and dilemmas which the superpowers face in the pursuit of their interests within various Pacific subregions and Australia, in particular.

Interests, Ambitions and Instrumental Objectives

In the most basic terms, the Soviet Union and the United States, like all nations, are motivated by defence-security and national development-prosperity impulses. These goals are interlocked. They subsume military, economic and political objectives and, in the Pacific as elsewhere, necessarily involve the influence of substantial other parties rather than simply their own bilateral calculations. Both wish to avoid general war. Neither blithely assumes that a limited conflict between them can be held in check. Both are mindful of the pitfalls inherent in the potential for escalation of disputes to which they may not be direct parties. Their reading of postwar history, the ideological gulf which divides them and their sense of global geopolitical imperatives have nonetheless dictated massive military preparations. On both sides, these are designed to impress and as appropriate to intimidate, to deter the other side and its coalition and, if necessary, to fight and hopefully to succeed.

In the Pacific context, the Soviets have by now assembled forces formidable in size and capabilities. As an extended land power with a Pacific flank exposure, they insist they must protect themselves against China as well as against the US and its regional allies. In the Pacific, their military reinforcement and logistics capabilities are, however, hampered by distance and climate, and their fleet movements constrained by the enclosing arc of the Japanese island chain. They, therefore, feel they must compensate with sizeable in-place forces and with naval and air facilities, the latter of which have been developed in Vietnam.

Depicting their own military efforts as defensive, the Soviets express apprehension over the large, mobile, highly capable and forward-deployed American naval and air assets in the Western Pacific. The Soviet sense of vulnerability is heightened by the immediate presence of actually, or potentially, dangerous neighbours such as China or Japan, by America's extended deterrence system of bases and other regional defence facilities and its alliance network. Accordingly, their objective is not simply to avert the remilitarisation of Japan or the reinvigoration of the Sino-American coalition, but to alter the currently adverse correlation of regional forces, through a decoupling of the US from its supportive friends and allies.

For its part, a major impulse behind America's effort to sustain a credible forward strategy is that Soviet behaviour has been interpreted as anything but benign and defensive. Although outright military confrontation with the USSR did not occur, America's most costly and frustrating post-World War II military operations - in Korea and Vietnam - were fought against forces abetted by the Soviet Union. The Soviet Union's occupation and militarisation of the Southern Kuril Japanese Islands, its military intervention in Afghanistan and basing of facilities in Vietnam have been construed as of hostile intent. The Soviet military build-up in the region is regarded as in excess of the dictates of prudent defence. In framing its strategic assessments, the US has generally felt that it could not afford to make allowances for distinctions such as whether Soviet behaviour is deliberately mischievous, part of a historical Russo-Soviet continuum, or not really all that dramatic.

In essence, the Soviets aim at sea denial in the Western Pacific, while the US aims at sea control over much of the area. A *de facto* American fall-back to Hawaii and the mainland, or even Micronesia, would be a strategic setback of global, as well as regional, proportions. American ability to countervail the Soviets in the Pacific demands capable, credible and flexibly deployable naval and air forces. This is viewed not only as a contribution to the central strategic balance, but to the insulation from intimidation, interdiction or other pressures levied at the very friends, allies, extended lines of communication and basing, surveillance, signal and other defense privileges which Moscow would wish to neutralise or overcome. Belatedly, to redress handicaps of distance and its own finite assets, the United States feels that it must count on the will of friends and allies to provide substantially for their own security, and to perform security tasks politically or materially not achievable through American resources alone.

Under Gorbachev, however, the Soviet Union has declared its intention for a major improvement of relations with the United States, including easing the arms race in the Pacific and elsewhere. A hallmark aim of this program is a lightening of the Soviet military burden. The Soviet economy is grossly inefficient, begetting increasingly adverse domestic political, as well as economic, consequences. The dividends of *perestroika* should in time pay off, but there is also a need for relief from a high and distorting defence budget. More directly, the Soviet leadership feels impelled to develop Siberia's vast natural resources, for the region's benefit and for the nation at large. Lacking the investment capital and technology to proceed alone, the Soviets are interested in turning to Western nations - among them Japan, whom they must persuade of the USSR's peaceful credentials. As a secondary step, the Soviet Union wishes to move beyond its presently minimal trade relations with Pacific basin countries; to establish a broader foothold for the region's products, resources and services; to ameliorate its substantially adverse balance of trade with the West; to earn greater political respectability and access to a region where the US is generally well-received and the Soviet Union is not.

In American quarters, concerned with broad strategic issues, the reaction to these overtures has been mixed. The particulars of a new *detente* apart, a tension-reduced climate in the Pacific is appealing. So is encouragement for a constructively-minded Soviet leadership which needs to demonstrate results to its often hard-line domestic skeptics. Also attractive, in principle, is the prospect of a reduction in America's own global and regional defence outlays. The US economy is strained by severe budgetary and foreign account deficits. Measures in defence have already been adopted, including the postponement of a 600-ship navy - the prime instrument in upholding an ambitious, forward-deployed Pacific strategy. Hence, in Robert Scalapino's terms, there is a seeming confluence of US and Soviet interests:

> The evidence is now overwhelming that the major powers without exception must give prior attention to serious economic problems, social as well as economic, that will not wait. This

requires a lower-risk, lower-cost foreign policy...and the great powers...are moving to that direction.[1]

As both superpowers recognise, the Pacific basin is the world's most rapidly expanding economic region. While broad Soviet security interests now mandate a closer economic alignment there, America's economic stakes are already immense. They reflect an interdependently woven fabric of investment, resource exploitation and transfer, trade, and assistance to poorer countries - conceived as a direct US benefit and as a contribution to regional national resilience and stability. For itself and others, the US understandably does not separate economic vitality from the will and capacity required to achieve security objectives.

From another American vantage point, deferring to the newly-packaged Soviet blandishments is either unnecessary or prejudicial to US interests. Will a reduction in Soviet arms expenditures be only temporary and cosmetic, awaiting resumption following the country's promised economic transformation of the Soviet Far East, including Siberia, which would add infrastructurally to the USSR's regional military capabilities? Should the Soviets succeed in an expanded, peacefully-conducted, politico-economic insinuation into the region? Would this deplete the security resolve of affected regional countries, including their facilitation of US military operations? Would all this amount to Soviet strategic gains won without coercive diplomacy? In an influential American view, what is happening is 'the addition of political and economic elements to the growing power projection capability [of the USSR] in East Asia and the Pacific, a capability clearly aimed at the US and its regional friends and allies'. [2] In this view, the fundamental Soviet aim - tilting the regional balance of power - remains; only means or inflections have changed.

Resources of Influence and Policy Instruments

The superpowers' mix of policy instruments designed to promote their overall regional interests is affected by the economic, military and political resources at their disposal. The Soviets have their Vietnamese ally, but China has long detached itself from its Soviet partnership. Soviet economic and historical contacts in the region are slight. The USSR's political appeal is minimal, if not negative. Both powers enjoy regional military power, but America's continues to be more sophisticated. It is far more regionally distributed, and welcome, whether through formal treaty/alliance connections or without. It is the US which holds the lion's share of regional resources of access and influence.

It is this traditional gridlock of regional weakness which the contemporary Soviet leadership has reasoned is in its national interests to break; to narrow the discrepancy between Soviet military power and politico-economic influence. The chosen policy tracks need to be complementary regarding what it says and does *vis-a-vis* the United States on the one hand and regional nations on the other. This is, in principle, a dictum appreciated by the United States, which needs to frame its own interest-promoting responses with equal complementarity; the bilateral relationship with Moscow is profoundly affected by the perceptions and behaviour of regional members. Ironically, the growing sense of confidence and independent-mindedness within Asia and the Pacific which, in part, complicates the American task, can be traced to a more salubrious security and economic climate cultivated by the United States itself.

As reflected in formulations announced by Gorbachev in his Vladivostok speech in July 1986 and in other venues, the Soviet Union has opted for a variety of tension-reducing security measures. It has suggested steps ranging from the negotiation of nuclear-free zones in Korea, Southeast Asia and the South Pacific, to limitations on regional US and Soviet surface and submarine deployments, to regional conferences on military-confidence building. It has been solicitous toward sub-regional initiatives which favour the banning of nuclear weapons. It has signalled its intention to retract great power presence by trading off its own facilities at Cam Ranh Bay for American facilities in the Philippines.

Throughout, the Soviet Union denies that it seeks 'any special rights for itself in the Asian-Pacific region. What it desires is to jointly build new and equitable inter-state relations. And, of course, the Soviet approach is based on the recognition and understanding of the *existing realities*' [emphasis added].[3] The American reaction has been deeply skeptical. On military strategic grounds, the US surmises that the Soviets are prepared to negotiate where they are weak or vulnerable, but would not forgo strength in their own backyard. Moscow's 'parity' spells Washington's disability. In effect, the Soviets are widely seen as wishing to undermine the forward-deployed strategy the US has assembled to counteract Soviet strategic assets. Trading off Vietnamese and Philippine installations is illusory, since the latter are far more elaborate and central to the US than the former are to the Soviet Union. A nuclear-free Korea would mean a removal of American theatre nuclear weapons, and the emasculation of the tripwire deterrent, but no change in the North Korean order of battle. Restriction of naval movements, as well as of Western Pacific basing of other defence facilities, for the US means falling back to Micronesia or Hawaii;

exposing Pacific nations, and undoing the delicate, interdependent Western security system at large. Much of American opinion concludes that, by speaking in ostensibly constructive terms, the Soviets hope to persuade regional countries that the US presence is unnecessary, even dangerous.

In the meantime, recent American security policies mostly reflect a number of on-going objectives. These include maintaining plentiful, modernised and forward deployed forces; protecting the integrity of the forward strategy's need for port access and basing; discouraging the spread of anti-nuclear sentiment through ostracising New Zealand for example, and refusing to adhere to the protocols of the new South Pacific Nuclear-Free Zone (SPNFZ); striving to maintain cordial political and military relations with a China still very suspicious of the Soviet Union; providing for contingencies by such means as pre-positioning equipment in Thailand and enhancing support capabilities in Alaska.

Both out of conviction, and to impugn Soviet assertions of non-hostile intent, the US has asked for concrete evidence of the Soviet Union's preparedness to match rhetoric with deeds, for example to end the military presence in Afghanistan and on the Japanese islands, to cause Vietnam to leave Kampuchea, and to abandon the threatening SS-20 missiles pointed at Asian countries. In part at least, the Soviets have replied positively. They have completed a military pullout from Afghanistan, and have dropped their earlier Intermediate Nuclear Forces (INF) Treaty reservations about withdrawing SS-20s from Asia. While Washington has waited for the Soviets to release such grips, it has taken note of Moscow's newly streamlined political and economic campaign directed at Pacific countries. For example, the Soviet Union has assiduously been rebuilding its relations with China, perhaps to put paid once and for all to Moscow's nightmare of a Washington-Beijing (and Tokyo) axis, and - in American eyes - as a Soviet effort to gain Chinese tolerance for a remodelled yet unswerving anti-American strategy. The Soviets have dispatched delegations in search of diplomatic and other official establishments where they are absent, extended offers of technical assistance and joint ventures, and entered into fishing and other commercial agreements.

The US is inclined to respond that much of this is not as normal and innocent for a great power, in the Soviet Union's position, as it seems. Diplomatic and economic access equals legitimacy and influence, at Western and US expense. An American-funded nuclear power plant in the Philippines is abandoned after being vehemently denounced by the Soviets, who then arrive with an offer to build a coal-fired installation. With critical US-Filipino base negotiations ongoing,

Soviet aircraft from Vietnam stage mock attacks off Philippine waters; to frighten the Aquino government into closing the bases, Washington reasons. The US has concluded further that the Soviet Union is not averse to supporting militants where this can be done with some circumspection, through, for example, the World Federation of Trade Unions, widely regarded as a communist front. The Soviets are heard selling peaceful discourse with ASEAN, but are prone to exploit ASEAN's trade disputes with the US. Equally they appear eager to associate themselves with multinational economic groupings such as the Asian Development Bank. Washington wonders whether these initiatives are made because the Soviets genuinely wish to incorporate themselves into a wider international economic system, or because they seek to interpose themselves into traditionally Western vehicles of economic influence? The Soviets signed fishing agreements, first with Kiribati, then with Vanuatu. These were purely commercial ventures, and consonant with the Soviet Union's pledges that it seeks no military footholds in the area. But American planners are disquieted, construing commercial and political footholds in the islands as meaningful cusps for fleet servicing, cross-Pacific transport and communications, and surveillance of Western naval manoeuvres, US naval movements and of such facilities as the missile testing range of Kwajalein, in the Marshall Islands.

Soviet and American Policy Tradeoffs and Prospects in Northeast Asia, Southeast Asia and the Pacific Islands

There are a number of circumstances in which superpower regional policy choices would appear to presage opportunity or difficulty. At present, it is the Soviet side which appears more venturesome, more involved in shifting, rather than sustaining, the regional security quotients. The Soviets have concluded that their interests require a more creative approach to the Pacific, with a tighter integration of military, political and economic policy and intentions. Apart from having built up considerable armed strength in and around their eastern reaches, they have traditionally been absent or only marginally successful in projecting objectives and influence into the Pacific basin at large.

In Washington, these changed circumstances are perceived as challenges to the interests of a United States which, unlike the Soviet Union, enjoys the standing of a substantial, influential and generally desirable regional actor The nervousness is compounded because, despite its current position, the US is by no means hegemonic nor able to escape nettlesome abrasions and setbacks in its dealings with Pacific nations. Its troubles are often not of Soviet doing, but illustrate a general global sense of *relatively* diminished superpower dominance, increased multipolarity, and national and sub-regional assertiveness. In the Pacific, resident states increasingly can, and do, insist upon following their own counsel and course, rather than tying themselves to the will of a great power, or for that matter, even middle powers. As a group, they are usually more absorbed with internal than with external concerns. But for the US, which essentially wishes to shore up its privileged position, and for a Soviet Union wishing to improve its own, the policy selection and management process designed to produce preferred outcomes becomes more taxing and uncertain. At base line, the Soviet-American rivalry in the Pacific is far from a one-on-one affair, since the affected resident nations are participant observers rather than spectators. The superpowers simply cannot by their own strokes fashion a climate favourable to one or the other. They must function within an environment which increasingly sets its own terms.

Northeast Asia is the site of the greatest Pacific basin Soviet and American geostrategic stakes, and of their force concentrations. The Soviet effort to enhance relations with China, to ease it away from overly close links with the United States and to afford some reduction of Soviet troop deployments on the Chinese border is complicated by Beijing's stiff terms for rapprochement. These focussed on the Soviet position in Afghanistan, Vietnam's occupation of Kampuchea, and on a proper and prior border settlement and Soviet military pullback. The Chinese also play off the US, holding out the olive branch of fully comfortable relations - but not anything like an informal security coalition. And, while they wish the US to help them modernise their defence establishment, such a prospect on a major scale frightens the basically pro-Western ASEAN nations, notably Indonesia, and of course the Soviet Union as well.

Japan's global status serves to define its keystone regional role. To preserve Japan's supportive, pro-Western disposition and its place in the structure of Pacific security, the US feels it needs to continue to demonstrate its alliance *bona fides*, which in turn stifle temptations of either recidivist Japanese rearmament or neutralism. But the US also needs to assuage sensitive Japanese, and other nations' feelings, that its forward-projection maritime strategy, which notionally includes rapid interdiction of Soviet nuclear submarines and air asset sanctuaries in time of conflict, is not in itself strategically escalative, destabilising, and therefore the potentially true 'threat' in the region.

The quality of Japanese-American relations is vulnerable on other grounds as well. The US accuses Japan of unfair commercial practices which it alleges contribute to unsustainable American trade deficits. This has resulted in retaliation, leaving both sides offended and suspicious. These commercial *contretemps*, in turn, affect the US desire for Japan to accept a relatively larger share of the regional defence sharing burden, which it feels Tokyo can well afford. The limits within which Japan is prepared to agree are narrow, and arm-twisting could exacerbate Japanese public hostility to the American military presence. Any significant Japanese rearmament program would alarm both China and ASEAN, engendering severe embarrassments for America's relations with them and thereby serving Soviet interests. Japan's rearmament could also endanger its substantial investment in economic development projects in Southeast Asia. This is a valued politico-strategically-related contribution which, owing to its budgetary and other economic frailties as well as some political limitations, the United States could not replace.

Signs of US-Japanese estrangement, especially in the form of reduced US markets for Japan, fuel incentives for Tokyo to accept Soviet invitations for broader economic relations. But the USSR faces its own, substantial, difficulties in cultivating Japan in a grand manner. The American pull remains strong. Major Soviet military forces are nearby. Soviet intransigence on the issue of the occupation and militarisation of the Southern Kurils, claimed by Japan, represents a vital and probably non-negotiable Soviet strategic asset and a factor which could temper the political climate needed for elaborate Russo-Japanese economic collaboration. Japan is, however, arguably the best Western source for Moscow's economic revitalisation program. If, for whatever reason, Moscow's hopes for Japanese and other nations' cooperation are dashed, the Soviets will need to address the option of scaling down their military investments. Would they choose this option? Some analysts think not, especially if the Soviet Union cannot negotiate sizeable arms control reduction measures with Washington - which for the most part believes that current proffered Soviet *regional* arms limitation enticements are asymmetrically flawed in Moscow's favour, and therefore unacceptable.

In Thomas Robinson's view, which encapsulates an important sector of American thinking, the Soviets simply cannot, without impressive counter-balancing concessions by the US, draw down their Asian-Pacific military establishment. To do so would not only make them more militarily vulnerable, but would also be an admission that they are something other than an Asian superpower, and reduce their capacity for various forms of influence extension. The dilemma which Robinson sees surfacing is that the Soviet economic up-grading, *perestroika* and all, cannot make much headway without an alleviation of the military burden: 'If the Gorbachev reforms at home fail, the Soviet influence in Asia will decline even further'.4 In the event, the Soviets face an exceptionally complex policy task of keeping the Asian situation fluid, undertaking to balance off a host of major regional actors, talking themselves into regional issues, addressing danger spots directly, and retaining their current gains.

Vietnam is a substantial Soviet asset, well beyond a validation that a fraternal, socialist system can sustain itself in the region or as a proxy buffer at China's side. Vietnam's naval and air facilities invest it with imposing and foreseeably irreplaceable value for the Soviets, for operations in the Pacific and Indian Oceans generally, and as both a military and political *point d'appui* opposite the Philippines and their American bases. The entire Indochinese situation also raises the importance of the Soviet Union as an actor-broker in Southeast Asia, regarding disposition of the Kampuchean issue or otherwise. But despite its economic dependence on Moscow, Vietnam is not a supine ally. Its continuing if reducing occupation of Kampuchea, on balance, detracts from the Soviet Union's own image and its prospects for warmer relations with ASEAN. Especially for Thailand and Singapore, the Soviets are not a force for peace, but unpalatable and dangerous.

America's position among the ASEAN nations, while undoubtedly firmer than the Soviet Union's, is nonetheless not without tensions. ASEAN has its own souring commercial quarrels with Washington. There are complaints over subsidised American rice exports, release of stockpiled tin onto the world market, copyright arguments, and bitterness over the allegedly punitive removal of Singapore from the list of the US Generalised System of Preferences. Moreover, ASEAN increasingly views the United States as being of little value in resolving the community's preoccupying Kampuchean issue. Its collective sense of trepidation over the major communist powers is mixed, with Indonesia and Malaysia more serious about Beijing than Moscow and reluctant to damage their nonaligned credentials.

To the US, ASEAN's strategic outlook seems frustratingly contradictory. An over-the-horizon American security shield is welcome, and there is even general support for the prospect of a continuing US base presence in the Philippines. Yet, ASEAN is unwilling to declare itself at this point emphatically and, particularly under Indonesia's inspiration, has been considering a nuclear weapons-free zone scheme. To the United States, even flirtation with such a proposal is troubling. The timing of ASEAN's consideration fails to serve American interests in negotiating Philippine base privileges on financially and militarily satisfactory terms. Moreover, ASEAN's in-principle opposition to foreign forces in the region appears to paint moral and strategic equivalence between Cam Ranh Bay and the Clark, Subic Bay and other Philippine facilities. It is also worrisome evidence of anti-nuclear and nuclear-free zone momentum throughout the Pacific basin, following as it does on what is perceived as New Zealand's apostasy and the SPNFZ established by the Treaty of Rarotonga.

Within the ASEAN context, America's dilemma is not which of several major policy options to take. It is rather how to patch, mend and plug holes; to avoid bumptiousness under stress; and to forgo demonstrations soliciting Chinese or Japanese militarisation. The US is still much better placed than the Soviet Union, but as many analysts and planners would concede:

> The Soviet Union has positioned itself in the region to be able to exploit future changes and is utilising the only advantage it has over its adversaries which is, ultimately, consistency of purpose and an ability to await opportunities.[5]

In a region where the Western market economies are increasingly in conflict, yet where development concentrates the mind more than grand strategy scenarios, the Soviets have arrived bearing gifts.

'Target of opportunity' has become an especially familiar phrase to describe Soviet policy calculations in the South Pacific. There, far more than in Northeast and Southeast Asia, the Soviet Union, until very recently, has been the distant outsider. What it might accomplish in the near future can, at probably very little material or diplomatic cost, be much less directed at consolidating a new influence of its own as at creating politico-strategic difficulties for Washington. In the South Pacific context, whose constituent entities are small, fragile, often parochial, anti-nuclear and anti-colonial by conviction and allergic to great power competition, the Soviet Union can confine itself to lofty declaratory policy and low-key policy instruments.

For example, when the United States earns a regional black eye for its dismissive attitude towards an island nation's Exclusive Economic Zone fisheries claims, the Soviets step in with commercial offers of their own. By the time the US reacts and signs its own fisheries agreement with the community, it is portrayed as having been pushed, responding not so much to the region's legitimate economic aspirations as to an ostensible Soviet security threat. As a global superpower, the US in its wisdom feels that it cannot antagonise the French. It is pictured as taking an unflustered stand on New Caledonia and - explicitly averring to its French alliance connections - demurs on the SPNFZ protocols. For their lingering colonial presence in New Caledonia and Polynesia, their nuclear testing at Muroroa, their tragi-comic blowing up of the *Rainbow Warrior* in Auckland harbour, the French are the region's unrivalled pariahs. But it is the USSR which can seek the high ground, condemn the French, accede to SPNFZ protocols, and voice anguish that Washington appears to lack respect for regional sensibilities.

The Soviets can sound morally incensed about the militarisation and nuclearisation of a region where they do not militarily deploy, and enjoy no facilities or other defence access. The Americans are there. The US Navy transits back and forth, visiting some island ports without challenge to their firm neither-confirm-nor-deny policy governing nuclear weapons aboard ship. There are important US tracking and communications installations in Micronesia, and the US may have to invoke contingency plans for fall-back to these bases if the Philippines bases become untenable. Here, quite starkly, is something on the order of a zero-sum game. If the US regional welcome becomes worn and its present, or foreseeable, Micronesian privileges and facilities become tenuous because of anti-nuclear and anti-great power sentiment, the strategic equation registers loss to the US and gain for the USSR. The last thing the Soviets would foreseeably want is to cast suspicion that they wish to insinuate themselves as an alternative military presence in the region. Much better to applaud the boldness and correctness of New Zealand's anti-nuclear position, and to recommend it as a model for the peace and safety of the neighbourhood. Unlike in other major Pacific basin sub-regions, few if any policy trade-offs are involved and there is no need to deal and bargain with the United States itself.

The cluster of American policy options is more tangled. The US can continue to warn regional states of the pitfalls of commercial or political contacts with the Soviets, but the argument becomes less plausible if the Soviets behave punctiliously. American strategic interests demand optimal, and worldwide, including the Pacific, capacity for deployments, basing and manoeuvre. The domino effect of anti-nuclear feeling among really significant friends and allies is a chilling prospect. So, to check the spread of such feelings, the US came down hard on New Zealand and, despite no codified impairment of individual treaty signatories to permit port entry, or to its general freedom of movement in the South Pacific, declined to ratify the SPNFZ protocols.

Soviet and American Policy Tradeoffs and Prospects in Australia

Australia is arguably the epitome of a Pacific basin nation which handsomely satisfies American interests. It is the first, or second, most important regional site of American investment, the world's second largest cash purchaser of American defence equipment, and a nation with which the US enjoys a favourable, two-to-one balance of trade margin. Australia is stable, sophisticated, developed, and uncommonly compatible in both a political and cultural sense. In the sense that it is not on the strategic front line and is far removed from direct risk, its protection does not call for the expenditure of significant American diplomatic or military resources.

Australia is a respected Western player in regional affairs, engaging in diplomatic and security activities which are generally congruent with American interests. It has stood by its American alliance despite New Zealand's deviation. It continues to extend exceptionally useful defence cooperation and facilities on its territory to an America whose other regional friends are almost without exception more timorous or selective. The US also takes comfort that both major Australian political party groups are on side. The US noticed and welcomed the observations of Prime Minister Hawke when he told a Moscow audience, speaking unapologetically of the American alliance, that 'Australians do not see [it] merely as a military alliance but as a partnership based on shared liberal democratic values; our deeply cherished values'.[6] It is in the clear interest of the United States that its policies sustain the benefits of the Australian connection.

What through its Australian connection is good for the United States, the Soviet Union regards as not good for itself, since Australia helps to underpin the Western coalition's efforts directed at Moscow. Both the logic of the situation, and the record of Soviet comment and conduct, indicate that the USSR does wish to decouple Australia from its American alliance. Such an achievement would be highly salutary in its own right, and serve to shake the confidence of Washington's friends and allies elsewhere. Whether to some degree the Soviets can, or will, succeed is another question. The answer depends on the style and content of *both* Soviet and American policies, and on Australia's own perceptions and circumstances.

The prevailing Soviet mix of policies toward Australia is emphatically in keeping with the spirit of cooperative reasonableness it is trying to project elsewhere. Plausibly, apart from what it might, or might not, achieve in attempting to wean Australia from its American orbit, the Soviet Union would wish that its very mode of approach would impress upon other, and basically pro-American, Asian-Pacific countries that it is possible and sensible for a major US ally and the USSR to enjoy friendly and even mutually profitable dealings. It would help to dissolve the Soviet Union's generally negative and clumsy image, prepare groundwork for more comprehensive involvement in regional matters, and open up economic opportunities sought by Moscow.

In its quest for closer and more sympathetic relations, there are various inducements, both articulated and non-articulated, which the Soviets can extend to Australia. The Soviet Union has reminded Australia that the hosting of American defence facilities exposes Australia to Soviet strategic targeting. Expressed in modulated terms, the message nonetheless is clear: no facilities, no targeting; the Soviets have no untoward designs toward Australia. Even if Australian governments are not readily diverted from established policy orientations by such a logic, there is a significant section of Australian opinion, in and outside the Australian Labor Party, which takes the Soviet rationale seriously. The prevailing national climate is one in which many Australians evince lower, and more relaxed, threat perceptions about the Soviet Union than tend to characterise American society. The US is itself widely viewed as guilty of exaggeration. Relatedly, it is often seen as pursuing counter-strategies, such as its surge-directed maritime strategy and toughness on arms control, which may carry more risk to regional and global security than being protective and war-avoiding. Soviet reassurances of international goodwill can therefore strike a responsive chord in the context of incentives for edging away from an over-zealous great ally in whose miscalculations and misadventures Australia could, to its regret, become caught up.

A second incentive extended for Australian consumption is that if the Australian Government varies its traditional outlook, listens to the Soviet Union's presentations and establishes meaningful new links with, or associates itself with some of its proposals, it would be doing something in which Australia could take justifiable pride. Australia would be gaining ground as the kind of independently-minded, unbeholden and nationally-spirited society it claims to have become and should continue to be. The South Pacific is one of the more promising sources of issue contention that allows the Soviet Union to play on this idiom. The South Pacific is a sub-region where Australia's stake is well-defined, and its efforts at building influence are concentrated. Moreover, much of US policy there has been seen as wrongheaded, insensitive to local sentiment, embarrassing to Australia and the course of its initiatives, and counterproductive to Western interests generally. The fisheries dispute, the French factor and the South Pacific Nuclear Free Zone Treaty have all been matters on which Australia has privately and publicly implored the United States to take a more accommodating approach. The Treaty of Rarotonga was launched and painstakingly crafted by the Labor Government to meet South Pacific community concerns, without inhibiting American security requirements. All the same, the US refused to ratify the protocols. From their strategically different and distant vantage point, the Soviets were able to present themselves as the truly understanding superpower on such issues. Moscow's original decision to sign the protocols incorporated reservations unbecoming to regional countries, including Australia. But the Soviets eventually rescinded their reservations, openly praising Australia's role in persuading them to do so.

The third incentive is economic. Part of this is intended as symbolism for the kind of self-confident Australia just alluded to. Australia is being offered an opportunity to deal pragmatically and unemotionally with an otherwise historical nemesis. Part of it is aimed at providing Australia with a direct opportunity to contribute to a worthwhile ideal assisting in the modernisation and supposed international domestication of a Soviet Union now reaching out to one and all. And, significantly, the Soviet appeal is designed as a tangible fillip to Australia's own economy. As perhaps only half-facetiously expressed by an Australian commentator, some tempting prospects lie ahead: 'it might not be too long before that symbol of Aussie culinary standards - a Four 'n Twenty Pie stand - joins McDonald's in the fast-food race on Red Square'.7 The Soviets wish to institutionalise a range of relationships with Canberra. Practical Soviet-Australian cooperation has occurred in a number of approved directions - in human contacts, consular arrangements, culture and sports as well as in trade, technical and scientific cooperation, Soviet investments in Australian mining and manufacturing, and collaborative development enterprises in Australia and in the Soviet Union, with emphasis on the Soviet Far East. With a shortage of hard currency, the Soviets wish to reduce their pronounced, 45-1 adverse trade balance with Australia. They see Australia as an advanced nation with selective, though significant, capabilities applicable to the USSR's economic rejuvenation.

In this context, international considerations blend with economic considerations. Soviet interests dictate that closer economic ties with Australia will occasion a more benign image of Soviet intentions and conduct. Their inducements need to be economically attractive to Australia itself. Such attraction, they reason, is enhanced by such Australian economic liabilities as severe current account deficits, constricting overseas markets and uphill efforts in opening substantial new manufactured, processed materials and technological export outlets. It is also enhanced by Australia's displeasure, which cuts across party and economic constituency lines, with American practices. While the US does not aim to harm Australia, its restrictive agricultural support and protectionist policies have damaged an Australia struggling to sell overseas at reasonable return. American reassurances have been of small comfort to Australia. The US is not just another international

actor, but a kindred society and a major ally. Hence the quip that while
the US now chooses to regard New Zealand as a friend rather than an
ally, it ironically treats Australia as an ally but not a friend. Australia
has not explicitly linked the continuation of American defence privileges
to improved American commercial policies, but it has made it plain that
the security relationship cannot but suffer gradual erosion under
continued economic stresses. Little imagination is required to
appreciate the Soviet Union's pleasure with such a prospect, and
thereby Moscow's concerted bid to ingratiate itself economically with
Australia.

Within the limits of being a superpower with global, rather than
just regional or Australian interests to sustain, the US cannot or will not
do much to alleviate Australia's economic complaints against it.
However, it holds policy options helpful to its reception in Australia.
This is especially true in Washington's relations with a Labor
Government which in the domestic policy context needs to exhibit
progressive and independently minded credentials. Extrapolating from
Coral Bell's insight:

> ...the Pacific alliance, like most alliances, lives by the political
> consent of its members, and the maintenance of consent
> depends on the credibility of Washington's reputation for
> prudence and good judgement during crises.[8]

To which can be added prudence between crises as well.

The United States already has some special, reputational and
image advantages from which to work. There is no wrenching conflict,
such as Vietnam had been, to corrode the relationship. The signing of
the INF treaty with the Soviets and the prospect for future arms
limitations softens criticism that the US is unbending and reflexively
anti-Soviet, and complements the Australian Government's commitment
to such ends. American reluctance to take exception to the Australian
Government's decision not to facilitate US testing of the MX missile is a
plus. So is its willingness to deal understandingly with new directions
in Australia's defence doctrine, including Canberra's reluctance to
become involved with American contingency planning far afield. Also a
plus is its sensitivity to Australian politics, manifested in American non-
support for the Opposition's summons for sterner measures against
New Zealand and its denunciation of Hawke's acquiescence in a
Gorbachev-led Soviet Union playing a constructive, non-military role in
the region.

Australia's freedom of action in dealing pragmatically with the
Soviet Union was widened by Hawke's visit to Moscow in late 1987
before an American Administration, of impeccable conservative

credentials, did much the same - and just after a British Government of even firmer conservative beliefs itself had a remarkably friendly meeting.[9] It is especially reassuring for the US that, while the Australian Labor Party has for years considered ways in which to curtail the alliance, Mr Hawke is not just supportive but relaxed and happy with the primacy of the US alliance.[10] It would be self-defeating for the United States to undermine this asset, be it through avoidable efforts of commission or omission.

Concluding Observations

Both Soviet and American interests, and policy options, in their dealings with Australia summarise much of their relative position within the Pacific basin generally. In terms of strategically-related indices, the Soviet position is measurably weaker than the American; its political access is smaller, and its reception and standing lower. It possesses formidable military strength in its eastern environs, but to date has lacked the means or finesse with which to move beyond its 'incomplete superpower' status. The Soviet Union is now striving to make corrections, playing on a combination of American policy and image problems, and on sub-regional states' sensibilities and desires for more self-direction. Its prospects for a genuine breakthrough are nevertheless doubtful, and its policy options often cross-hatched with dilemmas. It is worth noting Jonathan Pollack's assessment of the picture. The Soviet leadership:

> ...must do more than simply hope for tensions and disputes between the United States and its regional friends and allies. It must in time demonstrate Soviet credentials as a reliable partner, as well as to prove that Moscow seeks more in the region than domestic gains at the expense of the United States.[11]

The Soviets very likely cannot, in their own calculus, dispense with their regional military power. Yet if its military power continues to increase:

> Suspicions will undoubtedly grow that Moscow seeks little more than acquiescence to the permanence and irreversibility of its regional military presence.[12]

America's regional position remains on balance more imposing than the Soviet Union's. It is not, however, exactly buoyant, and is increasingly subject to slippages and uncomfortable policy choices driven by its own, domestic economic imperatives; by the region's general political maturation and diffusion of outlooks; and by the Soviet Union's refurbished rhetoric and policy toolkit.

The extent to, and manner in, which the US will foreseeably be able to remain the principal underwriter of regional security in the Pacific will depend on many familiar policy orientations. Although it still operates in a strategic environment relatively favourable to itself, the outcome will also depend on Washington's willingness to accept a somewhat less pervasive position, and to settle for a presence marked by bumping into arguments with friends and allies, across the Pacific's sub-regions. In sum, the scope for influence and for success will be smaller. To prevent it shrinking further, the US will probably have to resolve in the affirmative the question of whether a reformist-minded Soviet Union should be encouraged, including its collateral efforts at non-military projection into the area. Caveats about being guarded and watchful notwithstanding, the matter in large part comes down to whether the US and the West choose to venture on a course which will plausibly create a reduction in tension, and give a fair go to somewhat less-corseted approach to the conduct of their relationship. Also it, in part, comes down to whether in the eyes of the friends and allies on whose good will and support it relies, the US can cost-effectively afford to be carping and defensive, handing over initiative and moral high ground to a Soviet Union more than happy to accept.

Endnotes

1   Robert A. Scalapino, 'Asia's Future', *Foreign Affairs*, (Vol.66, No.1), Fall 1987, p.105.
2   Richard L. Armitage, Assistant Secretary of Defense for International Security Affairs, remarks in Honolulu of 27 February 1987; Department of Defense, *News Release*, No.98-87.
3   Evgeni Samoteikin, Soviet Ambassador to Australia, 'The Goals of Vladivostok', in Ramesh Thakur and Carlyle A. Thayer (eds.), *The Soviet Union as an Asian Pacific Power: Implications of Gorbachev's 1986 Vladivostok Initiative*, (Westview Press, Boulder, 1987), p.13.
4   Thomas W. Robinson, 'Soviet Policy in Asia: The Military Dimension', *Proceedings of the Academy of Political Science*, (Vol.36, No.4), 1987, p. 159.
5   Leszek Buszynski, *Soviet Foreign Policy and Southeast Asia*, (St. Martin's Press, New York, 1986), p.254.
6   Rt. Hon. Mr R.J. Hawke, Moscow address of 30 November 1987, cited in Department of Foreign Affairs and Trade, *Backgrounder*, (No.600), 2 December 1987, p.A17.
7   Sue Neales, *Australian Financial Review*, 8 January 1988.
8   Coral Bell, 'US Military Power in the Pacific: Problems and Prospects', *East Asia, the West and International Security: Prospects for Peace*, (International Institute of Strategic Studies, Adelphi Papers No.216, Part 1, London, Spring 1987), p.61.
9   *Australian Financial Review*, 11 November 1987.
10 Paul Kelly, *Weekend Australian*, 5-6 December 1987.
11 Jonathan D. Pollack, *Prospects for Stability and Security in East Asia*, (Pacific Forum, Honolulu, 1987), p.22.
12 *Ibid..*

BIBLIOGRAPHY

Chapter 1: Introduction to Strategic Thinking

Baylis, John et.al, *Contemporary Strategy - Theories and Policies* (London, Croom Helm, 1988, 2nd Edition, Volumes 1 and 2).

Beaufre, Andre, *An Introduction to Strategy* (London, Faber and Faber, 1965)

Earle, Eward M. (ed.), *Makers of Modern Strategy: From Machiavelli to Hitler* (Princeton, Princeton University Press, 1957).

Griffith, Samuel B., *Sun Tzu: The Art of War* (London, Oxford University Press, 1964).

Howard Michael, *The Causes of War and Other Essays* (Cambridge, Mass., Harvard University Press, 1983).

Howard, Michael (ed.), *The Theory and Practice of War* (London, Cassell, 1965).

Howard, Michael, *Clausewitz* (Oxford, Oxford University Press, 1983).

Paret, Peter (ed.), *Makers of Modern Strategy: From Machiavelli to the Nuclear Age* (Princeton, Princeton University Press, 1986)

Rappoport, Anatol, *Clausewitz, On War* (Middlesex, Penguin, 1968).

-------- *Journal of Strategic Studies* (Vol.9, Nos 2 and 3), June-September 1986, (Special Issue on Clausewitz and Modern Strategy).

Chapter 2: The Evolution of US Strategic Policy Since 1945

Ball, Desmond, *Deja Vu: The Return to Counterforce in the Nixon Administration* (California Seminar on Arms Control and Foreign Policy, Number 46, December 1974).

Ball, Desmond, Richelson, Jeffrey (eds.), *Strategic Nuclear Targeting* (Ithaca and London, Cornell University Press, 1986) pp. 57-83.

Ball, Desmond, 'US Strategic Concepts and Programs: The Historical Context' in Wells, Samuel F., Litwak, Robert S. (eds.), *Strategic Defenses and Soviet-American Relations* (Cambridge, Mass., Ballinger Publishing, 1987) pp. 1-35.

Ball, Desmond, *Politics and Force Levels: The Strategic Missile Program of the Kennedy Administration* (Berkeley, University of California Press, 1980).

Brodie, Bernard, *The Development of Nuclear Strategy* (University of California, Los Angeles, Centre for Arms Control and International Security, ASIC Working Paper Number 11, 1978).

Freedman, Lawrence, *The Evolution of Nuclear Strategy* (New York, St. Martin's Press, 1981).

Richelson, Jeffrey, 'PD-59, NSDD-13 and the Reagan Strategic Modernisation Program' *Journal of Strategic Studies* Volume 6, Number 2, June 1983, pp.125-146.

Rowen, Henry S., 'The Evolution of Strategic Nuclear Doctrine' in Martin, Laurence (ed.), *Strategic Thought in the Nuclear Age* (Baltimore, Johns Hopkins University Press, 1979) pp. 131-156.

Sagan, Scott D., 'SIOP-62: The Nuclear War Plan Briefing to President Kennedy' *International Security* (Vol.12, No.1), Summer 1987, pp.22-51.

Wells, Samuel F., 'A Question of Priorities: A Comparison of the Carter and Reagan Defence Programs' *Orbis* (Vol.27, No.3), Fall 1983, pp.641-666.

Wells, Samuel F., 'Sounding the Tocsin: NSC 68 and the Soviet Threat' *International Security* (Vol.4, No.2), Fall 1979, pp.116-158.

Chapter 3: The Development of Soviet Strategy

Adomeit, Hannes, *Soviet Risk-Taking and Crisis Behaviour - A Theoretical and Empirical Analysis* (London, George Allen & Unwin, 1982).

Ball, Desmond, 'Soviet Strategic Planning and the Control of Nuclear War' in Kolkowicz, Roman, Michiewicz, Ellen Propper (eds.), *The Soviet Calculus of Nuclear War* (Lexington, Mass., Lexington Books, D.C. Heath and Company, 1986) pp. 49-67.

Dibb, Paul, *The Soviet Union: the Incomplete Superpower* (London, Macmillan/IISS, 1986).

Grechko, A.A., *The Armed Forces of the Soviet Union* (Moscow, Progress Publishers, 1977).

Leebaert, Derek (ed.), *Soviet Military Thinking* (London, George Allen & Unwin, 1981).

MacKintosh, Malcolm, *Juggernaut: A History of the Soviet Armed Forces* (London, Secker and Warburg, 1967).

Miller, R.F., Miller, J.H., Rigby, T.H., (eds.), *Gorbachev at the Helm* (London, Croom Helm, 1987).

Morton, E., Segal, G., (eds.), *Soviet Strategy towards Western Europe* (London, George Allen & Unwin, 1984).

Scott, Harriet Fast, Scott, William F., *The Armed Forces of the USSR* (Boulder, Colorado, Westview Press, 1979).

Semmel, Bernard (ed.), *Marxism and the Science of War* (New York, Oxford University Press, 1981).

Steele, Jonathan, *The Limits of Soviet Power* (London, Penguin Books, 1985).

Chapter 4: The Future of the Global Strategic Balance

Ball, Desmond, 'Technology and Geopolitics' in Zoppo, Ciro E., Zorgibibe, Charles (eds.), *On Geopolitics: Classical and Nuclear* (Dordrecht, Boston and Lancaster, Martinus Nijhoff Publishers, Published in cooperation with the NATO Scientific Affairs Division, 1985) pp. 171-199.

Ball, Desmond, *Can Nuclear War be Controlled?* (London, International Institute for Strategic Studies, Adelphi Paper Number 169).

Carter, Ashton B., Steinbruner, John D., Zraket, Charles A., (eds.), *Managing Nuclear Operations* (Washington D.C., The Brookings Institution, 1987).

Gottfried, Kurt, Blair, Bruce G. (eds.), *Crisis Stability and Nuclear War* (Oxford and New York, Oxford University Press, 1988).

Lebow, Richard Ned, *Nuclear Crisis Management* (Ithaca, Cornell University Press, 1987).

May, Michael M., Bing, George F., Steinbruner, John D., 'Strategic Arsenals After START The Implications of Deep Cuts' *International Security* Volume 13, Number 1, Summer 1988, pp. 90-133.

Richelson, Jeffrey T., 'Evaluating the Strategic Balance' *American Journal of Political Science* (Vol.24, No.4), November 1980, pp. 795-819.

Stares, Paul B., *The Militarisation of Space: US Policy, 1974-84* (Ithaca, Cornell University Press, 1985).

United States Congress, House Committee on Armed Services, Defense Policy Panel, *Breakout, Verification and Force Structure: Dealing with the Full Implications of START* (Washington D.C., US Government Printing Office, 1988), pp. 21-23.

United States Department of Defense, *Soviet Military Power 1988* (Washington D.C., US Government Printing Office, Seventh Edition, 1988).

Chapter 5: Trends in Conventional Weapons Technologies

Ball, Desmond, (ed.), *Air Power: Global Developments and Australian Perspectives* (Sydney, Pergamon-Brassey's Defence Publishers, 1988).

Burt, Richard, *New Weapons Technologies: Debate and Directions* (London, International Institute for Strategic Studies, Adelphi Paper No.126, 1976).

Deitchman, Seymour J., *Military Power and the Advance of Technology - General Purpose Military Forces for the 1980s and Beyond* (Boulder, Colorado, Westview Press, 1983).

Digby, James F., *Precision-Guided Weapons* (London, International Institute for Strategic Studies, Adelphi Paper No.118, 1975).

Dudzinsky, S.J., Digby James F., 'The Strategic and Tactical Implications of New Weapons Technologies' in O'Neill, Robert (ed.), *The Defence of Australia: Fundamental New Aspects* (Canberra, Australian National University, 1977).

Kemp, Geoffrey, et.al., *The Other Arms Race* (Lexington, Mass., Lexington Books, 1975).

Paxson, E.W., Weiner, M.G., Wise, R.A., *Interactions Between Tactics and Technology in Ground Warfare* (Santa Monica, Rand Corporation, R-2377, 1978).

Perry, Robert, *The Interaction of Technology and Doctrine in the US Air Force* (Santa Monica, RAND Corporation, P-6281, 1979).

van Creveld, Martin L., *Technology and War* (London, Macmillan Press, 1989)

----- *New Conventional Weapons Technology and East-West Security Parts 1 and 2* (London, International Institute for Strategic Studies, Adelphi Paper Numbers 144, 145, 1978)

Chapter 6: Revolutionary Warfare

Adelman, Jonathan R., *Revolutions, Armies and War - A Political History* (Boulder, Colorado, Lynne Rienner, 1985).

Arendt, Hannah, *On Revolution* (New York, The Viking Press, 1963).

Atkinson, Alexander, 'Chinese Communist Strategic Thought - The Strategic Premise of Protracted War' *Journal of the Royal United Services Institute for Defence Studies* (Vol.118, No.1), March 1973, pp. 60-64.

Brinton, Crane, *The Anatomy of Revolution* (New York, Prentice Hall, 1952).

Fanon, Frantz, *The Wretched of the Earth* (Middlesex, Penguin, 1978).

LaFeber, Walter, *Inevitable Revolutions: The United States in Central America* (New York, W.W. Norton, 1983).

Laqueur, Walter (ed.), *The Guerrilla Reader: A Historical Anthology* (Philadelphia, Temple University Press, 1977)

Sarkesian, Sam C., *Revolutionary Guerrilla Warfare* (Chicago, Precedent Publishing, 1975).

Taber, Robert, *The War of the Flea, A Study of Guerrilla Warfare, Theory and Practice* (London, Paladin Press, 1970).

Tse-Tung, Mao, *Selected Military Writings* (Peking, Foreign Language Press, 1966).

Trotsky, Leon, *Military Writings* (New York, Pathfinder, 1971).

Chapter 7: Terrorism and Non-State Violence

Alexander Y., Carlton D., Wilkinson P. (eds.), *Terrorism: Theory and Practice* (Boulder, Colorado, Westview Press, 1979).

Alexander Y., Gleason, J.M., (Eds.), *Behavioural and Quantitative Perspectives on Terrorism* (New York, Pergamon Press, 1981).

Bowyer Bell, J., *A Time of Terror* (New York, Basic Books, 1978).

Crenshaw M. (ed.), *Terrorism, Legitimacy, and Power: The Consequences of Political Violence* (Middletown, CT, Wesleyan University Press, 1983).

George, A., Hall, D., Simons, W.R., *The Limits of Coercive Diplomacy* (Boston, Little Brown, 1971).

Slater, R., Stohl, M. (Eds.), *Current Perspectives on International Terrorism* (London, Macmillan, forthcoming).

Sloan, Stephen, 'International Terrorism: Conceptual Problems and Implications' *Journal of Thought* (Vol.17, No.2), 1982, pp. 19-29.

Taheri, Amir, *Holy Terror* (London, Sphere Books, 1987).
Wardlaw, Grant, *Political Terrorism* (Cambridge, Cambridge University Press, 1982).
Wilkinson, Paul, *Terrorism and the Liberal State* (London, Macmillan, Second Edition, 1986).
Wilkinson, Paul, 'The Future of Terrorism' *Futures* (Vol.20, No.5), October 1988, pp. 493-504.

Chapter 8: Alternative Defence Concepts

Barnaby, F., Ter Borg, Marlies, (eds.), *Emerging Technology and Military Doctrine: A Political Assessment* (London, Macmillan Press, 1986).
Boserup, Anders, Mack, Andrew, *War Without Weapons: Non-Violence in National Defense* (New York, Schocken Books, 1975).
Buzan, B., 'Common Security, Non-Provocative Defence and the Future of Western Europe' *Review of International Studies* Volume 13, Number 4, 1987, pp. 265-279.
Fischer, D., 'Invulnerability Without Threat: The Swiss Concept of General Defense' *Journal of Peace Research* (Vol.19, No.3), 1982, pp. 205-225.
Gates, D., 'Area Defence Concepts: the West German Debate' *Survival* (Vol.29, No.4), July-August 1987, pp. 301-317.
Johansen, M., 'A Bibliography of Alternative Defence' in Paul, D., (ed.), *Defending Europe: Options for Security* (London, 1985).
Mack, Andrew, 'The Strategy of Non-Military Defence' in Ball, Desmond (ed.), *Strategy and Defence: Australian Essays* (Sydney, George Allen & Unwin, 1982), pp. 148-169. (Also published as Peace Research Centre Reference Paper Number 5).
Stockholm International Peace Research Institute, *Policies for Common Security* (London and Philadelphia, Taylor and Francis, 1985).
Van Evera, S., 'The Cult of the Offensive and the Origins of the First World War' *International Security* (Vol.9, No.1), Summer 1984, pp. 58-107.
Windass, Stan, Grove, Eric, *The Crucible of Peace: Common Security in Europe* (London, Brassey's Defence Publishers, 1988).

Chapter 9: Arms Control

Ball, Desmond, Mack, Andrew (eds.), *The Future of Arms Control* (Sydney, Pergamon/Australian National University Press, 1987).
Bull, Hedley, 'The Classical Approach to Arms Control Twenty Years After' in Nerlich, Uwe (ed.), *Soviet Power and Western Negotiating Policies* (Cambridge, Mass., Ballinger, 1983, Volume II), pp. 21-30.
Bull, Hedley, *The Control of the Arms Race* (London, Weidenfeld and Nicolson, 1961).
Darilek, Richard, 'The Future of Conventional Arms Control in Europe' *Survival* (Vol.29, No.1), January-February 1987, pp. 5-20.
Findlay, Trevor, 'The Gorbachev Initiative' *Current Affairs Bulletin*, (Vol.64, No.1), June 1987, pp. 17-25.
Goldblatt, Jozef (ed.), *Non-Proliferation: The Why and the Wherefore* (London, Taylor & Francis, 1985).
Goldblatt, Jozef, *Agreements for Arms Control: A Critical Survey* (London, Taylor and Francis, 1982).
Lynn-Jones, Sean M., 'A Quiet Success for Arms Control: Preventing Incidents at Sea' *International Security* (Vol.9, No.4), Spring 1985, pp. 154-184.
Schelling, T.C., Halperin, M.H., *Strategy and Arms Control* (New York, Twentieth Century Fund, 1961).
Voas, Jeanette, 'The Arms-Control Compliance Debate' *Survival* Volume 28, Number 1, January-February 1986, pp. 8-31.

Chapter 10: The Evolution of Australian Defence Policy

Babbage, Ross, 'Australia's Defence After the Dibb Report' *Current Affairs Bulletin* (Vol.63, No.7), December 1986, pp. 16-23.

Babbage, Ross, *Managing Australia's Contingency Spectrum for Defence Planning* (Canberra, Australian National University, Strategic and Defence Studies Centre Working Paper No.108, 1986).

Babbage, Ross, *Rethinking Australia's Defence* (St. Lucia, Brisbane, Queensland University Press, 1980).

Ball, Desmond, Langtry, J.O. (eds.), *Problems of Mobilisation in Defence of Australia* (Canberra, Phoenix Defence Publications, 1980).

Ball, Desmond, Langtry, J.O., *Controlling Australia's Threat Environment: A Methodology for Planning Australian Defence Force Development* (Canberra, Australian National University Press, 1980).

Dibb, Paul, *Review of Australia's Defence Capabilities* (Canberra, Australian Government Publishing Service, Report to the Minister for Defence, 1986).

Langtry, J.O., Ball, Desmond (eds.), *A Vulnerable Country? Civil Resources in the Defence of Australia* (Canberra, Australian National University Press, 1986).

Millar, T.B., *Australia's Defence* (Melbourne, Melbourne University Press, 1965).

Minister for Defence, the Hon. Kim C. Beazley, MP, *The Defence of Australia 1987* (Canberra, Australian Government Publishing Service, A White Paper presented to the Parliament, 1987).

O'Neill, Robert (ed.), *The Defence of Australia: Fundamental New Aspects* (Canberra, Australian National University, Strategic and Defence Studies Centre, 1976).

Chapter 11: ANZUS: The Case For

Ball, Desmond (ed.), *The ANZAC Connection* (Sydney, George, Allen & Unwin, 1985).

Bell, Coral, *Dependent Ally: A Study in Australian Foreign Policy* (Melbourne, Oxford University Press, 1988).

Bercovitch, Jacob (ed.), *ANZUS in Crisis: Alliance Management in International Affairs* (London, Macmillan Press, 1988).

Burnett, Alan, *The A-NZ-US Triangle* (Canberra, Australian National University, Strategic and Defence Studies Centre, 1988).

McMillan, Stuart, *Neither Confirm Nor Deny: The Nuclear Ships Dispute Between New Zealand and the United States* (Wellington, Allen & Unwin, 1987).

Mediansky, F.A., Palfreeman, A.C. (eds.), *In Pursuit of National Interests: Australian Foreign Policy in the 1990s* (Sydney, Pergamon, 1988).

Rosecrance, R.N., *Australian Diplomacy and Japan, 1945-51* (Melbourne, Melbourne University Press, 1962).

Starke, J.G., *The ANZUS Treaty Alliance* (Melbourne, Melbourne University Press, 1965).

Chapter 12: ANZUS: The Case Against

Parliament of Australia, Joint Committee on Foreign Affairs and Defence, *The ANZUS Alliance* (Canberra, Australian Government Publishing Service, 1982).

Babbage, Ross, 'Australian Defence Planning, Force Structure and Equipment: The American Effect' *Australian Outlook* (Vol.38, No.3), December 1984, pp. 163-168.

Richelson, Jeffrey T., Ball, Desmond, *The Ties that Bind: Intelligence Cooperation Between the UKUSA Countries - Britain, the United States, Canada, Australian and New Zealand* (Sydney and London, George Allen & Unwin, 1985).

Else, Daniel H., 'America and Australia: Where the Future?' *Defence Force Journal* No.69, pp. 49-55.

Gelber, Harry, *The Australian-American Alliance: Costs and Benefits* (Ringwood Victoria, Penguin, 1968).
Martin, David, *Armed Neutrality for Australia* (Blackburn, Victoria, Dove Communications, 1984).
Renouf, Alan, *The Frightened Country* (London, Macmillan, 1979).

Chapter 13: Australian Defence Decision-Making

Ball, Desmond, 'Australian Defence Decision-Making: Actors and Processes' *Politics* (Vol.14, No.2), November 1979, pp. 183-197.
Behm, A.J. 'Australian Defence Policy: the Game and the Players' *Journal of the Australian Naval Institute* (Vol.12, No.4), November 1986, pp. 21-28.
Brown, Gary, 'The Management of Australia's Defence' *Defence Force Journal* No.70, June-June 1988, pp. 5-14.
Cheeseman, G.L. 'Interest Groups and Australian Defence Decision-Making' *Defence Force Journal* No.35, July-August 1982, pp. 23-32.
Defence Review Committee, (The Utz Committee), *The Higher Defence Organisation in Australia* (Canberra, Australian Government Publishing Service, 1982, Final Report).
Mediansky, F.A. (ed.), *The Military and Australia's Defence* (Melbourne, Longman Cheshire, 1979).
O'Connor, Michael, *Australia's Defence Policy: To Live in Peace* (Melbourne, Melbourne University Press, 1985).
Parliament of the Commonwealth of Australia, Joint Committee on Foreign Affairs, Defence and Trade, *The Management of Australia's Defence* (Canberra, Australian Government Publishing Service, 1987).
Parliament of the Commonwealth of Australia, Joint Committee on Foreign Affairs and Defence, *The Australian Defence Force: Its Structure and Capabilities* (Canberra, Australian Government Publishing Service, 1984).
Tange, Sir Arthur, *Australian Defence, Report on the Reorganisation of the Defence Group of Departments* (Canberra, Australian Government Publishing Service, 1974).

Chapter 14: Legal Aspects of the Employment of the ADF

Best, Geoffrey, 'Legal Restraints on Warfare: The Twentieth Century's Experience' *Journal of the Royal United Services Institute for Defence Studies* (Vol.122, No.3), September 1977, pp. 3-10.
De Lupis, Ingrid Detter, *The Law of War* (Cambridge, Cambridge University Press, London School of Economics and Political Science Monograph in International Studies, 1987).
Doogan, C.M., 'Defence Powers Under the Constitution - Use of Troops in Aid of State Police Forces - Suppression of Terrorist Activities' *Defence Force Journal* No.31, November-December 1981, pp. 31-38.
Draper, Colonel G.I.A.D., 'The New Law of Armed Conflict' *Journal of the Royal United Services Institute for Defence Studies* (Vol.124, No.3), September 1979, pp. 3-11.
Ewing, M.J., 'Military Aid to the Civil Power' *Defence Force Journal* No.57, March-April 1986, pp. 21-31.
Glover, Michael, *The Velvet Glove - The Decline of Moderation in War* (London, Hodder and Stoughton, 1982).
Lee, H.P., *Emergency Powers* (Sydney, Law Book Company, 1984).
Neate, Graeme, *Legal Aspects of Defence Operations on Aboriginal Land in the Northern Territory* (Canberra, Australian National University, Strategic and Defence Studies Centre Working Paper No.136, 1987).

Smith, Hugh (ed.), *Law, Change and the Services* (Royal Military College, Duntroon, Faculty of Military Studies, Department of Government, 1984).

Stephen, Sir Ninian, 'The Role of the Governor-General as Commander-in-Chief of the Australian Defence Forces' *Defence Force Journal* No.43, November-December 1983, pp. 3-9.

Chapter 15: Defence Force Personnel

Binkin, Martin, *Military Technology and Defence Manpower* (Washington D.C., Brookings Institution, 1986).

Bowman, William, Little, Richard, Sicilia, G. Thomas (eds.), *The All-Volunteer Force After a Decade - Retrospect and Prospect* (Washington D.C., Pergamon-Brassey's International Defence Publishers, 1986).

Downes, Cathy, *High Personnel Turnover: The Australian Defence Force is Not a Limited Liability Company* (Canberra, Australian National University, Canberra Paper on Strategy and Defence No.44, 1988).

Foster, Gregory D., Sabrosky, Alan N., Taylor, William J., (eds.), *The Strategic Dimension of Military Manpower* (Cambridge,Mass., Ballinger Publishing, 1987).

Moskos, Charles C., Wood, Frank W., (eds.), *The Military - More than Just a Job?* (Washington D.C., Pergamon-Brassey's International Defence Publishers, 1988).

Parliament of Australia, Joint Committee on Foreign Affairs Defence and Trade, *Personnel Wastage in the Australian Defence Force - Report and Recommendations* (Canberra, Australian Government Publishing Service, 1988).

Segal, David R., Sinaiko, H. Wallace, (eds.), *Life in the Rank and File - Enlisted Men and Women in the Armed Forces of the United States, Australia, Canada, and the United Kingdom* (Washington D.C., Pergamon-Brassey's International Defence Publishers, 1986).

Chapter 16: Defence Industry and Research Development

Bureau of Industry Economics, *The Australian Aerospace Industry: Structure, Performance and Economic Issues* (Canberra, Australian Government Publishing Service, Research Report 20, 1986).

Cooksey, R.J., *Review of Australia's Defence Exports and Defence Industry* (Canberra, Australian Government Publishing Service, 1986).

Department of Defence, *Directory of Australian Industry Defence Capability* (Canberra, DRB 29, December 1987).

Department of Industry and Commerce, *Annual Report 1986-87: Change and Adaptation in Industry* (Canberra, Australian Government Publishing Service, 1987).

Fox, J. Ronald., *The Defense Management Challenge - Weapons Acquisition* (Boston, Harvard Business School Press, 1988).

Gansler, J.S., *The Defence Industry* (Cambridge, Mass., The MIT Press, 1980).

Kiely, D.J. 'The Evolving Pattern of Naval Weapons Procurement' *Journal of Naval Science* (Vol.10, No.1), February 1984, pp.64-73.

Parliament of the Commonwealth of Australia, Joint Committee on Foreign Affairs and Defence, *Industrial Support for Defence and Allied Matters* (Canberra, Commonwealth Government Printer, Parliamentary Paper No.225/1977, 1978).

Parliament of the Commonwealth of Australia, Joint Committee on Public Accounts, *Review of Defence Project Management Report Number 243* (Canberra, Australian Government Publishing Service, Volume 1 - Report, (Vol.2) - Project Analyses, 1986).

President's Blue Ribbon Commission on Defence Management, *Final Report: A Quest for Excellence* (Washington D.C., US Government Printing Office, June 1986).

Chapter 17: The Defence Force and Australian Society

Albinski, H.S., 'The Armed Forces and the Community in Post-Vietnam Australia' *Politics* (Vol.14, No.2), November 1979, pp. 198-209.

Beddie, B.D., Moss, S., *Some Aspects of Aid to the Civil Power in Australia* (Canberra, University of New South Wales, Faculty of Military Studies, Department of Government, Occasional Monograph No.2, 1982).

Brown, G., 'Parliament and Defence; A Peep behind the Scenes' *Defence Force Journal* No.58, May-June 1986, pp.46-50.

Campbell, D., *Australian Public Opinion on National Security Issues* (Australian National University, Peace Research Centre, Working Paper Number 1, 1986).

Edmonds, Martin, *Armed Forces and Society* (Leicester, Leicester University Press, 1988).

King, P. (ed.), *Australia's Vietnam* (Sydney, Allen & Unwin, 1983).

Ross, Jane, *The Myth of the Digger* (Sydney, Hale & Iremonger, 1985).

Saunders, M., Summy, R., *The Australian Peace Movement: A Short History* (Canberra, Australian National University, Peace Research Centre, 1986).

Smith, H., Moss, S., (eds.), *A Bibliography of Armed Forces and Society in Australia* (Canberra, Australian Defence Force Academy, University College, Australian Defence Studies Centre, 1987).

Chapter 18: Security Policies in New Zealand

Ball, Desmond, 'The Security Relationship between Australia and New Zealand' in Ball, Desmond, (ed.), *The ANZAC Connection* (Sydney, Allen & Unwin, 1985) pp. 33-52.

Barnes, D.J. 'Logistics, Industry and Training' in Ball, Desmond (ed.), *The ANZAC Connection* (Sydney, Allen & Unwin, 1985) pp. 53-67.

Dodd, Norman L., 'New Zealand's Defence Problems' *Journal of the Royal United Services Institute for Defence Studies* (Vol.123, No.2), June 1978, pp. 49-56.

Jennings, Peter, *The Armed Forces of New Zealand and ANZUS Split: Costs and Consequences* (Wellington, New Zealand Institute of International Affairs, Occasional Paper No.4, 1988).

McGibbon, Ian C., *Blue-Water Rationale: The Naval Defence of New Zealand 1914-1942* (Wellington, New Zealand, Government Printer, 1981).

McGibbon, Ian C., 'The Defence of New Zealand 1945-1957' in *New Zealand in World Affairs* (Wellington, Price Milburn for the New Zealand Institute of International Affairs, 1977, Vol.1), pp. 145-176.

McGibbon, Ian C., *The New Zealand Army in Vietnam, 1964-1972* (Wellington, Ministry of Defence, A Report of the General Staff Exercise 1972, 1973).

Templeton, Malcolm, *Defence and Security: What New Zealand Needs* (Wellington, Victoria University Press for Institute of Policy Studies, 1986).

Tweddle, Grant, *The United States Military Presence in New Zealand* (Christchurch, University of Canterbury, M.A. Thesis, 1983).

Young, Thomas-Durell, 'New Zealand Defence Policy Under Labour' *US Naval War College Review* (Vol.39, No.3), May-June 1986, pp. 22-34.

Chapter 19: Indonesia and the Security of Australia and PNG

Budiardjo, C. Lion, Liem Soei, *The War Against East Timor* (London, Zed Books, 1984)

Crouch, H., *The Army and Politics in Indonesia* (Ithaca, Cornell University Press, 1978)

Leifer M., *Indonesia's Foreign Policy* (London, George Allen & Unwin for the Royal Institute of International Affairs, 1983).

Mackie, J.A.C., *Konfrontasi: The Indonesia-Malaysia Dispute 1963-66* (Kuala Lumpur, Oxford University Press, 1974).

May, R.K. (ed.), *Between Two Nations: The Indonesian-Papua New Guinea Border and West Papua Nationalism* (Bathurst, NSW, Robert Brown and Associates, 1986).

McDonald, H., *Suharto's Indonesia* (Blackburn, Victoria, Fontana/Collins, 1980).

Osbourne, R. *Indonesia's Secret War: The Guerrilla Struggle in Irian Jaya* (Sydney, Allen & Unwin, 1985).

Proklamasi, Yayasan, *Regional Dimensions of Indonesia-Australia Relations* (Jakarta, Centre for Strategic and International Studies, 1984).

Sundhaussen, U., *The Road to Power: Indonesian Military Politics 1945-1967* (Kuala Lumpur, Oxford University Press, 1982).

------ 'The Australian-Indonesian Relationship: A Current Assessment' *Australian Outlook* (Vol.40, No.3), December 1986, Special Issue.

Chapter 20: Indochina

Beresford, Melanie, *Vietnam: Politics, Economics and Society* (London, Pinter Publishers, 1988).

Brown, MacAlister, Zasloff, Joseph J., *Apprentice Revolutionaries: The Communist Movement in Laos, 1930-1985* (Stanford, Hoover Institution Press, 1986).

Chanda, Nayan, *Brother Enemy: The War after the War* (New York, Harcourt, Brace Jovanovich Publishers, 1986).

Chen, King C., *China's War With Vietnam 1979* (Stanford, Hoover Institution Press, 1987).

Duiker, William J., *China and Vietnam: The Roots of Conflict* (Berkeley, University of California, Institute of East Asian Studies, Indochina Research Monograph No.1, 1986).

Horn, Robert C., *Alliance Politics Between Comrades: An Analysis of Soviet Presence in Indochina* (Santa Monica, RAND/University of California, Los Angeles, Center for the Study of Soviet International Behaviour, 1987).

Johnson, Lieutenant Colonel Dion W., *Bear Tracks in Indochina: An Analysis of Soviet Presence in Indochina* (Alabama, Maxwell Air Force Base, Air University Press, 1987).

Marr, David G., White, Christine P., (eds.), *Postwar Vietnam: Dilemmas in Socialist Development* (Ithaca, Cornell University Southeast Asia Program, 1988).

Rowley, Kelvin, Evans, Grant, *Red Brotherhood at War: Indochina Since the Fall of Saigon* (London, Verso, 1984).

Stuart-Fox, Martin, *Laos: Politics, Economics and Society* (London, France Pinter Publishers, 1986).

Vickery, Michael, *Kampuchea: Politics, Economics and Society* (Sydney, Allen & Unwin Australia, 1986).

Zasloff, Joseph J., (ed.), *Postwar Indochina: Old Enemies and New Allies* (Washington D.C., US Department of State, Foreign Service Institute, Center for the Study of Foreign Affairs, 1988).

Chapter 21: South Pacific and Papua New Guinea

The Parliament of the Commonwealth of Australia, Joint Committee on Foreign Affairs, Defence and Trade, *Australia's Relations With the South Pacific*, (Canberra, Australian Government Publishing Service, 1989).

Kim C. Beazley, 'Australian Defence Policy', address to the Bicentennial Conference, *Australia and the World: Prologue and Prospects*, Strategic and Defence Studies Centre, Australian National University, 6-9 December 1988.

Muriel Brookfield and R. Gerard Ward (eds.), *New Directions in the South Pacific - A Message for Australia*, (Canberra, Research School of Pacific Studies, Academy of the Social Sciences in Australia, 1988).

Colin Clarke and Tony Payne (eds), *Politics, Security and Development in Small States*, (London, Allen & Unwin, 1987).
Commonwealth Secretariat, *Vulnerability - Small States in the Global Society*, (London, Commonwealth Consultative Group Report, Marlborough House,1985).
John Connell, *Sovereignty and Survival - Island Microstates in the Third World*, Research Monograph No.3, (University of Sydney, Department of Geography, 1988).
Gareth Evans, 'Australia in the South Pacific', Speech by the Australian Minister for Foreign Affairs and Trade, to the Foreign Correspondents Association, 23 September 1988, in *Backgrounder* (Australia, Department of Foreign Affairs and Trade), No.634, 28 September, 1988.
David Hegarty, *South Pacific Security Issues: An Australian Perspective*, Strategic and Defence Studies Centre Working Paper No.147, (Canberra, Australian National University, 1987).
R.A. Herr, 'Regionalism, Strategic Denial and South Pacific Security', *Journal of Pacific History*, (Vol.21, No.4), October, 1986.
R.A. Herr, 'Diplomacy and Security in the South Pacific - Coping With Sovereignty', *Current Affairs Bulletin*, (Vol.63, No.8), January 1987.
Talukder Manniruzzaman, *The Security of Small States in the Third World*, Strategic and Defence Studies Centre, Canberra Papers on Strategy and Defence No.25, (Canberra, Australian National University, 1982).
T.B. Millar (ed.), *International Security in the Southeast Asian and Southwest Pacific Region*, (St Lucia, Queensland, University of Queensland Press, 1983).

Chapter 22: China's Security

Barnett, A. Doak, *China's Economy in Global Perspective* (Washington D.C., Brookings Institution, 1981).
Fairbank, J.K., *The Great Chinese Revolution 1800-1985* (New York, Harper and Row, 1986).
Harding, Harry, Hewett, ed. A., 'Socialist Reforms and the World Economy' in Steinbruner, John D. (ed.), *Restructuring American Foreign Policy* (Washington D.C., Brookings Institution, 1989), pp. 158-184.
Harding, Harry (ed.), *China's Foreign Relations in the 1980s* (New Haven, Yale University Press, 1984).
Johnston, Alastair I., 'Chinese Nuclear Force Modernisation: Implications for Arms Control' *Journal of Northeast Asian Studies* (Vol.2, No.2), June 1983, pp. 13-28.
Muller, David J., *China as a Maritime Power* (Boulder, Colorado, Westview Press, 1983).
Qian, Wenyuan, *The Great Inertia, Scientific Stagnation in Traditional China* (London, Croom Helm, 1985).
Ross, Robert S., 'International Bargaining and Domestic Politics: US/China Relations Since 1972' *World Politics* (Vol.38, No.2), January 1986, pp. 255-287.
Segal, Gerald, Tow, William T. (eds.), *Chinese Defence Policy* (London, Macmillan Press, 1984).
The World Bank, *China: Long-Term Issues and Options* (Baltimore, Johns Hopkins University Press, 1985).
------'Gorbachev, 28 July Speech in Vladivostock' Foreign Broadcasting Information Service - Soviet Union, 29th July 1986, p. R14.

Chapter 23: The Superpowers in the Pacific

Albinski, Henry S., *ANZUS, the United States and Pacific Security* (Lanham MD, University Press of America for the Asia Society, 1987).
Babbage, R. (ed.), *The Soviet in the North Pacific in the 1990s*, (Sydney, Rushcutters Bay, Pergamon Press, 1989).

Ball, Desmond (ed.), *US Bases in the Philippines: Issues and Implications* (Canberra, Australian National University, Strategic and Defence Studies Centre, Canberra Papers on Strategy and Defence, Number 46, 1988).

Buss, Claude A., (ed.), *National Security Interests in the Pacific Basin* (Stanford, Hoover Institution Press, 1985)

Buszynski, Leszek, *Soviet Foreign Policy and Southeast Asia* (New York, St. Martin's Press, 1986).

Dibb, Paul 'Soviet Strategy Towards Australia, New Zealand and the South-West Pacific' *Australian Outlook* (Vol.39), August 1985, pp. 69-76.

Mediansky, F.A. 'The Defence of Australia and the American Alliance' *Australian Outlook* (Vol.41), December 1987, pp. 156-160.

Morley, James W. (ed.), *The Pacific Basin: New Challenges for the United States* (New York, The Academy of Political Science, 1986).

Pacific Forum (with the Australian Institute of International Affairs and the Australian Studies Centre, Pennsylvania State University), *Strategic Imperatives and Western Responses in the South and Southwest Pacific* (Honolulu, Pacific Forum, 1986).

Palmer, Norman D., *Westward Watch: The United States and the Changing Western Pacific* (Washington D.C., Pergamon-Brassey's International Defence Publishers, 1987).

Scalapino, Robert A., *Major Power Relations in Northeast Asia* (Lanham, MD., University Press of America for The Asia Society, 1987).

Thakur, Ramesh, Thayer, Carlyle A., *The Soviet Union as an Asian-Pacific Power, Implications of Gorbachev's 1986 Vladivostock Initiative* (Boulder, Colorado, Westview Press, 1987).

INDEX

armed forces, acquisition by, 53;
Soviet delivery systems, 54; Soviet
military strength, importance to, 55;
strategic stand-off, 14; strategic, use
by NATO, 165; submarine based
option mode preferred by NDP, 181;
tactical, 203, use by NATO, 165;
third generation, 78; US, numbers,
87; US development, 19; use in
general warfare, 57-8
Nuclear Weapons Employment and
Acquisition Master Plan (US,
1981)(NWEAMP), 39
Nuclear Weapons Employment Policy
(US)(NUWEP), 1974, 30, 31; 1977, 32,
34; 1980, 34; 1981, 38-9, 39; 1985-8,
41-5
Nulka anti-ship missile defence system,
334, 335
Nurrungar, 226, 228, 229 *bis*, 242, 245
NUWEP, *see* Nuclear Weapons
Employment Policy (US)(NUWEP)

O'Flynn, Frank, 370
Oberon, submarine replacement project,
294
Offensive strategy, advantages over
NPD, 177
Offensive-orientated theatre strategy,
changes under Gorbachev, 70
Office Cadet School Portsea, cadetship of
women, 347
Office of Defence Production, 326
Office of National Assessments, 263
Ogarkov, Nikolai, Marshal, 62, 63
Okhotsk, Sea of, submarine base, 81
Okuk, Iambakey, 393
Ombudsman Act 1976 (Australia), 275,
288n
'Operation Solarium', 19
Operational conflict, definition, 2;
military expertise, 3
Operational Manoeuvre Group (OMG),
Soviet strategy based on, 169
Organisasi Papua Merdeka (OPM), 393,
394, 395, 395-6
Orion aircraft, 237, 241
OTC (Australia), Indochina, in, 408
Over-the-horizon (OTH) radar, 81, 112;
Jindalee, 335; radar transmitters,
remote siting of, 123; US security for
ASEAN, 463
Outer Mongolia, reduction of forces, 66

P-3 Orion aircraft, 218
P-3C Orion aircraft, 373

Pacific, anti-nuclear and nuclear-free
zone proposals, 463-4; importance in
21st century, 229; questioning of
Soviet Union non-hostile intent, in,
459; strategic status in 1951, 230;
1990, 230; superpowers in, 454-74;
see also Asia-Pacific region; Northern
Pacific; South Pacific; Southwest
Pacific; Soviet Union in Pacific;
United States of America in Pacific;
Western Pacific
Pacific basin, economic expansion, 457;
Soviet security interests, *see* Soviet
Union in Pacific; US security
interests, *see* United States of
America in Pacific; Western Pacific
Pacific 'Exclusive Economic Zone'
fisheries claims, 464, 467
Pacific islands, battles for, 221;
sovereignty, 230; states and
territories, 414
Pacific Patrol Boat Program, 431-2
Pacific Rim security treaty, suggested,
432
Pacific War 1941-45, 412
Packard, David, 37
Palau (US Trust Territory), 413; political
volatility, 417
Palestine, cause, terrorism associated
with, 152; Irgun Zvai Leumi, 149,
157
Palestine Liberation Organisation (PLO),
149, 153
Palestine Mandate, end of, 157
Palestinian Liberation Army, 142
Palestinian terrorist activity, 153; Arab
support for, 160
Panin, V.I., Vice-Admiral, 68
Papua New Guinea, xxiii, xxiv, 240, 250,
412, 418 *bis*, 428; Australia and, Joint
Declaration of Principles, 432;
Australian commitment to, 228, 419;
battles for, 221; call-out of defence
force, 282-3; Chinese defence
modernisation, implications of, 451;
confrontation campaign against, 213;
defence, Indonesia, and, 378;
ethnicity, 428; Indonesia and, 378-97,
420, 431, 432, possible conflict with,
224, relations with, 430-1, treaty
(1986-87); Indonesian border, 387,
419, 420, 421; Irian Jaya, opposition
to Indonesian rule in, 393; Irian Jaya
border, Indonesian Army *Kostrad*
presence, 387; military capacity, 413;
OPM guerilla movement, Libyan
links, 425, support for, 393-4;

Sea-launched ballistic missiles (SLBMs), 58; Chinese, 440, 448; *see also* Submarine-launched ballistic missiles (SLBM)

Second Indochina War, 129

Second World War, *see* World War II

Second-strike retaliatory force concept, 45

Selective Attack Options (SAOs), 86-7

Self-defence, law of, 284

Self-deterrence, credibility, 166

Sendero Luminoso movement (Peru), 149

Sensor systems, long range battlefield, 127; nuclear warfare, development, 43

Sensor weapons, 112

Services Personnel Policy Committee (Australia), 304

Sex Discrimination Act 1984 (Australia), exemption of ADF, 348

Shafrir II, air-to-air missile, use in Israel-Arab conflict, 177-8

Sharapovo wartime relocation complex, 89

Shevardnadze, 422

Ship-borne electronic warfare (EW) systems, defensive measures against, 118

Ship-building and ship-repair in Australia, 324-5; economies of scale, lack of, 328-9; productivity, 328-9

Shipping Registration Act 1981 (Australia), 288n

Shortstop automatic gun systems, 118

Shultz, George, 432

Sidewinder, air-to-air missile, use in Israel-Arab conflict, 177-8

Signals Intelligence satellite systems (SIGINT), 42-3, 43, 78, 89; Soviet dependence on, 80

Sihanouk, Prince Norodom, 399, 406

Silent Pearl exercises, 240-1

Silkworm anti-ship weapon system, 442

Singapore, 451, 463; Australian exercises with, 240; British withdrawal from, 210; fall of, 209; Five-Power Defence Arrangements, 217-8; naval base, Australian reliance on, 209

Single Integrated Operational Plan (SIOP)(US), 22, 23, 25; Alert Response Plan, 88; controlled response doctrine, influence of, 86; Generated Operations Plan, 88; SIOP-5, 30-8; SIOP-6, 38-45; strategic nuclear forces, options for employment, 86-7; targets in, 87

Sino-Soviet relations, 449, 450, 459; *see also* Soviet Union, United States of America

Sino-US coalition, 455; relations, 449, 450

SIOP, *see* Single Integrated Operational Plan (SIOP)(US)

SLBM, *see* Sea-launched ballistic missiles (SLBMs); Submarine-launched ballistic missiles (SLBMs)

Sloss, Leon, 33

Small units, utility of, 122

Smart weapons, definition, precision-guidance techniques, 110

Social order, breakdown, terrorist tactic, 157

'Soft-kill' weapons, development, 44

Sokolov, Marshal, 62, 65, 68

Sokolovski, Marshal, 73

'Solarium', Operation, 19

Solomon Islands, 418; ethnicity, 428; negative growth, 428; population growth, 428

Sonar arrays, long-range, 112

Sonar equipment, towed array, US defence cooperation with China, 443

Sope, Barak, 417, 419, 425 *bis*

Sorokin, A.I., 68

Sorokin, M.I., General, 68

South Africa, African National Congress insurgency, 142

South America, terrorism, 153

South China Sea, Chinese navy and, 405

South East Asia Nuclear Free Zone, 405

South Korea, 450; invasion of (1950), Soviet Union complicity in, 54-5

South Pacific, ASEAN and, 416; Australia and, 412, 419, 421, 422, 433; Australian Defence Force and, 373, 374; decolonisation, 413, 414; diversity among states, 413; economic assistance to, 431; economic dependence, 421; economic pressures, 428-9; ethnicity, 427-8; exclusive economic zones, 416, 421, 431; external power interests, 416; future security, 432-3; information and intelligence exchange, 432; institutional weaknesses, 428; maritime surveillance, 366; natural disasters, 421; New Zealand, waning influence, 419; New Zealand defence aid, 432; New Zealand Defence Forces (NZDF) redirection to, 368-9; nuclear free zone negotiation, 458; Papua New Guinea-Indonesia border conflict, 430; political